A Su.. 428 GRA

Second Edition

'This second edition of *A Survey of Modern English* is an admirable achievement in providing its readers with concise, but nevertheless comprehensive and clearly written introductions to the main areas of English linguistics. Its coverage is most impressive, and this text is warmly recommended as an indispensable study companion and reference work.'

Bas Aarts, University College London, UK

'An indispensable companion for university students of English Language and Linguistics, with an accessible style and impressive range of subject matter.'

Howard Jackson, University of Central England, UK

A Survey of Modern English is the essential guide to modern English structure and usage.

Both comprehensive and accessible, *A Survey of Modern English* helps students and teachers navigate and explore the linguistic structure of present-day English and its varieties. The book starts with an account of modern English as a linguistic system, looking at grammar, vocabulary, pronunciation and spelling. It then moves on to consider the written and spoken use of language as well as social variables, including gender and ethnicity. The book concludes with an exploration of varieties of English – from the UK, North America, the Caribbean, Australia, New Zealand and South Africa, to West Africa, East Africa and Asia.

The new edition has been completely revised and updated, offering:

- a new introduction looking especially at Standard English, General English and variation in language
- an exploration of new developments in the study of modern English, such as corpus-based grammars
- a new section on dictionaries, vocabulary and new words in English
- a range of new examples illustrating topics from grammar to pidgins and creoles
- a new section on power, solidarity and politeness
- new 'further reading' sections, updated references and useful websites

Stephan Gramley and **Kurt-Michael Pätzold** are senior lecturers at the Faculty of Linguistics and Literature at the University of Bielefeld, Germany.

A Survey of
Modern English

Second Edition

Stephan Gramley and
Kurt-Michael Pätzold

Routledge
Taylor & Francis Group

LONDON AND NEW YORK

First published 1992 by Routledge
Reprinted 1995, 1996, 1999, 2002, 2005

Second edition first published 2004 by Routledge
2 Park Square, Milton Park, Abingdon, Oxon OX14 4RN

Simultaneously published in the USA and Canada
by Routledge
270 Madison Avenue, New York, NY 10016

Routledge is an imprint of the Taylor & Francis Group

© 1992, 2004 Stephan Gramley and Kurt-Michael Pätzold

Typeset in Times New Roman by
Florence Production Ltd, Stoodleigh, Devon
Printed and bound in Great Britain by
MPG Books Ltd, Bodmin, Cornwall

British Library Cataloguing in Publication Data
A catalogue record for this book is available from the British Library

Library of Congress Cataloging in Publication Data
A catalog record for this book has been requested

ISBN 0–415–30034–7 (hbk)
ISBN 0–415–30035–5 (pbk)

To Kurt Konrad Leo Pätzold
Hanna Pätzold, geb. Zielge
The first, if not the only, begetters

For Hedda

And for all our excellent students

Contents

Illustrations

MAPS

FIGURES

TABLES

Preface

A Survey of Modern English has grown, over twenty years, from a vague idea in the late 1970s, by way of our German language book *Das moderne Englisch* and the first, 1992 edition, to what it is here – a sometimes expanded, sometimes abridged and in any case very differently structured volume.

This book is to a large extent the product of teaching the subjects treated here to several generations of students in Bielefeld. We need, therefore, to thank them for reminding us again and again to keep our feet on the ground and to remember what they need and want: a view of the language related to what they know, explanations for phenomena that are new for them, insights into structures difficult to analyse immediately, and descriptions of varieties of English never before (or at least not extensively) encountered. It is because of our students, whom we have constantly had in mind in writing, that we have tried to be so relatively comprehensive and have made continual efforts to give straightforward explanations and to avoid too much unnecessary terminology. Where we have used the terms of the field, we have tried to be clear about what they designate either by using short glosses or by providing more extensive discussion.

We have also had our students in mind as we have made the often hard choices about what to include and what to leave out. Needless to say, the choices could have been different and not everyone who uses this book will agree fully. Nor, we know, will everyone agree with us in all of our interpretations. We know this from our own experience with each other. For although we divided up the work more or less according to themes and chapters (both: 1, 6, 12; KMP: 2, 3, 7; SG: 4, 5, 8, 9, 10, 11, 13, 14) and have read and discussed each other's work critically, there has not always been complete agreement between the two of us.

For this edition, the text of *A Survey of Modern English* has been carefully and completely revised. This has resulted in a tightened text, in which, however, nothing of importance has been left out. Some old chapters have been amalgamated while others have been substantially rewritten (new Chapters 1 and 2). All the chapters now end with notes on further reading and there are full references in the bibliography at the end of the book, which has been brought up to date to take account of developments over the past eleven years. Another new feature is a separate bibliography with a classified list of dictionaries and other reference works. We hope that our book in its new shape will continue to be found useful as an introduction to modern English and would be grateful for any suggestions for its improvement.

Extract from *Absurd Person Singular* by Alan Ayckbourne published by Chatto & Windus. Used by permission of The Random House Group Limited.

Abbreviations

AAVE	African American Vernacular English
AdjP	Adjectival phrase
AdvP	Adverbial phrase
AmE	American English
AusE	Australian English
BEV	Black Vernacular English
BrE	British English
CanE	Canadian English
CaribE	Caribbean English
EAfrE	East African English
EFL	English as a foreign language
ESL	English as a second language
ESP	English for special/specific purposes
EST	English for science and technology
FN	First name
GenAm	General American
GenE	General English
GVS	Great Vowel Shift
H	Hearer *or* High (language)
IndE	Indian English
IrE	Irish English
KT	Kinship term
L	Low (language)
LN	Last name
ModE	Modern English
NP	Noun phrase
NZE	New Zealand English
OE	Old English
PE	Pidgin English
PP	Prepositional phrase
RP	Received Pronunciation
S	Speaker
SAE	South African English
SingE	Singaporean English

SSE	Scottish Standard English
StE	Standard English
T	Title
VP	Verb phrase
WAfrE	West African English
WAPE	West African Pidgin English

Introduction

This is a book about the English language as it exists today. In Chapter 1 we set the scene by looking at ways in which people view and have viewed English, what kinds of attitudes they have towards the language and the type of variation which may be found in it. It is also the only chapter which goes into the historical dimension of the language at any length. Part 1 is the beginning of our survey of the current language, and each of the chapters in it deals with an important aspect of the linguistic system of English: its vocabulary (Chapter 2), including more complex lexical expression (Chapter 3); its pronunciation and spelling (Chapter 4); and its grammar (Chapter 5).

However, English is more than just the linguistic system. It is also a language used by all sorts of people in all sorts of situations, as we see in Part 2. How people use the language – whoever or whatever they are – depends on what purposes they are pursuing and who they are communicating with. This includes questions of medium, style, purpose, addressee, subject matter and more. Two chapters deal with English as it is used in the medium of writing (Chapter 6) and that of speech (Chapter 7). Chapter 5 also looks at the use of English for specific purposes (ESP), especially the English for science and technology (EST). English is used by the young and the old, by women and by men, by the rich and the poor, by people whose skin colour is black, brown, yellow, red or white, by illiterates and the highly educated, and so on. While it has not proven to be feasible – in this framework – to look at all of these types of users specifically we have chosen to touch on most of these (and some other categories) in an illustrative way in Chapter 8 and to deal extensively with one of them in Chapter 9.

Beyond the variation just touched on, English is also realized as an assortment of national and regional varieties, as discussed in Chapters 10 to 14 of Part 3. Note that this includes not only Britain and Ireland (Chapter 10), North America and the Caribbean (Chapter 11), Australia, New Zealand and South Africa (Chapter 13), where there are millions of native speakers of the language, but also East and West Africa and South and Southeast Asia (Chapter 14), where there are relatively few native speakers but millions of users of English as a second language. This even includes language forms which are only marginally English, namely Pidgin and Creole English (also Chapter 14). We have only drawn the line at looking at English as a foreign language, not because this does not belong here, but because it is too mammoth a task to include in this book. Within all the areas outlined above there is also a diversity of regional, social and ethnic varieties of the language, and we have endeavoured to provide a glimpse of this as well.

Accessing the material in this book can be facilitated by making good use of the index. But since this book is, of course, limited in what it can cover, we have tried to introduce you to the study of English by supplying bibliographical material which not only documents many of our sources, but also gives a starting point for further reading and research of your own. The bibliography of dictionaries is a new and useful addition to this volume which lists various types of dictionaries, thesauruses, usage guides and dictionaries of cultural knowledge. Both this bibliography and the general bibliography contain a short selection of useful websites.

Chapter 1

The English language

Standards and variation

1.1 STANDARD ENGLISH

There is little explicit agreement about just how Standard English (StE) should be regarded. Almost everyone who works with English assumes at least implicitly that it exists, but the descriptions made of it – for example, in dictionaries and grammar books, to say nothing of manuals of style – indicate that there is a certain amount of diversity in people's ideas about StE. Yet, there *are* dictionaries, grammars and manuals of style, and what they document – some would say prescribe – is what is most often understood by StE (see 1.3 and 1.4).

A standard language is used as a model in the speech community at large. In 1.3 you will read about four defining characteristics involved in the process of standardization: selection, acceptance, elaboration and codification. That this is necessary is evident in the cases of so many indigenous languages in Third World countries (see Chapter 14) which for lack of a native standard have adopted a standardized European language such as English, hoping in this way to ease the path to 'economic prosperity, science and technology, development and modernization, and the attractions of popular culture' and paying the price of loss of self-expression and diminishment in feelings of cultural worth (Bailey 1990: 87). The result is that 'the old political empire with its metropolis and colonial outposts has nearly disappeared, replaced by a cultural empire of "English-speaking peoples"' (ibid.: 83). This quotation indicates that codification can also be overdone if English becomes the instrument of cultural imperialism. In order for English to occupy a more deeply rooted position within post-colonial societies it must draw on the everyday usage of its speakers, and this includes the recognition not only of non-standard forms, but also of non-native ones. While this is a current which moves contrary to StE, it is also one which is likely to invigorate English worldwide and make it more flexible.

To look at it from another angle, StE is 'the kind of English which draws least attention to itself over the widest area and through the widest range of usage' (Quirk and Stein 1990: 123). It is most clearly associated with the written language, perhaps because what is written and especially what is published is more permanent and is largely free of inadvertent slips and is transmitted in spelling, which is far more standardized than pronunciation is. Compare the relatively few AmE–BrE differences in orthography (Chapter 12), but the numerous national and regional accent standards (Chapters 4, 10–14). Two criteria may be set to establish what 'draws least attention to itself' over the widest geographic spread and stylistic range. For one, there is the criterion of educated usage, sometimes broadened to include common usage and probably to be most reasonably located somewhere between the two (see 1.4). The other criterion is appropriateness to the audience, topic and social setting. However these criteria are finally interpreted, there is a well established bias towards the speech of those with the most power and prestige in a society. This has always been the better educated and the higher socio-economic classes. The speech – however varied it may be in itself – of the middle classes, especially the upper middle class, carries the most prestige: it is the basis for the overt, or publicly recognized, linguistic norms of most English-speaking societies. This is not to say that working class speech or, for example, what is called Black English (see Chapters 10 and 11) are without prestige, but these varieties represent hidden or covert norms in the groups in which they are current. Not to conform to them means to distance oneself from the group and its dominant values and possibly to become an outsider. Language, then, is a sign of group identity. Public language and the overt public norm is StE (see 9.2.3 for more on overt and covert norms).

Although a great deal of emphasis has been put on *what* StE is, including lists of words and structures often felt to be used improperly (see 1.2), it is perhaps more helpful to see *how* language use is standard. One useful view is that accommodation is what makes language usage standard as speakers communicate in a manner which is (1) socially appropriate (whether middle class or working class), (2) suitable to the use to which the language is being put (1.6.2) and (3) clear. Comments on points (1) and (2) have been made above, and these are important criteria underlying the description of StE in the first section of this book. This means that while we recognize the effects of the varying characteristics of users as well as the diverse uses to which the language is put, let us state explicitly that we have oriented ourselves along the lines of educated usage, especially as codified in dictionaries, grammars, phonetic-phonological treatments and a wide assortment of other sources. In doing this we are more Anglo-American than Antipodean, more middle than working class, and look more to written than spoken language (except, of course, in the treatment of pronunciation and spoken discourse).

The third criterion listed above, clarity, is often evoked. Its loss, and the resultant demise of English, is often lamented by popular grammarians and their reading public. This is best treated in connection with the question of language attitudes.

1.2 LANGUAGE ATTITUDES

Language can be evaluated either positively or negatively, and the language which is judged may be one's own, that of one's own group or that of others. It may be spoken or written, standard or non-standard, and it may be a native, a second or a foreign language variety. Whatever it is, an evaluation is usually reached on the basis of only a few features, very often stereotypes which have been condemned, or stigmatized, as 'bad' or have been stylized as 'good'. And because language is such an intimate part of everyone's identity, the way people regard their own and others' language frequently leads to feelings either of superiority or of denigration and uncertainty.

These feelings are strengthened by the attitudes prevalent in any given group. Sometimes a whole group can be infected by feelings of inferiority. It is reported, for example, that 'there is still linguistic insecurity on the part of many Australians: a desire for a uniquely Australian identity in language mixed with lingering doubts about the suit-ability and "goodness" of [AusE]' (Guy 1991: 224). Many Australians seem to feel that a middle class British or Cultivated Australian accent is somehow better, and they rate speakers with a Broad AusE accent less favourably in terms of status and prestige though more highly with regard to solidarity and friendliness (Ball *et al.* 1989: 94). In England the attitudes people have towards RP ('Oxford English', 'the Queen's English') vary from complete identification with it, including all sorts of attempts at emulation, to rejection of it as a 'cut-glass accent' or as talking 'lah-di-dah' (Philp 1968: 26).

Few people would hold up RP as a worldwide model and most seem to accept the many different English pronunciations used, hoping to understand them, joking about unexpected or odd differences, yet inadvertently judging people by the attitudes which these accents call forth. Matched guise tests, for example, have revealed many such attitudes. In these tests people are asked to judge certain features of 'each speaker' on the basis of their accent. In reality the same person has been recorded rendering a standardized text with various accents. The intention is to eliminate the effect of indi-vidual voice quality by using the same voice in each guise. Although there is the danger that such speakers will, in some cases, unwillingly incorporate mannerisms not attributable to accent and thus prevent a fair comparison, the results have revealed such things as the tendency of English speakers in England to associate speakers of RP with intelligence, speakers of rural accents with warmth and trustworthiness, and speakers of non-RP urban accents with low prestige (with Birmingham at the bottom). GenAm speakers enjoy relatively much prestige in England, but are rated low on comprehen-sibility. In the United States 'network English' (GenAm) – the variety most widely used in national newscasting – has high prestige; Southern accents, in contrast, have little standing outside the South; Black English has negative associations for whites. On American television British accents have increasingly replaced German ones for evil and/or highly intelligent characters in science fiction programmes. The list could easily be continued.

With the enormous variety and strength of feeling engendered, it is natural to ask where all this comes from. Fundamentally, attitudes are anchored in feelings of group solidarity or distance. It is normal to identify with one's own group; therefore, what is really curious is why some people have such negative attitudes towards the speech of their own group. To a large extent this is the result of the explicit and implicit messages which are constantly being sent out in the name of a single set standard. When this standard came into being in the centuries after 1600, it was the upper class, educated usage of southern England that was adopted. The force of the Court, the Church, the schools and the new economically dominant commercial elite of London stood behind it, and it was supported by the authority of a huge and growing body of highly admired prose (above all the King James (Authorized) Version of the Bible of 1611). To belong to this privileged elite, it was felt that a command of 'proper' language was necessary. This led to increasing codification and to the growth of a new class of grammarians who prescribed the standard. In this atmosphere keeping the standard became and still remains something of a moral obligation for the middle class and those who aspire to it; the bible of this cult is the dictionary; its present day prophets ('pop grammarians' such as Edwin Newman and Richard Mitchell, but also the authors of popular manuals of style such as Burchfield or Gower in Great Britain or Wilson Follett in the United States) condemn the three 'deadly sins', improprieties, solecisms and barbarisms.

Improprieties chiefly concern similar words which historically had distinct meanings, but which are commonly used as if identical. Most people, for example, use *disinterested* as if it were an alternate form of *uninterested*. *Imply* and *infer*, *flaunt* and *flout*, *lie* and *lay*, and many other pairs are often no longer distinguished in the way they once were. In a similar vein, *hopefully* as a sentence adverb (e.g. *Hopefully, you can follow this argument*) is widely attacked (see 12.4.1). Some of the many improprieties often named are **malapropisms** (see 2.4.2) which are due to ignorance or carelessness, but others are fully in the current of a changing language, which dictates that when enough (of the 'right') people are 'wrong', they are right (Safire quoted in McArthur 1986: 34).

Solecisms comprise what are felt to be violations of number concord (*A number of people are in agreement*), the choice of the 'wrong' case for pronouns (*It's him*; or: *between you and I*) and multiple negation (*They don't have none*). These are all phenomena which are considered to relate to logic. A singular pronoun such as *everyone* is said to logically demand continued reference in the singular (*Everyone forgot his/her lines*). But there is just as much logic in recognizing the 'logical' plurality of *everyone* as 'all people'; hence why not, *Everyone forgot their lines*? (see 9.1). The point is that an appeal to logic is not enough. Most people accept and use *That's me* (say, when looking at an old photograph of themselves) rather than the grammatically 'logical', but unidiomatic *That's I*; yet educated people would be hesitant to use multiple negatives (*Nobody didn't do nothing*) except in jest although they have no trouble understanding them. Multiple negation is, to put it directly, socially marked; it is non-standard. In this case the purist's idea of good English is also in line with what this book considers to be StE.

Barbarisms include a number of different things. For example, they may be foreign expressions deemed unnecessary. Such expressions are regarded as fully acceptable if there is not a shorter and clearer English way to the meaning or if the foreign terms are somehow especially appropriate to the field of discourse (*glasnost, Ostpolitik*). *Quand même* for *anyhow* or *bien entendu* for *of course*, in contrast, seem to be pretentious (Burchfield 1996). But who is to draw the line in matters of taste and appropriacy? Other examples of 'barbarisms' are archaisms, regional dialect words, slang, cant and technical or scientific jargon. In all of these cases the same questions ultimately arise. A skilled writer can use any of these 'barbarisms' to good effect, just as avoiding them does not make a bad writer any better.

Descriptive linguists, in contrast to the prescriptive grammarians or purists just treated, try to do precisely what the term indicates: describe. The aim is to discover how the language is employed by its users whatever their gender, age, regional origins, ethnicity, social class, education, religion, vocation, etc. Explicit evaluations are avoided, but implicit ones, centred on educated middle class usage are almost always present, since this provides the usual framework for reference and comparison. It is in this tradition that this book has been written.

1.3 THE EMERGENCE OF STANDARD ENGLISH

Although the focus of this book is on a synchronic presentation of present day English, it is useful to take a glimpse at its diachronic (historical) development since this makes the existence of the countless variants present in modern English more understandable. In this section we will trace out some of the factors which led to the emergence of the form of English commonly called StE (see 1.4). Standardization generally proceeds in four stages: selection, acceptance, elaboration and codification.

Selection   At the centre of the process of standardization lies power, be it military, economic, social or cultural. Those groups in a society which are the most powerful (richer, more successful, more popular, more intelligent, better looking, etc.) will be emulated according to the maxim 'power attracts'. As England began to develop into a more unified political and economic entity in the late medieval period, the centre of power began to concentrate more and more in London and the southeast. The Court had pretty well moved from Winchester to London by the end of the thirteenth century. Gradually the London dialect (or, more precisely, that of the 'east Midlands triangle', London, Oxford and Cambridge) was becoming the one preferred by the educated. This was supported by the establishment of printing in England in 1476 by William Caxton, for both had an east Midlands regional base. Furthermore, this was a wealthy agricultural area and a centre of the wool trade. With its commercial significance the London area was also becoming more densely populated, thus gaining in demographic weight. It was therefore inevitable that the English of this region would become a model with a wider geographic spread and eventually be carried overseas. Today it continues to exert considerable pressure on the dialects of England, which as a result are converging more and more toward the standard.

In this process variant forms were in competition with each other (see 10.2.2 on the Great Vowel Shift). Nonetheless by the end of the sixteenth century the preferred dialect was that of London, which itself existed in two standards: a spoken one and the written 'Chancery standard'. The latter moved more quickly toward what would be Standard English while the former was slower to lose its Middle English features. Chancery also differed from popular London speech by adopting characteristics from the northern dialects: two of the best known are the inflection of the verb in the third person singular present tense and the personal pronoun for the third person plural. This explains why we have northern *does* and not southern *doeth* even though the latter is familiar to many people even in the twenty-first century from the King James (Authorized) Version of the Bible. The southern third person plural pronouns were *hy*, *here*, *hem*; the northern and midland forms, which show Danish influence, give us the present day *th*-forms (*they*, *their*, *them*).

Acceptance   One historian of English, Leith, credits the acceptance of the east Midlands variety not so much to its use by the London merchant class as to its adoption by students from all over England who studied at Oxford or Cambridge. This gave the emerging standard an important degree of social and geographical mobility. A further significant point is 'its usefulness in communicating with people who spoke another dialect', especially the lower class population of London. Foremost among the reasons for its adoption, however, was surely its political usefulness as an instrument and expression of the growing feeling of English nationalism as well as its employment at the royal Court. Finally, we should mention its use by influential and respected authors, starting with Chaucer and continuing with such writers of the early modern period as Spenser, Sydney and, of course, Shakespeare (Leith 1983: 36–44).

The incorporation of characteristics of the northern dialect in the emerging standard was made possible by the extremely fluid social situation in the fourteenth century, which began with a rigidly structured society. This structure was changed by the population losses of the Black Death (30 to 40 per cent of the English population) and the Hundred Years' War, which cost the lives of much of the old nobility. Henry VII increasingly sought to fill offices with people from the middle classes who gave their own speech forms greater public currency. 'Most of the northern forms seem to be working their way up from the bottom, probably moving up into the upper class sociolect as speakers of the dialect move into the upper class' (Shaklee 1980: 58).

Elaboration   This term describes the spread of the use of the new standard into ever more domains of use, including those such as the Church and the Law, which were previously the preserve of Latin or French. In 1362, for example, Parliament was opened with an address held in English (instead of French) for the first time, and in the same year English was adopted as a language of the Courts. A century later the establishment of Caxton's printing press and the translation of the Bible into English continued the functional spread of the language.

As English expanded in the number of functions it might be expected to fulfil, there was a parallel expansion in the linguistic means required to carry this out. Most obviously the necessary vocabulary grew. The classical languages were the chief sources for new words and provided English with the means for stylistic differentiation – between the more common everyday words of Germanic (Anglo-Saxon) origin and those from Greek, Latin and French. For more detail and examples, see 2.4.1.

Codification   At the beginning of the seventeenth century grammarians were still relatively open to regional forms, but by the end of the century these forms were seen as 'incorrect'. Now grammarians 'were prescribing the correct language for getting ahead in London society, and standard English had risen to consciousness' (Shaklee 1980: 60). In their attempts to codify, the grammarians were continually trying to fix what was, by its nature, constantly changing. They thought that if they could record correct usage completely enough and teach it with rigour, it could be maintained unchanged. This did not work in earlier centuries and does not work today. The discrepancies between the grammarians' rules and actual usage continue to this day, and so the standard must and will change.

As the language grew more complex and the possibilities for making stylistic distinctions increased, and also as the number of people who aspired to use this new standard grew, there emerged an enormous need to know just what it consisted of, hence the advent of dictionaries, grammars and books on orthoepy (the study of correct pronunciation). The best known of the early dictionaries was that of Samuel Johnson, who produced his monumental two volume *Dictionary of the English Language*, which appeared in 1755. This dictionary stands at the beginning of a long tradition of lexicography which includes the incomparable twelve volume historical *Oxford English Dictionary* (1928; plus supplements; now in an Internet edition) as well as hundreds of further general and specialized dictionaries. The question of how to pronounce words 'properly' was addressed by numerous orthoepists: for example, John Walker's *Critical Pronouncing Dictionary* (1791) lent weight to the tendency to pronounce words in accordance with the way they were spelled, so-called 'spelling pronunciations'. Here, too, tradition has continued both with pronouncing dictionaries, now generally including at least the two major standard pronunciations, Received Pronunciation (RP) of England and General American (GenAm) of North America, and with linguistic descriptions such as those in the tradition of Daniel

Jones and A.C. Gimson (see the latter's *Introduction to the Pronunciation of English*). Grammar and usage was approached in grammar books by such venerable, though also prescriptive, grammarians as Bishop Lowth (1762) and Lindley Murray (1795). The latter's grammar became the school standard and went through innumerable editions. The writing of grammar books also includes such momentous works as Otto Jespersen's seven volume *Modern English Grammar on Historical Principles* (1940–2) or the *Comprehensive Grammar of the English Language* by R. Quirk *et al.* (1985). More recently, the *Longman Grammar of Spoken and Written English* by Douglas Biber *et al.* (1999) continues this tradition, based here on an extensive corpus of written and spoken usage in a variety of registers and usage drawn from BrE, AmE and other varieties.

1.4 STANDARD AND GENERAL ENGLISH

Before looking at StE and GenE let us point out that although both are dialects of English, they are not dialects in the full sense of the term, which includes vocabulary and grammar as well as pronunciation. StE and GenE are special cases. The main reason is that, since they are used widely throughout the English speaking world, they may be described in terms of their grammar and vocabulary only and not according to their accent or pronunciation. Both StE and GenE are, namely, pronounced with a great variety of different accents while staying within certain grammatical and lexical bounds. In contrast, the local speech-ways of the traditional dialects of Great Britain are all associated with specific local, dialect pronunciations. Nevertheless, StE in England is closely, though not necessarily, associated with one particular accent, RP, which is one of the standard accents on which the description of pronunciation in Chapter 4 is based.

The emergence of RP   RP is one of the products of the process of standardization. This pronunciation arose in the middle of the nineteenth century in the great public schools (in Great Britain not state run but private schools) of England, where it was and still is maintained and transmitted from one student generation to the next without being deliberately taught. It is maintained by virtue of the prestige and power of its speakers, who have traditionally formed the social, military, political, cultural and economic elite of England (and Great Britain). It is, for example, still practically a prerequisite for entry into the diplomatic service. As such it is a socially rather than regionally based accent. Although it has considerable (overt) prestige, there are signs that it is giving way to a more regionally based pronunciation, that of the lower Thames Valley, a variety (involving more than just pronunciation) sometimes termed 'Estuary English' (Rosewarne 1994; see Chapter 10.4.1).

In most of the other English speaking countries there is nothing quite like RP. There is a pronunciation which is recognized as the national standard in Scotland, the United States, Canada, South Africa and so on, but in all of these cases the basis of the standard pronunciation is regional and not social. Australia, however, comes close to the English situation because none of the three pronunciation types usually recognized, Cultivated, General and Broad, are regionally based.

Standard English   Standard English is a relatively narrow concept and the type of language associated with StE is closely associated with a fairly high degree of education. It represents the overt, public norm.

> Standard English is that variety of English which is usually used in print, and which is normally taught in schools and to non-native speakers learning the language. It is also the variety which is normally spoken by educated people and used in news broadcasts and other similar situations. The difference between standard and non-standard, it should be noted, has nothing in principle to do with differences between formal and colloquial language, or with concepts such as 'bad language'. Standard English has colloquial as well as formal variants, and standard English speakers swear as much as others.
>
> (Trudgill 1974: 17)

As an example of StE let us take the third person singular present tense form of the auxiliary *do*, which is *doesn't* as in *He doesn't care what you do*. Furthermore, double negation is not permitted, e.g. *Don't give me any of your sass*.

General English   General English, in contrast, is much wider and includes variants which are excluded from StE, but are widely used and understood. The choice of a given variant is more likely to be associated with solidarity. In this sense GenE represents a covert norm. However, since its possible variants include those which are associated with StE, we can say that GenE is the more general term and includes StE. As an example let us once again take the third person singular present tense form of the auxiliary *do*, which is, for most speakers of GenE, *don't* as in *He don't care what you do*. In GenE double (multiple) negation is commonly used (especially for emphasis), e.g. *Don't give me none of your sass*. (For further non-standard features of GenE, see 10.1.2 and 11.3.)

Traditional dialect   Traditional dialect, finally, is a term which covers varieties which are not so closely related as StE and GenE are. Examples which illustrate this can be found at all the systematic levels of the language. Compare:

	StE	Traditional dialect	
vocabulary	*dirty*	*mucky*	(Westmoreland)
pronunciation	juː məst iːt ɪt ʌp	ða mʊŋ gɛr ɪt ɛtn	(north of England)
grammar	*you must eat it up*	'thou must get it eaten'	

We can compare StE, GenE and traditional dialect using five criteria which are sometimes applied to language varieties: historicity, vitality, autonomy, reduction and purity.

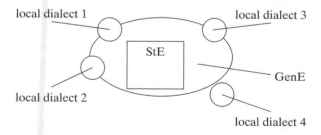

Figure 1.1   The relationship between GenE, StE and the traditional dialects

Historicity is similar for all three in the sense that they all may be traced back to earlier stages of the language. Only the English pidgins and creoles (see 14.3) are different in this point because they are the product of a relatively late process (in historical terms), which was independent of the historical dialects of English.

Vitality is a characteristic of StE, GenE and English pidgins and creoles, all of which have expanding groups of speakers. Only traditional dialects differ here since they are involved in a general pattern of decline.

Autonomy, which refers to whether the variety is regarded (by users at large) as an independent language, is doubtless the case for StE, which in fact is very often regarded as *the* language. In contrast to this some people regard GenE as somehow imperfect or 'substandard' and see the traditional dialects as antiquated. The pidgins and creoles are sometimes mistakenly regarded as non-languages.

Reduction includes reduction of status or form. Standard English has lots of 'dialects' and a well developed vocabulary of technical and similar terms; and it can be used in numerous registers (especially styles). It is certainly not reduced; however, this cannot be claimed for GenE, the traditional dialects, and pidgins and creoles, which are used for communication in fewer domains or areas of activity.

Purity is perhaps the one point where the traditional dialects have an advantage over StE. While StE includes thousands of borrowings from other languages, the dialects are generally regarded as pure – at least if we can find those mythical older, rural, uneducated, immobile speakers who still speak broad, or 'pure', dialect. Pidgins and creoles with their mixed origins are regarded as the very opposite of purity.

It is with all these remarks in mind that the reader should set out on the exploration of Modern English, as it is presented in this book.

1.5 SOCIOLINGUISTIC DIMENSIONS OF ENGLISH

Sociolinguistics is concerned with the social aspects of a language. It describes how social identities are established and maintained in language use. The area itself can be divided into the macro level of the sociology of language, 'primarily a sub-part of sociology, which examines language use for its ultimate illumination of the nature of societies' (Mesthrie *et al.* 2000: 5) and sociolinguistics proper, which is sometimes seen as involving the 'micro' patterns of language use in context: 'part of the terrain mapped out in linguistics, focusing on language in society for the light that social contexts throw upon language' (ibid.).

The sociology of language covers 'external' questions such as language planning and language policy, and also areas such as language birth, maintenance, shift and death, pidgins and creoles, language imposition, monolingualism, bilingualism and diglossia. Diglossia is the use of two languages or distinct varieties of one single language for, on the one hand, written literature, state institutions and established religion, and, on the other hand, for everyday, colloquial communication. The former is known as the diglossically High language; the latter, as the Low language (see Chapter 14). **Language planning** itself consists of **status planning** and **corpus planning**. The former is concerned with the domains, that is, the uses and functions of a language in a society, their relative prestige, and how the various languages in a society are acquired. Concretely, what is the language of the schools/education, administration, the media, etc. (see Chapter 14). The latter encompasses the selection of forms and varieties as well as language codification and modernization. This includes, among other things, devising a writing system, carrying out spelling reforms, coining and introducing new terms, and publishing grammars and other reference works (see 1.3).

Sociolinguistics proper examines the languages used by various groups – be they based on age, class, ethnicity, region, gender or something else. It looks into questions of group identities within societies according to these criteria and how variation in pronunciation, grammar, lexis or pragmatics (communicative strategies or speech acts) correlates with such groups. While the external perspective is more a matter of policy, the internal is more one of prestige.

Power and solidarity Both the external and the internal perspectives involve the central dimensions of social power and social solidarity. It is the aim of much language policy to create communities of solidarity and national identity, an important goal in many of the more newly independent states of Africa and Asia. Yet the instruments used are clearly ones of power, be they military, economic, social or cultural. The power of the state (or some other comparable institution) is the guarantor of an effective language policy: the goal is a reinforcement of the feeling of solidarity with the group in power, no matter whether its base is a region, a caste, a class, an ethnic group or some other group (including the dominant male gender). Frequently, language policy is enforced by the school system (access to literacy, access to the diglossically High language); other instruments are religious institutions, the military or the market place.

In many parts of the world where English is used, what language(s) road signs are in can be a highly political question (e.g. English and Gaelic in Northern Ireland or English and French in Canada). For many citizens in these countries it is not simply a symbolic point that state documents and information should be easily available in more than just English (e.g. voting ballots in the US in Spanish, Chinese etc. all depending on the demographic character of the population).

Within the world context the imposition of English is of great relevance. Planning recognizes the importance of acceptance, which means coming to terms with:

- linguistic assimilation – how likely is the adoption of a language (such as English) by everyone in a given society?
- linguistic pluralism – can different language groups/varieties coexist?
- vernacularization – is there a native language/variety which can serve as the vernacular?
- internationalization – what level of language uniformity is necessary to guarantee access to science and technology, international contact and communication on a widespread basis?

Historically some of the most important factors involved in language imposition have been: military conquest; a long period of language imposition; a polyglot subject group; and material benefits in adopting the new language. In the modern world further factors include: urbanization; industrialization/economic development; educational development; religious orientation; and political affiliation. The change from one language to another involves the central phenomena of bilingualism and code-switching, which are prominent in numerous societies where English is used (see Part 3). Attitudes within the various communities help decide which languages will be maintained and which may eventually die.

In sociolinguistics, solidarity is perhaps more prominent than power, yet the relationships between the various groups are very frequently governed by the relative power of the groups. Within the dominant groups in a given society there are conventions concerning what is politically correct, which is one of many ways of maintaining existing power relations: the dominant group defines what groups exist and how they should be regarded. In the United States, for example, the predominant, though not exclusive, ethnic-racial division is the Black-White divide (also Hispanic-White and Native American-White). South Africa under apartheid had a division into Black, Coloured and White (also Indian). For many years derogatory terms for American and South African Blacks (see derogatory AmE *nigger* or patronizing *darkie, colored* or derogatory SAE *kaffir*) were accepted, and they helped to cement attitudes on the part of both the dominant and the dominated. It is the relatively more **powerful groups** who are the source of **overt norms**. Public language is middle class language, is men's language, is white language, is the language of the relatively older (but only up to a certain age, after which increasing – or even abrupt – powerlessness sets in). Note, too, that certain text types are favoured, e.g. scientific, legal, economic ones. Often certain accents are given preference (e.g. RP, General Australian, GenAm).

The characteristic features of the language of a given group is determined by in-group solidarity or **covert norms**. In the case of slang the factor of **solidarity** is primary; slang is a case of group resistance to the language of power. Much the same is true of tabooed language as well as of many secret languages. Of course, the in-group language may, by chance, be the same as the powerful language of the overt norm; this 'default' language is, in countries like the United Kingdom, the United States, Australia, Canada, New Zealand and South Africa, most typically that of White, middle class males.

In sociolinguistics we correlate social/group features with language use. Gender is one such social feature. However, gender alone does not determine linguistic behaviour, but rather it is more fundamental social relations which are merely mirrored in gender: power and solidarity. In short, the male–female divide is characterized largely (though surely not exclusively) and probably most definitively by a power differential, while relations within each of the genders are often determined by solidarity. This does not mean that male–female relations cannot also be characterized by a high degree of solidarity. Furthermore, there are obviously male–female relationships in which the female is the dominant and more powerful figure. However, at a deeper societal level male dominance and power is almost an absolute – at least in Western society. This, we might say, lies in the basic economic hegemony of males in Western society, which cannot be changed, but may be covered over where superior female intelligence manifests itself, where individual females have better jobs than individual males, where females withhold sexual favours, where females are more wealthy, famous or successful – and so on. One of the things that sociolinguistics does, we see, is to offer a reflection of society and its inequalities.

Gender is significant for language inasmuch as males are many times more likely to identify with other males, including their economic and sexual rivals, than with women – just as women are equally likely to do the equivalent. Gender identity is based on solidarity. It is a fundamental identification which leads to imitation of behaviour. Yet within the framework of solidarity it is power which determines much of behaviour: those who are more powerful, more successful, more popular, more intelligent, better looking etc. – be they males or females – will be emulated by the other(s) according to the maxim 'power attracts'.

The complementary relationship, solidarity, is not without its attraction either. There are interpersonal relationships which are characterized by reciprocity, by a more or less balanced mutuality. One instance of this is the use of slang:

> The type of language referred to as *slang* is more than a level of formality. That is, slang cannot be understood simply as informal, colloquial, careless, sloppy language even though these notions are indelibly connected with the idea of slang in many people's minds. Slang is, rather, first and foremost, group language. This restriction – at least in its origins – is the key feature of slang. That is, slang has an extremely important social function to fulfil with regard to the groups that create it: it helps to establish solidarity and is associated with group identity. An elderly white American woman who talks about *dissing* ('to show *dis*respect toward someone') may be using (relatively) recent slang, but she is violating numerous restrictions on its use, chief among which is that this is typical of young black males. While slang usage such as this may drift upward into the language of the more powerful and outward into that of out-group users, this is far from automatic; and by the time this happens, the original group will probably have long since turned to a different expression.
>
> The fact that slang is typically connected with the subcultures of youth is perhaps what leads many people to see it as informal, colloquial, careless, or sloppy, for that is how many people evaluate young people's language, the language of the (as yet) weak, the (as yet) outsiders.

(Gramley 2001: 207f.)

1.6 WORDS IN USE: THE REGISTER APPROACH

This final section discusses a model that provides a systematic approach to the variation we find in English in terms of two large categories: the people who use the language and the situations in which people find themselves. The more permanent characteristics, those of the language users, are called **dialects**, while the various situational factors that influence language use are collectively referred to as **diatypes** or **registers**.

1.6.1 Dialect

Dialects come in various guises including temporal, regional, social and individual. We have made it clear that this book is centred on StE and GenE as the major default dialects, i.e. the ones most often meant when people talk about the English language. We are not directly concerned here with Old or Middle English. But this is not to say that some knowledge of the temporal dialects, or earlier stages of English, is not relevant to a full and correct understanding of the present day language. Reading Shakespeare or trying to understand items like *let* (in tennis), *kith and kin* and *ye olde tea shoppe* involves historical information of one kind or another which can be found in histories of the language and etymological dictionaries.

Regional and social dialects   Geographic variation is, as many of the previous remarks have indicated, extremely prominent in English. This may include regions within a single country or it may involve the national varieties of English. Furthermore, the urban–rural divide continues to be a major source of variation.

Regional dialects   Classical dialect studies in the United States and Canada (the Linguistic Atlas of the United States and Canada, LAUS) as well as in England (the Survey of English Dialects, SED, and the Lowman Survey of the Midlands and South of England) and Scotland (the Linguistic Atlas of Scotland) are the most important examples of regional studies of English. The SED (finished 1961) largely ignored age and social differences, emphasis being on farming culture (in nine main sections). The object was to determine 387 phonetic, 128 morphological, 77 syntactic, and 730 lexical points using such methods as naming, completing, talking, converting (for example, present to past tense) and reverse questions ('What does *corn* mean?') in direct interviews. The questions asked were exactly prescribed and formulated. Generally the most immobile, oldest and most poorly educated men were interviewed. In North America the Linguistic Atlas, which is a loose grouping of individual studies such as the LANE [Linguistic Atlas of New England] (Kurath *et al.* 1939–43) or the LAMSAS [Middle and Southern Atlantic States] (McDavid *et al.* 1980f), differs somewhat from the SED inasmuch as it takes the age and education (three levels) of the informants into account. The results showed larger differences according to education/class and smaller ones according to age. Even with their wider spread many of the American studies are methodologically weak and do not possess a high degree of validity and reliability.

Isoglosses and isogloss bundles   The product of such classical dialect surveys is a linguistic atlas which maps out the boundaries between geographical areas where different variants are used, for example where in England words like *farm* are pronounced with and without /r/. A line dividing places with form A from those with form B is called an isogloss. Several isoglosses running close together are called isogloss bundles. In this fashion dialect areas can be determined. But the divisions are seldom clear; rather, there are transition areas in which both forms may occur. Furthermore, sometimes an island of older usage is left behind while everything around it has changed; this is a relic area.

Other types of dialect   We will not be particularly concerned with regional dialectology in this book, but will be looking at the results of population movement, (a) from country to town and (b) from mother country abroad. Sometimes this has involved the maintenance of previously regionally based dialects as new social dialects, for example, when migrants of a particular regional origin make up significant parts of the new urban working class. This happened in the United States as southern workers entered the northern automobile industry in the first half of the twentieth century. Or there may be a levelling of dialect differences (known as **koinéization**), something which appears to be happening today with the emergence of Estuary English in the Thames Valley (see 10.4.1).

Geographical variation both within the various national types of English as well as the variation between the national varieties is the chief focus of Part 3 of this book. Traditional dialect, as discussed above, will play only a minor role (see 10.2.2). Social dialects will also be treated in Part 3; however, the link between pronunciation and the social class of speakers has also been mentioned in the discussion of RP above, and a number of class-related examples in the area of vocabulary are recounted in 2.10.

Idiolect   Idiolect or a person's **individual dialect** must be mentioned. This refers not so much to a different sort of dialect as to a selection from all of the above dialects, which together make up a large part of a person's linguistic individuality. Although idiolect can contain a few items that only this person or his or her family use, it usually consists of the established vocabulary common to most speakers of the person's speech community. It is no easy task to describe someone's idiolect as it tends to change over time and according to the circumstances he or she finds herself or himself in. Idiolect will, for example, reflect a person's gender in the choice of lexis (see 9.2.1) and it may well show regional mixes of one kind or another. American writers, for example, may use British items like *tarted up* or *roof rack*, or use native *faucet* beside British *tap*. Idiolects are therefore not fixed once and for all, but are dynamic, changing according to time, place, occasion etc.

1.6.2 Register

Variation in language clearly depends on when and where someone lives and on what his or her gender and social class identities are, but it is also a function of: 'what you are speaking about; who your addressees are; how well you know them; whether you are addressing them orally or in writing' (Quirk and Stein 1990: 41). This second set of factors relates not so much to the individual user as to language use in certain situations. Use varieties are called **diatypes** or registers and are treated under four aspects, all of which turn up again specifically in Chapter 6.

Field   Field is the first aspect and is also called **province**. It reflects the fact that one needs different words to talk about different subjects. There are many terms that characterize particular subjects: *folk etymology*, *lexeme* and *homograph* are found only in linguistics. Others take on special meanings, for example *boot* (verb), *hardware* and *window* in computing. There are also combinations of lexical items that are typical of certain fields, e.g. *desirable residence*, *tastefully modernized* or *compact patio-style garden*, which are found in the advertisements of property agents in England.

We are all perfectly capable of carrying on a general conversation about people, the weather, our holidays etc. These everyday uses of language, though essential to life in society, are easy because they do not make great demands on our minds or linguistic abilities. But when we move from the general field of everyday conversation to that of the Internet, genetic engineering or heart surgery, the number of people who understand the language, or could themselves use it, is rather more limited.

General language is most obviously distinguished from technical language by its lexis, though other factors are also important (see Chapter 6). While a command of various technical vocabularies is a matter of education and experience, their actual use is conditioned by various factors. Technical terms used by a surgeon in a hospital or a lawyer in a court of law are of course a convenient and precise means of communication. However, when experts use technical terms with members of the general public, things are rather different. They may be insensitive, or incapable of or unwilling to adjust their language – perhaps they want to put distance between themselves and their interlocutors in order to impress, exclude, intimidate or overwhelm them into willing submission. In short, we are talking here about language as social power. Solidarity with other people would show in words that everybody can understand.

Personal tenor   Also simply **tenor** or **status** or **style**, this refers to the formality of any given piece of language, for which dictionaries have labels such as formal, familiar, informal, colloquial or slang (see above for a discussion of slang). Most lexical items are not labelled because they are stylistically neutral. There is often little agreement on whether an item is colloquial or slang, or on how many levels ought to be set up. One quite well known model is the five term one proposed by Joos (1962), which Strevens (1964: 29) illustrates in this way:

Style	Example
Frozen style:	Visitors should make their way at once to the upper floor by way of the staircase.
Formal:	Visitors should go up the stairs at once.
Consultative:	Would you mind going upstairs, right away, please.
Casual:	Time you all went upstairs, now.
Intimate:	Up you go, chaps!

Notice that a change in tenor involves much more than a simple change in the stylistic level of the lexemes (*visitors* vs *chaps*). There is, for example, a change in the length and explicitness of the message: from *make their way* to *go*, and from *to the upper floor* to *up*.

Formality choices often go hand in hand with medium differences, but they are ultimately determined by the relationship between the people concerned. The closer the sender (speaker or writer) feels to his or her addressee(s), the more informal the language which the sender can use. Conversely, the more distant the personal relationship, the more formal the personal tenor is likely to be. The frozen and formal versions above are likely to be announcements over a ship's PA system, where the speaker does not see his or her addressees, while the other three versions can only be uttered when speaker and hearer see each other. Personal tenor is thus often determined by physical closeness or distance. It has to be stressed that speakers are free to stick to the generally accepted conventions or to flout them, for whatever reasons or purposes. Foreign learners should in any case be careful of using very informal or potentially offensive lexemes with people they do not know well.

Medium or mode   The five stylistic variants quoted above illustrate once again that there is no causal link between formality and medium, or mode (the five examples given all belong to spoken language). Although medial differences go far beyond lexical choices, the focus of the present discussion is on the lexis and syntax typical of the two media. First, however, a few more general notes are in order.

Speech is primary: it is acquired early in our lives more or less informally, while writing is learned much later and by far fewer people, usually in a formal educational establishment. Writing usually does jobs concerned with the transfer of information (technically called **transactional uses**) and confers greater prestige in society. Speech is typically used to create, maintain and enhance social bonds (**interactional uses**) and thus meets basic human needs, while writing satisfies less immediate ones, as becomes clear from the following list which starts with uses typical of the spoken language and ends with those that are exclusive to writing:

conversation in a pub, seminar, telephone conversation, personal letter, job interview, radio discussion, television advertisement, lecture, sermon, script of play, television news, newspaper, business letter, this book

(Leech *et al.* 1982: 140)

Speech, or more precisely spontaneous conversation, differs from writing in three major respects: there is a great amount of linguistic give-and-take (or **interactiveness**, to use a term from computer science); it is mostly, though not only, concerned with the lives and interests of the people who have the conversation, and it is produced as we go along (this has been called **on-line production**). At the other end of the spectrum are carefully thought out and edited written texts in which the author often does not mention her- or himself and has no specific addressees: indeed, they are monologues.

The interactive nature of conversation is clearly seen in the frequent use of items like *hm, ugh, yeah, right* and *well,* that have an emotional and interactional meaning, and are marked off from other utterances by pauses or their own intonation contours. There is a variety of labels for these, of which the most general and recent is **inserts** (see 7.5 for a discussion of the three **discourse markers** *now, you know* and *well*). Other features are tag questions and expressions like *I think, in my opinion* or *as far as I am concerned.* This ties in with the personal, interactive nature of conversation and explains the relatively greater use in written texts of items which have to do with impersonal, objective information.

Features determined by the situation are referring words (**deictics**) like *him* or *that one over there* and items of personal reference, such as first and second person pronouns. Participants in conversations share a geographical and temporal background as well as a lot of personal knowledge of each other so that allusions to places, persons and past times will be found that are unintelligible to outsiders. Writing has to be more explicit because writers are isolated from readers and cannot rely on the situation or on paralinguistic means to help make their message clear.

The spontaneity of conversation has the greatest number of linguistic consequences, in phonetics and syntax as well as lexis. Conversational pronunciations are characterized not least by contractions (*can't, won't*), reductions (**weak forms**, see 4.5.2), elisions and assimilation processes of many different kinds, which can present great difficulties to foreign learners.

The basic unit for syntactic descriptions is the sentence. In spoken English, however, there are many stretches of language where the concept of sentence makes no sense. Various alternative terms are in use for the units of spoken language, among them **information unit**, **utterance chunk** or **idea unit**. Spoken language units are short, having a mean length of approximately two seconds, which is about six words; they belong to a small set of syntactic structures and are much more predictable than written ones. Deletion of sentence elements such as the subject or the predicate is common. Speakers rely on well known structures that were learned early in life, such as paratactic constructions, while planned discourse uses those acquired at a later stage. Speech is untidy, full of mixed constructions (**syntactic blends**), false starts, repetitions (of words as well as constructions), digressions, loose ends, inconsistencies and changes of construction, none of which are permitted in formal written texts. There are, for instance, noun phrases in conversation whose function is to establish a topic first and then say something about it. This breaking down of the message into two distinct parts makes things easier for both speakers and hearers, as in: 'My wife, she only came later to the party.' This is called **left dislocation** in syntax and **preface** in discourse analysis. In the next example, a horrible murder has taken place and Larry King asks his guest (another talk show host on one of whose programmes the murder victim had appeared):

King: Did you remember the show? You do so many.

Springer: Yes, I honestly didn't. And I don't mean to sound insensitive about it. But the reality is, we do 200 shows a year. I have been doing it 10 years – not – finished 9 years already. That is 1800 shows. We have 10 guests a show. That is nearly 20,000 people. I didn't – you know, until obviously everyone has been showing me the tapes. At the time, when I heard about it, no I didn't remember it . . .

Springer has something similar to a preface, only here it is a temporal adverbial phrase (*at the time*) that is moved to the beginning of his utterance in order to make an emphatic contrast with the preceding clause *until obviously everyone has been showing me the tapes*. Notice that Springer first answers *yes*, which may be triggered by King's *you do so many*, but this sounds odd, as is shown later by normal *no I didn't remember it*. There is repetition of the lexical verb *do* and the constructions *that is* and *I didn't*. There is also an obvious break in his contribution after *I have been doing it 10 years*, where Springer hesitates and then changes his construction. Finally, the utterance *finished 9 years already*, where there is no subject and auxiliary, is an example of the deletion of function words in conversation and of how questionable it is to speak of 'sentences' in spoken language.

Noun phrases tend to be simple, as in Springer's answer, but are often modified in an afterthought by a following phrase. Clause-final, retrospective *though* (*It was nice, though*) in speech corresponds to written *although* at the beginning of a clause. Information density is lower in conversation, i.e. speakers use fewer lexical items than grammatical items. In all these respects writing is different: it uses highly structured syntactic forms that are less predictable; it knows anticipatory structures like *on the one hand*; it does not avoid subordinate constructions with causal or temporal sentence connectors like *because, since, therefore*. Recent research based on an extensive collection of data (what is called a **corpus**) has modified the received wisdom that speech and coordination go together as do writing and subordination: 'In fact, with the exception of *but*, the frequency of all coordinators is relatively low in conversation, while subordinators are more frequent in conversation than in news and academic prose' (Biber *et al.* 1999: 82f.). Nevertheless, writing demands greater attention from readers because it packs more information into its sentences, i.e. there is a higher percentage of lexical items. This fact is of course related to the main purpose of much writing: lexical items convey information. The differences are also well brought out by the distribution of inserts: while there are none in written texts, we find a good number of them in conversation, which ties in with conversation's interactional nature. Among other features particular to writing we find the passive rather than the active and relatively many declaratives but few imperatives, interrogatives and exclamations. Finally, processing a written text takes place at the leisure of the reader, who can skip pages, go back and forth or go over the same passage again as desired or needed. This is one of the factors that make literature and its appreciation possible.

Functional tenor While it is intuitively obvious that we use different means to instruct, threaten or persuade others, it is less obvious how many functions language can have and how to classify them. One approach distinguishes six functions, which are derived from six essential features of human communication:

- The *emotive* (or *expressive*) function is related to the sender, who wants to express emotions.
- The *conative* (or *directive*) function is addressee-related: it relates to attempts to influence others in order to achieve some goal, typically realized by orders and requests.
- The *meta-communicative*, or *meta-lingual*, function is related to the code used. It is involved in questions such as: 'What is the meaning of *let* in tennis?'
- There is a particularly close link between the message and the *poetic* or *aesthetic* function. This function can be defined as the use of language for language's sake, i.e. for a special aesthetic effect.
- The *informational* or *referential* function derives from the context or subject matter of communication and is concerned with information transfer.
- The final use of language is the *phatic* function, in which language is used to keep social relationships in good repair by ensuring that people keep talking with each other, as in small talk (see the interactional uses mentioned above).

Notice the contrast between phatic and aesthetic language: with phatic communion what is important is not the news value of what one says or the originality or creativity of the language used, but that something is said at all, that silence is avoided so that speaker and addressee feel at ease and can enjoy each other's company.

It should be noted that just as lexemes have different meanings, so one and the same phrase or expression can serve different functions: *I'm dying for a cup of coffee* can, in the right circumstances, be read as a piece of information, as an expression of the speaker's emotion, or as a veiled order to the addressee to get the speaker something to drink (see 7.2.1. on speech acts).

Evaluation and conclusion Registers have been divided into those where linguistic choice is limited (**marked registers**), e.g. greetings, forms of address and instructions, and those where there are more options available, for example, the language of journalism (**unmarked registers**). Much research has been concerned with looking at very general registers, such as the languages of journalism or advertising, and setting up subtypes within them. One approach to **advertising** differentiates between radio, TV and newspaper advertisements and discusses, in addition to the genre of traditional commercial consumer advertising, a new type which addresses more material needs in contrast to the social and symbolic needs met by many products. This type of advertisement is meant to sell goods and services presented as necessary whether they are or not – for example cars, suits, transatlantic flights and the latest colour TVs. These 'no-frills' advertisements are simple and factual; they mention the product's price and contain little hyperbolic language. Thus the difference in the perception of the product comes through in a no-nonsense style.

Another aspect in register research is the question of whether the four categories are always equally important. It has been said that the language of science is dominated by considerations of field, the language of diplomatic protocol by personal tenor, and the language of advertising by functional tenor. More generally, it has been claimed that it is genre or the type of text which determines choices in field, mode and personal tenor (see Biber 1988; Swales 1990). As a result, functional tenor as a category is not on a par with the other three. A great deal of research is being conducted at present and it is too early to say anything final about either the number of categories or possible hierarchies.

Finally, one should also ask whether the register model captures enough of the situational factors to be able to give an adequate description of language in use. Among the more permanent (dialect) characteristics, gender is treated in a substantial body of research (see Chapter 9). People's ages, ethnic and social affiliations (subcultures such as youth groups or Rastafarians) and sexual orientations have been given increasing attention in recent years. Some neglected (diatypical) factors are the settings of a situation, i.e. the physical and temporal contexts (see Biber 1988: 28–33 for a detailed list of situation components). If the register model is seen not so much as a closed system, but rather as an open approach which needs refining and extending, it will continue to be a very useful tool.

1.7 FURTHER READING

The contributions in Graddol, Leith and Swann 1996 are readable and useful supplements to much of the substance of this chapter. For a discussion of **improprieties, solecisms** and **barbarisms** see Nunberg 1983. Giles and Powesland 1975 explore **language attitudes** and report on matched guise tests. A very useful **history of English** is Baugh and Cable 2002.

Standardization is treated in: Leith 1983; Milroy and Milroy 1993. Shaklee 1980 and Fisher 1996 look specifically at the rise of Standard English. Leith offers a **social history of English** in his book.

Detailed treatments of **dialects** and **registers** can be found in: Crystal and Davy 1969; Biber 1988; Quirk and Stein 1990; O'Donnell and Todd 1991; Cook 1992; Thomas 1997. Research into register differences has taken off in the past 20 years or so.

Akinnaso 1985 investigates the differences between spontaneous conversation and scripted dialogue in the realization of such tasks as describing, explaining, arguing, protesting etc. and then analyses the linguistic means used in both **media**. Biber *et al.* 1999 is a treatment of spoken and written English which has set new standards in research linking grammatical structures with actual language use. The authors look at corpora representing four different registers (spontaneous conversation, fiction, newspaper language and academic writing) and catalogue the lexical items and syntactic structures. In many cases, their research has overturned the conventional wisdom.

Part 1

English as a linguistic system

Chapter 2

Vocabulary

In this and the next chapter the words of the modern English language will be at the centre of our discussion. Chapter 3 will focus on combinations of words (so-called **multi-word units** like idioms and proverbs). In this chapter the English vocabulary will be looked at from various points of view: the concept of *word* and the relationship between words and meaning; the major types of dictionaries; the structure and development of the English vocabulary; new words in the media and the Internet; euphemisms; non-sexist language; word formation; how words change their meanings; and a model commonly useful in the analysis of the English vocabulary.

2.1 WORDS AND MEANING

The vocabulary of the English language is conveniently recorded in dictionaries, of which the second edition of the *Oxford English Dictionary* (1989; abbreviated as *OED2* in the following) is the most recent and comprehensive. Although many people think it the greatest dictionary in the world, reviewers have no difficulty in pointing to words and phrases that are missing. Linguists draw a distinction between **dictionaries**, which are only incomplete recordings of the English vocabulary, and its total word stock, which they refer to as its **lexis** or **lexicon**.

It is not only because new words are coined all the time that it is impossible to say precisely how many words there are in English. It is also because of the vagueness of the everyday term *word*. For example, how often is the word *dictionary* used in the preceding paragraph? *Dictionary* (with a capital D) and *dictionary* are each found once while there are two examples of *dictionaries*. If we say that there are three different words (*Dictionary, dictionary, dictionaries*) we are simply referring to the physical shape of words, in this instance the black marks that appear on the paper of this book. Linguists have coined the term **word form** for this use of *word* (word forms are conventionally quoted in italics). From a different point of view we might say that there are two examples of *dictionary*, one in the singular and the other in the plural. Linguists use **word** to refer to this second, grammatical, use (no special conventions). If we say, finally, that there are four occurrences of the single word DICTIONARY we are basing our answer on the fact that, though different words and word forms are involved, they all show the same meaning. Word forms seen from the meaning point of view are called **lexemes** or **lexical items** (and are given in small caps). As lexemes can have many meanings, the need has been felt for a term which refers to the combination of one meaning with one word form. This is called a **lexical unit**. The lexeme OLD for instance represents at least two different lexical units. This becomes clear when you think of the opposite of OLD: one antonym is YOUNG, but OLD in *my old boyfriend* contrasts with NEW rather than YOUNG. What we find as main entries in dictionaries are lexemes, while each of the various meanings listed in these entries are lexical units. Having said all this, we will generally use the everyday term *word* in this book.

Words (in whatever sense) are, however, not the smallest meaningful units recognized in linguistics. Word formation goes beyond words such as {star} (called **free morphemes** because they can stand alone) and also recognizes forms such as {-dom} as meaningful. (Each of these morphemes is conventionally enclosed in braces or curly brackets.) The latter is a **bound morpheme**, which means it occurs only in combination with free morphemes (**combining forms** are an exception – they can combine with each other although they cannot stand alone, see below 2.7.4). On the other hand, it is no less important to recognize that there are combinations of more than one word, so-called **multi-word units**, like the idiom *pull someone's leg* or the proverb *he who pays the piper calls the tune*, which linguists regard as lexical items in their own right (see Chapter 3). Dictionaries often differ in whether they include not only free morphemes, but also bound morphemes, idioms and proverbs in their entries.

In the case of *dictionary* there is likely to be universal agreement that it is a word (in all of the senses), not least because it is easy to state its meaning. It is quite different for words like *the, mine* or *upon*. These **grammatical** or **closed set items** (e.g. articles, pronouns, prepositions) have grammatical functions rather than lexical meanings (e.g. the *to* in *he likes to play chess*). Indeed, they are also called **function words** because their grammatical function is often more important than their meaning. Lexical words, i.e. words with a distinctly lexical meaning, on the other hand, are members of the classes noun, verb, adjective and (partially) adverb: these are classes that do not have a limited set of members but which are constantly being added to. Such lexical items are therefore often called **open-class items**. Grammatical words can have weak stress and occur with high frequency; lexical items have strong stress.

The combination of word forms with meaning is also unproblematic in the case of *dictionary* because there are only one or two meanings (lexical units) involved. There are, however, many words which have a great number of meanings. Different linguists and lexicographers have different views on how many lexical units or lexemes to postulate in these cases. Table 2.1 shows how a few dictionaries deal with such a more complicated example, namely *romance*.

2.2 LEXICAL RELATIONSHIPS

Polysemy and homonymy   Table 2.1 mirrors the difficulties involved in deciding whether to view a given word form with several meanings as a case of polysemy (the existence of one lexeme with many related meanings) or of homonymy (the existence of different lexemes that sound the same (**homophones**) or are spelt the same (**homographs**) but have different, unrelated meanings). In the latter case we find separate main entries. Whereas AHD and COBUILD set up one main entry (= one lexeme), NODE offers two, while LDOCE has three main entries. Another finding is that LDOCE and COBUILD do

Table 2.1   Some dictionary entries for *romance*

	NODE	AHD	LDOCE	COBUILD
romance (noun)				
atmosphere	+	+	+	+
love (affair)	+	+	+	+
literary genre/work	+	+	+	+
medieval tale	+	+	+	+
exaggeration, falsehood	0	+	0	0
language family	R	+	R	0
piece of music	+	+	0	0
romance (adjective)				
relating to the Romance language family	R	+	0	+
romance (verb)				
exaggerate	+	0	r	0
court, woo	+	+	r	+

Notes: NODE = *The New Oxford Dictionary of English*, Oxford 1998. AHD = *The American Heritage College Dictionary*, 3rd edn, Boston 1993. LDOCE = *Longman Dictionary of Contemporary English*, 4th edn, Harlow 2003. COBUILD = *Collins COBUILD English Dictionary*, 3rd edn, London 2001

+	=	contained in main or only entry
r	=	additional main entry, small letter
R	=	additional main entry, capital letter
0	=	not recorded

not record three of the senses of the noun. This is because they are dictionaries for foreign learners that offer a more restricted coverage of lexical units. For more on types of dictionaries, see 2.3.

Synonymy   The distinction between homonyms and polysemous items has raised the question of semantic similarity and difference. Sets of lexical units that have identical, or near identical, meanings are referred to as **synonyms**. Theoretically they can take each other's place in any context but in practice there are always differences. Take the nouns *holiday, vacation, leave* and *furlough*, for example, which can all refer to a period of time when you do not do your usual work. Note how they differ in the words they occur with (their **collocations**, see Chapter 3): Sailors go on *leave*, but soldiers and people who work abroad go on *furlough*. *Leave* is often found in compounds such as *sick leave, maternity leave* and *unpaid leave*. *Vacation* is used in AmE like the GenE *holiday(s)* and can refer in both BrE and AmE to the time when no teaching is done at colleges and universities, although the informal short form *vac* for a university break (as in *long vac*) is restricted to BrE (the word form *vac* in AmE is an abbreviation of *vacuum cleaner*). Informal, short-ened *hols* is also BrE but is, in addition, somewhat old fashioned (public school) language. It is usual to say that synonyms share their **denotation**, or central meaning, while they differ in their **connotations**, whether regional, social, stylistic or temporal aspects.

Hyponymy and meronymy   Other relationships between words in **word fields** are **hyponymy**, or **inclusion**, which relates a general to a more specific term, e.g. *flower*, on the one hand, and *fuchsia, marigold* or *rose*, on the other. Lexical units such as *flower* are called **superordinate terms** while what they include are their **(co-)hyponyms**. **Meronymy**, in contrast, is a part–whole relationship with the parts being different from the (superordinate) whole, as in *church* versus *aisle, transept, chapel* and *steeple*.

Opposition   The relationship between the days of the week and the months of the year is called **incompatibility**, or **heteronomy**, and involves more than two members of a category which share one or more meaning elements and are mutually exclusive. **Antonymy** also holds between two or more members of the same category but here the members are arranged on a scale with clear end points, called **antonyms**, e.g. *hot* and *cold*, with *warm, lukewarm* and *cool* taking up positions between the extremes. It should again be noted that the same word form can be antonymous with more than one other word form: *old–new* (*car*) and *young–old* (*man*). This makes it clear that semantic relationships hold between lexical units, not lexemes. **Complementarity** is a distinct case of semantic opposition. It refers to absolute contrasts like *dead* and *alive, married* and *single*: if you use the one term then you have to deny the other. While antonymy allows comparatives (*hotter, colder*), complementarity does not (**deader*). Related to complementary pairs are **converses**, like *lend* and *borrow, husband* and *wife*, which look at the same relationship from different perspectives: the sentence *she is his wife* can be reversed to produce the reciprocal correlate *he is her husband*. When converses express movements in opposite directions they can be called **reverses**, e.g. *come* and *go, to* and *fro, up* and *down*. For an example of how lexical relationships work in texts see 6.2 and 6.3.

2.3 DICTIONARIES

Mental lexicon   It has been said that all dictionaries are out of date as soon as they are published: this is so because no dictionary can hope to include all the lexemes that are stored in the brains of its speakers. The vocabulary stored in the minds of the speakers of a language is called the **mental lexicon**. It is not only much larger than any published dictionary, it is also structured quite differently: its arrangement includes and goes beyond the alphabet and may be based on similarity (or contrast) in sound and, above all, meaning. This means that synonyms and antonyms are stored closely together in the brain, but also variants in syntax and pronunciation, information on the currency, frequency and social acceptance of lexemes as well as such features as the age, gender and social status of its speakers. The mental lexicon is therefore a complex, comprehensive and ever changing structure that no print or electronic dictionary can compete with, although thesauruses, field and learner dictionaries make use of some non-alphabetical structural principles.

An important general distinction is that between printed or **print dictionaries** and those on CD-ROM. **Electronic dictionaries** save space on your book shelves and tend to be quicker to use while perhaps giving less physical pleasure. What is crucial to realize is that there are different types of CD-ROM dictionaries. One type, often available for free, offers the text of a printed dictionary in electronic form and can only be used to access main entry words. Another type tends to make full use of the electronic medium by including visual and video materials and allows users to search for words in the complete text of the dictionary (this is called **full-text search**), which often finds more words than are listed as **head words**: *OED2*, for instance, has no entry for the verb *free up* but a full-text search comes up with two examples. Such a search gives you a complete set of examples (or **concordance**) in the context of the item searched for, which is invaluable for language teaching as well as a full linguistic description. This more sophisticated type of CD-ROM must usually be bought separately and can cost more than the print edition, but it is money well spent. In the following, dictionaries will be referred to by short titles, while a classified list of dictionaries with full references can be found in the Bibliography of dictionaries at the end of this book.

2.3.1 Dictionaries for scholars and native speakers

The two major groups of dictionaries for the purposes of this book are those that are published with a native speaker audience in mind and those that are meant for people whose first language is not English.

Historical dictionaries   *OED2* represents an outstanding lexicographic achievement. It offers the most up-to-date research into every aspect of lexemes: the history and present state of their spelling, pronunciation and meaning, together with their relationships with words in other languages and many examples, fully dated, referenced and arranged chronologically. The third edition, now being published on the Internet, makes up for former shortcomings with, for example, a better coverage of colloquialisms, native speaker varieties of English around the world and more careful and updated etymologies. Following the OED's model, many other English speaking countries have produced their national dictionaries on historical principles.

Desk dictionaries   For everyday use large, unabridged dictionaries are too unwieldy and extensive. In their place users turn to **desk** (the BrE term) or **college** (the AmE term) dictionaries, of which the American volumes had entries for people, places and events (so-called **encyclopedic entries**) long before their British counterparts, some of which still do not have this type of information (e.g. the *Concise Oxford Dictionary* and the *New Penguin Dictionary of English*).

Conceptual dictionaries and thesauruses   While the dictionaries mentioned so far are all arranged in alphabetical order, the **concept(ual)** or **thematic dictionary** arranges its words in groups by their meaning. The first fully-fledged work of this kind was published by P.M. Roget (*Thesaurus of English Words and Phrases*, 1852), and has appeared in many revised and expanded editions since then.

2.3.2 Non-native speaker dictionaries

The thesaurus type of dictionary is typical of native speaker dictionaries in that it usually gives long lists of words without illustrative examples or other information on how to use them. Thesauruses are for people who know their English, and they cannot be recommended to learners of English, who need to be shown how words behave in context so that they can really use them. The only thesaurus to do that is the *Longman Lexicon*.

Learner dictionaries   Desk dictionaries for people with English as their first language (or **L1-dictionaries**, to use the technical term) have word lists (referred to as the **macrostructure**) in excess of 150,000 items and usually give their etymologies. Dictionaries for foreign learners (or **L2-dictionaries**), on the other hand, have so far not offered etymologies nor do their word lists exceed 100,000 words and phrases. Again, native speaker dictionaries are meant for people who want to find out the meaning, pronunciation and spelling of words they do not know. In contrast, dictionaries for non-native speakers, while giving similar semantic, phonetic and orthographic help, also include information on how a word behaves syntactically, what word combinations or collocations it enters into and how it differs from words with similar meanings (synonym discrimination). While both dictionary types indicate whether a word is formal or informal, taboo or vulgar, the learner dictionaries take greater care to explain the meaning of words in simple English, often using a restricted number of words to do this (between 2,000 and 3,000 items). They also lead readers quickly to the various lexical units of lexemes, for which they use brief glosses that come before definitions; provide a great number of (sentence) examples, both British and American English equivalents in pronunciation and vocabulary (e.g. 'UK pavement, see *sidewalk* US'), and special usage notes, which demonstrate the correct, and warn against the incorrect, use of words. To make a pointed, if not wholly accurate contrast: L1-dictionaries are satisfied with helping you to find out about words (here one speaks of **decoding dictionaries**) while L2-dictionaries take much greater pains to help you produce correct and idiomatic English (**production dictionaries**, also referred to as **encoding dictionaries**).

Dictionaries of word combinations   These have a much reduced macrostructure but offer a detailed **microstructure**, listing the most important lexical and syntactic combinations, and often a good selection of fixed expressions such as **phrasal verbs** which are an important, because very frequent, type of verb in English.

Dictionaries of cultural literacy   Language is of course only one aspect of the culture of the countries where English is spoken. If you want to understand English language texts you also need to be aware of people, places, events, the arts, amusement and leisure activities, allusions to, or quotations from, mythology, the Bible, Shakespeare etc. and the meanings and connotations they have for native speakers.

Quite a number of dictionaries, both of the native and non-native speaker varieties are available on the **Internet** (for details see the Bibliography of dictionaries).

2.4 GROWTH AND STRUCTURE OF THE ENGLISH VOCABULARY

The English vocabulary, as with all languages, grows either by borrowing from external sources (these are called **loan formations**) or by internal means, using English word formation processes and, to a much smaller extent, by a combination of the two.

English has changed dramatically over the centuries from a language whose lexis was almost completely Germanic (in Old English times, that is, up to about 1100) to one which has taken in words from all the major languages of the world. Foreign influence shows in **loan words** as well as **loan translations** and **loan shifts**, where only the meaning, but not the form, has been borrowed, see OE *cneoht* 'farm hand' > ModE *knight* under the influence of Old French *chevaler*.

2.4.1 The three layers

By far the most important non-native items in English are those from French and the classical languages, Latin and Greek. Together they give us three historical layers: an Anglo-Saxon, a French and a classical one, each with its own characteristics. **French loans** have made their way into the language since the Norman Conquest of England in 1066; and although they were originally part of the class dialect of the new rulers, they have in the meantime, lost their connotations of prestige, social superiority or courtliness and have become part of the central core of English lexis. French-derived words are prominent for instance in the fields of art and architecture, fashion, religion, hunting, war and politics, but they are especially prominent in food and cooking.

How can the different strata be distinguished and characterized? English often uses Anglo-Saxon words for raw materials and basic processes while words for finished products and more complicated processes come from the French. A classic example of this, mentioned by Sir Walter Scott in the first chapter of his novel *Ivanhoe*, are the Anglo-Saxon animal terms *pig/sow*, *cow* and *calf* as opposed to their meat, *pork*, *beef* and *veal*. While *cook* is Anglo-Saxon, *boil*, *broil*, *fry*, *grill* and *roast* are French, as is *chef*. There is a similar division, this time between the names for the raw materials and the tradesmen, in Anglo-Saxon *beard*, *hair*, *cloth*, *meat*, *stone* and *wood* as opposed to *barber*, *tailor*, *butcher*, *mason* and *carpenter*.

While French contributed a great many terms from the realms of power and the higher arts of living and working, **classical loans** have provided English as well as most other (European) languages with countless technical terms in all branches of human knowledge, a need that was strongly felt by English humanists of the sixteenth century, who wanted English to become a medium capable of expressing the most refined thoughts, on a par with Latin and Greek (see also 6.6.2). *Lexis*, *lexeme*, *lexical*, *lexicographer*, *diction(ary)* and *vocabulary* are all derived from Latin and Greek elements, while only the rarer items *word book* and *word stock* are Germanic in origin.

An illustration of the interplay between Anglo-Saxon, French and Latin/Greek is provided by **kinship terms**, where the basic words go back to Anglo-Saxon times (*father, mother, husband, wife; son, daughter, sister* and *brother*), while *grandmother* and *grandfather* are **hybrid formations**, consisting of elements from more than one language, in this case French (*grand*) and Anglo-Saxon *father* and *mother*. *Aunt* (first recorded in the *OED* in 1297) and *uncle* (1290) come from the Latin via French as do *niece* and *nephew* (1297) while *family* (1545) has been imported directly from the Latin.

How does English form adjectives to go with these kinship nouns? One way is formations with the suffix {-ly}, of which only four are at all frequent, namely *fatherly, motherly, brotherly* and *sisterly*. They show meanings that range from neutral to (more often) positive: a *motherly woman* is kind and gentle, and so is *fatherly advice*. *Daughterly, sonly, husbandly* and *wifely* are old-fashioned and regularly used only when one wants to be humorous, ironic or self-consciously archaic or to characterize someone as pompous. Formations with {-like} (*daughter-, son-like* etc.), though listed in some dictionaries, do not seem to be in wide use either. Modern English uses genitive constructions (*a mother's love, father's behaviour, daughter's duty* etc.) in neutral contexts while it employs various Latin-derived adjectives in formal contexts, such as *filial* (= of a son or daughter), which is found in frequent combination with *love, obedience, piety*.

Avuncular (1831) goes with *uncle* but has the more general meaning of 'behaving in a kind way towards younger people, like an uncle does to his nieces and nephews'.

In addition, there are a number of quasi-synonymous adjectives: *maternal* competes with *motherly*, *paternal* with *fatherly*, *soror(i)al* with *sisterly*, and *fraternal* with *brotherly*. While *maternal* and *paternal* can have the same positive meaning as *motherly* and *fatherly* (*maternal/paternal affection*), they are perhaps more often used neutrally to refer to an ancestor, as in my *maternal/paternal grandmother*, i.e. my grandmother on my mother's/father's side. *Maternal* and *paternal* are also often used in scholarly and formal contexts, e.g. *paternal/maternal line* (in anthropology). *Fraternal* is perhaps most common in the collocation *fraternal twin*, where it contrasts with *identical twin*, while *sororal polygyny* is used in anthropology to refer to the custom of preferring the first wife's sister(s) as secondary wives. Similar differences in formality and meaning are found between *fatherhood* and *paternity*, *motherhood* and *maternity*. An abstract term to refer to the relations between members of a family is the French-derived *consanguinity* (*c*.1380), to which were added *blood-relationship* (1709) and *kinship* (1866) in mid Victorian England.

To sum up this discussion: most of the basic terms, simple and derived, are Anglo-Saxon, stylistically neutral and often associated with positive feelings, while the more peripheral and abstract terms come from French and Latin, are often found in formal contexts and carry specialized meanings. The English vocabulary is, then, a good example of a lexically mixed language, but that is true only with reference to the 616,500 word forms which we find in the *OED*. The three layers differ significantly in their share of the vocabulary and their frequency of use. It has been calculated that a majority of words, 64 per cent, in the *Shorter Oxford Dictionary* come from Latin, French and Greek while the Germanic element amounts to no more than 26 per cent. On the other hand, when we look at the items actually used in writing and speaking we find that the front runners are native English words. Of the roughly 4,000 most frequent words 51 per cent are of Germanic origin and 48 per cent of Latin and Romance origin while the Greek element is negligible. The 12 most frequent verbs in the *Longman Spoken and Written English Corpus* are all Germanic – *say*, *get*, *go*, *know*, *think*, *see*, *make*, *come*, *take*, *want*, *give* and *mean*. This shows the paramount importance of the inherited Germanic vocabulary in the central core of English. Loan words from French and Latin or Greek are, as we have seen, more peripheral, though relative frequencies vary by text type (see 6.3) and stylistic level: the more formal the style and the more specialized and remote from everyday experience the subject matter, the higher the number of loans will usually be. In everyday language, the English word will often be preferred because it is vague and covers many shades of meaning, while loan words tend to be more precise and restricted and so more difficult to handle. Thus, when faced with the choice between *acquire*, *obtain* and *purchase*, on the one hand, and *buy* or *get* on the other, most people will go for the short Anglo-Saxon words. In formal situations it may seem appropriate to *extend* or *grant a cordial reception*, while in less stiff situations you will *give a warm welcome*. The old-established items are usually warmer, more human, more emotional, while many (polysyllabic) loans from Greek, Latin or the Romance languages are cold and formal and put a distance between sender (speaker, writer) and addressee (listener, reader).

2.4.2 Hard words and their consequences

Several reasons have been put forward for the difference between overall distribution and actual use of the vocabulary. The emotional and everyday character of the native words makes them the words of choice for most situations. Another reason would seem to be the embarrassment of riches (a loan translation of French *embarras de richesse*) in English which can have two or three different lexemes (of different origins) to express a given meaning. This wealth of expressions is a welcome challenge for highly educated people with time on their hands but has always posed problems for the average native speaker. This is, incidentally, also one reason for the advent of English dictionaries at the end of the sixteenth century, at the height of the influx of learned loan words from the classical languages: they started as word lists that explained these difficult **hard words** to people with little formal education.

Besides being difficult to pronounce and spell, hard words are difficult for people without a knowledge of Latin because they often cannot easily be related to other words. Verbs like *defer, prefer, infer* or *assist, desist* and *insist* have to be learnt separately because English does not have the roots *{-fer} or *{-sist}. This also goes for such formally similar items as *pathos, pathetic* and the combining form {patho-} (as in *pathogen* or *pathological*).

The semantic difficulties of hard words are increased by formal problems. If you have social aspirations, you might well think a mastery of these erudite words the royal road to social status and advancement, as in this example where a socially adroit young American WASP (= *White Anglo-Saxon Protestant*) wants to impress his wife's senior colleague and his female partner, a head teacher:

> She should have known better than to doubt Jazz's social skills. . . . She did note, however, that he was aiming an inordinate number of four and five-syllable words at the headmistress when shorter ones would have done fine. Their discussion was fairly straightforward and . . . innocuous . . . such purposely inoffensive conversation did not require 'eventuate' and 'dissimilitude' on Jazz's part. Fortunately, he calmed down later, reverting to short, friendly words
>
> (S. Isaacs, *Lily White*, New York 1997, p. 429)

Jazz is only one of many fictional characters in English language literature since Shakespeare who try to make social capital out of their command of Latinisms. While Jazz is well educated and therefore brings off this linguistic feat – and, as he relaxes, returns to Anglo-Saxon words, which are much more appropriate to the party atmosphere – many other fictional characters are less certain of their hard words and are made fun of for getting their Latinisms wrong; for example, using *paradigm* where *paragon* is intended ('The Council is not a paradigm of virtue'). Huck Finn, knowing that difficult words are monstrously long, produces *preforeordestination* instead of comparatively humble *predestination* (*The Adventures of Huckleberry Finn*, Chapter 18). This blunder, called a **malapropism**, is not merely funny or confined to literature: an incensed crowd in England recently threatened a *paediatrician* (children's doctor) because they thought she was a *paedophile*, a person who is sexually attracted to children.

There can, then, be no doubt that hard words pose major problems. What have English speakers done to come to grips with these difficulties? There are various phenomena that have been linked to hard words. One of them is called **folk etymology**, in which the foreign form is changed to resemble English words or morphemes, as in *crayfish* for *crevisse* or *causeway* for French *chaussée*.

Another way of dealing with hard words is to shorten them and make them into mono-syllables, which are a characteristic feature of the English vocabulary: the most frequent 200 words in English consist overwhelmingly of one syllable; there are a few two-syllable ones (40 in AmE, 24 in BrE), and a handful of trisyllabic forms (3 in AmE, 2 in BrE), while only AmE has a single four-syllable item, the word *American* itself. Examples are *condo* < *condominium, pram* < *perambulator, pro* < *professional*, and *tec* < *detective*. These examples are exclusive to English while other clippings are shared with some European languages which also have, for example, *bus* < *omnibus*. It is not unlikely that some zero-derived forms, especially when they consist of one syllable, can also be explained as a means of avoiding overly formal Latinisms, e.g. *Petrarch's climb in 1353 of Mount Ventoux*, where *climb* is used instead of *ascent*.

Again, rather than employing polysyllabic Latinisms, English goes for the native form but adds native elements to create new meanings. This has resulted in **multi-word verbs**, or **phrasal verbs**, and the nouns derived from them, such as *A war would clearly set back the process of reform* and *the breakdown in talks represents a serious setback in the peace process*. Indeed, so strong is the pull of these phrasal formations that some simple verbs have formed new phrasal counterparts, often apparently without much of a meaning differ-ence, e.g. *They met up again for a glass of wine in the hotel bar*. Another aspect of this preference, and also perhaps sometimes the result of the avoidance of hard words, are lexicalized phrases such as *do one's hair, put someone on hold* (= make them wait on the phone), *do sums, have a think, give something a try* and *give someone a ring* (on the phone). The last three examples show that English sometimes prefers these phrases even where there is a synonymous simple verb (*think, try, ring*).

There is, moreover, the use of proper names for concrete nouns **(eponyms, toponyms)**, *china* (rather than *porcelain*), *Kleenex* (instead of *tissue* or *paper handkerchief*), *magnet, stetson* or *bowie knife*, all eponyms. A classic example is *Hoover* instead of *vacuum cleaner*, but this usage is restricted mainly to the UK, while AmE uses the shortened form *vacuum*. Examples of toponyms are *cashmere, champagne, damask, denim* ('of Nîmes' in France, and *jeans* (< Genoa).

A final note on hard words: they are often without the root word in English or other words that are derived from the same root (**word family**) that would define at least some of their meaning features. As a result, they have been freer to develop than their coun-terparts in other European languages where word families have often been preserved more completely. The meanings of such common European words as *actually, antic, mundane, pathetic, premises* and *sensible* differ famously between English and continental European languages (these words are called **false friends**).

2.4.3 Present day loans

It would seem that most new loan words nowadays refer to new things for which the foreign term has been taken over (so called **cultural borrowings**), while other factors are of minor importance today. Loan words were imported in the past because the terms arrived with new imports (e.g. Scandinavian *ski*, Russian *vodka*), or because of the tendency to complete word families (the Scandinavian verb *die* complemented the Old English adjective *dead* and the noun *death*). Borrowing also occurred, of course, out of sheer laziness or love of a new term (which may have sounded better, more learned or more fashionable). In more recent times, English has increased its range of donor languages, the main contributors being French, Japanese, Spanish, Italian, Latin, Greek, German, African, Yiddish, Russian and Chinese. The share of Indo-European loans has dropped in comparison with earlier times. The prominence of the Asian and African languages is qualitatively new. Often, loans are changed in form, and particularly in spelling. Finally, only the three major open word classes are represented, with nouns dominating massively over the few adjectives and even fewer verbs (for more detail see Cannon 1987).

2.5 NEW WORDS

While great numbers of foreign words have been taken into English from other languages, even more are formed by productive word formation processes from items that are already in the language. The first full length study of neologisms (Cannon 1987) presents the results of detailed investigations into 13,683 new items while Ayto 1999 affords decade-by-decade insights into what were the most important developments in the twentieth century. While the typical lexical growth areas of the 1980s were the media, computers, finance, money, environment, political correctness, youth culture and music, the 1990s saw significant lexical expansion in the areas of politics, the media and the Internet. In the first edition of this book we sketched some of the new environmental lexis; in this edition we give a brief description of developments in the media and the Internet.

The *digital revolution* has progressed far beyond the *PC* (*personal computer*) and given us the *digital compact disk* (*CD*) as well as the *digital video disk* (*DVD*). Information in all walks of life is *digitized* (= put into digital form) and *high-tech*(*nology*) *industries* have produced such things as *smart bombs and weapons* (that are fired from aircraft and guided by a computer), *smart buses* (equipped with all sorts of electronic devices to improve service and security) that can use *intelligent highways* (that monitor traffic flow and help drivers to avoid bottlenecks) and *smart cards* that will allow people to load their *mobile/cell phones* (or *mobiles/cellulars*) with *electronic cash* (also *e-cash*). There are concerns that while the West gets *wired* (= hooked up to the Internet), the poor countries of this world are in danger of falling ever further behind – this is the so-called *digital divide*. But as the cost of *ICT* (= information and communication technology) falls, poor countries stand a good chance of catching up.

As the telecommunications market has opened up with private competition challenging the old national monopoly carriers, the dream of merging telephones with computers and the Internet seems to be growing nearer. This has usually resulted in a lowering of costs and has led to the setting up of *call centres* which sell goods via the phone (*tele-marketing, telesales*). The major growth sector in telecommunications is however that of *mobile telephony*. In the not too distant past there were only *fixed* or *landline* telephones, which allowed people only to talk to each other while holding a *receiver* in their hand, while the main part of a mobile phone is a *handset*. So common are mobiles now in many countries that legislators have banned the use of *hand-held* phones while driving. To make *mobiles* (*cell[ular] phones* or simply *cells* in the US) indispensable to customers, their function is being vastly extended: Soon smart new phones will allow people also to check their e-mail, consult the Internet, shop (there is talk of *m-commerce* = *mobile commerce*), plan their schedules (up to now the job of an *electronic organizer* or *personal digital assistant* (*PDA*)), manage their bank accounts and load their phones with electronic cash (and thus make *ATM*s or *cash machines* superfluous), and send *text messages* or *text* them. To save time and money, the *digerati* (people who understand computers and high tech) use various *emoticons* (graphic symbols that are added at the end of a message and convey emotions), such as a smile [☺] (called a *smiley*). The same function is served by a great number of new abbreviations used in e-mail as well as in *SMS* (short messaging system): *AFAIK* = as far as I know; *GIGO* = garbage (= invalid data) in, garbage out; *ROTFL* = rolling on the floor (laughing).

The Internet, informally referred to as the *Net* or the *Web* (short for *World Wide Web*) has changed the way we live and learn, do business and keep informed. To make use of it, you need to sign up to an *access provider* (or *ISP* = *Internet Service Provider*) that will link (*wire*) your computer to the Net for a fee, and you also need specialized software (*a browser*) to view the billions of web pages. To save time and frustration, many people use *search engines* or *meta-engines* that allow classified searches by field of interest and come up with lists of web pages. More and more *portals* are set up that serve as gateways to other sites. Modern browsers are more than just *HTML* (= Hypertext markup language, used to produce pages that can be put on the Net) viewers; they are multimedia tools in their own right: they can play music and videos, allow you to handle e-mail, make safe connections to *e-commerce* (= *electronic commerce*) sites, *download* (= transfer) information from the Web onto your own computer and much more.

Two common elements used to produce new words related to the Internet are {cyber-} and {e-}: *cyber-* (*cybercafé* = a cafe that offers its customers computers with Internet access; *cyberfraud*; *cyberland*; *cyberterrorist* = a criminal who uses the Internet to do damage to computer systems; *cyberwidow* = the wife of a man who spends a lot of time with his computer rather than his wife); *e-*, short for *electronic*, which is almost universally combinable, as in: *e-hub* (a central site for a particular field); *e-cash*; *e-currency* (money that can be used only on the Internet); *e-money*; *e-signature* (a code that identifies the author of a document); *e-ticket*; *e-business*; *e-comm*(*erce*); *e-trade*; *e-tailer* (< electronic retailer); *e-fit* (a computer-generated picture of a suspect); *e-book* (that is not printed but can be read on a computer); *e-publishing*; and *e-zine* (< electronic magazine, which can be read on the Internet).

This fabulous new medium can also be a nuisance and is certainly open to abuse. *Screenagers* (< *screen* and *teenagers*) spend too much time with their computers; vain people go in for *ego-surfing* (checking how often their name or company is mentioned on the Web). More serious are *hackers* and *hacking*; *bugs* (see also *debug* = remove mistakes from a computer program); *spyware* (software concealed in other programs that reports back to its programmers how they are used); and all sorts of *viruses* (software that causes damage to computers). To combat these problems, one needs *cybercops* and *firewalls* (that control access between the public Internet and private *LAN*s = *local area networks*). The Internet has of course various sites where you can find out more about Internet language, such as *www.netlingo.com*, a site that is regularly updated.

2.6 EUPHEMISMS AND POLITICALLY CORRECT LANGUAGE

Euphemisms   Euphemisms are the result, not of changes in the real world, but of changes in the conscience of a society in areas where it feels guilt or is afraid to talk about a taboo subject. These areas have traditionally been the human body, death, sex, violence and money. But other fields are also involved – for example prisons, which have become *correctional centres* or *rehabilitative correctional facilities*, or menial jobs, so that servants can be referred to as *domestic engineers*, and refuse/garbage collectors as *disposal operatives* (BrE) or *sanitation engineers* (AmE). These euphemisms soon lose their force and new ones have to be created that are (as yet) free of the guilty or embarrassing association, and in this way euphemisms increase the word stock of English. Not only are euphemisms the cause of increased lexical turnover, but they can also cause the loss of a lexical unit. A recent case is that of *gay*, both noun and adjective, which is currently used almost exclusively in the sense of 'homosexual' and has almost completely lost its older sense of *happy*.

PC language   While euphemisms are universal, **politically correct (PC) language** (especially non-sexist; see 9.1) is employed to different degrees in English speaking countries. It was first developed, and is most regularly and frequently used, in the United States, particularly in official documents while Britain and other nations are less keen to right past wrongs in the language they use. A well known case is the terminology for people 'of African heritage' in the US. Some prefer to be called *African-American*, a word which has (partially) replaced *Afro-American*, which (partially) replaced the term *Black*, which (partially) replaced *Negros*, which in turn largely replaced *Coloured*, which replaced earlier *Black*. For people with disabilities, new phrasal adjectives like *hearing-impaired*, *mentally/physically challenged* and *visually impaired/challenged* have been coined, which are, however, also used to make fun of PC language, e.g. *residentially challenged* (= homeless), *vertically challenged* (= short) or *financially challenged* (= poor).

2.7 WORD FORMATION

Word formation processes account for almost 80 per cent of the new lexical items in Cannon's material (Cannon 1987: 279), as compared with new meanings (14.4 per cent) and borrowings (7.5 per cent). In this section we will look at the most productive word formation processes only, using the two operations of deletion and combination as the basis of the present treatment (see Algeo 1978).

Cannon has found that composite forms, which consist of derivations and compounds, take the lion's share with 54.9 per cent, followed by shifts (19.6 per cent) and shortenings (18 per cent), a ranking confirmed by Algeo 1998. Compounds (4,040, of which 3,591 are nouns) are the oldest category, and while they are still the largest class overall, as they have been throughout the history of the English language, Cannon thinks that 'shortenings provide the newest and perhaps potentially the most productive categories for the near future' (ibid.: 246).

Shifts and blends, as well as acronyms and back formations, are processes that few native speakers are aware of. Not many people will know, for instance, that the verb *beg*

Table 2.2　Word formation processes

process	combination	deletion	example
shift	–	–	(it's a big) *if*
blend	+	+	*infomercial* < information commercial
shortening	–	+	*tech*(nology)
composite forms	+	–	*swipe card, spammer*

is derived from *beggar* by back formation, or that the verb *beggar* (as in *they had been beggared by the war*) is a shift which comes later in time than the noun, or that *smog* combines *smoke* and *fog*. Speaking synchronically, we would analyse the *beg–beggar* relationship like any other pair such as *lie–liar* or *bake–baker* and assume that the noun is derived from the verb by adding a suffix. The word form *beggar* (noun and verb), we would say, shows multiple class membership, and *smog* is an unanalysable addition to the lexicon. On the other hand, composition, derivation and shortening, at least where the long form is retained, are more obvious as processes even to the lay person who only knows the contemporary language.

The following discussion, which relies heavily on Cannon's findings, does not always adopt his categories. Furthermore, not all the examples in Cannon's corpus or, for that matter, in the following pages will become a permanent part of the English language. They illustrate, however, certain trends and structural possibilities which are currently found in the English language.

2.7.1 Shifts

Shifts, like blends, are typical of English and were made possible through the loss of inflectional endings in the Middle English period (1100–1500). Shifts are lexemes that have been assigned a new word class without change in the form of the underlying lexeme. Various terms are used to refer to this process: **functional shift**, **conversion**, **multiple class membership** as well as **zero derivation**. The last term has been coined in recognition of the fact that this process can be seen as a kind of derivation without an affix: as *humid* (adj.) is to *humidify* (verb) (= make humid), so is *wet* (adj.) to *wet* (v.) (= make wet, as in *Wetting a paper towel, I wiped the blood off her arm*). The new items can share some (**partial conversion**) or all the features of the new word class (**complete conversion**). In some cases it will be impossible to decide which word came first but in many others we can look the words up in the *OED* and compare the dates of the first examples. Also, the source word is usually part of the definition of the later, derived item (*to party* = have a party; or *a swallow* = the amount that you can drink etc. in one swallow) but not the other way round (*party* = a social occasion when people get together to have a good time; *to swallow* = make drink go down your throat). Conversion most often results in nouns, followed by verbs (most of which are shifted from nouns) and adjectives.

Nouns: the *commute* is too long (= way to work); healthy *eats* (= food); give me a *for-instance* (= example); the replacements were a ragtag bunch of *has-beens* and *never-wases*; let's have an *update* on the traffic situation (= most recent information)

Verbs: the package had gone off to be fingerprinted and *DNA'd* and I was still being questioned; the audience do *intake* their breath when the women kiss; my mom *parented* six kids in Queens; the cruise missiles were heading for their targets, the aircraft *smart-bombing* from the skies; could you *video* the show for me at 7 p.m.?

Adjectives: He was a *can-do* guy; it was a *fun* party

This is perhaps a good place to mention **secondary shifts**, in which word forms move from one subclass to another within the same word class. Thus, *press* as in *the American press* or *meet the press* is a mass (non-count) noun, but the word can also be used as a count noun (*how many press* [= journalists] were there?). *Okay* has been in adjectival use for a long time, usually in predicative position (e.g. *don't worry, she's okay*), but it is now found in attributive position as well, i.e. before a noun, *Don't worry, Mom. I'm having an OK time.*

Two productive processes relate to verbs. First, the formation of new transitive verbs from intransitive ones where the new verb has a causative meaning: I will *drag on* this litigation forever (= make it go on); I grabbed him by the arm and *hurried him along* (= got him to hurry up); a shudder *chattered* my teeth and *shivered* my shoulders.

Second, a large number of intransitive verbs are formed from transitive ones, with a passive meaning. The best known example is perhaps the verb *sell*, as in *the book sells well*, which is also found in a more complex structure like *the novel has sold a million copies* (= a million copies of the novel have been sold). There are various labels for these verbs, among them **pseudo-intransitives**, or **notional or adverbial passives** (see 5.4.4), the latter because they often take an adverb of manner (*I don't anger/bruise/frighten easily*).

2.7.2 Blends

Blends (also called **telescope** or **portmanteau words**) are the fusion of the forms and meanings of two lexemes. The first item usually loses something at the end, and the second something at the beginning. Traditionally, blends have had at least one shared element (e.g. *motel* < *motor* and *hotel*) but more recent formations show no common elements (e.g. *brunch* < *breakfast* and *lunch*). They are characteristic of English, though they represent only a mere one per cent of new formations in Cannon's corpus. Blends are very popular in journalism, advertising and technical fields (especially names) and tend to belong to a more informal stylistic level. The majority of portmanteau words are nouns, with only ten adjectives and three verbs in Cannon's corpus:

Verbs: *gues(s)timate* < *guess, estimate*
            skyjack < *sky, hijack*

Adjectives: *glitzy* < *glitter, ritzy*

Nouns: *Chunnel < Channel, tunnel*
            edutainment < education, entertainment
            stagflation < stagnation, inflation
            three-peat < three, repeat (winning a competition three times)

2.7.3 Shortenings

Of the many processes which come under the heading of **shortenings** we will give examples for back formations, initialisms, clippings or stump words and ellipses. The smallest group is **back formations** which have lost what is mistakenly thought to be an affix or inflection, as in *edit < editor* and *buttle < butler*. Indeed, the major traditional class change found in Cannon's material is noun to verb; the remaining examples are new nouns and adjectives. The major patterns in the corpus are loss of {-ion} (e.g. *intuit < intuition*), {-er} or {-ing} in nouns, and loss of {-ic} in adjectives to form new nouns. There are also a host of new formations. Most striking among these are perhaps the result of the loss of {-y} (*complicit, funk, glitz, laze, raunch, sleaze*), the loss of a presumed prefix as in *ept* (*< inept*) and *flappable* (*< unflappable*), various additions after shortening (especially {-e}: *back-mutate, decapitate, enthuse*), and the rare loss of a root in *hyper* (*< hyperactive*). Native speakers get a lot of fun out of forming new back formations which might one day make it into the dictionaries: 'It had been a rough day, so when I walked into the party, I was very *chalant*, despite my efforts to appear *gruntled* and *consolate*. I was *furling* my *wieldy* umbrella for the coat check when I saw her . . . She was a *descript* person, a woman in a state of total *array*' (our italics; *chalant* is formed from *nonchalant*, *wieldy* from *unwieldy* etc; Burridge and Mulder 1998: 120).

   Initialisms are historically the most recent group; two types are usually distinguished, acronyms and abbreviations. Though both consist of a number of first letters, **acronyms** are pronounced as words (they are also called **syllable words**) whereas abbreviations are pronounced as a series of letters (**letter words**). Well established acronyms are *laser* (< lightwave amplification by stimulated emission of radar) and *scuba* (< self-contained underwater breathing apparatus); more recent are *AIDS* (acquired immune deficiency syndrome), *dinky* (< dual income, no kids + {-y}), *NIMBY* (< not in my backyard), *WYSIWYG* (= what you see is what you get) and *yuppy* (< young urban professional + {-y}). Cannon counts 153 acronyms (all but four of them nouns) as opposed to 460 **abbreviations**. Of the latter, all but three are nouns, consist for the most part of three letters, usually all capitals, and belong to fields like chemistry or health, transport, the military, computers and education. Examples are *AI* (Amnesty International; artificial intelligence); *ATV* (all-terrain vehicle in both AmE and BrE; Associated Television in BrE); *BP* (beautiful people in AmE; British Petroleum in BrE); *CAD* (computer-aided design); *CR* (consciousness raising).

   There are two major types of **clipping – front- and back-clipping**. The second is the more frequent, while medial and mixed shortenings, though not uncommon, are less frequent.

Mixed: *comp < accompany*; *van < advantage*
Medial: *vegan < vegetarian*; *veggies < vegetables*
Front: *fiche < microfiche*; *foil < hydrofoil*; *'tude < attitude*

Back: *autoland < automatic landing; detox < detoxification; flip < flippant; glam <*
glamorous; limo < limousine; lit(erary)-crit(icism); metro < metropolitan;
rehab < rehabilitation

In the case of **ellipses**, a new word has been formed by leaving out one of the two original words with the remaining part taking on the meaning of the whole. This is an extremely common process, typical of colloquial and informal English: *Alzheimer's*, *Parkinson's* <~ disease; a *non-profit* <~ organization (US); *anchor* < anchorman or -woman; *daily* <~ cleaning woman or newspaper; *life* <~ sentence, as in *he got life*; *mobile* <~ phone.

2.7.4 Composite forms

These can be roughly divided into compounds and derivations. **Compounds** consist of two or more free morphemes, which can be either simple (as are the morphemes in *book token*) or complex (*childhood sweetheart*). **Derivations** are made up of one or more free morphemes and at least one bound morpheme, e.g. *handy* < {hand} + {-y}. Bound morphemes in word formation are called **affixes**, of which **prefixes** come before, and **suffixes** after the free form. There are no bound **infixes** in English (affixes that are inserted into word forms), but highly informal English does know a few cases of insertion of free morphemes. Examples are usually of an objectionable (vulgar, obscene) nature:

> Up at three-**goddamn**-thirty in the morning, so I can drive to the Air-**god**-Force-**damn**-Academy to spoon-feed and clean up after these little dweebs; the world is full of lunatics and madmen and I've got to go see Miss Sai**fucking**gon.

There is also another type of bound form, called **combining form(s)**. These differ from affixes in that they tend to be of a technical nature (they are usually derived from Latin and Greek), are more recent and also can combine with other combining forms (as in *Afrophile*, *Anglophone*, *hologram*, *speleology* and *telethon*).

Compounds   Compounds are usually classified in semantic and syntactic terms. There are two types of semantic compounds, one where the compound as a whole is equivalent to (at least) one of its parts and the other where this is not the case. Thus, *goldfish* is a kind of fish, and *house party* is a kind of party. These compounds are called **endocentric** as opposed to the other type, called **exocentric**, where the compound meaning is 'idiomatic', i.e. where it is not equivalent to any of the constituent free forms. This is the case, for example, with *redcoats*, which are neither pieces of clothing nor colours, but English soldiers of the eighteenth and nineteenth centuries. Cannon has counted 3,579 new endocentric compounds as against 461 exocentric ones.

Syntactic compounds come in three types. Noun compounds constitute the over-whelmingly most frequent group (3,591), followed by adjectives (290) and verbs (135). Within noun compounds, the structure noun + noun is more than twice as common as that of adjective + noun. Also frequent are those beginning or ending with a particle (*hookup*, *standoff*). The frequency of compound nouns depends on the text type: in AmE for instance there are far fewer in conversation than in news reports.

Another frequent type is the **phrasal verb**, i.e. a simple verb plus a particle (*churn out*). In the 44 million word Lancaster Corpus of twentieth century English, these verbs are most common in fiction and conversation, as is to be expected from their colloquial nature and their use in directives such as imperatives, but are rare in newspapers and scholarly writing. The most frequently recurring phrasal verbs are formed by the lexical verbs *take*, *get* and *put*, in combination with the particles *up*, *out* and *on*.

Most compounds consist of two free forms but some items have three or more free forms. New developments in Cannon's view are exocentric structures of two words and endocentric structures consisting of more than three words.

New exocentric compounds:

Nouns:	*an around the world* (trip); *dog and pony show* ('elaborate sales or publicity campaign'); *freeze-frame*
Adjectives:	*before-tax* (income), *hatchback* (car), *on-the-job* (training); *off off Broadway* (production; = experimental, avant-garde); *larger-than-life* (leader; = very impressive)
Verbs:	*car-top* (= carry on top of a car), *blind side* (= attack critically), *nickel-and-dime* (= to ruin financially little by little)

New longer endocentric structures:

Four morphemes:	*combined-cycle gas turbine (CCGT)*; *sudden infant death syndrome*; *three-way catalytic converter*
Five:	*smaller European elm bark beetle*; *Washington-based public-policy group*
Six:	*experimental coal-fired combined-cycle plant*
Seven:	*National Abortion Rights Action League holiday sticker*

Derivations   There are almost as many derivations as compounds. Of these, derivations with prefixes (**initial affixations**) are more frequent than those with suffixes (**terminal affixations**). The main types of bound forms used in technical terms are combining forms, which are especially common in scientific/technical terms. Prefixes, suffixes and inflections, on the other hand, occur in less technical items. With regard to their word class effect, it can be said that as a rule suffixes produce word class change ({abnormal}+ {-ity}) while prefixes do not ({pre-} + {install}). It has been found for twentieth century English in general that academic writing has the most derived nouns, followed by news reporting and fiction, while spontaneous conversation has hardly any as it prefers simple nouns.

In **initial affixations**, there are six times more new items containing combining forms than prefixes. There is a strong word class link between combining forms and nouns on the one hand, and prefixes and the other open word classes on the other. Never before have so many combining forms in initial position been used in English. The most frequent of them are {micro-}, {bio-}, {immuno-}, e.g.:

{micro-}:	*chip, code, floppy, mesh, surgery, wave*
{bio-}:	*degradable, diversity, engineering*
{immuno-}:	*assay, chemistry, deficiency, suppression*

The few remaining native prefixes, {un-} and {mis-}, show low productivity. Most have been ousted by affixes of Latin and French origin, of which the most frequent are {anti-}, {non-}, {de-}, {pre-}, {super-}, {sub-}:

{anti-}:   *convulsant, depressant, hero, nuclear*
{non-}:   *art, Black, degree, event, hero, sexist, starter*
{de-}:   *regulate, selection, toxification*

Recent derivations with initial combining forms are more frequent than those formed with prefixes by almost three to two.

In **terminal affixations** the ratio between combining forms (407) and suffixes (906) is reversed. All but one of the 407 new formations involving combining forms belong to the sciences. The most frequent ones in Cannon's corpus are {-ology/-ologist}, {-in} (as in *sit-in*), {-genic}, {-meter}, {-emia}. However, some other combining forms are similarly productive and often more common, e.g.:

{-gate}   ('major political scandal', from the second element of Watergate): *Irangate, Koreagate*
{-scape}   (from the second element of *landscape*), as in *moonscape, seascape, street-scape, mindscape, dreamscape* and *sound-scape*
{-speak}   ('language of', used in a slightly derogatory way, e.g. Orwell's *newspeak*): *artspeak, computerspeak* and *winespeak*

There are more than twice as many different suffixes (98) as prefixes (42), but they are less productive (only 31 occur as many as 7 times vs 25 prefixes with at least 8 occurrences). Most productive is native {-er}, followed by {-ist}, {-ism}, {-ize}, {-ic}, {-in(e)}, and native {-y}. There is only partial overlap with the findings of Biber *et al.* 1999, who offer this list of relatively productive suffixes (again in decreasing order of frequency): {-ition}, {-ity}, {-er}, {-ness}, {-ism} and {-ment}. Examples are:

{-er}:   *backpacker, butterflyer* ('a swimmer who specializes in the butterfly'), *car pooler, flasher*
{-ist}:   *dartist, kineticist*
{-ism}:   *ableism* ('discrimination against handicapped people'), *ghettoism, middle-of-the-roadism*

Native suffixes such as {-ster}, {-ly}, {-ship}, {-dom}, {-ish} and {-hood} are hardly productive any more and have been supplanted by suffixes from Latin and French. There are a few examples of multiple affixation, with prefixes plus suffixes (*antifeedant, antifoulant, unflappable*). In other cases affixation takes place together with compounding: *wheeler-dealer*. This shows again that there is no absolute dividing line between the two types and that the term *composite form* used in this book serves a useful purpose. Other difficulties in definition are encountered with the distinction between compounds and derivations in items like *householder*: is this {household} + {-er} or {house} + {holder}? Composite forms of more than two elements often combine both processes, as in *baby boomer, gas-guzzler* or *ungentlemanly*.

Although they make up only two per cent in Cannon's corpus, **combining forms** are interesting because of their status between bound and free morphemes. They are like affixes in that they can be attached to a free morpheme, and they are like free morphemes in that one can be joined to another to form a new word, something that is not possible for affixes. The distinction between affixes and combining forms is, however, far from neat. **Initial combining forms** can be combined with established English words (*bio-chemistry, tele-conference, ethno-linguist*), sometimes in a shortened form, as in {e-} from *electronic* (*e-postcard*), {eco-} from *ecological* (*eco-activist, eco-freak*), or {Euro-} < *Europe(an)* (*Eurocheque, Eurogroup*). **Final combining forms** usually combine with another combining form, e.g. {-logy} requires an initial combining form such as {psycho-} or {socio-}. *Regicide* and *astronaut* are therefore regularly formed but what are we to make of *pigeoncide* and *spacenaut*, where the forms are combined with a free morpheme of a non-technical nature (*pigeon, space*)? Many linguists regard {-cide} and {-naut} as suffixes, a label that is also applied to {-thon} and {-aholic/-oholic}. These can combine with (English) free morphemes but are derived from the classical languages: the first is taken from *marathon* with the meaning 'something of specially long duration', as in *talkathon* (= long debate or discussion), *walkathon* (= long distance walk) or *romp-a-thon* (= an extended period of play). The second comes from *alcoholic* and has resulted in such words as *chocoholic, computerholic, spendaholic, shopaholic* and *workaholic*.

2.8 SHIFTS OF MEANING

Meaning in this section will be understood in the wider sense of the usage conditions of lexemes, which include not only semantic shifts, but also grammatical and **pragmatic shifts** (see Algeo 1998: 66ff.). A shift is called pragmatic for instance when a word is 'upgraded' from slang to colloquial to neutral, as has happened to *mob*, a shortened form (< Latin *mobile vulgus* = excitable crowd) which, although condemned by Swift in the eighteenth century, has established itself by now as a part of stylistically neutral English. The opposite has happened to *governor*, which developed a colloquial sense in the nineteenth century ('the person in authority, one's employer'), often spelled <guv'nor> or shortened to <guv>, especially as a form of address. Beside shifts in the level of formality there are those of acceptability, e.g. the use of *hopefully*, *like* as conjunction, or *flammable* (= easily set on fire) instead of historically correct *inflammable*. Next come changes in the geographical status of items, the most important type of which are nowadays AmE items that are accepted in ever increasing numbers into other national varieties, while there are many fewer British English items such as *fridge* (= shortened form of *refrigerator*) that have made it into AmE.

Semantic changes   Most **semantic changes** take place in small steps that can often be traced. Meanings are usually related by way of association, either because of their similarity or their nearness (*contiguity*). These associations can involve either the form of lexemes or their meaning; consequently, there are four different processes of meaning change:

Folk etymology   Folk etymology relates to the substitution of forms that speakers cannot (or can no longer) analyse by ones that are morphologically transparent. This has

Table 2.3 Processes of meaning change

	similarity	*contiguity*
form	folk etymology	ellipsis
meaning	metaphor	metonymy

happened to ME *bridegome* (*bride* = 'bride'; *gome* = 'man'), where the second element ceased to be understood and was altered to *groom*. A more complex example is the verb *depart* ('separate'), which was used in the wedding ceremony *till death us depart*. This meaning of *depart* became obsolete and the verb was re-analysed as *do* and *part*, and later the word order was regularized (. . . *till death do us part*). Though of considerable historical interest, folk etymology has never been a productive process.

Ellipsis　In ellipsis, part of a compound is deleted and the remaining part takes on the meaning of the whole; for examples see 2.7.3.

Metaphor　This usually involves deletion and/or addition of meaning elements (**semantic features**). *Mafia* as in *literary-mafia*, *mental health-mafia* or *office mafia* is no longer restricted to the meaning element [organized crime] and is now applied to any group that exerts an apparently sinister influence. When *dove* is applied to a politician, the meaning element 'peaceful' stays, but the feature [animal] is replaced by [human]. *Bank* in *blood-bank* or *bottle bank* has kept the element 'collection point', but has obviously lost the financial meaning. The language of computers is full of metaphors, e.g.: *breadboard* = board for making a model of an electric circuit; *mouse* = small device which controls the cursor; and *window* = any of the separate data displays on a single video screen. Metaphorical extension is also found in verbs: you can *launder* money, not just articles of clothing; you can *nurse* a drink; and you can *park* computer hard drive heads, chewing gum and even babies. Indeed, metaphors are as indispensable as our daily bread.

Metonymy　A common type of metonymy is that of a proper name which becomes used as the generic term for a commodity produced by a firm, e.g. *Xerox* or *Kleenex*. Other types of metonymy can be seen in *the leadership* = the leaders (abstract for concrete); he has no *date* for the prom (abstract for concrete: person for social occasion); *save someone's pocket* = save someone money (receptacle for content). Compare also *fare* (from money to person), *gossip* (from person to product, activity), and *shot* (as in *he is a good/poor shot*; from act to person).

2.9 MEANING CHANGE

Beside the four associative processes just discussed there are four types of meaning change which describe the semantic results: specialization (or narrowing, restriction), generalization (or widening, extension), deterioration (or pejoration, catachresis) and amelioration (a change for the better). Specialization and generalization are changes in the denotative meaning of words, while deterioration and amelioration concern their affective meaning. Cannon has found that generalizations are more numerous than specializations,

and ameliorations outnumber pejorations. Also, most changes in his corpus are from concrete to abstract meanings. In this process nouns (mostly composite forms) provide almost
two thirds of the new meanings; the remainder are accounted for chiefly by verbs and
adjectives.

Specialization and generalization   The adjectives *straight* and *bent* have, in
informal BrE, taken on specialized sexual meanings, with *straight* moving from 'conventional, respectable' to 'heterosexual', and *bent* from 'curved' > 'morally crooked' >
'homosexual'. Similarly, *glove box* has developed from 'a box for gloves' to 'a chamber
with sealed-in gloves for handling radioactive material' (metaphor). Finally, *wet* 'feeble,
weak' (informal BrE) refers to people without a strong character after having been first
applied to Conservative politicians who were suspected of Liberal tendencies (metaphor).
One and the same lexeme can undergo both these processes, witness *girl*, which in Middle
English referred to young people in general. While its present meaning is restricted to the
female sex, it can also be used to refer to adult women. A recent generalization or semantic
broadening has taken place in the phrase *you guys* in AmE, which is no longer restricted
to men and can refer to mixed company, or even women only. *Sell-by date* also shows
an extended meaning (metaphor) in *Kennedy kept Hoover on past his sell-by date*.

Amelioration and pejoration   The phrase the *state of the art* was originally a typical
(sub-) title of a report on what had been achieved in a particular field. The adjective *state-
of-the-art* has ameliorated from being neutral and merely descriptive to denote the latest,
and therefore the best of its kind (*state-of-the-art technology*). *Exposure* (= revelation of
an embarrassing truth) is no longer always something to be feared, e.g. *he had, in a few
short days of intense exposure, become a folk hero*. *Cowboy*, on the other hand, has come
via pejoration to refer to an unscrupulous businessman with little qualification. *Mental*
has developed the additional meaning of insane (*he's gone completely mental*).

Meaning and society   Changes in the affective meaning of words often reflect
changes in the evaluation that societies, or certain powerful groups in society, put on
them. It has been pointed out that some words referring to low social status have come
to express low moral evaluation, as in *churl, knave, villain*. High status terms, conversely,
now express moral approval, e.g. *free, gentle, noble* (see Hughes 1988 for more examples). To get publicity in the media nowadays, even if unfavourable, is regarded by some
people as desirable, which could explain the revaluation of *exposure*. English is in fact
rich in examples of lexemes referring to members of minorities or powerless groups that
have undergone pejoration (e.g. Blacks, homosexuals, women). Homosexuals have more
or less successfully fought this by consciously using *gay*, and Blacks have mounted a
campaign with the slogan *Black is beautiful*. The attempt to reverse the semantic status
imposed by the power elite can also be seen in the recent meanings of *bad* (= good, e.g.
He's a bad man on drums, and the fans love him), *tough* (= excellent) and *mean* (= skilful,
formidable; *she plays a mean game of chess*), which seem to have originated in the Black
community in the US.

Meaning and the language system   It must be stressed that semantic change does
not occur in isolation. Rather, semantic changes are conditioned by changes in society.
However, certain causes also lie in the language system itself, which may at least set the

scene for some meaning changes. When semantic fields adopt new members, or when established members develop new meanings, this often has consequences for other members of the field. It has been shown how the OE and early ME term for animal, *deer*, changed to its present meaning of 'ruminant animal, hooved, antlered, and with spotted young' under the pressure of the loans *beast*, *creature* and *animal*. On the other hand, when one lexeme develops a meaning that makes it a member of a new field, then other members of the original field can develop similar meanings. *Mad* and *crazy* mean not only 'insane' but also 'wildly excited', which is now one of the meanings of both *daft* and *mental* (as in *she is mental about punk rock*) in BrE. Some cookery verbs when accompanied by human beings as objects have developed meanings in the field of inflicting pain, discomfort or punishment: *grill* can mean 'interrogate', *fry* 'electrocute' and *roast* 'ridicule or criticize severely or mercilessly' (see Lehrer 1984 on lexical fields).

2.10 THE REGISTER APPROACH

2.10.1 Dialectal variation

Much has been made of the distinction in British English between U and non-U, that is, between what the upper class use and what they do not use. Almost everything and anything can indicate class: what names you give your children, where you live, your family and friends, hobbies and occupation, wealth, education etc. Meal names are well known class indicators: 'Any Englishman who does call lunch *dinner* indicates at once and for sure to any other Englishman that he hails from somewhere below the middle of the middle class' (Smith 1985: 153). Other, perhaps more contentious generalizations, which nevertheless contain a certain amount of truth, are that *afternoon tea* is U, starts at 4 p.m. and typically consists of tea, thin sandwiches and cakes. Non-U *tea* (south) or *high tea* (north) are middle and working class events starting at about 5 to 6 p.m. They are much more serious affairs and usually include one cooked course in the north. Mention should also be made of the suffix {-er(s)}, which is typical of public schools (in the BrE sense) and is used to produce informal variants of nouns and adjectives: *champers* (= champagne), *preggers* (= pregnant), *rugger* (= rugby football) and *starkers* (= stark naked, formed by ellipsis).

The upper and lower classes in the US generally also use much blunter language than the middle classes, who are insecure about their social status and therefore strive for elegance in their language, often ending up sounding pompous or affected. Thus, upper *boyfriend* and *driver* become middle *fiancé* and *chauffeur*, while *cross* can be replaced by the grand sounding *transit*, as in *several ships transited the area*. Pragmatic idioms like *goodbye* and *how do you do?* are upper and upper middle class, all others using *have a nice day* and *pleased to meet you*. These details need to be treated with some caution because they may be somewhat subjective and fashions can change quite rapidly. Also, the link between language and class is not always direct, as some non-upper class people affect certain U-usages while some (younger) upper class people in Britain seem to imitate non-U usage. All in all, however, there is no doubt that class connotations often attach to the choice of at least some lexical items just as they do to pronunciation.

2.10.2 Registers

Medium and style   Relatively little research has been carried out on spoken–written lexical differences. Biber *et al.* (1999: 65ff.), investigating the general distribution of lexical words, have found that: nouns are most common in news reports, less so in academic writing, and least frequent in conversation; adjectives are more highly represented in academic prose while rare in conversation; verbs and adverbs are most frequent in conversation and fiction, with the 12 most frequent verbs being much more common in conversation than in any other register. Conversation and academic prose differ distinctly in that scholarly writing, but not spontaneous speech, uses large numbers of verbs formed with derivational affixes, the most frequent of which being the suffix {-ize/-ise}.

Written language is primarily message oriented, often involving specific lexis. Spoken language is primarily listener oriented and shows a lack of specificity. Thus, writing is characterized by well established language that shows precise technical and specialized vocabulary items, such as polysyllabic hard words, while speech prefers short or monosyllabic words (see 2.4.1–2). Indeed, spontaneous conversation is held to be characterized by three lexical features: *imprecision, intensification* and *neologisms*. Imprecision, often due to emotional factors, loss of memory and lack of concentration or to the informality of the situation or the subject under discussion is visible in items like *things, thingy, whatsit(s)* etc., where a more exact word is not available to the speaker. Other imprecise items include vague, summary phrases at the ends of lists such as *and stuff/things, that sort of thing, and so on, and so forth*. There are also vague generic terms and collective nouns like *heaps of, bags of, oodles of* used in positive contexts, while *for anything, for the world* are found in negative contexts (*I wouldn't go there for the world*). Finally, there are many ways of expressing the concept of approximation in English. Particularly common are *about* and *or so*, while *odd* as in *sixty odd people* is fairly common in conversation. The suffix {-ish} (as in *Meet you sixish*) is infrequent and found only in spoken language (conversation and fiction) while *approximately* seems to be restricted to academic writing.

The second category of lexical items typical of spoken English, but equally of an informal conversational atmosphere, are words and phrases that express a high or exaggerated degree. Examples are adverbs and adjectives such as *absolutely, definitely, horrible, terrible* etc., and vogue words such as *ace, brill(iant), cool, great, super, smashing* etc. The turnover of these words is rapid: they soon become over-used and lose their force, so that speakers have to find new ones. Exaggeration in language is called **hyperbole** and has rather similar effects to euphemisms (see 2.6).

Most new meanings and new formations, **neologisms**, are created on the spur of the moment and are unlikely to be recorded in dictionaries. Frequently used word formation elements are {non-}, {mega-} and {semi-}, as well as the suffixes {-y}, {-like} and {-wise}, e.g. *weatherwise, we can't complain*. Note that few of the above listed categories and items are the exclusive function of the spoken medium, but rather a combination of medium and informality.

Functional tenor and field   The aesthetic function (1.6.2), though typically realized in poetry and fiction, is not restricted to poetry. Creative use of language is also often found in the field of English advertising, which serves a directive–persuasive purpose.

A characteristic feature is the use of puns: *Give your girlfriend a cheap ring*, a British Telecom advertisement, where *ring* equals both 'phone call' and 'piece of jewellery'; or *Flaming Tasty*, an advertisement on London cabs for a hamburger brand, where *flaming* refers to the grill one can see on the poster and also has an intensifying force. Other, less original features of advertising include the use of a few very common verbs (e.g. *buy, give, make, need, set, try*), typically in the imperative: this form is used less, however, in advertisements which sell their product more indirectly (the so-called *soft sell approach*). Also typical of the lexis of advertising is the occurrence of highly evaluative adjectives like *clean, fresh, soft* and, recently, *natural* and *organic*, which are often repeated to drive home the message. Short, one syllable lexemes and short sentences are preferred. Verbs are usually in the present tense. Readers/viewers/listeners are often engaged in a pseudo-conversation, the tenor of which is intimate and informal.

2.11 FURTHER READING

On **words** and **meaning** and **semantic relationships** see: Cruse 1986; Lyons 1995. On **dictionaries** see: Landau 1984; Hausmann 1989–91; for **learner dictionaries** see: Herbst 1996; Pätzold 1997. On the **mental lexicon** see Aitchison 2002.

For **histories of the English vocabulary** see: Graddol *et al.* 1996; Baugh and Cable 2002; McCrum, MacNeil and Cran 2002. Hughes 2000 gives analyses of how the three layers interact in many of the major English authors. On **hard words** and the **structure of the English vocabulary** see Leisi and Mair 1999. On **word formation** see: Marchand 1969; Cannon 1987; Bauer 1992; Katamba 1993.

On the vocabulary of **global English** from a dialect and register point of view see Gramley 2001. On **social dialects** see: Ross 1954; Cooper 1981; Fussell 1984. **False friends**: for a dictionary see Hill 1982; the *Cambridge International Dictionary of English* has short contrastive lists of false friends integrated into the main body of its dictionary.

New words and meanings can be studied in the *Oxford English Dictionary Supplement*, 4 vols, in the *Oxford English Dictionary Additions Series* and the *Oxford Dictionary of New Words*. See also the new words supplement in the 2001 edition of *Longman's Dictionary of Contemporary English*. For AmE see: the three *Barnhart Dictionaries of New English* (1973–90); the three supplementary collections to *Webster's Third New International Dictionary*; the journal *American Speech* (the section 'Among the New Words'); Algeo 1991; and the new words supplement in *Webster's Third New International Dictionary* (2000 edn).

Chapter 3

Words in combination

Language involves choice from among many possibilities which are restricted only by whether they are good grammar or not. But making a choice at one point often commits one to further choices which follow on from the first choice. Words are not independent of each other and, indeed, combine with each other to form new lexemes. The subject of this chapter is lexemes that consist of more than one word form, and, in the case of collocations, more than one lexical unit. These **multi-word units** are so common in normal language that they, rather than single words, should be considered the basic organizing principle in language production. They are well established and well known to every member of the speech community and are in constant use, so much so in fact that their use is often criticized, see 3.1 below. They are often contrasted with creative, original language such as can be found in fictional texts:

> Her clothes smell faintly of the Smeaths' house, a mixture of scouring powder and cooked turnips and slightly rancid laundry . . .
>
> (M. Atwood (1989) *Cat's Eye*,
> London: Abacus, p. 52)

> Alex was scared stiff and Joseph was scared sober for what would happen when Nora came to collect him.
>
> (C. Nolan (1988) *Under the Eye of the Clock*,
> London: Pan, p. 20)

The combinations *rancid butter* and *scared stiff* are expected, while *rancid laundry* and *scared sober* are highly unusual. This chapter cannot go much into the creative, unconventional use of language which is characteristic of poetry and prose fiction, where authors often attach greater importance to expressive language than to the desire to simply make themselves understood in conventional language. What is important here is that these examples can only be appreciated if readers know the established form – and it is clear that authors expect this knowledge on the part of their readers.

For our purposes, fixed expressions can be divided into two groups (see Table 3.1.), one of which expresses speech acts (see 7.2.1) such as promises, warnings, requests etc., while the other group does not. Another criterion is whether or not the expression is equivalent to a whole sentence (in the written language) or free utterance (spoken language). On the next level down, the left branch is subdivided by the semantic criterion of idiomaticity, i.e. a meaning which cannot be deduced from the meaning of the individual words. The right branch, on the other hand, is split into expressions which are used in set social situations and those which are not, a pragmatic criterion.

Table 3.1 shows the classification of the expressions dealt with in this chapter. Mention should also be made of what have been called **lexical bundles**, well tried combinations of three or more word forms which are used as building blocks in discourse, spoken as well as written. Bundles can be incomplete (e.g. *in addition to the, the point of view of*) or structurally complete (*in the same way, in the present study, on the other hand*), can occur in academic prose, as in the examples just cited, or in spoken discourse (e.g. *I don't know how/what, what's the matter with, what are you talking about*). Bundles are not tied to a specific situation, do not allow deletions, insertions or substitutions and are much more frequent than idioms. A complete list of fixed expressions would also include traditional phrases such as: **similes** (explicit: *as blind as a bat, as happy as a sandboy, as proud as a peacock*; implicit: *pitch black, squeaky clean, bone idle, snow white*); slogans, which have a definite purpose; and allusions and quotations, which have a known author, as opposed to the items listed, which do not. Also omitted are, for example, non-situational pragmatic idioms, such as discourse structuring devices like *well, I see, you know* (some of which are treated in 7.5).

Table 3.1   Some fixed expressions in English

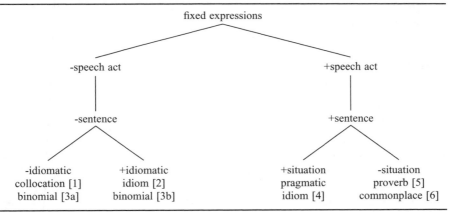

Examples:

[1]   collocation: *meet + demand; confirmed + bachelor; spring + leak*
[2]   idiom: *red herring; beat about the bush; put two and two together*
[3a] binomial: *bed and breakfast; bacon and eggs; forgive and forget*
[3b] binomial: *kith and kin; high and dry; head over heels*
[4]   pragmatic idiom: *say when; how do you do?*
[5]   proverb: *don't count your chickens before they're hatched; like father, like son; birds of a feather flock together*
[6]   commonplace: *orders are orders; you only live once; it's a small world*

3.1 FIXED EXPRESSIONS AS CLICHÉS

Clichés are routine or stereotypical forms that are found in many areas of life, e.g. art, thought, behaviour, visual images or urban architecture. In language, the use of fixed expressions is often criticized under the term of **cliché** by those who write about good English, who claim that people do not think when they use expressions like *acid test*, *psychological moment* or *leave no stone unturned*. While this has some truth in it, it can also not be denied that few people have the time and energy always to be original. Indeed, there are large areas where consciously thought out language is unusual, if not inappropriate. Redfern lists funerals, disasters, the writing of references and testimonials or letters of protest (1989: 20ff.). In much of everyday life, fixed expressions or clichéd language is not only unavoidable but can actually be assigned a more positive function. On everyday small talk Redfern remarks:

> chatter . . . indicates the dread of silence: clichés stop us thinking of nothing, of nothingness. If not life enhancing, they are life-preservers. 'Phatic speech', speech used as social cement . . . is not necessarily empty speech . . . It can be sorely missed, conspicuous by its absence.
>
> (1989: 22)

Not only do they help us to avoid awkward silences, clichés also have a warm, familiar ring about them. By using them you signal that you have acquired part of the culture of a given speech community and are on the verge of becoming one of its members. Far from always breeding contempt, clichés can help to create an in-group feeling of sympathy, solidarity and good will.

What can speakers do to escape being criticized for using clichés? The minimal strategy is to show that they are aware of the stereotypical nature of an expression and thus distance themselves from it. This is done, for example, by using such expressions as *proverbial* before nouns (*you were as blind as the proverbial bat*), noun phrases (*it's the proverbial can of worms, do you want to open it*), or (incomplete) proverbs (*human intervention would be the proverbial 'cure worse than the disease'*). The same function is also served by other expressions, e.g. *as they say*: *he could be, as they say, a danger to himself and others*; *he has come a long way, as they say*; *it's twenty-one billion dollars and counting, as they say at Cap Canaveral*. See also 3.6 on proverbial infixes.

A second option is to play with stereotypes in various ways. This method allows writers to have their linguistic cake and eat it: they use them as a foil that everybody knows, while at the same time changing them in ways that showcase their brilliant, inventive wit. For example, Ian Fleming, the creator of James Bond, has written novels with titles such as *Live and Let Die* and *You Only Live Twice*. However play with clichés is also found in restaurant names and above all in journalism. Burridge and Mulder (1999: 119) report these punning names (straight equivalents/meanings in brackets): *Beau Thai* (bow tie), *Eaternity* (eternity) and *Wok Inn* (walk in). *Time Magazine* had 'A crushing victory – a Spanish company will turn olive pulp into power' and headed a story about a dangerous computer virus 'Beware Geeks bearing gifts'. *The Economist* used 'Tyre Straits' for a report on a row over the recall of tyres. An article in the same magazine on exaggerated wage demands had the heading 'The sin of wages', a witty reversal of the biblical *the wages of sin*. In summary, clichés are employed universally, need not be avoided in social situations where they meet important needs and may be used creatively, so that each example of a cliché needs to be judged on its stylistic and other merits.

3.2 COLLOCATIONS

3.2.1 Definition

The term **collocation** is used differently by different linguists. As employed in this chapter, the term collocation refers to combinations of two lexical items each of which makes a distinct semantic contribution, belongs to a different word class and shows a restricted range. The first three criteria used (two items, not more; two lexical items, not grammatical words; independent meanings) distinguish collocations from other word combinations, such as idioms or proverbs, while the last two (word class and range) distinguish the central type (collocation: *drink heavily, confirmed bachelor*) from other lexical combinations.

A few explanations are in order. Note that the term has been used by other linguists to refer to combinations of three or more lexemes, as in *need badly*, which co-occurs frequently with a noun (e.g. *drink, money*), or *great big shame*, where **big shame* is an unacceptable combination. *Collocation* can also be used to refer to combinations of lexical and grammatical items or grammatical constructions, like *put on, put up with, proud of, interest in* and *finish/avoid* + *-ing* construction, in which case the term *grammatical collocation* is sometimes employed.

Meaning   The most important point about collocational meaning is that each lexeme makes an independent contribution to the meaning of the whole collocation. This recognizes the fact that lexemes can have meanings that range from normal to special or from restricted to idiomatic. Take the adjective *white* for example, the central and most frequent meaning of which is found, say, in *white paint* or *white snow*. Clearly, we are dealing with different meanings in *white coffee* ('with milk'), *white grapes* (which look more green than white) or *white wine*. Even more remote from the central meaning are *white lie* ('harmless') or *white night* ('sleepless'). In *white horses* ('foam-topped waves') and *white coal* ('water as energy source'), we have what look like exocentric compounds where it is possible to determine the meaning of both adjectives and nouns as metaphors. The combination of two lexemes can even appear contradictory at first glance, as in *rain solidly*, where *solidly* means 'continuously'. In addition to such physical meanings, collocations consisting of a verb plus a body part can express attitudes and emotions, e.g. *roll your eyes* (exasperation, irritation), *hang your head* (shame, embarrassment) or *curl your lip* (contempt, disdain).

Most research has concentrated almost exclusively on collocations of simple, non-idiomatic lexemes like *river-rise, agree-entirely* or *fine-heavy* (note that collocations will be quoted in this form from now on; see 3.2.3 for an explanation). This does not mean, however, that complex, idiomatic items cannot enter into collocations. Combinations like *it's raining cats and dogs*, often mentioned as a typical English idiom, do not qualify one hundred per cent for idiomatic status because the two constituents are independently meaningful (*rain; cats and dogs* = heavily). By the same criterion, even combinations of two idioms must be regarded as collocations, as in *to get on* (= have, start a relationship) in collocation with *like a house on fire* (= very friendly, easily).

Word classes   Another criterion for the central type of collocation is that the lexemes belong to different word classes, as in *demand-meet* (noun-verb), *hopes-high* (noun-adjective), and *apologize-profusely* (verb-adverb). The different word class criterion together with the lexical items only criterion excludes important noun-noun combinations such as *a pack of lies*, *a pride of lions* (collective nouns), *a cake of soap* (quantifying noun) or *a speck of dust* (unit noun) from the central class of collocations. Mention must also be made here of noun-noun expressions where the first noun corresponds to a verb that forms a central collocation with the second noun, as in *the howl of the wind* (*wind-howl*), *the deployment of troops* (*troops-deploy*) and *the publication of the novel* (*novel-publish*). Binomials like *bed and breakfast* and *bacon and eggs* are much more fixed and are altogether different (see 3.4).

Range   The final criterion, restricted range, helps to set up three different types of two lexeme combinations, namely **free combinations**, **collocations** and **fixed** (or **frozen**) **collocations**. Lexemes which belong to the core vocabulary of English are typically found in free combinations (e.g. *man, woman, house, night*), of which the number is enormous. *Need, condition, standard* or *requirement*, on the other hand, have fewer adjectives and verbs that combine with them (for example *meet, satisfy, fulfill*). When you discuss the number of lexemes (or **collocates**) that occur together (or **collocate**) with the lexeme under discussion (the **node**), then you are concerned with that lexeme's **range**. It is usual to express the difference between free combinations and collocations in terms of their ranges: the range of lexemes in collocations (also sometimes called **restricted collocations**) is smaller than that of lexemes in free combinations (also termed **unrestricted collocations**).

   In **fixed** (**unique, frozen**) **collocations** lexemes have only one collocate: the two items *like a house on fire* and *famously* (in the sense of 'very well') only seem to collocate with *get on*. Other examples are *ajar* plus *door* (*the door stood ajar*), *kick* and *foot, nod* and *head*, and *shrug* and *shoulders, sorely* (= very much) and *miss* (= feel the loss of). Frozen collocations are not numerous, and it would, in general, be rash to say that the range of any given lexeme is limited to one collocate only as lexemes can extend their range and individual usage varies. *Ajar* for instance also combines with such other nouns as *gate, lattice* or *window*. Note also that frozen collocations are frozen only when considered with the lexeme that has been mentioned first in the examples above. *Door, foot, head*, as well as *get on* and *miss*, enter of course into many other collocations. Further, it is important to distinguish between the lexical units of the same lexeme. *Nod*, for instance, means 'move one's head up and down' and enters into the unique collocation mentioned; but it also means 'indicate by nodding', as in to *nod one's agreement, approval, greeting* etc.

   Having made these distinctions, we must add that there is no dictionary or monograph yet that lists collocations according to their range. The two most user friendly dictionaries of collocations, *The BBI Dictionary of English Word Combinations* and *Oxford Collocations* list free combinations as well as collocations and frozen items. While there are practical difficulties, there are even greater theoretical ones: nobody has specified yet what 'limited range' means in absolute numbers.

1   **Fixedness**. Collocations show various degrees of fixedness.

2   **Morphology**. In some collocations the adverbs are not formally marked by the {-ly} morpheme: *drunk-blind, forget-clean, naked-stark, sober-stone cold.*

3   **Substitutability**. Some lexemes can be replaced by synonyms, e.g. *hardened criminal* is found side by side with *confirmed criminal* and *hardened outlaw*, though **hardened burglar* or **hardened murderer* are not found. *Conditions* can be *met, fulfilled* or *satisfied*. *Conflict* collocates with *end, settle* and *(re)solve*, though not apparently with **finish.*

4   **Additions**. Additions, most often pre- or post-modifiers, are normal:

> The oil-exporting nations ... may soon restrict production below the level needed to meet still rising world demand
>
> (*demand-meet*; B. Ward (1979) *Progress for a Small Planet*, Harmondsworth: Penguin, p. 15)

5   **Deletion**. Although deletions are not impossible they are much rarer than additions: *I have not got the faintest/foggiest* (sc. *idea*).

6   **Displacement**. Personal pronouns may replace the actual collocational items: 'Her heart wasn't very strong and her life assurance premiums weren't cheap. It can't have been easy to meet them.' (P.D. James (1981) *Death of an Expert Witness*, London: Sphere, p. 324).

7   **Separability**. In contrast to the majority of collocations, some **bound collocations** cannot be separated, e.g. *foot the bill* and *curry favour.*

8   **Distribution**. Finally, the word order or distribution of lexemes in collocations is relatively free: *they met their demands; their demands, which were not met completely; and it was these last demands which the parents did not want to meet.* Syntactic transformations are thus possible and do not change or destroy the meanings of collocations. On the whole collocations are less fixed than pragmatic idioms and the other types of expression discussed in this chapter.

3.2.2 Conditions and restrictions in collocations

In this section we discuss the influence syntax, phonology and semantics have on the formation of collocations. As we will see, all three levels of linguistic description have some role to play, but their influence is far from all pervasive.

As described in the last section, collocations are independent of word order but their frequency may depend on it. Greenbaum found that American students had lower scores than their British counterparts for such frames as *I badly* or *I entirely*, which he explains in the following way: 'It appears that American speakers prefer these intensifiers to be positioned finally ... Since the intensifiers were in pre-verb positions in the experiments, they did not evoke the verbs to the same extent as they might have done if positioned finally' (Greenbaum 1974: 85). Greenbaum also found that the choice of subject can similarly explain a difference in frequency: *I entirely agree* is more common than *my friend entirely agrees* (Greenbaum 1970). On the other hand, collocations are not conditioned by word classes (see *the argument is strengthened/is made more powerful, the strength/power of his argument, he argued strongly/powerfully*). By contrast, grammar does play a part in the acceptability of at least some collocations. While the collocations *he drinks heavily, he is a heavy drinker* and *he put in some heavy drinking* are grammatically acceptable, the collocation *the drinker is heavy, *heavy drink* or *heavily drunk* are not, at least not in the relevant sense of *heavy*. *The bachelor was confirmed, *the criminal was hardened* and ?*the pursuit was hot* are also unacceptable. And in *his socks are odd, odd* has a different meaning from *odd socks*. Syntax we see *may*, but does not always, play a role in the meaning and formation of collocations.

Phonology and personal tenor seem to have a more definite and far reaching influence. Take, for instance, *highly*, an intensifier of high degree typically used in academic prose. Here the phonology seems to require its collocates to be made up of more than one syllable (e.g. *authoritarian, centralized, fragmented, intelligent, publicized, selective*). *Dead*, although also a high degree intensifier, collocates with words that are similarly short and informal, e.g. *boring, certain, drunk, stupid, sure, tired* and *worried*. When dead is found in collocation with words of three and more syllables, these tend to be stylistically neutral or informal, such as *conventional, embarrassing, horrible, pathetic* and *threatening*. These phonological and stylistic tendencies can perhaps explain why *dead* does not seem acceptable in collocation with *mature, *positive, *exhausted* and *intoxicated*.

As to the influence of meaning, similar or identical meanings are realized by different lexical items. The meaning 'great amount' is expressed by *heavily* for the verbs *drink, smoke* and *rain*, but not *eat*, which takes *heartily* or *like a horse*. The meaning 'beginning' is expressed, for example, by *start/begin* (theatre performance etc.), *kick off* (soccer match), *fall* (night) and *break* (*day* or *dawn*, poetic language). Collocations are unpredictable not only in one and the same language but even more so between languages: of the two verbs used with French *nuit* ('night') *tomber* is predictable from English, *descendre* is not. German uses verbs that are all unpredictable when one equates English *fall* with German *fallen* (*die Nacht kommt, bricht an, sinkt hernieder, zieht herauf*; the last three are poetic).

While there seems to be no reason why *night* should collocate with *fall* rather than *break* or some other verb, this does not mean that semantics plays no role at all. In the frozen collocations above, there are semantic features in *kick* which demand *foot*, and the same goes for *nod* and *head*, and *shrug* and *shoulders*. These **inherent semantic features** have been distinguished from **selection restrictions**, which determine what may occur with given verbs. However, in this case the verb demands not a specific lexeme, but a whole class of semantically similar nouns, e.g. *spend*, which combines with numerous time nouns such as *day, evening, holiday, hour, life, spare time* etc. Other examples are provided by *eat*, whose objects must have the meaning element [solid], and *drink* plus nouns with the meaning element [liquid]. Similarly, some adverbs show a certain semantic bias in their collocates, e.g. *a bit* and *a little* tend to enter into collocations with adjectives that express something negative (*a bit*: *dull, frightened*; *a little*: *drunk, jealous, plump, tetchy, unkind*), while *highly* collocates perhaps more often with neutral to positive items (e.g. *accomplished, committed, educated, individual, likely, mobile, organized, paid, recommended*).

Finally, we want to report the findings of a classic study based on questionnaires (Greenbaum 1970). Greenbaum concentrates on only a few adverbs of degree (among others, (*very*) *much, greatly, utterly, completely*) and demonstrates convincingly that the choice of collocates is determined by semantic considerations in the majority of cases. *Utterly* and *completely* take pejorative verbs and adjectives (*detest, despise, indefensible, unsuccessful*), while *completely* collocates with *forget* and *ignore* as well. *Greatly* and (*very*) *much* are found above all with attitudinal verbs: *greatly* and *much* combine with *admire* and *enjoy*; *very much* on the other hand occurs more frequently with *like* and *enjoy*. *Greatly* also enters into collocation with attitudinal adjectives, many of them past participles like *appreciated, beloved, exaggerated* and *missed*.

3.2.3 Collocations and the needs of language production

Linguistic studies of collocations have in the past often focused on an adverb and then found out what its collocates are. This approach establishes links between lexemes, as reported above, but it does not consider what actually happens in language production. Here, a speaker starts, say, with the noun *debate* and looks for an adjective to describe the kind of debate which they have just had. It is rarely the case that one is thinking about what to do with the adjectives *bitter, heated, lively*, all of which collocate with *debate*. In the linguistic analysis of collocations, linguists can indeed make either the adjective or the noun the focus of attention, the **node**, but in language production learners as well as native speakers usually start from the base and look for acceptable partners. The linguistic, analytic approach is, in other words, often divorced from natural language use and therefore sees no need to set up a hierarchy among the members of a collocation. In both the *BBI* and *Oxford Collocations* dictionaries, however, a distinction is made between **base** and **collocator** in such a way that the entry for the base, the known word (*debate*), lists all its collocators. It is only when desperately looking for a suitable collocate that this immense improvement of the new arrangement in dictionaries of collocations is fully appreciated.

3.3 IDIOMS

3.3.1 Definition of idiom

In linguistics an idiom is defined as a complex lexical item which is longer than a word form but shorter than a sentence and which has a meaning that cannot be derived from the knowledge of its component parts. Meaning is thus the decisive, if not the only, criterion for idioms. The word forms in an idiom do not constitute lexical units and do not make an isolable contribution to the meaning of the whole, but show unitary meaning. As a consequence of this, some linguists also use a special term for the constituents of idioms, namely **formatives** (where *word form* would serve the same purpose). A test for a semantic constituent is that of recurrent semantic contrast (see Cruse 1986: 26–9). In the sentence *you need not jump down my throat* (= 'criticize me so fiercely'), take *need* and substitute for it the semantically different but syntactically identical item *may*. This changes the meaning of the sentence, of course, but the point is that the same substitution of forms in a completely different sentence will produce a parallel change of meaning, e.g. *they need/may not sit the exam*. The same test shows that *you* is also a semantic constituent, but that *throat* is not, e.g. semantically unacceptable **you need not jump down my windpipe*. In other sentence frames *throat* and *windpipe* are in recurrent semantic contrast, e.g. *he hit me on the windpipe/throat* and *they operated on my windpipe/throat.* In fact, *jump, down* and the possessive *my* are all part of the *idiom to jump down —'s throat.* Similarly, if *hit* and *pail* are contrasted with *kick* and *bucket* in the expression *to kick the bucket* it becomes clear that *kick the bucket* is an idiom. The same goes for an adjectival idiom like *red herring*: *red herring* is not to *green herring* as *red book* is to *green book.*

Recurrent semantic contrast does not mean that all idioms are equally difficult to decode. Idioms show different degrees of semantic opacity: *white tops* is less opaque than *white elephant* or *red herring.* Knowledge of the world will play a part in the degree to which speakers feel idioms to be opaque. Many idioms originated in metaphors which some speakers recognize while others remain unaware of their origin. Thus, while *bury the hatchet, give somebody the green light* and *gnash one's teeth* are likely to be intelligible to many, only few will know that *white elephant* ('some expensive but completely useless object') apparently derives from a king of Siam who used to make a present of a white elephant to people he wished to ruin. Dead metaphors often allow constituents to be replaced by synonyms, near synonyms or a semantic paraphrase, e.g. *tomahawk* instead of *hatchet* in *bury the tomahawk.* Some of the literal meaning is still relevant for the interpretation of, for example, *give someone a piece of one's mind,* but another part remains obscure, i.e. the pejorative, scolding meaning.

Few readers will apply the test of recurrent semantic contrast, so the question arises as to what other means there are to recognize that an expression is an idiom. Many expressions have two meanings, a literal and an idiomatic one (e.g. *kick the bucket, go to the country, pull someone's leg*). In such cases only the context will decide which meaning is intended. In other cases, when a literal reading does not make sense in terms of the world as we know it, the likelihood is that we are dealing with an idiom. This applies to *jump down someone's throat, fly off the handle* and *cats and dogs* (in *rain cats and dogs*). Irregular syntax can lead to the same conclusion, e.g. the definite articles in *kick the bucket* and *fly off the handle,* or *one* in *pull a fast one.* The definite article normally has the function of indicating that an item has already been mentioned or is considered unique in the context of the language community, while the pro-form *one* refers to a noun that must precede it. Neither of these conditions is fulfilled in the idioms just cited. Idioms can also be phonologically irregular in that they have an unpredictable stress pattern. In free syntactic groups, the last lexical item usually carries the tonic stress, e.g. *they ran into the 'house.* This is not so in *like a 'house on fire, you can say 'that again, learn the 'hard way* and *have a 'bone to pick with someone.* Also, in connected spoken discourse, idioms are often signalled by slight pauses or a clear intake of breath. Finally, there is a certain amount of lexical repetition in the environment of idioms, which makes for greater lexical cohesion. Often something is first described in non-idiomatic language, then the sender refers to it with an idiom, before it is picked up again by a non-idiomatic, literal lexical item.

3.3.2 Classifications of idioms

Idioms have been classified in applied linguistics according to the image or picture they evoke (e.g. *pull someone's leg* or *that is rather a mouthful* would appear under the heading of body idioms). This can hardly be called semantic of course, for none of the would-be body parts have that meaning in the idiom. Lattey (1986) divides the 500 idioms she has examined into four categories: those with a focus on the individual (*keep a stiff upper lip, throw in the towel, die a thousand deaths*); those with a focus on the world (*go down the drain, be touch and go, that takes the cake* (BrE *the biscuit*)); those that refer to the interaction of individuals (*lend someone a helping hand; someone is not fit to hold a candle to someone else*); and idioms which express the interaction between an individual and the world (*take up arms for something; know something inside out; be all Greek to someone*).

Idioms have been categorized by linguists according to various syntactic criteria. It has been mentioned above that idioms fall into two groups, depending on whether they are formed in accordance with the rules of present day English or not. Another classificatory scheme lists idioms according to their part of speech, e.g. nominal (*black market, red herring*), adjectival (*down-to-earth, happy-go-lucky*) or verbal (*go in for, put up with, cook the books, blow one's top*). More revealing about the structural characteristics of idioms at sentence level is Fraser's classification system which looks at what transformations they allow (1970). He set up a so-called **frozenness hierarchy**, in which idioms were arranged into six groups, ranging from those which are totally frozen, i.e. admit no transformation at all, to those at the other end of the scale which show almost no restrictions. Fraser considered, for example, insertions, transpositions, gerund use, passive and cleft sentence transformations. The fixed nature of idioms is shown by the fact that there are no idioms which allow all six transformations, while there are some which do not allow any transformation at all, e.g. *bite off one's tongue* and *face the music*. As we see, the more syntactically frozen, the greater the semantic opacity of the idiom.

Some of the reasons why certain idioms do or do not allow transformations seem to be idiosyncratic; for others semantic reasons can be given. Idioms will resist the isolation of one formative for emphasis, for example, in cleft sentence construction (**it was her throat that he jumped down*) as well as in adjectival and adverbial modification (**He jumped down her sore throat*) because both operations presuppose that word forms are semantic constituents, which they are not. *Throat* in *he jumped down her throat* has no isolable meaning in the idiom and can therefore not be modified. For the same reason substitutions are not usually possible in idioms, e.g. **kick the pail, *inter the hatchet, *leap down someone's throat*. Insertions are, however, possible in some cases (they are printed in bold here): *that rings a **faint** bell; he is going to come **a hell of** a cropper; the recipes are no great **culinary** shakes*.

3.3.3 Idioms and simple lexemes

As idioms show unitary meanings in the same way as single word lexemes do, linguists have wondered whether idioms behave more like simple lexemes or more like phrases or clauses. The answer is that they show characteristics of both. If *jump down —'s throat* behaved like a single word lexeme the past tense would be **he jump-down-my-throated*, which it is not. Neither **redder herring* nor **red herringer* are found, nor is **roll out the red carpets*, though *red herrings* and *John has bees in his bonnet about many things* are possible. It would seem, then, that nouns, adjectives and verbs in idioms are restricted in their freedom to share in the inflectional processes typical of their part of speech.

3.4 BINOMIALS

Binomials, like collocations, consist of two word forms (see Norrick (1988) for a recent discussion). These belong to the same word class and are linked by a grammatical item, frequently *and*. Their constituents can be independently meaningful (as in *bed and breakfast* or *hire and fire*), or they can be idiomatic (*bag and baggage*, *by and by*, *head over heels*). There are also three member combinations (**trinomials**, e.g. *left, right and centre* or *hook, line and sinker*), but these are much less numerous. The two constituents can be identical, as in *face to face* and *so-and-so*. The basic structure can be expanded, e.g. *from rags to riches*, *by fair means or foul* and *every Tom, Dick and Harry*. Binomials often preserve words which are rare (e.g. *hale* in *hale and hearty*) or only survive in the binomial expression (e.g. *kith* in *kith and kin*). The collocative potential of binomials varies as with other lexical combinations. *Bed and breakfast*, *high and mighty* and *odds and ends* enter into free combinations, while *high and dry* forms a collocation with *leave*, and *hook, line and sinker* with *believe (something)* or the synonymous verbs *accept, fall for, swallow* and *take (something)*.

Syntactically, the two constituents belong to the same word class and can have syntactic functions which neither constituent could have on their own, e.g. the three nouns *hook, line* and *sinker* function as an adverbial (*he accepted the story hook, line and sinker*), while the two adverbs *so-and-so* form a noun phrase (e.g. *what do you think of that old so-and-so?*).

The fixed expressions we are dealing with in this section are called **irreversible binomials** because their word order is, in contrast to collocations, completely unchangeable. This is no doubt connected to the fact that the second (or third in trinomials) constituent is usually phonetically more weighty, i.e. longer, than the first, *bacon and eggs* being one of the few exceptions. Also, none of the items can be exchanged for synonyms: there is no **help and abet* or **aid and help* or **kith and relatives*. Insertions are possible, though infrequent: *they really offered a marvellous bed and an even better breakfast* is a possible expansion of *bed and breakfast*, as is *they do you excellent bacon and not bad eggs*. On the other hand, **this is all an important part and even more important parcel of the whole initiation process* is not acceptable. This example would suggest that the nearer the binomials are to the idiomatic end of the semantic scale, the more fixed they become. The fixed nature of many binomials is heightened by assonance or alliteration. Rhyme is also not uncommon, e.g. *hire and fire*, *make or break*, *town and gown* and *wine and dine*.

Semantically, the two halves of binomials exhibit a whole spectrum of possibilities. They can consist of two near synonyms, which often complement or intensify each other, e.g. *rules and regulations, fuss and bother* and *over and done with*. They can also stand in semantic opposition to each other, as in *assets and liabilities, give and take* and *war and peace*. More generally, binomials range from completely transparent (*bed and breakfast, bacon and eggs, here, there and everywhere*) to semi-transparent (*kith and kin, left, right and centre, town and gown*) to opaque or completely idiomatic (*high and dry, hook, line and sinker, on the up and up*).

3.5 PRAGMATIC IDIOMS

In this section we will discuss lexical items and expressions whose use is determined by a particular social situation. We will refer to them as **pragmatic idioms** although there are many other terms such as **routines** or **social formulas** or **gambits**. Pragmatic idioms are not to be confused with pragmatic markers or expressions, often called discourse markers, such as *well, you know, I mean* etc., which are discussed in 7.5.

Among the many situations in which stereotypical, or routinized, language is used are the beginnings (greetings, introductions) and endings (leave takings) of social encounters and letters, eating and drinking, and all sorts of business transactions, as for example at a (railway) ticket counter (*Single or return?*), in a shop (*Can I help you?*, *Next, please*), or in a café (*Black or white?*) or wine bar (*White or red?*).

Situations differ in the degree to which the language used in them is predetermined. In many cases there is no choice, as in formal letters where one has to use *Dear* and *Yours* even when one has anything but friendly feelings for the addressee. In other situations, various options are available. When one first meets people and introductions are made one can use *How do you do?*, *Hello, Hi, Nice/Pleased to meet you* and *I have been looking forward to meeting you (for some time)*. How do these expressions differ from one another? First, they belong to different levels of personal tenor (see 1.6.2) with *How do you do?* at the formal end, *Hi (there)* at the informal end and *Hello* and the other two somewhere in the middle. *How do you do?* is becoming increasingly rare, not least because of the growing informality of English. When it is used, speakers often try to make it less distant and formal by combining it with *Hello* or *Pleased to meet you*. It is also felt to be typical of a certain social class (upper middle to upper), while *Pleased to meet you* is not so socially restricted. Other expressions are regionally marked, such as *Straight or handle?* (refers to whether one wants a glass with or without a handle in a British pub), or *Time, gentlemen please* (landlord's cry to get his customers to drink up and leave his pub). Another professional restriction can be seen in *Enjoy!*, used by waiters who have just served customers their food – the nearest that English gets to *bon appetit, buon appetito*, or *Guten Appetit!*

In contrast to the other types of fixed expression discussed in this chapter, pragmatic idioms often need the context of situation in order to be understood correctly. *Black or white?* in a different context (e.g. *Was the waiter black or white?*) has a completely different meaning. The difficult semantics results in many cases from omission: *Say when* is presumably shortened from *Say when I am to stop pouring* or *Say when you have enough*. Moreover, many situational idioms show a weakened meaning. This is obvious in both the *Dear* and *Your* discussed above and in *How are you?*, which is usually no more than a ritual recognition of the hearer's presence, and does not express a deeply felt interest in his or her well-being. *How do you do?* is semantically extreme in that it is difficult to state what meaning it has. Rather than state its meaning, many dictionaries describe its function ('used by people who meet for the first time').

All these aspects – regional and social class dialect and semantics – are still not sufficient when one wants to use them appropriately. It is also important to know the linguistic context. If introductions are made by a third party, and one speaker says *How do you do?*, how does the second person react? In most cases, she or he will reply with the same phrase, and the two people will shake hands. In other words, in order to behave correctly you need to know that *How do you do?* is only the second and third step in a sequence which involves three parties (the person introducing and the two being introduced to each other). Moreover, linguistic behaviour is accompanied by non-linguistic behaviour (the handshake). However, the increasingly informal social atmosphere in the English speaking world has caused a relaxation of these conventions and it is not uncommon for people to reply with other phrases than *How do you do?* and to refrain from shaking hands.

Hi and *Hello*, as well as being informal, also differ from *How do you do?* in that they can be used when meeting the same person or people on a later occasion (often with an added *again*, as in *Hi/Hello (there) again*), while *How do you do?* can only be used once. This also sets it apart from *How are you?*, which can be used more than once to the same person(s), though usually not on the same day.

To sum up, a full description of pragmatic idioms has to take into account: their register characteristics (e.g. regional and social distribution, personal tenor etc.); their semantic peculiarities; at what point in a social situation or sequence they come; whether they occur alone or whether reciprocity is usual or indeed necessary (and if so whether the same item or a different one can or must be used); whether there is a change of speaker; and, finally, whether the idiom can be used in an identical situation on a later occasion.

3.6 PROVERBS AND COMMONPLACES

Definition   Commonplaces in the form of truisms, tautologies and sayings (see below) are usually complete sentences, but this is not always the case with proverbs, where short-ened versions are quite common. Shortening and other changes (additions, variations, transpositions) do not necessarily affect the intelligibility of proverbs, presumably because they are so well known that even fragments and mutations are easily associated with the full form and, indeed, appreciated for their novelty by senders and addressees alike, e.g. 'I will write a long letter to my old mucker in Melbourne, I thought, and kill two birds with one tome. I'll get it all off my chest . . . ' (M. Frayn (1989) *The Trick of It*, London: Viking, p. 17; *tome* instead of *stone*). Mention should also be made of another type of fixed expression, the **proverbial saying**, which is similarly well established and metaphor-ical but differs from proverbs in that it is never equivalent to a sentence or utterance. For instance, the following three examples need a subject to form a sentence: *hit the nail on the head* and *carry coals to Newcastle*.

Proverbs as a class are not completely frozen, as is shown by the possibility of various additions and insertions. There are for example expressions that mark proverbs as such, e.g. *(as) they say*, *it is said* or *as the proverb goes*, which can precede, interrupt or follow the respective proverb; e.g. *as the old saw says* in: 'the man . . . took his mother's life insurance policy and unloaded every nickel of it . . . Easy come, easy go, as the old saw says' (P. Auster (1999) *Timbuktu*, London: Faber & Faber, p. 76). Norrick calls these **proverbial affixes** and contrasts them with **proverbial infixes** like *proverbial, everlovin'* and *(good) ol'* which 'can be inserted before any stressed noun phrase in a proverb' (1985: 45), e.g. *The proverbial pen is mightier than the sword*. Proverb collections often list a number of variant forms, which shows that variability is a characteristic trait of proverbs. Transformations like the cleft sentence construction do not change proverbs out of all recognition (e.g. *it is while the iron is hot that it should be struck*) in contrast to most idioms which would become meaningless if changed in this way or allow only a literal reading.

Proverbs often show irregular syntax (*Like father, like son* 'a son will resemble his father', *Handsome is as handsome does* 'what counts is not appearance etc. but one's actions'), while **truisms** conform to the syntactic rules of contemporary English. The vocabulary used in proverbs tends to be Anglo-Saxon or at least from everyday English and is more varied than that in truisms. Both proverbs and commonplaces are concerned with general rather than specific meanings, which is why the past tense is not normally found with them. Proverbs make a claim to wide, but perhaps not universal, validity while commonplace remarks are expected to apply everywhere and at all times. Proverbs are therefore sometimes syntactically restricted, which comes through in restrictive relative clauses, e.g. *He who pays the piper calls the tune.* Truisms do not have this feature, e.g. *You/we (all) live and learn, You only live once, Business is business.* Many proverbs are metaphorical and may pose problems for understanding while commonplaces are usually literal and easy to process. Proverbs also show features like hyperbole, metonymy and paradox. Proverbs survive because of their formulaic expression and memorable form (see below). While the proverb pattern is no longer productive, commonplaces flourish in everyday communication. Three patterns are distinguished: **tautologies** (*enough is enough, orders are orders*), truisms (*We only live once*) and **sayings** based on everyday experience (*Accidents happen, You never know, It's a small world*). Particularly productive is the pattern of tautologies, many of which can exist without making their way into the dictionaries. Proverbs, on the other hand, are well established and traditional, recorded in many collections and dictionaries.

Proverbs contain 'a good dose of common sense, experience, wisdom and above all truth' (Mieder 1989: 15). One, perhaps surprising, aspect of folk wisdom is that it expresses the complexities of life in sayings which contradict each other: compare *Opposites attract* and *Birds of a feather flock together* or *Fine feathers make fine birds* and *Clothes do not make the man.* Proverbs show structural patterns as well as prosodic features not (typically) found with commonplaces, such as its two part structure, alliteration, assonance, rhyme and lexical repetition: *once bitten, twice shy; easy come, easy go; a friend in need is a friend indeed; all that glitters is not gold.*

Proverbs, in the same way as collocations, binomials and idioms, are folklore items, have no known authors and cannot be traced to specific sources. As far as the users of both proverbs and commonplaces are concerned, they can be said to be associated with the older rather than the younger generation. A recent trend in written documents is play with the form and meaning of proverbs (see 3.1): while they shy away from straightforward use, the sophisticated still employ them to make a witty point, as in 'A Ms is as good as Male' (quoted in Mieder 1993: 71).

To sum up, commonplaces are: complete sentences; fall into three classes; claim universal validity; and are non-metaphorical. This explains both why they are easy to understand and why there is no need to list them in dictionaries. Proverbs are: traditional; express general ideas; and show non-literal meaning (metaphorical, metonymic); they can be added to, transformed and abbreviated. Proverbs are equivalent to a sentence and are also prototypically characterized by certain metrical, structural and prosodic features. Both types of expression tend to be used more by older speakers.

3.7 FIXED EXPRESSIONS IN TEXTS

The discussion so far has largely concentrated on the description of fixed expressions from a structural, systematic point of view. This final section will take a brief look at how these expressions function in texts. The first point is that one often finds more than one such expression in the same place, for example:

> *Ronald*: I think the bank could probably see their way to helping you out.
> *Sidney*: Ah well, that's wonderful news . . . that means I can put in a definite bid for the adjoining site – which hasn't incidentally come on the market. I mean, as I said, this is all purely through personal contacts.
> *Ronald*: Quite so, yes.
> *Sidney*: I mean, the site value alone – just taking it as a site – you follow me?
> *Ronald*: Oh, yes.
> *Sidney*: But it is a matter of striking while the iron's hot – before it goes off the boil . . .
> *Ronald*: Mmm . . .
> *Sidney*: I mean, in this world it's dog eat dog, isn't it? No place for sentiment. Not in business. I mean, all right, so on occasions you can scratch mine. I'll scratch yours . . .
> *Ronald*: Beg your pardon?
> *Sidney*: Tit for tat. But when the chips are down it's every man for himself and blow you, Jack, I regret to say . . .
> *Ronald*: Exactly.
>
> > (A. Ayckbourn (1979) *Absurd Person Singular*, in
> > *Three Plays*, Harmondsworth: Penguin, p. 38)

Here both speakers use fixed expressions, which characterizes an informal atmosphere (the scene takes place at a New Year's Eve party): *see one's way to doing something, help someone out, put in a bid, come on the market, strike while the iron is hot, tit for tat* etc. The massing of fixed expressions in Sidney's language is, however, unusual and reflects his desperate attempt to get Ronald's approval. What Sidney has in mind does not, however, seem to be entirely above board, and he uses all his rhetoric to convince Ronald that what he, Sidney, is planning to do is not only necessary but also common business practice, and therefore quite acceptable. He uses fixed expressions in the belief that Ronald will find it difficult not to agree with them because they express widely accepted maxims. Sidney speaks as one businessman to another, in the hope that this appeal to their common situation will win Ronald over to his side. Ronald's rather curt reactions suggest, however, that he does not see himself on the same level as Sidney (he is Sidney's bank manager), and perhaps resents Sidney's attempt at establishing common ground between them. As Ronald does not seem to be convinced by the first proverb (*strike while the iron . . .*) and idiom (*go off the boil*) Sidney pulls in one more proverb (*dog eat dog* = 'no quarter is given') to make his point. He also emphasizes the need for cooperation (proverb: *scratch my back and I'll scratch yours*). Sidney's final volley consists of another proverb (*tit for tat*) and a commonplace (*it's every man for himself*), a barrage which wears Ronald down so that he concedes the point. Proverbs and commonplaces are here used 'as silencers . . . the last word on the subject' (Redfern 1989: 120).

In this example, Ronald does not openly disagree with Sidney even though he does not seem to like him particularly. The social relationship of small business customer and bank manager puts certain restraints on possible behaviour, as does the party situation. In the next example we find serious disagreement between a wife, who wants a divorce, and her husband, who does not want to grant it:

Arnold: I can't bring myself to take you very seriously.
Elizabeth: You see, I don't love you.
Arnold: Well, I'm awfully sorry. But you weren't obliged to marry me. You've made your bed and I'm afraid you must lie on it.
Elizabeth: That's one of the falsest proverbs in the English language. Why should you lie on the bed you've made if you don't want to? There's always the floor.
Arnold: For goodness' sake don't be funny, Elizabeth.
Elizabeth: I've quite made up my mind to leave you, Arnold.

(S. Maugham (1931) *The Circle*, in *Collected Plays*, vol. 2, London: Heinemann, p. 56)

Why does Arnold use a form of the proverb *You've made your bed and you must lie on it*? A possible contextual paraphrase of the third sentence in his second speech would run *As you did [marry me], you must accept the consequences*. In comparison with the literal *marry*, a simple lexeme, *You've made your bed* is figurative language and a multi-word expression. Figurative language can be regarded as unusual when compared with literal language; it stands out and attracts attention to itself. Speakers are especially likely to use figurative language in situations where they want to highlight what they have to say. The proverb is also more weighty than *marry* as it consists of at least four word forms. It makes Arnold's refusal more emphatic. Furthermore, the relative position of literal and figurative expressions is important. When the figurative expression comes first, the literal counterpart has a rational function, usually to comment or provide a gloss. When the literal expression precedes, as here, the figurative item gives the message an emotional colouring. The meaning of figurative expressions is always more than the sum of their parts, so that by using the proverb after the literal counterpart Arnold avails himself of this semantic surplus. There is of course another proverb with similar meaning (*In for a penny, in for a pound*), but the bed proverb seems much better suited to the marital context and is in fact often used by or with reference to husbands and wives.

Proverbs are said to have a didactic tendency: they suggest a course of action. This is sometimes expressed directly (*When in Rome do as the Romans do, People in glass houses should not throw stones*), but more often indirectly (*The early bird catches the worm*). This indirect quality of the proverb suits Arnold's nature well; he does not need to show his anger openly but can be apologetic (*I'm awfully sorry*), although on stage his intonation and gestures may give him away. The proverb relieves him of the burden of thinking up a good argument for his refusal; it is there ready-made, waiting to be used. It also allows him to remain superficially nice to his wife, pretending to side with her against the moral demands of society (*I'm afraid . . .*), while at the same time making his point.

What has been said so far does not, however, explain Elizabeth's very emotional reaction. This is only understandable if she has been put under considerable pressure. Proverbs contain the practical wisdom of a culture as it has accumulated through the centuries. They are thus authoritative statements which it is difficult to contradict. Arnold hides behind the proverb, which he can expect to do a more effective job than he could by flatly refusing his wife's request. But how can Elizabeth hold her own against the overwhelming weight of proverbial wisdom? One possible move is to counter the proverb with another proverb which proves the opposite point (see above for examples of contradictory proverbs). Another possibility is to leave the level of direct interaction and talk about the (use of) the proverb and what it means. Elizabeth here takes this option and makes a meta-communicative statement about the validity of the proverb. But calling the proverb false will not on its own do the job of debunking the proverb. That is why she adds two more sentences. The first is a rhetorical question, quite suited to the emotional atmosphere. The second sentence, on the other hand, is thought highly inappropriate by Arnold. Elizabeth's use of wordplay to contradict him strikes him as frivolous and unacceptable. But it is of a piece with her overall strategy of fighting against conventions: just as she does not accept the truth of the conventional wisdom of the proverb, neither does she feel restricted to the conventional idiomatic meaning of the proverb and puts a literal interpretation on it. Arnold's use of the proverb, aimed at crushing his wife, has been foiled by the ridiculous effect achieved by Elizabeth, who reactivates the literal meaning of the proverb and thus robs it of any weight it might have.

The use of fixed expressions as foils for witty wordplay can be seen as characteristic of certain situations and text types. Punning is common in shop names, newspapers and commercial advertisements. Puns are also found in the titles of plays (e.g. Oscar Wilde's *The Importance of Being Earnest*) or works of fiction (e.g. A. Lurie's novel *Foreign Affairs*, which deals with the love affair of two Americans in England). Fixed expressions and wordplay based upon them are more frequent in social science texts than in the natural sciences, and more frequent in popular works on science than in technical scientific texts.

Fixed expressions can have several functions. They generally make people feel at ease and create an in-group feeling. This nearness between the sender of a message and its addressee can make it difficult for the addressee to disagree with the sender – this is clearly the effect that Sidney wants to exploit with Arnold. Fixed expressions (idioms, binomials and proverbs) provide stylistic variety and lend emphasis to statements. It has also been suggested that speakers use idioms to organize their discourse and to make evaluations. Proverbs and commonplaces deal with social situations, and their uses are manifold: 'to strengthen our arguments, express certain generalizations, influence or manipulate other people, rationalize our own shortcomings, question certain behavioral patterns, satirize social ills, poke fun of [sic] ridiculous situations' (Mieder 1989: 21).

3.8 FURTHER READING

For linguistic studies of **literary language** see: Leech 1969; Leech and Short 1981; Carter and Nash 1990.

General treatments of fixed expressions include: Alexander 1978/9; Burger, Buhofer and Sialm 1982; Norrick 1985; Tournier 1985; Gläser 1986; Redfern 1989; Everaert *et al.* 1995; Fernando 1996; Cowie 1998; Moon 1998; Lipka 2002.

On **lexical bundles** see Biber *et al.* 1999: 990–1024; for noun-noun combinations, see 248–59.

For **collocations** see: Hausmann 1984; Kjellmer 1994; *The BBI Dictionary* 1997; *Oxford Collocations* 2002. On **idioms** see: Cacciari 1993; Everaert *et al.* 1995; Fernando 1996; Moon 1998. Edmondson and House 1981 offer a treatment of **speech act idioms**. For study materials on **pragmatic idioms** see: Blundell, Higgens and Middlemiss 1982; Lee 1983.

The **discourse structuring function** of fixed expressions is treated in: Everaert *et al.* 1995; Moon 1998.

On **proverbs** see: Mieder 1989, 1993; Pätzold 1998; Charteris-Black 1999 is a corpus-based study of proverbs still in common use.

Chapter 4

The pronunciation and spelling of English

This chapter deals with the phonology of English together with a certain degree of phonetic detail and the essentials of English orthography. Naturally, a treatment of this length cannot take the place of a textbook in phonetics and phonology or a manual of spelling. Its aim is rather to present fundamental and systematic characteristics of, as well as tendencies in, the development of English pronunciation and to give the principles of English spelling in outline.

4.1 THE PHONOLOGY OF ENGLISH

In order to talk about the sound structure of English it is necessary to make certain abstractions from actual sounds. This means that the varied phonetic realization of the many speakers and the many varieties of English (idiolects, dialects, network standards, registers etc.) will be less at the centre of attention than the features these various pronunciations share. This procedure stands in contrast to an **acoustic**, **auditory** or **articulatory** description of a particular variety of English, which is what the discipline of **phonetics** would provide. Instead we assume a system that ignores the exact phonetic details of actual speakers, but rather deals with the meaningful sound contrasts or oppositions of the spoken language of as many varieties as possible. This is, then, a sketch of the **phonology** of English.

Fortunately for such a description, the inventory of the phonemes of those forms of English which speakers of Standard English (StE) use all over the world reveals only relatively small differences. This observation relies on the recognition of 'standard' pronunciations, particularly of the widely accepted ones called **Received Pronunciation** or **RP** in England and **General American (GenAm)** in North America. These and other standard accents such as Cultivated Australian (see 13.1.1), Conservative South African English (13.3.1), or Standard Scottish English (10.2.3) are in many respects artificial; for example, they gloss over a great many differences based on the class, gender, age or even region of the speakers. General American, for one, is ill-defined in the extreme and covers a wide of array of geographical areas. RP, for its part, is frequently divided into 'conservative', 'advanced' and 'affected', categories which correspond at least partly to age (see 10.1.3). In addition, studies all over the English speaking world have revealed class and male–female distinctions in pronunciation. Nevertheless, speakers everywhere do seem to recognize the existence of pronunciation norms and even to agree to an astonishingly high degree on what they are. However, this is *not* the case with numerous non-standard dialects such as Lowland Scots (10.2.2), Pidgin and Creole English (14.3), or English as a second or foreign language (14.1–2). It is because of this that we feel justified in proceeding as we do and outlining here, based chiefly on RP and GenAm, what we call 'the pronunciation of English'.

4.2 SEGMENTAL SOUNDS

It is possible to divide every linguistic utterance completely up into sequential sound segments which belong to a limited inventory of sounds. These sounds are called **phonemes**, and they are conventionally enclosed in slanted lines, e.g. /m/ for an 'm' sound as in *mat*. The concept of the phoneme is quite useful because it provides an abstract level of description which embodies the systematic sound contrasts of the language without becoming lost in minute phonetic detail. Nevertheless, it is not so abstract that it does not reflect the actual sounds of the language.

The segmental sounds are divided into vowels and consonants. A **vowel** is defined, *phonetically*, as a sound which is produced without audible friction or blockage in the flow of air along the central line of breath from the lungs through the mouth. To this must be added the *phonological*, or structural observation that vowels always form the centre of a syllable. All other sounds are consonants. Phonetically, this means only sounds which are produced with friction or blockage; but phonologically it includes sounds which are peripheral to the syllable. Note that these two approaches do not lead to the same results (see below **semi-vowels**). In this description, the phonemic view will generally be favoured.

For English it is possible to postulate 24 consonants (see Table 4.1 below) as well as 16 vowels in GenAm or 20 vowels in RP. Each of these phonemes is fully distinct from each of the others within its system. The idea behind the concept of the phoneme is that it designates the smallest unit of sound which causes a potential difference in meaning. This principle can be demonstrated through the use of what are called **minimal pairs**: if two words which differ with regard to one sound only have different meanings, then the two differing sounds are not the same phoneme. By a process of extension to ever more such oppositions in sound and meaning, it is theoretically possible to establish just which sounds are the phonemes of a given language such as English or a particular accent such as RP or GenAm. In Figure 4.1 *mat* differs from *gnat*, *met* and *mad* in meaning. This demonstrates that /m/ is not the same as /n/, that /t/ is distinct from /d/ and that /æ/ and /e/ are not identical. Eventually all the possible combinations might be tried out until it is established that English has the number of phonemes mentioned above.

In reality sounds occur which cannot always be clearly attributed to one single phoneme. For example, the second sound in the word *stop* is, despite the spelling, neither unambiguously a /t/ nor a /d/. This has to do with the fact that /p, t, k/, which are normally **aspirated**, i.e. pronounced with a brief puff of breath, are not aspirated after a preceding /s/ in the same syllable; as a result the correspondingly **unaspirated** sounds /b, d, g/ can no longer be distinguished from them. This is all the more the case since /b, d, g/, which are typically **voiced** (i.e. the vocal cords vibrate when they are pronounced), tend to lose their voicing (become **devoiced**) following /s/ and so to resemble /p, t, k/, which are always **voiceless**. Here, in other words, the difference between /t/ and /d/ is **neutralized**

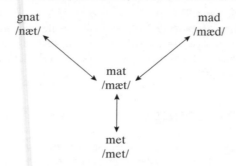

Figure 4.1   Examples of phoneme oppositions

(*disdain* is pronounced identically with *distain*, and *disgust* is indistinguishable from *discussed*). A sound which realizes two or more neutralized phonemes is sometimes referred to as an **archiphoneme** and transcribed with a capital letter symbol, in this case as /T/.

The example of neutralization shows that phonemes may have phonetic traits or characteristics in common; indeed, that is why /t/ and /d/ are so similar. An explanation for this may be seen in the fact that each phoneme is defined by a number of features which are characteristic of it and of it alone. For example, /t/ is (a) **alveolar** (articulated at the tooth ridge; see Figure 4.2), (b) aspirated, (c) voiceless and (d) plosive. A **plosive** phoneme (also called a **stop**) is one which is articulated by momentarily stopping the flow of air and then releasing the built-up pressure with a kind of explosive force. /d/ is also alveolar and plosive; however, it is not aspirated and, although sometimes voiceless, is typically voiced. Shared features characterize the similarities between phonemes while the particular combination of features distinguishes each from all the others.

Within the system of English consonants, three features are sufficient to distinguish all the consonants from each other: **place of articulation**, **manner of articulation** and **force of articulation** (hard or **fortis** versus soft or **lenis**). Lenis is regularly associated with voicing (vibration of the vocal cords) and fortis with voicelessness. For the vowels three features are also sufficient to make all the necessary distinctions of English: **the height** and **the horizontal position of the tongue** at its highest point and the **complexity of the vowel** (short vs long or diphthongized). The features named, which distinguish every phoneme from every other phoneme, are only a selection from the many possible features which any one of these sounds has; for this reason these features are called **distinctive features**. They have been chosen in such a way that they reflect the systematic, phonological oppositions within the sound system of English.

In the sense of phonetics, or actual articulation, any particular phoneme may sound very different from occasion to occasion. In particular, the phonetic environment in which a phoneme is produced may lead to noticeable differences in actual pronunciation. However, as long as the exchange of one such variant for another does not cause a difference in meaning, each of the realizations may be regarded as one and the same phoneme. Varying pronunciations of each 'single sound' are known as the **allophones** of a phoneme. It is usual to enclose the symbol for an allophone in square brackets, [ ].

A readily observable example of an allophone is /l/, which may be pronounced as a **clear** [l], as in *million* (it has some of the quality of the vowel /ɪ/ as in *fit* associated with it). This pronunciation typically occurs when /l/ precedes a vowel in RP. However, the /l/ may be **dark** [ɫ], as in *pull*, which means it has some of the sound quality of the vowel /ʊ/ as in *foot*. This is the way an /l/ is pronounced in RP when it is not followed by a vowel. The difference between the two is easy to hear; however, if they are exchanged one for the other, the words in which they occur do not become different words or unidentifiable sound sequences. (For more on /l/ see 4.3.1, p. 72.)

This is not always unproblematic, for in some accents of English (e.g. Cockney, various areas in the United States, New Zealand), /l/ is completely **vocalized**, that is, realized more or less like the vowel /ʊ/. In this case there is the possibility that new **homophones** (words which sound alike, but carry different meanings) may be created. The following words may, for example, be pronounced similarly in Cockney: *Paul* [pɔːʊ] or [pɔːə], *paw*, *pore*, *poor* [pɔː] or [pɔːə] (e.g. Wells 1982: 316). The theoretical question is whether the [ʊ] of [pɔːʊ] (*Paul*) is an allophone of /l/ or whether it has merged with the phoneme /ʊ/.

4.3 THE CONSONANTS

The inventory of English consonants has remained stable to a remarkable degree over several hundred years. As a result it is the consonants which contribute most to the phonological unity of the English language in its many and often quite different sounding accents throughout the world. The form of any English word is most easily characterized by the position and type of combination of its consonants.

Since the first Germanic sound shift (also known as Grimm's Law) in the third or second century BC, there have been no major changes. However, in the Middle English period (roughly between 1050 and 1500) the three sounds [ð], [ʒ] and [ŋ], which until then had been allophones of /θ/, /ʃ/ and /n/, became independent phonemes. In the same period the phoneme /x/ (the consonant sound of German *ach* or *ich*, which once regularly appeared in words still written with <gh> such as *right* or *thought*) disappeared in all but a few regions, most particularly the regional dialects of Scotland. In addition, the phoneme /hw/ (as in *which*) is presently losing its status as an independent phoneme for more and more speakers as it converges with /w/ (as in *witch*) – something that has already happened in RP and for most GenAm speakers.

The consonants may be divided up into the following types as far as the degree of their consonant-like nature is concerned.

Semi-vowels   Semi-vowels or **approximants** or **frictionless continuants** are consonants which are usually produced without audible friction in, or stoppage of, the air coming from the lungs; phonetically, therefore, they are vowel-like. However, they do not form the centre of a syllable, but are peripheral; that is, they are found initially or finally. In this phonological sense, therefore, they are consonants. The semi-vowels of English include /w, r, j/, though each also has variants (allophones) which involve friction and/or stoppage. /h/ may also be said to belong here; for, although it is not **sonorous** (that is, it is not produced with vibration of the vocal cords), it is voiceless and it has as many variants as there are vowels which may follow it. For this reason it will be called a **voiceless vowel** (i.e. it is whispered). However, it is also often termed **voiceless glottal fricative**, which would put it in the group of obstruents below.

Sonorant consonants   The **sonorant consonants** are those which are articulated with partial closure of the respiratory passage and vibration of the vocal cords. They are usually found at an initial or a final position in the syllable; however, under certain circumstances they may also be **syllabic**, i.e. central to a syllable. This is, for example, true of the /l/ in *bottle* [ḷ] (the small stroke under the *l* indicates that it is syllabic). In this sense sonorants sometimes resemble vowels phonologically. They include the nasals /m, n, ŋ/, which are articulated with closure of the mouth (the air stream is released through the nose), and the lateral /l/, which has partial closure of the mouth at the alveolar ridge with a lateral release of air around the sides of the tongue, which only touches the top of the mouth in the middle.

Obstruents   The **obstruents**, finally, are the 'true' consonants, which are produced with friction (the **fricatives**), e.g. /f, ð, ʃ/ or complete closure and blockage of the air stream (**stops** or **occlusives** or **plosives**), e.g. /p, d, g/, or a combination of the two (the **affricates**), /tʃ, dʒ/. Furthermore, they are always peripheral to the syllable.

Phonologically, the system of English consonants is characterized by a high degree of symmetry. We can distinguish 24 consonants (with /hw/ 25) according to 3 distinctive features, as mentioned above. These are:

1   **place of articulation**, of which there are four main ones: lips (**labial**); alveolar or tooth ridge (**alveolar**); the **post-alveolar** or **pre-palatal** region, also known as **alveolo-palatal** or **palato-alveolar**; and the palate itself (**palatal**); one less frequently used one, the teeth (**dental**); and possibly the glottis (**glottal**) in the case of /h/;
2   **manner of articulation**, of which there are seven types (stop or plosive, affricate, fricative, nasal, lateral, semi-vocalic and voiceless vocalic); and

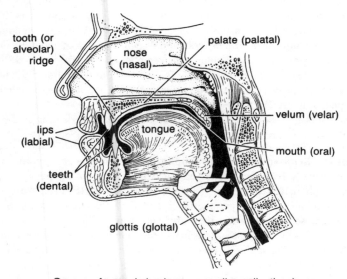

Organs of speech (and corresponding adjectives)

Figure 4.2   Places of articulation

Table 4.1   The consonants of English

Manner	Place					
	labial[1]	dental[2]	alveolar	post alveolar[3]	palatal	glottal
stop[4]	p b		t d		k g	
affricate[4]				tʃ dʒ		
fricative[4]	f v	θ ð	s z	ʃ ʒ		h
nasal	m		n		ŋ[5]	
lateral[6]			l		ɬ	
semi-vowel[7]			j[8]	r	w	
voiceless vowel[9]				h		

Notes:
1 /p, b, m/ are bilabial; /f, v/ are labio-dental.
2 /θ/ is called 'theta'; /ð/ is called 'eth' or 'barred d'.
3 There is a strong tradition in North America to use č, ǰ, š, ž (c-wedge, j-wedge etc.; the <ˇ> is called 'hachek') for tʃ, dʒ, ʃ ('esh' or 'long s') and ʒ ('yogh').
4 The left-hand symbol represents the fortis or voiceless phoneme; the one on the right, the lenis or voiced one. Sometimes /h/ is seen as a (voiceless) glottal fricative.
5 /ŋ/ is called 'eng'.
6 [l] and [ɬ] are allophones of /l/; see below.
7 /hw/ is present in some accents, e.g. Scots.
8 In North American traditions, often /y/.
9 /h/ is realized in numerous positional variants; see below.

3   **force of articulation**, which distinguishes soft or **lenis** from hard or **fortis**. This distinction generally coincides with voicing, that is, the distinction between **voiced** from **voiceless**. This third opposition involves only the stops, affricates and fricatives, i.e. the obstruents. In describing a consonant the usual order is force/voicing, place, manner, e.g. a fortis/voiceless, alveolar stop.

Despite the above-mentioned stability of the system many of the phonemes listed in Table 4.1 are involved in a noticeable process of change in the one or the other of the many varieties of English somewhere in the world. These changes are, however, seldom of phonological significance.

4.3.1 Manner and place of articulation

Obstruents   The high degree of symmetry in the occurrence of the stops and the fricatives is very noticeable. (Note that labio-dental /f/ and /v/ are classified as labial.) There are four pairs of stops and four of fricatives if the affricates /tʃ/ and /dʒ/, which consist of a close connection of a stop and a **homorganic** fricative (one produced at the same place or organ of speech), are counted with the stops. There has long been discussion about whether /tʃ/ and /dʒ/ are each a single phoneme or a combination of two. Phonologically, however, the freedom with which both may appear initially (*cheese, job*), medially (*bachelor, major*) or finally (*rich, ridge*) in words is a small indication of their unitary (one phoneme) status. Aside from this point note that there is a lack of balance between the stops and the fricatives, a 'mismatch' which is caused by the lack of the palatal fricatives /x/ and /ɣ/ and the presence of the dental fricatives /θ/ and /ð/. Note that the fricative /x/ (like the *ach* sound of German) with its allophonic variant [ç] (the *ich* sound) has, as already mentioned, been retained in the regional Scots dialects, for example in *night* /neçt/ or *loch* /lox/. Furthermore, many people use it in the pronunciation of foreign words or names such as *Bach* or the interjection *ugh* /ʌx/.

Nasals   The nasals do not occur in lenis-fortis (voiced-voiceless) pairs, for they are sonorants and therefore are, phonologically speaking, always voiced. There are only three nasals since the post-alveolar /ɲ/ of Spanish (*mañana*), Italian (*senor*) or French (*compagnon*) is not phonemic in English; instead, the analogous sound in English is seen as a sequence of two phonemes /nj/ as in *canyon* /kænjən/. Furthermore, the historically more recent addition to the nasals, the phoneme /ŋ/, is not fully equivalent to /m/ and /n/ since it cannot occur initially in a word, nor does it occur after all the vowels of English (in RP it follows /ɪ, æ, ʌ, ɒ/; in GenAm /ɪ, æ, ʌ, ɑː, ɔː/, e.g. *sing, sang, sung, song*, the latter with /ɑː/ or /ɔː/ in GenAm depending on the region).

The lateral   The lateral /l/ consists of two noticeably different allophones, clear [l] and dark [ɫ], which do not stand in phonemic opposition to each other. Indeed, there are accents such as those of southern Ireland or the southwest of England in which clear [l] appears exclusively, and accents from other areas, such as Scotland and some parts of the United States, in which only dark [ɫ] occurs. RP, as previously mentioned, is characterized by the **complementary distribution** of the two allophones. This means that in one set of circumstances only the one may occur and in another set of circumstances only the other. Concretely, clear [l] is used before vowels (e.g. *look, teller*) while dark [ɫ] appears before consonants (e.g. *help*) or at the end of a word (e.g. *goal*); this includes syllabic [ɫ̩] as in *bottle*).

The semi-vowels   The semi-vowels are difficult to adapt to the scheme of classification used here because they are, phonetically speaking, not consonants at all, but vowels which occur in the typical position of consonants, peripheral to the syllable (see 4.2). In many classifications /w/ and /hw/ are classified as bilabial. The rounding of the lips which is typical of /w/ and /hw/ is, however, of secondary importance and need not be present. Note that pre-vocalic /r/ is often produced with lip-rounding as well. The criterion which has been used in positioning the semi-vowels in the chart is the position of the tongue: /j/ corresponds to the high front vowel /ɪ/, because it has the same sound quality as /ɪ/. /j/ differs only inasmuch as it is extremely short (non-syllabic). Like /ɪ/ it requires a tongue position close to the alveolar ridge; hence it has been classified as alveolar. /r/ corresponds to the central vowel /ɜː/, which is more or less post-alveolar; and /w/ corresponds to /uː/, a high back vowel, which takes a tongue position close to the velum.

The voiceless vowel   /h/ occurs only before vowels and has a different resonance depending on what vowel follows it, hence the term 'voiceless vowel'. Preceding /iː/, as in *heat*, /h/ is [i̥ː]; preceding /æ/, as in *hat*, it is [æ̥] etc. The small circle ('under-ring') indicates devoicing; it is 'whispered'.

The glottal stop   [ʔ] does not have the status of a phoneme, but is so obvious in some accents of English that it will be treated below under 4.3.4.

4.3.2 Force of articulation and voicing

All of the obstruents are members of pairs of phonemes which share the same features with regard to place and manner of articulation. However, the members of each pair differ from each other in that the one is pronounced with more force or energy ('hard', 'fortis') and is always voiceless, i.e. the vocal cords do not vibrate while it is being pronounced; the other member of each pair is pronounced with relatively less force or energy ('soft', 'lenis') and is often, though not always, voiced. The pair /ʃ/–/ʒ/ differs from the other obstruent pairs because /ʒ/, which occurs relatively seldom, appears only at the beginning (e.g. *Zhivago*) or end (*rouge*) of words which have been borrowed from other languages and have been only incorporated into English imperfectly. In a medial position (*measure*) it is perfectly normal.

The nasals, semi-vowels and the lateral are always regarded phonologically as voiced, and indeed they usually are voiced phonetically as well. However, in a voiceless environment they may as a matter of actual phonetic realization become devoiced, e.g. *flee* [fl̥iː] or *twice* [tw̥aɪs]. /h/ is always voiceless. The voiced obstruents are fully voiced only in a voiced environment, such as between two vowels (e.g. /v/ in *giving* or /d/ in *sadder*). At the beginning of a word the sonority or voicing sets in gradually in the course of articulation, which means that voicing may be incomplete. In the final position of a word the voicing may be missing totally. In both of these cases the lack of voicing is not generally noticed because the distinction between the obstruent pairs is maintained more by force of articulation than by voicing. The /v/ of /laɪv/ is, for example, seldom voiced. The contrast to the /f/ of /laɪf/ is maintained, rather, because /v/ is lenis while /f/ is fortis. Furthermore, the length of the vowel differs since stressed vowels are longer before voiced than before voiceless consonants (see 4.4.2). In addition, the opposition between the 'voiced' and the 'voiceless' stops in initial position is supported by the aspiration which is associated with the fortis phoneme as opposed to the unaspirated lenis phoneme. In English no stops are aspirated after an /s/, as mentioned above in 4.2.

In AmE and increasingly in AusE the distinction between voiceless /t/ and voiced /d/ is neutralized in intervocalic position (provided the following syllable is unstressed); both are pronounced with voicing. Pairs of words such *latter-ladder* cannot, for this reason, be distinguished on the grounds of sonority or force of articulation. For some speakers the vowel preceding the stop may, however, be longer when a /d/ follows (see also 12.1.3).

4.3.3 Restrictions in distribution

The system of 24 consonants which has been assumed here does not mean that the various consonants are fully equivalent. The infrequency of /ŋ/ in comparison to /m/ and /n/ and that of /ʒ/ in comparison to /ʃ/ has already been pointed out. In much the same way initial /ð/ is restricted to the so-called grammatical or function words, which include pronouns (*they, thou* etc.), the definite article (*the*), the demonstratives (*this, that, these, those*) and basic adverbs such as *there, then, thus* etc. In addition, /ð/ never occurs directly before another consonant within the same syllable. The only exception is where an inflectional ending follows, but here the /ð/ is separated from the following consonant by a morpheme boundary, e.g. the regular inflectional {-D} (= /d/ of the past tense and past participle) as in *smoothed* or {-S} (= /z/ of plural nouns, possessive nouns or of the third person singular simple present of verbs) as in *paths, path's* or *breathes*.

4.3.4 Consonant changes

/hw/ is the only consonant which seems to be disappearing completely. Many speakers today use /w/ where once /hw/ was pronounced. In this way numerous <w-> and <wh-> words have become homophonous, so *wear* and *where*, *wheel* and *we'll*, *which* and *witch* etc. Nonetheless, many speakers still use /hw/ as an emphatic variant of /w/, as in *Why?!* /hwaɪ/. As a result there are cases in which people have been known to produce an un-historical /hwɑʊ/ *wow!*. The /hw/–/w/ opposition is still maintained in various American and British accents (e.g. the Northern dialect area in the United States and Scotland in Great Britain).

Especially noticeable is the disappearance of non-prevocalic <r> in many accents of English. While /r/ is pronounced wherever it is written in GenAm, in Irish English, in Scottish English and in various parts of the southwest of England, it is missing in such accents as RP, the English of New England and wide areas in the American South, Australia and New Zealand. In these latter accents an /r/ can occur only before a vowel. In talking about this split in the accents of English, it is convenient to speak of **rhotic** and **non-rhotic accents**, i.e. those which have and those which have not retained /r/ in all positions.

In those accents which have retained non-prevocalic /r/ the quality of this phoneme differs considerably. In America, Northern Ireland, parts of Scotland and the English southwest this /r/ is realized chiefly in the quality of the preceding vowel, which is **r-coloured**. In parts of southern Ireland and Scotland the /r/ may be rolled at the tip of the tongue, trilled [r] or flapped [ɾ].

Just as non-prevocalic *r* has become vocalic ('*r*-coloured vowels'), so, too, is non-prevocalic /l/ not only dark, as mentioned above, but completely vocalic in such widely separated accents as Cockney and Southern American: the tongue no longer touches the top of the mouth; instead, only the dark resonance of the back vowel /ʊ/, which is associated with it, remains (see the examples of homophonous *Paul* and *paw* given above for Cockney).

One of the stereotypes of BrE for an American is H-dropping, and, indeed, this is regularly the case not only for much of BrE, but for much of AmE as well as far as the change from /hw/ to /w/ is concerned. Beyond this, although an <h> is written in such words as *her*, *him*, *he*, all native speakers drop the /h/ when these words are unstressed (in the so-called weak forms). The stereotype which the Americans mean is the loss of /h/ in such stressed words as *hat*, *house*, *horse*. In a great many urban working class accents of England (but not of Ireland and Scotland) these words are pronounced *'at*, *'ouse*, *'orse*.

The simultaneous pronunciation (co-articulation) of /t/ and the glottal stop [ʔ] is typical of many urban accents of Great Britain and of GenAm as well. In BrE, however, it very often happens that /t/ is completely replaced by [ʔ]. It is this phenomenon which explains the humour of this remark made by a Glaswegian: 'My name's Pa'erson, with two ts' (McIntosh 1952: 53). In present day RP a /t/ is frequently realized as a glottal stop before consonants (except /l/) as in *hot day* /hɐʔdeɪ/.

The two dental fricatives /θ/ and /ð/ are often replaced by other fricatives. When this happens voicing/force of articulation retains its original distribution. The Cockney accent realizes the pair as /f/ and /v/ (*muvver* for *mother*, *nuffink* for *nothing*). New Yorkers often use /t/ and /d/ (*tanks* for *thanks*, *dis* for *this*) or the affricates [tθ] and [dð]; many Blacks in America have /t/ and /d/ at the beginning of a word, but /f/ and /v/ at the end (*dem* for *them, wiv* for *with*). In Ireland it is common to hear dental [t̪] or [tθ] and dental [d̪] or [dð] for /θ/ and /ð/ (the< >, which indicates dental articulation, is called a 'bridge'). In addition and independent of this, almost all speakers pronounce words like *clothes* or *months* without /ð/ or /θ/, namely as /kləʊz/ or /kloʊz/ and /mʌns/ when they are speaking casually.

Almost all accents of English have the pronunciation /juː/ for the spellings <u, ui, ew, iew/ieu, eu, ue> unless the preceding consonant is dental or alveolar. (An exception is the traditional accent of East Anglia, in which the /j/ does not occur for these spellings, e.g. *pew* /puː/.) When there is a preceding dental or alveolar consonant (/s, z, n, t, d, l, θ) as in *suit, exuberant, new, tune, dew, revolution, thews*, most accents of AmE have /uː/, the pronunciation varies between /uː/ and /juː/ in RP (see 12.1.3).

The sequence /h/ + /j/ as in *pew* [pʰjuː], *cue* [kʰjuː], *Hugh* /hjuː/ etc. is realized as [ç] (the sound of <ch> in German *ich*). (In *pew* and *cue* the [h] is the result of aspiration following /p/ and /k/ in word initial position.) [ç] is basically a voiceless fricative allophone of /j/; however, because of the meaningful opposition *who–Hugh–you* [huː]–[çuː]–[juː] the [ç] has marginal phonemic status.

4.3.5 Phonological processes

Palatalization   Wherever historical /j/ has occurred before an unstressed syllable, but especially in the suffixes *-ion* and *-ure* some degree of palatalization of preceding /s, z, t, d/ has taken place everywhere in the English speaking world, though not always in a fully predictable way. Such palatalization means that /s, z, t, d/ are pronounced slightly further back (at the palate rather than the alveolar ridge), as in the following examples:

	unpalatalized	palatalized
-ion:	/s/ (*missile*)	/ʃ/ (*mission*)
	/z/ (*fuse*)	/ʒ/ (*fusion*)
	/t/ (*motive*)	/ʃ/ (*motion*)
-ure:	/s/ (*fissile*)	/ʃ/ (*fissure*)
	/z/ (*please*)	/ʒ/ (*pleasure*)
	/t/ (*advent*)	/tʃ/ (*adventure*)
	/d/ (*verdant*)	/dʒ/ (*verdure*) (GenAm only)

In many accents the process of palatalization has been uneven, and there is change in present day RP (see 12.1.3).

Simplification of final consonant clusters   Whenever several consonants occur together at the end of a word, one of them is frequently left out. In the case of the few words which, according to the spelling and the phonotactics of English, can have a cluster of four consonants, such simplification is very common, e.g. *exempts* or *twelfths* are simplified from /egzempts/ and /twelfθs/ to /egzemps/ and /twelfs/. In addition, it is relatively normal, especially in casual speech, to drop final consonants in shorter clusters when the following word begins with a consonant as well, e.g. *west side* becomes *wes' side* [wesːaɪd] and *left leg* becomes *lef' leg* /lefleg/.

Assimilation   A number of the cases of consonant loss or change so far described are really cases of assimilation. A large part of the allophonic variation in English is due to this. The loss of the aspiration of fortis stops in word-final position, often even unreleased, or the voicing and flapping of intervocalic /t/ in AmE and AusE may, for example, be explained in this way. In the former case assimilation is in the direction of a pause or silence; in the latter, /t/ adapts to the sonority of the preceding and following vowels. These allophones are not consciously noticed as is also the case with the following: alveolar /s, z, t, d, n/ are dental [s̪, z̪, t̪, d̪, n̪] next to /θ/ or /ð/, as in *this thing*, *widths* or *right there*. In addition, the /t/ may have nasal release (the air is released through the nose; = [tⁿ]) before a nasal as in *button* and lateral release before /l/ (= [tˡ]) as in *bottle*. Or /k, g/ are pronounced with closure further forward against the palate when a front vowel follows (*king*, *get*) than when a back one follows (*could*, *good*).

Assimilation is also involved in palatalization. Indeed, whenever the pronunciation of one sound becomes in some way similar to that of a neighbouring sound, it is possible to speak of assimilation. Often only one single feature is changed. The following are well known examples in modern English of assimilation which occurred long ago and have remained frozen or irreversible:

- a change in voicing and force of articulation: in *have to* 'must' /hæftə/, the /v/ of *have* has become a voiceless, fortis /f/ due to the influence of the following /t/;
- a change in the manner of articulation: the original /d/ of *soldier* has become /dʒ/ under the influence of following /j/: (RP) /səʊldʒə/ (GenAm) /soʊldʒər/. (This is a case of palatalization; the place and manner of articulation have changed.)

Other instances of assimilation are dependent on the style of speech. What in careful, formal style is (RP) /ðɪs hɪə/ or /wɒt duː juː wɒnt/ and (GenAm) /ðɪs hɪr/ or /wʌt duː juː wɑːnt/ become (RP) /ðɪʃɪə/ or /wɒtʃə wɒnt/ and (GenAm) /ðɪʃɪr/ or /wədəjə wɑːnt/ in the casual style of colloquial language.

Morphophonemic alternations   If assimilation were seen as a purely sound conditioned phenomenon, many cases of alternation in form could not be explained because they are limited to certain grammatical and lexical classes of words. The form /beɪ/ *bay*, for example, is given the ending /z/ in order to form the plural *bays*. Since it is not possible to have a fortis /s/ here, this appears to be a case of assimilation to the preceding vowel. However, since there is also the word /beɪs/ *base*, in which there has not been a similar instance of assimilation, it becomes clear that the /z/ of *bays* is a case of assimilation restricted to particular circumstances. It involves only the inflectional ending and is therefore termed **morphophonemic**. It can be illustrated by the following examples.

(a) The ending {-S} (for the regular plural and the possessive of nouns and for the regular third person singular of the present simple form of the verb) as well as the {-D} (for the past tense, the past participle forms of regular verbs and the derivational morpheme {-ed} as in *blue-eyed* or *heavy-footed*) are realized in differing ways depending on what phonological environment they occur in. The morpheme {-S} is realized as:

/-ɪz/   when the word to be inflected ends in a homorganic fricative (/s, z, ʃ, ʒ, tʃ, dʒ/), e.g. *mixes* /mɪksɪz/, *bushes* /bʊʃɪz/;

/-z/ when the word to be inflected ends in any other phonologically lenis or voiced
      phoneme including a vowel, e.g. *boys* /bɔɪz/, *lugs* /lʌgz/, *child's* /tʃaɪldz/;
/-s/ when it ends in any other phonologically fortis or voiceless phoneme, e.g. *bikes*
      /baɪks/, *raps* /ræps/, *life's* /laɪfs/.

The morpheme {-D} is realized as:

/-ɪd/ when the word that is to be inflected ends in a homorganic (alveolar) stop (/t, d/),
       e.g. *headed* /hedɪd/, *heated* /hiːtɪd/;
/-d/   when the word to be inflected ends in any other phonologically lenis or voiced
       phoneme including a vowel, e.g. *allowed* /əlaʊd/, *rammed* /ræmd/, *saved* /seɪvd/;
/-t/   when it ends in any other phonologically fortis or voiceless phoneme, e.g. *licked*
       /lɪkt/, *brushed* /brʌʃt/.

Exceptions include such common, but irregular forms as *wife-wives* or *burn-burnt*.

(b) Lexical words of Latin origin are the second example of morphophonemic alternation. This has to do with the numerous words which end in the syllable /-ɪk/. Such words
as *public*, *historic* etc. show a change from /k/ to /s/ when a suffix beginning with <i> or
<e> is added. This alternation is due to assimilational processes in Latin and does not
apply to words of Germanic origin, e.g. RP:

public /ˈpʌblɪk/   *publicity* /pʌbˈlɪsɪtɪ/
                                     publisher /ˈpʌblɪʃə/ (here palatalized)
historic /hɪsˈtɒrɪk/   *historicity* /hɪstəˈrɪsɪtɪ/

but no such alternation in the following words:

stick /stɪk/   *sticker* /stɪkə/
picnic /ˈpɪknɪk/   *picnicker* /ˈpɪknɪkə/

English spelling, though inconsistent, makes the semantic–etymological relationships
involved in words derived from the Latin clear, inasmuch as the letter <c> can represent
both /k/ and /s/.

4.3.6 Phonotactics

Phonotactics is concerned with how sounds are distributed, that is, where they can occur
in a word (beginning, middle, end), which sounds can occur together, and in what relative order they can occur. Several points of distribution (involving /ŋ, h, ʒ, ð/) have already
been mentioned. To round out the picture in this area a few examples of regular combinations of sounds will be presented.

It is not possible, for example, to begin an English word with a combination of nasal
and stop (e.g. **mbit* /mbɪt/ or **dnime* /dnaɪm/). <Pn->, <gn-> and <kn-> are, as is well
known, only written: the stops are not pronounced. In the middle or at the end of a word
combinations of nasal plus stop are completely unproblematic in the case of the fortis

Table 4.2 Final and medial nasal-stop clusters

labial	*camp* /-mp/	*bomb* /-m/
	camping /-mp-/	*bombing*: /-m-/, but *bombard* /-mb-/
dental	*Lent* /-nt/	*land* /-nd/
	Lenten /-nt-/	*landing* /-nd-/
palatal	*think* /-ŋk/	*long* /-ŋ/
	thinker /-ŋk-/	*longing* /-ŋ-/; *singer*: /-ŋ-/ (but *longer* /-ŋg-/)

Notes:
Before the inflectional ending {-ing} the letters <mb> and <ng> are pronounced without the stops /b/ and /g/. The <g> of <ng> is, however, pronounced when followed by the comparative and superlative endings {-er} and {-est} as in *stronger*, *younger*, or *longest*. The <g> is not pronounced when the agent ending {-er} is added to a verb as in *singer*, *wringer*, *banger* etc.

In *bombard* /m/ and /b/ occur in two different syllables; cf. also *iambic*; /-mb-/ does not occur within a single syllable.

stops and of /d/, while nasal plus the lenis stops /b/ or /g/ can only appear in the middle of a word (see Table 4.2).

The phonotactics of English permits consonant clusters in which the semi-vowels /j, r, w/ and the lateral /l/ can occur after almost all the stops and some of the fricatives at the beginning of a word, e.g. /pr-, br-, fr-, tr-, dr-, θr-, ʃr-, gr-, kr-/. Only /s/ can occur before /p, t, k, m, n, f/ at the beginning of a word. At the end of a word considerably more combinations are possible. A large number of these consonant clusters are due to morphological endings like {-D} or {-S} discussed above or the {-th} (= /θ/) of many derived nominals (e.g. *twelfth*, *width*, *depth*).

4.4 THE VOWELS

Each of the vowels of English can be distinguished by three features: height of the tongue; horizontal position of the tongue; and the complexity of the vowel. In this brief presentation of the vowels, 20 in RP and 16 in GenAm, first the distinctive features (4.4.1 and 4.4.2) and then the status of non-prevocalic <r> (4.4.3) will be examined.

The nasality of a vowel (as in French, for example) is a further phenomenon; however, it is peripheral since its presence varies individually and regionally. Although it is typical of many varieties of AmE, it does not appear to be phonemic in any of them. Furthermore, lip-rounding, though not distinctive, is characteristic inasmuch as the front vowels are spoken with spread lips; the central ones with neutral lips and the back ones with rounded lips.

4.4.1 Position of the tongue

The sound quality of each vowel of English is determined by the horizontal position of the highest point of tongue, which can be in the front, centre or back of the mouth (the oral cavity). Three vertical levels are recognized: high, mid and low. Theoretically, a combination of these dimensions should provide for nine possibilities. However, among the short vowels of English only six of these are realized. A further short vowel is /ə/ (often called **schwa**); however, it is essentially different since it is always unstressed. (See below Figure 4.3.)

The system of the short vowels of English is of significance because it is the short vowels which have remained relatively stable over several centuries. With notable and clearly defined exceptions the short vowels are phonotactically limited to occurrence in **checked syllables**, that is in syllables which end in a consonant. This means that words cannot end in short vowels without a following consonant. Unstressed schwa /ə/ is not restricted in this manner. As a result there are no words of the form /be/ or /sæ/.

The notable exception to this phonotactic regularity is the use in RP (and the accents of northern England) of the vowel /ɪ/ as the realization of final <-y> or <-ie> in words such as *lazy* or *Suzie*. Most other accents (for example, in southern England, North America, Australia etc.) have long /iː/ here, and increasingly often RP does as well.

The vowel /ə/ is the form which many vowels may be regarded as 'taking' when they occur in unstressed syllables in the natural flow of speech. Schwa is never stressed. Because of the high incidence of unstressed syllables in English it is easily the most frequent vowel in the language.

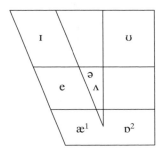

¹/æ/ is called 'ash'
²/ɒ/ is not present in GenAm

Figure 4.3 The short vowels

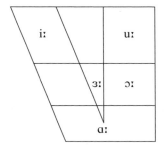

Figure 4.4 The long vowels

4.4.2 Complexity: length and diphthongization

Every deviation from the short nature of a vowel will be regarded here as a case of complexity. Length is one such deviation. Length is indicated by <ː>. Since, in addition, the long vowels have a distinct tendency in many varieties of English to be at least somewhat diphthongized, there is some justification for grouping length and diphthongization together. In addition, the short vowels are produced without special muscle tensing of the tongue (i.e. they are **lax**) while both the long vowels and the diphthongs are **tense**. The degree of diphthongization varies considerably, but it is usual to speak of three long **closing diphthongs** and two slightly diphthongized closing ones. Closing refers to the closing movement of the mouth during the articulation of these diphthongs. The arrows

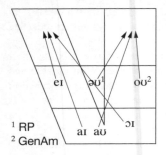

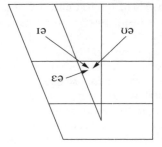

Figure 4.5 The closing diphthongs   **Figure 4.6** The centring diphthongs

in Figure 4.5 show the direction of the movement from the first to the second element of the diphthongs.

The two slightly closing diphthongs /eɪ/ and /əʊ/ (RP) or /oʊ/ (GenAm) are realized in many varieties (e.g. Standard Scottish English) or in certain phonetic environments (especially before fortis stops) in GenAm as long monophthongs, e.g. *gate* [geːt] or *goat* [goːt]. Three further diphthongs, /aɪ, aʊ, ɔɪ/ are pronounced as diphthongs in almost all accents. The centring diphthongs (see Figure 4.6) are present in RP, but not in GenAm (see below 4.4.3).

In addition to the phonological differences in length, which are of central importance here, there are also non-phonological length differences. All vowels, whether short or complex, are relatively shorter when followed by a fortis consonant and relatively longer when followed by a lenis one or, for those where this is possible, when no consonant follows (in free or unchecked syllables). For this reason the /eɪ/ of *late* is shorter than the /eɪ/ of *laid* or the even longer /eɪ/ of *lay*; the /æ/ of *back* is shorter than that of *bag*. This length difference may sometimes be used to distinguish *writer* from *rider* in GenAm, where both words have a voiced and flapped /d/ (= [ɾ]) in the middle. Since the /d/ of *writer* was historically a /t/, this means that for some (but not all) speakers the /aɪ/ of *rider* may be longer than the /aɪ/ of *writer*. Otherwise, the two words are indistinguishable. The same distinction may differentiate other pairs such as *latter* and *ladder*. It is not, however, clear whether such differences in length are perceived in normal speech.

4.4.3 Non-prevocalic /r/

Up to this point a system of 17 (RP) or 16 (GenAm) vowels has been assumed. This system and the comparability of these two standard accents becomes considerably more complicated when non-prevocalic *r* (traditionally termed 'postvocalic' *r*) is included. Non-prevocalic *r* refers to an orthographic <r> which is not followed immediately by a vowel (either within the same word or linked to an initial vowel in the following word); instead, it is followed by a consonant (*hard*) or comes at word end (*here*).

In the rhotic accents orthographic <r> is regularly pronounced in all environments. In many such accents the vowel system is noticeably simplified in the sequence vowel + /r/. (Note: this does not apply to all rhotic accents, for example, it does not apply to Scottish

Table 4.3 The vowels of General American and RP

Full system			Before <r> [in RP + consonant or zero]		
GenAm	RP	key word	GenAm	RP	key word
/iː/	/iː/	bead	/ɪr/ (or /Ir/)	/ɪə/	beard
/ɪ/	/ɪ/	bid			
/eɪ/	/eɪ/	bade			
/e/	/e/	bed	/ɛr/ (or /Er/)	/eə/ (or /ɛə/)	bared
/æ/	/æ/	bad			
/ɑː/	/ɑː/	GenAm: bod(y) RP: bar	/ɑːr/	/ɑː/	barred
–	/ɒ/	bod(y)			
/ɔː/	/ɔː/	bawd	/ɔːr/	/ɔː/	bored
/ou/	/əʊ/	bode			
/ʊ/	/ʊ/	Budd(ha), book			
/uː/	/uː/	booed	/ʊr/ (or /Ur/)	/ʊə/ (also: /ɔː/ sometimes: /ɔː/	boor your
/ʌ/	/ʌ/	bud	/ɜː/	/ɜː/	bird
/ə/	/ə/	baba	/ər/	/ə/	barbered
/aɪ/	/aɪ/	bide	/aɪr/, /aɪjər/[1]	/aɪə/, /aːə/, /aː/[2]	buyer
/aʊ/	/aʊ/	bowed	/aʊr/, /aʊwər/[1]	/aʊə/, /aːə/, /aː/[2]	bower
/ɔɪ/	/ɔɪ/	Boyd	/ɔɪr/, /ɔɪjər/[1]	/ɔɪə/, /ɔːə/[2]	Boyer

Notes:

1 The triphthongs /aɪr, aʊr, ɔɪr/ (= [aɪɚ, aʊɚ, ɔɪɚ]) are not stable and are therefore often pronounced as two syllables. This may result in an epenthetic [j] or [w] (= conditioned by movements necessary in articulation). Bronstein also counts [eɪɚ] as in *mayor* and [oʊɚ] as in *blower* as triphthongs (1960: 201).

2 There is a strong tendency towards simplification of the triphthongs in RP, called smoothing. Instead of the possible further triphthongs /eɪə/ or /əʊə/ one finds smoothed diphthongs as in the words *player* /eːə/ or *mower* /ɜːə/ or the monophthongs /ɛː/ or /ɜː/ respectively.

English.) In GenAm the oppositions that otherwise exist between /i/ and /ɪ/, between /eɪ/, /e/ and /æ/, between /ɔː/ and /ou/ and between /uː/ and /ʊ/ when /r/ follows are all neutralized. This leads to a system of just ten vowels (see Table 4.3).

Furthermore, in GenAm /r/ usually has the features of a vowel (it is a semi-vowel). (An actual consonant, such as rolled [r], occurs in few accents of English.) Combinations of vowel + /r/ in GenAm are often really phonetic diphthongs whose final element is an *r*-coloured schwa. This means the schwa has the sound quality of a retroflex [ɻ], produced with the tip of the tongue curled back towards the rear of the mouth, or a constricted [ɹ], articulated with lateral tension of the tongue. It is sometimes written with the symbol [ɚ]. This is the case, for example, with *fear* /fɪr/ = [fiɚ] or *cure* /kjʊr/ = [kjʊɚ]. The central vowel /ɜː/ is *r*-coloured without the need for a schwa [ɝ], e.g. *purr* /pɜːr/ = [pɝː]. This can be the case with /ɑː/ + /r/ as well, which may show up as in *car* /kɑːr/ = [kɑɹː].

Table 4.3 shows the full GenAm and RP systems of vowels on the left in comparison to the restricted system of vowels that occurs before non-prevocalic *r*. Note that the neutralized vowels may be transcribed with large capital letters, to indicate their status as archiphonemes. In the left-hand column there are only fifteen phonemes because /ɜː/ appears exclusively before an /r/ in GenAm. In the non-rhotic accents, in which non-prevocalic /r/ does not occur, there is also a reduced vowel system where non-prevocalic <r> is involved. Instead of the sequence 'vowel + /r/' RP has either 'vowel + schwa', schwa alone, or a long vowel alone (/ɑː, ɔː, ɜː/). The six sequences of vowel or diphthong + /ə/ are termed **centring diphthongs** or **triphthongs** because in each case their final element consists of the central vowel schwa. (Note, however, that /eɪ/ is generally realized as [ɛː]; more recently /ɪə/ is rendered as [ɪː] and /ʊə/ as [ʊː] or as /ɔː/.) This suggests that /r/ turned into /ə/ or, to put this somewhat differently, that GenAm /r/ and RP /ə/ are somehow equivalent in words with a postvocalic <r>. Such an assumption is, however, questionable in a synchronic description of present day RP (and other non-rhotic accents). The reason for this is that both /ɪ/ and /ɪə/ (the stressed vowels of *mirror* and *nearer* respectively) as well as /ə/, /eə/ and /æ/ (*merry*, *Mary* and *marry* respectively) appear in opposition before a following (intervocalic) /r/. Note that the schwa of the centring diphthongs is present together with /r/ in *nearer* and *Mary*. Consequently, it cannot be seen as a replacement for /r/. Furthermore, /ɑː/ as in *bar*, /ɔː/ as in *bore*, and /ɜː/ as in *purr* are all monophthongs without a second schwa-element which might be thought to 'replace' the /r/. When these forms occur prevocalically as in *barring*, *boring* and *purring* the /r/ is realized (see below 4.5.1). The oppositions /iː/–/ɪ/ and /eə/–/eɪ/–/æ/ only occur, however, before a prevocalic, i.e. intervocalic /r/:

spirit /'spɪrɪt/ – *spear it* /'spiːrɪt/
Harry /'hærɪ/ – *hairy* /'heərɪ/
herring /'herɪŋ/ – *hair ring* /ˌheə'rɪŋ/

In GenAm *spirit* and *spear it* are indistinguishable, but *marry* and *Harry* are often (regionally) distinguished from *Mary/merry* and *hairy*.

4.4.4 Transcriptional systems

Depending on the purpose which is being followed as well as the phonetic features which are considered important, the symbols used for a **broad** or **phonemic transcription** of the vowels of English vary considerably. Naturally, an analysis based on RP will differ from one based on GenAm for the simple fact that the number of vowel phonemes recognized will be different. Many dictionaries use symbols which are close to the sounds suggested by the spelling of English, e.g. <o> for /əʊ/ or /oʊ/and <a> for /æ/ etc. For use by non-native speakers, most learners' dictionaries employ a system based on the International Phonetic Alphabet (IPA). Table 4.4 provides a synopsis of the symbols used for the vowels of English in a number of important works.

4.4.5 Phonetic variety in the area of the vowels

The intention so far has been to present the vowels as phonemes. However, it is important not to forget that the phoneme is an abstract concept and that there are a large variety of differing realizations of each phoneme. It is this variety in pronunciation which often makes it difficult to understand an unfamiliar accent of English. To illustrate this, this section will take an exemplary look at one phoneme, /aɪ/, which will serve to show how varied actual pronunciation may be.

Table 4.4 Transcriptional systems

Key words		Based on RP			Neutral	Based on GenAm			
		Gimson 2001	Jones 1950	MacCarthy 1965	SAMPA 1995	Kenyon 1969	Trager/ Smith 1951	RHWCD 1991	MWCD 2001
bead	keyed	iː	iː	ii	iː	i	iy	ē	ē
bid	kid	ɪ	i	i	I	I	i	i	i
bed	kedge	e	e	e	e/E	ɛ	e	e	e
bad	cad	æ	æ	a	{	æ	æ	a	a
bard	card	ɑː	ɑː	aa	A:(r)	ɑr	ar	ä(r)	ä(r)
body	cod	ɒ	ɔ	o	Q	ɑ	a	o	ä
bawd	cawed	ɔː	ɔː	oo	O:	ɔ	ɔh	ô	ȯ
Buddha	could	ʊ	u	u	U	ʊ	u	o͝o	u̇
booed	cooed	uː	uː	uu	uː	u	uw	o͞o	ü
bird	curd	ɜː	əː	ee	3ː	ɝ	ər	ûr	ər
bud	cud	ʌ	ʌ	ʌ	V	ʌ	ə	u	ə
bet(deck)	c'ld	ə	ə	ə	@	ə	ə	ə	ə
bade	cade	eɪ	ei	ei	eI	e	ey	ā	ā
Boyd	cloyed	ɔɪ	ɔi	oi	OI	ɔɪ	oy	oi	ȯi
bide	Clyde	aɪ	ai	ai	aI	aɪ	ay	ī	ī
bode	code	əʊ	ou	ou	@U	o	ow	ō	ō
bowed	cowed	aʊ	au	au	aU	aʊ	aw	ou	au̇
beard	cleared	ɪə	iə	ie	I@	ɪr	ir	ēr	ir/er
bared	cared	eə	ɛə	ee	e@	ɛr	er	âr	er
board	cord	ɔː	ɔː	oo	O:(r)	ɔr	or	ôr	ȯr/ōr
boor	cured	ʊə/ɔː	uə	ue	U@	ʊr	ur	o͞or	u̇r/ōr
(bar)bered		ə	ə	ə	@(r)	ɚ	ər	ər	ər

Notes: Symbols from the International Phonetic Alphabet (IPA) are used in Gimson, Jones and Kenyon. The differing conventions reflect both phonetic differences between accents (RP vs GenAm) and changes in time (1950 vs 2001). The conventions employed by MacCarthy as well as Trager/Smith make use of only a limited number of special symbols, which made typewriter use feasible. In addition, Trager/Smith base their transcription on systematic considerations concerning English phonology (single symbols for short, simple vowels; double symbols for complex vowels, which are always a combination of a simple vowel and a high front element (/y/), a high back element (/w/), an element of length (/h/) or with /r/. SAMPA (Speech Assessment Methods Phonetic Alphabet) uses symbols that are available in the ASCII system and thus make transcriptions via e-mail possible. The final two systems given (*Random House Webster's College Dictionary* 10th edn, ed. by R.B. Costello, and *Merriam-Webster's Collegiate Dictionary* 10th edn, ed. by F.C. Mish) are typical of many dictionaries intended for native speakers (especially in North America); it uses the symbols, i.e. letters suggested by common English spellings and modified by such traditional conventions as diacritical marks for short (<˘>) and long (<¯>) vowels.

The phoneme /aɪ/ varies noticeably in the one or the other accent in one or more of the following four ways:

1   retraction of the first element;
2   raising of the first element;
3   weakening of the second element, resulting in some cases in a monophthong;
4   a split of the single phoneme into two distinct allophones in complementary distribution.

Retraction of the first element is noticeable especially in London Cockney and in the less prestigious accents of Australia, New Zealand and South Africa. Here the first element is frequently a back, open and, in some areas, slightly rounded vowel, resulting in something like [ɒɪ]. The settlement history of Australia, New Zealand and South Africa from the late eighteenth century, with a large number of immigrants from the home counties (around London) where Cockney is centred, offers an explanation for this wide ranging similarity. However, some other independent reason must be found to explain why [ɒɪ] is also the pronunciation traditionally found on the Outer Banks, the islands off the coast of North Carolina, which were settled considerably earlier. A degree of retraction, though less extreme, is also sometimes to be found in RP: [ɑɪ]. This is perhaps indicative of the way in which RP may develop, for various other developments in RP were first (and more extremely) observed in Cockney before they became the accepted realization in RP (see also 10.4.1).

Raising of the first element is to be found in Norwich, in the far north of England, in Wales, in Ireland, in New England and in Barbados and the Bahamas. The quality of the phoneme may be symbolized as [ʌi] (Norwich, Barbados, the Bahamas), [ʌɪ] (Ireland), [əɪ] (the far north of England), or [ɜɪ] (Wales, New England). Raising is also typical of Canada ('Canadian raising'; see 11.2.1) and in parts of Maryland, Virginia, North and South Carolina, Georgia and Florida (the Tidewater South). Here, however, [əi] or [əɪ] only occurs before a voiceless-fortis consonant. In other phonetic environments the pronunciation of /aɪ/ is [aɪ] (Canada) or [aːə] (for example, Virginia) or [ɑːɪ] (for example, South Carolina). This means that the vowels in *rice* and *rise* are clearly different:

rice [rəɪs]   *rise*   [raɪz] (Canada)
[raːəz] (Tidewater Virginia)
[rɑːɪz] (Tidewater South Carolina)

A split of /aɪ/ is also the case in Scotland and the Scots speaking areas of Northern Ireland. In Scotland a pronunciation without raising, [ae], is used in final position, before a voiced-lenis fricative, or before /r/, as in *buy*, *prize*, or *fire*. Otherwise [ʌi] or [əi], for example in *wipe*, *tribe*, occurs. Morphological boundaries also play a role here, which is the reason why, for example, *tied* [taed] and *tide* [tʌid] constitute a minimal pair.

In a final group of accents /aɪ/ is realized as a monophthong. Many speakers in the American South, for example, have exclusively [a(ː)] or lightly diphthongized [aᵉ]. However, other more prestigious accents of the South have [ae] or [aɪ] before voiceless-fortis consonants. For speakers of the latter type there is thus a split of /aɪ/ as illustrated by the two vowels of *night time* ['naɪtːam]. A further example of monophthongization of /aɪ/ may occasionally be found in Cockney; this leads to pairs such as *laugh* = *life*, both as [lɑːf].

Monophthongization is to be found for further diphthongs of both RP and GenAm such as /aʊ/, which is realized as [æ] in Cockney (*about* is pronounced as if it were spelled *abaht*). A further example is RP /ɛə/, which becomes [e] through the process of smoothing in Cockney, South African or Australian English so that *bed* and *bared* may be distinguished only by length (Cockney) or hardly at all.

4.5 SUPRASEGMENTALS

The suprasegmentals are those aspects of pronunciation which are realized over a range of more than one segmental sound. We will be concerned here with juncture, stress, rhythm and intonation.

4.5.1 Juncture

Juncture is the suprasegmental area which, perhaps, has the most to do with the segmental phonemes. Basically juncture has to do with the way neighbouring words are joined. A word sounds different depending on whether it is enunciated very carefully as a single word or uttered in the flow of speech. When a pause follows a word, there is what is called **open juncture**; otherwise, there is **closed juncture**. The distributional differences between clear [l] in prevocalic position and dark [ɫ] before consonants or open juncture as well as various cases of assimilation which have already been discussed are part of the area of juncture. When one word ends with a consonant and the next begins with a vowel, the final consonant of the first word is normally bound to the second word in what is often called **liaison** (or **linking**). When this liaison does not occur the speaker of English often uses a glottal stop [ʔ] to separate the two sounds. Glottal stops are particularly common in emphatic speech.

One particularly important kind of liaison in English is the use of what is termed the **linking *r***, which occurs in several non-rhotic accents (especially RP; the American South, for example, while frequently non-rhotic, does not have a linking *r*). This means that a word-final postvocalic <r> is pronounced if the following word begins with a vowel. By itself or before a word that begins with a consonant the word *Peter* takes the form /piːtə/; *Peter Andrews*, however, appears with a linking *r* as /piːtərændruːz/. For some speakers the pattern of the linking *r* leads to the articulation of /r/ where no <r> occurs in the spelling. This is especially the case following /ɔː/, /ɑː/ and /ə/ and is referred to as an **intrusive *r***, as, for example, in *I saw Ann* /aɪ sɔːræn/. Not all speakers of non-rhotic accents share this pattern, and for many speakers it is looked down upon. (See also the /j/ and /w/ mentioned in Table 4.3 which come about as a result of the linking of two vowels.)

Juncture seldom has a phonemic function. Nevertheless, it is not difficult to provide examples of minimal pairs such as *an oat – a note*, which are distinguished, it seems, on the basis of juncture and syllable boundaries.

4.5.2 Stress and rhythm

The phenomenon of stress is difficult to define acoustically. Functionally, it serves to emphasize something against the background of its environment. This can take place in the form of a change in loudness, a change in pitch, or a change in duration. Usually, two or three, sometimes four, distinct levels of stress are recognized, namely, primary <'>, secondary <ˌ>, tertiary (not used in the following) and unstressed (unmarked). Stress has an immediate influence on how a phoneme is realized inasmuch as unstressed sylla-bles tend to have vowels with a schwa. Note the initial vowel of '*atom*, which is (stressed) /æ/, while the unstressed first syllable of *a'tomic* is /ə/. The weak stress of some sylla-bles can lead to an identical realization of otherwise differing words, e.g. *drive* and *derive* may both be /draɪv/. Naturally, these words are hardly likely to occur in contexts in which they might be confused, and even if they did, speakers could easily remedy the possible confusion by using a more careful pronunciation of *derive*, /dəˈraɪv/.

Aside from its influence on the realization of phonemes, stress has two further important functions. For one thing it differentiates lexical pairs such as '*Main ˌStreet* and ˌ*main* '*street* or '*pass on* ('to judge' as in *we didn't feel capable of passing on her qual-ifications*) and ˌ*pass* '*on* ('hand to the next person').

Secondly, it marks (in connection with intonation) the word which carries the **syntactic** or **sentence stress**. In the careful style of spoken prose, e.g. a speech read at a meeting or the news read on radio or television, this is usually the last lexical word (noun, full verb, adjective or adverb) in a clause. Most frequently the rheme (see 5.4.4), or that part of the sentence which contains new information, carries the stress. If a different word, for example, a function word such as an article, a pronoun, an auxiliary verb, a preposition or a lexical word besides the final one is to be stressed, this will be a case of **contrastive stress**. This means that the item which carries the stress is consciously emphasized in oppo-sition to what might otherwise be the case, e.g. *Jerry doesn't eat pickled herring (even though Diane does)*. One author calls this second function of stress, in which a particular word which contains new information is emphasized, **tonicity** (Halliday 1970: 40ff.).

The connection between rhythm and stress is an important feature of English. All lexical words carry a primary or secondary stress. The pattern which arises from this series of stresses provides the skeleton of English rhythm, for all the remaining syllables are (relatively) unstressed. English (like German) is, for this reason, referred to as a **stress-timed** language as compared to a **syllable-timed** language (such as Spanish). It is often suggested that English has largely even rhythm, or isochrony, with each of the stresses occurring at equal time intervals.

Most lexical words contain only one stressed syllable. The remaining, unstressed sylla-bles tend to be reduced to a schwa. This makes for notorious spelling problems for native speakers of English, who have difficulty remembering how to spell these unstressed vowels (for example, *<attendence>* or *<attendance>*.) Yet, because there can be shifts in the syllable which carries the stress, the full value of many of these unstressed vowels must be restored, for example '*Jefferson* with final /-sən/ becomes *Jeffer'sonian* with final /-ˈsoʊniːən/, while *Dickens*, also with a final schwa /-ənz/ becomes *Dic'kensian* with final /-ˈenziːən/. In the following examples some of the endings which cause a change in stress are listed. We begin, however, with examples of derivational suffixes which cause no change and then go on to some which do cause a change as well as a few which some-times do and sometimes do not.

Stress neutral (the addition of the suffix does not affect the placement of stress):

+ {-ment}: 'govern, es'tablish, pro'nounce, reas'sure, 'settle, a'gree
+ {-ship}: am'bassador, 'scholar, 'friend, pro'fessor, 'workman
+ {-ness}: 'happy, satis'factory, 'genuine, 'literal, 'yellow, 'neighbourly
+ {-al}: de'ny, ap'praise, with'draw, re'fuse, re'mit, ac'quit

Stress switch:

+ {-ation}: con'tinue–continu'ation; 'justify–justifi'cation; ac'cuse–accu'sation
+ {-ic(al)}: 'photograph–photo'graphic; 'analyze–ana'lytic; 'acid–a'cidic; 'ocean–oce'anic
+ {-ity}: 'lethal–le'thality; 'universe–uni'versity; u'nanimous–una'nimity
+ {-y}: 'photograph–pho'tography; a'ristocrat–aris'tocracy; 'democrat–de'mocracy

Uncertain behaviour:

+ {-ous}: 'courage–cou'rageous; 'moment–mo'mentous; 'outrage–out'rageous
but: 'prosper–'prosperous; 'mountain–'mountainous
+ {-ive}: 'subject–sub'jective; 'object–ob'jective
but: 'substance–'substantive; 'predicate–'predicative; 'lucre–'lucrative

Weak forms   One of the further consequences of the stress pattern of English is that monosyllabic, non-lexical, i.e. grammatical or functional, words are fully unstressed. They are, for this reason, termed weak forms. In the normal flow of speech, that is, if they are not in a position in the sentence such as the final position, where they cannot be reduced, the vowels of these words are rendered as schwa or the words are contracted. Here are some examples with their reduced forms indicated:

pronouns: *he* /iː/; *him* /ɪm/; *you* /jə/; *her* /ə(r)/ (e.g. *Did you see 'er?*); etc.
determiners: *the* /ðə/; *a/an* /ə/, /ən/; *some* /səm/; etc.
auxiliaries: *shall* /ʃəl/; *will* [ɫ]; *can* [kn̩]; *am* [m̩]; *is* /z/ or /s/; *are* /ə/ or /ər/; *have* /əv/ (e.g. *should of*); etc.
conjunctions: *or* /ə/ or /ər/; *that* /ðət/; *and* [n̩] (e.g. *rock 'n' roll*)
adverbs: *then* /ðən/; *there* /ðə/ or /ðər/
prepositions: *at* /ət/; *for* /fə/ or /fər/; *of* /əv/ or /ə/ (e.g. *helluva* or *kinda*); *to* /tʊ/ or /tə/ (e.g. *hafta* 'have to'); etc.

Under contrastive stress it is possible that normally weak forms may carry stress as well.

4.5.3 Intonation

The final major area of phonology is intonation or the use of changes in voice pitch (high or low). There are numerous variations in the details of its use from region to region. Nevertheless, the basic function of intonation is probably very similar for most varieties. Intonation has an affective, a grammatical and a discourse function. Thus it is possible to use the same sequence of words to express a wide range of feelings such as joy, indifference, sarcasm etc. by employing what often amounts to only the finest of differences in intonation. Intonation can also be used grammatically to signal whether a particular sequence of words is to be understood as a statement or a question, as a list of single features or a combination of common characteristics. Finally, it has also been pointed out that intonation is used pragmatically to add 'specific interactional [discourse] significance to lexico-grammatical items' (Coulthard 1987: 46).

English employs four basic intonational contours, referred to as **tones**. They are:

[1]   fall
[2]   rise
[3]   fall-rise
[4]   rise-fall

There are numerous variations which can occur, but which cannot be presented here. For example, the intensity, duration and range of the pitch change. Pitch change usually occurs within a single syllable, which is called the **nucleus** or **tonic syllable** or **tonic segment**. It may, however, be spread over further syllables which follow the actual nucleus and are called the **tail** or the **enclitic segment**. This is especially the case for the complex tones (tones [3] and [4]), where the speed of the fall or rise or the abruptness of the change from fall to rise (as in tone [3]) or from rise to fall (as in [4]) is involved. If one or more stresses are present, the whole stretch from the first stressed syllable (the head) to the nucleus is called the **body** (sometimes simply the **head**). For example, in answer to the question with rising intonation, *When did they leave?* [2], someone might say *They left at five* [1]. Here *five* would be the nucleus with [1], a fall; *left* is the head; *at*, the body (alternatively *left at* is the head); and *They*, the pre-head. In a simplified reply consisting only of the words *At five*, *At* is the pre-head; *five*, the nucleus; and there is no head or body. The affective function of a low pre-tonic and relatively level nucleus might be to convey lack of interest. In *They left at five* [2] a jump from a high pre-head to a low head leading into a rise on the nucleus could signal mild astonishment, as if to say 'Didn't you know?' Almost needless to say, the number of variations that actually may occur are so great that there has been little agreement about what the significant contours are, what meaning they convey and why this is so.

There do, however, seem to be two things of significance which can be said. One has to do with the general meaning of rises and falls, and the other has to do with how intonation serves to structure information in discourse, such as when a fall to low signals 'that a particular mini-topic is ended' (Coulthard 1987: 60).

The general meaning of falling and rising intonation   Halliday's analysis and interpretation of the intonation of English comes to the following conclusion: 'Tone marks the kind of activity involved, by a complex pattern built out of a simple opposition between certain and uncertain . . . If . . . certain, the pitch of the tonic falls; if uncertain, it rises' (1973: 124). In this way it is possible to understand both the affective and the grammatical functions of intonation as aspects of the same general criterion. A series of examples may serve to clarify this.

Statements are usually spoken with falling intonation [1] because they expresses certainty; if, however, the speaker is less certain or wants to appear less certain or dogmatic, this attitude can be conveyed by means of a final rise, as in *It's getting pretty late* [3] as opposed to the same statement with [1]. (See 13.1.1 on Australian Question Intonation, itself by no means limited to AusE; also 9.2.3 on women's intonation.)

A *yes-no* **question** is in order if a speaker is not sure whether something is the case or not. The appropriate intonation will normally be rising [2]. Even a sentence without the inversion of subject and auxiliary verb will probably be interpreted as a question or at least as contradiction, astonishment, or similar, if it is uttered with rising intonation, as with *It's getting pretty late* [2].

Wh-**questions** differ from *yes-no* questions in containing a premise which is in any case asserted. In the question *Where is your sister?* [1], the assumption is made that you do, indeed, have a sister. For this reason *wh*-questions always contain an assertion, and it is understandable that they take falling intonation. However, a low rise at the end is not unusual: it permits a question to sound more open and friendly, less absolute. Thus a low rise together with the sequence of words *When are you going home?* [2] is less certain than the same with falling intonation [1]; the result is that the speaker comes across as more polite and friendly, because a rise [2] leaves more room for the addressee to answer freely, even, for example, by perhaps remarking that he/she is not planning to go home at all right now (see also 8.2.2 on politeness).

An interesting alternative to Halliday's general principle is that of Brazil which can be stated as follows:

> We can generalize . . . that a basic function of the fall-rise tone is to mark the experiential content of the tone unit, the *matter*, as part of the shared, already negotiated, common ground, occupied by the participants at a particular moment in an ongoing interaction. By contrast, falling tone marks the matter as new.
>
> (Coulthard 1985: 105)

In these terms a statement with falling intonation, *It's getting pretty late* [1] is rather more peremptory because it *proclaims* something new to the hearer. The same statement with fall-rise [3] creates more social solidarity because it *refers* to common knowledge. When applied to questions, the same principle is valid. A referring tone, [2] or [3], 'projects the speaker's wish to have his assumptions confirmed with respect to a truth which he presents as having been negotiated'; proclaiming tones, [1] and [4], 'project a wish that the respondent should provide a selection from a thus far unnegotiated set' of choices (Brazil 1985: 171). In this sense, *wh*-questions usually have falls because the information asked has normally not yet been negotiated. Rising *yes-no* questions suggest: 'I think I know the answer: please tell me whether I am right' (ibid.: 172f.). Perhaps the greatest disadvantage to this approach is that it applies better to RP than to other accents of English. The widespread use of [3] described here is, for example, relatively unfamiliar in American English as well as in areas in the British Isles outside southern England.

The approach espoused by Brazil includes the idea of **pitch concord**, which helps to predict what type of response will follow. A nucleus which falls from a high or mid pitch level will suggest a response which starts on the corresponding level. A rise which ends high or mid will tend to have a similar effect. Ending a statement at a mid level pitch has the effect of asking for agreement [3] (a common ground is assumed); ending it at a high level would tend to call forth a definitive statement [1] (*yes?* or *no?*). A fall to low or a rise from low does not have the same constraining effect on the response: the hearer is free to respond as he or she wishes or not at all. Note that in BrE a perfunctory *Thanks* which falls to low releases the other from any obligation to reply and may therefore terminate an encounter. In AmE in the same situation *Thanks* is more likely to end at mid or even high, which allows for the more usually American *You're welcome* or the like.

Tonality   The information expressed by a sentence may be affected not only by the choice of tones and by the distribution of stress in the sentence, i.e. tonicity, but also by the number of intonational contours which correspond to a clause (according to Halliday (1970): tonality). Tonality affects the structure of information. When a simple sentence or a single clause corresponds to a single intonational contour, Halliday speaks of **neutral tonality**, which is the 'normal' or unmarked case. However, an intonational contour can be longer or shorter than a clause.

Non-restrictive (or non-defining) **relative clauses**, for example, can have their own separate contour, something which is not possible with **restrictive** (or defining) relative clauses, which must share a contour with the sentence they are embedded in. If someone has only one brother, then the sentence given below is non-defining and may appear as either (a) or (b), i.e. either with or without a separate contour for the non-restrictive relative clause, and the (b) version will be with a comma. If the speaker has several brothers, the relative clause serves to identify which is meant and is defining; hence only one contour, as in (b), is possible (and the comma is not permitted):

(a) That's my brother [1], who lives in Oregon. [1]
(b) That's my brother(,) who lives in Oregon. [1]

Alternative questions have different interpretations depending on which contours they have and whether or not they have more than one contour. *Can you speak Spanish or French?* may have the following interpretations depending on the tones and the tonality:

(a) Can you speak Spanish or French? [2] neutral: 'Can you speak either one?'
(b) Can you speak Spanish [2] or French? [1] 'Which of the two?'
(c) Can you speak Spanish [2] or French [2] 'Or maybe another one?'
(d) Can you speak Spanish [1] or French [1] 'Do you know any foreign languages at all?'

In conclusion, it should be pointed out that the relationship between tone, tonicity and tonality is complex and that the global interpretations presented here are far from being universally accepted. Despite the fact that intonation and stress are of central importance, not enough is known about either. Both contribute to the expression of speaker attitude and speaker intention and to the information structure of the sentence; however, **tempo** and **voice quality** are two further factors, not dealt with here, which play a similarly significant role.

4.6 THE ORTHOGRAPHY OF ENGLISH

Orthography refers to the set of conventions which are employed when writing a language. Since written conventions are not sufficient to express all the information which the spoken word transmits and because the written language has a long tradition and a set of regularities of its own, the two systems, that of speech and that of writing, correspond only imperfectly (for more discussion, see 1.6.2). To begin with, almost everything which is written is a part of StE and presumes a certain minimum degree of education. In addition, the written language cannot reflect the many elements which in the spoken language identify the emotional state and the regional and social origins as well as the sex and age of the speaker. (Of course, handwriting may offer some hints, for example young children or less highly educated writers of the language may be fairly readily identified. Some (especially fictional) writers also use dialect spellings for the regional and/or educational classification of people.) When such information about language users is to be expressed in writing, it is best done explicitly, for example, by saying in so many words that someone is male or female, is tired, angry, happy, or is old, young, poorly educated etc. Clearly, everything which has to do with accent and voice quality is lost in the written language. Only the choice of vocabulary and use of syntax remain as elements of style which may contain hints as to region, class, sex or age.

4.6.1 Punctuation

As one part of orthography punctuation serves two main purposes:

a)   it separates units;
b)   it specifies grammatical function.

Punctuation is governed largely by conventions but individual preference is also important.

The separating function is probably clear without further explanation. Included here are: indentation or free lines to mark paragraphs; spaces between words and the full stop (BrE) or period (AmE) <.>; the semi-colon <;>; the comma <,>; the dash <—>; brackets (BrE) or parentheses (AmE) <( )> etc. Commas, dashes, brackets/parentheses and inverted commas (BrE)/quotation marks (AmE) <' ' or " "> are generally used in pairs when they mark embedded material.

The grammatical function of punctuation includes the following: the use of the question mark <?>; the exclamation point/mark <!>; the apostrophe <'> as a marker of possessive case; underlining (in handwriting) or italics (in print) for emphasis or to mark the use of linguistic material or foreign words; as well as other less central conventions.

4.6.2 Spelling

English spelling has a bad reputation. This is partly because numerous words have more than one spelling, partly because many phonemes can be represented by a whole series of different **graphemes** (units of spelling consisting of a letter or sequence of letters), and partly because one and the same grapheme may represent various phonemes. Emery quotes the following sentence:

> In a *cozy* house *cater-cornered* from the palace a *finicky caliph* who maintained that a *jinni* had revealed to him the secrets of the *cabala*, spent much of his time smoking *panatelas* – sometimes *kef* – and training his pet *parakeet*.

and remarks that if all the permutations and combinations of different spellings for the nine words in italics as given in five different American dictionaries were added up, there would be 11,197,440 different *correct* versions of this sentence (Emery 1975: 1f.).

This kind of variation is interesting to note, but is trivial, for the spelling of English is fundamentally based on phonemic principles. However, there is an imperfect degree of correspondence between sound and sign due to such factors as

- historical spellings which have been retained (e.g. *cough, plough, knight, write*);
- etymological spellings (e.g. *subtle* and *doubt* with a <b> despite the lack of /b/ in the pronunciation; this is based on the model of Latin *subtilis* and *dubitare* even though older English had *sutil/sotil* and *doute* without a <b>); and
- a variety of foreign borrowings (e.g. *sauerkraut, entrepreneur* or *bhang*).

The spelling of the consonants   The situation is less complicated in the area of the consonants than with the vowels. In most cases there is a fixed correspondence between one letter and one sound; <k> represents /k/ and <b>, /b/. The exceptions are relatively few and easy to remember: the <k> of <kn-> (*know, knife* etc.) and the <b> or <-mb> (*comb, lamb* etc.), for example, are never pronounced (see above 4.3.6).

When there is no letter available in the Latin alphabet to represent a particular phoneme, a combination of two letters is used, for example the graphemes <th>, <ch>, <sh> or <zh> (<zh> in foreign words for /ʒ/). The fact that <th> is used for both /ð/ and /θ/ and that <ch> is used for /tʃ/, /k/ and /ʃ/ is, of course, inconsistent, but the principles behind this are easy to grasp. Initial <th> represents

- /ð/ in grammatical or function words, i.e. pronouns (*they, them, their, this, that* etc.), the basic adverbs (*then, there, thus*), or the definite article (*the*);
- /θ/ in all the other (lexical) words, e.g. *thing, think, theatre, thunder, thin*;
- /t/ in a few exceptional cases such as *Thomas, thyme, Thames, Thailand*.

In the middle of a word <th> is /ð/ if it is followed by <e(r)> as in *leather, weather, father, brother, either, other* etc. Only a few words of Greek origin such as *aesthetic, anthem* or *ether* are exceptions to this. When no <e> follows, <th> is /θ/, as in *gothic, lethal, method, author, diphthong, lengthy, athlete*. Exceptions with /ð/ are the result of inflectional endings which have been added on, especially <ing>, e.g. *breathing* (from *breathe*), but also exceptionally *worthy* (from *worth*).

At the end of a word /ð/ is sometimes marked by a following silent <e>, e.g. *seethe, bathe, breathe, teethe, clothe*, but individual words such as *mouth* (verb) are not differentiated in this way. There is also an alternation between voiceless-fortis singulars and voiced-lenis plurals for some words, e.g.

path /θ/   paths /ðz/
bath /θ/   baths /ðz/
mouth /θ/   mouths /ðz/ etc.

However, there are also numerous exceptions to this, e.g. *math–maths*, both with /θ/ or *lath–laths*, both with either /ð/ or /θ/.

The use of <ch> for three different phonemes can be explained by reference to the history of the language: words which were present in Old English have <ch> at the beginning of a word to represent /tʃ/, e.g. *cherry, cheese, church, cheap* etc. Words which entered the language from French after the Middle English period are by and large pronounced with /ʃ/ though spelled with <ch>, e.g. *chalet, champagne, chef, Chicago, chic* etc. In learned words, finally, which ultimately stem from Greek or Latin, initial <ch> is pronounced /k/, e.g. *chaos, character, chemistry, chorus, chord* etc.

Two letters are sometimes used for a single consonant phoneme when one would be sufficient. For example, final /k/ can be spelled <k>, <c> or <ck> (*took, tic, tick*); <g> and <gh> both stand for /g/ (*ghost, goes*); <j>, <g>, <dg> all represent /dʒ/ (*jam, gem, bridge*); <f> and <ph> are both possibilities for /f/ (*fix, phone*); and <s> and <ss> may be used for /s/ (*bus, dress*), just as <z> and <zz> may be for /z/ (*fez, fuzz*) etc. The reasons for this are sometimes of an etymological nature (for example, <ph> for /f/ in words from Greek). Often, however, the use of a single **graph** or letter versus a **digraph** (a two letter combination) is important because it provides information about how the preceding vowel grapheme is pronounced, as will be illustrated in the following.

The spelling of the vowels   When one of the single letter-vowels of the alphabet, namely <a, e, i/y, o, u>, occurs singly (i.e. neither doubled nor together with another letter-vowel as in <ee, ie, ea> etc.) and is the vowel of a stressed syllable, its phonemic interpretation is signalled by the graphemic environment. When a single letter-vowel is followed by a single letter-consonant plus another letter-vowel, it has the phonemic value of the alphabet name of the letter, i.e. 'long' <a> = /eɪ/, 'long' <e> = /iː/, 'long' <i> = /aɪ/ (also for <y>), 'long' <o> = /əʊ/ (RP) or /oʊ/ (GenAm) and 'long' <u> = /(j)uː/, as in the words *made, supreme, time/thyme, tone* and *mute* (see Table 4.5).

When, however, two letter-consonants or one letter-consonant and the space at the end of a word follow, the letter-vowels are interpreted (in the same order) as /æ/, /e/, /ɪ/, /ɒ/ (RP) or /ɑː/ (GenAm) and /ʌ/. Examples are *mad(den), pet(ting), hit(ter), hot(test), run(ner)*. In a number of words <u> is not /ʌ/, but /ʊ/, e.g. *bush, push, bull, pull, bullet, put, cushion, butcher, puss, pudding*. It is interesting to note that in all those words where /ʊ/ rather than /ʌ/ occurs there is a /p, b, ʃ, tʃ/ immediately next to the vowel and each of these consonants is pronounced with lip-rounding, as is /ʊ/. This seems to be a necessary, though not a sufficient condition since quite a few words have central, unrounded /ʌ/. Note, for example, *put* /ʊ/ vs *putt* /ʌ/ or *Buddha* /ʊ/ vs *buddy* /ʌ/ (see Tables 4.6 and 4.7).

Table 4.5   The 'long' vowels: spellings and pronunciation

Spelling	Pronunciation	Examples	Some exceptions
<a> + C + V =	/eɪ/	rate, rating	have, garage
<e> + C + V =	/iː/	mete, scheming, extreme	allege, metal
<i/y> + C + V =	/aɪ/	ripe, rhyme, divine	machine, river, divinity[1]
<o> + C + V = RP	/əʊ/	joke, joking, verbose	come, lose, gone,
GenAm	/oʊ/		verbosity[1]
<u> + C + V =	/(j)uː/	cute, nuke	–

Note:
1 Words which end in <-ity>, <-ic>, <-ion> (*divinity, mimic, collision*) have a short vowel realization of <a, e, i, o, u> as a result of historical processes (cf. Venezky 1970: 108f).

Table 4.6 The 'short' vowels: spellings and pronunciation

Spelling	Pronunciation	Examples	Some exceptions
\<a\> + C + C/∅ =	/æ/	rat, rattle[1]	mamma
\<e\> + C + C/∅ =	/e/	set, settler,	–
\<i/y\> + C + C/∅ =	/ɪ/	rip, ripping, system	–
\<o\> + C + C/∅ = RP	/ɐ/	comma	gross
GenAm	/ɑː/		
\<u\> + C + C/∅ =	/ʌ/	cut, cutter	butte
	/ʊ/	put, bush[2]	

Notes:
1 In RP and RP-like BrE numerous words follow a special rule for \<a\>; see Table 4.7.
2 See text for discussion.

Table 4.7 Words with /ɑː/ in RP, but /æ/ in GenAm

Spelling		Examples	Some exceptions (all with /æ/)
\<a\> +	\<f\>	after, daft	baffle, raffish
	\<s\>	ask, pass	gas, as, basset
	\<th\>	path, rather	math, hath
\<a\> +	\<m\> + C	example, sample	ample, ramble
	\<n\> + C	advance, trance	random, Atlantic
\<a\> + \<l\> + \<f\>		half, calf	Talmud, Alfred

In a final set of circumstances an \<r\> follows the letter-vowel. In such cases a whole new system of correspondences applies. One type involves \<r\> followed by two letter-vowels (e.g. *various*) or a single letter-vowel and a space (*Mary*); a second type provides for \<r\> followed by a letter-vowel plus a letter-consonant (*arid*) or double \<rr\> (e.g. *marry*); and a third type has \<r\> followed by a letter-consonant or a space (*part, mar*) (see Table 4.8).

There are, of course, numerous exceptions to these rules, as has been indicated. In addition, there are all those representations of vowels which make use of combinations of two letters (digraphs). Venezky (1970: 114–19) refers to these as 'secondary vowel patterns' and distinguishes between major correspondences and minor correspondences. **Major correspondences** include the use of \<ai/ay/ei/ey\> for /eɪ/ (*bait, day, veil, obey*) or of \<ea/ee\> for /iː/ (*each, bleed*) or of \<oo\> for /uː/ (*boot*). **Minor correspondences** involve such 'exceptions' as \<ai\> for /e/ (*said*) or \<oo\> for /ʊ/ (*book, good, wool, foot* etc.).

Spelling reform   English spelling seems to be regular and systematic enough to resist any serious attempts at reform. Nevertheless, two important tendencies may be noted. Popular spellings – especially in America and in the language of advertising – affect numerous words, in particular ones with \<-gh\> such as *do-nut* (*doughnut*), *nitelite* (*nightlight*), *thruway* (*throughway*), but also such expression as *kwik* (*quick*) or *krispy kreme*

Table 4.8 a–c   The pronunciation of vowels before <r> (cf. Venezky 1970: Chapter 7)

	Spelling	RP	GenAm	Examples	Some exceptions
(a)	<ar> + V + (V/∅) =	/eə(r)/	/er/	ware, wary, warier	are, aria, safari
	<er> + V + (V/∅) =	/ɪə(r)/	/ɪr/	here, cereal	very
	<ir/yr> + V + (V/∅) =	/aɪə(r)/	/aɪr/	fire, inquiry, tyre	–
	<or> + V + (V/∅) =	/ɔː(r)/	/ɔːr/	lore, glorious	–
	<ur> + V + (V/∅) =	/ʊər/	/ʊr/	bureau, spurious	bury, burial

	Spelling	RP and GenAm	Examples	Some exceptions
(b)	<ar(r)> + VC =	/æ/	arid, marriage	catarrh, harem
	<er(r)>	/e/	peril, errand	err
	<ir(r)/yr(r)>	/ɪ/	empiric, irrigate, lyric	GenAm squirrel
	<or(r)>	RP /ɒ/;		
		GenAm /ɑː/ or /ɔː/	foreign, oriole, borrow	worry, horrid
	<ur(r)>	/ɜː/	burr, burry, purring	urine
				RP hurry, turret

	Spelling	RP and GenAm	Examples	Some exceptions
(c)	<ar> + ∅/C	/ɑː/	par, part	scarce
	<er>	/ɜː/	her, herb	concerto, sergeant
	<ir/yr>	/ɜː/	fir, bird, Byrd	–
	<or>	/ɔː/	for, fort	attorney
	<ur>	/ɜː/	cur, curd	–

(*crispy cream*). Besides these unofficial reforms, a certain regularizing tendency has been standardized in AmE spelling with the levelling of <-our> to <-or> (*honour > honor*), <-re> to <-er> (*centre > center*) etc. (see 12.2.1).

Spelling pronunciations   Spelling also exerts a certain influence on speech habits so that so-called spelling pronunciations come into existence. Traditional /fɒrɪd/ (RP) or /fɔːrɪd/ (GenAm), for example, becomes /fɔːhed/ (RP) or /fɔːrhed/ (GenAm) and the previously silent <t> in *often* is pronounced by many speakers. Of this Potter writes: 'Of all the influences affecting present day English that of spelling upon sounds is probably the hardest to resist' (1979: 77).

There are, in other words, tendencies for people to write the way they speak, but also to speak the way they write. Nevertheless, the present system of English spelling has certain advantages:

> Paradoxically, one of the advantages of our illogical spelling is that . . . it provides a fixed standard for spelling throughout the English-speaking world and, once learnt, we encounter none of the difficulties in reading which we encounter in understanding strange accents.
>
> (Stringer 1973: 27)

A further advantage (vis-à-vis the spelling reform propagated by George Bernard Shaw) is that etymologically related words often resemble each other despite the differences in their vowel quality. For example, *sonar* and *sonic* are both spelled with <o> even though the first is pronounced with /əʊ/ or /oʊ/ and the latter with /ɐ/ or /ɑː/. Remember also the comment on <c> to represent both /s/ in *historicity* and /k/ in *historic* above in 4.3.5.

4.7 FURTHER READING

Van Riper 1986 discusses the **concept of GenAm** critically; **RP** is treated in Wells 1982. A readable introduction to **phonetics and phonology** is Roach 1991; a more technical overview is provided in Clark and Yallop 1995; for **phonetics** see Gimson 2001 and, less technically, Knowles 1987 (RP oriented); Kenyon 1969 or Bronstein 1960 (GenAm oriented). For extensive presentations of **generative phonology** and a critical discussion of **morphophonemic alternations** see: Chomsky and Halle 1968, especially Chapter 4; Shane 1973; Sommerstein 1977. Among the various useful **pronouncing dictionaries** of English, Wells 2000 can be recommended.

For a general introduction to **stress**, see Brinton 2000. For a detailed treatment of word stress, see: Fudge 1984; Poldauf 1984.

Intonation is covered by Brazil *et al.* 1980 and Brazil 1985; Cruttenden 1986; Crystal 1975; Halliday 1967a, 1970, 1973; Gimson 2001; Kingdon 1958; O'Connor and Arnold 1961; Pike 1945; Roach 1991. On tonicity see Halliday 1970 and 1973; for a more recent differentiated view see Maidment 1990. Coultard 1985, 1987 integrates intonation in discourse.

Spelling and punctuation: Many modern monolingual dictionaries of English contain a presentation of the rules and conventions of English punctuation. In addition, special books such as Carey 1972 or Partridge 1963 may be consulted. See also Salmon 1988 or Carney 1994. Venezky 1970 provides an excellent structural overview of spelling (see also Venezky 1999). For a history of English spelling, see Scragg 1974.

Chapter 5

Grammar

This chapter deals with the grammatical structure of StE. It is however impossible to do this without, on the one hand, making comments on other aspects of the structure of English (phonology, lexis, text types) and without, on the other hand, making at least occasional reference to regional and social variation in syntax and morphology. Note that a more detailed treatment of American and British differences in grammar is to be found in 12.3.

The following pages will concentrate on a presentation of English grammar which begins on the level of individual words, moves on to make some observations about functional word groups or phrases and then explores the fundamental syntactical relations of English at the clause or sentence level. The first level, that of the word, is concerned with an identification of word classes or parts of speech, and it briefly reviews the inflectional morphology of English. The second step introduces functional groupings of words, the noun, verb, adjective, adverb and prepositional phrases. The third stage goes more extensively into the way sentences in English are constructed; it identifies and comments on the various clause elements and both how clauses vary and how they are combined into more complex structures. The role of grammatical processes in texts is treated in Chapter 6.

5.1 WORD CLASSES

Within English grammar nine word classes are traditionally recognized: nouns, pronouns, verbs, adjectives, adverbs, prepositions, conjunctions, interjections and articles/determiners. While this division is useful, it also has several drawbacks. Among the advantages is the fact that these classes are familiar and widely used – including their employment in the description of numerous other languages – and the fact that their number is manageably small. What is problematic is that many of these parts of speech include subclasses which are often dramatically different from each other. As a result, it is sometimes difficult to find a clear common denominator and to make definitive judgements about class membership (see below).

Open and closed classes   One of the most noticeable disparities within the traditional classes is that between open classes and closed sets. This is the case, for example, with the verb. Most English verbs are lexical items, which means that they prototypically have relatively concrete content, often but not always easily visualized, e.g. *run*, *read*, *stand*, *investigate*, *take out*, *consist of*. New verbs can be added to the language and the meanings of old ones can be extended as needed to name new concepts such as *biodegrade* or *recycle*. These are examples which show that lexical verbs are part of an open class – 'open', because their number can be extended. Other verbs belong, however, to groups which may not be added to in this way; they are members of closed sets. Prominent examples are the auxiliary verbs, both non-modal (*be*, *have*, *do*) and modal (*must*, *can*, *shall*, *will*, *may* etc.). The items in these sets may be listed in their entirety. Furthermore, none of them are easy to picture: for they are not content or lexical words; rather, their meaning is grammatical. They are commonly referred to as **function**, **grammatical** or **structure** words.

Nouns consist exclusively of lexical words since the grammatical words with a noun or nominal function have traditionally been separated out into the class of pronouns. Adjectives are also a lexical class, but adverbs consist of both lexical and functional items (see below 5.1.5). Prepositions are usually regarded as grammatical, but there is, in fact, a wide range of types within this class stretching from the highly grammatical (for example, *of*) to the highly lexical (say, *to the left of* or *at the foot of*). Conjunctions and articles are functional classes, though conjunctions have important lexical dimensions to them (time, cause, concession, condition etc.). Interjections, finally, are a ragbag of linguistic and non-linguistic items; they include single nouns and verbs (*Hell!*, *Damn!*), phrases and clauses (*Good morning!*, *Break a leg!*), special interjectional items (*Wow!*, *Whew!*) and sounds such as whistles, coughs and sighs. They may mark surprise, disgust, fear, relief and the like; or they may function pragmatically as greetings, curses, well wishes and so on. They will not be considered in the following since they are governed less by formal consideration of syntax and morphology than by expressive and situational demands.

Morphological and syntactic criteria   Word classes may be determined by observing their possible inflectional morphology and syntactic position. Morphology is the more restricted criterion since several of the word classes have no inflections at all (conjunctions, prepositions and articles). Not even all nouns, pronouns, verbs, adjectives and adverbs can be inflected. In the sections on the individual parts of speech below, the inflectional paradigms will be presented in tables.

Syntactic position means that the part of speech of a word can typically be identified by word order. Concretely, a noun, for instance, can appear by itself immediately after an article (*the lamp*, *an expression*, *a book*). Prepositions appear before nominal expressions (*after the show*, *because of the accident*, *in spite of them*). Adjectives may appear after articles and before nouns, (*the red car*, *an unusual sight*, *a heavy load*). There are some problems involved in this way of defining word classes. Not all members of each class conform to the positional criteria. For example, some nouns are seldom if ever preceded by an article (proper nouns like *Holland* or *Lucy*; or nominalized forms such as gerunds, e.g. *working* or *being happy*). Some prepositions follow their objects (*two years ago*). Some adjectives are not used attributively (**the ajar door*). Furthermore there is overlap since, for example, some nouns take the same position as adjectives (*the dilapidated* (adj.) *house* vs *the brick* (noun) *house*). Similar objections apply to positional definitions of the other parts of speech. Furthermore, each of the definitions presumes an understanding of some of the other word classes. What this means is that we are dealing with somewhat vague classes grouped around typical members of the various word classes.

5.1.1 Nouns

At the centre of the class of nouns are those items which fulfil the positional requirements described above; added to this is the typical inflection of a noun (possessive {-S}, plural {-S}); and finally, semantic criteria may be applied: a noun is the name of a person, place, or thing. Obviously there are numerous nouns which do not inflect and/or do not fulfil the positional criteria, as mentioned in the previous paragraph; furthermore there are also innumerable abstract nouns, i.e. ones which are not designations for concrete persons, places or things, e.g. *truth, warmth, love, art*.

Words that do, however, conform to the characteristics mentioned are prototypical nouns. They may be simple, consisting of one word (*bird, book, bay*), or complex (*string bean, sister-in-law, sit-in*). Grouped around them are further items which conform only partially, yet are regarded as nominal because they can be part of the kind of phrases noun occur in, namely noun phrases, or NPs (see below 5.2). It is this functional similarity which serves most broadly to define the limits of the class of nouns.

Inflection Nouns are prototypically concrete ('persons, places, things') and, as such, refer to objects which can be counted. As a result they characteristically take the inflectional ending {-S} for plural number. Inasmuch as they refer to something animate they take a further inflection for possession (also {-S}). This results in the paradigm shown in Table 5.1. The spellings *'s, -s, -s'* are not differentiated in pronunciation; hence these three forms are **homophones**. The way {-S} is realized phonologically (as /z/, /s/, or /ɪz/) depends on the preceding phoneme (see 4.3.5). In addition, there are a small number of inflectional exceptions in plural formation (e.g. *child/children, man/men, deer/deer, goose/geese*). Non-animate nouns are seldom found in the possessive (exceptions are time expressions: *a day's wait*). Numerous mass or non-count nouns (ones not normally used to designate discrete, countable units) have no plural, e.g. *snow, water, accommodation* (always singular in BrE; but usually plural in AmE), *information, advice, furniture*, though the last three are frequently pluralized in non-native second language varieties of English in Africa and Asia (see Chapter 14).

Table 5.1 Noun inflections

	singular		*plural*	
common case[1]	president	/prezɪdənt/	presidents	/prezɪdənts/
possessive case	president's	/prezɪdənts/	presidents'	/prezɪdənts/

[1] **Common case** in the table contains all the non-possessive occurrences of a noun such as what is traditionally called the nominative or objective/accusative.

Table 5.2 The English personal pronouns

	1st person		2nd person	
	singular	*plural*	*singular*	*plural*
nominative	I	we	you	you
objective	me	us	you	you
possessive	mine	ours	yours	yours
reflexive/intensive	myself	ourselves	yourself	yourselves

3rd person singular	*masculine*	*feminine*	*neuter*	*plural*
nominative	he	she	it	they
objective	him	her	it	them
possessive	his	hers	its	theirs
reflexive/intensive	himself	herself	itself	themselves

5.1.2 Pronouns

Those words which can replace noun phrases (NPs) are called pronouns. They are a closed class, and they are divided into several well known subsets: the personal (including reflective and intensive pronouns), impersonal and reciprocal, demonstrative, relative, interrogative and indefinite pronouns.

Personal pronouns   The **personal pronouns** are used to distinguish the speaker (first person), the addressee (second person) and a further or third party (third person). They have, for English, a fairly elaborate set of case, number and gender forms.

   Case in English does not reflect grammatical function (subject, object) strictly. Predicative complements after copular verbs (*be, seem, appear, become* etc.) occur most frequently and naturally in the objective case (*That's **me** in the picture*). This may well be because the position after the predicator (= the verb) is the typical object position. Objective case forms can be subjects as well, especially if two are joined together, e.g. ***Me and him**, we're going for a swim*, even though such forms are often regarded as non-standard and the subject forms (*He and I*) are preferred by prescriptive grammarians. This may be attributed to the disjoined or **disjunctive** position of the two objective form pronouns in the example. Finally, the objective occurs as a disjunctive pronoun when the pronoun stands alone, e.g. Q: *Who did that?* A: ***Me**.* (but *I did*, where the pronoun does not stand alone).

   Two further pronouns are closely related to the personal pronouns. The first is the third person singular pronoun *one*. It is used for general, indefinite, human reference and frequently includes the listener implicitly, as in ***One** does what **one** can*. It is often regarded as socially marked, namely affected. Like the other indefinite pronouns which end in *-one*, it has a possessive (*one's, everyone's, someone's, no one's*, but also *(n)either's*). It differs from the other indefinite pronouns, however, in also having a reflexive form: *oneself*.

   The second type closely related to the personal pronouns consists of the reciprocal pronouns *each other* and *one another* (which are virtually interchangeable). They have

Table 5.3 The pronouns *who* and *which*

	animate/personal	*inanimate*
nominative	who	which
objective	who(m)	which
possessive	whose	whose

possessive forms (*each other's, one another's*), but no reflexive, which is logical since they function much like reflexives, referring to a previous referent. In contrast to the reflexives they must have a plural subject (e.g. *we, you* or *they*); the verbs they occur with express a mutual relationship (*we saw each other = I saw you + you saw me*).

Relative and interrogative pronouns Specifically *who* and *which*, these are the only other pronouns which have case distinctions. The interrogative *what* is used for a person or persons when the desired answer is a class of people, for example, a vocation (***What** is she? She's a chemist*), rather than a particular person (***Who** is she? She's my sister/Susan*). The determiner (see 5.5.2) *what* may be used not only for things, but for persons as well. Asked about their sister someone who has no sisters might say, *What sister?* This stands in contrast to someone with several, who might say *Which sister?* There is one other relative pronoun in common use in modern English: *that*; it may refer to animate or inanimate antecedents; it is never inflected. For more on relative pronouns (and relative adverbs) see 5.5.5.

The demonstrative and indefinite pronouns The former are inflected for number (*this, that, these, those*). Some of the indefinite pronouns are inflected like adjectives for the comparative and superlative (*(a) few, fewer, fewest; little, less, least; many, more, most*); the remainder are not inflected (*some, any, both, all, each* etc.) except for those mentioned above which take a possessive {-S}.

One special case is that of the pro-form *one*. The NP *the red house* can be replaced by the pronoun *it*, however the replacement for the single noun *house* is the pro-form *one*: *the red one*. This pro-form is inflected for number and possession like a noun (*one's, ones, ones'*), as are the forms of *other*, which may also replace single nouns, but which, unlike *one*, may not be modified by an adjective (e.g. *the (*red) others*).

5.1.3 Verbs

Lexical verbs **Lexical verbs** are an open class. They follow NPs in patterns such as: *the government **issued** a statement; my left foot **hurts**;* or *that symphony **is** a masterpiece*. Prototypical verbs designate actions (*issued*), but, other verbs also refer to states (*hurts*) or relations (*is*). They inflect for person (third person singular, present tense), for tense (past) and as present participle (*issuing, hurting, being*) and past participle (*issued, hurt, been*). This provides the paradigm shown in Table 5.4.

On the pronunciation of the regular morpheme endings {-S} and {-D}, see 4.3.5. As for the irregular verbs, there are various inflectional patterns for the approximately two

Table 5.4   Verb morphology

	irregular verbs	regular verbs
infinitive and present (not 3rd person singular)	write	fix
3rd person singular	writes	fixes
past	wrote	fixed
present participle	writing	fixing
past participle	written	fixed

hundred of them in English. Among other things, some verbs have no distinct past and past participle forms (e.g. *hurt, set, let, burst*). The verb *be*, on the other hand, has eight distinct forms (*be, am, are, is, was, were, being, been*). See also 12.3.1.

Verbs may be complex, consisting of more than one word. At least the following types are distinguished:

a)   **Verb + adverbial particle**: *put up, set out, hand over* etc. For example, *put up* in *they put up my cousin* means 'to provide with a place to stay'. The particle is stressed in pronunciation, which indicates that it is lexical rather than grammatical (see below b). If the verb is transitive and the direct object is a noun, the word order is variable: *they **put** my cousin **up***. This word order is normally the only kind possible with pronouns: *they put him up*, but not **they put up him*.

b)   **Verb + preposition**: *look at, count on, reckon with* etc. For example, *count on* in *we are counting on you* means 'to trust in, depend on'. The prepositional particle is not stressed, which indicates that it is more grammatical than lexical. Word order is invariable.

c)   **Verb + particle + preposition**: *put up with, stand up for, run out on* etc. This is a combination of (a) and (b). Since the preposition is always the element before the object, word order is invariable as in *they are standing up for their rights*.

d)   **Verb + noun**: *take a bath, give a talk, do (some) work* etc. For example, *take a bath* is one of the meanings of 'to bathe'. The noun is syntactically restricted (*take a bath, take two baths* etc. are possible, but *?*take the bath* is not normally used). This is part of what is referred to as nominal style (see 6.5.2).

e)   **Verb + adjective**: *be satisfied, become angry, turn sour* etc. A copular (linking) verb and a predicative adjective express a unitary meaning, which it is generally not possible to express with a single word in English (but *grow red* = 'to redden').

Auxiliary verbs   The **auxiliary verbs** are, as has already been pointed out, a closed set of function words. The non-modal auxiliaries are *be* (eight forms, see above), *have* (four forms: *have, has, had, having*) and *do* (three forms as an auxiliary: *do, does, did*). The modal auxiliaries are defective. None of them has the {-S} inflection of the third person singular present tense. In fact, some have only one form, *must, ought (to)*. This applies to *dare, need, used (to), had better* inasfar as they are modal verbs at all.

There are four paired sets of modals: *shall, should; can, could; will, would; may, might*. These pairs are seldom related to each other in the same way as the present and past tenses of lexical verbs (see 5.4.5).

A final unusual formal feature of some of the auxiliaries is the pronunciation many of them have in RP when combined with the contraction of *not*: *do* /duː/ becomes *don't* /dəʊnt/ (the vowel of *do* becomes /ʌ/ in *does*); *will* /wɪl/ becomes *won't* /wəʊnt/; *shall* /ʃæl/ becomes *shan't* /ʃɑːnt/; *can* /kæn/ becomes *can't* /kɑːnt/ (in RP); *am* /æm/ becomes *aren't* /ɑːnt/ (for some speakers). In GenAm the /əʊ/ of *don't* and *won't* is, of course /oʊ/, and the /ɑː/ of *shan't, can't* is /æ/. Furthermore, there is no contracted form **mayn't* in either variety for most speakers.

Syntactically, the auxiliaries differ from the lexical verbs in four ways, the so-called NICE features. First of all, Negation: they may be negated directly, e.g. auxiliary *I couldn't come* and lexical **I camen't*. Second, Inversion: auxiliaries may invert with the subject (for example, in interrogatives), *Could you come?*, but not **Came you?* Third, Code: this refers to reduced, elliptical forms, possible with auxiliaries (A: *Could you come tomorrow?* B: *Yes, I could*), but uncommon with lexical verbs alone (A: *Did you come yesterday?* B: *?Yes, I came*). Finally, Emphatic affirmation: auxiliaries can freely and easily be stressed, as in *I could come*, which is possible but not very common with lexical verbs alone.

These NICE-operations require an auxiliary, which means that if there isn't one in the sentence the dummy auxiliary *do* must be introduced. This results in negative *I didn't come*, interrogative *Did you come?*, emphatic *I did come* and elliptical *Yes, I did*. The only lexical verbs which allow direct negation and question inversion are the lexical verbs *be* and, for some speakers in some cases, *have* (*Aren't you afraid?* or *Haven't you an idea?*). In order to be able to refer easily to verbs with the NICE-syntactic features, whether an auxiliary or lexical *be* or *have*, the term **operator** is sometimes used.

Catenative verbs   A number of lexical verbs are semantically very similar to auxiliaries. We see this in pairs like *must : have got to* (*Must we do that?* : *Do we have to do that?*) or *will : want* (*He won't go : He doesn't want to go*). These lexical verbs, which, like auxiliaries, are followed by non-finite verb forms (infinitives, gerunds, participles) or by indirect statements and questions in the form of finite *that-* and *wh-*clauses, are here called catenative verbs (see 5.7).

5.1.4 Adjectives

Adjectives are an open class with numerous semantic subgroups (terms of colour, size, age, weight, value etc.). They typically attribute qualities or properties, which are gradable in terms of more or less. These properties and qualities may be **stative**, i.e. not subject to wilful control. An example of this is *tall*; either a person is or is not tall. It is not possible to direct someone (**Be tall!*), nor can a person be temporarily tall (**She's being tall today*). Other adjectives may be **dynamic** and hence subject to will (*Be careful!* or *We're being very careful with the good china*). It is chiefly dynamic adjectives which can be made into adverbs by adding *-ly* (see next section).

Attribution of quality or property may be to a noun; here adjectives generally appear before the noun (attributively), e.g. *an old man*. Or it may be to a whole NP; in this case they appear most commonly after a copula (predicatively), e.g. *the left-over milk turned sour*. Some adjectives can only be used attributively; others, only predicatively: in *the system of criminal justice* 'the court system for dealing with crime' the adjective has a different meaning and it should be regarded as a different lexical item (lexeme) from the same word form used predicatively in *the system of justice is criminal* 'the court system is unjust/dishonest'. Some adjectives occur after nouns (post-positively), either in fixed expressions (*secretary general*, *court martial*) or as the head of a complex adjectival construction (*an author famous for her/his words*).

The inflection of adjectives is restricted to those which express some kind of relative degree (gradability) and it is realized either by the endings {-er}, {-est} or by the periphrastic elements {more}, {most}. Only monosyllabic and some bisyllabic adjectives, those ending in an unstressed syllable (< -y>, <-ow>, <-le>, <-er>, <-ure>, e.g. *prettier, mellower, littlest, cleverest, obscurest*) take the endings (for exceptions see most grammar books): *cute – cuter – cutest*; *pretty – prettier – prettiest*; but *beautiful – more beautiful – most beautiful*). All negative forms use *less* and *least* regardless of the number of syllables (*less cute, least beautiful*). There are also some adjectives with irregular comparatives and superlatives, e.g. *good – better – best*; *bad – worse – worst*; *much – more – most*. A few have no comparative, but superlatives only, e.g. *inner – innermost, outer – outermost* etc. Where degree is not involved comparatives and superlatives do not exist, for example with adjectives of material (usually derived from nouns), such as *atomic, metal, wooden* etc., where there is *an atomic power plant* but no **a more atomic power plant*.

5.1.5 Adverbs

Adverbs are more difficult to define than nouns, verbs and adjectives because there are so many subclasses and positional variations. Some of the basic semantic areas are those of time, place and manner, as represented by the adverbial pro-forms *then/now*, *there/here* and *thus/so*. However, intensifiers (such as *very, awfully, hopelessly*) and conjuncts (connective adverbs such as *however, nevertheless, furthermore* etc.) also belong here.

Endings are involved in two ways. First, numerous adverbs are derived from the corresponding dynamic adjectives by adding the ending {-ly}. This is the case with **adverbs of manner** (*quick → quickly*), which tell how something is done (*He left quickly*). This also includes **sentence adverbs**, or **disjuncts** (*hopeful → hopefully*), which modify a whole sentence (*Hopefully, it won't snow*). Note that adverbs are not derived from other classes of adjectives; hence there is no **oldly* or **greenly*.

The second type of ending is the inflection involved in connection with the comparatives and superlatives of adverbs of degree (*quickly – more quickly – most quickly*). In addition, a few adverbs have comparatives and superlatives with the endings {-er} and {-est} (*[to work] harder/hardest*); however, this is not common since these endings can only be used with adverbs which do not end in {-ly}.

Adverbial expressions derived from adjectives in {-ly} (*friendly*), {-like} (*ladylike*), {-style/-fashion} (*western-style*) must be constructed periphrastically, e.g. *in a friendly way/manner/fashion, in the style of the west*.

Some adverbs are not derived from adjectives. Generally these are parts of various closed (sub-)sets, for example, time adverbs like *yesterday – today – tomorrow*, place adverbs like *here – there – yonder*, but also numerous adverbs identical in form to prepositions or derived originally from prepositional phrases (*above, ahead, behind, outside, upstairs* etc.).

5.1.6 Prepositions

Prepositions are often close to adverbs because they, like adverbs, express time, place and manner/modality. In addition, they are used for degree (*over two hours, under twenty pounds, about sixty years old*) and comparison (*like, as*), subject matter (e.g. *about*) and motivation/contingency (*because, despite, in case of*). As a group they are more a closed than an open class, but it is hard to draw the line between complex prepositions and similar constructions which are not prepositional. That is, the commonest simple prepositions, *about, at, by, from, for, in, of, on, over, through, to, with*, are clear cases, and so are such highly fixed complex prepositions as *in front of* or *in regard to*. More marginal are *at the front of* or *in sight of*. At the further extreme are clearly non-prepositional constructions, such as *in the considered opinion of* or *at the new shop of*, which consist of individual units joined by normal syntactic processes, which are signalled in part by the presence of the article (*the*) and of an adjective (*considered, new*).

Prepositions have no inflectional morphology to define them. Perhaps the most satisfactory criterion is positional: they are followed by an NP, together with which they form a prepositional phrase (PP). This distinguishes them from (subordinating) conjunctions, which are followed by clauses (preposition *after the party* vs conjunction *after we left the party*). It also distinguishes them from adverbs, which are not followed by any particular types of word or phrase (preposition *they dropped a letter in the box* vs adverb *they dropped in*). However, this also means that items such as *e.g.* or *namely*, must be included because they are regularly followed by NPs, even though they are not traditionally considered to be prepositions.

5.1.7 Articles/determiners and conjunctions

These are the final parts of speech to be considered. They may be defined positionally by their occurrence before (adjective and) noun, e.g. ***the*** *large basket*. Since there are only two words which are articles, definite *the* and indefinite *a/an*, the simplest definition is simply to name them. However, a large group of **determiners** might be included here. These consist of: the demonstratives *this, that, these, those*; possessive determiners (*my, your, our, her* etc.); interrogatives and relatives (*what, which, whose* etc.); and quantifiers such as *some, any, no, all, double, half, both, (n)either, each, every, many, more, most, enough* etc. as well as both cardinal (*one, two, three, . . .*) and ordinal (*first, second, third, . . .*) numerals. They all share the feature of appearing before attributive adjectives as part of an NP. Furthermore, they are subdivided by position into **pre-determiners**, **central determiners** and **post-determiners** (see 5.5.2).

Conjunctions are basically of two types, coordinating (*and, or, nor, but, yet, for*) and subordinating (e.g. *after, because, although* etc.). Both groups consist of relatively limited sets. They include not only single word items but also double (correlative) forms such as *both . . . and* or *either . . . or* as well as phrasal constructions such as *ever since, in case,* or *as soon as.*

5.2 FUNCTIONAL PHRASES

In the preceding section the focus of attention was on individual words, even though they are sometimes actually complex (*string bean, one another, put up, ever since* etc.). This section will point out that words do not so much occur individually as in groups of syntactically related items, called **phrases**. Nouns, for example, may appear in such phrasal structures as determiner + adjective + noun + prepositional phrase (e.g. *the large apples on the table* or *a weak spot in your argument*). Phrases of this sort are referred to as noun or nominal phrases (NPs) because the noun is the member (or constituent) which must be present. The noun phrase may, however, appear with or without a determiner, adjective or prepositional phrase. Hence in the following even the single word *apples* is an NP:

NPs: the large apples on the table ⎫
       the large apples   ⎬ are delicious
       the apples   ⎪
       apples   ⎭

An NP always consists of at least a noun (or nominal or pronoun) which is its **centre** or **head**. Determiners and modifiers are optional.

Three other types of phrases also consist of either single words as minimal obligatory elements or of these plus further accompanying words. They are the verb phrase (VP), the adjective phrase (AdjP) and the adverb phrase (AdvP), e.g.

VP: *go, will go, would have gone*
AdjP: *green, amazingly green, amazingly light green*
AdvP: *gently, very gently, very gently indeed*

The final type of phrase, the prepositional phrase (PP), as understood here, differs from the others inasmuch as it must consist of at least two elements, a preposition and an NP. Without the preposition this would be an NP; without the NP, an adverb (see 4.1.5).

PP: *in trouble, in big trouble, in very big trouble*

Phrases occur within other phrases. For instance, PPs may be part of a higher level NP (e.g. *the small dog **on the porch***, where the PP *on the porch* belongs to the whole, which is an NP) and so too may AdjPs (*small* in the previous example is at one and the same time an adjective and a (simple) AdjP). In the following, however, the chief concern will be with phrases as the realization of the functional elements which make up the parts of a sentence or clause, e.g. subject, object, predicator. These elements are realized exclusively and completely by the phrase types just enumerated. Before looking more closely at the two most important and complex phrasal types, the VP and the NP, the functional elements of English sentences as well as a typology of English sentence patterns will be introduced.

5.3 FUNCTIONAL SENTENCE ELEMENTS

5.3.1 The predicator

Within the description of the structure of English in this Chapter the clause or sentence is the highest level unit (for larger units see Chapter 6). It consists for our purposes of a **predicator**, which consists of or at least contains a verb. There are, however, sentences without predicators, for example, *The sooner, the better*. These are called **minor sentence types** and will not be treated here. The predicator is the central syntactic element in a sentence. This is the case because it is the predicator which determines the number of complements that will occur and, indeed, whether a particular element is a complement or an adjunct (see below).

5.3.2 Complements

Connected with every predicator is at least one kind of element which serves to complete the predication. Such elements are called **complements**. If there is only one it will be the *subject* of the predicator and therefore of the sentence/clause (*She fell asleep*). If there are two the second will be either the *direct object* (*She lost **her keys***) or the *predicate complement* (*She became **a specialist***). If there are three such complements, there will be a subject, a direct object and either an *indirect object* (*She gave **us** her report*) or a predicate complement (*She named him **her assistant***). There are never more than three.

In addition to filling the grammatical functions of subject, object, indirect object and predicative complement, the complements also realize a variety of differing **semantic roles** or relations depending on the verb involved. The most common of these roles are the following, but note that the number and the names of the roles vary considerably from author to author.

agentive: the deliberate instigator of an act or activity (***My brother** has gone to Chicago*);
cause: the inanimate source of an event or process (***The storm** ruined the harvest*);
experiencer (or **dative**): the animate subject of thoughts, feelings, sensations (***We** think you're right*);
instrument: the inanimate tool used to do something (*I used **a pen** to make my notes*);
objective: the goal affected by a predication (*I read **the book***);
factitive: the object created by the activity of the predicator (*I baked **a pie***).

These roles are not necessarily associated with any particular sentence function (such as subject or object); rather, any one verb will have a certain constellation of roles associated with it. For example, the verb *make* will have an agentive (e.g. *the carpenter*), a factitive (*a table*) and an instrument (*the tools*). The preferred subject is the agentive with the factitive as the object and the instrument as a prepositional phrase (*The carpenter made a table with the tools*). Other constellations are also possible such as passive *The table was finished by the carpenter with the new tools*.

5.3.3 Sentence patterns

Just how many complements there are in a sentence depends on the type of verb in the predicator. The following are the major types of verbs:

A **Predicators with one complement only**:

   I   **Intransitive verbs**: *sleep* (*I was sleeping*), *walk* (*She walked to work*), *be worried* (*He's worried*).

   II   **Impersonal (weather) verbs**: *rain* (*It was raining*), *snow* (*It's going to snow*). These verbs are often regarded as having no complement at all on semantic grounds since the subject *it* has no reference and is only a 'dummy' which must appear because predicators in finite sentences must have (grammatical) subjects.

B **Predicators with two complements**:

   III **Transitive verbs**: *read* (*Did you read the report?*), *carry* (*She was carrying the groceries*), *delight* (*The weather delighted me*).

   IV **Copular verbs with predicative complements**:
      a) **With an NP identical to the subject**: *Bill is my brother*; subject and predicate complement are reversible: *My brother is Bill*.
      b) **With a predicative nominal or NP**: *be* (*I'm a student*), *become* (*The teacher became a bore*), *sound* (*That sounds a mess*). Verbs of physical appearance such as *sound, look, feel* etc. cannot be followed by a predicate noun in AmE; a PP with *like* must be used in AmE (see 12.3.1).
      c) **With a predicative adjective (AdjP)**: *be* (*We were tired*), *get* (*They got drunk*), *look* (*You look happy*).
      d) **With a predicative adverbial (of place)**: *be* (*Who's in there?*), *live* (*She lives in Wilmington*), *there + be* (*There was no one at home*). The immediately preceding example (the 'existential *there*' construction) consists regularly of a 'dummy' subject *there*, some form of the verb *be*, which is the 'logical' subject, and an expression of place. Although verbs other than *be* may occur and the place expression may be missing occasionally, the pattern given is the predominant one.

   V   **Intransitive verbs + adverbial complement**: *last* + duration (*The concert lasted (for) two hours*), *weigh* + amount (*My brother weighs 200 pounds*), *cost* + value (*The peaches cost $2.00 a pound*), *walk* + distance (*We walked 20 miles*).

C **Predicators with three complements**:

   VI **Ditransitive verbs**: *give* (*We must give her a party*), *show* (*Who showed you the way?*), *tell* (*I told him a joke*). The indirect object often appears after the direct object and is introduced by the preposition *to* or *for* (*We must give a party for her, I told a joke to him*).

VII **Transitive verbs with predicative complements**:

a) **With a predicative nominal (NP)**: *call* (*She called me a weakling*), *elect* (*They elected her captain*), *declare* (*The newspaper declared you an enemy of the people*).

b) **With a predicative adjective (AdjP)**: *call* (*She called me stupid*), *make* (*That made me mad*), *find* (*The court found them guilty*).

c) **With a predicative adverbial**: *spend* + place (*He spent the day in bed*), *put* + place (*Who put the peanut butter in the fridge?*), *behave/treat* + manner (*The CD player is behaving (itself) capriciously/in an unpredictable way*).

If any of these predicators are used in the imperative form, the subject, of course, does not appear and the number of complements is lessened by one (e.g. *Give the money to her*). The same applies when a transitive predicator (III, VI, VII) is passive (*She was given the money*).

The complements are usually NPs, as the examples have shown, but in a number of cases they are also PPs and AdvPs and of course the predicate adjectives are AdjPs. In fact, as a rule, subjects are NPs; direct objects usually are as well. Indirect objects vary between NPs and PPs with *to* or *for*. Adverbial complements may be PPs, AdvPs, or NPs.

5.3.4 Adjuncts

The third type of functional sentence element is the adjunct. As its name suggests, it is adjoined or added to the sentence. This means that its status is one of optionality. In other words, an adjunct, however important it may be for the *meaning* communicated, is not *grammatically* necessary: if it is left out the sentence is still 'well formed'. A complement, on the other hand, may not be omitted without the sentence becoming ungrammatical or having a grammatically different structure. The predicative adverbial, a complement, in *The waiter set the plate on the table* cannot be left out, e.g. **The waiter set the plate*; the adjunct of place in *I cut the meat on the table* may be, e.g. *I cut the meat*.

Adjuncts and complements are thus theoretically distinguishable according to the criterion of omissibility. In reality this criterion is extremely hard to apply. Indirect objects as complements, for example, are part of the 'essential' structure of sentences with ditransitive verbs, yet they can often be left out without the sentence becoming ungrammatical (*I told (him) a joke*); the resulting sentence is, however, perhaps a different structure: type VI (ditransitive) has become type III (transitive).

Adjuncts may be realized as NPs, AdvPs, PPs and even as subordinate clauses: *They drove the car **two miles*** (NP); *They drove the car **too fast*** (AdvP); *They drove the car **to town*** (PP); *They drove the car till it got dark* (subordinate adverbial/temporal clause). Adjuncts may indicate time, place, manner, means, agent, instrument, cause, condition, purpose, concession etc. What is a complement in one sentence may be an adjunct in another. Status as a complement or as an adjunct is a syntactical question, not one of semantic role: *The craftsman* [agent, complement] *used a special tool* [instrument, complement] *to cut the tiles* as compared to *The tiles were cut by a craftsman* [agent, adjunct] *with a special tool* [instrument, adjunct].

5.3.5 Connectors

The final sentence element is the connector (or **connective**). It is used to connect sentence elements with each other, or to link clauses with each other. Connection can be realized by conjunctions, but also by PPs, AdvPs, relative pronoun NPs and some special elements called complementizers, which will be introduced later (5.6). Here are some short examples of all but this last type:

Conj: *John **and** I played tennis* (coordinating conjunction) *I left **as** it was late* (subordinating conjunction)
PP: *We went skiing; **in addition**, we did some skating*
AdvP: *It was cold; **nevertheless**, we went skiing*
NP: *I just met someone **who** knows you*

5.4 THE VERB PHRASE (VP)

The verb phrase may be subcategorized into two major types, finite and non-finite. The difference between the two is that finite ones always occur as clause predicators, always include tense and always have a (nominative) subject. For example, in *I was looking for a solution* the finite VP *was looking* is the clause predicator, it is in the past tense, and it has a subject (*I*).

Non-finite VPs, in contrast, need not be clause predicators and need not have a subject of their own. For instance in *He seems to like me*, where *like* is the predicator of the infinitive clause *to like me*, it has to 'share' its subject (*he*) with *seems*. In other cases, non-finite forms may be **modifiers** instead of predicators and therefore adjectival in nature, e.g. the past participle in *a broken window*, the present participle in *a raging fire*, or the infinitive in *the way to do that*. Furthermore, non-finite forms can also be nominal in nature, e.g. the infinitive subject in *To err is human* or the gerund prepositional object in *She is in charge of **renting** additional office space*.

The following section deals exclusively with finite VPs. Non-finite forms will be taken up again in a later section on catenative verbs (5.7).

5.4.1 Finite VPs

Every finite VP consists of at least one and as many as six elements. The six can be illustrated by the following sentence, in which each of the elements represents one of the grammatical choices of English in the area of the verb, always in the same relative order:

[Henry] might have been being entertained [royally].

   might: expresses modality; this takes the form of a modal verb, which is followed by an infinitive; if a modal verb is present, it always occupies the initial position;

   might: also expresses tense, here the past of *may*; the first element in every finite VP must be either past or present;

have:	expresses perfect aspect; this is always introduced by *have* and followed by a past participle;
being:	expresses (passive) voice; passive is frequently introduced by *be*, but sometimes by *get* or *have* followed by a past participle;
been:	expresses progressive aspect, which is always introduced by *be* and followed by an {-ing} form;
entertained:	expresses the predication; this may appear as any lexical verb and may consist of more than one word; it may also appear as one of the pro-forms, *do* or *so*, where appropriate.

VPs in which all five categories are represented are highly infrequent. However, any combination of the categories may occur so long as the relative order is not changed. In the vast majority of cases the lexical verb, indicating the predication, will be present, but in cases of repetition, it is often elided or replaced by a pro-form (*do* and with inversion *so*), e.g. A: *Have you turned in your paper?* B: *Yes, I have* (or, *Yes, I have done*, a form more common in BrE than in AmE, see 12.3.1) A: *So have I*. Note that more than just the lexical verb is elided (or replaced by *done* and *so*): the direct object is as well.

5.4.2 Tense

This is the category of the verb which was described above as being obligatory in the finite VP. In terms of form alone, the first element in every finite VP will be one of two tenses, present or past. In this sense a sentence with *will* (often called the 'future tense'), such as *When will you get an answer?*, is really present, because *will* is the present tense form just as *would* is the past tense form of *will*. The same applies to all other initial forms. Hence the present also includes, for example, *it's raining*, *it has rained* and *it must have rained*; and the past includes *it would be nice*, *it had been nice* and *it was nice*. (Note that modals such as *must*, *dare* and *need* have only one form and therefore only one tense.)

Concord   All the verbs of the language except the modals have an inflectional {-S} in the third person present singular. This is all that is left in English of a system of marking agreement between subject and verb, a system which was at one time considerably fuller and which served to mark the subject and the predicator as belonging together through concord or agreement in person and number. Besides the single instance of third person singular present tense {-S}, there are the further special forms of *be* (*I am*, *he/she/it is*, *we/you/they are* in the present; *I/he/she/it was*, *we/you/they were* in the past). The fact that inflection has grown so weak in modern English, has been compensated for by relatively strict word order. The subject is usually the NP which comes directly before the VP.

The subject normally determines concord according to its own grammatical number. This is called **grammatical concord**. If the subject is singular, the verb is singular and if it is plural, so too is the verb. However, not only the grammatical number of the subject, but also the concept of number which lies behind the form of the noun subject may determine concord. This is called **notional concord**. Since a team consists of various members, it is possible for singular *team* to have a plural verb, e.g. *The team **are** playing Bristol next week*. This type of concord is more prevalent in BrE (especially with subjects like *government, committee, family*) than in AmE, although it is not unknown in the latter (see 12.3.1). Conjoined subjects are often notional units, such as *apple pie and cheese* or *bread and water* and may therefore sometimes have singular verb concord as in *Bread and water **is** good for you*. Plural amounts are usually singular (and sums of money almost always are), as in *$2 **is** a lot*. Furthermore, a subject such as *a number of people* is usually regarded as plural according to *people* rather than singular according to *number*. The nouns *people* and *police*, although unmarked, are always plural just as apparent plurals such *the United States* or *news* are always singular. A third principle is **concord by proximity**. This principle may be partly responsible for concord of the type just mentioned, as in *A number of people **are** waiting*, where both the plural notion in *number* and the nearness of *people* to the verb have the same (plural) effect. Proximity is clearly the determining factor in the *there is/are* construction, in which the first noun after the verb determines the concord, e.g. *There **is** a plate and three forks on the table*. A second instance is with conjoined *either . . . or* subjects, in which the second element conventionally decides the concord, e.g. *Either you or I **am** mistaken*.

Time and tense   There is little doubt that tense is related to time. However, the relationship is not one-to-one. In everyday thinking the continuum of time is commonly divided up into three: past, present, future. Tense, as has been pointed out, is binary (divided into two): present and past. Furthermore, the present tense may be used for non-present time (see below **Future**), and the past tense has a function which is wider than that of marking time (see below **Past**).

Present   **Present** is the 'unmarked' tense. This may be understood morphologically as the general lack of a special ending such as the past {-D} (except for the third person {-S} discussed above). However, it also refers to the fact that the present may be used to designate something temporally unrestricted. In the following examples, text (1) is an example of present tense used for general situations which extend beyond the present into both the past and the future; they sometimes include 'general truths'; more suitably, they may be called characterizing statements. Text (2) is an example of what is sometimes called the 'historical present', which is typical of an especially immediate or vivid style of storytelling. Note that here the present may be used for past reference, though the converse (past for present) is not possible.

1   **Characterization [habitual action]**. *High summer and Friendship's* [name of a town] *quiet. The men **tend** the shimmering fields. Children **tramp** the woods, **wade** the creeks, **sound** the cool ponds. In town, women **pause** in the heavy air of millinery, **linger** over bolts of yard goods, barrels of clumped flour.* (Stewart O'Nan (2000) *A Prayer for the Dying*, New York: Picador, p. 3)

2   **Narration [historical present]**. *But they **don't say** anything after I **tell** them what I do, so while Tamsin and India **talk** about the celebrity chef who invented*

tonight's fish and while Josh and Dan **bellow** *at each other about various areas of commercial law, I* **sit** *silently on the sofa, slowly getting completely and utterly stewed.* (Tony Parsons (2002) *One for My Baby*, London: HarperCollins, p. 157)

In addition, the present tense is used in the following ways: for reporting something just as it takes place, as in sports broadcasting or in stage directions.

3   **Report [stage directions]**. *Light* **rises** *on the kitchen.* WILLY, *talking,* **shuts** *the refrigerator door and* **comes** *downstage to the kitchen table. He* **pours** *milks into a glass.* (*Death of a Salesman* Act I, in J. Gassner (ed.) (1960) *A Treasury of the Theatre*, New York: Simon and Schuster, p. 1068)

It is also used for reporting or explaining what one thinks or feels (4), for performing a (speech) act (5), for comments immediately accompanying a demonstration and explaining the individual acts involved (6), and even for future time, especially in temporal clauses such as the following one introduced by *before* (7) (see also below **Future**).

4   **Mental or emotional state**. *Between you and me, Reverend, I* **do** *not* **think** *the people here are looking for your kind of salvation. I* **think** *they are looking for Patrice Lumumba, the new soul of Africa.* (Barbara Kingsolver (1999) *The Poisonwood Bible*, New York: HarperPerennial, p. 122)

5a   **Performative act**. This includes both extremely formalized acts such as the performance of a marriage: *In the Name of God, the Father, the Son, and the Holy Ghost, I now* **join** *you together to live in holy wedlock as husband and wife.* (*Hymnal and Liturgies of the Moravian Church* (1948), Bethlehem, PA, p. 42)

However, it also includes more everyday acts such as explicitly apologizing, promising or, as in the following example, averring:

5b   **Speech act**. *I didn't do anything, I* **swear**, *Dad. Dad. Cross my heart and hope to die. Look. – I crossed my heart.* (Roddy Doyle (1994) *Paddy Clarke Ha Ha Ha*, London: Minerva, p. 79)

6   **Demonstration**. *Now watch – I* **drop** *the tablet into this warm water, and you see it* **dissolves** *quite nicely.* (Joos 1968: 105)

7   **Simple present for the future**. *To accompany me I have chosen three men. I call them together the afternoon before we* **leave** *[future reference].* (J.M. Coetzee (1982) *Waiting for the Barbarians*, Harmondsworth: Penguin, p. 58)

Past   The past tense has three clearly distinct functions. The easiest to recognize is its use to mark a situation as having taken place in the past time.

8   **Narration**. *I **took** a deep breath to ease the pressure in my chest. Then in one quick movement I **pulled** the front part of the blue cloth on to the table so that it **flowed** out of the dark shadows under the table and up in a slant on to the table in front of the jewellery box. I **made** a few adjustments to the lines of the folds, then **stepped** back.* (Tracy Chevalier (2000) *Girl with a Pearl Earring*, London: HarperCollins, p. 142)

The second function is to mark indirect speech after a reporting verb in the past tense (9) (see 5.7.3).

9   **Reported speech**. *Joyce Johnson said she **didn't know** what **had come** over her last night, but she felt okay, though her husband **was** mad at her. He said she **had barked** like a dog.* (G. Keillor (1986) *Lake Wobegon Days*, New York: Penguin, pp. 412f.)

The final use is in unreal (10) and contrafactual (11) conditional constructions (see 5.4.5).

10   **Unreal condition**.
     *'You know, if you **weren't** so mysterious –'*
     'I'm not "mysterious."'
     *'If you **weren't** so secretive,' Gary said, 'maybe you **wouldn't have** this problem.'*
     (Jonathan Franzen (2002) *The Corrections*, New York: Picador, p. 228)

11   **Contrafactual condition**. *THE SILVER FOX. What sort of man would write that on his car? If only he just **hadn't** . . . **stenciled** those stupid words on the side of the van, Janine thought.* (Richard Russo (2002) *Empire Falls*, London: Vintage, pp. 64f.)

What each of these three seemingly different uses of the past tense have in common is the idea of **remoteness**. First of all it is remote in time, as in (8). Second, what is reported is put at a distance to the person reporting, as in (9). Interestingly enough, the temporal **backshift** of **indirect speech** to the past need not be made when the speaker identifies with what he or she reports. Accepted facts, for example, do not normally undergo a backshift to the past (e.g. *He pointed out that blood is* [not necessarily: *was*] *thicker than water.*). In the third case, the past tense indicates remoteness to reality, as in (10) and (11). A likely condition (a 'real conditional') has the present tense and differs from an unreal conditional insofar as there is less likelihood that the latter will be realized. Compare *If I had time, I'd write* [unreal conditional, writing is unlikely] with *If I have time, I'll write* [real conditional, writing is less unlikely].

One further use of the past tense that may well be related to this is the past tense for politeness as in:

12   **Politeness**. *'Dad, I **was** just wondering,' Aaron's voice trails off. He holds up the guitar case.* (Myla Goldberg (2000) *Bee Season*, London: Flamingo, p. 75)

With a first person subject, as in this example, the past expresses more tentativeness and unobtrusiveness. This is accomplished thanks to the remoteness of the past, which puts greater distance between the speaker and his/her request (= 'I was wondering, but I am not necessarily any more'), which is reinforced here by the use of the progressive to indicate something on-going and therefore less complete and definite. This distance makes a refusal on the part of the addressee easier.

Future   Tense consists of only two options, as mentioned above: past and present. For lack of a special future tense, the language must resort to a number of different constructions to express future time, which we have chosen to illustrate from Michael Frayn's novel *Headlong* (London: Faber and Faber, 2000), in which the conventionally moral and bourgeois protagonist finds himself trying to cheat a neighbour out of a valuable painting while betraying his wife Kate with the neighbour's wife. The first five possibilities of expressing the future, (1)–(5), are by no means freely interchangeable. They fall more or less roughly into two groups, those which stress intention and those which express prediction. Intention is strongest with (1) and (3); prediction is more prominent with (2), (4) and (5).

(1)   ***Be going to***: *I'**m going to** sit down beside Kate at the kitchen table and take her hand, and kiss it. I'**m going to** confess that I've behaved wrongly, and ask her forgiveness* (*Headlong*, p. 130). The form with *be going to* is used with wilful agents to indicate that a course of action has been decided on. When the subject is determined, only this form is appropriate (*I'**m going to** sit down beside Kate*). *Will* in the 'same' sentence (*I'll sit down beside Kate*) is inappropriate because it is merely a vague declaration. However, the full form *will* spoken emphatically (*I **will** sit down*) might be used by some speakers to indicate great wilfulness. With inanimate or non-volitional subjects, in contrast, *be going to* makes predictions, but ones of great certainty, e.g. the speaker and his wife about their little baby Tilda: *I get up again to go, because at any moment Tilda's grizzling **is going to** change into a full-scale howl* (*Headlong*, p. 132). Here again, *will* cannot be used.

(2)   ***Will* and *shall***: *Then I **shall** tell her everything – the whole plan, with nothing kept back. Perhaps, when she sees how contrite I am, . . . she'**ll** make a huge leap of faith and trust me to do as I think best* (*Headlong*, p. 130). *Will* and the less frequent *shall* (restricted to the first person; chiefly heard in southern England) make predictions, but ones which are vague, relatively uncertain. If someone says *she'll make a huge leap of faith*, this is said without the certainty of *be going to*. Often this form appears after an introductory expression which indicates this vagueness (*I think I'll . . .*) or spontaneity, e.g. *I jump up as hurriedly as someone with the runs. – '**I'll** check Tilda,' I mumble* (*Headlong*, p. 27).

(3) **Present progressive**: *'You're selling the Giordano? How? What do you mean? Why didn't you tell me? What else have you arranged with him?'* (*Headlong*, p. 131). The progressive form is used to indicate something which is going on (see 5.4.3). If the actual act lies in the future (*selling the Giordano*), then the current activity can only be seen in the fact that a decision (= intention) to sell it has at present already been made. This expression of the future is frequently supported by a future time adverbial.

(4) *Will* **+ progressive**: *So if I buy them, I **shall be receiving** stolen property* (*Headlong*, p. 216). *Will/shall* + the progressive, in contrast, comes close to being a 'pure' future since this construction is used for future situations which are set and will take place as a matter of course. It indicates certainty (here indicated as conditional) without suggesting intention, see also *You'll **be taking** your exam in just two days and I know you'll **be quivering** in your boots.*

(5) **Simple present**: *'Tomorrow afternoon,'* I assure him. *'I'll put the money in your hands. You **put** the pictures in mine.'* (*Headlong*, p. 338). The simple present (always used with an adverbial expression of future time) is another way of expressing the certainty of a future event. This is basically the report function of the present which was mentioned above; here, however, something in the future is being reported. This works best with verbs which express dynamic acts (*meet, depart, decide* etc.) rather than general activities (*discuss, read* etc.).

The simple present is also the usual form found in temporal clauses referring to the future, e.g. *Before I **say** a word to her I'm going to have to do some careful research* (*Headlong*, p. 50). The verb *say* is clearly future in reference; none of the other four forms (1, 2, 4, 5) could replace it. The same holds for the *if*-clauses (including ones introduced by *suppose*) of real conditionals, *'Suppose Tony Churt simply **asks** [not *will ask] you? . . .' – But if he **does**? If he **says** [not *will say], "Is this a Bruegel?" ' – 'I'll tell him the truth.' – 'That it's a Bruegel?'* (*Headlong*, p. 127). Only if volition is explicitly expressed does a *will* or *would* appear in the *if*-clause, *'If you'd like to bring it* [the painting to the dealer's] *in some time . . .'* (*Headlong*, p. 324).

In addition, what has not (yet) taken place is regularly referred to by the following:

(6) **Other modal verbs besides *will* and *shall***: *'Are you selling the other two pictures?' – 'I **might**. I'll see'* (*Headlong*, p. 132).

(7) **Semi-modal verbs**: *I remember I still haven't looked up the Giordano. But by this time the exact figures involved in the stupendous deal I'**m about to** do seem to me of remarkably little importance* (*Headlong*, p. 183).

(8) **Imperatives** and (9) **numerous lexical verbs**: *'**Wait, wait**. What about the other two pictures we saw? Does he **want you to** sell those as well?'* (*Headlong*, p. 132).

5.4.3 Aspect: perfect and progressive

The tense system of English as presented in the previous section cannot really be understood without including the category of aspect. Both tense and aspect have to do with time, but in differing ways:

tense is a deictic category, i.e. locates situations in time, usually with reference to the present moment ... Aspect is not concerned with relating the time of the situations to another time-point, but rather with the internal temporal constituency of the one situation; one could state the difference as one between situation-internal time (aspect) and situation-external time (tense).

(Comrie 1976: 5)

In English there are two types of aspect, the perfect and the progressive.

The perfect   This form is more closely related to tense than the progressive is. Situations which are reported in the present perfect refer, for instance, to the past. If *someone has bought a sweater*, then the act of buying is over. What is of importance as far as aspect is concerned is that the implication is different when the same act is reported in the past (*someone bought a sweater*). The difference is frequently described as involving **current relevance** in the case of the perfect; this is a kind of expansion of the actual event (its situation-internal time) to include the present. The past, on the other hand, as the unmarked form may but need not necessarily involve such relevance. This might be explained as follows: if someone says they have bought a sweater, they are making the purchase the theme of conversation and probably expect an interested comment or question from their interlocutor (*Oh, really, show me* or *Where did you find it?*). The use of the past might, of course, provoke a similar reaction, but what it is primarily doing is reporting something which happened in the past.

There are two different ways in which the perfect may be relevant to the present. If the verb in the predicator indicates a completed act or event (e.g. *buy something, arrive somewhere, read something, meet someone* etc.) it may be referred to as the **resultative perfect**. Something has happened and the results are of current or present interest, e.g. *In past years, electricity prices **have been kept** low by abundant rainfall at the region's hydroelectric dams* (*Time*, 3 March 2003: 36, about electricity shortfalls in Scandinavia). The other possibility is that the verb designates an activity or process which does not presuppose completeness or a conclusion (*sleep, read, live somewhere, learn, grow wise* etc.). When there is no result, furthermore, the activity or process can be reported in the perfect progressive and will indicate something which began in the past and is still going on, *'The market mechanism **has for the past 12 years worked** (also possible: *has been working*) [= is still working] according to expectation,' Norwegian Petroleum and Energy Minister Einar Steensnaes told TIME. But opponents say the jump in prices **has been** [= still is] outrageous* (ibid.). This is what is called the **continuative perfect**. While the continuative perfect may occur in both the simple and the progressive form with dynamic verbs like *work*, the resultative perfect can only occur in the simple form. If a verb which indicates an unfinished activity occurs in the simple perfect, it will either be nonsense (*?I have slept*) or will be reinterpreted in a resultative sense (*He has grown wise* = 'he is now wise') (see Table 5.5, p. 120).

Adverbial specification   The occurrence of the perfect is restricted not only by the type of verb in the predicator, but also by the adverbials used. Most past time adverbials (e.g. *last year, an hour ago, formerly*) cannot occur together with the perfect; there is no **He has done it **yesterday***. (But, *She has talked with him **in the past*** – known as the **experiential perfect**.) As a result when there is an indicator of past time, current relevance cannot be expressed with the present perfect. A speaker would have to indicate relevance lexically, such as with an explicit statement (*He talked to her yesterday, which I find very interesting for us*).

Just as there are adverbials which are incongruent with the perfect, there are a few which demand the perfect. These are ones whose scope includes not only the past, but also the present. The most prominent of these is temporal (not causal) *since*. Examples are *The weather has been rainy since we arrived*, or *I haven't seen them since last year*. Note that both sentences would be ungrammatical in the past tense. Occasionally *since* occurs with the present tense (*I like French cooking since our vacation in Burgundy*). It may even be used, exceptionally, with the past to avoid ambiguity, as in *I was in America since we met last* (implies one visit) vs *I have been in America since we met last* (implies a continuous stay).

Several other adverbials have a strong, but not necessarily absolute tendency towards use with the perfect; they include *still, (not) yet, already, just, so far, up to now*, adverbials of indefinite past time such as *ever* and *never* and *recently*. BrE tends to employ the present perfect more strictly with these than AmE does. A few adverbials, especially those containing a referentially ambiguous use of *this* are sometimes past in reference and demand the past tense and sometimes present in reference and allow the perfect. For example, if someone says *this morning*, and it still is the morning, the adverbial is present in scope; in the afternoon of the same day, however, it is a past adverbial.

Thus far the comments made on the perfect have been concerned with the present perfect (e.g. *have gone*). In the case of the past perfect (*had gone*) and the future perfect (*will have gone*), there are no adverbial restrictions of the types just outlined. Indeed, both sometimes express relevance with regard to a past or future time point just as the present perfect does to the present; but sometimes they are more tense-like and provide further levels of temporal differentiation, such as a 'deeper' past (e.g. *Fifty years ago this week, on Feb. 28, 1953, Francis Crick walked into the Eagle pub in Cambridge, England, and announced that he and James Watson **had 'found** the secret of life'* (*Time*, 3 March 2003, p. 41)). Indeed, the perfect of non-finite forms seems to be one alternative way of indicating anterior time in non-finite VPs, which cannot otherwise be marked for tense (see 5.7.3).

A final remark about the perfect is that it is often used within texts, especially narrative or reporting texts, to provide background information while the actual report is in the past:

> Slumping share prices and the spectre of war have blighted the market for initial public offerings (IPOs). This year began with America's first IPO-free January since the bear market of 1974.
>
> (*The Economist*, 1 March 2003, p. 69)

Progressive aspect   The progressive (or **continuous**) form in English is closely related to the idea of incompletion. It distinguishes **acts** and **events**, which are complete, from **activities** and **processes**, which are not. If someone is reading a book, reading is an activity that this person is not yet finished with. If, however, someone has once read a book, then this is an act which they are through with. From this distinction it is only a small step to the frequent characterization of the progressive as a form which marks limited duration. Progressive aspect is concerned with the internal constituency of an activity such as reading – how it looks, so to speak, from the inside, where it is still going on. It therefore emphasizes the duration of an activity. When the non-progressive form is used, an act or event is simply reported as completed, regardless of how much time it may, in actual fact, have taken. In addition, a speaker often has a choice whether he or she wants to express one and the same happening as having temporary duration (and therefore in the progressive) or as permanent (and therefore in the simple form), as in *I am living in Utah* vs *I live in Utah*. The simple form is once again the unmarked form. Using it does not exclude the possibility of temporary duration, while the progressive marks precisely this aspect of meaning explicitly.

Narration and background description   The most impressive evidence for the distinction between the simple and the progressive forms can be observed in narrative texts. When someone tells what happens, one event after the other, each of these events is regarded as an individual step in a sequence and each is reported in the simple form (usually simple past, sometimes simple or historical present). What lies outside this narrative chain is background information which overlaps with the narrative events. From the perspective of these events, it is therefore incomplete. Consequently, this background information is presented in the progressive form:

> Robbie made a great show of removing his boots which weren't dirty at all, and then, as an afterthought, took his socks off as well, and tiptoed with comic exaggeration across the wet floor. . . . He was play-acting the cleaning lady's son come to the big house on an errand. They went into the library together, and when he found his book, she asked him to stay for a coffee.
>
> (Ian McEwan (2002) *Atonement*,
> London: Vintage, p. 27)

In this passage the play-acting is the initial background activity which consists of individual acts: *make a show – took his socks off – tiptoed*. Then the narrative chain continues with: *went – found – asked*. All the acts are in the simple past and might be linked in each case by the phrase 'and then'; they are treated as uniform points in a sequence regardless of whether one was longer or shorter than another. They are the focus of attention in the narrative foreground. In each case 'the whole of the situation is presented as a single unanalysable whole, with beginning, middle and end rolled up into one' (Comrie 1976: 3). The activity of play-acting, in contrast, goes on as a kind of backdrop; its duration is the central feature emphasized by the choice of the progressive.

Stative and dynamic verbs   The use of the progressive is rendered more complicated by the fact that not every verb may occur freely in this form. Verbs which express states, for example, are restricted to the simple form. One of the main verbs of state is *be* (*The sky is cloudy*, not **The sky is being cloudy*). Yet almost any verb may be used in the progressive under the appropriate circumstances. With *be*, for example, we find *You're **just being** polite*, which indicates that the politeness of the addressee is temporary and perhaps not fully sincere. A convenient test to see whether a state verb is being used dynamically is to try it out as an imperative. If this is grammatical, the verb is dynamic (***Be** polite*); if not, it is stative (**Be six feet tall*). This is the case because issuing a command presumes intention and control over action on the part of the addressee.

Most verbs are dynamic, which means that they can easily appear in the progressive if that is what is called for. Verbs of movement are clear examples (e.g. *run, jump, build, write* etc.), but numerous others are also dynamic (*read, sleep, talk*). For the non-progressive or non-dynamic verbs it is convenient to make a subdivision into two classes. The first of these is the **private verbs**, so called because they refer to what an individual alone can experience in his or her sensations, thoughts or feelings. When any of these are expressed, they are essentially reports, and like all other reports, appear in the simple form. Verbs of perception, cognition and evaluation (e.g. *see, hear; know, believe; want, love* etc.) belong here. It is normal to hear a child say *I **love** my mummy*; but **I'm loving my mummy* is unacceptable. A verb of evaluation may be found in the progressive, but chiefly to indicate a growing intensification (*Are you **smoking** more and **enjoying** it less?*). Note, however, that some private verbs, such as *feel, itch* and *ache* may be used in both forms (*How are you feeling?* or *How do you feel?*).

The second subclass is that of **verbs of state**. These are verbs which designate relationships not regarded as temporary, even if they eventually turn out to be so: *equal, resemble, seem, cost, depend, adjoin* and many others. Clearly two plus two equals four, and no one would venture to say **two plus two is equalling four*.

Perfect and progressive   The progressive and the present perfect can occur together as was pointed out above (see 'The perfect'). However, not every type of verb may appear in this combination. Verbs which designate undifferentiated activities, that is, activities which do not logically include the idea of completion, must occur in the present perfect progressive and cannot appear in the present perfect simple. Compare *I have been thinking* vs **I have thought*. These verbs may be used in the present perfect simple only as expressions of general experience (*?I have slept*), but people seldom feel the need to say such self-evident things.

In contrast to verbs of undifferentiated activity there are verbs which are intrinsically perfective; that is, they designate an act which necessarily presupposes its conclusion, e.g. **I have been discovering the answer to the world's energy problems*. Since *discover the answer* expresses completeness it does not fit with the idea of incompleteness contained in the present perfect progressive. The sentence marked as ungrammatical by

Table 5.5   Verb types and the present perfect

verb types	present perfect	present perfect progressive
undifferentiated activity (*read, sleep, dream, talk*)	no	yes
perfective acts, events (*arrive, eat something up, find the solution*)	yes	no
ambiguous for the above (*listen to the news, eat supper, read a book*)	yes [= resultative]	yes [= continuative]
state verbs (*know something, resemble someone, contain something*)	no	no

the asterisk is, of course, acceptable if the speaker is using it to make a declaration about what that person thinks he or she is doing.

State verbs cannot, of course, occur in the present perfect progressive because they never occur in the progressive. In addition, state verbs cannot be in the present perfect simple either, for a state is something unchanging, while the present perfect simple is used for something which by implication has been completed in the past (though relevant in the present), e.g. *I have been six feet tall or *Two plus two has equalled four or *I have known the answer.

Most verbs, however, allow both a perfective and a non-perfective interpretation. In the former case they are examples of the resultative perfect (I've done my homework); in the latter they are instances of the continuative perfect (I've been doing my homework). Table 5.5 sums up the different verb types.

5.4.4 Voice

This category consists of the contrast between active and passive. The use of the passive causes a change in perspective, not in remoteness, current relevance or limited duration, but in the **sentence theme**. The passive is favoured in informative texts, especially academic and scientific ones (see 6.7).

Active and passive sentences are related to each other syntactically. What is the object of an active sentence is the subject of a passive one (*Frayn wrote **the story** ↔ **The story** was written by Frayn*). Conversely, the subject of the corresponding active sentence, which is usually the agent (often referred to as the 'logical' subject), may be expressed in a passive sentence in a *by*-PP (*by Frayn*). However, this is the case only approximately 20 per cent of the time. There are several reasons for this low frequency. For one thing, there is a strong tradition of apparent objectivity in scholarly texts, in which the first person point of view is regarded as stylistically inappropriate (e.g. *In this section the passive is discussed*; less formal, *In this section we will discuss the passive*). In addition, the 'logical' subject may be non-existent (e.g. *Many factors are involved in the passive*) or it may be unknown or indefinite (e.g. *Many texts are written with a high percentage of passives*).

Not every predicator can appear in the passive. Those without an object (intransitive, copular and weather verbs) can only be active. The verbs listed in Table 5.5 above as verbs of state do not have a passive, e.g. *He resembles you*, but not **You are resembled by him*; *The box contains two dozen pieces*, but not **Two dozen pieces are contained by the box*. On the other hand, ditransitive sentences (e.g. *We gave her the book*) have two passives, one less frequent one in which the direct object is the subject (***The book** was given to her*) and a more common one in which the indirect object is the subject (***She** was given the book*).

Statal and dynamic passives   While passives most frequently appear with the auxiliary verb *be*, two others are also common, *have* and *get*. The latter is particularly important because passive constructions with *be* are often ambiguous between the occurrence of an act and the result of such an occurrence. The first is called the **dynamic passive**, the second the **statal** (or **stative**) **passive**. As an example note that *John was hurt* can refer to a dynamic act in which someone inflicted damage or insult on John.

It can also refer to the state or condition of being injured or insulted. The sentence *John got hurt*, in contrast, has only the dynamic meaning.

Despite the advantage of its clearly dynamic meaning, *get* also has a disadvantage: it may only be used with certain verbs (*get married, get involved, get done*; not **?get seen, *?get aided, *?get instructed*). *Get* is only suitable when a change of state is involved. Furthermore, style is also a factor: in more formal usage *get* is less acceptable than in casual conversation.

Other 'auxiliaries': the semi-passive   In some cases *get* is less a passive than a copula followed by a participial adjective. This can be confirmed by the fact that an intensifier such as *very, awfully* or *extremely* may precede the participle (*Towards midnight I got (terribly) tired*). Much the same thing is true of *become, grow, feel, seem* and a number of others. They resemble the passive, but are not usually regarded as true passives.

Passive-like structures   Both *get* and *have* are used in a structure in which the subject is the experiencer (but not the agent, see 5.3.2) of a passive act: *John got/had his arm broken in the fight*. Here John experienced something, but did not actually do it. In a different interpretation of this structure, the subject may be understood as the person who caused or instigated what was done (*John got/had his tonsils removed*, meaning 'asked the surgeon to do this').

Active constructions with passive meaning   In conclusion it should be pointed out that there are a number of constructions in which the subject of an active sentence is the 'logical' object of the predicator. This gives these sentences a passive-like interpretation, and is possible with such verbs as *blow, burn, ring, break, open* etc. (*The leaves blew in the wind*, 'were blown by the wind'; *The house burned down*, 'was burned down').

A similar pattern applies to verbs which usually occur with an adverbial. Here the agent can be left out and the object can then become the subject; hence *We **are selling** that book awfully fast* becomes the passive-like *That book **sells** awfully fast*, 'is being sold fast'. This is not truly a passive, for note that the same relationship holds with intransitive *You **can write** well with that pen*, which becomes *That pen **writes** well*. Here no passive paraphrase is possible, for the subject has the semantic role of instrument. There do not seem to be any obvious restrictions on what predicators permit this so long as they: (a) (usually) contain an adverbial of manner and quantity; and (b) what is promoted to subject is an objective or instrumental semantic role.

The communicative structure of sentences   One final, extremely important question remains: what function does the passive fulfil? In English what comes early in a sentence is its **theme** or **topic** and what follows is the **rheme** (from the Greek word meaning 'what is said') or **comment** on this topic. Since subjects usually come at the beginning of sentences, they also normally designate the theme. Sometimes, however, the object is the theme. By using the passive the object can become the subject and take the thematic position at the beginning of the sentence. For example, in *John's in the hospital. Someone hurt him in a fight*, the theme of the second sentence is John, as established by the first sentence. The two sentences would have more **cohesion** if the expected theme came first in the second sentence and the new material, the comment, towards the end. This can easily be accomplished with the passive: *John's in the hospital. **He** got hurt in a fight*.

Other devices are also available to change the placement of elements. One of these means of highlighting information is by **fronting** (*Roses, I like; **violets**, I don't* or *He didn't go gracefully, but **quickly** he did go*). Notice that fronting is used especially for contrast. **Left-dislocation** is a variation on this in which the usual, or canonical, position of the element which is moved to the front/left is marked by a pronoun, e.g. ***Roses**, I like them*; ***John**, he didn't go gracefully*.

Another way of contrasting elements is by means of **contrastive stress**, which can be indicated only imperfectly in writing by using italics or underlining for what, in speech, would be realized by loudness, pitch change or similar (see 4.5.2).

In formal writing especially, but not only there, use is made of **cleft** and of **pseudo-cleft sentences**. In the first type the rheme is introduced by *It is/was* and the theme follows in a relative clause (*It was my car keys which I lost*). This reversal of the usual theme-rheme order has, once again, a contrastive function. Any sentence element or part of a sentence element except the VP may be made the rheme in this way:

it is the **second question** which concerns us [subject];
it is **statements of this sort** which the author deals with [object];
it was **in a flash** that they left [adjunct].

In the pseudo-cleft construction, even a VP may be highlighted. Here the element which is to be emphasized is preceded by the appropriate sort of relative clause and the verb *be*. The element highlighted may be

a verb:	*What we did was **(to) leave** as fast as possible*;
a noun:	*The person who got hurt was **John***;
a manner adverbial:	*The way (in which) he did it was **by dishonesty***;
a place adverbial:	*(The place) Where we met was **(in) Ohio***;
a time adverbial:	*The day (when) we left was **Tuesday**.*

A further means of changing the relative order of elements in a sentence is **extraposition** (see 5.8.7).

5.4.5 Modality

Modality in English has to do with the world, not so much the way it is as the way it might potentially be. This may revolve around people's beliefs about it or around their potential actions in it. There are various linguistic means of expressing this in English, e.g. with AdvPs and PPs (***Probably** he's coming*; *It's **in their power** to decide the issue*), with AdjPs (*It's **likely** that he's coming*; *They're **able** to decide the issue*), with NPs (*the **probability** of his coming*; *their **capability** to decide the issue*) and with VPs (*He **might** come*; *They **can** decide the issue*). Here we will concentrate on the modal verbs.

Morphology and syntax   The modal verbs form a closed class whose central members are *will, would, may, might, can, could, shall, should* and *must*. Somewhat less central are *need, dare, ought to, used to* and *had better*. All the modals share the NICE syntactic features of the auxiliaries/operators (see 5.1.3). The central modals retain these features under all circumstances, however the less central ones do not always exhibit them. *Dare*, *need* and *used to* may appear with *do*-periphrasis. For example, *I needn't ask* is virtually the same as *I don't need to ask*. In addition, *had better* seems to have no widely acceptable interrogative form (*?Had I better buy a new one?* sounds awkward). In addition, none of the modals has the third person singular {-S} (*she may*, never **she mays*), and all take the bare or unmarked infinitive except *ought (to)* and *used (to)*. For these reasons *needs/dares to* are often not regarded as modals; no further notice will be taken here of any of the more peripheral modals except for *needn't* as a negation of *must*.

The defective nature of the modal verbs vis-à-vis lexical verbs can be seen in the fact that none of them (as modals) have either a present or a past participle. As a result they cannot appear in the perfect, progressive or passive forms. Furthermore, while four of the modals do form present-past pairs (*will-would, shall-should, may-might, can-could*), the past tense forms function as markers of past time only in the most restricted of circumstances (see below 'Tense').

Proposition and event orientation   There are two major types of modality in English. The one, propositional, has to do with beliefs and knowledge about logically possible or logically necessary situations, and it commonly referred to as **epistemic**. The other, event-oriented, has to do with potential actions and is frequently called **deontic**.

Epistemic modality indicates the degree of probability of a fact or proposition. Take a proposition such as *Sally is 170 cm tall*. This can be viewed as relatively unlikely or convincingly plausible or, of course, somewhere between the two. Expressed with modals this produces *Sally **might be** 170 cm tall* at the unlikely end and *Sally **must be** 170 cm tall* at the certainty end. Each of these could be paraphrased as follows: *It is **just possible** that Sally is 170 cm tall* and *It is necessarily true that Sally is 170 cm tall*. Since epistemic modality is also often based on evidence, it is sometimes termed **evidential**.

The epistemic modals can be arranged on a scale from low to high probability: *might-may-could-can-should-ought to-will-must*. This scale is a somewhat subjective estimate and is not always accurate. The modals are too vague to allow a more precise calibration. *Will*, for example, makes a prediction, sometimes on the basis of evidence (*The phone's ringing; that'll be my sister*) and sometimes 'out of the blue' (*It'll be nice at the party, I hope*).

Deontic modality has to do with ability, permission, volition and obligation with regard to an action. If you can or may do something, i.e. are allowed to do it, the possibility exists that you will carry out this action. If you must do it, there is an obligation or a necessity, rather than a possibility. The key terms are permission and obligation. Ability and volition are variants of permission (they are sometimes referred to as a further type of modality, **dynamic**). While permission comes from outside the agent, ability and volition are internal to the agent (see below 'Subjective and objective').

Time and tense   Deontic and epistemic modality have different structures for expressing the past. For epistemic modality reference to the past is realized by means of the perfect infinitive, e.g.:

it might be true now	:	it might have been true back then
it may be true now	:	it may have been true back then

it could be true now	:	it could have been true back then
it must be true now	:	it must have been true back then

Note that all of the epistemic modals, even the past tense forms, have a present (sometimes future) meaning when used with the simple infinitive; furthermore, all of them may be used with the perfect infinitive to express conjecture about the past. In addition, the past form of the modal in connection with the perfect infinitive has a contrafactual or condition-contrary-to-fact effect, which may make them ambiguous, e.g. *they could/ might have done it, (but didn't)*; or, *but I don't know if they did* (see below 'Conditional Sentences').

In reported speech there is no backshift of those modals which are already past in form or which have no past form, i.e. *might* remains *might* and *must* remains *must*; epistemic *will*, *can* and *may* can be shifted to *would*, *could* and *might*, though this need not be the case.

In their present tense forms the deontic modals have future or potential reference. For past time reference there are substitute forms available; they include *be permitted/allowed to* for *may* and *can*, *be able to* for *can*, *be willing to* or *be going to* for *will*, *be supposed to* for *should* and *have (got) to* for *must* (also possible for epistemic *must*).

The two (dynamic modality) past tense forms, *could* and *would*, are the only ones which fulfil all of the remoteness functions of the past tense: past time reference, distance in reported speech, unreality in conditional sentences, and politeness and tentativeness in statements (see 5.4.2). However, past time reference is not completely unrestricted. Note that both auxiliaries have past time reference chiefly in non-assertive contexts such as negation and questions and only in ability and volitional meanings. That is, it is the ability meaning which is carried by the past negative *couldn't*. For *will*, it is the volition (rather than prediction) meaning which *wouldn't* conveys. The unnegated past of *can* ability is usually not expressed by *could*, but by *be able to* and the volition sense of *will* not by *would*, but by *want to* or *be willing to* (negative *He **couldn't** solve the problem* as compared to positive *He **was able to** ...*; and negative *She **wouldn't** sell her stock* as opposed to positive *She **wanted to** ...*). The past permission meaning of *can* is never expressed by a modal as in *He was **permitted/allowed** to stay up late*, while *He **could** stay up late* has an ability meaning. Likewise the future-in-the-past of *will* must be the non-modal *She **was (not) going to** sell* and not the volitional *She **would(n't)** sell*.

Should, though past tense in form, never has past time reference. Past deontic time reference is possible either with the perfect infinitive, which has a contrafactual effect (*should have done* = 'was/were supposed to, but did not'), or with the substitute forms *was/were supposed to do/have done*, which is not restricted to a contrafactual interpretation. The same applies to *ought to*. *Should* is not used as the tentative or unreal form of *shall*, either; however, it is employed as a backshifted form in reported speech, e.g. A: *Shall I leave?* B: *She asked if she should (*shall) leave.* Much the same sort of thing applies to *might*, which is almost never found for past time reference and seldom as the unreal or tentative form of *may*. It can, however, be used for backshifted *may* in reported speech, e.g. A: *You may have some cake if you wish.* B: *She said we might* (more likely: *may*) *have some cake if we wished.*

Negation   Besides the effects of negation just mentioned for the past tense of *can* and *will*, there are some important complications that have to do with the question of whether *not* negates the modal or the following infinitive. Sometimes this is unimportant inasmuch as, for example, not having permission to smoke (*You can't smoke in here*) is what would usually be said. Having permission not to smoke (*You can not smoke in here*), which sounds strange, would very likely be interpreted in the same way as the former utterance. Much the same applies to the *should* and *ought* of obligation. The most complicated case of negation is with deontic *must*. The negative of the modal is *needn't* (*You needn't go*, 'it is not necessary that you go'). The negative of the lexical verb, in contrast, is *mustn't* (*You mustn't go*, 'it is necessary that you not go').

Subjective and objective   As mentioned above, the sentences *We said they were able to help out* and *We said they could help out* do not mean the same thing. In the first case the ability to help out is introduced as an objective possibility. In the second case the subject of the main clause (*we*) attributes this ability to the subject of the reported clause *they*; it is an assessment and as such subjective.

There are several such pairs, for example: subjective *must* and objective *have to*; subjective *needn't* and objective *not have to/not need to*; subjective *can* and objective *be allowed to*. The distinction is, however, not always clearly maintained, and this can lead to ambiguity, as when the Australian Prime Minister said of a politician who was accused of deceiving the Parliament: *Senator Withers may have misled Parliament.* As a case of subjective modality the Prime Minister would be committing himself to this possibility; as a case of objective modality [the actual intention] the Prime Minister would merely be admitting that others had made this accusation (example from Huddleston 1984: 167).

The deontic modal *must* is subjective, which means that it imposes an obligation stemming from the speaker; hence it is relatively forceful. Objective *have to* invokes an outside obligation, which takes the onus off the speaker. This may well be the reason why some dialects of English (for example, some varieties of Scottish English) do not have *must*, but only *have to*. Certainly, the difference between the impolite sounding *You must leave immediately* and the more neutral *You have to leave immediately* is evidence for this. If, however, something pleasant is expressed as an obligation, *must* is unproblematic (*You must try our new sauna*).

Conditional sentences   Four types of conditional sentences may be distinguished in English, and the modals play an important role in all of them. The types are given in Table 5.6. Modals do not normally appear in the *if*-clause. However, *will* may when it expresses volition. Generally, the modal auxiliaries are restricted to main clauses. **Real conditional** clauses refer to the future; since the modals are commonly used for future reference, they appear frequently in such sentences. *Will* is the most common, but other central modals occur in real conditional clauses as well. **Unreal conditional** sentences differ from real ones only inasmuch as they express less likelihood. The use of the past tense therefore fits very well as a marker of remoteness.

Contrafactual conditionals, the third type, are used to say something about the past. Here a conclusion is drawn about a hypothetical state of affairs. The main clause always contains a modal (chiefly *would*, often *could*, sometimes *might*) plus a perfect infinitive. This combines the remoteness of the past with epistemic modality, which expresses the likelihood of something given the right conditions in the past. Since the past is not repeatable and cannot be changed, this is 'contrary to fact' or contrafactual.

Table 5.6   Conditional clauses

Type of conditional	if-clause	main clause
I **real condition**	present	*will* (or other modal)

Ex: *If you study hard, you will/can get a good grade.* [= future]

| IIa   **unreal condition** | past | *would* (or other modal) |

Ex: *If I studied hard, I would/might get a good grade.*

| IIb   **stronger unreal condition** | *were* + infinitive | *would* (or other modal) |

Ex: *If I were to study hard, I would . . ..*
[*were* is a subjunctive form indicating unreality]

| III   **contrafactual condition** (contrary-to-fact; irrealis) | past perfect | *would* (or other modal) + perfect infinitive |

Ex: *If I had studied hard, I would/could have had a good grade.*

| IVa   **implicational condition** (no tense restrictions) | present | present or *must* + infinitive |
| | past | past or *must* + perfect inf. |

Ex: *If that is the evening star, it is (must be) Venus.*   [modal of logical necessity]
If you studied hard, you got (must have gotten)
    good grades.

| IVb   **implicational condition** (iterative) | present | present |
| | past | past |

Ex: *If (= Whenever) I study hard, I get a good grade.*

Also possible with habitual *would*: *If (= Whenever) I studied hard, I got/would get*
    good grades.

The final type, the **implicational conditional**, states a relationship which the speaker logically supposes to be true. It is basically a variant of the real condition. The *if*-clause represents not a possibility but a circumstance whose truth is not definitively known. Hence *if it's raining* implies that the speaker does not know whether or not it is raining. However, if the condition is true, then by logical implication it is also true that *they must be getting wet*. Note that the predicator in the main clause will either be the epistemic *must* of logical necessity or it will be the straightforward indicative (i.e. *they are getting wet*).

Conjunctions   Conditional clauses have, for convenience and clarity, been referred to as *if*-clauses. While it is true that *if* is the most common conjunction employed, others are also to be found, for example: *supposing, suppose, in case, allowing that, in the event that, on (the) condition that* (all stylistically formal); *unless*, negative (= 'if not', e.g. *This can't be true unless I'm dreaming!*); *lest* ('in order that not'; extremely formal, chiefly AmE, e.g. *Plan in advance lest ill fortune bring you to a fall*, 'if you do not want ill fortune to . . .'). In addition, conditional clauses may be introduced by subject-operator inversion, (e.g. *Were he to agree/Should he agree*), *I would be very astonished*; also

Had he agreed I would have been . . . . Finally, *conjoined clauses* (chiefly second person and frequently imperative) may have a conditional effect, e.g. [threat]: *(You) come here again and you'll get to know me.*

The semi-modals This label is used to refer to a number of (non-defective) verbs which have meanings parallel to those of the modal auxiliaries. They include, above all, the substitute forms mentioned above: *have (got) to, be willing to, want to, be allowed/ permitted to, be supposed to, be able to* and *be going to*. Evidence for the auxiliary nature of many of these may be seen in the irregularity caused by the assimilation of the infinitive marker *to* with the preceding element to form a single phonetic unit, i.e. *have to* is really *hafta* /hæftə/ (*has to* is *hasta* and *had to* is *hadda*), *have got to* is *gotta*, *supposed to* is *supposta*, *going to* is often *gonna*, *want to* may be *wanna*; even the less central modals with *to* have *usta* for *used to*, a possible *needa* for *need to* and *oughta* for *ought to*. This kind of reduction does not apply to other verbs followed by an infinitive; there is no **beginna* for *begin to* or **lofta* for *love to*.

5.5 THE NOUN PHRASE (NP)

The NP can consist of up to four parts: the obligatory noun head, pre-head determiners with several different positional possibilities, pre-modifiers and, finally, post-modifiers, also consisting of several possible elements.

5.5.1 The noun head

Nouns can be divided into common nouns, themselves subdivided into count and non-count, and proper nouns.

Count and non-count nouns Count nouns are prototypical nouns because they have plurals and, in many cases, possessives (see 5.1.1). They also take all forms of the determiner (*the, a/an* and *zero*). Non-count nouns, in contrast, have no plural and an individualized singular. As a result they cannot appear with the indefinite article (e.g. there is no **a snow*). They may, instead, have either the definite article with specific reference or zero article with generic reference (see below). Non-count nouns may be concrete and include such mass nouns as *coffee, sand, wheat* or *mud*. More often, however, they will be abstract nouns such as *loudness, strength* or *entrepreneurship*. Furthermore, a large group of nouns includes both concrete and abstract nouns which are sometimes count and sometimes non-count, e.g. *cabbage, denial* or *sound*, as in *I bought a cabbage* (= a head of cabbage), where *cabbage* is a count noun, and *I don't like cooked cabbage*, where it is a non-count mass noun. In addition, mass nouns may be used as count nouns, when, for example, you order *two coffees* or a writer talks about the *snows* of yesteryear. Normally, however, this is accomplished by prefixing some measure or quality expression as in *two cups of coffee, a kind of snow*, or *a grain of sand*. Article usage with count and non-count nouns is summarized in Table 5.7.

Nounds used in a **generic** sense refer to typical representatives of a class. With count nouns there are three common ways in which generic reference is realized, namely, the

Table 5.7 Articles with count and non-count nouns

definite	count	non-count	indefinite	non-count
singular	the (song)	the (music)	a (song)	music
plural	the (songs)	–	(songs)	–

singular with the definite article (***The unicorn*** *is a mythological beast*), the singular with the indefinite article (***A unicorn*** *has a single horn*) and the plural with no article (***Unicorns*** *do not exist*). The three differ from each other in that ***the* + singular** refers to the class represented; it has an informal alternative with *your* (*Your unicorn is a mythological beast*). *A* + **singular** is used much like *any*. It may only occur in subject position. **Zero article and the plural**, also restricted to subject position, is the same as saying *all* (or *no*, if negative). A variant of this is the definite article and plural nouns of nationality (*Germans are orderly = The Germans are orderly = All Germans are orderly*). Non-count nouns are generic when they occur without an article (*Snow is white*).

Proper nouns can be identified as those which are capitalized. Capitalization is a sign that each such noun refers to a unique entity (even if, in fact, there is more than one, say, Joe or Barbara in the world). Because the people, places or things referred to are unique, they cannot be further specified and therefore occur without an article. There are two important exceptions to this. The first and most general is that a name of a person can occur more than once. If we want to distinguish between two people with the same name we can specify further by using the definite article and a post-modifying phrase and saying, for instance, ***the** Joe **I know*** or ***the** Barbara **with the red hair***. In this case plurals are also possible, e.g. ***the** Anna's **of this world***. The second exception involves places. Many place names which are derived from common nouns retain their article, so *the United States, the Metropolitan (opera), the Mississippi (river)* etc. Unfortunately, there is no easy rule to distinguish between, for example, *Buckingham Palace* (no article) and *the White House* (with the definite article).

5.5.2 Pre-head

The elements of the pre-head are divided first into those which specify (tell which of a group) or quantify (tell how many or how much). These are the **pre-determiners**, **central determiners** and **post-determiners**, the last of these divided into two subgroups. Following the determiners come the adjectives and participles, which are all designations of quality.

Determiners Many of the determiners are uncountable (*much, less (snow)* – the latter increasingly plural as well, e.g. *less people*), singular (*a/an, every, each, this, that*), dual (= reference to two: *both, either, neither*) or plural (*all, many, fewer, these, those*).

The most common **central determiner** is the article as in *all **the** fresh eggs* or *what **a** nice car*. There are, however, various other sets of central determiners, for example:

demonstrative determiners:	*this, that, these, those*
possessive determiners:	*my, your, her; Ruth's, (the) boy's, whose*
indefinite determiners:	*some, any, no, every, each, (n)either*
relative determiners:	*which(ever), what(ever)*

Both the demonstrative and the possessive determiners may be preceded by the **pre-determiners**, which are quantifiers of scope (sometimes with, sometimes without *of*), for example *all, half, a/one third, both, double, twice* etc. (e.g. *both (of) the* students). There is, in addition, the quantifier *many* and a small set of qualifying pre-determiners (*such, quite, what*) which may precede the indefinite article (*such a day*). With *so, how, too* and *enough* adjectives are moved in front of the indefinite article along with the determiner (*so/how/too big a problem/big enough a problem*). The **post-determiners** are exclusively expressions of quantity. They consist of relativizing items including the ordinal numbers, e.g. *first, second, third,* but also *next, last, further, additional, other* etc., which precede the cardinal numbers and a few other quantifiers of number (*one, two, three, few, several*). No more than one representative of each of the four positional classes may appear in any one NP, e.g. *half (of) the next three (weeks)* or *all (of) her second three (attempts)*.

5.5.3 The order of adjectives

This is not strictly fixed, but the dominant principle is that the more accidental, subjective and temporary qualities are named before the more essential, objective and permanent ones. This means that evaluative adjectives (*beautiful, important, stupid*) tend to come first, and those which name the substance out of which something is made (*wooden, metal*) or the subject matter something refers to (*economic, religious*) come last. In between come size (*tiny, tall, fat*), then shape (*round, flat, sharp*), then participles (*blazing, ruined*) followed first by age (*old, new, young*) and then colour (*red, green, blue*). After that comes nationality or provenance (*British, American, African*). Adjectives which are gradeable may be preceded by adverbial intensifiers (*somewhat, astonishingly, pretty, very*). Here are some illustrative examples (more than three or four adjectives in one NP would be rare in actual use):

both my last two very worthless old British pennies;
all your shapeless old-fashioned felt carpet slippers;
the second dozen small somewhat wilted yellow roses;
his confusing modern poetic works.

5.5.4 Post-modifiers

The noun head can be followed by several types of modifying expression. A few adjectives can be post-positive, be they fixed expressions (*secretary **general**, president **elect***) or adjectives and participles with complements (*a woman true **to her principles**, a jacket **made to order***). Those adverbs of time and place which can modify nouns also follow (*the valley **beyond**, that car **there**, years **before***). Many of these adverbs are variants of PPs, which are the most frequent post-modifiers (*the valley **beyond ours**, a story **about*** *love and war, a person **of distinction***). PPs themselves are sometimes, but by no means always variations of clauses, both non-finite (*the valley **situated beyond ours**, the woman **sitting beside you**, the valley **to visit***) and finite (*the valley **which is situated beyond ours**, a student **who comes from Ghana***).

The relative order of post-modifiers is generally from short to long. The main exception to this is that PPs which provide information about the nature or provenance of the head noun (*a woman **of virtue**, the currency **of Japan***) come before participles and adverbs (*a friend of the family waiting outside in the yard*).

Post-modifiers can be restrictive (defining) or non-restrictive (non-defining), whereas pre-modifiers are more likely to be restrictive only (on restrictive and non-restrictive, see 5.5.5). As restrictive elements they often introduce new and distinguishing or identifying features. On further mention these restrictive, defining elements, now known or given, may become the initial member of a compound in much the fashion of the theme-rheme, given-new distinction (see 5.4.4). For example, a program may be introduced as *a program using a computer*; further mention can then be of *the computer program*. More detail may be added as in *a computer program for the checking of spelling*, which can then lead to *the computer spelling-check program* and so on. This is parallel to the way information is introduced via a predicative complement: *Her car is black* which then becomes *her black car*.

5.5.5 Relative clauses

The restrictive vs non-restrictive distinction just mentioned is also made by relative clauses. Restrictive relative clauses are used if the identity of the referent is not clear. If someone says, 'my mother', it is not possible to ask 'Which of your mothers?'; the identity is clear, so a post-modifying relative will be non-defining (*My mother, who loves flowers, is president of the garden club*). However, if someone says 'my brother' or 'my sister' and has more than one, the relative clause may be necessary to identify which one of them is meant (*My sister who is at university just turned 20, but my other sister is only 16*). However, the distinction between referents which are already identified and ones which need further definition is often far from clear. One result is that many writers fail to indicate the distinction, namely that non-restrictive clauses are conventionally separated off by commas while restrictive ones are not.

Non-restrictive pronominal relatives consist of only the items *who(m)*, *which* and *whose*. Restrictive relative pronouns include these as well as *that* and zero relative [= Ø] (e.g. *the book that/[Ø] I read*). Non-restrictive relative clauses are always finite. Restrictive pronominal clauses, in contrast, may be finite (*We don't like people who complain all the time*) or non-finite (*the hotel at which to stay/the hotel [Ø] to stay at*).

Sentential relative clauses   In this type of construction, the antecedent is a whole clause and only *which* can be used (*Grammar is interesting, which is why I study it*). It is always non-defining. This is, of course, not a post-modifier in an NP, but a kind of sentence adverbial.

A further important distinction between relatives is that there are both pronominal relative clauses, that is, ones which are introduced by a relative pronoun (*who(m)*, *whose*, *which*, *that*) and adverbial ones, introduced by a relative adverb (*when*, *where*, *how*, *why*).

Pronominal relative clauses   These distinguish what they post-modify (their antecedents) according to whether this is personal or non-personal. *Who(m)* is used for the former (*the friend who(m) I met*) and *which* for the latter (*the computer which I use*). This distinction is neutralized in the possessive since *whose* refers to both (*the friend whose computer I use*; *the computer whose printer is so noisy*). It is also neutralized with the relative pronoun *that* (*the friend that . . ., the computer that . . .*). The restrictive relative pronoun does not need to appear when it is not the subject of its own clause (*the friend [Ø] I met*; *the computer [Ø] I use*).

Relative adverbial clauses   These are similar to pronominal relatives because temporal *when* is equivalent to *the time in/at which* and local *where* to *the place in/at which*. Both can be defining or non-defining, as in non-restrictive *London, where Parliament sits, is the capital of the UK* as opposed to restrictive *The city where the meeting was held is somewhere in Illinois*. Those of manner (*how*) and reason (*why*) are always defining. If the antecedent is indefinite (*the place, the time, the way, the reason*) the relative *that* is also employed (*the last time that I saw you*). Manner relatives never occur with both antecedent and relative (**the way how*), but only either with the one (*He saw the way I did it*) or the other (*He saw how I did it*). When there is no antecedent, which can also be the case with time, place and reason clauses, the adverbial relative can be considered to be fused (see following paragraph). In such cases *how, when, where* and *why* are sometimes indistinguishable from indirect questions.

Fused relatives   Fused relatives are called this because the antecedent and the relative are, as it were, fused into a single whole (*You must return what you borrow* = 'return that which you'). This type is not a nominal post-modifier because there is no separate antecedent for it to modify.

5.6 NOMINALIZATION

While many nouns are 'typically' concrete and countable, not all of them are. In addition to the uncountable mass nouns already mentioned there are many abstract designations such as *liberty, relationship* or *art*. Furthermore, acts, events, activities, processes and states, which are usually expressed by verbs, can be nominalized – that is, put into a noun form. Such forms are called **nominals** (in contrast to nouns). Five types of nominals will be recognized here:

1   derived nominals: *agreement, hardness*
2   action nominals: *the solving of problems*
3   gerunds: *your singing popular songs*
4   infinitives: *for them to complain*
5   nominal and interrogative clauses: *that they agreed*; *whether the police know*

Nominals are somewhere between noun on the one hand and verb or adjective on the other. Semantically they all refer more to time (occurrences; verb-like, e.g. *agreement*) or to properties (adjective-like, e.g. *hardness*) than to space (objects; noun-like, e.g. *car*).

Derived nominals and action nominals are the most noun-like. The former may be pluralized in concrete reference, for example, *the governments of the EU countries*. Note that the abstract act of *government* 'governing' cannot be plural. Both (1) and (2) may be preceded by an article (*a/the refusal*). Furthermore, both (1) and (2) may be followed by PPs (*the interviewing **of people**, the hatred **of evil***). Most important, however, both nouns and nominals form the centre (or head) of NPs. As such, they may, for example, be the subject of a sentence as in ***His writing of poems** keeps him busy*.

The gerund and the infinitive are both particularly verb-like since they can take a direct object, e.g. *Singing **songs**/To sing **songs** is fun*. Gerunds and infinitives take the verbal categories of aspect and voice (*writing, having written, having been writing; being written, having been written* and *to write, to be writing, to have written, to have been writing; to be written to, to have been written to* etc.). The gerund is perhaps more noun-like than the infinitive because only it may appear freely after prepositions (*by doing that*; but not: **by to do that*).

The gerund, infinitive, as well as nominal and interrogative clauses (*that*- and *wh*-clauses) are associated with what are called **complementizers**. These are markers which signal the presence of a clausal nominalization. For the gerund it consists of the (optional) possessive determiner, e.g. *she likes **our** cooking supper* (instead of *us cooking supper*); for the infinitive it consists of an initial *for*, which precedes the subject of the infinitive in at least some cases, e.g. *it is nice **for** you to type so quickly*. For the nominal clause the complementizer is the optional element *that*, e.g. *(that) I came*; and for the interrogative clause it is the mandatory presence of a *wh*-word (*when, where, why, whether, how they did it* etc.).

Nominals form NPs, but they cannot freely occur in all the same places that noun-headed NPs can (few will ever appear as indirect objects). All of them occur frequently as subjects if lexically appropriate (*To go jogging is healthy*). However, long, 'heavy' subjects may be moved to the end (**extraposition**), leaving the 'dummy' subject *it* behind, e.g. *It was great that you remembered Mother's birthday* rather than *That you remembered Mother's birthday was great*.

What is most intriguing and complex about the nominals is the use of gerunds, infinitives and nominal and interrogative clauses with the verbs referred to as catenatives. The following section is devoted to them.

5.7 CATENATION

Catenatives are those predicators which can have gerunds, infinitives and nominal or interrogative clauses as complements. Examples are *I remember **seeing** them* (gerund), *They told you **to return** the book* (infinitive), *My uncle said **that we should go now*** (nominal clause), *I doubt **whether he's right*** (interrogative clause). In describing how these verbs and their complements are used together it is necessary to: (1) distinguish verbs by their semantic classes; (2) differentiate the internal forms of each of the nominal types; and (3) recognize the time relationships between the predicators and their complements.

5.7.1 Verb classes

There are perhaps some 30 different classes of catenatives, each of them defined by meaning. All in all some 500 to 600 verbs (not including verb + adjective combinations like *be afraid* [*to do something*] are involved. Some are polysemous and occur in more than one class (see 5.7.4)

It does not seem reasonable to attempt an even moderately complete review of the classes; however, a look at some of the more important ones can serve to clarify the way in which catenation functions. The following classes (with examples) will be observed:

perception:	*see, hear, feel*
cognition:	*think, remember, suppose, see*
speech:	*say, declare, suggest*
command and request:	*ask, demand, remind, suggest*
volition:	*agree, love, wish*
evaluation:	*like, love, hate*

What all of these verbs and verb classes have in common is that they say something about either a state or an action/happening. They may say something about the possibility that a state existed or an action occurred (it began or ended, was caused, observed, wanted, demanded etc.).

5.7.2 Internal formal differentiation

An infinitive is not just an infinitive. As the following examples reveal, there are important formal differences (aside from possible progressive, perfect and passive forms):

I can **come**	subjectless bare infinitive
I hope **to come**	subjectless *to*-infinitive
I saw **you come**	bare infinitive with subject
I asked **you to come**	*to*-infinitive with subject
I planned **for you to come**	complementizer *for* + *to*-infinitive with subject

Just as there are five different kinds of infinitives there are three kinds of {-ing} forms (again without considering aspect and voice; the term {-ing} form is being used because it covers both gerunds and present participles):

I began **working**	without a complement subject
I saw **him working**	with object case subject
I minded **his working**	with possessive case subject

Nominal clauses may also be differentiated:

I like **it that he came**	*it* + complementizer *that*
I established **that he came**	complementizer *that*

I thought **(that) he came**	no complementizer necessary
I told him **(that) he should come**	modal predicator; no complementizer necessary
I recommend **(that) he come**	subjunctive predicator; no complementizer necessary

Interrogative clauses, finally, are differentiated by the variety of different *wh*-words which can occur as introductory complementizers. In the following, interrogative clauses (indirect questions) will not be pursued any further.

5.7.3 Time relations

There is a basic temporal distinction between the infinitive and the {-ing} form. Non-finite complements which refer to a time before that of the main or catenative predicator are exclusively expressed by {-ing} forms (e.g. *I remember **doing** it*; *She admits **going***; *They deny **being** there*). An infinitive complement can indicate past relative to the main verb only by appearing in the perfect form. This is really a report of a present state which has resulted from a past occurrence (e.g. *We seem **to have done** something wrong*; *They happen **to have gone***; *He is rumoured **to have overslept***).

Non-finite complements which are future with regard to the catenative are infinitives (*Please remember **to mail** the letter*; *We wish **to go** early*; *You promised **to come***). Only a relatively small group of verbs does not follow this pattern: *recommend **doing** something*, *urge **doing** something* etc.

Those complements, finally, which designate a state or action which is simultaneous with the main verb may be followed by either. One difference between the two involves progressive aspect (*see someone **leave*** vs *see someone **leaving***; *begin **to know*** vs **?begin **knowing***, where stative *know* resists use in the progressive). A second distinction is that of factuality (past/present) vs potentiality (future), as in *I tried **smoking**, but didn't like it*, 'actually smoked' vs *I tried **to be** on time, but didn't manage to*, 'did not actually arrive on time'.

Finite *that*-clause complements are, of course, freer in their temporal relations to the catenative which embeds them because they contain a finite verb. The tense of the predicator is, however, not fully free. Recall the rules of sequence of tenses which apply to indirect speech (see 5.4.2). In general, a past tense form in the main clause will normally require a past tense in the *that*-clause of the reported speech; for example: *will go* becomes *would go*; *goes* becomes *went*; *have gone* becomes *had gone*. Furthermore, the imperative verbs which take *that*-clause complements are restricted to the mandative subjunctive or to the deontic modal of obligation *should* (see 'Suggest' in 5.7.4).

5.7.4 Examples

To illustrate how this works four verbs have been selected (*see, remember, love, suggest*), all of which take a variety of different complement types. As the complement observed changes, it is also possible to see that the verb itself changes classes in accordance with the status of the complement.

See   Note the contrast between *I saw them crossing the bridge* and *I saw them cross the bridge*: in the first case it is the *activity* of crossing which is witnessed by the subject by means of physical perception. No conclusion can be reached about whether the people crossing ever finished crossing, that is, got to the other side. The second case focuses on the *act*, namely something completed. It is clear that the crossing was finished. As a cognitive verb *see* may also take a *that*-clause complement (*I saw that they have found a cure for the common cold*). Here the subject did not necessarily see any direct evidence which might have led to the conclusion; instead, he or she may simply have read this in the newspaper and accepted it because someone said that this was the case. What is expressed is not an activity or an act which has been perceived, but a proposition which has been cognitively accepted.

Remember   *I remember doing my homework* (or with a subject: *I remember him doing his homework*) refers to an activity which the subject (or someone else) carried out at an earlier time. This stands in contrast to a present or continuing state as in *I remember him to have red hair*, where a conclusion is drawn about a present state on the basis of memory. In both cases *remember* is a verb of cognition. Other verbs of this class (for example, *believe, find, know*; *I believed him to be friendly, she found the bread to be stale*) frequently take complements of this sort, sometimes called the **accusative with infinitive** or **a.c.i.** (from the Latin *accusativus cum infinitivo*). When the main clause predicator is put into the passive, the subject of the infinitive becomes the subject of the whole sentence (*They were seen to have crossed the bridge*). This is sometimes called the **n.c.i.** (*nominativus cum infinitivo*). In *I remembered to do my homework*, finally, doing the homework is future with regard to the remembering. In this third example *remember* is like an imperative verb (= 'remind'), as can be seen more clearly when a subject and the *for . . . to* construction occurs (in those varieties of English which have such a construction): *I remembered for him to do his homework* = 'I reminded him to do it'.

Love   There is a contrast between *I love sitting there* ('I have sat there/am sitting there/sometimes sit there and love this') and *I love to sit there* ('I may do it [again]'). In the first instance *sitting* is a gerund and names an actual act or activity, and *love* is a verb of evaluation. When the infinitive is used, the verb is volitional and directed towards what is desired in the future. A final variation is *I love it that I am sitting here*. Here *love* is a verb of evaluation, and the *that*-clause complement is the proposition which states that the subject is, in fact, sitting 'here'. The proposition is presupposed to be factual and then positively evaluated ('I love it'). This is much like the gerund with the difference that tense and aspect can be specified in the *that*-clause complement.

Suggest   This verb may be followed by a gerund or an infinitive complement. In the former case (*I suggest our taking a long walk*) it is a proposal about a future activity and is unusual, as gerunds are used for future reference with only the verbs of this class (*propose, intend, recommend, advocate* and *oppose*). The sentence *John suggested taking a long walk* may, but need not mean that John goes along.

In some varieties of English the *for . . . to* construction is possible after *suggest* (*I suggested for us to take a long walk*). A similar restriction to certain varieties is true of the construction with no subject and the simple infinitive (*I suggested to take a long walk*). These sentences are used to report a potential act. In such cases *suggest* may be regarded as a manner of communication verb such as *whisper, yell, moan* etc. as well as *say*, where this type of complement is common (*He screamed (for us/to us) to pay attention*).

The mandative subjunctive is a further form which is possible after *suggest* (*I suggested that he take a long walk*). An alternative complement is with the modal *should* (*that he should take*). Both are the reported form of an imperative. The mandative subjunctive is used after predicates which introduce a demand or proposal (the verbs *demand, insist, order, request* etc.; the adjectives *important, mandatory, imperative, advisable* etc.; and even the nouns *decision, requirement* etc.).

Syntactically, this subjunctive is marked by having the base or infinitive form after the subject in all persons (*It is desirable that he/they **be** informed*). Furthermore, negation is realized without *do*-periphrasis, but rather with simple pre-posed *not* (*I prefer that he/they **not** learn what happened*). In BrE the subjunctive is restricted more to formal contexts. In this variety the form with *should* is very common, but the indicative is found as well (*I suggest that he takes a walk*). The latter form is likely to be misunderstood in AmE as a verb of speech (*suggest* = 'insinuate') which is followed not by an imperative, but by a proposition ('In my opinion this is what he did').

5.8 THE CLAUSE

Among the phenomena which are relevant at the level of the clause are illocutionary force, sentence patterns/mood and complexity. Furthermore, some phenomena such as clause pro-forms, negation, thematic focus and word order are best observed at this level. The major syntactic or sentence patterns have already been introduced (5.3.3). We will continue here with mood.

It is well known that many a statement really pursues a different purpose than just, say, giving information. *I've just mopped the floor* may be intended as a prohibition ('Don't walk on it yet') or a request ('Say thanks'). In the appropriate setting the statement *It's warm and sunny* may be taken as a question ('Shall we go for a stroll?'), which is used in the sense of a directive (see 7.2.1).

5.8.1 Clause types

As far as this chapter is concerned, each of the traditional **moods** is associated with a particular sentence type. The **indicative** is rooted in the **declarative** sentence and this is the type used in 5.3.3 to illustrate sentence patterns: the subject comes first, followed by the predicator and then by whatever further complements may be called for (direct object, indirect object, predicative complement).

The interrogative provides a variation on this inasmuch as most questions involve a *wh*-question word (*who, what, where, when, why, how* etc.) and operator-subject inversion. For example, the declarative *She left us at noon* becomes the question ***When** did she leave us?* in which the operator *do* is introduced since the declarative in the example has no operator. Of course, inversion does not always occur (***Who** left us at noon?* where the *wh*-word is subject); nor is there always a *wh*-word (*yes-no* questions such as *Did she leave at noon?*). If such a *yes-no* question is reported, however, the *wh*-word *whether* or *if* is used (*They asked **whether/if** she left at noon*). In reported questions there is usually also no inversion (*They asked when she left*). However, there is a tendency to retain inversion in informal usage (*They asked when did she leave*). Sometimes there is neither inversion nor a *wh*-word as in *She left us at noon?* spoken with rising intonation. In writing, direct questions always have a question mark at the end.

The imperative typically appears as the base form of the verb without a subject (*Speak up, please*). Imperatives are, despite the lack of a subject, clearly second person, addressed to a hearer/reader. This is evident both in reflexive forms and anaphoric pronoun reference (*Help **yourself** to more potatoes if **you**'re still hungry*; *Give me a hand, will **you**?*). Imperatives never contain modals, and there is never perfect aspect in imperatives. The lack of the perfect clearly has to do with the fact that imperatives refer to the future. The progressive is possible though infrequent (***Be working** when the boss comes in*). Passives are found, but most often in the negative (***Don't be fooled** by her*), or with the auxiliary *get* (*Come on! **Get organized***). Note that *be* is negated with the auxiliary *do* in imperatives (***Don't** be late*) and uses emphatic *do* and takes a tag question with *will* (***Do** give me a hand, **will** you?*).

Although typical imperatives are second person forms, the imperative construction with *let* is sometimes thought of as a first person variant as in *Let's give a party* or as in the reflexive ***Let me [Lemme]** treat **myself** to a cup of coffee* or *Let's leave early, **shall we?*** with a pronoun tag. Sometimes third person forms are also found (e.g. *If they have no bread, **let them** eat cake*). The negative is either *Let's not go* (AmE and BrE), *Don't let's* (BrE) or *Let's don't go* (AmE).

Exclamatory mood may be imposed on practically any syntactic form if emphatic stress and strongly rising or rising-falling intonation is used. However, there is also one exclamatory sentence type, namely independent utterances introduced by *what* or *how* with or without a predicator, e.g. *What a day (it was)!* or *How nice (they are)!* An exclamation point is often but not invariably used in writing.

5.8.2 Complexity

Clauses can also be linked by **coordination** and **subordination**. When two main clauses are connected, this is referred to as a **compound sentence**. Subordination may, as 5.7 has shown, involve finite and non-finite clauses embedded within main clauses, including reported speech. Relative clauses can expand NPs as post-modifiers (5.5.5). Furthermore, a subordinate (adverbial) clause may be joined to a main clause. These instances are all called **complex sentences**. A combination of the compound and complex sentences are referred to as **compound-complex**. Complexity is one means of establishing cohesion within texts (see Chapter 6).

Two main clauses can be coordinated by means of the coordinating conjunctions *and*, *or*, *nor*, *but*, *for* and *yet* (*It's warm, **and** the sun is shining*). There is also the possibility of using correlative coordinating conjunctions, *both . . . and*, *(n)either . . . (n)or*, *not only . . . but (also)*, in which one member comes at the beginning of the first and the other at the beginning of the second clause (***Not only** is it warm, **but** the sun is **also** shining*).

Coordination can also be achieved with **conjuncts**, i.e. adverbials which have a connecting function. They tend to be relatively formal in style. Some of the most common are *however, nevertheless, moreover, therefore, in other words, on the other hand*; but there are many more. In writing, if the two clauses do not appear as separate sentences, the convention is to use a semi-colon before and a comma after them (*Conjuncts are connectors; **nevertheless**, they are not conjunctions*). If a conjunct occurs within the second clause the punctuation is as follows: *Conjuncts are connectors; they are, **nevertheless**, not conjunctions*. In addition, coordinating conjunctions may also link subordinate clauses, phrases or individual words with each other. A final means of coordinating two clauses in writing is by simply putting them next to each other and connecting them with a semicolon or colon (*The word 'but' is a conjunction; the word 'however' is a conjunct*).

Subordinate adverbial clauses fulfil much the same function as adjunct AdvPs and PPs. They are usually introduced by a subordinating conjunction which may express time (e.g. *when, before, as soon as*), cause (*because, as, since*), concession (*although*), condition (*if, supposing, unless*), purpose (*so that, in order that*), comparison (*as, like*) and a few other relations (see 5.3.4)

A subordinate adjunct clause may follow or precede the main clause; that is, the sub-ordinating conjunction may occur initially in the sentence or between the two clauses (*We went swimming **as** it was hot* or ***As** it was hot, we went swimming*). A coordinating conjunction, in contrast, may only come between the clauses it joins (*We went swimming, **for** it was hot*; **For** it was hot, we went swimming*).

The content of an introductory subordinate clause tends to be thematically given and therefore less prominent vis-à-vis the new information of the main clause. In the sentence *Although it was late, I read for a while before I turned off the light* the lateness of hour is treated as if already known, and the focus is on the continued reading. The final temporal adjunct clause carries more weight than the initial concessive one without having quite the same character of given-ness; yet it definitely is not highlighted. If the two subordinate clauses are exchanged (*Before I turned off the light, I read for a while although it was late*), it is the temporal clause which is the given and the concessive one has more weight.

5.8.3 Pro-forms

Do is used as a pro-form when the predicate itself and all the complements which follow it are elided (*Jack hurt himself fetching water, and Jill **did**, too*). If another auxiliary is present, the pro-form *do* is less common (*Has Jack hurt himself? Yes, he **has**; also, Yes, he has **done**; see 12.3.1). Note that the pro-form *do* is not the same lexeme as the auxiliary *do*; the latter has only the forms *do, does, did* while the pro-form has these as well as *done* and *doing*.

The pro-form *so* is used for the complements which follow the predicator, as in *Jack broke his crown, and Jill did **so**, too*. Its negation would be . . . *but Jill did **not**. Alternative negative forms are with *neither, nor* and *not* . . . *either* (*Jack didn't hurt himself and **neither/nor** did Jill* or *Jack isn't a child and Jill isn't **either**). *So* is especially common as a pro-form for *that*-clauses after verbs of speech and cognition, e.g. A: *Do you believe they're here?* B: *I'm not sure, but I believe **so**; negative: *but I believe **not**, or *but I don't believe **so**).

5.8.4 Negation

Elements of all sorts can be negated at all levels and in a variety of different ways, namely words (*partisan* : *non-partisan*; *skilled* : *unskilled*), phrases (*with malice* : *without malice*; *very carefully* : *not very carefully*) and clauses (*Someone yelled* : *No one yelled*; *I went* : *I didn't go*). At the clause level, it is normally the predicator which is negated. And this is normally done with the word *not*.

The use of *not* to negate a finite VP is always realized by putting this word after the operator (*I am working* : *I am not working*). If there is no operator in the unnegated version, an appropriate form of *do* is inserted (*I left* : *I didn't leave*). Two exceptional usages are worth mentioning. The first is the negation of an imperative, in which even the verb *be* (although an operator) takes a pre-posed *don't* or *do not* (*Don't be upset*). The second is the negative of the subjunctive and of infinitives and *-ing* forms, all of which have *not* without *do* (*I suggest that you not be late again*; *To be or not to be*; *Not eating sweets is my New Year's resolution*).

5.8.5 Non-assertive contexts

A number of items are restricted to contexts in which there is negation or some other form indicating uncertainty about the truth or reality of a situation (this includes questions, conditionals and some instances of modality). Many of the words which occur in such contexts correspond to others which appear in positive or assertive contexts. Such assertive: non-assertive pairs include *some*: *any*, *too*: *either*, *already*: *yet* and *sometimes*: *ever*. Hence there is assertive *He's already bought some*, *They sometimes go*, or *She did it, too* and non-assertive *He hasn't bought any yet*, *They don't ever go*, or *She didn't do it, either*. This alternation is most stringent under negation. In questions, in conditionals and with modals the non-assertive member of each pair is not always necessary (*Has he bought any yet/already?* or *Do they ever/sometimes go?*). *Either* may not, in fact, occur except with negation (*Did she do it, too/*either?*). Furthermore, the whole series of words formed around *some* and *any* involve numerous complications which depend on such things as the scope of negation and the meaning of *some* (quantifier or marker of indefiniteness)

A special effect of non-assertive elements is the occurrence of negative elements (*never*, *not once*, *at no time* etc.) and semi-negative ones (*barely*, *hardly*, *infrequently*, *rarely*, *seldom*, *scarcely*) at the beginning of a sentence. When this happens there must be inversion of subject and operator (*Rarely did the sun appear that afternoon*).

5.8.6 Word order

The arrangement of words in sentences is one of the most important means of establishing grammatical cohesion in English (see Chapter 6). Often word order is grammatically fixed. This has been mentioned above at various points, such as 5.3.3 on sentence patterns. In 5.8.1 on mood it was pointed out that there is subject-operator order in declaratives and inversion in interrogatives. The effect of initial negatives and semi-negatives appeared in the preceding paragraph (5.8.5). The relative order of determiners and of adjectives has also been sketched out (5.5.2). Furthermore, word order is obviously an important factor in the way in which theme-rheme works, both in the communicative structure of sentences (see 5.4.4) and also in that of NPs (5.5.3). The two guiding principles of cohesion are, in brief, those just mentioned: grammatical restrictions on word order and thematic focus.

The relative position of adjuncts   The order of adjuncts is perhaps the most diffi-cult to present concisely. The overriding principle is that of focus. An adjunct which is to carry more weight will come at the beginning (thematic) or at the end of the sentence (rhematic). Very few restrictions can prevent this from happening. This does, of course, take for granted that the element which is fronted or which occurs finally would not normally be found there. In other words, it presupposes some kind of unmarked or normal word order from which it departs.

The usual position of adjuncts is after the predicator and its complements with place before manner and manner before time (*We drove the car home* [place] *in a hurry* [manner] *before the storm broke out* [time]). There are several reasons why this pattern is seldom found. First of all, all three types of adjunct are not often likely to appear together in a single sentence. Second, manner adjuncts, especially in the form of single adverbs, such as *quickly* instead of *in a hurry*, will occur before the lexical verb (*We **quickly** drove . . .*). Third, time adjuncts freely appear in initial position, especially if this prevents the occurrence of a series of sentence-final adjuncts (***Before the storm broke out**, we drove the car home quickly*). Finally, the greater length or weight of an element will lead to its appearance closer to the end (*Yesterday we drove the car quickly **to the place where we last remembered seeing the picnickers***).

Displacement of a long element to the end of a sentence is virtually a grammatical requirement in some instances. *That*-nominal clauses and infinitives which are the subjects of sentences are often felt to be too weighty and so are moved to the end. When this happens they leave the pronoun *it* behind to supply the necessary grammatical subject (*It was nice that you called* or *It was great to hear from you*). With several common verbs this movement to the end, called **extraposition**, is grammatically obligatory (*appear, seem, happen, occur, turn out*) as in *It happens **that she likes you***.

Extraposition can apply to sentence objects as well as subjects. Where a nominal clause is displaced, *it* may be introduced immediately after the predicator (*We consider it important that you report to headquarters immediately*); more usual is *We hope very much that you have a safe journey home*).

5.9 FURTHER READING

For more detail see any one of the numerous **grammars** available. The following short list may be of help. Quirk *et al.* 1985 is the most comprehensive modern grammar of English and covers most of the topics discussed in this chapter; see also Greenbaum 1996. Biber *et al.* 1999 is similarly comprehensive and is based, in addition, on extremely useful corpus-based observations on regional (AmE–BrE) and stylistic (academic prose, news, fiction, conversation) usage. Useful handbooks include: Alexander 1988; Baker 1995; Berk 1999; Brinton 2000; Close 1975; van Ek and Robat 1984; Greenbaum 1991; Greenbaum and Quirk 1990; Leech, Deuchar and Hoogenraad 1982; Huddleston 1988; Thomson and Martinet 1983.

For a non-traditional discussion of **word classes** see Fries 1952, Chapters 5–7; otherwise, see Huddleston 1984, Chapter 3. On **verb types** see: Bolinger 1971; Cowie and Mackin 1993; Taylor 2000; Palmer 1987, Chapter 10. The criteria for **prepositions** are discussed in Quirk and Mulholland 1964.

Phrasal units are treated in Huddleston 1984; also Quirk *et al.* 1985. For more on **sentence elements** and **sentence patterns** see van Ek and Robat 1984 or Quirk *et al.*1985. Dirven and Radden 1987 apply Fillmore's concept of **case** to English.

Joos 1968, Palmer 1987 and Leech 1987 all offer comprehensive discussion of the **categories of the verb**. For more on the **future** see: Wekker 1976; Close 1988. **Tense** in the languages of the world is the subject of Comrie 1985; the same for **aspect** in Comrie 1976. For more extensive treatments of the **perfect** see: McCoard 1978; Fenn 1987. The **passive** is treated in: Stein 1979; Svartvik 1966. For **modality** see Palmer 1990, 2001.

Theme-rheme and the communicative structure of sentences are treated in: Halliday 1967b; Duškova 1971; Erdmann 1990. On the **imperative**, see: Davies 1986; Hamblin 1987.

Part 2

Uses and users of English

Chapter 6

Written texts and English for specific purposes (ESP)

The importance of texts is self-evident when we remember that all language occurs in communicative units usually larger than single words or sentences. All the same, texts have proven to be the hardest units to describe, perhaps because of the seemingly endless variations texts present us with. Nevertheless, this chapter shows that a number of meaningful things can be said about texts. The phenomenon *text* will be treated from two points of view. The first half of the chapter defines (in 6.1 and 6.2) what qualities linguists have in mind when they speak of texts and then attempts a classification of text types (6.3), which is applied to the discussion of a concrete example (6.4). The second half of the chapter (6.5–6.7) deals with ESP, which is the use of English in a restricted set of social and thematic areas chiefly for the unambiguous transfer of technical information. Here we give special attention to one particular genre of written texts, that of English for science and technology (EST).

This chapter and Chapter 7, 'Spoken discourse', complement each other: the discussion of cohesion and coherence in this chapter is also relevant for spoken language, while the discussion of speech act theory (7.2.1) and global knowledge patterns (7.4.2 'Schemas') has a direct bearing on the production and reception of written language. The chapter titles 'Written texts' and 'Spoken discourse' have been chosen for practical reasons rather than terminological precision – many linguists use the two terms *text* and *discourse* interchangeably, as is done on occasion in this book. However, a distinction is often made between *text*, as a unified stretch of language without regard to situational context, and *discourse*, in which situational factors are taken into account.

6.1 TEXTUALITY

What distinguishes written (or spoken) texts from a random collection of sentences (or utterances) is the quality of **textuality**. Textual units are connected with one another by means of what is called **connectivity**, **connexity**, or **continuity**. Textuality is the result of the seven factors discussed below and depends on both the writer and the reader to varying degrees.

(1) Cohesion and (2) coherence   Textual unity manifests itself at different levels. Writers link text sentences above all using grammatical and lexical means (sometimes termed the **co-text**, Werlich 1983: 80) which prompt readers to interpret them as belonging together. This is called **grammatical** and **lexical cohesion**. A deeper, semantic level is involved in **coherence**, which refers to the continuity of subject matter (see 6.2).

(3) Intentionality and (4) acceptability These relate to the attitudes of writer and reader. Writers intend to produce cohesive and coherent texts, and readers accept them as such, showing a certain tolerance towards texts where writers' intentions may be less than perfectly realized. Both writer intention and reader acceptance are not based solely on knowledge of the language system but also on the ability of the sides to bring their knowledge of the world to bear on text production and reception (see 6.4.2. on schemas). Of particular interest is the way addressees fill in gaps or breaks in the surface continuity of texts in order to make them cohesive and coherent (see 7.2.2. on inference).

(5) Informativity This is reader centred and refers to the degree to which the text produced is expected or unexpected, and whether it repeats what is known already or provides new information. No text provides only old or only new information, but the ratio of the two can vary considerably and depends on the writer's intentions and assessment of the reader. Texts about well known things are easy to produce and understand, but can also easily bore the reader. Texts that give a lot of new information, on the other hand, are more difficult to understand, though they are likely to be of greater interest to readers. There is, then, an inverse correlation between minimum writer and reader effort (efficiency) and maximum impact of the message (effectiveness). In general, writers focus on the problematic or variable aspects of a topic because only they provide new information (de Beaugrande and Dressler 1981: 189). For instance, the midday meal is a well established institution in many countries: therefore, when writing about lunch in England one will concentrate on what is different from lunch in other countries, namely the class connotations that attach to it (see the text in 6.2).

(6) Situationality This concerns factors of appropriateness and relevance. This includes such aspects as using informal vocabulary and short sentences in informal situations. It also has to do with discourse **strategies**, for example the selection and sequencing of text units in such a way as to achieve the writer's goal.

(7) Intertextuality This stresses the fact that the production and reception of texts and text units often depend upon both the writer's and the reader's knowledge of other texts or text forms and their patterns or ways of expression.

The presence or absence of these seven aspects depends on the individuals involved. Different people will see different things in the same text and in different situations: Textuality is not an inherent property of a collection of sentences or utterances, but is attributed to it by a reader. Furthermore, it is not necessary to realize all seven for textuality to be present. This seems to be a subjective matter. As regards informativity, it has been shown that readers will try to make a text relevant and informative even if it is far from clear what it is meant to communicate. So, one needs to question the degree to which the sender and addressee might be aware of the connections of any one particular text with other texts. For example, in the cases of *Vanity Fair* (by Thackeray – an allusion to an episode in John Bunyan's novel *The Pilgrim's Progress*) and *Ulysses* (by Joyce – the Latin name of the hero in Homer's *Odyssey*) the significance of the titles for the interpretation of the novels depends on the literary education of the reader. Yet a text which is not dependent on other texts in an obvious way would not be without textual status either. It is obvious that people vary in the extent to which they can decode the information in a text successfully.

6.2 COHESION AND COHERENCE

We will illustrate **cohesive devices** from the following text (the numbers in brackets are used in the subsequent discussion to refer to the headword and each of the sentences):

[1] **Lunch** [2] The word – and the thing itself – cause endless trouble still in England at that join in the class pyramid where it is still called dinner. [3] Any Englishman who does call lunch dinner indicates at once and for sure to any other Englishman that he hails from somewhere below the middle of the middle class. [4] The difficulty is relatively new in the long vista of English history, since the word till quite recently meant a snack between proper meals. [5] There was a time when everyone in England who could afford to do so dined in the afternoon and supped in the evening. [6] Then, with ease and affluence, lunch began its metamorphosis to a meal in its own right: an agreeable pause in the rhythm of the working day for deals and dalliance. [7] It is now a social divider of infinite power. [8] It distances husbands from their wives (he had roast beef in the cafeteria, she had cottage cheese salad in the kitchen). [9] It distances bosses from their workers (grouse and claret in the boardroom, sandwiches and tea on the building site). [10] It separates the employed from the unemployed (steak and kidney in the pub, baked beans by the telly). [11] The proliferation of the expense account has allowed a whole clutch of restaurants to spring up serving meals customers would never dream of eating at home. [12] Whether much business is achieved at these festivals of cholesterol is a moot point: in certain flash callings like showbiz and publishing the point is not so much what you eat but with whom you eat it. [13] It has become a handy way for royalty to entertain foreign potentates who are not worth putting up and for government to entertain middling visiting politicians; a convenient means for business to coddle new clients and a continuing solace to underdogs for their meagre rewards. [14] There may be no bonus at Christmas again but at least there's lunch to look forward to with old Ronnie at L'Escargot (see *Soho*). [15] Though a socialist government did its best to discourage lunch by making meals no longer tax-deductible it has had little effect. [16] In any event, the left seems as keen to go out to lunch as anyone else. [17] Lunch will cease to be a problem in England when it means the same to every Englishman as *déjeuner* does to every Frenchman.

(G. Smith (1985) 'Lunch', The English Companion,
Harmondsworth: Penguin, p. 153)

6.2.1 Lexical links

For many text types, lexical or semantic ways of creating cohesion and coherence are more important than syntactic means, especially in non-narrative texts. Lexical links will therefore be discussed first. There are many ways vocabulary items contribute to cohesion and coherence. Most importantly: they constitute lexical fields; they establish semantic relationships; and they can activate larger text patterns, thus imposing structure on a whole text.

Lexical fields   The text under consideration deals with lunch in England. This is reflected in lexical sets which refer to the food consumed at lunch, to meal names and to typical places of eating:

food and drink:	*roast beef, cottage cheese salad, grouse, claret, sandwich, tea, steak and kidney [pie], baked beans*
meal names and verbs:	*lunch, dinner, snack, meal; sup, dine; have, serve (a meal); go out to lunch*
places:	*cafeteria, kitchen, boardroom, pub, restaurants.*

These sets of lexical items activate in readers stored knowledge of things, places, people and their roles (see 7.4.2), with which they flesh out what is said in the text, and thus make the text coherent in their minds.

Semantic relationships   The most obvious means of continuity is perhaps the exact **repetition** of a word. *Still* is thus repeated in [2], as is *Englishman* [3, 17] and *meal* [4, 6]. *Simple repetition* is found in *called* [2] and *call* [2], as well as *meals* [4] and *meal* [6]. This all seems straightforward to the point of triviality. But it is far from clear what can count as repetition and what kinds of repetition should be distinguished. In our text, it is necessary to differentiate at least between the examples just mentioned, in which both word form and meaning seem to be identical, and the various occurrences of *lunch* [3, 6, 14–17], where this is not the case: *lunch* has the modern meaning of 'meal' in [3, 14–17] but refers to a snack in [6], where it cannot count as a repetition of *lunch* in [3] because the information contained in the two identical word forms is different.

Close in meaning, if not identical, are *difficulty* [4] and *problem* [17], both of which link with *trouble* in [2]. While *difficulty* and *problem* are loose **synonyms** independent of context, *distance* [8, 9] and *separate* [10] are made synonymous only for this passage. The same contextual synonymy is found in *handy* and *convenient*, and *way* and *means* in [13]. Also to be noted is the contextual synonymy of *meals* in [11] with the unmentioned compound *business lunch*, which is implied by the mention of *expense account* in [11], and *business* in [12].

Repetition in the sense of identical information content is also present in words which stand in the semantic relationship of **hyponymy**, provided that the more general (**superordinate**) term follows the more specific. Thus, *meal* in [4] follows *lunch* and *dinner* in [3], as well as *snack* in [4]; furthermore, it does not add any information that was not contained in the three earlier words. The same goes for *the left* [16] and its hyponymous expression *socialist* (*government*) [15]. *Word* and *thing* [2] can also be seen to repeat *lunch* [1], though much more general than *meal*.

A further instance is the example of words which, though they do not contain the same information, are related in meaning. Here there is hyponymy with an increase of information, as in *calling* (superordinate) and *showbiz* and *publishing* [all 12]; see also *rewards* [13] and *bonus* [14].

The final group of examples all illustrate the relation of **opposition** as with the notions 'continue' and 'cease' contained in the words *still* and *cease* (*cause endless trouble still* [2] and *will cease to be a problem* [17]), or in the **complementary** (or **binary**) **pair** 'male' and 'female' contained in *husbands* and *wives* in [8] and *the employed–the unemployed* [10]. Examples of less exclusive forms of opposition are *lunch–dinner* [3], *lunch* [3, 14–17] and *lunch* [6], *dine–sup* [5], *bosses–workers* [9]. Of the pairs of places which are contrasted in [8–10], perhaps only *boardroom* and *building site* could be seen as opposite in meaning (in terms of social class) outside of a specific context, while the others (*cafeteria–kitchen, in the pub–by the telly, restaurants–home*) do not really exhibit either striking similarity or opposition in meaning in isolation. Finally, a contrast seems also to be involved in *discourage lunch* 'stop people from wanting to go out to lunch' and *seem keen to go out to lunch* [15–16].

Larger text patterns   Certain vocabulary items have the function of linking larger segments of text. Examples are *problem, issue, approach, solution, difficulty, drawback* and *question*. The function of these **procedural lexical items** is to organize and structure a text, to indicate the 'larger text-patterns the author has chosen, and build up expectations concerning the shape of the whole discourse' (McCarthy 1991: 76). The word *trouble* in [2] has great cohesive power because it activates in the reader what has been called the *problem–solution pattern*. The full pattern consists of the steps *situation, problem, response, result, evaluation*. The word *trouble* makes the reader expect to be told at least what the problem is and, possibly, how to resolve it. Sentence [2] is a brief statement of the situation, and [3] and [7] through [12] give detailed descriptions of the problem. An actual response to the situation, and its result, is mentioned in [15]. The final text sentence [17] can be seen as a sort of evaluation. The problem–solution pattern, signalled by *trouble* [2], *difficulty* [4] and *problem* [17], is thus a device which helps to establish the unity of the text.

Among the conceptual, and more broadly semantic, relations that are often found in argumentative texts, three are evident in the lunch test: **opposition, value** and **reason** (see de Beaugrande and Dressler 1981: 184). The most important semantic relationship is that of **contrast** or **opposition**. The most comprehensive contrast in our text is between the harmful effects of lunch [7–11] and the useful functions it fulfils [13–16]. The pros and cons also differ in degree. The lexemes indicating a positive evaluation (and thus realizing the conceptual relation of **value**), *handy, convenient* and *continuing solace* [13] express a low or middling degree, while the negative evaluations are located near the middle or the top of the scale: *endless trouble* [2], *difficulty* [4], *social divider of infinite power* [7], *a whole clutch of restaurants . . . meals customers would never dream of eating* [11], *festival of cholesterol* [12], *problem* [17].

Englishmen in general are set in opposition to one another in [3] and in [8] to [10]. In [17] the English are contrasted with the French. A further series of contrasts clusters around the concept of *lunch*. Elaborating on the contrast between *word* and *thing* in [2], the author first mentions the changes in the meaning of the word in [4] and [6] before he proceeds to detail the differences in the thing itself, using places and foods to point up the contrast in [8] to [10]. The final contrast is between the *action* (*discourage* [15]) and the *state* (*be keen* [16]). The frequency of semantic contrasts on the levels of concepts, lexical items and text sentences reflects a view of lunch as something which creates divisions and sets people against one another. Oppositions are therefore particularly appropriate for the theme chosen.

Only slightly less important is the relationship of **reason** or **causality**. Thus, [3] provides the justification for the statement in [2], just as the second half of [4] and [5–6] give the grounds for the statement in the main clause of [4]. The same goes for the examples in [8–10] in relation to [7] and for the clause after the colon in [12] with respect to the statement before the colon. The frequency of the reason relation demonstrates once again that the author wants to win over his readers to his view of lunch in England.

6.2.2 Syntactic links

Other, syntactic, means also create links between text items: co-reference is established by using pro-forms and articles, ellipsis, connectives, tense and time adverbials.

Co-reference Pronouns, articles and other pro-forms cannot be interpreted in their own right, but rather direct the reader to look elsewhere (either in the text or outside it) for their interpretation. The relation between pro-forms and articles, on the one hand, and the text items referred to, on the other, is called **co-reference** and is distinct from **reference**, which is the function of lexical items which writers and speakers use to indicate what they are writing or talking about outside the text (Brown and Yule 1983: 205). Pro-forms and articles have two different uses, **anaphoric** and **cataphoric**: when they follow the items which explain them, they have anaphoric force; when they precede them, they are cataphoric.

Pronouns and pro-forms *It* has only anaphoric uses in the text about lunch, but its scope varies considerably. The first instance of *its* in [6] refers to *lunch*, and the second instance to *meal*. In other cases the pronoun does not follow immediately on its referent, see *it* in [2] where one has to go back to *the word – and the thing itself*. Close contiguity is no help either in deciding on the referent for *it* in [7]: in making the connection with *lunch* in [6] one has to cross the sentence boundary. *It* refers of course to *lunch*, the central topic, and picks up the pattern of initial *it*, which is used in [7] through [10], but we need our knowledge of the text topic and the text as a whole to be sure of this. The almost exclusive co-referential function of *it* with *lunch* (exceptions are [12] and [15]) provide the text with strong cohesive force. In all the sentences except [5] *lunch* is present either in the form of lexical reference or co-reference with *it*.

All the other pronouns used in the text co-refer with something in the same sentence. Most of them are also anaphoric (e.g. *he* [3], *their* [8], *its* [15]). Note that *he* and *she* in [8] pick up *husbands* and *wives* respectively. An indefinite meaning ('one, people in general') attaches to *you* in [12].

There are only two cataphoric uses of pro-forms in the text. One is *that* [2], which points forward to *where it is still called dinner*. In the other example, *do so* [5] refers to *dined in the afternoon and supped in the evening*, the new information in the sentence. A change in word order would have destroyed the thematic structure by putting the semantically empty pro-forms in the informationally most prominent position at the sentence end.

No final answers can be given to the question why one form of reiteration is chosen rather than another – why, for example, a pronoun is preferred to a lexical item. One criterion is distance: there is a limit, though this may vary from case to case, to the distance across which a pronoun can still successfully co-refer to its antecedent. Furthermore, there are stylistic grounds which may prevent the repetition of (lexical) items and require synonyms etc. to be used. For both these reasons one might have expected *lunch* rather than *it* in [13]: the nearest instance of *lunch* in [6] is quite a distance away, and sentence [12] ends with *it*, which does not link with *lunch*. The explanation lies perhaps in a different syntactic direction: when *it* co-refers with *lunch* in this text, it is identified with sentence-initial position and the subject function. This makes it easier to understand *it* in [13] and also accounts for the fact that the objects in [11], [12], [14] and [15] are realized not by *it*, but by lexical items. In cases where an item is stressed, only a lexical item, not a pronoun, is normally possible. This seems to be the more general reason behind the use of *lunch* in [14]. The same thing applies particularly to [17], which closes the topic in this text: it has been suggested that pronouns keep a text sequence open, while lexical items indicate the end of a text sequence.

The definite article   In [2], the definite articles in *the word* and *the thing* also have anaphoric force, making it clear that the *word* and *thing* meant is *lunch* in [1]. In [4], *the difficulty* co-refers, presumably, to the whole of [3], and *the word* points back to *lunch*.

   In other examples co-reference is to things that are not mentioned in the text itself. Here the article signals 'you know which one I mean', implying that there is only one – or only one that is appropriate in the context. The author relies on the reader's knowledge to make the text cohesive. Types of knowledge can range from worldwide (*the afternoon, the evening* [5]) to very local. The author does not expect his readers to know the restaurant L'Escargot in London's Soho district, so he makes a cross-reference to his entry for *Soho*. This creates a minimal link (of repetition) between two articles in *The English Companion*. In contrast, there is no cross-reference to *class* for *the class pyramid* [2] or to *pubs* for *the pub* [10], for a full understanding of which readers need to activate their knowledge of English society and institutions. Other concepts like *the cafeteria, the kitchen* [both 8], *the boardroom, the building site* [9], *the telly* [10] and *the left* [16] are not restricted to England in the same way and therefore can be expected to be meaningful to a wider readership.

Ellipsis   The reader is also called upon to become active in several places and provide missing sentence parts. Subject and predicator are deleted in the brackets in [9] and [10], but can easily be supplied in analogy with [8]. In [13], *it has become a handy way* is not repeated before *for government*, and subject and verb must be supplied to complete the subject complements in the second half of [13].

Conjunctions and connectives   What is striking in the 'Lunch' text is the lack of explicit markers of relationships between sentences and parts of sentences. There is only one connective (*in any event* [16]) and two conjunctions (*since* [4] and *though* [15]). The author uses formal markers sparingly and relies instead largely on the readers' ability to provide the missing links themselves.

Tense and time adverbials   The author is careful to mark temporal relationships clearly. He starts out in the present, but *still* [2] establishes a link between present and past, which is taken up again in *relatively new* and *till quite recently* [4]. A kind of natural order is then established from past back to present, and it ends with a reference to the future. The past tense indicates past time in [4] to [6], and this is underlined by the time adverbials *there was a time* [5] and *then* [6]. The return to the present is signalled by the present tense and by *now* in [7]. The text stays with the present tense from then on, including the present perfect, in [11], [13] and [15]. The only exception is the past tense form in [15], which is devoted to an action in the past, but is made relevant to the present by the perfect *has had little effect* [15]. The text ends with the only reference to future time. (This text is further discussed in 6.4 below using the criteria established in 6.3.)

6.3 A TYPOLOGY OF TEXTS

The typology presented in the following should be regarded only as a practical means of producing, predicting and processing texts and not as a theory which lays down hard and fast rules for the distinction of text types: 'The conditions of communicating are simply too diverse to allow such a rigorous categorization' (de Beaugrande and Dressler 1981: 186).

6.3.1 Functions

The first, or highest, level of observation consists of the various functions that language serves in human communication. While the functions mentioned are not exclusively linguistic (traffic lights have informational and directive value), language is the primary means used to perform them. Among the many functions that have been distinguished (see 1.6.2) four will be regarded as basic in this chapter. These are the **expressive function**, the **phatic** or **social-interactive function**, the **informative** and the **directive functions**. A fifth primary function is the **aesthetic function**, which relates above all to literature, but also, for example, to advertising. It may include elements typical of any of the other functions since it is usually subject to little restriction although there are some literary forms (e.g. the sonnet, the limerick) which follow conventions of uncommon rigour. (See also 6.7.3 on text models.)

All expressions of emotions (joy, anger, frustration) are subsumed under the expressive function. It is the most basic or general because all the other functions (the phatic or interactive, the informative, the directive) always include some expression of self. Note that actual texts (both spoken and written) often realize more than one function. Conversations or personal letters, for example, contain much interactive language (what is called **phatic communion**) in which the social bonds between writer and addressee are reinforced (see 7.3.1), but they can also contain a part in which some business is transacted, as when news is exchanged (informative) or plans or instructions are discussed (directive).

Only a few examples will be given here, and none for the first function, as it is realized implicitly in all the others. Phatic texts relate to social or seasonal occasions (births, deaths, anniversaries, Christmas). The majority of texts are informative or directive.

Text types   When the informative and the directive functions are grouped together five major text types are often recognized: **descriptive**, **narrative**, **directive** (also called **instructive**), **expository** and **argumentative**.

Table 6.1   The categories of text types

	concrete	*cognitive*
real, actual	narrative (time) descriptive (space)	expository
potential	directive	argumentative

The text types under discussion are general functional concepts and are not to be confused with such realizations as advertisements, editorials, sermons, shopping lists, poems, telephone books or novels, which are here referred to as **text forms** (see 6.7.2) The five types are examples of different realizations of the register category of **functional tenor** or **purpose** (see 1.6.2 and 6.4); and although further types may exist, these five are general enough for the classification of most texts. In addition, the five may be sorted into four basic categories according to the two criteria of concrete vs cognitive and real or actual vs potential. The actual dimension is centred on entities, events and states located in the 'real world', whether it is the time–space continuum around us (= concrete) or a part of our mental reality (= cognitive) which we describe, narrate or explain. The potential dimension has to do with something which is not regarded as established, but which can be accomplished (directive, concrete) or which can become a part of the addressee's cognitive reality. This is represented graphically in Table 6.1.

Narrative texts have to do with real world events in time. It is immaterial whether a narrative is fictional (as in a fairy tale or novel) or non-fictional (as in a newspaper report). What is characteristic is the sequencing of events in which dynamic verbs (see 5.4.3) occur in the simple form and in which sequencing adverbials such as *and then* or *first, second, third* provide the basic narrative structure, e.g. *First we packed our bags and then we called a taxi. After that we* . . . etc.

Descriptive texts, in contrast, are concerned with the location of persons and things in space. For this reason they will tell what lies to the right or left, in the background or foreground, or they will provide background information which, perhaps, sets the stage for narration. Once again it is immaterial whether a description is more technical-objective or more impressionistic-subjective. State or positional verbs plus the appropriate adverbial expressions of location are employed in descriptions (*the operation panel is located on the right-hand side at the rear*; *New Orleans lies on the Mississippi*). Perfect and progressive forms typically give background information (*he was peacefully dreaming when the fire broke out*; *as the cabinet has agreed on the principles, an interministerial committee will work out the details*).

Directive texts are concerned with concrete future activity. Central to such texts are imperatives (*Hand me the paper*) or forms which substitute for them, such as polite questions (*Would you hand me the paper?*) or suggestive remarks (*I wonder what the paper says about the weather*) (see 7.2.1). Stage directions, though phrased in the simple form like narrative texts, are normative statements and, for this reason, have the effect of directives (*The maid enters, opens the door and admits a visitor*). Assembly and operation instructions use sequences of imperatives (*Disconnect the 15-pin D-shell connector* . . . *and secure the signal cable firmly* . . . ; *Shake well before using. Do not ingest with alcohol*).

Each of the three types just discussed are centred around concrete events and things, whether realized or potential. In contrast, expository and argumentative texts are cognitively oriented. This is the case because they are concerned with the mental processes of explanation and persuasion, although the former may include a considerable amount of description and the latter may have consequences in future action.

Expository texts identify and characterize phenomena. As such they include text forms such as definitions, explications, summaries and many types of essay. Once again they may be subjective (essay) or objective (summary, explication, definition). They may also be analytical, starting from a concept and then characterizing its parts, as in definitions and the 'Lunch' text. On the other hand, expository texts may proceed in the opposite, synthetic direction as well, recounting characteristics and ending with an appropriate concept or conclusion, as in summaries, which exist as the sum of their parts. Typical syntactic constructions which may be appropriately expanded when forming expository texts are identifying statements with state verbs (*Pop music has a strong rhythmic beat*), or epistemic modals (*Texts may consist of one or more sentences*), or with verbs indicating characteristic activities or qualities (*Fruit flies feed on yeast*; *Most geraniums are red*).

Argumentative texts start from the assumption that the reader's beliefs must be changed. A writer might therefore begin with the negation of a statement which attributes a quality or characteristic activity to something. Even when a scholarly text provides positive support for a particular hypothesis there is almost always at least implicit negation of previous assumptions. Advertising texts, often at the extreme opposite pole of academic texts in terms of style, also try to persuade their readers that a particular product is somehow better than others, at least implicitly.

Mixtures of text type elements   Few texts are pure realizations of a single type. Advertisements, for instance, are frequently both argumentative/persuasive (*This is good because*) and directive (*So buy now!*; *Click here!*). The 'Lunch' text is expository (text form, definition), but also argumentative inasmuch as it implicitly pursues the thesis, '*Lunch* is not what you think it is; it's really a socially problematic phenomenon'.

Expository texts can be neutral or contain evaluative elements (reviews, references, letters to the editor, rules and regulations etc.). Whether or not they have directive force depends: in a review or newscast the information given is primary; a set of instructions contains information, but the directive function predominates. Laws, decrees and treaties fulfil the double function of informing the members of the society in question as well as directing their behaviour. They are thus partially expository and partially directive texts.

The 'Lunch' text shows some features of the aesthetic, the argumentative and the informative functions. The frequent repetitions, the alliteration (e.g. *cafeteria and kitchen*) and the wide use of parallel structures are evidence of delight in language for its own sake, which is no doubt part of the author's intention to entertain. Such features of the aesthetic function can also be seen in the well turned phrase *festivals of cholesterol* [12] and in speech rhythms, e.g. *with ease and affluence . . . for deals and dalliance* [6]. Although there are features which show that it is argumentative (the writer wants his readers to share his belief that lunch poses a problem in English society), the overall function of the text is to inform readers, not to get them to do something. While the text is nearest to exposition (definition of lunch), it also has features of the other text types: In common with narrative texts it has the chronological progression from past [4–6] to present [7–16] to future [17]. However, the majority of its text units are not located in the past, as is the norm in narrative texts, but in the present, and the present tense system is characteristic of expository texts. Another feature shared with expository texts is a clearly stated theme or point of view, which is expressed in the first sentence of the main body of the text [2]. As is often the case in factual reports, the first sentence is particularly important because it summarizes the whole text. A further aspect is the list of the various forms that 'Lunch' can take (see the brackets in [8–10]).

6.3.2 Situations

Any given text is not only a realization of a particular text type (including mixed forms), but is also the product of the further register categories of **medium** (spoken or written), **field** (see 6.4–6.7) and **personal tenor** or **style**, where in making a request, for example, writers have to decide on such matters as the degree of directness and politeness. Additional criteria are whether texts are part of non-verbal activities and whether they are used to accompany or accomplish practical or theoretical activities. A letter asking for a social security number for instance is characterized by these features: directive function; field of public (social) administration; medium of writing; personal tenor of communication between two persons in a social relationship with noticeable status differences including, conventionally, the use of relatively formal language.

The stylistic **informality** of the 'Lunch' text is signalled by both grammatical and lexical means. Among the grammatical means are the lack of explicit markers of the semantic relationship between sentences and the various ellipses. The lexical means include ellipsis (*steak and kidney*, namely *pie* [10]) and **hyperbolic expressions** such as *endless* [2], *once and for all* [3] and *infinite* [7]. Also important are mixtures in the register categories: formal or neutral words are found beside informal items, just as archaic or neutral forms can be contrasted with coinages of more recent origin. 'Serious', academic texts would perhaps stay within the same stylistic level and temporal dialect. **Informal items** are: *telly* [10], *clutch* [11], *festivals of cholesterol* [12], *showbiz* [12], *old Ronnie* [14], *though* [15]; and a number of idioms and phrasal verbs of a more or less informal nature: *spring up* [11], *put up* [13], *look forward to* [14], *do one's best* [15]. **Formal words** are: *vista* [4]; *solace* [13]. The two levels clash in the combination *flash* (informal) *callings* (formal) [12]. *Sup* [5] is an **archaic item**, and a clash is seen again in *deals and dalliance* [6]. The author very appropriately chooses the only retrospective passage in the text for these obsolete terms. A further level is that of **hard words** *metamorphosis* [6], *proliferation* [11] and *tax-deductible* [15] which contrast with such **(Anglo-Saxon) monosyllabic words** as *word*, *thing*, *pub*.

6.3.3 Strategies and structure

On the level of strategy, writers have to make decisions on how to present their message in a way that is most likely to achieve their goal. Writers must not only be clear about their intentions (functional tenor, text types) and take into account other situational factors (field, medium, personal tenor), but also ensure that the addressee can process the message easily. The relative easiness (or difficulty) of a text depends, among other things, on: the number of participants mentioned in a text (i.e. the fewer people involved, the easier the text); on whether the features that distinguish between characters in, say, a story are memorable; on the simplicity and symmetry of spatial structures; on the simplicity and sequencing of temporal structures; and on whether writers give explicit hints for interpretation.

A high level strategic decision relates to what means writers employ in the pursuit of their intentions. The step-by-step exposition is, for example, found in many expository texts, and similar strategies have long been established in classical rhetoric. In narration, events are presented in 'ordered sequences linked by time proximity and causality' (de Beaugrande and Dressler 1981: 90). This is basic to the overall structure of text types such as chronicles, histories and much narrative fiction. Descriptive texts centre on objects and situations and how they relate to each other. A general aspect of the matters to be described or a particular point of view or vantage point provides the organizing principle for the writer's presentation. Guidebooks are spatially oriented, but can also have passages that are temporally dominated. Note that biographies are agent dominated texts, but that they are also temporally structured. Texts, in other words, can contain one, two, or more strategies simultaneously. It also follows that the mix of strategies can vary considerably. Long texts are more likely to be multi-strategic than short passages. As pointed out in 6.7.3, texts may even be organized cyclically, moving from one strategy to another in repeated waves.

The 'Lunch' text uses the **stack strategy**, which is marked by a predetermined unity, clearly visible in the thematically central sentences [2]–[7]–[17]. However, in this text the stack method of exposition contains elements of a **step-by-step** procedure in the brief historical sketch in [4–6] as well as of the **balance strategy**: the case against lunch [7–11] is contrasted with the various uses it has [13–16]. [12] provides the transition between the pros and cons.

6.3.4 Language patterns

The choice of appropriate language for a particular type of text is partly a matter of individual preference, but partly also a matter of convention, which writers can of course flout if they think it will help them to achieve their goal. General maxims valid for an application for a social security number, for example, are: (a) factual approach; (b) concise style; and (c) polite tone (see preceding section). More specific patterns relate to typical lexical items and combinations of lexical items. In a description of elections in Great Britain there will be such expressions as: *proportional representation*; *redraw the boundary*; *go to the country*; *go to the polls*; *declare the result*; *return an MP to parliament*. Also of great importance to the reader are so-called **text structuring devices**. These can give a preview of what is to come (e.g. *Let us now turn to X* [new topic]; or *This Chapter consists of five parts. The first . . . The second . . .*), or refer to what has already been dealt with (*So much for X*). Here too belongs the class of **procedural lexical items** like *problem*, *issue* etc. (see 6.2.1).

6.4 ESP AND THE REGISTER MODEL OF LANGUAGE

Understanding the ways in which English varies according to its use in particular situations lies at the centre of a major field of endeavour, namely **English for special/specific purposes (ESP)**. As English has expanded to become the preferred language of international communication in more and more fields, the needs of ever more non-native users of English have become evident. The important assumption has been made that these users, as well as their native speaker colleagues, employ English in a restricted range of social and thematic areas. Why, after all, should an Egyptian or Brazilian technician bother with the language of English poetry if what he/she is interested in is, say, a set of technical specifications or instructions? What is important for this technician is the communication of information, which necessitates the use of unambiguous terminology and clear grammar. This clarity and lack of ambiguity are desirable from the perspective of both the writer and the reader.

Special Englishes are, in the sense of the preceding paragraph, instances of registers. Two criteria within this model which are frequently used to classify ESP are **field of discourse** and **purpose** (or **functional tenor**). Discourse and genre analysis as well as computer-based analyses reflect these directions. In addition, the further criteria of **personal tenor** or **style** (relationship of the speaker/writer to addressee) and **medium** (spoken/written) are also significant. However, the latter seldom show up as the major criteria for the classification of ESP.

Field   Dividing up use according to field has the advantage of following the relatively easily observable criterion of shared vocabulary. However, there is no agreement on the appropriate size of the fields. Major areas such as science, technology, law, medicine, the social sciences, business and economics are commonly named. However, finer (for example, biology, chemistry and physics) and ever finer divisions (such as biophysics, zoology, biochemistry, gene technology etc.) can also be made (one author speaks of up to 300 fields, Beier 1980: 25); yet it is not clear where the point is beyond which further distinctions cannot be expected to be helpful.

Purpose or functional tenor   **Purpose** or **functional tenor** crosses the boundaries of the individual disciplines, providing for such types as English for business and economics (EBE), English for legal purposes, English for vocational purposes or English for academic purposes (EAP). Within the last, the English for science and technology (EST) is recognized as an important subdivision. Even within and across these areas more specific communicative purposes can be distinguished. These consist of the **text types** or **rhetorical functions** of description, report/narration, exposition, direction/instruction and argumentation discussed above.

Style or personal tenor   EST texts are characterized by the neutral, unemotional and objective tone of scientific and academic prose. The writer–addressee relationship will be different in scholarly prose used in learned journals compared with that of popular science publications (such as *The Scientific American*), or science reports in general newspapers, or magazines (such as *The New York Times* or *The Atlantic*).

Medium or mode   So far it has been exclusively the written language which has been referred to; yet a wide range of spoken usage belongs here as well, stretching from scholarly colloquial to technical training classes to salesroom explanations. ESP/EST will probably be more strongly oriented towards written forms.

Special vs General English   One of the major difficulties in describing ESP, regardless of how it is subdivided, is deciding what the nature of the difference between it and everyday or GenE is. Since, for instance, the latter includes *all* the regularities of the grammar of English, the area of grammar offers no absolute criteria for making a distinction. Nevertheless, there is 'the intuitive notion of an everyday language and we would wish to uphold its existence' (Sager *et al.* 1980: 3), and there are meaningful distinctions which can be made (see below).

Part of this general–special/specific distinction is the question whether the 'S' of ESP means 'special' or 'specific'. The earlier designation was 'English for *special* purposes'. Since the late 1970s, however, the term 'English for *specific* purposes' has displaced it. The rationale behind this is that 'special' implies restricted languages, while English for *specific* purposes focuses attention on the purposes of performing a task in English. These determine the selection of skills needed (reading, listening, writing, talking), the text types involved, as well as the vocabulary and grammar necessary for this. Practically speaking, this means that:

1   the complete grammar of English belongs to ESP; and
2   the same processes of morphology and word formation apply to it that are found in GenE.

Yet this also recognizes that:

1   there may be distinctly different frequencies in the use of individual syntactic and morphological constructions as well as of word formation processes;
2   the selection of vocabulary will be influenced by field;
3   terminology will be at least partially standardized to eliminate ambiguity;
4   certain conventions will be observed with regard to the elements and structure of written texts;
5   special visual phenomena (symbols, graphs, tables etc.) may be employed in written texts that are not a part of everyday English.

In other words the Englishes involved here are indeed restricted, selective and special. Yet they should not be dismissed as non-essential: these features belong firmly to their genres.

6.5 SYNTACTIC FEATURES OF ENGLISH FOR SCIENCE AND TECHNOLOGY (EST)

The remainder of the chapter will deal with some of the typical characteristics of those ESPs which have been most commonly studied, namely academically oriented English for science and technology, or EST. A number of studies of its syntax point out such features as:

1   the greater frequency of the passive;
2   the greater frequency of non-defining relative clauses compared to defining ones;
3   specific, frequently employed, rhetorical devices such as anaphora, parallelism, parenthetical elements, emphatic inversion, rhetorical questions and ellipsis;
4   nominal style (see 6.5.2);
5   the selection of pronouns employed (more frequent than in General English: *we*, *this/these*; less so: *I*, *he*; and even less so *she*, *you*);
6   the occurrence of new plurals (e.g. *fats*, *oils*, *greases* etc., see Gerbert 1970: 40) and Latin and Greek plurals (*mitochondrion/-ia*; *bacterium/-ia*);
7   the use of telegram style (see 6.5.2).

6.5.1 The verb

Voice   What is typical of the form of the verb in EST is, more than anything else, the frequency with which the passive voice occurs. Studies show frequencies of passives among the total finite verb forms ranging from about one quarter to about one third, sometimes even as high as 40 to 45 per cent. The comparative figures for literary texts lie between 2 and 3 per cent. This might seem to be all there is to say; however, two important additions must be made. For one, figures suggest an accuracy and objectivity which is illusory. The representativeness of the corpora used is unlikely to be more than approximate and, in addition, the values given will vary depending on whether a percentage is taken of all the finite verbs in a corpus or only those which could potentially appear in the passive, such as transitive and prepositional-transitive verbs.

The second point has to do with when and why the passive is used. One common explanation is that the passive allows the author to step back so that the work reported on stands at the centre of attention. According to one study 'author's passives' make up one third of the total. These are passives which involve the action of the author(s), e.g. *Several interviews were conducted to substantiate this hypothesis* ('We conducted several interviews . . .'). Passives which replace other agents account for approximately one tenth of the cases. A few passives can be explained by difficulties in expression using an active construction or similar problems. About half, however, are used for generally unspecified non-human causes. The motivation here is likely to have to do with the thematic focus of a sentence. In English, the topic of a sentence is usually named at the beginning and what is said (predicated) about it, at the end (see 5.4.4). The passive allows a direct or an indirect object which is the topic to occupy the initial thematic position and thus helps to realize the desired thematic focus of the sentence. A study of the use of the passive in two journal papers on astrophysics confirms the validity of this principle. In addition, however, the same study offers three further explanations of the use or non-use of the passive: (1) standard procedural choices in astrophysics research are reported in the passive while unique procedures chosen by the authors of the articles are reported in the active (with the subject *we*); (2) previous work in the same field is reported in the active *we*-form if it is the author's own and in the passive if it is by others and stands in contrast to the author's own work; if other work agrees with or supports the author's research the active is used; (3) work which the author proposes to do in the future is referred to in the passive (Tarone *et al.* 1998).

These three explanations from the astrophysics papers cannot be generalized to other fields or other text forms besides journal papers without further studies. However, there seems to be a deeper principle involved here which might usefully be pointed out. This is the use of voice for deictic purposes. In the astrophysics papers the active serves to highlight (bring closer) the author's procedures and decisions. The passive is used to express the writer's greater distance.

Tense and aspect   The same deictic functions can also be expressed through the appropriate use of tense. For example, the present tense is normally used to describe scientific apparatus. However, if the apparatus is historical and no longer in use, the past will be used. Furthermore:

> if writers use the past tense in reporting research done previously by themselves or others then that research is of secondary importance to the current work being reported on. If, on the other hand, the writer uses the present perfect or the present tense, then the research is of more direct and primary importance to the writer's work.
>
> (Trimble 1985a: 126)

Above and beyond these points, it has also been established that the simple past far outnumbers other verb forms and that the progressive is especially infrequent.

Modal verbs   A final point is that modal verbs may occur in meanings which are relatively rare in GenE, such as the 'non-standard uses of *should* and *may*' to mean *must*. Here they indicate that there is no choice, rather than the standard meaning, 'desirable but not necessary' in sentences such as:

> Steel weld backing *should be* [= must] sufficiently thick so that the molten metal will not burn through the backing. . . . For steel thicknesses other than gage material, a relief groove *may be necessary* [= must be used].
>
> (Trimble 1985a: 119f.)

6.5.2 The nominal

The nominal differs in several ways, one of which is that EST has a higher proportion of nouns (but also prepositions and adjectives); in one count this is 44 per cent of all words in EST vs 28 per cent in general texts (Sager *et al.* 1980: 234).

Nominal style is, in part, understood as the tendency to use combinations of function verb + noun instead of simple verb. In these structures function verbs are 'general purpose verbs' with little meaning of their own such as *do, make, take, have* or *give*:

to work	→	to do some work
to investigate	→	to make an investigation
to photograph	→	to take a photograph
to hypothesize	→	to have (or make) a hypothesis
to report	→	to give (or make) a report

Nominalization refers to the replacement of clauses which contain finite verbs with complex structures consisting of nouns and noun adjuncts, e.g. *because the surface of the retina is spherical* → *because of the sphericity of the retinal surface*; or, *[something] is near the nucleus* → *[something] occupies a juxtanuclear position* (examples quoted from Gerbert 1970: 36). In a similar fashion, prepositional phrases 'disappear': *experiments of transfer of momentum* becomes *momentum transfer experiments*; and *a vessel for storage of liquids* takes the compact form *liquid storage vessel* (examples quoted from Trimble 1985a: 132f.).

Nominalization and thematic structure   The formation of complex noun phrases is itself a part of the theme-rheme structure of English. What appears in pre-nominal position may represent information shared by sender and addressee; it is, in other words, presupposed information. In contrast, what is new and is being introduced occurs in post-nominal position. In a neurological text in which the branchlets of nerves are discussed, mention may, for example, be made of a *posterior branchlet of the saccular nerve*. At a later stage the information – now given and no longer new – that it is the saccular nerve that is being referred to can be placed in pre-nominal position as the *posterior saccular branchlet* (Dubois 1982: 53–63).

The article   A further feature involving the nominal is the use or non-use of the article. On the one hand, the definite article is often dispensed with in instructions written in telegram style, e.g. *Insert red tab into red slot and blue tab into blue slot*. The opposite tendency can also be observed, namely the 'overuse' of the definite article as in the following description of a process: '*The gas turbine engine fires continuously. The engine draws air through the diffuser and into the compressor, raising its temperature.*' The first use of *the* is generic and might, but need not, be replaced with the indefinite article *a*; the third and fourth instances could appear as indefinite articles in GenE. The indefinite article is, after all, usual when something is mentioned for the first time in a text (see 5.5.1). Native language text users regularly interpret the third and fourth instances of the article differently, however. Here, for example, engineers reading the description of the gas turbine engine 'took the use of the definite article . . . to indicate that the machinery being described contained *only one* of whatever part was being marked by the article' (Trimble 1985a: 122).

6.5.3 The sentence

The sentence as a whole differs between GenE and ESP. Sentences in ESP are, on average, longer and more complex. Furthermore, the frequency of occurrence of clause types is different: relative clauses are particularly frequent; declarative sentences clearly predominate; imperatives are regularly found for giving instructions; while interrogatives are limited to use as rhetorical questions and to study questions at chapter ends in textbooks.

6.6 LEXICON AND WORD FORMATION IN EST

'. . . the lexicon of special languages is their most obvious distinguishing characteristic' (Sager *et al.* 1980: 230). While their syntax is distinguished from that of GenE only in the relative frequencies of constructions, the vocabulary of ESP will often contain words which cannot be found outside the given field. No one can say how many such special words there are, but there are several million for chemical compounds alone. The numerous dictionaries, terminological clearing houses, databases etc. clearly indicate that the number is large. Here is one example of each. A general dictionary of science is *The Longman Dictionary of Scientific Usage* (1988). It contains 1,300 terms basic to all branches of science and 8,500 technical terms from biology, chemistry and physics. The terminological clearing house Infoterm was established within UNESCO in 1971 for the coordination of work on terminology on an international basis; it cooperates with the International Organization for Standardization (ISO), the Association for Terminology and Knowledge Transfer (GTW) and the International Institute for Terminology Research (IITF) among others. Important characteristics of the vocabulary of EST are the following:

1   it is international, often based on Greek or Latin elements;
2   it is standardized and as unambiguous as possible;
3   it is non-emotive in tone;
4   it favours certain processes of word formation;
5   it incorporates symbols.

6.6.1 Terminology

Terms are special items of vocabulary whose meanings are fixed by convention. They are necessary in order to avoid the ambiguity which a variety of regional, non-standardized meanings could lead to. Needless to say, ambiguity poses a threat not only to the success of experiments and manufacturing processes, but also to health and safety. Among the qualities associated with systems of terminology are that they are:

1   exact, i.e. they designate a particular meaning;
2   unambiguous, i.e. they cannot be confused with the meanings of any other terms;
3   unique, i.e. one and only one term is available;
4   systematic, i.e. they are part of a larger, ordered system of terms, preferably in a clearly structured terminological hierarchy;
5   neutral, i.e. they are oriented towards cognition and objective processes and do not include aesthetic or emotive elements;
6   self-explanatory or transparent, i.e. they include elements which reflect the important features of the concept designated (see Beier 1980: 31f.).

These features are, of course, ideals that cannot always be realized. The demand for economy may, for example, be sacrificed to the greater need for exactness, lack of ambiguity and uniqueness. Furthermore, scientists and technicians may often use vocabulary which is more informal, at least in oral communication. This might include clippings and metaphors from everyday language, such as *streps* for *streptococci, mag sulf* for *magnesium sulphate* or *juice* for *electrical current* (examples from Beier 1980: 35f.).

A special sub-area of terminology is that of the signs and symbols employed in the various fields. The fact that they do not always have a widely accepted pronunciation indicates once again that EST is, to a large extent, a written language. Examples of signs and symbols drawn from EST are Σ, $\sqrt{}$, $+$, $=$, $>$, μ, $°$, π.

6.6.2 Borrowing and word formation

Borrowing and word formation are of central importance because of the absolute quantity of terms needed and the qualities expected of them. Terms are, in some cases, borrowed from General English, e.g. metaphorical *memory* for *computer storage capacity*. More often, however, they are derived from other languages, especially Latin and Greek. In addition to direct borrowings, such as *apparatus*, *matrix* or *phenomenon*, this involves morphological elements including, for instance, prefixes ({aero-}, {astro-}, {baro-}, {cryo-}, {ferro-}, {gyro-}, {hydro-} etc.) and suffixes ({-gram}, {-graph}, {-ology}, {-scope}, {-tomy} etc.). In chemistry, for example, the order and status of roots and affixes are strictly provided for:

> Thus eth + an + ol signifies, in that order, a structure with two carbons, simply linked together and with one of these linked to a hydroxyl (—O—H) group, and no other combinations of these morphemes describes that structure.
>
> (Dermer *et al.* quoted in Beier 1980: 32)

In addition to the ubiquitous elements of Latin and Greek, EST, of course, also uses the normal derivational processes of General English (see 1.4) with or without Latin-Greek elements, be they:

1   prefixing ({anti-}, {in-}, {mis-}, {non-}, {semi-}, {un-})
2   suffixing ({-ar}, {-al}, {-ed}, {-er}, {-less}, {-ment}, {-ness})
3   conversion/zero derivation (*to dimension < dimension*)
4   back formations (*to lase < laser*)
5   clippings (*lab < laboratory*)
6   abbreviations (*FBR < fast breeder reactor*)
7   acronyms (*laser* 'light amplification by stimulated emission of radiation')
8   blends (*pulsar* 'pulsating radio star')
9   composite forms (*aeroplane*).

Perhaps most distinctive in the field of word formation is the extremely high frequency of compound nominal phrases (or noun compounds). They were found to occur as follows in corpora of ten two thousand word texts in each of three areas:

General English	0.87 per cent
Medical English	9.76 per cent
Technical English	15.37 per cent
	(Salager 1984: 138f.)

The high percentage figures for medical and technical English are to be understood as a consequence of the exactness, non-ambiguity and uniqueness of technical terms:

compounds are mainly used to refer to something which is conceived of as a single entity, as an item in a class of its own. This underlines the difference between the compound and the relative clause. ... There is a semantic difference between ... *banana curve* and the related but not synonymous phrase *a curve shaped like a banana*.

(ibid.: 141f.)

6.6.3 Frequency

The proportion of technical words in EST texts has been estimated at approximately 25 per cent. In a count of the 1,000 most common words one comparison revealed 339 words in EST which were not among the first thousand words of General English. In addition, there is a difference in distribution, which is also due to the higher frequency of what are called semi-technical or sub-technical words. While words from the closed classes (auxiliaries, pronouns, articles, demonstratives, prepositions) have approximately the same frequency in GenE and in EST, there are noticeably more lexical items in EST associated with:

1   exposition (e.g. *discussion, argument, result, conclusion*);
2   procedure (*analysis, experiment, measurement, observation, test*);
3   statistics (*sample, probability, distribution, significance*);
4   classification (*class, type, group, species, item, unit*); as well as
5   relational words (*similar, distinct, average, relative, normal*).

(Johannson 1975: 22).

Furthermore, relatively less use is made of the shorter, everyday words as compared to longer, more formal words: for example, EST *also* rather than General *too*; *certain* vs *sure*; *determine* vs *decide*; *large* vs *big*; *obtained* vs *got*; *thus* vs *so* (ibid.: 25f.).

The fact that we are looking at more formal, written texts in EST also accounts for such differences in style as: the lack of contractions; the greater use of cohesive devices, e.g. *this/these, above, below, preceding*, or *following*, for reference within a text; and the greater occurrence of such relatively formal adverbs as *moreover, overall, primarily, therefore* and *however*.

6.7 THE EST TEXT

Text type is an important factor in the linguistic characterisation of EST. The closer a text is to the thematically non-specific, to the personally informal, to the temporally and spatially immediate (the 'here and now') and to the subjective-conversational, the more likely the text is to be General English. EST, in contrast, is oriented towards the formal, the written, towards independence of the immediate moment and place, and objectivity. While there are exceptions and mixed forms (talking shop, lecturing, note-taking, popular science writing etc.), this observation is basically accurate.

6.7.1 Types of message

One approach to texts which takes these factors into account suggests five basic message types: dialogue, memo, report, schedule and essay. **The dialogue**, as an exclusively spoken form, will not be considered here. **The memo**, characterized as demanding a response of some sort, encompasses a wide range of text forms. A large number of its realizations are administrative (minutes, business letters, invoices, contracts) or journalistic (advertisements). However, textbooks, manuals and handbooks may be regarded as part of it. **Reports**, which are records of acts or processes produced at someone's request, include, for example, the laboratory report. **Schedules** order and classify material. They include such important instances of written EST as bibliographies, indexes, tables of contents, glossaries, the valency table of the elements, or the Linnean system of biological nomenclature. **Essays**, finally, are central to EST in the form of dissertations, journal articles and university theses (see Sager *et al.* 1980: 104–23).

Typical EST texts will therefore be found in published writing. More popular science texts will be relatively more accessible to the general public and hence less specifically cases of ESP.

6.7.2 Text forms

Well over one hundred traditional text forms can be enumerated, such as *address*, *agenda*, *aide-memoire*, *announcement*, *article*, *bibliography*, *blurb*, *book review*, *brochure*, *bulletin* etc. (Sager *et al.* 1980: 148–81). Gläser 1990 examines 35 text forms primarily arranged according to whether they are meant for academic peers, students and the lay public, or (potential) users. Just how many text forms may usefully be distinguished is not known; indeed, not even the criteria for a typology have been agreed upon. What is available is, rather, a number of individual studies of what have intuitively been viewed as distinct text forms. These include, for instance: articles in learned journals; dissertations; laboratory reports; MS theses; and university level textbooks. It is these texts which have been drawn upon most often for the syntactical features of EST described above.

6.7.3 Text models

EST texts are also relatively strongly formalized: it is possible to expect a number of rather highly conventionalized text models. Journal articles normally have the following five divisions:

1   an introduction, in which the purpose pursued/hypothesis investigated is presented;
2   a review section, in which previous work is summarized or evaluated;
3   a methods part, in which procedural sequences, criteria etc. are evaluated;
4   a results section, in which the findings are presented;
5   a discussion part, in which the findings are evaluated in the framework of the initial hypothesis.

Longer texts such as textbooks and dissertations will be cyclically organized repetitions or partial repetitions of such sequences. Note that, although the order of the five divisions is fixed, not all texts will necessarily contain all five steps. Studies of individual divisions have also proved fruitful. Swales 1981 investigates article introductions, which, regardless of the discipline involved, fall into a structure containing a series of four moves: establishing the field; summarizing previous research; preparing for the present research (motivation); and the introduction of present research. A study of discussion sections has revealed the presence of corresponding moves, but in the reverse order: statement of the results of the present study; re-description of the motivation; review of the literature; and implication for further research (Huckin quoted in Dudley-Evans 1989: 75).

The five textual divisions mentioned can each be given partial linguistic profiles. For example, introductions-cum-reviews as well as conclusions make great use of *that*-clauses (a third and a quarter respectively). This is logical since both reported findings, and findings themselves, are typically presented in reported speech, which uses *that*-clauses. Result sections have fewer *that*-clauses (about a sixth) and methods sections have virtually none (1.33 per cent) (West 1980), which can be explained by the varying rhetorical purpose of each of the sections, for example reporting vs describing. A high proportion of the simple present tense correlates with the expository function of introductions. Passives are by far more common in methods sections (two thirds vs one third elsewhere), at least in chemistry and biology papers, in which procedures and experiments are prominent. The danger of over-generalizing from field to field is demonstrated by the fact that in physics, which often remains highly theoretical and argumentative, the methods sections are hardly different from the other sections (Hanania and Akhtar 1985: 54).

Just as symbols are a special aspect of the lexis of EST, its texts very often contain visual material such as diagrams, graphs, outlines, formulas, charts and tables. These visual elements, as well as the various sections of EST texts, are given textual cohesion by means of the conventionalized occurrence of the individual sections, which is often reinforced by the editorial requirements of journals publishers. Other cohesive devices include:

1   the use of referential vocabulary (adverbs, demonstratives);
2   the deictic use of tense and voice;
3   the employment of enumeration, advance labelling, reporting, recapitulation, hypothesizing and rhetorical questions (Tadros 1989: 18);
4   adopting recognizable patterns of logical development, such as problem and solution, statement and justification, generalization and exemplification.

(ibid.; see also 6.2.1; 6.3.3)

While the specific field may cause some of the variation in components, there is an astonishingly high degree of similarity over a wide spread of fields. This is probably due to shared text types.

6.8 FURTHER READING

General treatments of **text linguistics** include: de Beaugrande and Dressler 1981; van Dijk and Kintsch 1983; Werlich 1983; van Dijk 1985; Brinker 1988; Petöfi 1988 and

1990; Heinemann and Viehweger 1991; McCarthy 1991; Martin 1992. On the continuity of forms and meanings necessary for **textuality** see: Halliday and Hasan 1976; also de Beaugrande and Dressler 1981: Chapters 4–5; Brown and Yule 1983: Chapter 6; Quirk *et al.* 1985: Chapter 19 on grammatical means.

For a detailed discussion of meaning relationships in **lexical semantics** see: Lyons 1977; Cruse 1986. In this book we can give only a brief, text based introduction to **anaphora**. For more detail see: Brown and Yule 1983: Chapter 6; Fox 1987; Hofmann 1989. For problems with pronominal substitution see Brown and Yule 1983.

Text types and typologies are dealt with in: Heinemann and Viehweger 1991; Brinker 1988; and Werlich 1983. For **text strategies** see: Enkvist 1987; de Beaugrande and Dressler 1981; Swales 1981; Dudley-Evans 1989; Hopkins and Dudley-Evans 1988. Fortanet, Posteguille, Palmer and Coll 1998, as well as Swales 1990 and Bhatia 1993, deal with **genre studies**.

Sager, Dungworth and McDonald 1980 is a good comprehensive introduction to **ESP**; see also Dudley-Evans and St John 1999. For a short overview, see Robinson 1989. *English for Specific Purposes. An International Journal* (since 1981) is a good source for contributions to this field; Coleman 1989 and Flowerdew and Peacock 2001 contain collections of articles. Much of the literature in this field is teaching oriented, e.g. Hutchinson and Waters 1987 or Jordan 1997. **Syntactic features** of ESP are dealt with in: Hoffmann 1987 (general); Cheong 1978g (general); Hanania and Akhtar 1985 (verb); Heslot 1982 (tense); Huddleston 1971 (the sentence); Master 1987 (the article); Tarone, Dwyer, Gillette and Icke 1998 (passive); Chih-Hua Kuo 1999 (personal pronouns). For a further characterization of nominals see: Williams 1984 and Salager 1984 (both on compounds); West 1980 (*that* nominal clauses). **Vocabulary** is treated in Johansson 1975. Dictionaries include: *Larousse Dictionary of Science and Technology* (1995); *Chambers Science and Technology Dictionary* (1999); and *The Longman Dictionary of Scientific Usage* (1988).

Chapter 7

Spoken discourse

In Chapter 1 we discussed some of the differences between spoken and written English in general (see 1.6.2). In this chapter we will look at one variety of spoken language, spontaneous conversation. Naturally occurring conversation has received a great deal of attention over the last twenty years from scholars in such varied fields as speech act theory, the ethnography of communication, pragmatics, conversation and variation analysis. We will try to indicate the underlying shared assumptions that make conversations possible (7.1), how meaning is built up by speakers and perceived by hearers (7.2), how conversations are structured in interactional terms (7.3), how speakers negotiate whose turn at talk it is and how they select what they want to say (7.4). In conclusion, the major functions of words like *well* and *you know* in spoken discourse will be discussed (7.5). To save space, S will be used for speaker and H for hearer.

7.1 GENERAL CONSIDERATIONS

Conversation is a social activity in which language plays a decisive, if not exclusive, role. Non-verbal ways of communication such as gestures, body language and eye contact can underscore or contradict what is said, show whether someone likes people and is attentive to what they say, or, indeed, it can signal whether someone is willing to talk to them in the first place. While non-verbal aspects of speech are of great importance, the focus of this chapter will largely be on the verbal aspects of conversation (for non-verbal behaviour see 9.5).

Many of the rules that make for smooth social intercourse in general also apply to talk between two or more people. Among these are, above all, showing consideration for others. In most cases, people are assumed to be honest, reasonable, truthful and trust-worthy individuals. If life in society is to be tolerable, not to say profitable, then people must try to accept others the way they are or at least the way they choose to present themselves, avoid offending them and help them to preserve face. For conversations this means that each S should accept the other's topics, let him/her have their say and give their opinions a fair hearing before challenging them. Hs should make Ss feel at their ease, let them have their turn at talk (by uttering things like *uh, huh, mmhm*), agree with Ss and appreciate what Ss say (*how awful, wonderful*), express their surprise (*really!, is it!*) and show their interest by asking for further details or clearing up misunderstandings. These are aspects of what has been called the **hearer support maxim**. If Ss do not receive feedback, support and encouragement, they cannot be expected to return the same (see 7.3.5 on uptakers).

A further aspect of polite behaviour is that one should repay compliments or other verbal behaviour with which people show that they are interested in us. Awareness of the H also shows in the choice of when to talk and when to be silent. Silence can cause embarrassment because it usually indicates a conversational breakdown. People who can only talk and not listen (conversational bullies or 'steamrollers'), or who can only listen and not talk, make others feel uncomfortable and are in danger of being shunned. How to begin a conversation, what topics to introduce and what particular aspects to mention – all these are matters of convention, which may differ from society to society. In many English speaking countries, for instance, it is usual in everyday conversation to keep away from areas of potential conflict and to avoid introducing too many new ideas or going too deeply beneath the surface. Over and above grammatical (i.e. syntactic, phonetic, phonological, lexical and semantic) knowledge of the language in question, non-native speakers have, therefore, to acquire what has been called a **communicative competence** in the foreign culture, memorably summed up by Hymes: 'competence as to when to speak, when not, and as to what to talk about with whom, when, where, in what manner' (1972: 277).

An amusing example of an unproductive conversation comes in the children's classic animal fable *Charlotte's Web*. The young lamb has just said that it does not want to play with Wilbur, the pig, because 'Pigs mean less than nothing to me.' This is a very blunt refusal, to which Wilbur makes this angry reply:

> 'What do you mean, less than nothing?. . . I don't think there is any such thing as less than nothing. Nothing is absolutely the limit of nothingness. It's the lowest you can go. It's the end of the line. How can something be less than nothing? If there were something that was less than nothing, then nothing would not be nothing, it would be something – even though it's just a very little bit of something. But if nothing is nothing, then nothing has nothing that is less than it is.'
> 'Oh, be quiet!' said the lamb. 'Go play by yourself!'
>
> (E.B. White (1980) *Charlotte's Web*, New York: HarperCollins, p. 28)

This exchange between the lamb and the pig flouts many of the norms we have mentioned. It is confrontational instead of cooperative, blunt and direct instead of tentative and indirect and contains what amounts to a short philosophical treatise on the precise meaning of *nothing* instead of accepting the lamb's loose, everyday use of the word. Conventionally, people do not ask searching questions that might embarrass others but stay with what is generally known and accepted, which is arguably the best method of establishing common ground with interlocutors. Banal, stereotypic thoughts and statements, though unacceptable in intellectual discussions, have their legitimate place in everyday talk (see 3.1 on clichés).

Finally, mention must be made of humour. Humour arises in conversation from differences in perception, conflicts, tensions; and it serves various purposes. It creates a relaxed atmosphere; it allows people to talk about serious topics while being able to distance themselves from them and disguise the fact that serious things are being talked about; it allows speakers and hearers to position themselves not just with regard to their conversational partners but also to the culture of the speech community at large. Humour can thus be a veiled instrument of power to assert one's views in conversation which allows speakers at the same time to hide this fact from others (see Eggins and Slade 1997: 155–67).

7.2 MEANING

Every communicative act can be regarded both from the point of view of interaction between the partners in a conversation and with regard to the meanings that Ss want to express and Hs are intended to understand. Interaction will be dealt with in the next section while this section is concerned with how meaning is built up and perceived in conversation.

7.2.1 Speech acts

It is often not difficult to understand what is meant if one knows the meaning of a word or phrase and the rules of how words are put together to form sentences. In particular, there are a number of verbs which are used to perform certain public acts and which leave no doubt about the intended meaning. Examples are *I hereby pronounce you husband and wife*; *I name this ship* Cutty Sark; *I sentence you to five years in jail*. These verbs show that language can be used not just to talk about things, but also to do things. Such acts performed by language have been called speech acts, and the verbs used are known as speech act or performative verbs. What can be questioned is not the meaning of these performative utterances (**performatives** for short), but whether they are carried out appropriately or not. To be judged appropriate, performatives must meet certain conditions (technically called **felicity conditions**): they must be part of some ritual or well established procedure, like marrying, naming ships or passing sentences in court, as in the examples above. Other restrictions concern the people and the place: only certain, authorized people are allowed to make these utterances (in the first person, simple present tense), and they can usually make them only in certain officially established places (e.g. churches or registry offices for weddings). The procedure must also be executed fully and correctly: if a priest leaves out the crucial words, the wedding ceremony is not valid, and the resulting offspring illegitimate.

Speech acts have been divided into those in which a performative verb actually appears (they are called **explicit**) and those which do not have one in their surface structure. The latter are called **primary** because they are far more frequent than the other type. There are two tests to determine whether an utterance is to be considered an explicit speech act. When the first person is present and the word *hereby* can be inserted, the utterance is a speech act (*I hereby agree, declare, refuse* etc.). However, the presence of the first person simple present active is clearly not a necessary condition, for example *Patrons are kindly asked to refrain from smoking*, or *Guilty*, as pronounced by the jury foreman in a court of law. The second test says, therefore, that utterances count as explicit (performative) speech acts if they are reducible, expandable, or analysable into the form 'I + present simple active verb', as in *I state that the jury finds the accused guilty*.

Speech acts used in conversations are understood much more widely and can be divided into three basic categories, **meta-interactive**, **turn-taking** and **interactive**. The first concerns the organization of the conversation itself, i.e. the marking of beginnings and endings (e.g. *now*, *right*), the opening or closing of a conversation (e.g. *hello*, *bye*) or the structuring of the conversation in some way (*Sorry, I'm afraid I must go now*). Turn-taking speech acts are used to pass on, hold or obtain the floor in public speaking (*what do you think?*; *if I may just finish this*; *could I come in on this?*). Interactive acts are of four types: **eliciting acts** require some linguistic response, such as asking for information, a decision, agreement or the clarification or repetition of an utterance; **informing acts** offer information or respond in other ways to eliciting acts, such as agreeing, confirming, qualifying or rejecting; **acknowledging acts** provide positive or negative follow-up or feedback; and **directing acts** ask for an immediate or future action.

If all utterances do something, the question arises *what* it is that they do. Three aspects have been distinguished. First, utterances perform a **locutionary act**, whose interpretation is concerned with meaning, for which both knowledge of the language system as well as extra-textual knowledge of the world is necessary. Second, by making an utterance Ss perform an **illocutionary act**. This is a linguistic act whose interpretation is concerned with the force of the utterance, e.g. advising, ordering, urging or warning somebody. Third, utterances can have an effect on people, for instance persuading or dissuading them. This non-linguistic act is called the **perlocutionary act**, and the effect is referred to as **perlocutionary force**. Illocutions are (potentially) under the control of Ss; perlocutions never are: 'I may warn you hoping to deter you but in fact succeed only in encouraging or even inciting you' (Coulthard 1985: 19). Two effects have therefore been distinguished according to whether they are intended by the S (**perlocutionary object**) or not (**perlocutionary sequel**).

There are various difficulties about these distinctions, the most important of which relates to the illocutionary force of utterances. Indirect ways of getting things done by language, called **indirect speech acts**, are particularly difficult to process, though they are more frequent in everyday talk than direct and unambiguous statements. If I am sitting at the only fast computer in the department at 9.50 a.m. and a colleague comes in and asks 'Are you teaching at ten?', the question is what does he want? When I answer 'No, I am not' and he goes away without saying anything else, it is likely that he wanted to get on the computer to deal with his e-mail (his own machine being much slower) but did not want to ask me directly. Another indirect way to ask would be 'Are you going to be long?', which also avoids the direct question 'Can I get on the machine?'

Indirect speech acts often show a discrepancy between grammatical form and communicative function in that the declarative, interrogative and imperative moods do not consistently realize statements, questions and orders. In particular, in situations where the role relationships between participants are not clear, an S may well choose indeterminate expressions like *Is that the phone?*, which the H can interpret as a genuine question or as a veiled order. Ss can thus get around imposing their will on others too openly and directly, and an unpleasant confrontation is avoided (for an example of how to distinguish genuine questions from veiled orders in classroom interaction see Coulthard 1985: 130–1).

Statements and exclamations can also present problems. Consider a husband who writes to his wife, 'I'll be back next Thursday': this may be no more than a piece of information, but he may well be asking her to meet him at the station, cook them a nice dinner etc. and be disappointed when none of these things happen. For exclamations, there is the famous case of Henry II's apocryphal utterance, 'Will nobody rid me of this turbulent priest?' This may have been no more than an angry exclamation (in question form), but some of his knights took it to be an order and went to Canterbury and killed Thomas à Becket. Henry may, of course, have deliberately exploited the illocutionary indeterminacy of his exclamation so as to claim later that he had not given an order. This ambiguity explains why it is sometimes necessary to point out explicitly how the H is meant to understand an utterance, e.g. an added *I was only joking* or *this is an order*. These phrases prove the general point that meaning is an interactive category: it is the H who at any given time determines the meaning of utterances, not the S, though the S may be more explicit in a later contribution to the conversation. This has been called the **hearer-knows-best principle** and applies to the interpretation of spoken discourse just as much as to literary works.

7.2.2 Conversational principles

Searle has said that to derive the meaning of indirect speech acts such as *Can you pass the salt?* Ss need 'a theory of speech acts, a theory of conversation, factual background information, and general powers of rationality and inference'(1969: 176). In his seminal article of 1975 Grice sets out to explain the inference process through which Ss derive meaning from H utterances. He starts from the basic assumption that people work together to achieve some goal in a conversation. This **cooperative principle** manifests itself in certain consequences, which he summarizes in four '**maxims**'.

1   Quantity:
    (i)   Make your contribution as informative as is required (for the current purposes of the exchange).
    (ii)   Do not make your contribution more informative than is required.

2   Quality:
    (i)   Do not say what you believe to be false.
    (ii)   Do not say that for which you lack adequate evidence.

3   Relation: Be relevant.

4   Manner:
    (i)   Avoid obscurity of expression.
    (ii)   Avoid ambiguity.
    (iii) Be brief (avoid unnecessary prolixity).
    (iv)   Be orderly.

(ibid.: 46)

There are, of course, activities in which these maxims apply only in a limited way, e.g. discussion between enemies, political speeches, press conferences or police interrogations. Parliaments which allow filibustering clearly suspend maxims 3 ('Be relevant') and 4 ('Be brief'). Grice recognizes that Ss can choose not to stick to the maxims, and therefore his point is rather that 'people will interpret what we say as conforming to the maxims on at least some level' (Levinson 1983: 103). Take this example, which seems to be in breach of the maxim of quantity ('Be informative'), since it is obvious from the answer that B is also aware of the low temperature:

A: Cold in here, isn't it?
B: Okay, I'll shut the window.

A's utterance is apparently not informative because it contains no new information for B. According to Grice, B will interpret A's utterance as implying that A wants B to do something about the low temperature, in fact, that A is uttering some sort of request. This is the obvious interpretation when B assumes A to be relevant despite surface appearances. Here is a further example involving the maxim of relevance:

A: Can you tell me the time?
B: Well, the milkman has come.

The chain of inference is described by Levinson as follows:

> Assume B's utterance is relevant; if it's relevant then given that A asked a question, B should be providing an answer; the only way one can reconcile the assumption that B is co-operatively answering A's question with the content of B's utterance is to assume that B is not in a position to provide the full information, but thinks that the milkman's coming might provide A with the means of deriving a partial answer. Hence A may infer that B intends to convey that the time is at least after whenever the milkman normally calls.
>
> (Levinson 1983: 107)

According to Grice's inference scheme, therefore, Hs usually make the assumption that though Ss seem to be breaking the cooperative principle, at a deeper level they are not doing so. Grice's maxims are to be understood as a device to move from what people say to what they really mean. It can be doubted whether inference sequences like the second one above take place very frequently. In the *Cold in here, isn't it?* example a scheme like Grice's becomes unnecessary when the conversational inference becomes a conventional one.

Although the Gricean principle with its associated maxims can be useful in selecting and rejecting possible readings of utterances, it does not address the question of why speakers are so often indirect in expressing what they have in mind. To go back to *Cold in here, isn't it?*, why does A not say *Could you close the window?* or even *Close the window!*? The answer seems to be that A wants to get B to do something and to be polite at the same time, and so chooses a form of expression which does not impose on B too much, thus giving B a certain freedom to react to this veiled order. A could have been more informative, but only at the cost of being rude to B. In this case, as in many others, the **politeness principle** overrules the cooperative principle with its four maxims, including the quality maxim. Other examples include white lies (*I'm terribly sorry but we've got something on already tonight*), which can be used to avoid having to do something without giving offence. As Leech points out, the more indirect a speech act is, the more polite it tends to be, because indirect speech acts 'increase the degree of optionality, and . . . because the more indirect an illocution is, the more diminished and tentative its force tends to be' (1983: 108). He lists these examples (in increasing order of indirectness and politeness): *Answer the phone*; *I want you to answer the phone*; *Will you answer the phone?*; *Can you answer the (tele)phone?*; *Would you mind answering the phone?*; *Could you possibly answer the phone?* (ibid.).

Irony is also sometimes linked to the politeness principle: in cases where one cannot avoid giving offence one should at least do it in a way that does not obviously clash with the politeness principle. Fixed expressions like *That's all I need* ('Why did this have to happen to me?') or *that's a fine/pretty kettle of fish* ('a messy, confusing situation') clearly mean the opposite of what they seem to be saying and thus go against the quality maxim. As there is often no reason why speakers should not be cooperative, the obvious explanation is that they say untrue things to save the politeness principle. This comes out even more clearly where the ironic expression is a comment on people and their actions, e.g. *You're a real genius* (= 'You're an idiot') or *How brilliant!* ('How stupid'). It has to be admitted, however, that avoiding the offending terms does not mitigate the strong impression on the part of the H that the S thinks he or she is the one who is wiser and superior to the H – an implication no doubt resented by H.

The politeness principle can account for some of the S-choices that Grice's maxims do not explain – as can other principles not discussed here (for example the charity principle 'Construe the speaker's remarks so as to violate as few maxims as possible' and the morality maxim 'Ss should not do things, or make Hs do things, that they ought not to' mentioned in Bach and Harnish 1979: 68). But neither speech act theory nor the various inference schemes seem to be able to explain how utterances that can have many meanings in isolation come to have only one in a particular context. It has been said of the example *Cold in here, isn't it* that it can be an indirect request to close the door, but, as Sadock points out, it is infinitely flexible: 'But it can also convey a request to open a door or to bring a blanket or to pay a gas bill. In fact it's difficult to think of a request that the utterance could *not* convey in the right context'(1978: 286). It should be added, however, that the speech context (or co-text) often constrains the interpretations that can be put on an utterance (see 7.4.1. on the concept of the adjacency pair).

7.3 CONVERSATIONAL INTERACTION

Every utterance in a conversation has a double status. Seen from the point of view of speaker meaning, it expresses what the S has in mind; seen from the point of view of the interaction between conversational partners, it is a move in the conversational game that S and H jointly play. In this section we will discuss some aspects of the interactional structure of conversations, basing our treatment on Edmondson (1981) and Edmondson and House (1981).

Conversations are made up of **encounters**, which can be divided up into **phases**, which, in turn, consist of at least one **exchange**. Exchanges have two or more **moves**, which themselves consist of one or more **acts**.

7.3.1 Encounters

Encounters are the highest unit of conversational structure. It is usual to distinguish three phases within them: an opening phase, a central phase in which the main business of the respective encounter is dealt with, and a closing phase. While conversational partners are fairly free to negotiate the topics for the substantial part of the encounter, they are much more restricted in the choice of things that can be mentioned in the opening and closing phases, which are marked by a high degree of conventionality.

7.3.2 Phases

Openings   The opening phase consists of exchanges in which the partners in a potential conversation acknowledge one another's presence, decide whether they want to enter into a longer conversation and explore whether the other person is available for conversation. There are three types of expressions that can be used as openers: expressions directed to the other (*Sleep well?*; *Have a good journey?*); self-oriented expressions (*Before I forget*; *Thirsty work this*); and neutral remarks (on the weather etc.) In **non-solidary encounters** where the social status of speakers differs, social superiors will use other-oriented expressions while social inferiors produce self-oriented ones. This is so because social inferiors 'are not allowed to invade the psychological world of the superior, as this would infringe the status rules which hold between them' (Cheepen and Monaghan 1990: 33). However many conversations are also started with **shared world tokens**, expressions which are both self- and other-oriented (e.g. *Excuse me*; *Sorry to bother you*; *I've been longing to meet you*).

Encounters can be divided into **transactional encounters**, which have some business other than a simple social meeting (a job interview, a loan application, a purchase of some kind), and **interactional encounters**, whose sole purpose is the establishment and confirmation of social bonds. In both types the exchange of greetings belongs to the pre-opening phase. On the other hand, while **small talk** (about the weather, a new dress or car, the behaviour of the cat/dog, or the height of a child) provides the topics in interactional encounters, it must be regarded as a pre-topic in transactional encounters, which move on to the real purpose of the encounter in the central phase. In interactional encounters with strangers, the opening phase involves a gradual, step-by-step disclosing of and request for more or less personal details about the other person, for example, where they live, come from, went to school etc., after which the conversation can move on to matters of mutual interest such as films, restaurants, a foreign country, a book, flying experiences, hobbies etc. Topic changes are frequent and usual. People not only direct their efforts in the opening stage towards establishing common ground by choosing safe topics, but also refrain from introducing controversial ideas or from disagreeing with their interlocutor, who might feel threatened. This is again in keeping with the general maxim that one should support the H. Disagreements or contradictions, if they come up at all, tend to be introduced by appropriate softening devices or will be kept back until a later stage in the encounter when enough common ground and mutual goodwill have been established.

Endings   As a conversation is nearing its end, participants often make a comment about the quality of the current encounter (*it's been nice talking to you* or *it was nice meeting* *you)* and refer to possible future meetings. Phrases such as *I mustn't keep you*; *I'd better let you go*; *I'm afraid I must get back to work* are used in order not to appear too ready to close the encounter. It can be difficult to get out of boring or unproductive conversations, so that you might have to use strong signals like standing up or tidying up the scene of action, which will bring the conversation to its end even if your partner should not want to finish it just yet. As the ending of conversations is also a cooperative undertaking, both must agree to stop, usually by using such tokens as *right (then)*, *okay* or hesitations and references to some other topic or activity. It is only in extreme cases that you leave using a direct excuse like *Sorry, I've got to run* or *Sorry, I must rush*. In this situation there is rarely the time, or the desire, to reassure the other that you like his/her company and looks forward to renewing the contact (*I hope we'll meet again*; *hope to see you again soon*; *I'll be in touch*; or *I'll write soon*). It is also quite common to find pre-final side sequences, in which an earlier topic is briefly mentioned again. Final goodbyes come in various forms depending on the tenor of the social relationship of the speakers, e.g. *(good)bye now, so long, cheerio, see you, be seeing you* etc.

It should be stressed that many of the speech acts mentioned, though they may appear banal and trivial at one level, are an important part of the social competence of all native speakers. This becomes immediately apparent when you come across someone who does not make the appropriate social noises. Some people do not feel like engaging in small talk, either because they think it silly or because they are not aware that it is expected of them. Such people are likely to be perceived as strange and difficult, if not unfriendly or threatening.

Central phase   While some research has been carried out into the **boundary sequences** (openings and closings), not much has been done on the central section of conversations. Cheepen and Monaghan 1990, however, have found that the central phase in interactional encounters (which they call *conversation*) consists of two main elements, speech-in-action and stories. **Speech-in-action** occurs at, or near, the beginning of an encounter and consists of comments by the participants on various aspects of their immediate environment. Comments on the nature of the social encounter (e.g. *how nice to see you*) are less common than those which relate to objects and conditions that are observable by the participants (such as the weather, the scenery, pet animals, the speakers themselves; see the discussion on openings above). Speech-in-action functions 'as a base for the telling of story, to which the speakers refer between instances of story, and from which the bulk of new conversational topics arise' (ibid.: 45).

Stories are extended stretches of speech and consist of more than one turn. Stories can feature the storyteller (this has been called a **recount**), or can focus on other people (**narrative**) or a specially remarkable event (**anecdote**), and can have a particular moral point (**exemplum**). At the workplace, anecdotes, recounts and exemplums (in this order) are more frequent in casual conversation than other forms like jokes, comments, observations or opinions. There are marked gender differences: men's stories tend to be about a 'hero' overcoming a particular difficulty, while women are more likely to tell anecdotes that involve embarrassing, humiliating or worrying situations. While male stories are calculated to elicit admiration, women's stories provoke laughter.

In telling stories, special care must be taken by Ss because other participants are likely to break in at possible finishing points. Storytellers therefore often get permission to tell a story by using a **story preface** (e.g. *you know what happened to me this morning?*

or *have you heard the one about x?*). Ss must ensure that stories fit well into the conversation and are clearly marked off from other talk. They can achieve this by using a disjunct marker (e.g. *oh*) to indicate that what follows is not directly related to the preceding utterance and/or by repeating a word, phrase etc. which links the following story to earlier talk. The stories themselves tend to have clearly marked beginnings and endings and some general point or message. Speech-in-action is used to bring the listeners back to the present time so that other Ss can then tell their stories, which often show similarities (in content, specification, moral) to the preceding story – another instance of hearer support in operation. This telling of parallel narratives enhances the point of the first story and thus achieves a **shared world** view, perhaps the most important function of conversations.

Stories generally have the structure of state–event–state, i.e. they narrate an event, which arises out of a particular state and which brings about a change in the world, a new state. Stories in naturally occurring conversation are specifically about clearly defined human beings, are told in dialogue form and allow participants to agree on evaluations, which contribute to **social bonding** between co-conversationalists, which is the ultimate goal of interactional encounters. As participants can take control of the conversation at different times, they feel they are equals, which is another condition for good social relationships.

The main body of the conversation can also contain passages in which conversational trouble arises. Sometimes this is overt and has to do with the wrong choice or the misunderstanding of lexical items, which temporarily interrupt the smooth flow of conversation and bring about side sequences. More serious trouble is covert and arises either because one or more of the participants feel threatened in their conversational status or because of a failure to agree on an evaluation. This trouble can be repaired by a negative evaluation sequence of a highly exaggerated nature, in which all speakers make comments on, for example, an absent person. This scapegoat repair helps speakers to create unity and harmony again. After a scapegoat repair speakers often move back to an earlier topic (this is called a **topic loop**). Presumably even more effective in re-establishing good relationships are delayed repairs in which conversational trouble is put aside until a later stage in the conversation, when it can be fitted into some earlier topic and dealt with in such a way that the offended parties are reconciled and interactional harmony restored. Both side sequences and the sequence trouble – repair – topic re-run/topic loop show that naturally occurring conversation is not an unstructured activity, as has often been asserted, but that conversations have a goal and that conversationalists monitor closely the way conversations develop and try to find the right moment for what they want to say.

7.3.3 Exchanges

A **phase** consists of one or more **head exchanges**, in which the main business is transacted. Related but less important matters are dealt with in minor exchanges, which occur before or after the head exchange. These **pre-** and **post-exchanges** are optional, although it is not uncommon to find more than one such subordinate exchange, especially in the case of post-exchanges.

Pre-exchanges   **Pre-exchanges** have various functions; for example, they introduce a topic (*I've got a bit of a problem*) or seek advance commitment (*Could you do me a favour?* or *Could you spare a moment?*). They are also commonly employed by Ss to check on possible objections by Hs before they make their main move:

pre-exchange	A:	Have you got anything on tonight?
	B:	No, not really.
head exchange	A:	Well, would you like to go to the cinema?
	B:	I'd love to.

A can be sure that, whatever else B may come up with, B will at least not be able to say that he or she has other plans. If B had answered in the positive, A might well not have invited B in order to avoid the danger of being turned down. The benefits of pre-exchanges are, however, not all on S's side: B is also spared the potentially embarrassing situation of having to turn down an invitation. This example also shows that pre-exchanges lead directly to head (or other) exchanges and that the S who initiates a pre-exchange also produces the first move in the directly following (head) exchange.

While Ss use pre-exchanges in order not to be turned down, Hs use them before they commit themselves one way or another (this is called a **pre-responding exchange**):

A: Have you got anything on tonight?
B: Why do you want to know?

Post-exchanges   **Post-exchanges**, on the other hand, confirm or make more precise the outcome of a preceding exchange. Examples with more than one post-exchange are quite frequent (A and B have just reached a solution to a baby-sitting problem):

A: . . . I'll bring my friend round tonight.
B: Yeah okay.
A: What time would you like?
B: Oh any time about eight thirty'll be fine.
A: Oh, yes alright fine. Well, I'll bring her round tonight.
B: Yeah.

(adapted from Edmondson 1981: 102)

This example shows that post-exchanges are often employed to bridge the central or business and closing phases of an encounter. Here the first post-exchange confirms the outcome reached in the preceding conversation, while the second settles a detail of the outcome and the third closes the conversational encounter. We can therefore say that post-exchanges can be either *substantial* (the second exchange in the example) or *ritual* (exchanges one and three), where the outcome of the exchange is the same as that of the previous exchange.

So far we have dealt with one way of linking head exchanges to pre- or post-exchanges, that of subordination. Edmondson also proposes a second type, that of coordination, which takes either the form of **chaining** or of **reciprocation**. The following question-answer sequence illustrates the chaining process:

A: Well, can you prescribe anything for the allergy?
B: Does it itch at all?
A: Yes, it itches quite a lot.
B: Do you get scabs forming on it . . .?
A: No.
B: Hm hum. It's just on your face and hands, is it?
A: And my arms.
B: And your arms. Is it on any other place of the body?
A: Well, it's spreading, yeah.
B: Well, I think I can prescribe some ointment for you . . .

(adapted from Edmondson 1981: 110)

This question-answer sequence shows all the conditions for chaining: the exchanges all have a common topic, a skin problem; the information asked for by the doctor could have been got in one block question which would have contained all the other questions; the pre-responding exchanges are of the same type (question-answer), and B's intentions are the same in all the exchanges (eliciting information).

Reciprocation is commonly found in small talk, where the partners to a conversation are nice to each other, asking about one another's health (*How are you?. . . And how are you?*), volunteering information about themselves etc. Reciprocal exchanges illustrate again the hearer support principle, can be started by either partner and can appear in chained sequences.

7.3.4 Moves

Exchanges consist of two or more **head moves**, in which at least one partner in the conversation engages in talk in order to achieve some result. Once this goal is obtained, the participants can either embark on a new exchange or end their conversation. It is the conversational goals by which exchanges are defined while the individual moves are characterized by the role they play in reaching these conversational goals. We will distinguish the head moves **initiate, satisfy, counter** and **contra** and three **supporting moves**, namely **grounders, disarmers** and **expanders**.

Head moves   In the simplest case, an exchange consists of two moves only, a stimulus and a response: S initiates a conversation and H reacts positively to this move. The move that gets the conversation going is an **initiate**, and the H's positive reaction to it is a **satisfy**:

A: Excuse me, could you tell me the time?
B: It's half past three.

Moves need not always be realized, as is the case with B's satisfy in the next example:

A: Have you got coffee to go?
B: Milk and sugar?
A: Yes, please.

This example can be made explicit as follows:

A: Initiate
B: [Satisfy;] Initiate
A: Satisfy

The positive answer, the satisfy to A's initiate, remains unspoken; otherwise, B's question, the second initiate, would not make sense. On the other hand, just as a satisfy can be omitted, whole sequences may be added in an exchange before the outcome is achieved.

Another way of responding to an initiate is with a refusal, either a final or a provisional one. The first, called **contra**, realizes an ultimate reaction in the negative, and it is quite possible to find exchanges with more than one contra, as in

Initiate	A:	Coming to Alan's party tonight?
Contra	B:	'Fraid I can't, I have to finish this essay.
Initiate	A:	But the whole gang are coming.
Contra	B:	Sorry, I really must hand it in first thing tomorrow morning.
Initiate	A:	What a shame, we specially asked Susan to come along for you.
Contra	B:	Yeah, well, I'd love to come but I really can't.
Satisfy	A:	Oh well, some other time then.

B maintains his/her contra until the exchange is eventually closed by A, who takes back his/her initiate by offering a satisfy to B's third contra.

The second negative move, the **counter**, is valid only for a certain time and is taken back in the course of the exchange:

Initiate	A:	I think we should invite the whole family.
Counter	B:	Oh God their kids are so loutish.
Satisfy	A:	Yeah I agree they're pretty horrible – but
Initiate		you know – they did put up with our lot last time.
Satisfy	B:	Oh God alright – invite them then – and the bloody dog.

(adapted from Edmondson and House 1981: 40–1)

B's first reaction is provisional (a counter), not a contra, because it is taken back in B's second contribution. Note also that although A agrees with B's counter (i.e. satisfies it), A does not give up her/his initiate. Contrast the following exchange, in which again B's first reaction must be classified as a counter:

Initiate	A:	I think we should invite the whole family.
Counter	B:	Oh God the kids are so loutish.
Contra	A:	Oh come on – they're not that bad.
Satisfy	B:	Yeah perhaps you're right – but even so – I
Contra		don't want to have to cook for the whole family – I'll be exhausted.
Satisfy	A:	Oh well – if you feel like that about it – let's forget the whole business.

(adapted from Edmondson and House 1981: 40–1)

Here A gives up her/his initiate in the last move, thus offering a satisfy to B's contra of the preceding move. A counter is, then, only a provisional negative reaction, and it also differs from a contra in its potential consequences. First (as in the first example of a counter above), the acceptance of a counter does not necessarily mean that the S who offers a satisfy to a counter takes back the initiate. Second, as in the second example of a counter, if the counter is met with a contra and the S who has produced the counter goes on to take back this counter, i.e. produces a satisfy to the other's contra, this does not necessarily mean that he or she accepts the original initiate. It should also be noted that a satisfy always refers to the immediately preceding move, and that while no exchange can be closed by a move other than a satisfy, producing one does not always bring the total exchange to an end. Thus there are, in the last two examples quoted above, two non-closing satisfy's, one responding to a counter and the other to a contra.

There seem to be very few restrictions on the order in which moves can follow on one another. In theory, any move can be combined with any other move, with the exception of the satisfy, which must follow on one of the other moves. There are, however, restrictions on the number of moves Ss can make in any one contribution. The normal **turn** (see 7.4.1) consists of one of the moves mentioned so far. Ss can make more than one move in any given turn only if their first move is the satisfy of a counter or contra. After the satisfy of an initiate, however, there is again competition between both participants, i.e. either speaker can make a move. Change of speaker within the exchange is thus determined by interactional structure, but conversationalists are free to negotiate whose turn it is outside the exchange structure.

Supporting moves   The basic move inventory is to be distinguished from supporting moves, which are relevant, but subsidiary to head moves. Their function is defined in terms of their semantic relationship to head moves. **Grounders** give reasons for (conversational) behaviour; **disarmers** are used to apologize for a possible offence before it is committed; and **expanders** provide more than the absolute bare minimum of information asked for. Whether speakers make use of these moves depends on how they view the situation, and in particular on how appropriate, or necessary, they think them for their conversational goals. Though supporting moves are thus partly a matter of speaker strategy, there are strong social pressures which make their use almost obligatory. Normal politeness would require speakers to produce reasons for requests, or to apologize for potential offences. Indeed, speakers may well feel they have to use more than one of these supporting moves, e.g. grounders in this example:

> The woman stopped at her husband's shoulder. 'If the king of kings is ready it's high time we were going. Cathy's had quite enough sun for one day and the tide's coming in fast. And we're late for tea already.'
> A nice voice, less refined than the expression, with affection taking all the sting out of the marching order.
>
> (A. Price (1977) *Our Man in Camelot*,
> Sevenoaks, p. 23)

Apart from showing the importance of non-verbal means (affection) in interaction, the last example also illustrates that Ss employ supporting moves strategically to anticipate possible wishes, doubts, questions or hesitations by H with respect to a head move.

Put in interactional terms, a supporting move is a satisfy to an anticipated initiate, which H might otherwise be expected to produce before he or she reacts to S's initiate. Grounders can be placed either before or after the head move. They can be so conventionalized that they are interpreted to convey that which they would normally serve to ground:

A: Can you come and see me tomorrow morning?
B: The buses are on strike.

Here the negative answer *I'm sorry, I can't* is missed out and only the grounder remains.

Disarmers are used to make it difficult for others to take offence. Without appearing unfriendly and uncooperative S tries through self criticism to prevent H from claiming that a real offence has taken place. Commonly used tokens are *Sorry to interrupt but . . .*; *I don't want to sound bossy but . . .*; and *I hope I'm not disturbing you. . . .*

Expanders typically occur at the beginning of an encounter in what is called small talk. Here participants show that they are well disposed towards each other and are prepared to enter into a real conversation. Generally speaking, people who only answer *yes* or *no* will be interpreted as unfriendly and uncooperative because they do not provide enough information, as in this example (note: the conversation is between Dr Harley and Harold, who has been sent to the doctor at his mother's insistence):

'You don't seem to be listening, Harold. I asked you, do you have any friends?'
Harold abandoned his musings and concentrated on the question. 'No,' he answered.
'None at all?'
Harold considered. 'Well, maybe one.'
'Would you care to talk about this friend?'
'No. . . .'
'I see.' Dr Harley ran his hand over the back of his head. He decided on a new tack.
'Were you happy at school ?' he asked.
'Yes.'
'You liked your teachers?'
'Yes.'
'Your classmates ?'
'Yes.'
'Your studies?'
'Yes.'
'Then why did you leave ?'
'I burned down the chemistry building.'
Dr Harley stood up slowly and walked to the window. He adjusted the venetian blind.
'We are not relating today, Harold,' he said.

(Colin Higgins (1971) *Harold and Maude*,
London: Pan, pp. 28–9)

The use of supporting moves is a matter of knowing about and wanting to keep to the social rules of English speaking countries. The maxim behind the use of disarmers might be said to be, 'When your action is likely to give offence, make sure you apologize for it.' Another such rule, one governing the employment of expanders, is to give information freely when asked for it. Harold does not conform to this norm of social behaviour because he is not willing to cooperate with Dr Harley.

7.3.5 Acts

The smallest units in Edmondson's model are called **acts**. One or more head acts, which are optionally accompanied by preceding or following elements (pre- and post-head acts), combine to form a move. Interaction in the full sense of the word cannot be said to take place in individual acts or moves, but only at the level of the conversational exchange, for which at least two moves are necessary. Still, there is structure discernible at the level of the act and a list of interactional units would be incomplete without a description of it.

Three elements can be distinguished at this lowest level, a **head act** or **head**, which can be preceded by a **pre-head act** or **uptaker** and followed by a **post-head act** or **appealer**. Head acts are the same as head moves insofar as they realize illocutionary acts like request, permission, invitation, apology etc. By contrast, uptakers and appealers do not constitute speech acts (or, to put it differently, do not to have illocutionary force). They do, however, serve important interactional functions: uptakers establish a link between the preceding move and the ongoing move; and appealers connect the current move with the following one.

Appealers are used by Ss to get agreement, most often to a move that conveys some kind of information. They include tokens like *okay, (all) right, don't you think?* as well as question tags and non-linguistic *eh, uh* and *mhm*.

Uptakers (also known as **back channel behaviour**) are signals of active listening on the part of H. Typical tokens include *hmm, uhum, aha, ah, uh*. The most frequent uptakers in English are *yes* or *yeah*, not to be confused in this function with their use to signal agreement. Beside these neutral tokens there are a number of more emotional items (*really, you don't say, good heavens, terrific, not again, bloody hell* etc.). An important interactional use of uptakers occurs when they do not precede a move but are used on their own, as in this example (uptakers in parentheses):

> . . . she's a very unique type, very very upper middle class English (yes yes) you see (yeah) – er sort of the general's daughter sort of type (yes yeah) and he was erm from Essex somewhere (yeah). . .
>
> (after Crystal and Davy 1975: 62)

This class of uptaker does not interrupt (called a *go-on gambit* by Edmondson and House 1981: 73) but clearly supports S as they indicate to S that he or she can go on with his/her turn. In fact, when Hs do not produce them, Ss are likely to stop talking altogether and ask whether something is wrong or, on the phone, whether the H is still there. By using an uptaker a person shows that they accept the other's contribution, but also indicates that they are ready to take a turn themselves (see 7.5 on discourse markers).

Uptakers and appealers are optional elements because many head acts/moves contain them implicitly or presuppose them. If, for example, you refuse a request or agree to one, this obviously presupposes that you have heard the request, and therefore it may seem unnecessary to make this fact explicit. However, even if uptakers and appealers are structurally optional, they often play an indispensable interactional role, as the example of the go-on gambits illustrates.

7.4 TURNS, SCHEMAS AND TOPICS

This section is concerned with how Ss choose what to tell and to whom, that is, how they select 'tellables' from the mass of potentially interesting things and how they decide who to communicate them to.

7.4.1 Turns

Naturally occurring, spontaneous conversation differs from other types of spoken language in two important respects. First, the roles of speaker and hearer frequently change, and second, neither the change nor the size or order of turns are predetermined but are a matter for negotiation. The turn-taking mechanism describes how speakers get a turn, how they keep it and how they hand it over to the next speaker.

A common definition of **turn** states that a turn consists of all of one S's utterances up to the point when another person takes over the role of S. This definition raises the question of what an utterance is. Utterances can be defined in terms of syntax: a stretch of talk that is an independent clause (including elliptical sentences like *Super!* or *How?* and expressions like *No, really!*), a term of address or a tag (*you know?*, *Doesn't he?*). Utterance boundaries also tend to be marked by intonation contours and terminal junctures: low pitch on the final tone unit of an utterance is a signal that a speaker has reached a point of semantic completeness. Finally, utterances express **propositions**, i.e. they assert (or predicate) that there is some relation of the subject to an attribute or some other entity. There is some disagreement over the status of items typical of conversation like *well, hmm, erm*, which have no propositional content, even though they fulfil important communicative functions as discourse lubricants 'for both the speaker (to cover his confusion, uncertainty and so on) and for the hearer (reassuring him, seeking to persuade him and so on)' (Edmondson and House 1981: 66). We will say that turns consist of one or more utterances that have semantic content (called **illocutionary acts**; see 7.2.1). In actual fact, because there is great competition for turns they usually consist of a single sentence only, unless an S has been granted permission to tell a joke or a story (see 7.3.1).

How do participants in conversations get their turn at talk? Sacks *et al.* 1974 found that there are two ways of getting your turn. Either the current S passes his/her turn on and names the next S, or the current S simply stops and allows the next speaker to self select. The next S may, of course, be identical with the current S when nobody else takes up the turn. These possibilities apply again at the next point in the conversation where speaker change can take place (called a **transition relevance place**). Changeover places in conversations are signalled above all by linguistic means. *If I may come in here* or *Excuse me but* are among the phrases commonly used to get a turn. Ss may complete the sentence begun by the previous S, but though this is less hostile than interrupting, it too must be used sparingly. Possible linguistic devices to signal that one is coming to the end of what one wants to say are: pauses; a rising or falling intonation at the end of an utterance; expressions like *you know, but, so*; an increase in volume and/or a drop in pitch together with these expressions; the completion of a clause; and, of course, expressions that make the end of a turn explicit. These last are rare because they are considered too formal for spontaneous conversation. Non-linguistic means include relaxing one's body, stopping the movements of one's hands and starting another activity, e.g. eating, drinking or smoking. When Ss want to keep a turn they will fill their own pauses (e.g. with a *well*) and leave the clauses incomplete. Ss can also use structural pointers like *first of all, then, next, finally*, or *to sum up*, which will allow them to say everything they have to say.

In rare cases it may be necessary to break somebody's flow of speech and be un-cooperative. A permissible interruption is one in which H asks S to explain something that H has not understood, using such tokens as *Excuse me, what did you say?*; *Would you say that again?*; *Sorry, you've lost me*; or *Sorry, I missed that*. On the other hand, interrupting to correct Ss or to question the truth of what they are saying is a much more delicate matter as it endangers the conversational standing of the Ss. Such hostile inter-ruptions can be warded off by: using structuring remarks that show how long you intend to speak (e.g. *I would like to comment on two points*; *I just have a few comments*); using complex sentences; saying *Let me finish*; *If I may just finish this*; or raising one's voice to drown the other out.

All this may explain why conversations go on with remarkably little overlap and few awkward silences. When overlap does occur, it is likely to be unintentional, because Hs usually recognize when an utterance is complete. The reason for two participants speaking at the same time often is that the current S has not selected the next S. But this situation is quickly remedied: typically, the participant who was the first to speak continues with his/her turn. Silences between turns are filled by questions (e.g. *Didn't you hear me*) or by repetitions on the part of the current S. The new S will use starting noises (*erm, um, mm*).

The rules outlined above do not take into account, however, that meaning can be important for the placing of utterances: 'turns initiated with *but* are more likely to occur at non-transition relevance places than turns initiated with either *so* or *and*' (Schiffrin 1988: 268). Also ignored in this approach is the fact that overlap, and its evaluation, is culturally determined: 'members of some ethnic groups interpret overlap as evidence of cooperative involvement and enthusiasm' (ibid.). It seems therefore that a rule based account of turn-taking needs to be supplemented by a description of the roles that are played by social meaning.

Most turns consist of single sentences, and conversations consist minimally of two turns. The ties between turns vary a good deal. They can be very close for what are called **adjacency pairs**, which consist of two utterances successively produced by different speakers in a fixed order. Examples of first parts of pairs are such speech acts as complaints, greetings, invitations, offers and questions. The first part of the adjacency pair requires a following speech act. What follows a complaint, invitation etc. will be interpreted as a response to that first part. Thus, a move which comes after a complaint will be understood as an apology, justification etc. Likewise, Hs will go to great lengths to interpret the move following on an invitation as expressing acceptance or refusal. Second parts can also be reciprocal (greetings are answered by greetings). Sometimes there is only one appropriate second part (a question can be reacted to appropriately only by an answer), while at other times there is not so much restriction (complaints can be followed by apologies, denials or justifications).

Several qualifications must be made about this characterization. Second parts do not always follow immediately because other conversational matter is inserted, while in other cases there is no second part at all. For instance, second parts in a thank-you sequence (like *no problem* or *you're welcome* in AmE, or *don't mention it* in BrE) seem to be more regularly used in the US than in Great Britain. Usually, however, Ss expect a second part and when no answers are forthcoming to questions or when greetings are not returned, Ss will comment on this behaviour as rude or impolite. Another problem is that the predictive power of first parts is diminished, and with it the importance of adjacency pairs for the organization of conversation, if there are many alternatives for second parts. This number can, however, be limited because certain realizations are preferred, as mentioned above: requests have grants as their second parts of choice, and offers and invitations prefer acceptances and not refusals. In other words, **preferred seconds** are unmarked and are the most frequent alternative, while unpreferred seconds are marked, unusual and structurally more complex. They are distinguished by various features such as: delay (a pause before delivery as well as displacement over a number of turns); the use of markers or announcers (like *uh*, *well*); the production of appreciations (for offers, invitations etc.); the use of apologies (e.g. in the case of invitations or requests); or the giving of reasons for why the unpreferred alternative is chosen:

A: Uh if you'd care to come and visit a little while this morning I'll give you a cup of coffee. [invitation]
B: Hehh [delay] Well [marker] that's awfully sweet of you [appreciation] I don't think I can make it this morning [refusal = unpreferred second] hh uhm I'm running an ad in the paper and uh I have to stay near the phone [reason].

(adapted from Coulthard 1985: 71)

This principle of **preference organization** can also be invoked in the case of other behaviour, e.g. when questions or invitations are met with silence, which will be interpreted as a negative answer or a refusal.

7.4.2 Schemas

How do Ss select what they want to tell Hs, and how do Hs process both what they are told and what they are not told? As a general rule, Ss will avoid speaking about events and situations which they can expect Hs to know. But how can they know what Hs know? Look at the following example:

I woke up at seven forty. I was in bed. I was wearing pyjamas. After lying still for a few minutes, I threw back the duvet, got out of bed, walked to the door of the bedroom, opened the door, switched on the landing light, walked across the landing, opened the bathroom door, went into the bathroom, put the basin plug into the plughole, turned on the hot tap, ran some hot water into the wash basin, looked into the mirror . . .

(Cook 1989: 69)

This illustrates the fact that even if asked to tell the truth, the whole truth and nothing but the truth, witnesses in court will not produce texts like this when they have to account for their movements on a particular morning. They can assume that the information contained in the example is known to every person in court, so that its recital is superfluous, irrelevant and probably boring. People have stored in their brains knowledge about what getting up in the morning involves so that only those features need to be listed which are not in the expected getting up schema, for example, what one had for breakfast and when one left for work. Details not mentioned by speakers will be assumed to be present unless this assumption is explicitly cancelled. Other schemas include the motor car, the restaurant and the waiting room schema. What all patterns have in common is that they are knowledge structures which tie together information in our memories about things, sequences of events and actions, about goals and motivations, plans and interests. Various patterns have been distinguished, as follows.

- **Frames** consist of common sense knowledge about some central concept, for example a restaurant. They store all the things that belong together, but do not specify the order in which they will be done or mentioned.
- **Schemas**, on the other hand, provide order for states and events and are arranged in a progression.
- **Plans** are defined by the goal that events and states lead up to and must be made under consideration of all the relevant elements according to the criterion of whether they help to achieve the goal.
- **Scripts** are well established plans which specify the roles of participants and their actions.

Global knowledge patterns thus incorporate **background knowledge** (classes of relevant objects and participants; principles of possible actions; values attached to objects, actions etc.) and **action knowledge** (description of circumstances or conditions; sequences of actions or events; possible choices).

The great advantage of having knowledge patterns like these stored in our memory is that they reduce the complexity of life and allow us to keep a great deal of information ready for use. Applied to written and spoken texts this means that speakers have stored patterns of jokes, stories, fairy tales or crime novels, as well as other text types which predict, for example, participants, their roles and plot development. Speakers also have patterns of turn-taking, length of turn and the general goal and development of conversation.

These global knowledge patterns are activated in Ss and Hs alike and thus help them to select what is relevant, both as Ss and Hs of discourse. It has been pointed out that global knowledge patterns go a long way towards explaining Grice's maxims. Communication can be economical because Ss will give us only new information after taking into account what Hs know already in their schemas. The maxim of brevity may be violated because Ss assume too little knowledge in Hs; the clarity maxim may be broken because Ss make wrong assumptions about shared schemas.

7.4.3 Topics

When Ss have made their selection of what to tell Hs with the help of the various knowledge schemas, they must decide whether what they have chosen to communicate is of
potential interest to Hs. The concept of **newsworthiness** is not easy to apply to a given
situation, and Ss can make wrong assessments, but it is obvious that an S makes
constant assessment of H with regard to the what and when, not to mention the how, of
communication:

> For instance, if one's sister becomes engaged, some relatives must be told immedi-
> ately, others on a first meeting after the event, whereas some of one's friends might
> not know the sister or even that one has a sister, and for them the event has no import-
> ance or even interest.
>
> (Coulthard 1985: 79)

The topic that is the first to be mentioned in a conversation is of special importance
as it is the only one which Ss are free to choose; all others are determined to a greater
or lesser extent by what has gone before. The initial topic of conversation usually has to
do with the reason for the encounter. It is very likely that Ss will say why they are seeking
an encounter, as is borne out by cases where people are just paying social calls without
any ulterior motive. In these cases they will say something like *I was just passing* or *I
wanted to see how you are*. Some Ss will, of course, hold back the real reason until they
can fittingly mention it.

A conversation, if it is to be satisfactory to participants, proceeds from topic to topic
in such a way that Hs take up what Ss have said (**linked transition**). We can all think
of unrewarding conversations where there was no close fitting of topics but rather **abrupt
topic changes.** To make participants enjoy conversations, Ss and Hs must be willing to
talk not only about similar topics (i.e. where they went on holiday) but about the same
topic (e.g. how holiday costs have gone up). Another unsatisfactory, though not infrequent type of conversation, is when Ss are unwilling to take up the previous utterance
but stick to their own topic and refer back to their own contribution (this has been called
skip connecting).

Topics can, but need not be, marked off from one another in various ways. Common
tokens include *OK, well, right, now,* or *good* uttered with strong stress and high falling
intonation and followed by a pause (this has been called a **frame** or **framer**). Another
means of indicating a topic boundary is for one S to produce a brief summary (often in
the form of a common saying, such as a proverb) with which the H can and, indeed, is
expected to agree.

7.5 DISCOURSE MARKERS

This section provides a brief summary of the major aspects of discourse by discussing
items that perform a number of different discourse functions. We will first introduce a
discourse model in which five different components are distinguished. Then we will look
at the main characteristics of discourse markers and round off our discussion by treating
three such markers in greater detail, namely *now, you know* and *well*.

7.5.1 Discourse components

Schiffrin 1987 sees discourse as made up of five components: exchange structure, action structure, ideational structure, participation framework and information state. The first two components lie in the pragmatic area because S and H are centrally important in determining their organization. The units of the **exchange structure** are variously referred to as *turns* and *adjacency pairs* (see 7.4.1), or *moves* and *exchanges* (see 7.3.2 and 7.3.3). As we have seen, Ss and Hs negotiate whose turn it is and use signals to indicate the beginning and end of their contributions as well as their willingness to listen. **Action structure** is also non-linguistic because it emerges through (perlocutionary) acts, i.e. units which are realized by means of language but which are not themselves linguistic. This has to do, for example, with the sequence of acts, what actions are intended and what actions actually follow (see the distinction between *perlocutionary object* and *perlocutionary sequel* in 7.2.1).

The third dimension, **ideational structure**, consists of linguistic units, ideas, topics or propositions; it concerns the organization of discourse into these units and how they relate to each other.

The **participation framework**, the fourth component, refers to two different aspects. First, it concerns the ways in which S and H can relate to each other; hearers can, for example, be differentiated into those who are intended to receive a message (addressees) and those who are not (overhearers). It also encompasses the various social role relationships such as teacher–pupil, doctor–patient, shop assistant–customer, which influence the roles Ss and Hs can assume. Second, it refers to mode (or orientation), that is, the relations between Ss and utterances. This includes such aspects as whether Ss use direct or indirect speech acts to realize their meanings. Another aspect of S stance is the transition from the narration, or neutral presentation, of a story to its evaluation or interpretation.

Information state, the fifth component, concerns what Ss and Hs know (knowledge), and what they know about their respective knowledge (meta-knowledge). S and H information determines, to a large extent, how Ss shape their message and how Hs receive it. Knowledge and meta-knowledge are differentiated by degrees of certainty and of saliency or relevance. The function of discourse markers is to make the various levels explicit by integrating them to create coherent discourse, i.e. talk that is unified because it shows connections on the various discourse planes.

7.5.2 Discourse markers

Discourse markers such as *now, right, well, you know, you see, I mean* etc., share various features. First, they relate utterances to the **textual coordinates, participants** (speaker, hearer), on the one hand, and to the **text**, on the other. Markers refer either to preceding discourse (anaphoric reference) or to following discourse units (cataphoric) or to both. This reference function is called the **indexical function**. Second, markers appear at the boundaries of discourse units, but 'are not dependent on the smaller units of talk of which discourse is composed' (Schiffrin 1987:37). Schiffrin calls this the **sequential dependence** of markers and illustrates this aspect of the definition, for example, by pointing to combinations which are only acceptable at the discourse level. In 'Now these boys were

Table 7.1 Some discourse markers and their functions

	now	*you know*	*well*
Exchange structure		+	+
Action structure		+	*+
Ideational structure	*+	+	+
Participation framework	+	+	*+
Information state		*+	+

Note: the asterisk indicates the primary function (adapted from Schiffrin 1987: 316).

Irish. They lived different [sic]' (ibid.: 38), *now* cannot be a temporal adverbial, because that meaning of *now* cannot easily co-occur with the past tense. Discourse markers are thus independent of syntactic organization (i.e. they are not attached to sentences). Other features are: they are commonly used at the beginning of utterances; they show certain prosodic characteristics (e.g. tonic stress followed by a pause or phonological reduction); and they have no or only vague meaning, which allows them to function on different planes of discourse.

7.5.3 *Now*

The main function of *now* is in the ideational structure of discourse and consists in marking 'a speaker's progression through a discourse which contains an ordered sequence of subordinate parts' (Schiffrin 1987: 240). Comparisons, either explicit or implicit, completed or unfinished, and the expression of opinions are some of the larger structures in which *now* focuses on one of the subordinate parts:

- **Explicit comparison**: 'They used t'keep them trimmed. Now, for us to do that oh it's gotta be a hundred dollar bill!' (adapted from ibid.: 232).
- **Implicit comparison**: 'They have an open classroom at Lansdon. Now there's lots of the mothers in that room are very upset about it. I'm not' (ibid.: 234). Here the topic statement is absent (*parents feel quite differently about this new type of classroom*) in relation to which the *now*-utterance contains an implied comparison.
- **Opinion**: 'He was giving a spelling test. Now to me, if you're inviting parents t'come observe, y'don't give a spelling test!' (ibid.: 236). Here the S sets up a contrast between what she feels and what other people may feel, and this implicit comparison is introduced by *now*.

The other function of *now* relates to shifts in the participation framework, such as a change from statements to questions, or from narration to evaluation. *Now*, because of its cataphoric reference, is also used 'when the speaker needs to negotiate the right to control what will happen next in talk' (ibid.: 241). Tokens like *now listen to me and do what I tell you* show how Ss try to get back their turn at talk. *Now* also prefaces the most important move by the S in an argument, often indicating prior resistance to a command:

And my mother says, 'Now Jerry, and this is the God's honest truth, I'm not gonna hold no punches . . . I don't want you to marry that [girl] – and I want you to break it off right now.'

(adapted from ibid.: 243)

The last two examples show that *now* focuses on the S's next contribution to the discourse rather than on the H's reaction to it. This reflects the deictic use of *now* as a temporal adverb, which also expresses speaker nearness. In some cases *now* can display as many as three different shifts: in the ideational structure; in speaker orientation; and in the hearer/speaker footing, as in this example:

Henry: Value. Your sense of value is lost. Now you take your father's a dentist.

(ibid.: 244)

First, the ideational shift is here from general (*your sense of value is lost*) to specific (*you take your father*), with *now* focusing on the new item, the example. Second, S stance, and thereby the S–H relationship, changes from making a statement to involving the H in the assessment of this statement. Third, S moves from the declarative mood to the imperative, which implies a change in his attitude towards H.

7.5.4 *You know*

The basic function of *you know* derives from the meaning of the phrase. *Know* is a stative verb meaning 'have something in one's mind or memory'. *You* can either refer to the addressee or hearer, or it can have indefinite reference 'one, anyone, a person'. *You know* therefore marks meta-knowledge about either what speaker and hearer share or what is generally known.

Ss use *you know* to 'create a situation in which the speaker knows about . . . knowledge which is shared with the hearer' (Schiffrin 1987: 268). This is why the main function of *you know* lies in the information state. However, as *you know* often causes Hs to react, *you know* can also function in the action structure as an interactional marker. Schiffrin thinks that *you know* derives from *do you know*: it can therefore be regarded as the first part (question) of an adjacency pair, which sets up the strong expectancy of a second part. This is why it is marked in Table 7.1 as having a function in the participant framework and the exchange structure.

Jack: And when you're a cripple [. . .] they're cripples because they're so religious is what – is the point I'm trying to make. In other words they're sick. Religiously. Like the . . . you know what Hasidic is?

Debby: Umhmm.

Jack: The Hasidic Jew is a cripple in my eyes, a mental cripple.

(adapted from ibid.: 269)

This example clearly illustrates that it depends on the H whether the S has to provide information so that S and H share the same knowledge. As Debby has the information in question, Jack can go on and make his point.

In many other examples *you know* is used as a marker of general truths (*You know when you get older, you just don't keep socializing anymore*; ibid.: 277), which can take the form of fixed expressions such as proverbs, commonplaces etc. The appeal to shared knowledge is used to win confirmation of one's own point of view or to win over an opponent in an argument (see 3.7). With one exception all of Schiffrin's examples of the marker prefacing general truths show falling intonation while all cases, again with one exception, where the marker refers to what S and H share have rising intonation. Schiffrin concludes that rising intonation indicates that Ss are less certain about shared knowledge than falling intonation (see 4.5.3). This seems plausible because the more general a truth is, the greater the likelihood is that it is universally known.

Finally, the marker also functions in the ideational structure of discourse. *You know* causes Hs to focus on a particular piece of information (*Y'know what I like the best? I like the seashore area*; ibid.: 289). In storytelling *you know* helps Hs to focus either on what is important for the understanding of the point or on evaluations (*Like out of the clear blue sky!*; *Y'know they just have such an arrogant air about them!*; ibid.: 289). *You know* thus often 'focuses on the centrality of a single proposition for the overall idea structure of a text' (ibid.: 317).

7.5.5 *Well*

In contrast to *now* and *you know*, where the semantic content influences the function which the marker has, *well* has no meaning which could restrict its use to any one plane of discourse. Its primary function is in the participation framework: the main participant role it defines is that of the respondent in an exchange. It is particularly frequent in question-answer as well as request-compliance pairs.

Schiffrin has found that the syntactic form of questions influences the use of *well*. It is rare after *yes-no* questions and tag questions but more frequent after *wh*-questions, which give Ss a greater range of answer options. Another frequent use is in cases where Ss do not limit themselves to the options offered in questions, or where they delay the core of their answer. The following is an example of a complex deferral where Zelda uses a story to give an answer:

Debby: What happened?
Zelda: Well . . . at one time he was a very fine doctor. And he had two terrible tragedies. [story follows]

(ibid.: 110)

In general, *well* is used by Ss when they have difficulty finding an answer because what they want to say does not fit the explicit or implicit semantic options mentioned in the question. This is also the reason for the marker's use in request sequences, where it is more likely to be employed to mark non-compliance than compliance. Put differently, *well* prefaces a dispreferred second, such as an insufficient answer, denial or disagreement. Let us look at the five tokens of the discourse marker in the following extract:

B: So we'll have to try and do something about the allergy and get your rash cleared up first, won't we?

A: Well [1], can you prescribe [. . .] anything for the allergy [. . .]?
B: Does it itch at all?
A: Yes, it itches quite a lot.
B: Do you get scabs forming on it or anything?
A: No.
B: Hm hum [. . .]. It's just on your face, is it?
A: And my arms.
B: And your arms. Is it on any other place of the body?
A: Well [2], it's spreading, yeah.
B: Hm hm (begins writing)
A: All over.
B: And is it painful at all?
A: Well [3], only – well [4] if I scratch it, yes, it becomes very painful.
B: [. . .] Well [5], I think I can prescribe some ointment for you . . .

(adapted from Edmondson 1981: 182–3)

A's first *well* prefaces an answer which does not consist of a simple *yes* or *no* and also demonstrates a lack of appreciation of B's contribution, perhaps even resentment of the *we* often used by doctors: it is not *we*, but the doctor whom A expects to do something about his rash. The context for the second use is again a contrast between B's question (*any other place*) and A's answer, which informs B that the rash has in fact spread all over his or her body. *Well* can be viewed, both here and in the first use, as a means of softening disagreement or deferring an embarrassing answer. This seems to apply also to the third and fourth tokens. But, more importantly, the fourth illustrates the use of the discourse marker in contexts where it introduces responses not to another participant's utterance but to one's own. Self-repairs are thus signals of a shift in speaker orientation and belong the participation framework.

The tokens discussed so far are all placed in contributions immediately next to the utterance which solicited them. This is different for the fifth token, which looks back to the beginning and answers A's first question, a request for a prescription. This second major use of *well* is in the action structure: put in interactional terms, *well* functions in head exchanges which are preceded by a number of pre-responding exchanges. Another non-local use of *well* has already been mentioned (see 7.3.2): *well* can bridge the business and closing phases of an encounter. *Well* has therefore functions at both the local level of the exchange or adjacency pair and the global level of discourse phases.

7.6 FURTHER READING

See Schiffrin 1994 for a critical assessment. For **conversational texts** see: Crystal and Davy 1975; Svartvik and Quirk 1980; Cheepen and Monaghan 1990; Carter and McCarthy 1997; and Eggins and Slade 1997. For **comprehensive treatments** see: Brown and Yule 1983; Coulthard 1985; van Dijk 1985; McCarthy 1991; Martin 1992; Schiffrin 1994; Eggins and Slade 1997. On **communicative competence** see Hymes 1972. On typical **hearer roles** and their linguistic realization see Gardner 1994. **Speech acts** are dealt with in: Austin 1962; Searle 1969; Grice 1975; Leech 1983; Levinson 1983; de Souza Filho 1985; Flowerdew 1988. On **indirectness** see Thomas 1995, Chapters 2, 5 and 6. For

politeness see: Leech 1983; Brown and Levinson 1987;Thomas 1995. On **stories** see: Cheepen and Monaghan 1990; Coates 1996; Eggins and Slade 1997; on **closings**: Schegloff and Sacks 1973; on **turn-taking** see Sacks, Schegloff and Jefferson 1974. For **global knowledge patterns** see: Schank and Abelson 1977; Johnson-Laird 1983; van Dijk and Kintsch 1983; and on **discourse markers** Schiffrin 1987. On **relevance** (Grice's maxim number three) see Sperber and Wilson 1995.

Chapter 8

Modes of address, power, solidarity and politeness

Language use can reflect the social and linguistic background of its speakers and addressees, be it the gender of the participants (see Chapter 9), or their age, status, education, regional background, race, religion or whatever. It will also reflect aspects of the situation in which that language is used, be it a special English (see Chapter 6), or the emotional content, number of participants, or nature and purpose of the occasion. As a central indicator of social relations between people language use also reveals relations of power and of solidarity and serves as a vehicle for politeness in our behaviour towards others. One of the most illuminating ways to show the multiplicity of factors involved is to observe how people address each other.

There are two very prominent aspects to address. The first is the speaker's evaluation of the addressee (and situation), on the one hand, and what we can learn about the speaker's social background as revealed in his or her use of a particular form of address, on the other. The second aspect is linguistic and systematic, namely what forms of address the language makes available to its users, for example, what second person pronouns are available. We will look first at the types of elements involved in the system of address and then to exemplify the ways in which the major social categories listed in the first paragraph may be observed in the way people address one another.

8.1 THE LINGUISTIC ELEMENTS OF ADDRESS IN ENGLISH

The forms of address of English include the pronouns used in the second person and vocative forms. The former offer very little variation in comparison with other languages, being largely restricted to *you*; the latter carry the burden of social differentiation. Pronouns themselves are divided, on the one hand, into those which are syntactically **bound**, that is, those which carry a syntactic function such as subject or object. On the other hand, there are syntactically **unbound** pronouns, which are used as vocatives. Since **vocatives** are not integrated into the structure of the clause, they have variable word order: they may precede, follow or interrupt a clause. They also have separate intonation. Furthermore, there are some grammatical restrictions on them. For example, they may not contain a definite article, e.g. **Come here, the friend*. Nor can they include any (unbound) personal pronouns other then the second person, **Hey them, come here*; indefinite pronouns, however, do occur in vocatives, e.g. *Hey everyone, come here*.

There are a number of word forms which are exclusively vocative in the sense that they cannot also be used as syntactically bound forms (i.e. subjects and objects). This is especially true of common nouns without an article, such as *captain, professor, son* etc. as well as specifically vocative forms such as *sir* and *ma'am/madam* and the M-forms, *mister, missus* and *miss* (not to be confused with the titles *Mr, Mrs, Miss, Ms,* see below). Some (especially) BrE speakers, however, treat *captain, miss* etc. as proper names; in such cases the word form without an article may also occur as a non-vocative, e.g. *Captain says you are to come immediately.* Vocatives may be divided up into five distinct classes: pronouns, names, kinship terms, titles and descriptors.

Pronouns   For all intents and purposes English has only one second person pronoun, *you.* Only in the reflexive (*yourself, yourselves*) is the singular and plural differentiated, but reflexives are not very frequent forms. The regional plural *you all* (especially American South) is convenient but not consistently used and dialectal forms like *youse* or colloquial ones like *you guys, you fellows, you people* etc. are restricted stylistically. And in no case does GenE distinguish between a polite and a familiar singular form on the model of French *vous* and *tu,* Italian *Lei* and *tu,* German *Sie* and *du,* Russian *vy* and *ty* or Spanish *Usted(es)* and *tu.* The historical second person singular form *thou* is no longer in use in current StE (but see 8.3.7 and 8.3.8). The linguistic system provides, in other words, for no socially meaningful pronoun choices but this does not mean that the language cannot express differences in politeness, respect, intimacy etc.

A minor possibility of bound address in English is by means of the third person. This does not involve pronouns, but is restricted to honorifics and titles like *your excellency, your highness* etc. or *colonel* (e.g. *Does Your Honour wish me to continue?*). Kachru gives the following IndE example with the term *huzoor,* which is reserved for superiors: *Would huzoor like to sleep in the veranda?* (1966: 273). In the military, third person address is also common in formal situations when addressing a superior officer, e.g. *May I have the General's indulgence for a few minutes?* (Jonz 1975: 73).

Pronouns are then, as might be expected, of minor importance. Really the main contrast here is between *you* and no pronoun at all, as in *Hey you, watch out!* vs *Hey, watch out!* The use of *you* without the introductory *hey* in the example above to soften its effect would be considerably more direct and therefore less polite (e.g. the same sentence with rude *You there*). The use of vocative *you* is, consequently, infrequent. It is the noun vocative (names, kinship terms, titles and descriptors) which bear the burden of making social distinctions.

Names   As forms of address there are the following common types of names: the full form of a first name (FN), *Stephen, Elizabeth*; familiar forms, *Steve, Liz*; diminutive forms, *Stevie, Lizzie*; nicknames, *Tiger, Bunny*; and last names (LN), *Smith, Windsor.* LN alone is not a particularly common form of address. It seems to be used chiefly among men, particularly in the military (Jonz 1975: 74) and in British public schools. The diminutives include phonetic-morphological variations on names, *Stevio, Lizzikins.*

This final point is impressively illustrated for AusE, for which there is a sizable list of suffixes including {-y}, {-o}, {-a}, {-s}, {-ers}, {-kin}, {-le}, {-poo}, {-pops} as well as multiple suffixing *Bobbles* {-le + -s}, *Katiekins* {-y + -kin + -s}, *Albertipoo* {-y + -poo}, *Mikeypoodles* {-y + -poo + -le + -s}. However, it is not possible to combine just anything: {-kin(s)} cannot follow on a /k/ (**Mikekins*) and {-y} cannot be appended to a vowel (*Di-y). The {-o} suffix is only masculine; furthermore, most suffixes to male names are monosyllabic. The suffix {-y} is usually restricted to children's names (exceptions: *Terry, Tony*); forms like *Jimmy* will, as a rule, be used for adult males only by their mothers and girlfriends or for teasing. In addition, there is 'a phenomenon regarded by many as peculiarly Australian, but not in fact limited to Australia, . . . the truncated forms of certain names whose initial syllable is open and whose second syllable commonly begins with *r*' (Poynton 1989: 62). Here the shortened form closes with <z>, producing forms like *Baz* from *Barry*, *Shaz* (see also BrE, with the variant *Shazzer*) from *Sharon* and *Taz* from *Terence* or *Teresa* (ibid.: 61–4). A related case is BrE *Chas* from *Charles* or *Gaz* from *Gary*.

Multiple naming refers to a practice in which people move freely from one form to another, whether first names, full or familiar, nicknames or last names. This seems to indicate a great deal of intimacy.

Generic names, i.e. ones applicable to any male regardless of his actual name, e.g. *bud/buddy, mack*, or *jack*, are applied to a few limited vocations, such as taxi drivers, or to express belligerent feelings; they can also be used as markers of masculine solidarity, as what might be called **camaraderie forms** (see 8.3.5).

Kinship terms   A kinship term (KT) may function as a name or as a title. *Grandmother, father* and diminutives of them, *Granny, Dad*, are used as names (notice that they are always capitalized in this use). Some KTs may combine with a name in the manner of a title, e.g. *Aunt Liz, Uncle Steve, Granma Brown*. Generally KT's are used upwardly only, from a younger towards an older relative; however, older and rural usage may sometimes include *cousin* + FN.

Titles   This type of vocative is probably most often used with a last name (T + LN = TLN). Titles may be classed as vocational (*Dr, Prof., Senator* etc.), as ranks in the military or police (*Lt, Capt., Gen., Constable, Officer, Sheriff* etc.), or as religious (*Father, Brother, Sister, Mother Superior*). Most common, however, are the M-forms (*Mr, Mrs, Miss, Ms, Master*), which are generic 'titles' applicable to anyone within the bounds of conventions regarding age, gender and marital status.

Although these titles, as vocatives, are usually combined with LN (sometimes with FN alone; see below 'Region' and 'Age'), most of them can be used alone. However, not all of them can stand alone, for example *Pope (instead of Your Holiness)*, *King (for Your Majesty)*, *Representative (for Congressman, Congresswoman)*. Quite a number of these titles have alternative vocative forms, for example, a more informal *Judge* next to the distinctly formal courtroom *Your Honour*, or similarly *Prince* next to *Your Highness*. The M-forms, *Mr* and *Mrs*, are used without LN only in relatively restricted circumstances (and then they are spelled out in writing): *Mister* sounds rude by itself; *Missus*, uncultivated. Instead, it is usual to hear the polite forms *sir* and *ma'am* (or the more formal *madam*, especially in BrE).

Descriptors   **Descriptors**, the final category of vocatives, are forms of address which, as the term suggests, contain an element of description. Among these there are numerous general terms for males only (*buddy, chum, fellow, mate, old bean, pal* etc.), some for females only (*babe, sister, toots*, e.g. the movie *Tootsie*) and some for both (e.g. plural *folks, guys* and *people*). Besides these there are thing designations for people such as *taxi* or *room service* as well as vocations and functions (e.g. *waiter, operator, nurse* etc.), sometimes even prefixed by an M-form as in a note with the salutation *Dear Mr Milkman* or the traditional parliamentary address *Mr Chairman* or *Madam Chairman* (see also *Mr/Madam President* or *Mr/Madam Secretary*). Furthermore, there are numerous vocative terms of insult such as *stupid, jackass, dolt* etc., on the one hand, and terms of endearment, on the other, such as *dear, honey, darling* etc. These latter two categories allow further lexical subclassification. Most prominent are animal terms of endearment, some masculine, some feminine, some either (*bear, tiger, kitten, puppy, ladybird* etc.) and of insult (*dog, swine, bitch, minx, vixen* etc.). National and ethnic names used as vocatives are almost always insults (*nigger, Paddy, wog, wop, Yank, Brit* [perceived by 'Brits' as insulting though hardly meant that way by non-Brits], *yid* etc.). Numerous insulting vocatives are tabooed; not only the ones just listed, but also obscene and scatological terms of address, e.g. *ass(hole), bastard, cunt, dyke* etc.

8.2 POWER, SOLIDARITY AND POLITENESS

The use of the wealth of vocatives available in English depends on a wide variety of features of the users, both of the speaker and the addressee as well as the situation of use. Before these are characterized more closely, let us make a summary of some of the general principles which lie behind the use of forms of address.

8.2.1 Power, solidarity and reciprocal use

Vocatives indicate the nature of relationships between people. Of primary importance is whether the terms are used reciprocally or non-reciprocally. **Reciprocal** forms indicate some kind of equality, and often solidarity, while **non-reciprocal** ones indicate an imbalance in power or prestige. Examples of non-reciprocal relationships are parent–child, in which a parent is given KT (*Mom, Dad*), but gives FN (*Steve, Liz*). Another example is teacher ↔ student, which typically has TLN ↔ FN. This dimension is called the **power semantic**.

Reciprocal dyads (a **dyad** is a pair of participants interacting with each other) are common within a status group. Children, students, fellow workers are all likely to exchange mutual first names (FN ↔ FN). However, there is also the possibility of mutual TLN ↔ TLN when people who are not well acquainted with each other interact, say employees from different departments in a large firm or military officers. Reciprocal relations are examples of what is called the **solidarity semantic**. Just how the power and the solidarity semantics are applied varies by region/nation and according to the status, education, vocation, age, sex, race, religion, ideology and kinship of speaker and addressee. Furthermore, they reflect the situation of use.

8.2.2 Politeness

Politeness is a category which is closely related to power and solidarity, but is not to be equated with either of these. Politeness is oriented according to what is called 'face'. This can be positive face, as when we offer our addressee support by emphasizing our admiration for something accomplished or possessed or for the way the person addressed appears (clothing, hair, behaviour). Positive face is supposed to *make the hearer feel good*. Under the perspective of negative face we refrain from intruding on the other or limit our intrusion by using mitigating linguistic expressions, for example, the indirectness mentioned in 5.4.2. Power-driven politeness and solidarity-driven politeness can both can be realized by positive or negative face. Many of the non-reciprocal, power-driven forms of address which we look at in this chapter are determined by the power norms of society (including slurs and derogatory epithets). This covers the *sir*'s and *ma'am*'s as well as the *ass*'s and *idiot*'s of much of our social interaction.

The second type of politeness, which is solidarity-driven, makes use of positive hedges, boosters and compliments, and is also found in the negative politeness strategies of apology. Women practise positive politeness by intensifying their interest in the hearer via the use of tag questions, words signalling group identity and negative politeness by practising disagreement avoidance. Men's politeness is more restricted to patterns of negative face, which means they seek to minimize imposition (Brown and Levinson 1978). Men are more often task-oriented, giving opinions, providing information, disagreeing; they are interested in maintaining status. Women, on the other hand, want to maintain respectability, and they display socio-emotional behaviour, dramatizing, agreeing, showing tension. Empirical studies indicate that men use politeness strategies much less than women (in a variety of languages and situations) (Talbot 1998: 91). We will illustrate this by looking more closely at one of these areas, compliment behaviour, which functions in a manner similar to forms of address.

Both power and social distance play a role in how people pay compliments. Basically, compliments are examples of positive face, but how they come across depends on the power relationship between complimenter and receiver. 'That's really good' when used from a teacher to a student differs from when used between two equals. It is praise when it comes from a superior, but between equals it is an expression of friendship and solidarity. In other words, a compliment may be used to assert power over the recipient, even if not meant this way. 'It is possible to interpret a compliment as a patronizing "put-down"' (Talbot 1998: 92). In such a case it may even take on the character of a **face threatening act (FTA)**, and it seems that men are more likely, perhaps because of their socialization in terms of hierarchy, to be wary of compliments as assertions of power. This may help us to understand gender differences better (see Chapter 9). Men in general and American men in particular engage in complimenting behaviour far less than women, and when they do so, the nature of their compliments differs from that of women. First of all, men seldom pay compliments to other men, perhaps because of their potential FTA nature. Compliments are, for most men, expressions of praise, and praise is evaluation, and evaluation implies power. In hierarchical situations people pay compliments more rarely, and those who pay them are the more powerful. However, 'it is not *only* men who can interpret compliments as threatening or patronizing, as any woman will attest who has been congratulated for successfully parking her car' (Talbot 1998: 93).

The second way of using compliments is as an expression of solidarity. 'Holmes found that by far the largest proportion of compliments were between people of equal status' (ibid.: 94). As instruments of social solidarity compliments are almost exclusively female. Males pay compliments in AmE less frequently and use them less often to negotiate social relations. Female AmE compliments are produced more as tokens of good will. They elicit a lot of history type responses from other women (e.g. where something comes from), which makes them conversational. Male compliments elicit mere acceptance (e.g. *Thanks*), which is less satisfying conversationally (Herbert 1998: 72).

Is this to say that men cannot express solidarity? Certainly not, but while compliments are an important strategy for showing solidarity among women, men resort more to sparring and criticizing. Competitive mock verbal insults are widely practised by men, often in a ritualized manner, for instance the insulting vocative the villain, Trampas, addresses to the hero, the Virginian in the following:

> It was now the Virginian's turn to bet, or leave the game, and he did not speak at once.
> Therefore Trampas spoke. 'Your bet, you son-of-a____.'
> The Virginian's pistol came out, and his hand lay on the table, holding it unaimed. And with a voice as gentle as ever, the voice that sounded almost like a caress, but drawling a very little more than usual, so that there was almost a space between each word, he issued his orders to the man Trampas:
> 'When you call me that, *smile*!' And he looked at Trampas across the table.
> Yes, the voice was gentle. But in my ears it seemed as if somewhere the bell of death was ringing; and silence, like a stroke, fell on the large room.
>
> (Owen Wister (1902) *The Virginian*, New York:
> Macmillan, pp. 28–9)

This is certainly not polite behaviour; it is clearly a matter of power. But had it been said with a *smile*, the matter might have been different. While insults hardly seem to qualify as polite behaviour, they often have much the same effect as compliments do among women: they may be perceived as friendly signals which create or express solidarity. 'This presents an intriguing mirror image of the pattern Holmes found about women . . . Men are threatened by compliments, but use insults to cement friendship' (Talbot 1998: 97).

8.3 DOMAINS OF MODES OF ADDRESS

We now return to examples of the use of address, but we always with the underlying dimensions of power and solidarity and the strategies and conventions of politeness in mind.

8.3.1 Nation

Britain and the United States   If we abstract from the great variety of user characteristics (status, age, sex, race etc.), we find that the AmE address system is basically a two term system: either FN or TLN. The latter includes KT as a form of title. Non-reciprocality is the rule across generations within the family with the older generation receiving KT (*Granma*) or KT + FN (*Uncle Steve*) from the younger generation and giving FN in return. Likewise, teacher ↔ student is TLN ↔ FN; often boss ↔ employee is TLN ↔ FN as well.

Adults are frequently introduced with mutual TLN, but the switch to mutual FN is rapid, especially among the young and where the dyads are of the same sex. In many familiar or informal situations introductions are in the form of mutual FN + LN and are followed by immediate use of FN ↔ FN. In cases of doubt, no naming is a common strategy. The following precepts offer general guidelines. One may readily use FN with everyone except: with an adult (if one is an unrelated child); with an older adult (if one is markedly younger); with a teacher (if one is a student); with a clergyman or religious person (particularly Roman Catholic and Orthodox); with a physician (Hook 1984: 186).

Despite the impression that outsiders might have, FN does not necessarily indicate intimacy; it is simply a feature of American society. In fact, to refuse FN could be interpreted as unfriendly or snobby. 'First names are required among people who work closely together, even though they may not like each other at all' (Wardhaugh 1986: 260). For intimacy, either nicknames or multiple naming is employed in AmE. In BrE the pattern is generally similar although the move from mutual TLN to mutual FN may proceed at a slower pace, or may require some special formula, as in 'Dear Steven and Mike (if I may)', which was the address used to the present writers by an unacquainted British colleague. The 'bonhomie' connected with instant first naming is still regarded by some people in England as very American.

University use   There are some BrE–AmE contexts in which there are differences. Ervin-Tripp mentions a three option system in connection with British universities in which T (*Dr*, *Prof.*) + LN is used for most deference, the M-forms (MLN) as an intermediate stage and only then FN. In addition, males may engage in mutual last naming (without a title or M-form); such male LN ↔ LN is also practised at some private schools (1974: 274f.).

In North American universities one study shows that there is little use of overt address between professors (= teaching staff) and students at all; when there is any, TLN is used to the professors and FN address is rare: 'More than one informant spoke of the need to avoid expressing intimacy which does not exist, or indicated that such expression would be inappropriate so long as the student–teacher relationship pertains' (McIntire 1972: 290). Where there is movement to addressing a professor by his or her FN, the initiation does not come, as expected, only from the more powerful or superior, but in most cases from the inferior. The most important factor is age. Older male graduate students are the ones most likely to initiate FN with their professors and then more easily with professors under 40 (ibid.: 289). A later study reveals that students, especially female ones, addressed young female professors (aged 26–33) by FN more often than they did their male teachers (Rubin 1981: 966). There were also some differences in the use of TLN. Male students preferred M-forms and *Dr* + LN while women students preferred *Prof.* + LN for male professors. For female professors women students used M-forms and *Dr* + LN most often while male students used M-forms + LN or FN. 'Thus, female students seem to be affording more status to their male professors' (ibid.: 970).

Australia   The AusE use of address follows the same general lines as in AmE or BrE. FN has been widely adopted without necessarily implying equality or solidarity.

> Sellers of cars and real estate assume the social utility of addressing potential buyers by personal name [i.e. FN], while the would-be Don Juan who uses diminutive forms to newly-met potential bedfellows can be seen as preparing the ground for physical intimacy by decreasing social distance linguistically.
>
> (Poynton 1989: 57)

India   Countries such as India, where English is used as a second language, provide a real contrast. IndE, for example, uses forms of address which come from the non-native use of English in the context of Indian culture (Kachru 1966: 268).

> It is customary in Indian languages to avoid the use of the second person pronoun in favour of some honorific title when face to face interaction occurs between a person and his menial servant or someone of similar low status. In *Train to Pakistan* [by Khushwant Singh (1956), p. 77] a bearer addressing his boss says: 'Sahib's bed has not been laid yet . . . would huzoor like to sleep on the Verandah.'
>
> (Mehrotra 1989: 431f.)

Such third person address may be by kinship terms: *chacha, bhaiji, beybey*; name: *Juggat Singji, Jugga, Juggia*; occupation (with or without honorific): *bairah, lambardara, brother policeman, magistrate sahib*; but also by words of abuse: *you swine, ass, bastard*; or interjection: *oye* (ibid.: 429). Special terms are used to express social relations such as master–servant and age–youth. While these relations exist in native speaker English language societies (however attenuated they may appear), the further vocatives below, given according to several important social categories, are specific to IndE (Kachru 1966):

caste: pandit, thakur, jamadar;
profession: havaldar, inspector (sahib);
honorific: babu sahib, huzoor, government, king of pearls (Mehrotra 1989: 429). Note: *babu* or *baboo*: 'A term of respect used frequently in the north of India. In the south of India it is used as equivalent to *sir, your honour*' (Kachru 1966);
religion: khwaja, pandit, sardar;
kinship: brother-in-law, mother, sister, grandmother, father. Note: 'A term restricted to the kinship system of a [particular] language may be used with extended meaning in another culture and transferred to an L2' (ibid.: 272). Hence IndE has '*mother* as a term of respect, *sister* of regard and *father-in-law* in the sense of abuse. *Bhai* ("brother") is used for any male of equal age, *father* for all elder persons and an uncle may be referred to as *father*' (ibid.: 273f.);
superiority: cherisher of the poor, king of pearls, huzoor, ma-bap ('mother-father'), friend of the poor;
neutral: babu-sahib, bhai, master, dada (male), didi (female), sab.

Singapore   Differences in forms of address transferred to English may also be illustrated by the usage of polite forms in Singapore English. Polite reference (not address) is via T + FN + LN (*Mr Arthur Orton*), but if well known T + FN (*Mr Arthur*). A woman who is unmarried is, for example, *Miss Tan Mei Ling* [*Tan* = LN]. If she marries Mr Lim Keng Choon [*Lim* = LN], she has three options: she may be called *Mrs Lim Keng Choon* (rarely) or *Mrs Lim Mei Ling* or *Madam Tan Mei Ling*. Quite obviously, 'the conventions governing naming and forms of address in Malay, Chinese and Indian languages are quite different from those in English' (Tongue 1974: 104).

Nigeria   In Nigeria, finally, KT's may be used as they are in the West, but they may also be applied to the polygynous family, so that children of one father may address his several wives all as *mother*. Furthermore, *Father/Daddy* and *Mother/Mommy* are also used for distant relations or even unrelated people who are treated with deference and are of the appropriate age. 'Immediate bosses in their places of work get addressed as either *Daddy* or *Mommy* by subordinate young officers' (Akere 1982: 96). A further difference in modes of address in Nigerian English is that TLN is often reduced to simple T; the M-forms, including the Muslim title *Malam*, can be used for direct address without the LN. Furthermore, multiple titles are also used, e.g. *Chief Doctor Mrs* + LN (ibid.), a practice which is rare in GenE.

8.3.2 Region

Only a few examples of differences in usage due to regional factors will be mentioned. One relatively significant difference concerns the southern United States, where the use of *ma'am* and *sir* is particularly common. In the South the usage balance between *ma'am* and endearments such as *honey* or *dear* in what are called service encounters (e.g. at gas stations, stores etc.) is 83.1 per cent to 16.9 per cent while in the northeast it is 24.5 per cent to 75.5 per cent for equivalent types of speakers (Wolfson and Manes 1980: 82f.). *Ma'am* may even be used seriously (and not jokingly or ironically) among intimates. Indeed, it is so general in the South that it can be considered formulaic and, therefore, not necessarily to convey respect. It may even indicate people's momentary attitudes as people may omit it when they feel annoyance. 'In general, however, the use of *ma'am* does indicate that the addressee is either of higher status or older than the speaker' (ibid.: 85).

Note that *ma'am* and *sir* are not used just as forms of address in the South. For one thing 'the single term *ma'am* [and *sir*], with rising intonation, can indicate that the speaker has not heard or understood what was said'; it is equivalent to saying *Pardon?*. In addition, a use of '*ma'am* [and *sir*] which is specific to the south is the phrase "yes, ma'am" which function[s] as a variant of "you're welcome"' (Wolfson and Manes 1980: 84).

Finally, note the colloquial, especially southern and western AmE use of emphatic *yessir* or *yessiree* to signal agreement.

A further aspect of address in the American South is the use of T + FN. This usage is regarded as quaint or old-fashioned outside the South, but it offers a compromise between intimacy and respect for its users. Inasmuch as it is a relict of the older racially tainted master/mistress–servant dyad with TFN ↔ FN (e.g. the film *Driving Miss Daisy*), it is certainly not acceptable to most people today. Where it exists independent of race it may be viable (President Carter's mother was widely known and addressed as *Miz Lillian*).

Other regional differences which are frequently encountered are ones involving the use of regionally marked descriptors. For example, *lass* is found most frequently in northern England and Scotland; *guv'nor* is Cockney; *stranger* or *partner* are stereotypical for the American West.

8.3.3 Status, education and vocation

There is frequently a general, though not absolute, correlation between level of educa-tion, prestige of vocation and power of status. Where these factors do not correlate, it is generally the case that vocational status (achieved status) tends to override attributed status, including age. However, age is usually a powerful predictor of non-reciprocal relationships. Hence in the business world the higher someone's position, the more likely they are to receive TLN and the more likely they are to give FN. In cases of mutual FN it is the more highly placed person who will probably allow a switch either from non-reciprocity or from mutual TLN to FN ↔ FN. For purposes of 'team spirit' superordinates may permit wide liberties otherwise not tolerated from their subordinates.

It is worth mentioning that there is more to deference than the choice of a respectful form of address. The type of salutation (*Hi!* to intimates and subordinates, but *Good morning* to superiors), or the use of touch (superior to subordinate, not vice versa) are two further examples. Furthermore, a businessman can ask an elevator operator about his/her children, but not vice versa. Some titles allow a compromise position between deference and intimacy, so the use of *Skipper* to a marine captain or *Doc* by an attendant to a physician.

8.3.4 Age

After status, age is the most potent factor in determining address relationships. It may mitigate the effect of status, and it is also crucial to the use of KT's, where the older generation receives KT or KT + FN (*Granma, Aunt Lizzie*), but gives FN. Age differ-ences seem to be meaningful if they are approximately 15 years or more. If they are less, FN ↔ FN seems to be no problem (unless there are major status distinctions). Even a KT will probably be dispensed with where, for example, aunts and uncles are of much the same age as their nieces and nephews. A compromise form (England, the American South) for an old servant to the son or daughter of an employer is M + FN.

While there is only the single deference form *sir* for men, there are two for women, *miss* and *ma'am* (not counting the formal and infrequent variant *madam*). Young women receive *ma'am* if well dressed (status!); otherwise, *miss*. Women over 30 are more likely to get *ma'am* than *miss* from men (Kramer 1975: 204). There still is a special M-form, *Master*, which is sometimes used in postal addresses when writing to young boys.

8.3.5 Gender

Address directed to men and women is far from equivalent. In service encounters (stores, public services, hospitals) women direct endearments (*sweetheart, honey, dear, love* etc.) to women who are total strangers more frequently than to men; men also address women in this way, but they may never do so to other men. With the exception of female sales personnel the use of endearments towards a man on the part of a woman is likely to be perceived as a sexual advance. Endearments by men to women in service encounters, on the other hand, are, for some men, their standard form of address; for others it seems to be a way of putting women down, of showing 'the customer to be somewhat less than totally competent' (Wolfson and Manes 1980: 89). A further indication that women are treated as incompetent or immature is that 'women are addressed as *girls* very much more frequently than men are addressed as *boys* and when men are so addressed it is usually in contexts where they are relaxing, not playing serious adult roles' (Poynton 1989: 59).

Camaraderie forms   What men can receive from total strangers instead of endearments are camaraderie forms such as *buddy, buster, mac* etc. All of these, as designations of manliness, show male solidarity when supplied by other males; women are hardly likely to use such forms towards men since they are 'rough' terms (and not 'sweet' ones) and are therefore reserved for men.

When endearments and camaraderie forms as well as the deference forms *ma'am* and *sir* are used in service encounters, they are seldom reciprocal. However, it is not alone the gender of the members of the dyads which is decisive; it is also nearly always a question of role relationships. It is almost exclusively the service giver who uses a vocative. Cases in which the person being served is the one who uses a vocative are restricted to *sir* and *ma'am* from persons seeking help from public agencies (the police, health services, welfare bureaus). Furthermore, endearments and camaraderie forms, on the one hand, and the deference forms *ma'am* and *sir*, on the other, stand in complementary distribution to each other inasmuch as both are not used together by the same speaker in a single situation. What determines which will be employed depends on both social and individual aspects of the service giver. The status of the institution in which the encounter takes place reflects the former: in 'classy' establishments the deference forms are used towards the customers, patients or clients unless the addressee is sufficiently young or obviously lacking in status. The latter, individual factor may be related to the relative egalitarianism of the service provider: many people (outside regions such as the American South) find the deference forms hard to use. Hence if they use any vocatives at all to strangers, these will be endearments or camaraderie forms.

The area of sex also supplies the vocatives of strongest abuse; what is said of AusE in the following quotation is true of AmE and BrE as well, though the specific terms employed may vary:

> Among the potentially most seriously insulting terms of address in Australian English are those impugning the heterosexual identity of males (such as *poofter, fag*), those attributing promiscuous sexual behavior to women (*moll, tart*) and identifying males or females (but particularly insulting when directed at males) in terms of female genitalia (*cunt*).
>
> (Poynton 1989: 60)

Semantic inversion   Males have a richer inventory of terms including the {-o} suffix to names, the camaraderie terms and the possibility of semantic inversion, i.e. using insulting terms to each other as a sign of solidarity. For example they may greet one another with an insult such as jovial, *Well, you old son of a bitch, I haven't seen you for at least a year!* There are, in contrast, no exclusively female morphological forms and no generic camaraderie names for women, with hardly any ritual inversion, but many more endearments.

Fun naming **Fun naming**, which has nothing to do with a person's real name, also expresses solidarity and is practised by both males and females. It takes the form of appellations which rhyme with the last syllables of routine formulae or particular key words. Examples include the venerable *See you later, alligator* to which the standard response is *In a while, crocodile*, but also *I'll be back, Jack*; *Alright, Dwight*; *No way, José; That's the truth, Ruth*; or *Here's the money, honey*.

8.3.6 Race and ethnicity

Differences in address based on racial or ethnic identity are highly ostracized today, yet there is little doubt that insulting epithets (*Chink, Jap, nigger, spick* etc.) are often used. Similarly, some older non-reciprocal usage can still be heard in the American South, where Blacks once regularly received FN and where black men were addressed as *boy* (a practice once common in many parts of the English speaking world for non-Whites), but where Blacks had to give TLN or, perhaps, the more intimate form TFN. Even today continuing status differences often insure that Blacks give, but do not receive, *sir* and *ma'am* when dealing with Whites. A variation on this is the use of generic names for members of an ethnic group in situations of powerlessness, as when a male Mexican or Chicano migrant worker in California is addressed as *Pedro* or an Irishman in England as *Paddy* or *Mick*.

8.3.7 Religion and ideology

The field of religious language is the only one in which the obsolete second person singular pronoun *thou* is still used by non-dialect speakers of GenE. Note that some dialect speakers in the British Isles and some Quaker fellowships still use parts of the old second person singular forms in addressing some people. People invoke God with it, above all in liturgical language and in the still popular King James (Authorized) Version of the Bible, e.g. *Our Father which art in heaven, Hallowed be thy name* (Matthew 6: 9).

Vocatives specific to religious groups include, in particular, the KT's *Father* for God and for priests, *Brother* and *Sister* for members of religious orders and *Mother (Superior)* for heads of female orders. In the Roman Catholic Church these KT's may be followed by FN in the case of *Brother* and *Sister* and by LN in the case of *Father*. In many Protestant bodies fellow members are addressed with their LN preceded by *Brother* or *Sister*. Blessings may be addressed to a *son, daughter* or *child*, the faithful being regarded as the children of God. See also the religious terms used in IndE above.

Ideological fellowships of a non-religious sort may also use special terms of address, be they any one of numerous lodges with a variety of titles, or members of trade unions and socialist or communist groups, who use the term *comrade*, either by itself or before a LN.

8.3.8 Literature

Special features of the literary use of address is the old-fashioned no longer productive use of *thou*, e.g. *Shall I compare thee to a summer's day* (Shakespeare, Sonnet 18) and the vocative *o* or *oh* in poetry which is still read, e.g. *O Love, if death be sweeter, let me die* (Tennyson, 'Elaine's Song' from *The Princess*).

8.3.9 Kinship

The basic system of giving FN name to the same or a younger generation and giving KT or KT + FN to an older one influences practice in non-kinship areas (see above 'Religion'), perhaps because family is so basic to interpersonal relations. It is worth remarking, however, that its customary practice is not immutable, for many parents who consider themselves progressive encourage and accept FN from their children. This may be part of the general trend towards the suppression of asymmetric (non-reciprocal) relations which can be observed throughout the Western world. On the other hand, many mothers assert authority or express an uncompromising attitude by reverting from FN, diminutive or similar to FN + LN or even first, second and last name (FN + SN + LN).

In addition, many children learn to address unrelated friends of their parents as *Aunt/Uncle* + FN. Furthermore, older people, especially men, patronizingly address boys and young men as *son* or *sonnie*; *son* is also used by rank superiors in the military towards the lower enlisted ranks. While *sis* is a friendly, informal term used between sisters, *sissy* derived from *sister*, has become an insult directed to boys who do not show the degree of masculine behaviour which their peers expect of them.

8.4 SITUATION OF USE

The pragmatics of address, i.e. why people use vocatives in the first place, obviously involves deixis, i.e. the singling out of one or more addressees within a larger group; but it is influenced by the choice of a particular form which may indicate solidarity or power. Yet, factors in the communicative situation may be decisive. While titles and deference forms may serve to flatter an addressee or to insinuate the user into the addressee's good graces, how a student and a professor address each other may be very different in and outside of class. Officers of differing rank may stick strictly to TLN or at least to title alone while on duty, especially in the presence of either senior officers or enlisted men, but use mutual FN in their private quarters; when under fire all or almost all distinctions fall (Jonz 1975: 70, 75).

It might be mentioned here that, beyond deixis, the decision to use any vocative at all has to do with interpersonal dynamics. Relatively constant naming among children at play, for example, is used to guide play; adults may use naming to control behaviour. Kramer (1975: 200f., 207) notes that in literary works address may be aggressive and is often coupled with an exclamation point or a question mark. Furthermore, she notes in this connection that men address women more than women do men. Fasold, finally, mentions that speakers often avoid address altogether because they are confused about what the appropriate or expected form is or because they do not know the name of their addressee (1990: 15).

In conclusion it is necessary to point out explicitly that no sure predictions about usage can be made. For one thing, the interplay between the various factors discussed is fluid; second, the participants in a dyad may well share more than one type of relationship.

8.5 FURTHER READING

Braun 1988 is a broadly focused cross-cultural study of **terms of address**. A very read-able treatment of the variety of **vocative forms in** English is Whitcut 1980. Brown and Ford 1964 is an older, but quite useful treatment of **address in AmE**, which is nicely supplemented by Ervin-Tripp 1974. Poynton 1989 is a discussion of **address in AusE**. **Gender and address** are dealt with in Kramer 1975 and Rubin 1981. An important seminal contribution to **power, solidarity and modes of address** can be found in Brown and Gilman 1972. Hook 1984 applies this nicely to English. Brown and Levinson 1987 and Holmes 1995 are fundamental treatments of **politeness**.

Chapter 9

Language and gender

Among the many different ways in which English varies, the gender of the speaker is one of the features in which there is currently a vast amount of interest and one which makes itself felt in many ways. Not the least of these is the widespread concern of many people that English not be used in the sense of sexism, which 'may be defined as words or actions that arbitrarily assign roles or characteristics to people on the basis of sex' (NCTE Guidelines 1977: 182) rather than assessing people individually.

Concepts of gender   Gender as it is used here should not be confused with **grammatical gender**, which is the association that we find in languages like Latin, German, Spanish, French and so on of the categories masculine, feminine and (sometimes) neuter with whole classes of nouns. Rather, gender is a social attribute of human beings. Yet it does not necessarily stand in a one-to-one relation with the sex of the speaker. Gender is a question of people's role perceptions and their behaviour in social interaction. Special codes of linguistic behaviour are associated, for example, with gay language. And female language behaviour is often identified with politeness and reciprocal behaviour. However, it is not gender alone which determines linguistic behaviour, but more fundamental social relations which are merely mirrored in gender (as well as in age and ethnicity and so on): power and solidarity. In short, the male–female divide is characterized most definitively (though surely not exclusively) by a power differential while intra-gender relations are often determined by solidarity. This is significant for language inasmuch as males are many times more likely to identify with other males – including their economic and sexual rivals – than with women, just as women are more likely to do the same among themselves. This is a relationship based on solidarity. It is a fundamental identification which leads to imitation of behaviour. Yet within this framework of solidarity it is power which determines much of behaviour: Those who are more powerful, more successful, more popular, more intelligent, better looking etc. – be they males or females – will be emulated by other(s) according to the maxim 'Power attracts'.

The ways in which the sociolinguistic category of gender shows up is by no means fixed. It can influence a wide variety of behaviour, verbal and non-verbal, such as topics of conversation, styles of speech, pronunciation, grammar, vocabulary choice and much else. Yet despite wide areas of differentiation along the lines of gender identity, all the differences that show up in English are relative. That is, there are quantitative tendencies for males and females to give particular forms their preference. For this reason it is common to speak of 'sex preferential' differences rather than absolute (or 'sex differential') ones. This should not blind us to the fact that there is also much variation among men as a group and women as a group. In this chapter we will be looking first at how language is used to make reference to males and females and then how it is differently employed by males as opposed to females.

9.1 REFERENCE TO MALES AND FEMALES

Investigations have revealed that the sexist use of language is or has been commonplace in a wide of variety of words. In general, dissatisfaction with sexist language leads to the replacement of lexical items considered exclusively male in reference and of ones with a pejorative meaning or connotation with regard to women. To begin with there has been considerable interest in unpaired words ending in -*man*, for which there are no traditional equivalents with a suffix designating a female. One of the demands of reform minded language users has been to replace such exclusive terms with more inclusive ones. So it is that for many people *firemen* have become *firefighters*, American *mailmen* have become *letter carriers* and *chairmen* have become either *chairwomen* or *chairpersons*. There are other terms which do not end in -*man*, but which are also unpaired. For some of these there are no generally accepted non-exclusive equivalents (but note the alternatives in parentheses): *bachelor's degree* (but *BA*), *master's degree* (but *MA*); for *university fellowship* and *liberty*, *equality and fraternity* there are no solutions readily available.

In English a large number of designations for persons are paired. This includes areas such as religion (*nun/monk*, *prioress/prior*, but *priestess* is not equivalent to *priest*!) and aristocratic titles (*duke/duchess*, *king/queen*, *prince/princess*, *count/countess* etc.) and kinship (*sister/brother*, *mother/father*, *aunt/uncle* etc.). In these examples feminine and masculine terms are roughly equivalent. However, a great number of further pairings are one sided with the masculine term being positive and the feminine 'counterpart', pejorative: *major* (an officer) vs *majorette* (a woman dressed in a short skirt and marching ahead of a band); *courtier* (an officer of the court) vs *courtesan* (a prostitute with wealthy or aristocratic clients); *master* (boss, expert etc.) vs *mistress* (lover); *governor* (high political office holder) vs *governess* (private teacher).

It is, of course, debatable whether such asymmetrical pairs are the results of structural features of English or the way in which the language is used. It seems, in any case, to be possible to 'repair' many of these imbalances. The counterpart of a governor who is male, for example, may be called a *woman governor* if it appears necessary to indicate the sex of the governor at all. This seems to indicate that the alleged sexism of the language is, to a large extent, the result of sexist usage, and this usage is rooted it would appear in the linguistic stereotypes of the users. For example, women are often thought of as friendly, gentle, enthusiastic, smooth and who talk gibberish on trivial topics, while men can be thought of as forceful, loud, dominating and who get straight to the point (Scott 1980: 200). Studies such as those reported by Condry and Condry (1976) also indicate that we attribute specifically male and female traits to very young children. In this particular study people observing the same videotape of an infant of nine months interpreted one and the same reaction (the child's startled reaction to a jack-in-the-box) as anger if they thought they were watching a boy and as fear if they were told it was a girl.

Just how pervasive stereotyping in language can be has been pointed out by studies of dictionaries. Nilsen reports on 385 dictionary entries which are clearly male oriented (e.g. *son*) and 132 which are similarly female oriented (e.g. *daughter*). Despite the larger number of terms for males there were more negative female designations than negative male ones. Male designations were six times as likely as female ones to include an element of positive prestige (1977).

Perhaps the most perfidious tendency in the language is what has been called **semantic derogation** or **pejoration**. Stanley (1977) collected as many words as she could for both females and males as 'sexually available', for example, *honeypot* or *hustler*. She found that: (a) there are far more for women (220) than for men (22); and (b) all but four of the female terms (*lady of the night, entertainer, concubine, mistress*) are derogatory, i.e. demeaning and shameful (*leasepiece, loose woman*); and they often involve allusion to cost (*put out, giftbox*) and frequently rely on metonymy, in which a part of the body stands for the whole (*ass, tail*), or on metaphor, especially animal metaphor (*bitch, bird*). Again and again in the history of the language, one finds that a perfectly innocent term designating a girl or woman may begin with neutral or even positive connotations, but gradually it acquires negative implications, at first perhaps only slightly disparaging, but after a period of time becoming abusive and ending as a sexual slur (Schulz 1975: 65).

Along with terms which designate people, there is the related field of vocatives, or terms used to address people (see 8.1). Once again there is a certain asymmetry to the language system inasmuch as the title for a man is simply *Mr* while a woman is *Mrs* if married and *Miss* if unmarried. For many language users (but by no means all) this disequilibrium has been remedied by the introduction of the new title *Ms*, the abbreviation of *Miz* /mɪz/, the Southern American pronunciation of both *Mrs* and *Miss* for all women.

Generic reference   A final look at the use of language to refer to males and females focuses what is known as 'generic reference'. This has to do with the use of a particular term for people without regard to their sex. It is said that the word *man* is such a term when it means any human being. The problem is that *man*, in fact, suggests men rather than both men and women. Hence the (unintended) humour of a biology textbook which speaks of 'pregnancy in man' (Silveira 1980: 168).

At the centre of the discussion of generic reference is the use of *he*. According to the grammatical category of gender, the pronoun *she* is used to mark referents who are female while *he* is employed for males, for both, or for indeterminate referents. However, many people argue that the so-called generic *he* excludes females; and, indeed, studies have shown that this is the case: Graham counted 940 uses of *he* in a sample of 100,000 words. Of these 744 referred to male humans, 128 to male animals, and 36 to persons presumed to be male, such as sailors or farmers. This left only 32 as indeterminate and hence generic (1975: 58). One interpretation of this is that people, but especially males, will consequently tend to interpret generic *he* as masculine. Furthermore, the choice of the pronoun has an effect on attitudes: for example, women are reported to get better results on mathematical problems which use female oriented situations and language (Martyna 1980: 71ff.).

That *he* is not neutral may be further illustrated by noting how it is used in personification in children's literature. MacKay and Konishi counted 35,000 occurrences of *he*, *she* or *it* in an anthology. Animals were *he* 76 per cent of the time and *she* 24 per cent. The masculine pronoun was typically used for large mammals such as lions, gorillas and wolves; the feminine, for small ones such as small birds or insects (bees, ladybugs).

MacKay and Konishi point out, among other things, that a switch to *it* would have the disadvantage of lessening the emotional and personal involvement of the reader (1980: 152ff.).

Bodine (1975) has made the interesting point that none of the grammatical categories of the English personal pronouns, namely person, number and gender, are strictly observed in actual usage. It is, for example, well known that *we* may be used singularly in the so-called royal *we* (e.g. Queen Victoria's *We are not amused*) or editorial *we* (*We shall be looking at language and sex in this chapter*). Impersonal *you* is regularly used as a third person form (*How do you* [= anyone] *get from here to the airport?*), but sometimes also as a first person form (*As tired as I am, you* [= *I*] *can't stand any extra noise*). On the basis of this rather loose and pragmatic application of categories Bodine argues for the use of singular *they* as a non-sexist generic. This not only works (*Ask anyone; they'll agree*), but is also natural to most speakers when they refer to indefinite antecedents such as *anyone*, *someone, no one*. This also makes logical sense since such pronouns, while grammatically singular, are notionally plural because *anyone*, for example, means 'all people'.

A number of people have suggested adopting a new sex neutral third person singular personal pronoun, a neologism, and these suggestions have included candidates such as *thon, co, hir, e* or *E, tey, hesh, po, re, xe, jhe, per*. None of these has been accepted, nor are they likely to be, because none of them are natural or easily available to speakers, even though they have the advantage of being sex neutral. Since pronouns belong to those words which are integrally part of the structure or grammar of the language, change is not likely to come easily.

What seems to have more chance of success is the adoption of the double pronoun, *he or she*, or the use of a plural antecedent, such as *writers*, which then allows the use of sex neutral plural *they*. This is the approach that many of the now numerous guidelines for the avoidance of stereotyping or for the improvement of the image of women suggest.

9.2 LANGUAGE USE OF MALES AND FEMALES

In the following comments on the differing use of English by males and females it is important to remember that there are, in reality, far more similarities than there are differences. Furthermore, the variable gender is only one of several including age, geographic region, socio-economic class, ethnic identification, occupation and specific social situation and is seldom the sole factor influencing usage.

9.2.1 Vocabulary use

Vocabulary differs significantly from pronunciation and grammar inasmuch as people are not only aware of their choice of words but also because they exercise greater control over their vocabulary than they do over pronunciation and grammar. In addition, words also clearly carry elements of referential content that grammar and pronunciation do not. Yet there have been relatively few studies in the field of vocabulary choice. Nevertheless, a few areas have been investigated, including: topics of discussion; emotive, supportive and polite language; colour terms; taboo words; and exclamations.

Topic   Findings indicate that women seem to avoid certain subjects such as money, business and politics while concentrating more on people (men, other women, themselves), clothing and decoration. Men favour topics such as money, business and sports. To some extent, this is not unexpected, for traditionally there has been greater engagement of men in paid employment, politics and sports and of women in person-oriented domestic (family) situations. This, of course, is a product of economic and educational opportunity (or its lack) as well as socialization and expectations.

Emotive language   Somewhat indirectly related to the alleged greater preference among females for talk about people is the often expressed feeling that women use more emotive language than men do. Indeed, a great deal is made, especially by feminists, of the supposedly less assertive, more supportive language and behaviour of women as opposed to the more competitive and dominating behaviour of men. This belief is also behind attempts to rehabilitate the traditionally negative term *gossip* as a positive feminine phenomenon in which concern is more about social interaction than the exchange of concrete information (see below).

Colour words and taboo language   One of the main theses that is pursued with regard to sex specific vocabulary is that there are features which are said to be typical of female use, such as more exact colour terms, e.g. *chartreuse* rather than male *greenish yellow*, or *beige* instead of *light brown*. Furthermore, women are credited with using such intensifiers as *so*, *such*, *quite* and *vastly* and adjectives such as *adorable, charming, sweet, lovely* or *divine*. 'Masculine' counterparts of such feminine adjectives are definitely rarer, though ones like *helluva* or *damn good* might come close (e.g. 'We had such a lovely time.' vs 'We had a helluva good time.'). This may well be true but so far there is little empirical research that confirms this.

The single area which seems to have attracted the most attention is that of taboo language. In the extensive annotated bibliography in Thorne *et al.* 1983 in the section on word choice and syntactic usage, 13, or well over a quarter of the 43 references listed, have to do with profane/obscene items or tabooed words referring to sex related acts or the genitals. By and large, these, as well as further studies, show that men are more likely than women to use obscene expressions and that women are more likely to employ impersonal or clinical terms. It is perhaps fruitful in this context to recall the remark above about possible 'masculine' adjectives such as *helluva* or *damn good*: both are mildly profane, mild enough to be used in mixed company and profane enough to be regarded as masculine. Although much of what has been reported is taken from the realm of speculation, it may be noted that overly positive (euphemistic and superlative) and therefore semantically empty terms are *viewed* as feminine while abusive and obscene language is often *regarded* as masculine.

9.2.2 Grammar

Imperatives   Among the tendencies towards divergence we find that males may, for example, use more straightforward imperatives and other directive forms than females do. This is, of course, not only a question of grammar, but also one of speech style and power (see 8.2 and 9.3). In an investigation of the language used by two- to five-year-old children in play situations in which two children of the same sex played doctor it turned out that the girls had a clear tendency to soften their directives: 'many more of the girls' utterances were mitigated (65 per cent as compared with 34 per cent for boys)' (Sachs 1987: 184). For example 25 per cent of the boys' commands/requests were straightforward imperatives ('Bring her to the hospital') and 11 per cent were prohibitions ('Don't touch it'), while for girls the results were 10 and 2 per cent respectively. On the other hand, girls used more joint directives ('Now we'll cover him up'), namely 15 per cent as compared to the boys' 3 per cent (ibid.: 182). Girls also use more instances of *let's*, which boys almost never use, a form which explicitly includes the speaker in the proposed action (Coates 1995: 23). Gleason found that mothers were more likely to use directives in the question form while fathers employed a higher proportion of direct imperatives and indirect speech acts such as 'Your car is blocking mine', which suggests that the other move his/her car). By the age of four children were following the speech patterns of their same sex parents (Gleason 1987: 197f.).

The patterns reported by Sachs and Gleason for largely white, middle class American children are substantially confirmed by Goodwin for working class black children in Philadelphia. She found that in a cooperative play situation girls' imperatives are suggestive rather than demanding, that the right to give directions rotates in a group of girls and that when imperatives are used by girls, they are modified in some way (emphasizing group benefits or accompanied by laughter) as opposed to the boys' unmitigated forms (1988: 88).

How effective and powerful imperatives are is called into doubt by findings that the bare imperatives used by male doctors found less compliance (47 per cent) than female doctors' proposals for joint action (*let's*) at 67 per cent; suggestions for action (*You could try 'x'*) had a 75 per cent success rate (West 1990: 108).

Tag questions   A further syntactical phenomenon which has generated a great deal of attention is Lakoff's impression that women use many more tag questions of the sort which seek confirmation of a personal opinion (e.g. 'The way prices are rising is horrendous, isn't it?') (1976: 16). In an attempt to check this Dubois and Crouch counted the number of tag questions used in an academic conference and found that all of them were used by men. They then preceded to interpret this by writing that these tags were, 'far from signalling lack of confidence, . . . intended to forestall opposition' (1975: 292).

There seem to be two issues involved. The first is whether men or women use more tag questions. Dubois and Crouch, for example, found men using more in formal talk, while the study by Sachs quoted above revealed girls to use twice as many as boys (1987: 184). Other studies have not clarified this question since the conditions of the setting vary considerably. The second question has to do with the purpose which tag questions serve. Some say they are used to sustain communicative interaction, for example, by women to elicit a response from an uncommunicative male conversational partner. In the opinion of one writer:

1   Women do not use more tag questions than men.
2   Even if they did, it would not necessarily mean they were seeking approval, since tag questions have a wide range of uses.
3   In any case women's use of tag questions will always be explained differently from men's, since it is cultural sex stereotypes which determine the explanation of linguistic phenomena, rather than the nature of the phenomena themselves.

(Cameron 1985: 56)

This display of evidence and interpretation reveals that numerous factors must be taken into account, such as the sex, age, relative status etc. of the conversational participants, the nature of the setting (formal/academic, informal/chatty), the topic and the purpose pursued by the person who uses a tag question and more.

Non-standard grammar A widely discussed question with regard to sex differential use of English has to do with how standard or non-standard a person's utterances are. There seems to be a connection in the minds of speakers of English between non-standard English and masculinity. Cheshire reports a much greater tendency for boys who are firmly embedded in local vernacular culture to use local non-standard forms than for girls to do so in Reading, England. The non-standard forms of the verbs investigated seem to reflect 'toughness' for the boys (1978: 64f.). Much the same result has been established for speakers of American Black English in Detroit, where men have been found to use multiple negation ('Ain't nobody going nowhere noways') 30 per cent more often than women (Shuy *et al.* 1967).

The association between 'non-standard' and 'masculine' has been advanced especially with regard to non-standard accents (see 9.2.3); however, this is not the only association which is feasible. The non-standard is also often identical with the vernacular and therefore may have strong associations with local culture. This would fit the association between broadest Black English Vernacular (the basilect) in Washington, typically used in the family, and 'little boy' language. 'Big boys' from the age of seven or eight reject it, possibly because it is associated with the culture of the home (Stewart 1964: 17). Here a masculine identity may work against the non-standard. In another American Black English community in South Carolina, it is the young men who turn out to maintain the broad vernacular because their work and social lives are shared with other men from the local community (Nichols 1984: 34ff.).

9.2.3 Pronunciation

The final systematic level of language use is pronunciation. Here, once again, many of the same tendencies can be found which have already been mentioned. This seems to be especially true of the findings of a number of important sociolinguistic studies of pronunciation variables with regard to the standard/non-standard distinction just discussed.

Pitch and voice quality Even the idea that male voices can be distinguished from female voices because of the lower pitch of the former is not all there is to the picture. Experiments show that girls and boys who have not yet entered puberty and whose vocal tracts do not yet differ in size can nevertheless be distinguished by sex. It seems to be the case that young boys typically speak as if they were larger than they really are and that young girls speak as if they were smaller (see Sachs *et al.* 1973: 75; Sachs 1975: 154). This may be due to distinctive configurations in the relative distance between the bands of sound frequency produced when articulating vowels: the upper bands of vibrations, the formants, are closer to the lowest band, the fundamental, for boys than for girls. The result may be a configuration similar to that of adult males. Other factors may, of course, also be involved in the successful identification of the sex of pre-adolescent speakers, ones such as voice quality, loudness, speed, intonation or fluency (see Lee *et al.* 1995).

Women do, of course, have higher overall pitch; in addition, the range of their pitch is also wider, as a study of American speakers reveals:

> Men consistently avoid certain intonation levels or patterns: they very rarely, if ever, use the highest level of pitch that women use. That is, it appears probable that most men have only three contrastive levels of intonation, while many women, at least, have four.
>
> (Brend 1975: 86f.)

Men who have or adopt a similarly wide range of intonation are perceived as effeminate.

Women are reported to use a higher percentage of final rises than men do in Tyneside Speech (England) (Pellowe and Jones 1978: 110), and Brend reports similar findings for American English (1975: 87). Above and beyond this, speakers of English identify final falling intonations significantly more often as masculine and rising ones as feminine (Edelsky 1979: 22). The interpretation often given to rising intonation is that it shows a greater degree of uncertainty and/or a greater degree of reserve and politeness (see 4.5.3).

Addington's report (1968) on the assessment given to each of seven different voice qualities (breathiness, thinness, flatness, nasality, tenseness, throatiness, orotundity plus speed and pitch) shows that people can perceive a great variety of differences, though it is not easy to verbalize just what lies behind each of these labels. His investigation reveals that breathiness is a feminine feature (suggesting prettier, more petite, more effervescent, more highly strung) and that breathy males are regarded as younger and more artistic. Flatness is masculine and comes over negatively (sluggish, cold, withdrawn) for both sexes. Throatiness is also masculine – more positive in a male (older, more mature, realistic, sophisticated, well adjusted) while negative for a woman (less intelligent, more masculine, lazier, boorish) (1968: 499ff.). Although Addington's findings are controversial (see Smith 1985: 76), there can be little doubt that people evaluate male and female speakers differently on the basis of features of pronunciation other than individual, segmental sounds.

The pronunciation of individual sounds   The relatively large number of sociolinguistic studies of pronunciation variation in a large variety of urban areas has revealed that women adopt pronunciations which are relatively closer to the accepted public norms of the given region while men of the same social class tend to be closer to the non-standard or vernacular norms. By no means all the sounds of the language are affected. While men and women may have a tendency towards differing pronunciations of one particular phoneme in one speech community, they may well have indistinguishable pronunciations of the same segmental sound in other regions. Occasionally a sex preferential difference is nearly universal in the English speaking world. The verbal ending {-ing} illustrates this. Everywhere the pronunciation considered to be standard or 'correct' has the velar nasal /ŋ/, while the alveolar nasal /n/ is considered inappropriate in more formal situations requiring Standard English. Fischer, looking at children of three to ten years old in New England, reported that a 'typical' boy ('physically strong, dominating, full of mischief, but disarmingly frank about his transgressions') used /n/ more than half the time, but especially with informal verbs, e.g. *punchin'*, *flubbin'*, *swimmin'*, *hittin'* (formal verbs had /ŋ/, e.g. *criticizing*, *reading*, *visiting*) (1958: 49ff.). Girls typically used more /ŋ/ endings, a result that was substantiated for adult speakers in Norwich, England (Trudgill 1972: 187).

It is not only the gender of the speaker but also socio-economic class which correlates with an orientation towards the standard or non-standard form of pronunciation. In Norwich women classified as upper working class share the pronunciation norms of men classified as lower middle class. This pattern repeats itself throughout all the classes investigated with women typically using pronunciations credited to the men in the class immediately above them. Trudgill speaks of a greater status consciousness of women than men in English society. As a result they tend to adapt 'upwards' towards the public norm, which possesses **overt prestige**. Trudgill finds confirmation for this in the fact that women, when asked to tell what pronunciation they themselves use, report more use of the overt norm than is actually the case; this is called 'over reporting'. Men behave in the converse fashion: they use more standard forms while claiming to use fewer; this is referred to as 'under reporting'. On the basis of this, the non-standard, non-prestige accent used by men, but especially working class men, is said to have **covert prestige**. For these under reporting men it may be assumed that working class speech has positive connotations of roughness and toughness (Trudgill 1972). Conclusions of this sort, especially that females conform more to the prestige pronunciation, have been made about English speakers in many other parts of the world as well.

Nonetheless, there are results which do not conform to this pattern. One of the best known divergences is that of young women in a section of west Belfast known as the Clonard. These women were more likely than men of the same area, age and class to realize the variable 'a' = /æ/ as in *hat* or *man* as non-standard [ɒ], i.e. with a higher degree of backing (Milroy and Margrain 1980: 66). The explanation given for this is that this particular group of women are part of a highly integrated social network, that is, one in which the members share mutual acquaintanceship in a variety of ways, at work, in place of residence, in leisure time activities, as kin. The social network is, in other words, a thick ('**multiplex**') meshing of shared relationships (as opposed to a simpler perhaps singular ('**uniplex**') relationship). This has the consequence of causing a mutual reinforcement of all sorts of values and behaviour, including language. What is unusual here is that this sort of mutual reinforcement of the local vernacular in both traditional rural and working class industrial environments is normally more typical of men than of women. In the Clonard widespread male unemployment had caused a thinning out of male social networks: there was no workplace to share; as a result local speech norms would be reinforced less strongly than with women and their intact social networks. Nichols applied this type of explanation to speakers in two communities in South Carolina, one black and one white, to make the dynamics of speech change clearer (Nichols 1984: 40f.). In working class communities men's speech differs from women's less because of gender than because of the tight-knit nature of men's networks.

The social network may be **multiplex** relationships, such as shared neighbourhood, work, kin and activities, or a **uniplex** relationship. The more firmly people are enmeshed in a network, the more likely they are to share values, including language use. With such an approach the ideas of prestige consciousness, as in the first explanation above, appear somewhat one sided. Obviously, they can still be meaningful, but prestige now is clearly a group norm and may dictate language forms which conform to the overt standard *or* the local covert norms depending on the nature of the social network involved; the gender of the group members is not necessarily the most relevant factor.

The perception of pronunciation   A final point about pronunciation differences is the way in which speakers with various accents are perceived. This tells less about how males and females actually speak, of course, than about the stereotypes of male and female speech which people have. Elyan *et al.* used what is called the matched guise technique 'to determine evaluative reactions to RP versus Lancashire (Northern) accented female speech' (1978: 125). In a matched guise test, one and the same speaker produces samples of speech with differing accents. These are then played from tape to judges who evaluate the supposedly differing speakers according to scales of personality traits. While this technique is used to eliminate idiosyncratic voice features which might influence the listeners' judgments thus leaving accent alone as the variable to be evaluated, it can never fully guarantee that the speakers may not be unconsciously switching implicit stereotypes in voice quality as well as accent. Bearing this in mind, the results of Elyan *et al.* may be considered:

> RP-accented females in Britain are upgraded in terms of competence and communi-cative skills but downgraded in terms of social attractiveness and personal integrity relative to regional accented females. ... RP women are expected to bear fewer children, to create a more egalitarian relationship with their husbands and are seen to be more masculine in their sex traits (positive and negative) while at the same time being rated higher on the femininity trait than Northern accented females.
>
> (ibid.: 129)

9.3 COMMUNICATIVE STRATEGIES

It is uncontroversial to say that women and men communicate differently. The disagree-ment comes in explaining why. Three approaches to this question are generally recognized. The first suggests that women are at a linguistic disadvantage vis-à-vis men because of their socialization. The emphasis on disadvantage has given this approach the designation 'deficit model'. The 'dominance model' moves the blame to men, whose power is revealed in their linguistic behaviour – interrupting, determining the topic of conversation, speaking more. Women are forced to adapt to this situation. The third view finds its expression in the 'difference model', which sees the two genders as acting and interacting linguistically in their own ways. In the words of Cameron 'men boast and women gossip. Each sex engages in the sort of talk which secures the rewards they prefer – status for men, connection for women' (1995: 35). While this third approach corres-ponds to the descriptive approach of modern linguistics and accepts both styles of communication, it must by the same token ignore the social inequality involved. Certainly it is not enough to advise women not to use tag questions, rising intonation in statements, whiny, breathy or high pitched voices and not to talk 'all the time'. In looking at some of the ways speakers use the language to communicate we will pick up the theme of power introduced in 8.2. In asymmetrical communication it is the powerful who ask the most questions, who can use unmitigated forms of directives (treated in 9.2.2), who may interrupt in public and professional situations and who speak the most. As we will see, there is more to it than this.

9.3.1 Topics and text types

We begin by picking up the word 'gossip', which was just mentioned. Within feminist discourse this term has been reassessed to encompass a number of genres more typical of women. Deborah Jones is quoted as identifying:

> four distinct kinds of conversation among women, which she views as different varieties of gossip. These are 'house-talk', occupational talk which is the housewife's equivalent of 'talking shop'; 'scandal', which involves the verbal policing of other women's behaviour; 'bitching', a form of troubles-talk involving complaints about men to other women; and finally 'chatting', which is purely phatic.
>
> (Talbot 1998: 81)

Here gossip is pretty obviously established as a female genre of its own, independent of the public genres in which men so frequently predominate. It emphasizes the binary oppositions between women's and men's styles which are often referred to and very instructive, but are unlikely to lead anywhere since they do nothing about the inequalities of the status quo: female intimacy, rapport and supportiveness vs male independence, status consciousness and oppositional attitudes (ibid.: 98).

There seem to be other distinct types of texts produced by males and females. For example, there is far more evidence of men than of women engaging in verbal duelling and ritual insults (see 8.2.2). In a similar vein joke telling seems to be more a male than a female domain, especially in the case of dirty jokes. Men are credited with jokes which are more competitive and aggressive (and dirty jokes, which frequently have women as their butt, are certainly aggressive). Yet women tell bawdy jokes as well.

There is a related phenomenon in men's greater use of witty remarks. At staff meetings in a mental hospital 'men made by far the more frequent witticisms – 99 out of 103 – but women often laughed harder' (Coser 1960: 85). Humour and wit, which 'always contain some aggression' (ibid.: 83), originated more often from senior staff than from junior staff or paramedical workers and was never directed upwards in the hierarchy (ibid.: 85f.). What determined this outcome was the higher status of the men (all but two of the psychiatric staff while the paramedics were all women) and the fact that women are not expected to be witty. Their humour may be acceptable in some situations, but it is disapproved in those social situations in which there is danger of subverting implicit or explicit male authority (ibid.: 86).

9.3.2 Dominance behaviour

The example of laughter just quoted touches on the important question of who controls conversational interaction. Although the evidence is not unambiguous, there are indications that males dominate in the amount of speaking they do and in the ways they control topics.

Amount of speaking There is a stereotype of the talkative and gossipy female: Q: *What are the three fastest means of communication?* A: *Telegraph, telephone and tell a woman.* Yet, it seems to be males who speak most, both with regard to the number of turns they take and the average length of turns. In a review of the research findings on this question James and Drakich stress the importance of the context and structure of the social interaction including status differences between the men and women and their dissimilar cultural expectations with regard to abilities and areas of competence (1993: 301). While some studies find no differences or even a greater amount of speaking by women, far more studies show men to produce more speech than women. In more formalized settings in which hierarchy and power are more obviously relevant, such as staff meetings, male dominance is almost paradigmatic. Eakins and Eakins report an American college departmental faculty meeting as follows:

> in average number of verbal turns per meeting, the men, with the exception of one male, outweigh the women in number of verbal turns taken. The women with the fewest averaged 5.5 turns a meeting, whereas the man with the fewest turns had over twice as many and exceeded all the women but one.
>
> (1978b: 57)

The number of turns was also positively related to the hierarchy of status and power, rank, importance and length of time in the department. The length of turns for the males ranged from 17.07 to 10.66 seconds. For the females it was 10.00 to 3.0 seconds (ibid.: 58). Swacker (1978) found similar results with regard to questions asked in discussion periods at a scholarly conference. The stereotype of the talkative women may be based on:

> the fact that men have more frequently interacted with women in informal than in formal interactions. Therefore, men have experienced women as talking at times when they would be less likely to choose to talk themselves, and about matters about which men would be less likely to choose to talk about themselves.
>
> (James and Drakich 1993: 302)

A final remark: silence is not in itself a sign of powerless; in fact, many men use it to dominate and control (Tannen 1993: 178).

Topic control: interruption   The rudest, most direct way of determining who will speak and what the subject of discourse will be is through interruption, which is one way of exercising power and control in conversation. Again, while the evidence is mixed, more studies show men interrupting women than vice versa, and the social setting is obviously an important element in this variable. In a widely reported investigation of conversations involving male–female couples in a California coffee shop 'virtually all the interruptions and overlaps are by male speakers (98 per cent and 100 per cent respectively)' (Zimmerman and West 1975: 115). The conclusion drawn that females' 'rights to speak appear to be casually infringed upon by males' (ibid.: 117) may not be justified without further qualification. Beattie found no such male dominance in conversational behaviour during university tutorials in England (1981: 22ff.) and suggests that other factors may be of importance such as the need for social approval, i.e. to make a 'good impression', which might deter interruption by a female in an informal social encounter such as those investigated by Zimmerman and West. Or, of course, interruption may be a sign less of dominance than of enthusiasm and involvement. Kennedy (1980) goes into the question of interruption further and establishes, for a group of undergraduate students, that the following grounds account for interruption:

agreement	38 per cent
subject change	23 per cent
disagreement	19 per cent
clarification	11 per cent
tangentialization	8 per cent

James and Clarke, in a review of the research, found that it definitely is not the case that men interrupt more than women (nor vice versa). However, there is some evidence of the differing overall behaviour of women, who seem to engage in more overlapping or simultaneous speech than men: 'women are more likely than men to use simultaneous talk to show involvement and rapport' (1993: 232).

Topic control: questions Differing overall strategies of topic control can be seen in the tendency of women to approach this problem from a completely different angle. They have been found to use up to three times as many questions as men do. This suggests a strategy in which questions function as 'sequencing devices' in conversation: because they demand a response, they may well serve to keep a conversation going: 'A question does work in conversation by opening a two-part (Q–A) sequence (called an **agency pair**). It is a way to insure a minimal interaction – at least one utterance by each of the two participants. By asking questions, women strengthen the possibility of a response to what they have to say' (Fishman 1983: 94). However, the function of questions is not necessarily identical from situation to situation: 'information-seeking questions are . . . rare in all-female discourse. Instead, interrogative forms are used to invite others to participate, and to check that what is being said is acceptable to everyone present. They are also used as part of a general strategy for conversational maintenance' (Coates 1995: 22).

Minimal responses Fishman's explanation above gets a certain amount of reinforcement from the observation that women are more likely than men to produce minimal responses, or go-on gambits (see 7.3.5), that is, those *mm*'s, *uhuh*'s and *yeah*'s which indicate active listening and encourage the speaker to go on. Apparently, women are more willing to play a supportive conversational role (Fishman 1983).

9.4 LANGUAGE ACQUISITION AND DEVELOPMENT

A look at language acquisition in children leads to the central question whether the differences are genetic or social, in other words, due to nature or nurture. While there is, indeed, evidence of girl–boy language differences, especially with respect to the age of acquisition (a result of girls' earlier maturation), there is an even greater amount of evidence which demonstrates the immense influence of socialization in the development of language patterns. Certainly the influence of adults, especially parents, is unquestionably great. By the age of two or three children were learning politeness patterns, with girls showing more cooperation (Ervin-Tripp *et al.* 1984: 134f.). At age four, boys are imitating male forms and girls are imitating female patterns, a process which may begin as early as at eighteen months (Gleason 1987: 198). Note also the greater number of unmitigated imperatives and other types of directives used by boys (discussed in 7.2.1), just as fathers use particularly many of them with their children, especially their sons (see below). Boys also talk more about sports and transmit more information while girls talk more about school and sitting games, use fewer direct requests, laugh more and are more compliant. At nursery school age and beyond (three to seven), for example, children portray fathers' speech as straightforward, unqualified and forceful; mothers' speech, as talkative, polite, qualified and higher pitched. This shows how unerringly children imitate gender role models.

The models available have traditionally been considered to vary so much between men and women that the adult input language is often termed 'motherese', for it is mothers, above all, who simplify their language according to the child's age. Motherese involves slowness, redundancy, simplicity and grammaticality. Utterances are shortened: mothers stay about 1.5 words in length ahead of the child. There is a great deal of repetition. There is present orientation, and there is control. Fathers have fewer exchanges with their children but tend to introduce more new words, to use more imperatives, to ask fewer questions and to make fewer repetitions. Nevertheless, motherese, in the sense of simplified language, is used by both parents (Gleason and Greif 1983).

9.5 NON-VERBAL BEHAVIOUR

Communication takes place not only by means of language, but also through other non-verbal channels such as gestures, mimicry, posture, eye contact, smiling, touch and so on. Non-verbal communication is implicit, compared to explicit communication with words. Indeed, so important is non-verbal behaviour for communication that the signals it provides may override the actual words a person uses. For example, we are all aware of the false smiles we sometimes encounter and are wary of their bearers, however friendly their words. 'In general, it was found that, when there was inconsistency among components, the implicit cues dominated the verbal cues in determining the total impact' (Mehrabian 1972: 103).

As far as gender behaviour is concerned, it seems that women are generally more sensitive to non-verbal signals than men are. This may have to do with the fact that women have less power and status in society and are therefore in greater need of interpreting implicit messages (Eakins and Eakins 1978a: 149) or it may be due to the requirements of motherhood, i.e. the need to respond to non-verbal signals from children (ibid.: 66).

Smiling   Women have been found to smile more than men, even when the smile has nothing to do with whether the person smiling is happy. Just why this is the case is not clear, but explanations tend to emphasize either the greater politeness of women or the relatively weaker social position most women have.

> The traditional female role demands warm, compliant behavior in public situations; the smiling facial expression may provide the mask to convey this impression. . . . For her, the smile may be situationally or role defined, rather than being relevant to the immediate verbal interchange.
>
> (Bugental *et al.* 1971: 315)

Touch   Closely related is the area of touch. In general it seems to reflect socio-economic status: the higher the status, the more liberty one can take in touching others. It likewise reflects age, with the older person generally having the greater freedom to touch. Since women are generally touched more and do less touching, this fits the pattern established: women have less status and are often classed with children. Think of the use of modes of address (see Chapter 8), where the socially more powerful or the older has the right to initiate the use of first names. Touching behaviour is, however, further complicated by the factor of sex: if a woman touches a man, her touch is very likely to be interpreted as a sexual gambit.

Proximity and body posture   In a similar manner women are approached more closely in comparison to men, thus underlining the fact that women are allowed less personal space. Women are expected to move out of the way of men in passing on the streets. Body posture emphasizes this, too: men hold their arms and legs at a wider angle than women do. In other words male territoriality is greater than that of females.

Eye contact   People look at higher status speakers more than lower status ones, and women maintain more eye contact than men do. One study of visual behaviour closes among other things with this remark:

> An understanding of how power, dominance and status are communicated has practical value as well as theoretical importance. If, because of traditional socialization processes, men typically assume a dominant visual display and women adopt a submissive posture during mixed-sex interaction, then nonverbal cues can contribute to the perpetuation of perceived status differences between the sexes.
>
> (Dovidio and Ellyson 1985: 146)

9.6 FURTHER READING

General introductions. On gender (and language) Crawford 1995. On language: Coates 1986; Eakins and Eakins 1978a. Lakoff 1976 is a seminal, though somewhat intuitive book.

For an example of **guidelines** on the use of inclusive language see Linguistic Society of America (1995). Recent books containing articles (reprinted) on a wide selection of topics are: Cheshire and Trudgill 1998; Coates 1998. Note also Johnson and Meinhof (1997) on language and masculinity.

Sociolinguistic variationist approaches can be seen in: Labov (NYC) 1972a; Macaulay (Glasgow) 1978, Trudgill (Norwich) 1972. An influential alternative **social network approach** (Belfast) is presented in Milroy and Margrain 1980. See Lanham and McDonald for white English speaking South Africans (1979) and Levine and Crockett for Piedmont North Carolina (1966). **Socialization and gender differences** among children are, for example, nicely illustrated in the titles listed in the bibliography by Sachs 1987. See also Swann 1992. On **discourse**: Coates 1996 (articles). On **politeness**: Holmes 1995; and Harper *et al.* 1978: 216–18 for a review of the literature on gender specific **non-verbal behaviour**.

National and regional varieties of English

Chapter 10

English in the British Isles

English is the primary language of both Great Britain (England, Scotland, Wales) and Ireland (the Republic of Ireland, Northern Ireland). There are, of course, numerous other languages which are spoken by the citizens of these various countries, and some of these will be mentioned briefly below. Yet it is English which predominates. In fact, English is native to England and a major part of Scotland, from where it was transplanted to the other native English speaking areas in the British Isles and around the globe. It is perhaps because its origins are here that this variety, **British English (BrE)**, is often regarded by English learners in many parts of the world as somehow the 'best' English. This is reason enough to examine English in the British Isles more closely and to try to find out more about its nature.

BrE comprises numerous, often greatly differing regional variants. Furthermore, in England, Scotland and Ireland there exist what are called **traditional dialects**. These are the regional dialects of England and the Scots dialects of Scotland and Ireland (see 10.2.2). They grew up over centuries of relative geographic isolation and exhibit fairly obvious lexical, morphological, syntactic and phonological differences from each other and from GenE. Furthermore, a particular type of pronunciation, Received Pronunciation (or RP), which enjoys special prestige in England and other parts of the UK, is in wide use and will be discussed below once again (see also 1.4).

10.1 ENGLAND AND WALES

The vast majority of the inhabitants of England (approximately 48 million) and Wales (approximately 3 million) speak English as their first language; yet there are considerable minorities who do not. This is perhaps most obvious in Wales, where around 20 per cent of the population speaks Welsh. In addition, there are large minorities in urban centres throughout Great Britain who immigrated from the Indian subcontinent or Cyprus and whose mother tongues are not English.

10.1.1 Wales

Wales is the only area in the British Isles where one of the original Celtic languages has been able to survive as the daily language of a large number of people: just under one fifth use Welsh; of these about 70 per cent use it as their exclusive home language and a further 13 per cent use both it and English as their home languages (MacKinnon 1997). Although the future of Welsh is by no means assured, its use seems to have stabilized somewhat vis-à-vis English. There are Welsh language schools in the predominantly Welsh speaking areas in the north, and a fair amount of broadcasting is carried out in Welsh as well.

Welsh English shares many of the linguistic features of southern England (see 10.1.2). What marks it off from the English of England is the effect of the Celtic substratum, which shows most obviously in its sing-song intonation, presumably influenced by Welsh. In monolingual areas such as the southeast, the influence of Welsh is considerably weaker. Here, for example, monolingual English speakers generally have non-rhotic accents, while bilingual ones further to the west are more likely to have rhotic ones. Throughout Wales clear [l] is the rule, whether prevocalic or postvocalic. This, too, may be due to the substratum, but it is also typical of the English southwest.

In grammar Welsh English is, for the most part, similar to GenE. However, Welsh influenced English grammar (and vocabulary) is more likely to be heard in non-anglicized areas. Moreover, non-standard Welsh English has additional forms for habitual aspect constructed with the uninflected auxiliary *do* (present) or *did* (past) plus the infinitive (*He do go to the cinema every week*) or with an inflected form of *be* plus an *ing*-form of the verb (*He's going to the cinema every week*). The latter construction correlates well with the equivalent Welsh form while the *do*-form, which is predominant in the southeast, is an English construction apparently originally borrowed from the neighbouring English counties, but which is spreading into the *be* + V-*ing* area in the west. Fronting for topicalization (*Singing they were*) is common in Welsh English and is a reflex of the substratum. The same is true of the practice of reporting indirect questions in the same word order as direct questions (*I'm not sure is it true or not*). Furthermore, possession can be expressed by using a prepositional construction (*There's no luck with the rich*, 'they have no luck'). All of these examples have parallels in IrE (see 10.3.4). A further instance of influence from the substratum is the use of *there* in exclamations where GenE would have *how* (*There's young she looks!*, 'How young she looks!'). The use of an all-purpose tag question *isn't it?*, finally, is reminiscent of the same construction in second language Englishes in Africa and Asia (see Chapter 14). All examples are from Thomas 1984; 1985. Further non-standard grammatical features of Welsh English, as mentioned in Thomas 1985, are no different from many of the widespread non-standard forms of England as listed and illustrated under (2), (3), (6), (9) and (10) in the following section on England.

10.1.2 England

The regional dialects of England   As one moves from area to area in England the variety of local forms in use can be impressively different. It may be difficult, for example, for Somerset and Yorkshire people to understand each other. Yet lack of mutual comprehension does not actually occur very frequently. The reasons for this lie in the fact that almost 90 per cent of the population of Great Britain lives in cities and towns and the speech forms of urban populations are less noticeably different from each other than those of traditional rural communities. Furthermore, speakers of the traditional dialects almost always have a command of GenE.

The traditional dialects are fairly distinctively divergent from GenE in grammar, morphology, vocabulary and pronunciation. Usually these divergences are unpredictable because they do not stand in a regular correspondence with GenE. In this chapter we will not be looking at them any further. A comprehensive investigation of English dialects was carried out in the Survey of English Dialects (SED), which was conducted in England and Wales in the 1950s and early 1960s.

Within the cities there has been a great deal of levelling (**koineization**) to a common denominator of forms, and here the more common, overarching, public, media-oriented linguistic culture of General English has become dominant. This is not to say that there are no regional distinctions between the areas. For although there are, they are hardly as extreme as those between many of the traditional dialect areas.

The major division within England is between the north and the midlands, on the one hand, and the south, on the other (see Map 10.1 below). The chief differences lie in several features of pronunciation. In southern England, the vowel in such words as *luck, butter, cousin* or *love* is pronounced with a low central or fronted vowel /ʌ/ and is therefore distinctly different from that of *pull, push, could* or *look*, all of which have /ʊ/. In the north the two groups of words have an identical vowel, namely /ʊ/, so that *look* and *luck* are homophones. A second distinction involves the distribution of /æ/ and /ɑː/. In such words as *bath, after, pass, dance* and *sample* the realization in the north is a phonemically short vowel as in GenAm (see Table 4.7 and section 12.1.5) though the quality of /æ/ is nearer [a] in northern England. The south, in contrast, has a long vowel, either [aː] or [ɑː]. In a third group of words, namely *quarry, swath, what*, which have a /w/ preceding the vowel, the northern vowel is fronted [a] while the south has back /ɒ/. A final distinction is the presence of the short low back vowel /ɒ/ preceding a voiceless fricative in words like *moss, off, broth* in the north. The south has a long vowel here, /ɔː/. (RP once had /ɔː/, and some older speakers still use it while younger ones use /ɒ/). Other important distinctions within the regional accents of England are the exclusive use of a clear [l] in the southwest and the presence of rhotic areas both in the southwest and in Lancashire in the north.

Regional variation in vocabulary is infrequent outside the traditional dialects. Where it does exist, it is often restricted to the domestic, the local, the jocular or the juvenile. A wide display of different terms is provided, for example, by children's words for 'time out' or 'truce' in games: *fainties* (southwest and southeast), *cree* (Bristol), *scribs* (mid southern coast), *barley* (western midlands and northwards to eastern Scotland), *exes* (East Anglia), *crosses* (Lincolnshire), *kings* (Yorkshire and southwards), *skinch* (Durham–Newcastle) (Trudgill 1990: 119).

Grammatical variation within GenE is probably less a regional dimension, though this can be the case, than it is an educational one. Those who value education are likely to use StE habitually while those whose orientation lies elsewhere are more likely to use non-standard GenE, which shares a number of characteristics which transcend not only the regional boundaries of England, but its national borders as well and are to be found among native speakers of the language all over the English speaking world. These features include the following:

1   third person singular *don't* (*she don't know*);
2   non-standard past and past participial forms (*they come to see us yesterday*; *you done a good job*; *have you went to see them yet?*);
3   multiple negation (*she don't have none*);
4   widespread use of *ain't* for *be* and the auxiliary *have* (*I ain't interested*; *he ain't comin'*; *we ain't seen him*);
5   *never* for (*do*) *not* (*Did you take them sweets? No, I never*);
6   various non-standard relative pronouns such as *what* or *as* (*he was the man what/as did it*); or none at all as the subject of a restrictive relative clause (*he was the man did it*) (see 5.5.5);
7   the demonstrative determiner *them* (*where did you get them new glasses?*);
8   the reflexive pronouns *hisself* and *theirselves* (*he hurt hisself playing football*);
9   no plural form after numbers (*she's five foot five tall and weighs eight stone*);
10 not quite so widespread is the use of the ending {-S} for all persons in the west of England (*I likes it, you likes it, she likes it*), but the lack of any {-S} in East Anglia (*she like it*).

10.1.3 The RP accent

In England there is one accent which is not connected with a specific locality though it is rather more southern than northern in its overall character. This is RP, which is short for Received Pronunciation, where 'received' originally meant 'accepted' in the sense of being the accent current in the 'best' social circles. This rather restricted reference is hardly appropriate in present day English society, for RP is not limited in such a strict way any more. This is not to say that there are no social distinctions connected with it, for clearly there are. RP is closely associated with education itself as well as with the kind of higher social position and responsibility which is often associated with education. Ramsaran remarks that RP may be viewed:

> as a kind of standard, not necessarily deliberately imposed or consciously adopted, not a norm from which other accents deviate, nor a target towards which foreign learners need necessarily aim, but a standard in the sense that it is regionally neutral and does undeniably influence the modified accents of many British regions.
>
> (1990b: 183)

Despite the advantages of RP as a regionally neutral accent, it has not displaced the local accents of England. Estimates about the number of people who speak RP 'natively' (i.e. who learned it at home as children and not later in life) are usually set at three to five per cent of the population. As such, RP is clearly a minority accent. However, its speakers occupy positions of authority and visibility in English society (government and politics, cultural and educational life, business and industrial management) far out of proportion to their actual numbers. Until the Second World War RP was also the exclusive accent of the BBC.

Perhaps because of its one time dominance in broadcasting RP is sometimes referred to as BBC English, even though a wide range of English and non-English (Scottish, Irish, North American, Australian) accents can be heard daily on the BBC and other television channels and radio stations. Further designations for this accent include **Public School Pronunciation, the King's/Queen's English** and **Oxford English**. In linguistic treatments of the accent, 'RP' has become the usual label.

The accent itself is neither changeless nor uniform, nor is there complete agreement about just what it is. Nevertheless, **General RP** is a useful concept and is adopted in Chapter 3 on pronunciation as the descriptive basis together with GenAm, with which it is compared and contrasted in Chapter 12. With perhaps a few concessions to local pronunciation habits, it might be possible to extend the number of speakers to whom RP applies; within England this would include a total of perhaps ten per cent, but it would also include many of the most prestigious accents in countries like Australia, New Zealand and South Africa. Such an extended accent is called **near-RP** by Wells and is somewhat vaguely defined to refer 'to a group of accent types which are clearly "educated" and situated well away from the lower end of the socio-economic scale, while differing to some noticeable degree from what we recognize as RP' (1982: 301).

Within RP itself there are several streams. For one there is **Refined** or **U-RP** (= Upper Class RP). Among the various characteristics which Wells cites for it the most likely diagnostic feature is a single tapped [ɾ] in intervocalic position, which is recessive in General RP. The Refined variety has sub-varieties which Gimson once called **Conservative** and **Advanced RP** (1980: 91). The former counts as old-fashioned and will most likely be heard only among older speakers. It is characterized by a diphthongization of /æ/, something like [eæ]. Furthermore, /ɔː/ may still be realized as the centring diphthong [ɔə]. The centring diphthongs themselves end closer to [a] than to [ə]: [ɪa], [ɛa] and [ʊa]. /əʊ/ may be [oʊ], and, finally, the vowel in words of the type *moss, off* and *broth* can be old-fashioned /ɔː/ rather than General /ɒ/. As for Advanced RP, many people consider it affected. However that may be, it often shows the way that General RP may develop. Its features might include the fronting (and unrounding) of /uː/ and /ʊ/ to [ʉː] or [ɨː] and [ɨ]; the vocalization of [ɫ] to [ʊ]; or the use of [ʔ] for /t/ before accented syllable or pauses as in [nɒʔ iːvn] (*not even*) or [siː ɪʔ] (*see it*). A second major strand within RP is **Adoptive RP**. This is the accent of someone who has learned RP as an adult, perhaps for vocational reasons. If well learned, it is no different from General RP. However, it may well be that such speakers retain their 'native accents' for more informal registers and that they have difficulty using RP in informal speech styles (Wells 1982: 284).

Justifying the choice of RP   Just what is the basis for the primacy of RP, especially in foreign language teaching? In the vast literature in which this question has been batted around four major positions have evolved.

The aesthetic argument   An early stance maintained that RP 'is superior, from the character of its vowel sounds, to any other form of English, in beauty and clarity' (Wyld 1934: 606). This position can hardly be seriously defended, for it would find /paɪnt/ aesthetically pleasing when it is the RP pronunciation *pint*, but unaesthetic as the Cockney pronunciation *paint*. Furthermore, it is based completely on social prejudice that cannot be substantiated by native speakers of English who are unfamiliar with RP. North Americans, for instance, are not only incapable of distinguishing RP from near-RP; they cannot even be counted on to distinguish it from Irish, Scottish or Welsh English (all are equally foreign and British sounding).

The intelligibility argument   When, early in the century, Jones chose RP as the basis for his description of English pronunciation, one of his arguments was that RP and near-RP are easily *understood* almost everywhere that English is spoken. It is certainly true that RP is frequently heard in the media and is therefore easily accessible to many students of English as a foreign language (EFL). Furthermore, familiarity helps to guarantee comprehensibility. Yet this should not be overvalued, for in the words of Trudgill, 'Differences between accents in the British Isles are hardly ever large enough to cause serious comprehension difficulties' (1975: 53). In addition, it is conceivable that people in parts of the world where RP is not familiar (particularly in the sphere of influence of AmE) might find RP less intelligible than GenAm.

The scholarly treatment argument   RP has long been the basis of linguistic treatments of English pronunciation and has been used in EFL teaching materials (including tape recordings and pronunciation exercises) to a degree that far outdistances any other accent. Hence for purely practical purposes RP has a lot to recommend it. Material based on other accents, mainly GenAm, is also available. Most teachers see the advantage in using a single standard in the initial stages of EFL teaching, whichever it is, but few would dispute the necessity of exposing more advanced students to both RP and GenAm, at least, and preferably to other important accents as well.

The social argument   As the introductory remarks to this section indicate, RP does have social associations. While it is not exclusive to any particular class, it is, nonetheless, typical of the upper and the upper middle classes. In sociolinguistic studies such as that of Trudgill in Norwich it has become clear that RP is the overt norm in pronunciation for most of the middle class (and especially for women). On the other hand, in Norwich local speech forms and London vernacular forms were said to be the covert norms in the working class (particularly strongly among men; see also 9.2.3). This fact should not be lost on the foreign learner, who needs to be aware of the connotations of accent within English society, not only to understand how the English see (hear) each other, but also to realize what the accent he or she has learned may suggest to his or her interlocutors.

In actual fact people seldom choose an accent. Rather, they have one. (EFL students, of course, get one – initially, at least, their teacher's.) What counts is the norms of the group they belong to or identify with. People have the accent they have because they are where they are in society. However, a few who move up in society 'modify their accent in the direction of RP, thereby helping to maintain the existing relationship between class and accent' (Hughes and Trudgill 1996: 8).

In other words, some people aspire to 'talk better' and are or are not successful; others disdain this as 'talking posh' or using a 'cut-glass accent'. Just how strong the social meaning of accent is has been repeatedly confirmed by investigations designed to elicit people's evaluations. In so-called matched guise tests subjects were asked to rate speakers who differed solely according to accent (often the speaker was one and the same person using two or more accent 'guises'). The general results of such tests reveal that in Britain RP has more prestige vis-à-vis other accents, is seen as more pleasant sounding, that its speakers are viewed as more ambitious and competent, and as better suited for high status jobs. On the other hand, RP speakers are rated as socially less attractive (less sincere, trustworthy, friendly, generous, kind). It is reported, for example, that the content of an

Map 10.1 Great Britain

argument on the death penalty, identically formulated, but presented in four different accent guises, was more positively evaluated in the RP as opposed to three non-RP guises. Interestingly enough, the regional voices were, nevertheless, more persuasive (Giles and Powesland 1975: 93). Other experiments showed that people are more willing to comply with requests (e.g. filling out questionnaires, including the amount of written information provided) that are framed in an RP accent. Such results indicate the type of danger involved here. The expectation is that a distinctly non-RP accent may signal lack of competence and authority, an attitude hardly justified in times such as these when education is no longer a class privilege. What is even less justified is the expectation of many teachers that children with the 'right' accent who use StE are more intelligent or capable than those with a local accent and non-standard GenE forms. Yet no investigations have indicated that the use of non-prestige forms correlates with less intelligence or capability. What they do correlate with is class. Of course, imparting knowledge about the social evaluation of language is a legitimate educational goal, but this is different from wasting time trying to eliminate non-prestigious speech forms well anchored in regional peer groups. The latter is unlikely to meet with success. The need is really for greater linguistic tolerance in society coupled with more widespread training to a reasonable level of competence in StE, which is becoming absolutely necessary for more and more jobs.

10.2 SCOTLAND

10.2.1 The languages of Scotland

The move from England to Scotland (population: just over 5 million) is one of the linguistically most distinct that can be made in the British Isles as far as English is concerned. StE itself is well established throughout Scotland in government, schools, the media, business etc. in the specifically Scottish variety of the standard, which is usually referred to as **Scottish Standard English (SSE)**. Yet in many areas of everyday life there is no denying that forms of English are used in Scotland which are often highly divergent from the English of neighbouring England. These forms are ultimately rooted in the rural dialects of the Scottish Lowlands, which differ distinctly from the dialects south of the Border: there is 'a greater bundling of isoglosses at the border between England and Scotland . . . than for a considerable distance on either side of the border (Macaulay 1978: 142). (Note: an **isogloss** represents the boundary line between areas where two different phonetic, syntactic or lexical forms are in use.) The traditional rural dialects as well as their urban variations are collectively known as **Scots**.

Besides SSE and Scots one further non-immigrant language is spoken in Scotland. That is Scottish Gaelic, a Celtic language related to both Welsh and Irish. At present only a small part of the population (no more than 1.5 per cent) speaks Gaelic; the Gaelic language areas are located in the more remote regions of the northwest and on some of the Hebrides. Since 40 per cent of Gaelic native speakers live today in urban (= English language) Scotland, their continued use of the language is questionable. However, the situation of Gaelic has stabilized somewhat since the 1960s largely due to: the teaching of Gaelic in schools; bilingual primary education; the Gaelic playground movement;

Gaelic residential areas in Glasgow, Inverness, Skye, Lewis etc. Those who speak Gaelic are, in any case, bilingual and also speak English; their English is often influenced by their Celtic substratum (see 10.2.3).

10.2.2 Scots

Scots is frequently seen as slovenly and does not enjoy high overt prestige. While the language is undoubtedly widely used,

> social pressures against it are so strong that many people are reluctant to use it or have actively rejected it. . . . The only use of it made regularly by the media is for comedy. . . . [It] is repeatedly associated with what is trivial, ridiculous and often vulgar.
>
> (McClure 1980: 12)

While this statement is valid, it is also necessary to note that there are several different types of Scots, each with a different status and prestige. The variety so often and so subjectively regarded as vulgar is urban working class Scots; considerably more positive are the often romanticized rural dialects; a third type is literary Scots (sometimes termed **Lallans**, 'Lowlands'). This final variety is also sometimes pejoratively referred to as synthetic Scots because it represents an artificial effort to re-establish a form of Scots as the national language of Scotland and as a language for Scottish literature (much as was the case before the union of the crowns in 1603, when James VI of Scotland became James I of England, which eventually resulted in a linguistic reorientation of Scotland towards England).

Scots is commonly subdivided into four regional groupings. **Central Scots** runs from West Angus and northeast Perthshire to Galloway in the southwest and the River Tweed in the southeast. It contains both Glasgow and Edinburgh and includes over two thirds of the population of Scotland; it also includes the Scots areas of Ulster (see 10.3.2). **Southern Scots** is found in Roxburgh, Selkirk and East Dumfriesshire. **Northern Scots** goes from East Angus and the Mearns to Caithness. **Island Scots** is the variety in use on the Orkney and the Shetland Islands. The Shetlands are further distinguished by the continued presence of numerous words which originated in Norn, the Scandinavian language once spoken in the Islands (see Map 10.1).

The situation of Scots vis-à-vis SSE may be usefully summarized with regard to its historicity, its standardization, its vitality and its autonomy, all criteria useful in assessing language independence (see Macafee 1981: 33–7 for aspects of the following).

The **historicity** of Scots as the descendant of Old Northumbrian is clearly given, and Scots is consequently a cousin of the English of southeastern England, which was the basis of StE. Of course, Scots has been highly influenced by StE, not least in the form of the King James (Authorized) Version of the Bible (1611). Perhaps it is the success of the English Bible which has inspired the various more recent translations of the Scriptures into Scots (see Lorimer 1983). Lallans, as a language with literary ambitions, has drawn heavily on the older Scots language for much of its vocabulary, but this is not a natural process and the words it has adopted have no real currency, for few will seriously use *scrieve* rather than *write* or *leid* rather than *language*.

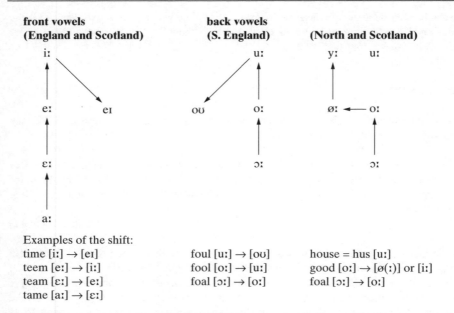

front vowels   **back vowels**

(England and Scotland)   **(S. England)**   **(North and Scotland)**

Examples of the shift:

time [iː] → [eɪ]   foul [uː] → [oʊ]   house = hus [uː]
teem [eː] → [iː]   fool [oː] → [uː]   good [oː] → [ø(ː)] or [iː]
team [ɛː] → [eː]   foal [ɔː] → [oː]   foal [ɔː] → [oː]
tame [aː] → [ɛː]

Figure 10.1 The Great Vowel Shift (GVS) in southern England and in northern England and Scotland

Part of the difference between English and Scots is due to changes in the long vowel system in the period between Middle and Early Modern English, known as the Great Vowel Shift (GVS). This shift ran differently in southern England from in northern England and Scotland. While the long front vowels changed in much the same manner in both places, the long back ones did not, giving us a fronted vowel [øː] in *good* and leaving [huːs] for *house* unchanged (see Figure 10.1)

Standardization is the goal of the creators of Lallans, but the tendencies of its champions are to reject as vulgar the Scots forms which have the most **vitality** or actual currency in everyday speech, namely those of the urban working class. A limited amount of success within the Lallans effort has been achieved in the area of standardization of spelling.

> For *good*, a Glaswegian says 'guid', a Black Isle speaker 'geed', a northeasterner 'gweed', and a man from Angus or the Eastern borders 'geud', with the vowel of French *deux*, but each could readily associate the spelling *guid* with his own local pronunciation.
>
> (McClure 1980: 30)

In a similar fashion <aa> is widely accepted as the spelling of either Central Scots /ɔ/ or Northern /a/ as in *ataa* 'at all'. But note that the common word /ne/ 'not' is spelled either as *na* or as *nae*.

The **autonomy** of the Scots dialects is, in general, least visible in vocabulary, for virtually all Scots speakers have long since orientated themselves along the lines of

English, even though Scots has retained numerous dialect words such as *chaft* 'jaw', *lass* 'girl', *ken* 'know', or *ilka* 'each, every'. The lack of a Scots standard is also reflected in the fact that there is sometimes a variety of local words for the same things, e.g. *bairn*, *wean*, *littlin*, *geet* ('child') or *callant*, *loon*, *chiel* ('boy'), or *yett*, *grind* ('garden gate') without there being any generally recognized Scots word.

More divergent, and hence more autonomous, are some of the grammatical forms. Among these note, for example, such non-standard morphology as the past and past participle forms of the verb *bake*, namely, *beuk* and *baken* or those of *work*, where both forms are *wrocht* (sometimes also spelled *wrought*). A few words also retain older plural forms: *coo* 'cow', plural *kye* 'cows' (see English *kine*), *soo* 'pig' (see StE *sow*), plural *swine* 'pigs', or *ee* 'eye', plural *een* 'eyes'.

The second person pronoun often retains the singular–plural distinction either using *thou/du* vs *ye/yi/you* or *yiz/youse*. Instead of StE relative *whose* one may find *that his* or *that her*. Furthermore, the demonstratives comprise a three way system: *this/that/yon* and *here/there/yonder* (for close, far and even further). Prepositions beginning with *be-* in StE often begin with *a-* in Scots, so *afore, ahind, aneath, aside, ayont* and *atween*. The verb is negated by adding *na(e)* to the auxiliary, e.g. *hasna(e), dinna(e)*. Furthermore, the auxiliaries are used differently; for example, *shall* is not present in Scots at all.

The syntax of Scots includes the possibility of an {-S} ending on the present tense verb for all person as a special narrative tense form, e.g. *I comes, we says* etc. (see 11.4.3 for a similar feature in American Black English).

The pronunciation of Scots, finally, is also tremendously important in defining its autonomous character. Quite in contrast to the other varieties of English around the world, 'Scots dialects . . . invariably have a lexical distribution of phonemes which cannot be predicted from RP or from a Scottish accent [i.e. SSE]' (Catford 1957: 109). By way of illustration, note that the following words, all of which have the vowel /u/ in SSE, are realized with six different phonemes in the dialect of Angus: *book* /ʊ/, *bull* /ʌ/, *foot* /ɪ/, *boot* /ø/, *lose* /o/, *loose* /ʌʊ/ (ibid.: 110).

The list given below enumerates some of the more notable features of Scots pronunciation:

- /x/ in *daughter*; in *night* it is [ç]
- /kn-/ in *knock, knee* (especially Northern Scots)
- /vr-/ in *write, wrought/wrocht* (especially Northern Scots); Island Scots: /xr-/
- the convergence of /θ/ and /t/ to /t/ and of /ð/ and /d/ to /d/ in Island Scots (the Shetlands)
- /uː/ in *house, out, now*; Southern Scots: /ʌu/ in word-final position (see GVS above)
- /ø/ or /y/ in *moon, good, stool*; Northern Scots: /iː/
- /eː/ in *home, go, bone*; Northern Scots: /iː/
- /hw-/ in *what, when* etc.; Northern Scots: /f-/

In Urban Scots many of the features listed are recessive, for example, /x/, /kn-/, or /vr-/. However, /hw/ is generally retained; furthermore, Scots remains firmly rhotic. Yet some younger speakers do merge /w/ and /hw/, and some also delete non-prevocalic /r/. Glasgow English is a continuum with a variety of forms ranging from Broad (rural) Scots to SSE. This involves a fair amount of code-switching as the following exchange overheard in an Edinburgh tearoom illustrates:

A: Yaize yer ain spuin.
B: What did ye say?
A: Ah said, Yaize yer ain spoon.
B: Oh, use me own spoon.
            (from Aitken 1985: 42)

Often pronunciations in which only certain lexical items retain a more traditional Scots pronunciation are found with only selected words while other words have an SSE realization. For example, the vowel /ɪ/ is found in the items *bloody*, *does* and *used*; /i/ in *bread*, *dead* and *head*; /u/ in *about*, *around*, *brown*, *cow*, etc; and /e/ in *do*, *home*, *no* etc.

Glasgow speakers have lost much of the traditional vocabulary of Scots; in its place, so to speak, they have available an extensive slang vocabulary of varying provenience, but it does include such Scots expressions as *plunk* 'to play truant' or local Glasgow *heid-banger* 'lunatic' (Macafee 1983: 43). Grammatical features of Glasgow English which differ from StE are a mixture of Scots forms such as verb negation using enclitic *-nae* or *-ny* (e.g. *isnae* 'isn't') and general non-standard forms which can be found throughout the English speaking world (e.g. multiple negation, as in *canny leave nuthin alane*, 'cannot leave anything alone').

10.2.3 Scottish Standard English (SSE)

StE in Scotland is virtually identical to StE anywhere else in the world. As elsewhere, SSE has its special national items of vocabulary. These may be general, such as *outwith* 'outside', *pinkie* 'little finger', or *doubt* 'think, suspect'; they may be culturally specific, such as *caber* 'a long and heavy wooden pole thrown in competitive sports, as at the Highland Games' or *haggis* 'sheep entrails prepared as a dish'; or they may be institutional, as with *sheriff substitute* 'acting sheriff' or *landward* 'rural'.

Syntactically, SSE shows only minor distinctions vis-à-vis other types of StE. For instance, in colloquial usage, the modal verb system differs inasmuch as *shall* and *ought* are not present, *must* is marginal for obligation and *may* is rare (Miller and Brown 1982: 7–11).

SSE has its own distinct pronunciation as is the case with all national or regional varieties of English. Some of its features are similar to those of Scots: It maintains /x/, spelled <ch>, in some words such as *loch* or *technical*. /hw/ and /w/ are distinct as in *wheel* and *weal*. /l/ is dark [ɫ] in all environments for most speakers though it is clear everywhere for some speakers in areas where Gaelic is spoken or was earlier; it is also clear in the southwest (Dumfries and Galloway) (Wells 1982: 411f.). This variation in the pronunciation of /l/ is rooted in the fact that SSE includes two very different traditions. One of these is the Lowlands Scots background, discussed above. The other tradition is that of Gaelic as a **substratum**. This means that the phonetic habits of Gaelic are carried over to English. The more immediate the influence of Gaelic, the more instances there will be of English influenced phonetically by Gaelic.

Outsiders are often struck by the fact that the glottal stop [ʔ] is widespread for medial and final /t/ in the central Lowlands, including Glasgow and Edinburgh. In Glasgow its use has been shown to vary with age, sex and social class, being more frequent among the young, among males and in the working class (Macaulay 1977: 48). This is, therefore, arguably not a feature of speakers of SSE.

SSE is a rhotic accent, pronouncing /r/ wherever it is written. The articulation of the /r/ is sometimes rolled or trilled [r], sometimes flapped [ɾ], sometimes constricted [ɹ]; however, some speakers even have non-rhotic realizations. Whatever the case, SSE differs considerably from other rhotic accents because it preserves the /e/–/ɪ/–/ʌ/ distinction before /r/ in words like *heard–bird–word*, where in RP and GenAm these vowels have all merged to central /ɜː/. Note, however, that there are a number of local differences within Scotland. Moreover, Scottish English also distinguishes between /o/ and /ɔ/ before /r/ as in *hoarse* and *horse*.

The vowel system of SSE does not, on the other hand, maintain all the vowel contrasts of RP. Where the latter has /uː/ in *fool* and /ʊ/ in *full*, SSE has undifferentiated /u/ in both and often central [ʉ] or even fronted [y]. Not quite as widespread is the loss of the contrast between /ɒ/ and /ɔː/ (*not* vs *nought*) and the opposition between /æ/ and /aː/ (as in *cat* and *cart*) are missing as well, though even less frequently. It has been suggested that these three stand in an **implicational relationship**, which means that whoever neutralizes /æ/–/aː/ also neutralizes the other two pairs. And whoever loses the opposition between /ɒ/ and /ɔː/ also loses that between /ʊ/ and /uː/, but not necessarily the /æ/–/aː/ one.

Scottish English does not rely on vowel length differences as both RP and GenAm do. Length does not seem to be phonemic anywhere. However, there are interesting phonetic differences in length which have been formulated as **Aitken's Law**. According to this all the vowels except /ɪ/ and /ʌ/ are long in morphemically final position (for example, at the end of a root such as *brew*, but also at the end of bimorphemic *brew + ed*). Vowels are also longer when followed by voiced fricatives, /v, ð, z/ and /r/. Because of this, *brewed* contrasts phonetically with *brood*, which has a shortened vowel (Wells 1982: 400f.). Closely related to this are the differing qualities of the vowels in *tied* and *tide*. The former is bimorphemic *tie + ed* with /ae/. *Tide* is a single morpheme in which the vowel is not followed by one of the consonants which causes lengthening; it has the vowel /ʌɪ/ (see Aitken 1984: 94–100).

10.3 IRELAND

Ireland is divided both politically and linguistically and, interestingly enough, the linguistic and the political borders lie close together. Northern Ireland (the six counties of Antrim, Armagh, Down, Fermanagh, Londonderry and Tyrone), with a population of approximately 1.5 million, is politically a part of the United Kingdom while the remaining 26 counties form the Republic of Ireland (population of about 3.5 million). Although Irish English (IrE), which is sometimes called Hiberno-English, shares a number of characteristics throughout the island, there are also a number of very noticeable differences (see 10.3.2 and 10.3.4). Most of these stem from fairly clear historical causes. The northern counties are characterized by the presence of Scots forms. These originated in the large scale settlement of the north by people from the Scottish Lowlands and the simultaneous displacement of many of the native Irish following Cromwell's subjection of the island in the middle of the seventeenth century. In what is now the Republic, a massive change from the Irish language (a Celtic language related to Welsh and Scottish Gaelic) began around the year 1800. The type of English which became established there stems from England and not Scotland and shows some signs of earlier settlement in the southeast by people from the west midlands of England. Most characteristic of southern IrE, however, are the numerous features in it which reflect the influence of Irish as the substratum language. In a few areas in the west called *Gaeltacht*, Irish is still spoken; and Irish is the Republic's official language (together with English, the second official language). The percentage of population who actually speak Irish is, however, very low (around two per cent).

10.3.1 Northern Ireland

The split in Ireland as a whole is reflected once again within the historical province of Ulster, which is partly in the Republic (the three counties of Cavan, Donegal and Monaghan) and partly in Northern Ireland. The population of Northern Ireland itself is divided very much along confessional lines, somewhat under one half Roman Catholic (the Republic is over 90 per cent Catholic) and the remainder chiefly Protestant. This, too, reflects the historical movement of people to and within Ireland. The northern and eastern parts of the province are heavily Scots and Protestant; the variety of English spoken there is usually referred to as Ulster Scots or, sometimes, Scotch-Irish. Further to the south and west the form of English is called Mid-Ulster English, and its features increasingly resemble those of English in the South, with South Ulster English as a transitional accent.

The same split, but also new, mixed or compromise forms, can be observed in Belfast, which at approximately half a million is the largest city in Northern Ireland and second only to Dublin in all of Ireland. Although there is a great and ever growing amount of sectarian residential patterning, speech forms in the city as a whole are said to be merging (Barry 1984: 120). Harris, for example, states: 'The vowel phonology of Mid Ulster English can be viewed as an accommodation of both Ulster Scots and south Ulster English systems' (1984: 125). Phonetically, however, there are distinct Ulster Scots and South Ulster English allophones in Belfast. One of the most potent reasons advanced for the increasing levelling of speech forms is the weakening of complex ('**multiplex**') social networks (with shared family, friends, workmates, leisure time activities). Especially in the middle class, where there is more geographical mobility, and in those parts of the working class where unemployment has weakened social contacts (in the non-existent workplace), there is a move away from complex local norms and distinctions, one of which is shared language norms (see Milroy 1991: 83f.). The practical consequence of the interplay of socio-economic patterns, regional origin and social networks of varying complexity in Belfast is a zigzag pattern of linguistic variants representing reality in which there is no unambiguous agreement on prestige models of speech (whether overt or covert). Furthermore, political affiliations (pro-British unionists vs Republican nationalists), especially where residence patterns, schooling and workplace are so highly segregated, help to reinforce this diversity of norms (Harris 1991: 46).

10.3.2 Characteristics of English in Northern Ireland

Northern Ireland has a number of distinct speech areas (see Map 10.2). In the north and the east there is a band of Scots speech areas running from County Down through Antrim and Londonderry to Donegal. Its linguistic features are similar to those described in 10.2.2, including Aitken's Law. Notably different is the lack of dark [ɫ] (see Harris 1985: 18–33). Generally to the south of these areas comes Mid-Ulster English, which is also the variety spoken in Belfast. In the very south of Ulster there is what has been called South Ulster English, a 'transitional dialect' (Harris 1984: 118) between Ulster English and Ulster Scots and southern Hiberno-English (see 10.3.4). The differences between these varieties are especially noticeable in their vowel phonologies. Harris (1985: 10) also emphasizes that the phonetic conditioning of vowel length in the Scots varieties as opposed to the phonemic length of the English varieties is mixed in Mid-Ulster English and Belfast Vernacular, 'the dialect upon which the regional standard pronunciation is based' (ibid.: 15). Belfast has also introduced some innovations, for example, more instances of dark [ɫ], the loss of the /w/–/hw/ distinction and some glottalization of voiceless stops before sonorants (*bottle* [baʔtɫ]. Ulster Scots has considerably more glottaling. Belfast also has local forms for *mother*, *brother* etc. without the medial /ʔ/ as in [ˈbrɔ͡ər]. Among the specifically northern grammatical forms the best known is probably the use of the second person plural pronoun *youse*. For other points see Harris 1984: 131–3.

10.3.3 Southern Ireland

In general, it seems that Southern Irish English has more features in common region-ally than it does differences; nevertheless, a speaker's origin is usually localizable. Social distinctions are, in contrast, much clearer. At the top of the social pyramid there is an educated variety, sometimes termed the 'Ascendancy accent', which is relatively close to RP. However, this accent does not serve as a norm. Indeed, if there is a standard of pronunciation, it is likely to be based on that of Dublin. English in Dublin is, of course, far from uniform. Bertz recognizes three levels: **Educated**, which is reserved for more formal styles and used by people with academic training; **General**, which is found over a wide range of styles and is used by the more highly trained (journalists, civil servants etc.); and finally, **Popular**, which is again stylistically more restricted, namely, to informal levels and which is typically heard among speakers with a more limited, elementary education.

Further distinctions in IrE are those which run along urban–rural lines. Filppula (1991) found that three typically IrE constructions (clefting, topicalization and the use of the subordinate clause conjunction *and*; see 10.3.4) were significantly more frequent among rural than among Dublin speakers. The explanations offered are: urban speakers are further from the Irish substratum; there were lower frequencies in rural Wicklow, which has long been English speaking, than in Kerry and Clare, where change has been more recent; furthermore, Dubliners have more contacts with the non-Irish English speaking outside world.

Map 10.2 Ireland

10.3.4 Characteristics of English in the south

In most general terms IrE in the Republic is characterized by the influence of the Irish language.

Pronunciation In the area of the vowels there is phonemic identity with RP which is only disturbed by the fact that IrE, which is rhotic, does not have the centring diphthongs. Nor does it have /ɜː/ since words with it in RP such as *purr* are phonemically analyzed in IrE as /ʌr/ (see Wells 1982: 420). The fact that there is such overall phonemic agreement between IrE and RP does not, of course, mean that the two actually sound alike. For one thing, the vowels of *gate* and *goat* are commonly the monophthongs /eː/ and /oː/. For another, the distribution of particular phonemes in various words may often differ. It is stereotypical of IrE, for example, to render a large number of words spelled with <ea> and pronounced in RP and GenAm as /iː/ with /eː/ in IrE: e.g. *tea, meat, easy* and also

Jesus. In addition, /ʌ/ and /ʊ/ are distributed in different and unpredictable ways so that /ʊ/ may occur in words such as *mother, sup* or *cut.* In addition, there is reportedly a great deal of variation between /ɒ/ and /ɔː/ in such words as *cross, loss, lost, often, cost.* Also /ɪ/ and /e/ regularly merge before a nasal so that *pin = pen.*

The actual quality of further vowels may differ markedly. /ɒ/ is usually unrounded [ɑ], more like the GenAm realization than the RP version. /æ/ is more open [a], and /ʌ/ is further back [ɜ]. The diphthongs /aɪ/ and /aʊ/ tend to have higher initial elements: [əɪ] and [əʊ], respectively; and /ɔɪ/ is not distinguished from /aɪ/ in all environments by all speakers.

The 24 consonants of RP and GenAm are matched by 22 in some varieties of IrE and the full 24 in others. The difference of two lies in the fact that for many speakers (in Cork and parts of Dublin) /θ/ and /ð/ have merged with /t/ and /d/ respectively. Most speakers, however, distinguish these phonemes, even though the distinction may not be recognizable to non-Irish ears: /t/ is articulated at the alveolar ridge while /θ/ is commonly dental [t̪], sometimes the affricate [tθ] and, in more sophisticated speech, [θ]; in the same fashion /d/ is alveolar, and /ð/ is [d̪] as well as [dð] and [ð]. The general lack of phonetic [θ] and [ð] as well as the split between dental and alveolar-palatal /t/ and /d/ can be attributed to the influence of the phonology of Irish. Furthermore, a final /t/ (sometimes even a prevocalic /t/) may be realized as a voiceless alveolar slit fricative [ṱ] as in *hit* [hɪṱ]. Note that intervocalic /t/ may be flapped and voiced [t̬] (as in GenAm) or even [r] or it may be glottalized [ʔ] (as in much popular urban speech in England and Scotland). Indeed, there seems to be increasing influence from urban British usage due to the great amount of emigration to Britain (with the consequent return visits in Ireland) and also due to a certain amount of permanent resettlement in Ireland after a period of work in Great Britain.

In IrE the two palatal stops, /k/ and /g/, are differentiated into the velar allophones [k] and [g] and the more palatal ones [kj] and [gj] as in [kjar] *car* or [gjardən] *garden* in some of the more conservative accents. The latter, 'palatalized' realizations are conditioned by a following front vowel and hence correspond to the phonotactic regularities of Irish. Other instances of the influence of Irish phonology in IrE are the realization of /w/ as a voiced bilabial fricative [β] and a clear [l] everywhere. In words borrowed from Irish /x/ may be retained (*Taoiseach* 'Prime Minister' [ˈt̪iːʃəx]).

A final interesting example of the influence of the substratum on pronunciation is the carry-over of what might be called consonant harmony within consonant clusters. In Irish the last consonant in a cluster determines whether the cluster as a whole will be made up of palatalized or unpalatalized consonants. In this sense the following consonants of IrE count as palatal: /t, d, ʃ, ʒ, n, l/ and the following as non-palatal: /t̪, d̪, s, z, r/. Concretely this means that a cluster such as /str/ (*strong*) will be non-palatal because of cluster-final /r/. /s/ is already non-palatal and is unproblematic, but /t/ is palatal and will therefore be realized as [t̪] thus producing [st̪raŋ]. Most non-Irish will not notice this, but more obvious is the following case: /l/ and /n/ and /t/ are palatal, hence a preceding /s/ in, say, *slow* or *snow* or *stop* must be palatal /ʃ/. The result is [ʃloː] and [ʃnoː] and [ʃtɑp].

Vocabulary   The vast majority of words in IrE are identical with those in other varieties of StE. In non-standard usage IrE does, however, include a number of words which represent older or regional usage in Great Britain or which reflect the effects of the Irish substratum. Examples of older items are *cog* 'to cheat on an exam', *airy* 'gay, light-hearted', or *bowsey* 'a disreputable drunkard'; instances of dialect words are *kink* 'spasm of laughter or coughing' or *blather* 'to talk nonsense at length'; illustrations of words borrowed from Irish are found in *spalpeen* 'rascal' or *sleeveen* 'sly fellow'. The ending {-een} comes from Irish and is a diminutive frequently added to words for something small or young as in *girleen* 'a small or young girl'.

Idioms and other expressions are frequently translations of Irish ways of saying things. The directions of the compass can therefore be *above* ('north') and *below* ('south'), *back* ('west') and *over* ('east'). The fact that Irish *fiadh* means both 'deer' and 'God' together with the fact that English has both the expressions *Oh dear* and *Oh God* makes the IrE extension *The Dear knows* 'God knows' all the more easy to use.

Grammar   In this area the influence of the substratum is once again obvious (for the following see especially Bliss 1984): 'Southern Hiberno-English has precisely the same range of tenses as Irish has, but the forms are built up out of English material' (Bliss 1984: 143). This means that the present perfect for reference to the recent past is periphrastic-ally realized as the preposition *after* + an {-ing} form of the verb as in *All the week it's after being cold*. This construction is, of course, not employed to the exclusion of the StE form. In a study of Dublin usage, the *after* construction appeared to be used most frequently in friendly encounters among family and acquaintances (Kallen 1991).

Another important consequence of the fact that IrE is modelled so closely on Irish is that the progressive is more widely used than in standard BrE or AmE. The restriction of the progressive to dynamic predicators is, as a result, not so absolute, e.g. *Who is this book belonging to?*

The use of habitual tense-aspect forms (the **consuetudinal**) is an expansion of the StE system. This provides for *I do be* ('I usually am') next to simple *I am* ('I am right now'). This can be extended to all the verb forms as in *He bees writing* vs *He does be writing* 'He usually writes'.

Sentence structure also differs at various points. IrE does not, for example, dictate changed word order in indirect questions (*They asked when would you be back*) nor is *if* or *whether* necessary to report *yes-no* questions (*I wonder does she honestly mean it*).

Several structures which are particularly Irish include changes in theme–rheme structure. For one thing this involves the relatively frequent use of fronting of elements to topicalize them (*A pastime he used to have*). Even more well known is the use of clefting, very much parallel to usage in Irish, to bring an element into topic position, e.g. *It's looking for more land a lot of them are.* Filppula (1991) found both to be common in all the areas he investigated (Counties Kerry and Clare; County Wicklow; Dublin), but more common in the rural areas where the influence of Irish is still strong in comparison to Dublin.

The use of *and* with the effect of a subordinating conjunction is frequently met with. How the conjunction is to be interpreted depends very much on the context, but usually it is temporal. In *He fell and him crossing the bridge* the effect is the same as that of *when*. Filppula, who investigated this construction as well as clefting and fronting, found that it is rarer than the other two (1991: 57).

IrE is further characterized by the extensive use that it makes of prepositions on the model of Irish. Possession is expressed by the verb *be* plus *on*, *at*, *near* or *by* (*There weren't any candles by this man* 'he didn't have any'; *It was a custom by them to go out on Christmas Eve* 'it was their custom . . .'; *It is not any common sickness that is on him* 'he doesn't have any . . .'). Existence is also expressed this way (*Sure there's no daylight in it at all now* 'there's none left'). A third typical use of prepositions is the dative of interest with *on* (*He was murdered on me one St Patrick's Day fair* 'this affected me'). For these and other examples see Bliss 1984: 149f.; Barry 1984: 108.

10.4 URBAN BRITISH ENGLISH

Throughout this chapter the English of a number of cities has been referred to. These varieties have enjoyed increasing attention from linguists in the past few decades. Some of the better known investigations have had to do with Norwich in East Anglia (Trudgill 1974), Glasgow (Macaulay 1977) and Belfast (J. Milroy 1981). Urban language surveys have not only provided a great deal of systematic, empirical data; they have also helped to advance insights into how people identify themselves linguistically and into some of the roles which language plays in modern urban society. Among the general conclusions which can be drawn from the work that has been done are the following (for discussion of some of these, see 9.2.3):

1   Urban accents are related to the pronunciations of the regions in which they are situated, with a sometimes high degree of koineization.
2   There are relatively few local lexical items.
3   Non-standard grammatical features are often shared over a wide geographic range (nationally or even internationally) (= GenE).
4   Phonetic variables are particularly revealing as sociolinguistic indicators of class, gender and age.
5   Sociolinguistic indicators are most visible for pronunciations currently involved in change.
6   Phonetic realization correlates highly with speech style (word list style, reading style, interview style, casual conversation).
7   Stigmatized pronunciations are most subject to variation according to style since they are most closely monitored.
8   Sociolinguistic indicators are not absolute, but functions of the frequency of occurrence.
9   Pronunciation change comes either from above (the overt norm) via the middle class or from below (the covert norm) via the working class.
10   Middle class women are most often leaders in change towards the overt norm; working class men are most often the initiators of changes towards the covert norm.

10.4.1 Cockney

Of all the urban varieties of English in the British Isles, Cockney, the one urban variety we will look at a bit closer, is doubtless the best known, not least because of its use in *My Fair Lady*. Traditionally, a Cockney is an inhabitant of London's East End. But from the point of view of language Cockney or near-Cockney can be heard throughout the city. In general, it is a working class accent, and as such it has little or no overt prestige. Its covert prestige is, however, enormous. In the form of it which Wells describes under the label London English, it 'is today the most influential source of phonological innovation in England and perhaps in the whole English-speaking world' (1982: 301).

The grammar of Cockney is basically of the non-standard vernacular type sketched out in 10.1.2. Its vocabulary is equally unexceptional. However, it is well known for its **rhyming slang**. This is not an exclusively Cockney feature, nor is it typical of the everyday speech of most Cockneys. But it does help to contribute to the image of Cockney as colourful. In rhyming slang a word is replaced by a pair of words, the second of which rhymes with the one replaced. For example, *my wife* may disappear in favour of *my trouble and strife* or, positively, *my fork and knife*. The new pair is often shortened so that someone may say *Use your loaf* instead of *Use your loaf of bread*; both mean the same: *Use your head*. The expression *Let's get down to brass tacks* ('Let's get down to business') is originally rhyming slang (*brass tacks* = *the facts*), though few people realize this.

What is most distinctive about Cockney is its pronunciation; and what is significant about this is the fact that Cockney pronunciations have often indicated the way in which RP was eventually to develop. This does not mean, of course, that RP will indeed adopt all of the points which are discussed below; for many of them are so highly stigmatized that adoption of them in RP and near-RP varieties is, in many cases, virtually inconceivable in the immediate future (H-dropping, Cockney vowels, more extreme forms of the use of the glottal stop etc.). For the following (and more) see Wells 1982: chapter 4.2.

Among the consonants, Cockney is characterized by H-dropping, as just mentioned. While the spelling <h> at the beginning of words such as *hour* and *honour* is never pronounced in any standard variety and while its pronunciation in some items is variable (*hotel, herb, human*) depending on the region or the individual, there are no limits in Cockney on the words beginning with <h-> which may sometimes occur without /h/, e.g. *'ouse* for *house* (see 3.3.4). The voiceless stops /p, t, k/ are frequently more strongly aspirated than in RP or GenAm. They are affricates in some cases: [tˢəɪ] (*tea*) or [kˣoʊ] (*call*). Furthermore, in final position the same stops may have glottal coarticulation, i.e. a glottal stop just before the oral one, e.g. [ɛʔt] (*hat*). It is also possible for the glottal stop to replace /p, t, k/ completely. This could lead to a loss of the distinctions between *whip*, *wit* and *wick*, all as [wɪʔ]. In addition, intervocalic /t/ may be realized as tapped [ɾ] or as the glottal stop. The former is making inroads into RP; the latter is found in numerous urban dialects in Great Britain (but seldom in Ireland). The fricatives /θ/ and /ð/ are very frequently, but not exclusively pronounced as /f/ and /v/ respectively, i.e. *three* = *free* and *mother* rhymes with *lover*. One exception is that initial /ð/ is not realized as /v/; instead /d/ may be used (*these* = *D's*). Following /t, d, n/ Cockney may have /uː/ instead of /juː/ (*tune* = *toon, dune* = *doon, news* = *noos*). In the case of /t/ and /d/ there seems to be a switch in progress towards a following /j/ which is then palatalized, e.g. /t/ + /j/ → /tʃ/ (*Tuesday* = *Chewsday*). One last point about the consonants is the vocalization of /l/ (see 4.2). Here words like *milk* may be pronounced with new diphthongs, e.g. [mɪʊk]. The same sort of thing is happening in Australia and New Zealand (see 13.1.1 and 13.2.1) and in the American South.

The traditional complex vowels (long vowels and diphthongs) of Cockney are noticeably different from their RP and GenAm equivalents. Those which are front or have a front second element in RP start at a progressively lower or more greatly backed position (see Figure 10.2). Those which are back or have a back second element in RP start at a progressively lower or more fronted position (see Figure 10.3). One of the consequences of these shifts in articulation is that RP *light* sounds virtually the same as Cockney *late*. (For other vowel shifts, see 10.2.2, 11.2.2 and 13.1.1.)

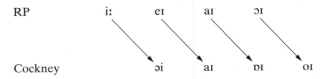

Figure 10.2 Cockney diphthongs with a front second element in comparison with RP

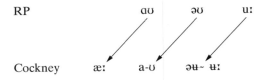

Figure 10.3 Cockney diphthongs with a back second element in comparison with RP

Estuary English (London regional English) is a koineized form of English that seems to be developing in London and its vicinity (the Thames Estuary and the lower Thames valley). It shares the less stigmatized features of Cockney and may be on its way to becoming competition to RP as the pronunciation norm in Britain, as evidenced by the spread of some of its features to cities far removed from the London area (e.g. Bristol, Hull, Liverpool, Manchester, Glasgow). Like Cockney it shows a move of /eɪ/ to [aɪ] and /aɪ/ to [ɑɪ], L-vocalization, the palatalization of initial /tj-/ and /dj-/, the loss of /j/ in words like *new* etc. increasing replacement of /t/ by [ʔ]. It does not, for example, have H-dropping or the replacement of /θ, ð/ by /f, v/. And in contrast to Cockney the real-ization of /r/ in Estuary English may be [ɰ] and /s/ may be rendered as /ʃ/ at the beginning of consonant clusters, e.g. /stuːdənt/, /stɒp/ and /əbˈstrʌkt/ become [ʃtuːdənt], [ʃtɒp] and [əbˈʃtrʌkt].

10.4.2 British Black English

Since the early 1960s the ethnic make-up of most British cities has changed enormously. High levels of immigration from Commonwealth countries which are not primarily ethnic-ally European have produced a 'multicultural Britain'. As positive as *multicultural* sounds on paper, the reality has been different. Prejudice and discrimination, subtle and open, have prevented the full assimilation of many of these 'New Commonwealth citizens'. While it is presumptuous to assume that these immigrants and their children want to become replicas of the English people around them, economic integration requires a command of GenE. This means that there are two forces pulling on them. The one, the overt norm, is towards General English, be it StE or the local vernacular. In the case of the descendants of black Britons from the Caribbean, the other force, the covert norm, is pulling them towards the ethnic variety or '**patois**', London Jamaican. The latter is a koineized form of West Indian Creole used by second generation British Blacks. It resem-bles Jamaican Creole more closely than it does the Eastern Caribbean varieties. Although it differs from Jamaican Creole in avoiding many of the 'deeper' creole forms (see

Sutcliffe 1984: 220–9), it has an overall resemblance to the Caribbean creoles treated in 11.7 and 14.3.3.

Sebba reports that there is 'considerable peer-group pressure' on young black males to learn it (1986: 156). However, there is far from complete agreement about what London Jamaican (also known as British Jamaican Creole) is like. Sebba thinks London Jamaican is nothing more than 'a set of rules applied to a London English "base" to "convert" London English to London Jamaican' (1986: 160). Sutcliffe, in contrast, speaks of British Jamaican Creole as having 'its own grammatical stability and separate integrity' (1984: 231).

To what extent the children of West Indian immigrants are Creole or GenE speakers has not been clearly established. What does seem fairly clear, however, is that most of these people regularly speak the English vernacular of their region and the patois only on certain occasions, but the majority of them can speak patois if they wish. In regard to young London Blacks Sebba writes:

> most of them are, first and foremost, speakers of London English. Among women nearly all conversation seems to be carried on in London English except in certain, reasonably well defined, circumstances, when Creole is used. Among males the situation is different . . . In formal situations, such as at school and when white people are present, London English is likely to be used.
>
> (1986: 151)

Various investigators have suggested that the vernacular as spoken by black Britons is hardly different from that of their white peers. Yet the few differences which do crop up may be particularly significant as markers of identity. Sutcliffe calls this variety, located between the creole and the English vernacular, British Black English; Sebba uses the term Afro-Caribbean London English. Both seem to agree that the differences are small. Possibly the difference lies in something in the tone of voice which has not been further defined (Sebba 1986: 152). A particularly indicative syntactic item is the use of *se* after verbs of speech and cognition in the same function as English *that* (*An all white jury found out se 'e was guilty*).

Young Blacks may indulge in code-switching involving the vernacular and the patois. Since their interlocutors often understand both codes, the question is why they do this. Sebba suggests that 'code-switching is used as a strategic and narrative device, as well as an additional resource for conveying affective meaning, i.e. for giving information about the attitude or state of mind of the speaker' (1986: 164). A switch may serve to show solidarity or distance, to mark off speech acts, to report speech, to frame a narrative (vernacular) or to create a black narrative persona (patois) (Sebba 1986: 163–7).

10.5 FURTHER READING

A recent popular book on BrE, including sections on Welsh, Welsh Gaelic and Scottish Gaelic, is Bartsch-Parker *et al.* 1999. A comprehensive collection of contributions on all sorts of English around the world, including of course BrE, is Burchfield's *English in Britain and Overseas*, 1994.

Wales   For more detail on Welsh English pronunciation see: Russ 1984; Thomas 1984; and contributions in Coupland 1990. On attitudes towards Welsh English, see Giles 1990.

England   Features of StE are treated in a comparison with AmE in Chapter 11. Pronunciation in English dialects in Wakelin 1983. Attitudes towards accents in Giles *et al.* 1990 and the literature cited there.

BrE dialects   For a short overview of English dialects see Wakelin 1984 and the bibliography there; Trudgill 1999 is a readable introduction. Useful collections of articles which are, however, not limited to England nor always to traditional dialects, are: Wakelin 1972; Viereck 1985; Trudgill and Chambers 1991. A very readable introduction to the diversity of urban speech is Hughes and Trudgill 1996. Milroy and Milroy 1993 is a collection of studies on non-standard grammar. Dialect pronunciation is also treated in Foulkes and Docherty 1999.

Scotland   The languages of Scotland are documented in *The Linguistic Atlas of Scotland* (Mather and Speitel 1975–7); see also Aitken 1979; Romaine 1984; Macafee and Macleod 1987; McClure 1994. For grammar, see Miller 1993. For pronunciation see: Catford 1957; Macafee 1981; Murison 1977. Macaulay 1997 looks at Scots urban speech. Görlach 2002 deals with Scots in Ulster. See also the journal, *Scottish Language*.

Ireland   Kallen 1997 is a collection of contributions on IrE. Northern IrE pronunciation is reviewed in: Harris 1984 and 1985; and Barry 1984. The linguistic situation is covered in part in insightful local studies such as: Bertz 1975; Filppula 1991; Kallan 1991; pronunciation in: Bliss 1984; Wells 1982. There is little information available about the suprasegmental features of IrE. On grammar see: Bliss 1984; Barry 1984; Filpulla 1991.

Urban English   L. Milroy (1984) and Cheshire (1991b) provide very useful overviews of the work done. **Cockney**, see: Barltrop and Wolveridge 1980; Wright 1981. Wells 1982 is, as usual, extremely useful on pronunciation; see also Gimson 2001. Hughes and Trudgill 1996 offer a brief characterization with a recording. On **Estuary English** see Coggle 1993; Rosewarne 1994; a brief characterization of its pronunciation may be found in Gimson 2001. **British Black English**. For linguistic details see: Sutcliffe 1984; Sebba 1986; Sebba's *Corpus of Written British Creole* is at http://www.ling.lancs.ac.uk/staff/mark/cwbc/cwbcman.htm.

Chapter 11

English in America

English is spoken as a native language in two major spheres in America. The larger one covers the United States and English speaking Canada; the other, lesser, sphere is the Caribbean area, centring on Jamaica, the Lesser Antilles and Guyana. A few peripheral areas, the creole speaking sections along the Atlantic coast of Central America and the Gullah area of South Carolina and Georgia, will be considered in Chapter 14 on pidgins and creoles; Puerto Rico is mentioned only in connection with Puerto Ricans living in the mainland United States.

These two areas are distinguished according to two linguistic criteria. The first is that educated Caribbean usage is relatively clearly oriented towards BrE while United States and Canadian English together make up AmE (despite numerous BrE features to be found in CanE). The second criterion is rooted in the Creole-English linguistic continuum which exists in CaribE, but not in AmE. A **continuum** is a spectrum of language forms between two extremes, but with only small, incremental differences as one moves from one point on the continuum to the next. At the one extreme, correlating with the lowest socio-economic and educational level of society, lie creole forms of English; at the other extreme there is StE in its West Indian form.

Both spheres, AmE and CaribE, encompass a fair amount of internal variation and the overview in this chapter will attempt to distinguish the most important regional, social and, above all, ethnic varieties of AmE, especially American Black English Vernacular (BEV), also known as African American Vernacular English (AAVE).

11.1 THE LANGUAGES OF THE UNITED STATES AND CANADA

The largest single English speaking area in the world is that formed by the United States and Canada. Approximately 85 per cent of the 275 million Americans and almost two thirds of the Canadian population of about 31 million had English as their native language in 2000. This is a sum total of approximately a quarter of a billion speakers. Many, but by no means all, of the inhabitants of Canada and the United States who do not have English as their first language, nevertheless use it in a multitude of different situations. The United States does not have an official language despite efforts by the 'English Only' movement; however, some 23 states have passed laws making it their official language (see McArthur 2002: 205f.). In Canada both English and French are official languages.

The next most widely used languages are Spanish and French. Significant numbers of Spanish speaking residents, many of whom are recent immigrants (both legal and undocumented), live in Miami (especially from Cuba) and New York (especially from Puerto Rico), as well as in neighbourhood pockets in many large American cities (generally from Mexico and Central America). Others live in communities whose Spanish language traditions go back hundreds of years (chiefly Chicano communities of the southwest).

French is the majority language of Quebec (almost 6 million native speakers with an English speaking minority of approximately 600,000). Ontario and New Brunswick also have sizeable francophone minorities; relatively few French speakers live in the remaining provinces and territories. In the United States the only concentrations of French are in New England, close to French Canada and in Louisiana, where speakers are divided into those of the standard metropolitan variety (descendants of the original French settlers), of Cajun French (descendants of the Acadians, expelled from what was then renamed Nova Scotia) and speakers of Creole French (mostly descendants of slaves).

Needless to say, countries of immigration such as Canada and the United States have large numbers of speakers of other mother tongues. Few of them, however, have settled in such a way that their languages have also been able to serve as community languages. Nevertheless, there are rural communities in both countries in which immigrant languages have been maintained over several generations (e.g. the German speaking Amish of Pennsylvania and the Russian speaking Doukhobors of Saskatchewan), and there are urban communities such as the numerous Chinatowns and Little Italy's, where languages besides English, French and Spanish are maintained.

Non-immigrant and non-colonial languages are still in daily use in some Native American environments. Perhaps 0.5 million of the 2 million American Indians and Alaska Natives in the United States can speak their traditional languages. In Canada approximately 62 per cent of the more than 0.5 million Native Canadians and Inuits (Eskimos) now have English as their native tongue (and 5 per cent have French); less than 200,000 speak their native languages.

Despite the large number of non-English native speakers (over one half in New Mexico, over one third in Hawaii, California, Arizona and Texas and over one quarter in New York), there are few places in the United States and Canada where it is not possible to communicate in English. (Note that, despite highly developed French–English bilingualism, there are some 4.25 million monolingual French speakers in Canada.) Language retention for English in Canada is given as 111.4 per cent, which means that English is spreading at the cost of other languages; for Canadian French the rate is 95.9 per cent; for all other languages, just over half (54.9 per cent). In the United States several non-English speaking groups are expanding noticeably, above all Spanish and Chinese; but the retention rate for native born children is generally not much higher than 50 per cent in the first American born generation.

11.2 NATIONAL AND REGIONAL VARIETIES OF AmE

11.2.1 Canada

CanE is solidly part of the American variety of English. Yet there are important features of CanE which distinguish it as an independent sub-variety of AmE. 'What is distinctly

Canadian about Canadian English is not its unique features (of which there are a handful) but its combination of tendencies that are uniquely distributed' (Bailey 1984: 161). Not the least of the factors contributing to the independence of CanE are the attitudes of anglophone Canadians, which strongly support a separate linguistic identity.

The effect of attitudes on language behaviour is revealed in a study in which Canadians with relatively more positive views of the United States and of Americans are also more likely to have syllable reduction in words like the following: *mirror* (= *mere*), *warren* (= *warn*), or *lion* (= *line*). They also have fewer high diphthongs in words such as *about* or *like* (see below) and are more likely to voice the /t/ in words like *party*, *butter* or *sister*. Finally, they use more American morphological and lexical forms. Pro-British attitudes correlate well with a preservation of vowel distinctions before an /r/, such as *spear it* vs *spirit*, *Mary* vs *merry* vs *marry*, *furry* vs *hurry* and *oral* vs *aural* as well as distinct vowels in *cot* vs *caught*. Pro-Canadian attitudes mean relatively more levelling of the vowel distinctions just mentioned, more loss of /j/ in words like *tune*, *dew*, or *new* (also true of speakers with positive attitudes towards the United States). Canadianisms are heard more among such speakers as well. A number of surveys have been conducted to register preferences with regard to the pronunciation of various individual words (*tomato* with /eɪ/ or /ɑː/, *either* with /iː/ or /aɪ/, *lever* with /e/ or /iː/ etc.) as well as spellings. Approximately 75 per cent say *zed* (BrE) instead of *zee* (AmE) as the name of the letter and just as many use *chesterfield* (specifically CanE) for *sofa* (AmE and BrE). Two thirds have an /l/ in *almond* (GenAm), but two thirds also say *bath* (BrE) the baby rather than *bathe* (AmE) it (Bailey 1984: 160). BrE spellings are strongly favoured in Ontario; AmE ones in Alberta. Indeed, spelling may call forth relatively emotional reactions since it is a part of the language system which (like vocabulary use) people are especially conscious of, in contrast to many points of pronunciation. This means that using a BrE spelling rather than an AmE one can, on occasion, be something of a declaration of allegiance. As the preceding examples indicate, differences between CanE and US AmE are, aside from the rather superficial spelling distinctions, largely in the area of pronunciation and vocabulary. Grammar differences are virtually non-existent, at least on the level of StE.

Vocabulary provides for a considerable number of Canadianisms. As with many varieties of English outside the British Isles, designations for aspects of the topography and for flora and fauna make up many of these items. Examples are: *sault* 'waterfall', *muskeg* 'a northern bog', *canals* 'fjords' (topography), *cat spruce* 'a kind of tree', *tamarack* 'a kind of larch', *kinnikinnick* 'plants used in a mixture of dried leaves, bark and tobacco for smoking in earlier times' (flora); and *kokanee* 'a kind of salmon', *siwash duck* 'a kind of duck' (fauna). The use of the discourse marker *eh?* is also considered to be especially Canadian (on discourse markers, see 7.5.2), for example:

> I'm walking down the street, eh? (Like this, see?) I had a few beers, en I was feeling priddy good, eh? (You know how it is.) When all of a sudden I saw this big guy, eh? (Ya see.) He musta weighed all of 220 pounds, eh? (Believe me.) I could see him from a long ways off en he was a real big guy, eh? (I'm not fooling.) I'm minding my own business, eh? (You can bet I was.)
>
> (McCrum *et al.* 1992: 264)

Many words peculiar to Canada are, of course, no different in status than the regional vocabulary peculiar to one or another region of the United States, and much of the vocabulary that is not part of BrE is shared with AmE in general.

The pronunciation of CanE (sometimes called General Canadian) applies to Canada from the Ottawa Valley (just west of the Quebec–Ontario border) to British Columbia and is similar to what has been described as GenAm (see Chapters 4 and 12). It shares the same consonant system, including the unstable contrast between the /hw/ of *which* and the /w/ of *witch*. Its vowel system is similar to that of the northern variety of GenAm, which means that the opposition between /ɑː/ and /ɔː/ as in *cot* and *caught* has been lost (except by the Anglophiles mentioned above). The actual quality of the neutralized vowel is said to vary according to the phonetic environment, for example [ɔ] (exclusively) as a possible regional realization in Edmonton. The distinctions between /iː/ and /ɪ/ (the stressed vowel of *beery* vs that of *mirror*), between /eɪ/, /e/ and /æ/ (*Mary* vs *merry* vs *marry*) and between /ɒ/ and /ɔː/ (*oral* vs *aural*) are rapidly dying out in CanE as they are in most varieties of AmE.

What shows up as the most typical Canadian feature of pronunciation is what is generally called 'Canadian raising'. This refers to the realization of /ɑʊ/ and /aɪ/ with a higher and non-fronted first element [ʌu] and [ʌi] when followed by a voiceless consonant. Elsewhere the realization is [au] and [aɪ]. Hence each of the pairs *bout* [bʌut] – *bowed* [baud] and *bite* [bʌit] – *bide* [baɪd] have noticeably different allophones. While other varieties of English also have such realizations (e.g. Scotland, Northern Ireland, Tidewater Virginia), the phonetic environment described here is specifically Canadian. One of the most interesting aspects of Canadian raising is its increasing loss (levelling to /ɑʊ/ and /aɪ/ in all phonetic environments) among young Canadians. This movement may be understood as part of a standardization process in which the tacit standard is GenAm and not General CanE. This movement has been documented most strongly among young females in Vancouver and Toronto and is indicative of a generally positive attitude towards things American, including vocabulary choice. However, an independent development among young Vancouver males, namely rounding of the first element of /ɑʊ/ before voiceless consonants as [ou], is working against this standardization and may be part of a process promoting a covert, non-standard local norm (Chambers and Hardwick 1986).

Regional variation in CanE   The emphasis in the preceding section was on the English westwards of the Ottawa Valley (sometimes called Central/Prairie CanE even though it reaches to the Pacific). It is an unusually uniform variety, at least as long as the focus is on urban, middle class usage – and Canada is overwhelmingly middle class and urban – and the bulk of the English speaking population lives in the area referred to. Working class usage is said to differ not only from middle class CanE, but also in itself as one moves from urban centre to urban centre. Woods shows working class preferences in Ottawa to be more strongly in the direction of GenAm than middle and upper class preferences are, at least in regard to the voicing of intervocalic /t/ and the loss of /j/ in *tune*, *new* and *due* words. Working class speech patterns also favour /ɪn/ over /ɪŋ/ for the ending {-ing} and tend to level the /hw/–/w/ opposition more completely (1991: 137–43).

Eastwards from the Ottawa Valley and including the Maritime provinces of New Brunswick, Nova Scotia and Prince Edward Island is the second major region of CanE. Here the norms of pronunciation are varied. For the Ottawa Valley alone Pringle and Padolsky distinguish ten distinct English language areas. Much of the variation they

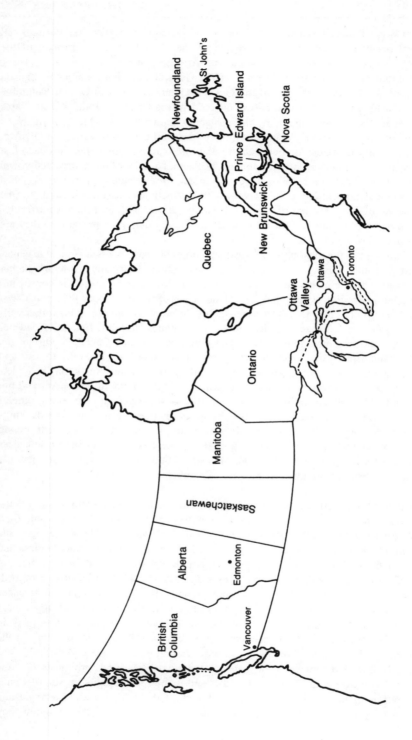

Map 11.1 Canada

recognize may be accounted for by the settlement history of the Valley: Scots, northern and southern Irish, Kashubian Poles, Germans and Americans (especially Loyalists who left the United States during and after the War of Independence) (Pringle and Padolsky 1983: 326–9). Although there is also much variation in the Maritime areas as well, the Eastern Canadian region is perhaps best characterized overall as resembling the English of New England, which is where many of the earliest settlers came from; there is, for example, less /ɑː/–/ɔː/ levelling, yet the English of this area is, like all of Canada, rhotic (/r/ is pronounced where spelled), while Eastern New England is non-rhotic.

The final distinct region of CanE is Newfoundland (population approximately 570,000). Wells even speaks of the existence of traditional dialects in Newfoundland, something which exists in the English speaking world only in Great Britain and Ireland and perhaps in the Appalachian region of the United States. The linguistic identity of Newfoundland is the result of early (from 1583 onwards) and diverse (especially Irish and southwest English) settlement, stability of population (93 per cent native born) and isolation. Since it joined Canada in 1949 its isolation has been somewhat less and the influence of mainland pronunciation patterns has become stronger. Yet the distinct phonological identity of Newfoundland English is well rooted. Southwestern English influences have been observed in the voicing of initial /f/ and /s/. IrE influences include clear [l] in all environments; also monophthongal /e/ (for /eɪ/) and /o/ (for /əʊ/ or /oʊ/); /ʌ/ is rounded and retracted. Some speakers neutralize /aɪ/ vs /ɔɪ/, realizing both as /aɪ/. The dental fricatives /θ/ and /ð/ are most often /t/ and /d/ (but also dental [t̪] and [d̪]). Furthermore, *pate* /pɛːt/ and *bait* /bɛɪt/ do not traditionally rhyme; /h/ is generally missing except in standard speech; and consonant clusters are regularly simplified, e.g. *Newfoun'lan'* or in *pos'* (= 'post') (see Wells 1982: 498–501). 'Canadian raising' is universal in all phonetic environments for some speakers (Chambers 1986: 13).

Many of these features are typical only of older Newfoundlanders, 'while the speech patterns of certain teenage groups would be, to the untrained observer at least, virtually indistinguishable from those of teenagers in such major Canadian centres as Toronto or Vancouver' (Clarke 1991: 111). In other words, considerable change is taking place in Newfoundland English, and 'age is by far the most important' (ibid.: 113) of the socio-linguistic factors involved, with females generally taking the lead. In contrast, 'loyalty to the vernacular norm is most evident among older speakers, males, and lower social strata' (ibid.: 116).

11.2.2 The United States

The regional varieties of English in the United States consist of three general areas (see Map 11.2): Northern, of which CanE is a part, Midland and Southern. Each of these may be further differentiated into subregions. Grammar is of relatively little importance for these three areas; most of the dividing and subdividing is based on vocabulary and pronunciation, though the two may not lead to identical areas. However, the lexical distinctions are themselves most evident in the more old-fashioned, rural vocabulary which is investigated in the various dialect geographical projects in or related to the 'Linguistic Atlas of the United States and Canada': The earliest to be carried out was the *Linguistic Atlas of New England* (LANE; Kurath *et al.* 1939–43), which was followed by numerous other regional *Linguistic Atlas* studies. Increasingly, general North American terms are replacing such distinctions as Northern *(devil's) darning needle*, or Midland *snake doctor/snake feeder* or Southern *mosquito hawk* 'dragon fly'. However, some urban terms continue to reinforce the older regional distinctions. For example, *hero* (New York), *sub/submarine* (Pittsburgh), *hoagie* (Philadelphia), *grinder* (Boston), *po' boy* (New Orleans) and a number of others all designate a roughly similar, over-large sandwich made of a split loaf or bun of bread and filled with varying (regional) goodies. Each of the cities just mentioned is, more or less coincidentally, also the centre of a subregion. On the whole, vocabulary offers distinctions which are often infrequent and which can usually easily be replaced by more widely accepted terms.

Pronunciation differences, in contrast to lexis, are evident in everything a person says and less subject to conscious control. The Southern accents realize /aɪ/ as [aˈ] or [a], that is, with a weakened off-glide or no off-glide at all, especially before a voiced consonant, and /uː/ and /ʊ/ are being increasingly fronted. Lack of rhoticity is typical of Eastern New England and New York City, but not the Inland North. It is also characteristic of Coastal Southern and Gulf Southern, even though younger white speakers are increasingly rhotic, while Mid Southern (also known as South Midland) has always been rhotic. Northern does not have /j/ in words like *due* or *new*, nor does North Midland, but /j/ may occur throughout the South. The /ɑː/–/ɔː/ opposition is maintained in the South (with tendencies towards its loss in parts of Texas), but has been lost in the North Midland and is weakening in the North. 'Canadian raising' is a Northern form which, despite its name, is common in many American cities of the Inland North (see 11.2.1).

The Northern Cities Shift is a demonstration of changes within AmE pronunciation. It is taking place in the northern dialect area of the United States (including Detroit, Chicago, Cleveland, Buffalo) and affects the short vowels. As the diagram shows, this involves a chain-like movement in which realization of each of the phonemes indicated changes, but the distinctions within the system are maintained (see 10.2.2, 10.4.1 and 13.1.1 for further chain shifts).

The pronunciation of the Northern Midland area more or less from Ohio westwards, has often been referred to as **General American** (GenAm). This label is a convenient fiction used to designate a huge area in which there are numerous local differences in pronunciation, but in which there are none of the more noticeable subregional divisions such as those along the eastern seaboard. Furthermore, the differences between North Midland and Inland North are relatively insignificant. Both areas are rhotic, are not likely

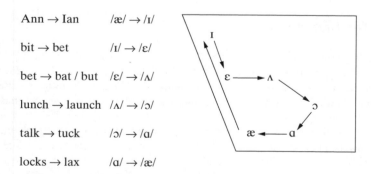

Ann → Ian	/æ/ → /ɪ/
bit → bet	/ɪ/ → /ɛ/
bet → bat / but	/ɛ/ → /ʌ/
lunch → launch	/ʌ/ → /ɔ/
talk → tuck	/ɔ/ → /ɑ/
locks → lax	/ɑ/ → /æ/

Figure 11.1 The Northern Cities Chain Shift

to vocalize /l/, have /aɪ/ as [æɪ] or [aɪ], do not distinguish /ɑː/ and /ɔː/ (or increasingly do not; note, however, that this opposition is still recognized in this book) and no longer maintain the /j/ on-glide in the *due* words. Most significant of all for the selection of North Midland for the label GenAm is the fact that it is this type of accent more than any other which is used on the national broadcasting networks.

The most noticeable regional contrast is that between North and South. This division is, in addition to vocabulary and pronunciation differences, underscored to some extent at least by grammatical features. It seems that it is only in Southern varieties, including Black English Vernacular (or African American Vernacular English; see 11.4.3), that such admittedly non-standard features occur as perfective *done* (e.g. *I done seen it*), future *gon* (*I'm gon* [not *goin'*] *tell you something*) and several more far reaching types of multiple negation, such as a carry-over of negation across clauses (*He's not comin', I don't believe* = 'I believe he's not coming').

It is also in the South that an area is to be found with speech forms approaching the character of a traditional dialect (such as otherwise found only in Great Britain and Ireland, and possibly also in Newfoundland). The dialect which is meant is Appalachian English and the related Ozark English, which are found in the Southern Highlands (Mid Southern on Map 11.2). The English of these regions is characterized by a relatively high incidence of older forms which have generally passed out of other forms of AmE. Examples include syntactic phenomena such as *a*-prefixing on verbs (*I'm a-fixin' to carry her to town*), morphological-phonological ones such as initial /h/ in *hit* 'it' and *hain't* 'ain't' and lexical ones such as *afore* 'before' or *nary* 'not any'.

11.3 SOCIAL VARIATION IN AmE

Besides differences according to the gender of the speaker (see Chapter 9) and race or ethnicity (see 11.4), there are significant differences according to the socially and economically relevant factors of education and social class. In North America socio-economic status shows up in pronunciation inasmuch as middle class speakers are on the whole more likely than those of the working class to adopt forms which are in agreement with the overt norms of the society. The now classic investigations of Labov in New York City in the 1960s provided a first insight into these relations (Labov 1972a). This may be illustrated by the finding that initial voiceless <th-> (as in *thing*) is realized progressively more often as a stop [t] or an affricate [tθ] than as a fricative [θ] as the classification of the speaker changes from upper middle to lower middle, to working to lower class (Labov 1972b: 188–90).

Although variation is usually within a range of regional or local variants, it may in some cases be a non-regional standard which is aimed at. For example, New Yorkers increasingly (with middle class women as leaders) pronounce non-prevocalic <r> even though rhoticity was not traditionally a feature of New York City pronunciation. Since younger speakers also favour pronunciation of this <r>, this is not only an excellent example of the differing speech habits of differing social classes and the greater orientation of women towards the overt norm, but also the gradual adoption of rhoticity by a new generation, a fact that indicates a probable long-term change in the regional standard.

Map 11.2 The United States

Social distinctions are especially perceptible in the area of grammar, where a remark-able number of stigmatized features (often referred to as *shibboleths*) apply supra-regionally. All of these features are within the scope of GenE. Nevertheless, a person is regarded as uneducated, unsophisticated and uncouth who uses

1   *ain't* (e.g. *I ain't done it yet*)
2   a double modal (*I might could help you*)
3   multiple negation (*We don't need none*)
4   *them* as a demonstrative (*Hand me them cups*)
5   no subject relative pronoun in a defining relative clause (*The fellow wrote that letter is here*)
6   *don't* in the third person singular (*She don't like it*)
7   *was* with a plural subject (*We was there too early*)
8   *come, done, seen, knowed, drownded* etc. for the simple past tense
9   *took, went, tore, fell, wrote* etc. as a past participle.

Investigations of usage have revealed that these and other non-standard forms are used most by the less well educated of the rural and urban working class (e.g. Feagin 1979). Users are also frequently the oldest and most poorly educated rural speakers such as were often sought out for studies in the framework of the *Linguistic Atlas* studies. It would be a mistake, however, for the impression to arise that such non-standard forms are somehow strange or unusual merely because StE, and therefore the written language, does not include them. The contrary is the case. All of them are very common. Indeed, many of them may be majority forms. In Anniston, Alabama, for example, third person singular *don't* was found to be used by all the working class groups investigated more than 90 per cent of the time, except for urban adult males, whose rate was 69 per cent. The use of singular *don't* by the Anniston upper class, in contrast, ranged from 0 to 10 per cent (Feagin 1979: 208). This type of situation seems to be the case wherever English is spoken.

11.4 ETHNIC VARIETIES OF AmE

As might be expected in countries of immigration, in the immigrant generation and some-times in the second generation many people speak an English which is characterized by first language interference. Experience has shown, however, that by the fourth generation most of the descendants of immigrants have become monolingual English speakers (Valdés 1988: 115f.), and virtually all signs of interference have vanished. There are then no grounds for speaking of an ethnic variety. Recognizing such a variety would be justi-fied only if it could be viewed as distinct from mainstream AmE and as self-perpetuating.

Yet there are some groups of native English speakers in North America who: (a) have an ethnic identity; and (b) speak a type of English which is distinct in various ways from the speech of their neighbours of comparable age, class, sex and region. For two of these groups it is uncertain whether it is really suitable to speak of ethnic rather than inter-ference varieties of English: Native American Indians and Chicanos. The third group, African Americans, include a large number who speak the ethnic dialect African American Vernacular English (see 11.4.3).

11.4.1 Native American English

Today the majority of American Indians are monolingual speakers of English. For most of them there is probably no divergence between their English and that of their non-Indian peers. However, among Native Americans who live in concentrated groups (on reservations) there are also 'as many different kinds of American Indian English as there are American Indian language traditions' (Leap 1986: 597). This is seen as the result of the on-going influence of the substratum (the traditional language) on English, even if the speakers are monolingual. Many of the special features of this English are such familiar phenomena as word-final consonant cluster simplification (e.g. *west* > *wes'*), multiple negation, uninflected (or invariant) *be* (see below 11.4.3), and lack of subject-verb concord. Although mainstream non-standard English has the same sort of surface phenomena, those of American Indian English may be the products of different grammatical systems (Toon 1984: 218). It is suggested, for example, that it is because a traditional language requires identical marking of subject and verb that Indian English may have such forms as *some peoples comes in* (ibid.).

11.4.2 Spanish influenced English

Hispanic Americans are one of the two largest ethnic minorities in the United States (Blacks are the other; each makes up approximately one eighth of the general population or about 35 million each in 2000). They consist of at least three major groups, Cubans, Puerto Ricans and Chicanos (or Mexican Americans; but many Central American immigrants are grouped with them as well).

Cubans   Approximately 600,000 of the roughly 1 million Cuban Americans live in Dade County/Miami in Florida; another 20 per cent in West New York and Union City, New Jersey. Because of this areal concentration they have been able to create unified communities with ethnic boundaries. Nonetheless, integration with the surrounding Anglo community is relatively great (a high number of inter-ethnic marriages), perhaps because Cuban Americans, due to the nature of emigration from Cuba, encompass all levels of education and class membership and are not relegated to an economically marginal position vis-à-vis the greater outside society. Only six per cent of the second generation of Cuban Americans were monolingual Spanish in 1976 (García and Otheguy 1988). 'Second-generation Cubans, as is usually the case with all second-generation Hispanics, speak English fluently and with a native North American accent' (ibid.: 183). Indeed, perhaps only the presence of loan words and calques/loan translations such as *bad grass* (> Span. *yerba mala* 'weeds') may indicate the original provenance of the speakers.

Puerto Ricans   Puerto Ricans have, as American citizens, long moved freely between the mainland United States and Puerto Rico. Most originally went to New York City (see, for example, *West Side Story*), and although many have moved to other cities in the meantime, approximately 60 per cent of mainland Puerto Ricans are still to be found there, where they often live in closely integrated ethnic communities. Many members of these communities are bilingual (only one per cent of second generation mainland Puerto Ricans are monolingual Spanish speakers; García and Otheguy 1988: 175), and there are a number of differing Spanish–English constellations of language usage within families.

One investigation showed that those 'reared in Puerto Rico speak English marked by Spanish interference phenomena, while the second generation speaks two kinds of non-standard English: Puerto Rican English (PRE) and/or black English vernacular (BEV)' (Zentella 1988: 148).

Chicanos   Chicanos make up by far the largest proportion of the Hispanic population of the United States and are a rapidly growing group. They include recent immigrants as well as native born Americans who continue to live in their traditional home in the American Southwest (Texas, New Mexico, Arizona, Colorado and California), which was conquered from Mexico and annexed in the middle of the nineteenth century. Chicanos are most numerous in California, where they are an urban population, and in Texas, especially southwest Texas, where they are often relatively rural. Spanish is more commonly maintained in the Texas than in the California environment. Furthermore, large numbers of Mexican and Central American Hispanics live in urban centres throughout the United States.

The type of English spoken by many of these people – some bilingual, others mono-lingual English speakers (5 per cent of second generation Mexican Americans remain monolingual Spanish speakers; García and Otheguy 1988: 175) – consists of several vari-eties. Among bilinguals it is characterized by frequent code-switching (sometimes referred to as Tex-Mex). For many speakers English is a second language and contains numerous signs of interference from Spanish. However, whether an 'interference variety' or a first language, the linguistic habits of a large portion of the Chicano community are continu-ally reinforced by direct or indirect contact with Spanish, whose influence is increased by the social isolation of Chicanos from Anglos. Most important for regarding Chicano English as an ethnic variety of AmE is that it is passed on from generation to generation and serves important functions in the Chicano speech community. The maintenance of Chicano English as a separate variety 'serves the functions of social solidarity and supports cohesiveness in the community' (Toon 1984: 223). It can be a symbol of ethnic loyalty as when Chicanos use it as one means of Chicano identity vis-à-vis both Mexicans and Anglos.

The linguistic features of Chicano English are most prominently visible in its pronunciation, including stress and intonation. There seems to be little syntactic and lexical deviation from GenE. As with Puerto Ricans, contact with Blacks may result in the use of various features of Black English among working class Chicanos.

Pronunciation (with obvious signs of Spanish influence):

1   stress shift in compounds (*'miniskirt* → *mini'skirt*)
2   rising pitch contours (independent of the final fall) to stress lexical items
3   rising pitch in declarative sentences
4   devoicing and hardening of final voiced consonants (*please* → *police*)
5   realization of labio-dental fricative /v/ as bilabial stop [b] or bilabial fricative [β]
6   realization of /θ/ and /ð/ as [t] and [d] (*thank = tank*; *that = dat*)
7   realization of central /ʌ/ as low [a] (*one = wan*)
8   simplification of final consonant clusters (*last = las'*)
9   merger of /tʃ/ and /ʃ/ to /ʃ/ (*check* → *sheck*)
10 merger of /iː/ and /ɪ/ to /ɪ/ (*seat = sit*) and of /eɪ/ and /e/ to /e/ (*gate = get*) and occa-sionally of /uː/ and /ʊ/ as /ʊ/ (*Luke = look*).

The final two points distinguish Chicano English from the second language 'interference' variety. The predictable interference pattern would be a realization of /ʃ/ as /tʃ/, of /ɪ/ as /iː/, of /e/ as /eɪ/ and of /ʊ/ as /uː/ since Spanish has only the latter member of each pair. As pointed out above under 9 and 10, Chicano speakers often realize the member of each pair which is not predicted, and this is what distinguishes such Chicano speakers from both Mexicans and Anglos.

Various studies have shown that there are considerable obstacles in the way of general acceptance of Chicano English as equivalent to other accents of StE. A matched guise test, for example, in which the participants were told that all the voices they heard were those of Mexican Americans showed a clearer association of pejorative evaluations (stupid, unreliable, dishonest, lazy etc.) with a Chicano voice than with a near-Anglo accent (Arthur *et al.* 1974: 261).

11.4.3 Black English (BEV/AAVE)

The most widely recognized and widely researched ethnic dialect of English is Black English Vernacular, also known as African American Vernacular English. Before looking at it more closely, it should be pointed out that many middle class Blacks do not speak BEV/AAVE, but are linguistically indistinguishable from their white neighbours. Rather, it is the poorer, working and lower class African Americans, both in the rural South and the urban North, who speak the most distinctive forms of this dialect. It is often distinctly associated with the values of the vernacular culture including performance styles especially associated with black males in such genres as the dozens, toasting, ritual insults etc., but also chanted sermons (Abrahams 1970; Kochman 1970; Rosenberg 1970).

One of the main debates which have raged in connection with BEV/AAVE concerns its origins. Some maintain that it derives from an earlier Plantation Creole, which itself ultimately derives from West African Pidgin English (see Dillard 1972; Burling 1973; Labov 1998; Rickford 1998; see also Chapter 14.3). This would mean that BEV/AAVE contains grammatical categories (especially of the verb phrase) which are basically different from English. The converse view is that BEV/AAVE derives from the English of the white slave owners and slave drivers, which ultimately derives from the English of Great Britain and Ireland. BEV/AAVE, so conceived, is only divergent from StE in its surface forms. It is, in addition, possible to take a position in between these two, maintaining that both have had influence on BEV/AAVE.

In evaluating the question of origins it has generally been conceded that BEV/AAVE has a phonological system which is often greatly different from that of GenAm, though often remarkably similar to White Southern Vernacular English. Since BEV/AAVE has its more immediate origins in the American South, pronunciation similarities between the two are hardly astonishing. This explains the followed shared features:

1   realization of /aɪ/ as [a] before voiced consonants (*I like it* sounds like *Ah lock it*);
2   convergence of /ɪ/ and /e/ + nasal (*pin = pen*);
3   merger of /ɔɪ/ and /ɔː/, especially before /l/ (*boil = ball*);
4   merger of /ɪ/ and /æ/ before /ŋk/ (*think = thank*);
5   merger of /i(r)/ and /e(r)/ (*cheering = chairing*) and of /ʊ(r)/ and /ɔ(r)/ (*sure = shore*).

Furthermore, both are historically non-rhotic (though White Southern Vernacular English is increasingly being rhoticized; see Bailey/Thomas 1998: 91), both vocalize /l/ (*all* = *awe*), and both simplify final consonant clusters (*best* → *bes*; *hand* → *han*) (for further points of difference and similarity, see Bailey/Thomas 1998).

It is this final point which, in the end, also distinguishes the two accents, for BEV/AAVE carries the deletion of final consonants much further than Southern White Vernacular does. While both might simplify *desk* to *des'* (and then form the plural as *desses*), BEV/AAVE deletes the inflectional endings {-D} and {-S} more frequently so that *looked* becomes *look* and *eats*, *tops* and *Fred's* become *eat*, *top* and *Fred*. Some people have called the existence of the category of tense in BEV/AAVE into question because the past tense marker {-D} is so frequently missing. However, the past tense forms of the irregular verbs, where the past does not depend only on {-D}, e.g. *catch* – *caught* or *am/is/are* – *was/were* are consistently present. Hence any conclusion about the lack of tense would be mistaken. Indeed, the tense and aspect system of BEV/AAVE is remarkably complex and allows its speakers to make distinctions which speakers of StE cannot make within the grammatical system of StE (see the list below).

Furthermore, there are some remarkable grammatical differences between BEV/ AAVE and comparable forms of Southern Vernacular White English. The absence of third person singular present tense {-S} is far reaching. One study shows 87 per cent deletion of BEV/AAVE versus 11 per cent deletion for Southern White Vernacular (Wolfram 1971: 145; see also Fasold 1986: 453f.). Consequently, it is not unreasonable to conclude that it is not well anchored in BEV/AAVE ('AAVE shows no subject-verb agreement, except for present-tense finite *be*' Labov 1998: 146). This, of course, is not a terribly serious loss since there is no potential confusion of meaning as there can be when {-D} is lost. With plural {-S}, which does carry important meaning, there is much less frequent deletion than with the verb ending {-S} (Fasold 1986: 454).

A number of grammatical features specific to BEV/AAVE have been pointed out. They include

1   **stressed *béen*** (sometimes given as *bín*) as a marker of the remote past (e.g. *The woman béen married*, which does not mean 'The woman has béen married (but no longer is)', as a StE speaker might assume, but indicates something which happened in the more distant past and whose results are in effect: 'The woman has been married a long time' (see Martin and Wolfram 1998: 14; Green 1998: 46f.; Labov 1998: §5.5.4);

2   **non-finite *be*** as a marker of habitual aspect, e.g. *he be eating* 'he is always eating' (see e.g. Green 1998: 45f.; Labov 1998: §5.5.1 gives a slightly different view); this stands in contrast to *he eating* 'he is eating (right now)';

3   **perfective *done*** (sometimes given as *dən*) for perfective or completive aspect as when an event has taken place and is over (even though its effects may still be in effect), e.g. *they done washed the dishes* 'they have already washed the dishes'; like the StE present perfect this form does not co-occur with past adverbials nor with stative verbs (see e.g. Green 1998: 47f.; Labov 1998: §5.5.2);

4   **sequential *be done***, often as a future resultative marker, shows one of several possibilities of combining the aspectual markers just given, e.g. *I'll be done killed that motherfucker if he tries to lay a hand on my kid again* 'I'll kill him if he should try to hurt my kid' (Labov 1987: 7f.; 1998: §5.5.3);

5   **no** or **infrequent third person singular present tense {-S}** as explained above; where the verb *be* appears as an inflected form we find *I* + *am*, but *you, he/she/it, we, y'all, they* + *is* (Green 1998: 42);

6   **third person singular present tense {-S}** used as a marker of narrative in contrast to unmarked non-narrative usage; this is viewed as a recent development (Labov 1987: 8f., but see 10.2.2. for a similar feature in Scots);

7   **the past and the past participle** are frequently identical, e.g. *I ate* 'I ate' or 'I have eaten'; the two are distinguished when emphatic (*I DID eat* vs *I HAVE ate*) or when negated (*I didn't eat* vs *I ain't/haven't ate*) (Green 1998: 40f.);

8   some young speakers form the **simple past of a verb** using *had* + lexical verb as in *I had got sick* 'I got sick') (ibid.: 43);

9   **relative clauses** (virtually exclusively defining ones, since non-defining relatives are typical of rather formal, especially written language) are seldom formed using *who, which* and *whose*; zero relative is preferred, even when the relative element is the subject of the relative clause, e.g. *That's the man [Ø] come here the other day* (Mufwene 1998: 76f.);

10   **plural marker** and **demonstrative** *them* is widely used (as elsewhere in non-standard English), e.g. *them/dem boys*; this includes what is known as the **associative plural**, a form of *them* added to a definite noun, e.g. *Felicia nem* (< *and them*) *done gone* 'Felicia and the others have already gone' (Mufwene 1998: 73);

11   **negative concord** (also known as **multiple negation** or **pleonastic negation**) allows not just one single negation, as in StE, but permits the negation to be copied onto all the further indefinite (so-called **negative polarity items**), even in cases where the negation is copied onto a subordinate clause as in *He don't think nothing gonna happen to nobody because of no arguments* (Martin/Wolfram 1998: 23);

12   **question formation** may occur without inversion both in indirect questions, e.g. *They asked could she go to the show*, and in direct questions (though less frequent), e.g. *Who that is? Why she took that?* (ibid.: 27ff.);

13   **double modals** (as are frequently used in Southern AmE), e.g. *I might could of (= have) gone.*

The most discussion has centred around what is called **non-finite** or **invariant** or **distributive** *be* (2 in the preceding list). In order to understand what this is, it is first necessary to note that there are two distinct uses of the copula *be* in BEV/AAVE. The one involves zero use of the copula, e.g. *She smart* = 'She is smart', which describes a permanent state or *She tired* 'She is tired', which names a momentary state. Here colloquial white English might use a contraction (*She's smart*); BEV/AAVE may be thought of as deleting instead of contracting. Where contraction is not possible in StE, neither is deletion in BEV/AAVE, e.g. *Yes, she really is*. Invariant *be*, in contrast, is used to describe an intermittent state, often accompanied by an appropriate adverb such as *usually* or *sometimes*, e.g. *Sometimes she be sad*.

The major question is where this form comes from (origins again). It seems that invariant *be* does not occur in the most extreme creoles, though it does in some de-creolized forms. Therefore they are an unlikely source. Some studies of White Southern Vernacular: (a) show it to be rare; and (b) do not indicate clearly whether it carries the same meaning as in BEV/AAVE or whether it is not merely an instance of *will/would be* in which *'ll* or *'d* have been deleted (Feagin 1979: 251–5). The White Vernacular is therefore also not a very likely source of this construction. One investigation of southern BEV/AAVE even reveals it to be something of a rarity there, too (Schrock 1986: 211–14). However, the *Linguistic Atlas of the Gulf States* turns up instances of it in both black and (a very few instances of) white vernacular speech. In this data invariant *be* sometimes represents deletion of *will* and *would*, but more often it is used for an intermittent state (including negation with *don't*: *Sometime it be and sometime it don't*) and, with a following present particle, for intermittent action (*How you be doing?*) (Bailey and Bassett 1986). If invariant *be* is an innovation of BEV/AAVE, then this would speak for an increasing divergence of BEV/AAVE from white vernacular forms. This question has been hotly, but inconclusively, debated (*American Speech* 1987; see also Butters 1989). Whatever its source may actually be, invariant *be* is a construction that speaks strongly for the status of BEV/AAVE as an independent ethnic dialect of English.

11.5 THE LANGUAGES OF THE CARIBBEAN

The Caribbean stretches over a wide geographical area and includes, for our purposes, at least 19 political units which have English as an official language (see Map 11.3): Anguilla, Antigua-Barbuda, The Bahamas, Barbados, Belize, the British Virgin Islands, the Cayman Islands, Dominica, Grenada, Guyana, Jamaica, Montserrat, Puerto Rico (with Spanish), St Kitts-Nevis, St Lucia, St Vincent, Trinidad-Tobago, the Turks and Caicos Islands and the American Virgin Islands. In addition to these countries and territories there are numerous others with Spanish as the official language (Costa Rica, Cuba, Columbia, the Dominican Republic, Guatemala, Honduras, Mexico, Nicaragua, Panama, Puerto Rico (with English) and Venezuela), as well as a few with French (Guadeloupe, Haiti, Martinique) and Dutch (Aruba-Bonaire-Curaçao and Surinam). Although the majority of the islands are anglophone, the largest are not (Cuba and Hispaniola [the latter with the Dominican Republic and Haiti]); and Puerto Rico is chiefly Spanish speaking. The mainland all the way from Guyana to the United States is hispanophone with the exception of Belize. In the sub-US Caribbean the 5 to 6 million inhabitants of the anglophone countries are greatly outnumbered by their Spanish speaking neighbours.

Below the level of official language policy lies the linguistic reality of these countries. Here English is truly a minority language, for the vast majority of people in the anglophone countries are speakers not of StE or even GenE, but of English creoles. In addition, Guyana and Trinidad-Tobago have a number of Hindi speakers. Guyana also has Amerindian language speakers. Belize has Amerindian as well as Spanish speakers. Spanish is used by small groups in the American Virgin Islands and Jamaica. French Creole is widely spoken as a vernacular in Dominica and St Lucia as well as by smaller groups in the American Virgin Islands and Trinidad-Tobago. English creoles are, however, the major languages on most of the anglophone islands; furthermore, they are in use on the Caribbean coast of several Central American countries besides Belize.

English creoles refer to vernacular forms which are strongly related to English in the area of lexis, but which diverge from it syntactically, so strongly, in fact, that it is not unjustified to regard them as separate languages rather than dialects of English (see 14.3). The various English creoles not only share a similar historical development; in addition, migration patterns between the various Caribbean countries as well as with West Africa may have further heightened their mutual resemblance. More recently migration to and

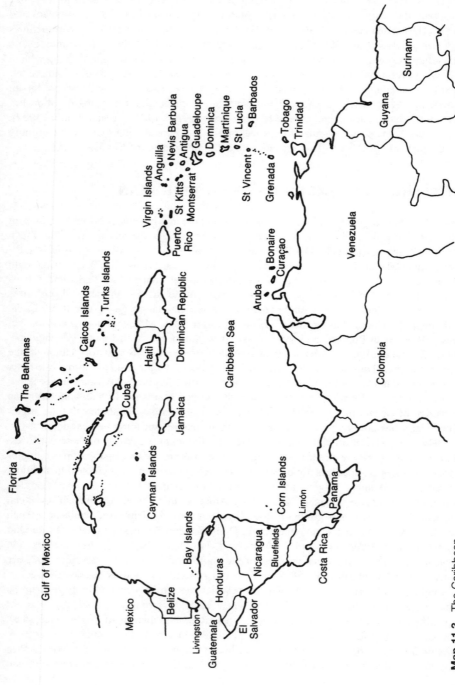

Map 11.3 The Caribbean

from the US, Canada and Great Britain have had an added unifying factor for many West Indians. Furthermore, tourism has increased exposure to AmE speech. Despite all of this the various English creoles are, in actual fact, often so different that mutual comprehension between, for example, Guyana and Barbados cannot be taken for granted, sometimes not even between StE speakers and creole speakers within a single country such as Jamaica.

The explanation lies in the fact that each of the territories has its own history. In the case of Barbados, for example, the vernacular has de-creolized more strongly than the relatively conservative varieties of Guyana and Jamaica. Special factors influencing Barbados are the higher rate of British and Irish settlers in the early colonial period, the greater development of the infrastructure and relatively small size of the island, and the high degree of literacy (97 per cent). Jamaica, in contrast, received slave imports for a much longer period than Barbados; this led to a lengthening of the pidgin phase and a subsequent strengthening of the creole. Guyana is linguistically similar to Barbados because there was a great deal of immigration there from Barbados. However, besides its black population Guyana also has an approximately equal number of East Indians (most of whom have, in the meantime, adopted the creole for daily use); their arrival (between 1838 and 1924) slowed down the de-creolization process by acting as a buffer between the StE top of society and the creole bottom.

11.6 THE LINGUISTIC CONTINUUM

Regardless of whether the various English creoles are more or less mutually comprehensible, more or less creolized, they all have one thing in common: all of them are diglossically Low languages in relation to the High language, which is StE in the anglophone countries, Dutch in Surinam and Spanish in Honduras, Nicaragua, Costa Rica and Columbia. This means that StE (and Dutch and Spanish) are used in government administration and state schools (although changes are in progress in the direction of more use of the creoles, especially in Belize, Jamaica and Trinidad). StE dominates in most of the printed media and all but a little of the electronic media. The creoles are the language of everyday life, the home, family and neighbourhood. Church sometimes uses the vernacular, sometimes the High language. Literature makes a few forays into creole. Only Sranan, a creole relatively distantly related to English, is used widely for literary (and religious) purposes.

If it is not unjustified to regard the English creoles as separate languages, as remarked above, it is also not fully justified to do so. Many people see StE and the creoles as two extremes related through a spectrum or **continuum** of language varieties, each of which is only minimally different from the nearest variety upward or downward from it on the scale. The lowest or broadest form is called the **basilect**; the highest, StE, the **acrolect**. In between lie the **mesolects**, which are any of numerous intermediate varieties. Evidence of a linguistic nature indicates, however, that there is a fairly strong, perhaps substantial break between the basilect and the mesolect. The underlying grammatical categories shared by the mesolect and the acrolect (though realized in distinct forms) are essentially different from those of the basilect (see below for exemplification).

The basilect lacks overt prestige while the acrolect commands respect. The lower a person's socio-economic status and the poorer his or her education, the more likely that person is to speak the basilect. Rural dwellers will also be located closer to the basilect than the urban part of the population. Age is an additional factor, since younger speakers generally seem more likely than older ones to adopt the more standard forms, which, however, need not be all the way up to the level of StE.

Despite the overt prestige of the acrolect, individual and group loyalties may lead to more use of basilect for some speakers. There are covert local norms which favour creole language and culture. Indeed, certain speech genres, especially those associated with performance styles, can hardly be imagined apart from the vernacular: teasing, riddles, traditional folk tales such as the Anansi stories with their spider hero, ritual insults and the like (see also similar uses in BEV/AAVE). Furthermore, the forms people use with one another may be a good indication of both where they feel they belong on the social scale and how they feel towards their conversational partners:

> The speaker of Jamaican creole who controls a substantial segment of the linguistic spectrum on the island knows when he meets an acquaintance with the same control speaking with another speaker who controls a lesser range, that if his friend uses *nyam* and *tick* he is defining the situation on the axis of solidarity and shared identity whereas if he is using *eat* and *thick* he is interested in the maintenance of social distance and formality.
>
> (Grimshaw 1971: 437)

The continuum is not the same in all the territories mentioned. The English of Barbados, Trinidad and the Bahamas is so de-creolized that it is possible to say there is, relatively speaking, no basilect. In countries where English is not the official language, the opposite might be said to be the case: there is no acrolect. This is actually the case only for Surinam, where Sranan has gone its own way, no longer oriented towards English.

11.7 LINGUISTIC CHARACTERISTICS OF CaribE

StE in the Caribbean area is syntactically the same as other standard varieties. Where there are BrE–AmE differences CaribE is oriented towards BrE; only in the American Virgin Islands and Puerto Rico – to the extent that English is spoken in the latter – is AmE the model. The creole forms, on the other hand, offer an enormous contrast in grammar (see 14.3).

The vocabulary of CaribE contains a considerable number of terms not widely known outside the area. Inasmuch as its speakers move easily between the acrolect and the mesolect, it is only natural that standard CaribE draws on these lexical resources. The special regional (or subregional) vocabulary of the Caribbean draws ultimately on two major sources: the African languages of the slaves and non-standard regional English of the early settlers from Britain and Ireland. A number of creole words of Scottish origin have become part of standard CaribE, e.g. *lick* 'to hit, strike', *dock* 'to cut the hair', *heap* 'a great deal'. Examples of Africanisms tend to be calques (loan translations) rather than direct borrowings. For example, *eye water* 'tears', *sweet mout'* 'flatter' and *hard ears* 'persistently disobedient, stubborn'. Reduplication (*little-little* 'very small') is also probably an African carry-over. An example of a direct borrowing from an African language is *John Canoe*, the term for the mumming parade at Christmas time. Its source is the Ewe language, but re-analysed after the fashion of folk etymology. Cassidy explains it as follows:

> The chief dancer in the underlying African celebration seems to have been a medicine man, and in Ewe we find *dzonc* 'a sorcerer', and *kúnu* 'a cause of death', or alternatively *dzonkc* 'a sorcerer's name for himself', and *-nu*, a common suffix meaning 'man'. Some African form or forms of this kind meaning 'sorcerer-man' has been rationalized into *John Canoe*.
>
> (Cassidy 1986: 137)

There are two norms, a local one and StE. 'Despite consciousness of two different norms within each of the relevant territories, there is, in reality, no simple juxtaposition of unrelated language varieties in any of them. The continued influence of English throughout the years has blurred the distinction between what must once have been more easily separable varieties' (Christie 1989: 247). Here are some examples from Christie:

> *scratch* 'itch' (My hand is scratching me)
> *care* 'care for' (Care your books)
> Word with counterparts in StE generally known in CaribE:
> *foot-bottom* 'sole' (The corns on my foot-bottom are painful)
> *hand-middle* 'palm' (Show me your hand-middle and I'll tell your fortune)
> Words with additional meanings or different ones:
> *hand* 'arm, hand' (She has her left hand in a sling)
> *tail* 'hem' (The tail of her dress has come loose)
> Words belonging to a different grammatical category:
> *grudge* 'envy . . . for' (The woman grudge me my big house)
> *sweet* 'give pleasure to' (The joke sweets him)
> Collocations:
> *best butter* 'butter' (I don't want margarine. I must have best butter)
> *tall hair* 'long hair'(John's girl-friend is the one with tall hair)
> Idioms:
> *work out* 'outside the home' (Since my parents work out, I go to me aunts)
> *keep a party* 'have one' (John kept a party at his house on Friday)
> Intra-regional differences in lexis:
> *trace* (Trinadad-Tobago) = *gap* (Barbados) = *lane* (Jamaica) 'narrow street'
> *callaloo* a different stew (crab meat and leafy vegetables) in Trinidad-Tobago from the spinach-like plant and soup made from it in Jamaica

The pronunciation of CaribE marks it as regional more than anything else. Here the carry-over between basilect and acrolect is especially prominent. One of the most noticeable features is the stressing, which gives each syllable more or less equal stress (syllable timing). In addition, in a few cases pitch may play a decisive role in interpreting a lexeme; *kyan* with a high level tone is positive 'can', while the same word with a high falling tone means 'can't'.

The consonants in comparison to RP and GenAm include the following particularly noticeable differences:

1 /θ/ and /ð/ are freely, but not exclusively realized as [t] and [d] (*tick* for *thick*; *dem* for *them*);
2 /v/ may be a [b] or a bilabial fricative [β] (*gib* for *give*, *bittles* for *vittles*);
3 the ending {-ing} is regularly /-ɪn/ (*talkin'*);
4 simplification of consonant clusters, especially if homorganic and voiced after /n/ and /l/ (*blind* → *blin'*); in the basilect even initial clusters are sometimes simplified (*string* → *tring*)
5 palatalization of /k/ and /g/ + /aː/: *car* /kjaːr/
6 clear /l/ in all phonetic environments

Some territories are rhotic (Barbados); some are non-rhotic (Trinidad, the Bahamas); and some are semi-rhotic, i.e. stressed final *r* as in *near* is retained (Jamaica, Guyana) (Wells 1982: 570); in the basilect /r/ is sometimes realized as [l], *flitters* for *fritters*, but this is becoming less common.

The vowels differ most vis-à-vis RP and GenAm. In Jamaica, for instance, /eɪ/ and /əʊ/ are the monophthongs [eː] and [oː]. /æ/ is realized as [a], which is also the realization of /ɒ/, so that *tap* and *top* are potential homophones. Both are distinguished by length from the vowel of *bath* [aː]. Central vowels are less a fixed part of the system; hence schwa is often [a] as well as [e]; /ʌ/ may be back and rounded; and /ɜː/ may be [o] (e.g. Jamaican Creole *boddem* 'birds'). In the basilect /ɔɪ/ sometimes merges with /aɪ/, making *boy* and *buy* homophones.

11.8 FURTHER READING

Algeo 2001b and the articles in it (several listed below) cover a great many aspects of North American English. See also Schneider 1996 and McArthur 2002. For a history of AmE, see Dillard 1993. For a summary of the varied history of the term **General American**, see Van Riper 1986. Lippi-Green 1997 looks at attitudes towards English accents, American and other. A reasonable sample of contributions to **variation study** in North American English is Glowka and Lance 1993; see Pederson 2001 on American dialects. The **vocabulary of AmE** is entertainingly presented in Flexner and Soukhanov 1997; see also Cassidy and Hall 2001; and Lighter 2001 on slang as well as Bailey 2001 on AmE abroad. Gallegos 1994 deals with the movement to establish English as the official language of the US. The website of the American Dialect Society http://www.americandialect.org/ offers a great deal of information on American English. See also http://us.english.uga.edu/ and http://polyglot.lss.wisc.edu/dare/dare.html for the *Dictionary of American Regional English (DARE)*. The *Phonological Atlas of North America* can be accessed at http://www.ling.upenn.edu/phono_atlas/home.html.

For **CanE** see: Edwards 1998; Brinton and Fee 2001; *The Canadian Oxford English Dictionary* (1998). The *Dictionary of American Regional English* (1985, 1991, 1996) lists regional vocabulary. See also the *Longman Dictionary of American English* (1997).

Cities in which **sociolinguistic studies** have been carried out include: New York (Labov 1972a); Detroit (Shuy *et al.* 1967); Philadelphia (Labov *et al.* 1972); and Anniston, Alabama (Feagin 1979). Butters 2001 treats vernacular AmE. Kroch 1996 is a rare study of upper class speech.

Native American English is treated in Leap 1993. **Spanish influenced English** is dealt with in contributions by García and Otheguy, Valdés, and Zentella in McKay and Wong 1988. A recent collection of contributions on **BEV/AAVE** is Mufwene *et al.* 1998, which contains Martin and Wolfram; Green; Mufwene; Labov; Rickford; Bailey and Thomas, all quoted in §11.4.3; see also Rickford and Rickford 2000. Wolfram and Clarke 1971 is older, but contains a readable collection of articles dealing with both sides of the question of the origins of BEV. For a good non-technical introduction and a compromise view of BEV origins see Burling 1973. On consonant deletion: see Fasold 1972; this also treats invariant *be*, as does Feagin 1979. Dozens, toasting, ritual insults etc. are well treated in Abrahams 1970 and Kochman 1970; for chanted sermons see Rosenberg 1970. The question of the convergence or divergence of BEV and white vernacular English is discussed in 'Are Black and White Vernaculars Diverging?', *American Speech* 62 (1987): 1–80; and in Butters 1989. A possible entry to BEV/AAVE is http://www.arches.uga.edu/~bryan/AAVE/.

A general treatment of CaribE is Holm 1994. For more on the spread of **English in the Caribbean** see Holm 1985. The pronunciation of CaribE is treated in Lawton 1984: 257 and Wells 1982. Roberts 1988 is a non-technical treatment which contrasts the features of the major territories grammatically, lexically and phonetically. Chapter 14 deals with, among other things, English creoles in the Caribbean. Two links to **Jamaican Creole** are http://www-user.tu-chemnitz.de/~wobo/jamaika.html and http://www.jamaicans.com/speakja/glossary.htm.

Chapter 12

Standard British and American English in comparison

Although by far the majority of linguistic forms in the English language are common to both BrE and AmE (as well as AusE, NZE, SAE, WAfrE, EAfrE, IndE, SingE and Philippine English) there are a considerable number of points at which the two major varieties diverge. Chapters 1 through 5 concentrated on a systematic presentation of StE largely ignoring possible variation. The purpose of this chapter, then, is to look at the differences between the two major varieties, BrE and AmE, in their *standard* forms.

12.1 PRONUNCIATION

It is in the area of pronunciation that BrE–AmE differences are most obvious. While divergent patterns of grammatical usage, of vocabulary choice and of spelling preference crop up only sporadically, pronunciation pervades and colours every aspect of oral communication. Some of this is due to the differences in what is called articulatory set, the predisposition to pronounce sounds and words in a particular fashion. This includes much that is difficult to describe, yet contributes to the typical voice quality of an accent. Many American speakers, especially from the Middle West, for example, have a 'nasal twang'. This is caused by the articulatory habit of leaving the velum open at all (or most) times so that the nasal cavity forms a (near-)constant further resonance chamber. Coupled with this is a narrowing of the pharynx which occurs because the root of the tongue is pushed backwards more strongly; this gives the voice a tenser, darker quality. Southern American speakers, in contrast, are stereotyped for their drawl by other Americans. This drawing out of sounds is due perhaps to an overall lack of tension in articulation. British accents are often thought of as 'clipped' by Americans, possibly because of the greater tension and lesser degree of lengthening in stressed vowels.

In addition to these overall contrasting features there are a number of more specific differences. In the following, differences in the phoneme inventories in BrE as represented by RP and in AmE as realized by the GenAm accent will be recounted first; then the major differences in phonetic (or articulatory) realization and the phonotactic (or distributional) differences will be reviewed; and after that divergent patterns of phoneme use in whole sets of words will be mentioned as will a small list of individual words which differ in their pronunciations only by chance. A few remarks on differences in stress and intonation will close this section.

12.1.1 Differences in phoneme inventory

The consonants of RP and GenAm are identical. Both varieties contain the same 24 phonemes (see 4.2). The only possible difference lies in the maintenance of the /hw/–/w/ distinction (as in *where* vs *wear*) in some of the regions where GenAm is spoken, though the use of /hw/ seems to be recessive. Some RP speakers also retain this distinction through a conscious effort to do so, feeling perhaps that this is somehow 'more correct'.

With the vowels there is a clear difference in the number of phonemes available: RP has 20; GenAm 16. This may be attributed to the fact that GenAm, which is a rhotic accent (see 4.4.3 and 12.1.3), has no centring diphthongs. While GenAm has the combinations /ɪr, er, ʊr/ as in *lear*, *lair* and *lure*, RP has the phonemes /ɪə, eə, ʊə/, though /ʊə/ is merging with /ɔː/ in many words such as *sure* and /eə/ may be rendered as [ɛː]. This latter change is one of the most widespread currently in progress in RP and is what Wells calls **smoothing**. It is the simplification of a diphthong to a monophthong, or of a triphthong (/aɪə, aʊə, ɔɪə/) to a diphthong or a monophthong. It leads to the reduction of the vowels of *tower* and *tire* to the monophthong [ɑː] and [aː] respectively, sometimes even going so far as to produce homophonous *tower*, *tire* and *tar*, all as [tɑː] (Wells 1982: 292f.).

In addition, GenAm does not have the phoneme /ɒ/. Wherever RP has this sound GenAm has either /ɑː/ or /ɔː/. This as well as RP non-rhoticity lies behind the following story:

> *American* (to an Englishman): Say, what's your job?
> *Englishman*: I'm a clerk.
> *American* (astonished): You mean you go 'tick-tock, tick-tock'?
> [RP klɑːk/ 'clerk' = GenAm /klɑːk/ 'clock']
>
> (Strevens 1972: 68)

Corresponding to RP /ɒ/ GenAm has only /ɑː/ in some regions (for example, in parts of the Middle West and neighbouring Canada); in other areas two distinctive phonemes are retained. The distribution of RP /ɒ/ between GenAm /ɑː/ and GenAm /ɔː/ varies regionally in America; the following is one common example of this split: before /l, m, n/ (*doll*, *bomb*, *don*) GenAm has /ɑː/; the same is true before the stops as in *top*, *rob*, *dot*, *God*, *dock*; however, before a voiced velar stop as in *dog* or *fog* /ɔː/ is widespread. The same is true of the position before the velar nasal /ŋ/ (*song*), before /r/ (*orange*) and before the (unvoiced) fricatives /f, θ, s/ (*off*, *moth*, *moss*). However, GenAm has /ɑː/ before /ʃ/ as in *posh*, *slosh*, *gosh*. This distribution and regional modifications of it apply only to words with /ɒ/ in RP. It does not mean that GenAm never has /ɔː/ when a stop follows (e.g. *gaudy* or *taught*) nor /ɑː/ when /r/ (*far*) or a fricative (*father*) follow.

12.1.2 Differences in the phonetic quality of phonemes

The chief consonant which may be noticeably different in its realization in the two accents is /r/. In GenAm there is a strong tendency for /r/ to be retroflex [ɻ] (made with the tip of the tongue turned backwards), while it is often the constricted continuant [ɹ] in RP (made with the tongue raised and tensed in the area just behind the alveolar ridge with relatively little retroflexion). In addition, an /r/ between two vowels (as in *very*) is sometimes articulated with a single flap of the tongue against the alveolar ridge [ɾ] in RP even though such a realization is increasingly rare after an accented syllable. It is also not particularly unusual to hear RP speakers who realize /r/ with a /w/-like sound (actually [ɰ]), so that *rap* sounds a bit like *wap*.

The /l/-sound differs inasmuch as GenAm tends to use a dark [ɫ] in all positions in contrast to RP, which has clear [l] before vowels (*loop*) and dark [ɫ] before consonants (*help*), at word end (*sale*), or where /l/ is syllabic [ḷ] (*bottle*) (see 4.3.1 'Lateral').

Among the vowels there are far more examples of different articulations. Most are slight, yet some are readily noticed. The first element of /əʊ/ is a central vowel (schwa) in RP, but a back vowel in GenAm, hence [oʊ]. In fact, the degree of diphthongization of GenAm [oʊ] may be almost non-existent, namely [oː], just as /eɪ/ may be [eː]. In RP /ɔː/ may be so close as to sound almost identical with GenAm [oː]; in GenAm, on the other hand, /ɔː/ is relatively open.

/ʌ/ (as in *cut*) is more or less mid central in GenAm, but more open and fronted in RP. Both GenAm and RP have a long, mid, central vowel realization of /ɜː/ (as in *bird*); however, in RP this vowel is almost never followed by an /r/ (exception bimorphemic: *furry* /fɜːrɪ/; see 12.1.4), while in GenAm it always is (and therefore might be regarded as an allophone of the central vowel /ʌ/ before /r/).

In GenAm /æ/ is usually longer than in RP. One of the consequences of this is that it is frequently at least somewhat diphthongized in stressed syllables in GenAm. Where the first element of the resulting diphthong is a high front vowel, as in New York City, the girl's name *Ann* and the (British) name *Ian* may become synonymous /ɪən/. In addition, GenAm /æ/ is often subject to nasalization if a nasal consonant follows. For some speakers the following nasal disappears completely leaving only the nasalized vowel, for example, *bank* /bæŋk/ first becomes /bæ̃ŋk/ and then possibly /bæ̃k/, which itself is distinguished from *back* /bæk/ only by its nasalized vowel. RP /æ/ is also undergoing change, but chiefly in the other direction: it is becoming more open [a] and thus more like the realization in northern England.

In both varieties /uː/ is being increasingly fronted to [ʉ] and in RP often unrounded to [ɨː] (and /ʊ/ to [ɨ]).

12.1.3 Phonotactic differences

Rhoticity   RP has an /r/ only where there is a following vowel (*red*, *every*). When this includes a vowel in the following word (*tear + up*), what is known as a '**linking r**' may link or connect the two words into a single phonetic unit. Such linking may also occur where no *r* is present in the spelling (*law officer* /lɔːrɒfɪsə/); this is called an '**intrusive r**' and may be found after final /ɔː, ə, ɑː/ before a vowel in the following word. GenAm regularly pronounces /r/ where the spelling indicates; it does not know an intrusive *r* (see also 4.4.3).

Intervocalic /t/   GenAm realizes what is written as a <t> with a flap of the tongue tip against the alveolar ridge when it comes between two voiced sounds. Phonetically this is very much like the flapped [ɾ] of RP *very*, but it is perceived as /d/. Indeed, intervocalic /d/ is also flapped in GenAm, which means that *latter* and *ladder* sound identical, both with flapped intervocalic [t̪]. Further examples of the resulting homophony include *hurting* = *herding*; *helter* = *held'er* ('held her'), *totem* = *towed'em* ('towed them') or *futile* = *feudal*. This voicing of intervocalic <t> does not apply if the syllable following the <t> is stressed, hence '*a-tom* = '*A-dam*, both with a flapped [t̪], but *a-'tom-ic*, with /t/. In RP the realization of /t/ is variable before an unstressed syllable. In words like *butter* it may be tapped [ɾ] much as in GenAm. However, there can also be the glottaling of /t/ as in (*hatrack* = *ha'rack* [hæʔræk]), something heard in many (non-RP) urban accents of England and Scotland as well (see 4.3.4). This is seen as a change currently in progress in RP (Ramsaran 1990b: 183).

Post-nasal /t/   In words like *winter* or *enter*, where an unstressed vowel follows, the <t> is frequently not pronounced at all in GenAm. As a result *winter* = *winner* and *intercity* = *innercity*. When the following syllable is stressed, /t/ is pronounced as in *in-'ter*; /t/ is also pronounced if a consonant follows as in *intra-city*.

Dental and alveolar consonants + /j/   The combinations /nj, tj, dj, sj, zj, lj, θj/ do not occur in GenAm, while they may in RP. Hence all those words spelled with <u>, <ew>, <eu>, <ui> and <ue> and a few other combinations containing <u> (words such as *tune*, *thews*, *deuce*, *suit*, *neutral*, *lieutenant* etc.) have simple /uː/ in GenAm, but /juː/ in RP (for *lieutenant*, see 12.1.5). Sometimes, especially after /s, z, l/ (as in *suet*, *presume*, *lute*) there is free variation in RP between /juː/ and /uː/ with the latter being the majority form in present day RP, and this is increasingly the case after /n/ as in /nuː/ *new*. Both RP and GenAm agree in having /uː/ where the spelling has <oo> (*noose*, *loose*, *doom* etc.). Note that the combinations /n+j/ and /l+j/ are possible in GenAm if there is an intervening syllable boundary, e.g. *Jan-u-ary*, *mon-u-ment*, *val-ue*, all with /juː/.

Palatalization   The lack of /j/ before /uː/ as described in the preceding paragraph represents a relatively late development in GenAm. Evidence that an earlier /j/ must have been present can be seen in the palatalization which took place in words such as *feature*, *education*, *fissure* or *azure*, in which original /t, d, s, z/ as reflected in the spelling have moved slightly backwards in the mouth to a more palatal place of articulation. In addition, the stops /t/ and /d/ frequently changed to the affricates /tʃ/ and /dʒ/ while /s/ and /z/ merely became the palatal fricatives /ʃ/ and /ʒ/. In GenAm palatalization is regular when the following syllable is unstressed. Before a stressed syllable there are a few well known cases of palatalization such as *sure*, *sugar*, *assure*. RP agrees in most cases with GenAm, but it has the additional possibility of unpalatalized /dj, tj, sj, zj/ in those cases where a <u> follows. This is phonotactically impossible in GenAm. Hence GenAm has only the palatalized version of *education* and *issue* while RP *education* may be /edjuːkeɪʃən/ or /edʒəkeɪʃən/ and *issue* may be /ɪʃuː/ or /ɪsjuː/ though the palatalized form is the general form in present day RP when followed by an unaccented syllable. Note that both RP and GenAm agree in using unpalatalized forms for *Tuesday*: RP /tjuːzdɪ/ and GenAm /tuːzdiː/ (GenAm with no /j/ cannot undergo palatalization); yet many non-RP speakers and some RP speakers of BrE have the palatalized form even here, where the following syllable is stressed as /tʃuːzdɪ/ (*Chewsday* as it were) or /dʒʊərɪŋ/ (*during*). On the other hand, while *literature* is generally pronounced as palatalized /lɪt(ə)rətʃə(r)/ in both varieties, some (American) accents have unpalatalized /lɪtərətuːr/.

When a <u> is not involved, but rather /iː/ or /ɪ/ + unstressed vowel, the situation is less predictable. RP has, for example, both unpalatalized *Indian* /ɪndɪən/ and (old-fashioned) palatalized /ɪndʒən/, unpalatalized *immediately* /ɪmiːdɪətlɪ/ and palatalized /ɪmiːdʒətlɪ/. GenAm has only the unpalatalized versions of each. A number of place names are unpalatalized in RP and palatalized in GenAm, e.g. *Tunisia*, RP /tjʊnɪzɪə/ and GenAm /tuːniːʒə/, or *Indonesia*, RP /ɪndəniːzɪə/ and GenAm /ɪndəniːʒə/ (see 12.1.4 for voicing differences, e.g. RP /ʃ/ vs GenAm /ʒ/.) Both agree in having palatalized *soldier, auspicious, financial* etc; and both have unpalatalized *easier, Finlandia* or *rodeo*.

Vowels   In the area of the vowels only two frequent and very noticeable points will be mentioned. GenAm does not allow any short vowels except for unstressed schwa to occur in unchecked syllables (ones that do not end with a consonant). This means that the only vowels which can come at the very end of a word are long vowels, diphthongs and schwa. RP makes an exception to this rule by allowing final unstressed /ɪ/. As a result, all those words ending in unstressed <-y> and <-ie> such as *cloudy* and *birdie* have /ɪ/ in RP, but /iː/ in GenAm. /ɪ/ is retained even when an ending follows, hence in RP *candied = candid* /kændɪd/. However, there is a tendency among younger RP speakers to lengthen this /ɪ/ in the direction of /iː/.

The other point about vowels also involves unstressed syllables. GenAm has a much greater tendency to reduce unstressed vowels to schwa while RP retains /ɪ/, especially where the endings {-D} and {-S} are pronounced with a vowel. This distinguishes *boxes* /bɒksɪz/ from *boxers* /bɒksəz/; however, unstressed /ɪ/ is increasing realized as /ə/ in RP as well. GenAm has schwa in both cases, but this causes no confusion because *boxers* is pronounced with an /r/.

12.1.4 Divergent patterns of phoneme use in whole sets of words

Among the consonants of English there is a notable difference in the way intervocalic <-si-> is realized before an unstressed syllable (see the remarks on palatalization in the preceding section). While all the following have /ʒ/ in GenAm, only those under (a) have this consonant in RP; the ones under (b) have either /ʒ/ or /ʃ/ in RP; and the items in (c) have only /ʃ/ in RP:

a)   *vision, confusion, decision, measure, treasure, pleasure, usual, seizure*;
b)   *Asia, aversion* (GenAm: /ʒ/ or /ʃ/), *immersion, magnesia* (GenAm: /ʒ/ or /ʃ/), *Persia, perversion*;
c)   *version, aspersion*.

In addition, *Malaysia, Melanesia, Micronesia* have /-zɪ-/ in RP and either /ʒ/ or /ʃ/ in GenAm; *Indonesian* has /ʃ/ or /-zɪ-/ in RP and /ʒ/ or /ʃ/ in GenAm; *euthanasia, Polynesia* and *Tunisia* have RP /-zɪ-/ and GenAm /ʒ/.

At least some areas of America, especially the South, have an /l/ in words with <-alm> (*alms, balm, calm, palm, psalm, qualms*). Furthermore, in those varieties in which there is an /l/, the vowel is not /ɑː/ but /ɔː/. In varieties of GenAm without an /l/ either vowel may occur. RP never has /l/ and always has /ɑː/.

There are four important sets of words in which RP and GenAm generally differ in the vowel chosen. The largest and best known is the set of so-called *bath* words, which have /æ/ in GenAm and /ɑː/ in RP. This set of words is defined by the occurrence of a spelling <a> followed by <s>, <f> or <th>, as in *pass*, *after*, *path* or *rather*; in addition, the <a> may be followed by <m> or <n> plus another consonant, as in *example* or *dance*. Approximately 300 words fulfil these conditions, but only about one third have /ɑː/ in RP; the remainder have /æ/ in both varieties (e.g. *ass*, *traffic*, *math(s)*, *gather*, *trample*, *Atlantic*). One word has /ɑː/ in both varieties (*father*), and some vary in RP between /æ/ and /ɑː/ (*lather*, *mass*).

The second set of words which vary between the two varieties comprises those in which an intervocalic /r/ follows a mid central vowel, as in *borough*, *burrow*, *courage*, *concurrent*, *curry*, *flurry*, *furrow*, *hurricane*, *hurry*, *nourish*, *scurry*, *thorough*, *turret*, *worry*. Here GenAm has /ɜː/ while RP has /ʌ/. RP can have the combination /ɜːr/ only when a word otherwise ending in /ɜː/ has been given an ending beginning with a vowel, as in *furry*, *deterring* or *referral*.

The third set includes those words derived from Latin which end in <-ile>. In RP the usual pronunciation is /aɪl/ while in GenAm it is /ɪl/ or /əl/, e.g. *febrile*, *fragile*, *futile*, *missile*, *puerile*, *tactile*, *virile*. Note, however, that individual words in GenAm may vary so that, for example, *textile*, *reptile* and *servile* commonly have either /aɪl/ or /ɪl/.

The final set of words includes names of countries, such as *Slovakia*, *Nicaragua*, *Rwanda*, *Surinam* or *Vietnam*. Here GenAm usually has /ɑː/ for the <a> in the stressed syllables while RP has /æ/, e.g. /nɪkərægjʊə/ vs /nɪkərɑːgwə/.

12.1.5 Individual words which differ

A few words have differing pronunciations in the two varieties without this divergence being systematic or belonging to a larger set of words. In the list first the RP and then the GenAm pronunciation is indicated for each item or group of items:

	RP	GenAm
schedule	ʃ	sk
lieutenant army: left-; navy	luːt-	luːt-
erase and *parse*	z	s
gooseberry	z or s	s
herb	h	no h
geyser	iː	aɪ
quinine	ɪ + iː	aɪ + aɪ
stressed *been*	iː	ɪ
aesthetic, evolution, era	iː	e
squirrel	ɪ	ɜː
(n)either	aɪ	iː
tryst	aɪ	ɪ
dynasty, midwifery, privacy, viola (musical instrument)	ɪ	aɪ
progress, process	əʊ	ɑː
data, apparatus, status	eɪ	eɪ or æ or ɑː
leisure, zebra, zenith	e	iː
wrath	ɒ	æ

quagmire	ɒ or æ	æ
produce (noun), *shone, scone,*		
yoghurt	ɒ	oʊ
tomato, strafe	ɑː	eɪ
what, was, of	ɒ	ʌ
vase	vɑːz	veɪz or veɪs
plaque	ɑː or æ	æ
clerk, Berkeley, Derby	ɑː	ɜːr
route	uː	uː or aʊ

Stress and intonation The stress patterns of RP and GenAm are generally the same. One well known difference is in the pronunciation of words ending in <-ary>, <-ery> or <-ory>. In RP they contain a single stressed syllable, which is the first or the second one in the word, and the second to last syllable is frequently elided. In GenAm the stress is on the first syllable; in addition, secondary stress falls on the next to last syllable, for example:

	RP	GenAm
secretary:	'sec-re-t(a)ry	'sec-re-ˌtar-y
library:	'li-br(ar)y	'li-ˌbrar-y
stationery:	'sta-tion-(e)ry	'sta-tio-ˌner-y
laboratory:	la-'bor-a-t(o)ry	'lab-(o)-ra-ˌtor-y
corollary:	co-'rol-la-ry	'cor-ol-ˌlar-y

A number of individual words also carry their stress on different syllables in the two varieties. Here is a short list, always with the RP form first:

RP	GenAm		RP	GenAm
ad'vertisement	adver'tisement	the <i> is	ɪ	aɪ
arti'san	'artisan	the second <a> is	æ	ə
'ballet	bal'let	the <e> is	eɪ or ɪ	eɪ
'baton	ba'ton	the <a> is	æ	ə
'chagrin (n.)	cha'grin	the <a> is	æ	ə
'detail	de'tail	the <e> is	iː	ɪ
doc'trinal	'doctrinal	the <i> is	aɪ	ɪ
'frontier	fron'tier		'frʌntʃə	frʌn'tɪr
				(also RP)
'garage	ga'rage	the first <a> is	æ	ə;
		the second is	ɪ or ɑː	ɑː
'lamentable	la'mentable		'læmənt-	lə'ment-
'résumé (noun)	resu'me	<re-> is	re or reɪ	re
re'veille	'reveille		rɪ'væliː	'revəliː
'valet	va'let		'væ-lɪt or -leɪ	və'leɪ
				(and as in RP)

The intonation of both accents functions according to the same basic principles. Yet the intonation of RP is often characterized as more varied, that of GenAm as flatter. Some of the individual points of difference include the following. RP more frequently uses sharp jumps downwards, but has more gradual rises than does GenAm. In lengthy sentences GenAm will repeat the overall contour, leaving the final rise or fall until the very end; RP, in contrast, draws out the rise or fall in small increments from stressed syllable to stressed syllable. GenAm generally has falling intonation in *wh*-questions while RP frequently uses an alternative pattern with a low rise at the end, something which is perceived as friendlier. *Yes-no* questions have a rapid rise in GenAm, remain high and finish with a further small rise. In RP the final rise may be preceded by a falling contour.

12.2 SPELLING AND PUNCTUATION

Spelling and punctuation differences are, in the same way as most differences in pronunciation, not merely haphazard and unsystematic. Instead, the principles of simplification, regularization, derivational uniformity and reflection of pronunciation are used. Of course, there are a number of individual, unsystematic differences in addition. Although it is not always easy to attribute British–American divergences unambiguously to a single principle, the following presentation will proceed as if this were no problem.

12.2.1 Spelling

Simplification   This principle is common to both the British and the American traditions, but is sometimes realized differently. AmE has a greater reputation for simplification as often attested by such standard examples as *program* instead of *programme* (but note that BrE has *program* for computer software). Compare also measurement words ending in <-gram(me)> such as *kilogram(me)* etc., where the form with the final <-me> is the preferred, but not the exclusive BrE form. Likewise, BrE *waggon* is still found next to AmE (and, increasingly, BrE) *wagon*. AmE has *counselor, woolen, fagot* as well as common *counsellor, woollen* and *faggot*.

Simplification of <ae> and <oe> to <e> in words taken from Latin and Greek (*heresy, federal* etc.) are the rule for all of English, but this rule is carried out less completely in BrE, where we find *mediaeval* next to *medieval, foetus* next to *fetus* and *paediatrician* next to *pediatrician*. We also find AmE forms with simple <e> compared to the non-simplified forms of BrE in words like *esophagus/oesophagus; esthetics/aesthetics* (also AmE); *maneuver/manoeuvre; anapest/anapaest; estrogen/oestrogen; anemia/anaemia; egis/aegis* (also AmE); *ameba/amoeba*. Note, however, that some words have only <ae> and <oe> in AmE, e.g. *aerial* and *Oedipus*.

A further simplification in AmE is one which has not been adopted at all in BrE: the dropping of the *-ue* of *-logue* in words like *catolog, dialog, monolog*. This simplification, which does not extend to words like *Prague, vague, vogue* or *rogue*, is not fully accepted for use in formal AmE writing. Note also the simplification of words like (BrE) *judgement* to (AmE) *judgment; abridg(e)ment; acknowledg(e)ment*.

BrE employs some simplified spellings which have not been adopted in AmE, such as BrE *skilful* and *wilful* for AmE *skillful* and *willful*. BrE *fulfil, instil, appal* may be interpreted as simplification, but AmE double <-ll-> in *fulfill, instill, appall* may have to do with where the stress lies (see below 'Reflection of pronunciation'). Nevertheless, AmE uses common *fulness* alongside (AmE) *fullness*; other words which have both forms in AmE are *instal(l)*, *instal(l)ment* and *enthral(l)*.

BrE simplifies <-ection> to <-exion> in *connexion*, *inflexion*, *retroflexion* etc. Here AmE uses *connection* etc. thus following the principle of derivational unity: *connect* > *connection*, *connective*; *reflect* > *reflection*, *reflective*. For more on 'Derivational uniformity' see below.

Regularization This principle is again one which has been employed more completely in AmE than in BrE. It shows up most obviously in the regularization of the endings <-or> and <-our> to the single form <-or>. This seems justified since there are no systematic criteria for distinguishing between the two sets in BrE: *neighbour* and *saviour*, but *donor* and *professor*; *honour* and *valour*, but *metaphor*, *anterior* and *posterior*; *savour* and *flavour*, but *languor* and *manor*; etc. Within BrE there are special rules to note: the ending <-ation> and <-ious> usually lead to a form with <-or-> as in *coloration* and *laborious*, but the endings <-al> and <-ful>, as in *behavioural* and *colourful*, have no such effect. However, even AmE may keep <-our> in such words as *glamour* (next to *glamor*) and *Saviour* (next to *Savior*), perhaps because there is something 'better' about these spellings for many people. Words like *contour*, *tour*, *four* or *amour*, where the vowel of the <-our> carries stress, are never simplified.

Note that, although unrelated to the preceding, AmE also has *mold*, *molt*, *smolder* and *mustache* where BrE has *mould*, *moult*, *smoulder* and *moustache*. Similarly AmE has *gage* where BrE has *gauge*.

The second well known case concerns <-er> and <-re>. Here BrE words in <-re> are regularized to <-er> in AmE. For example, BrE *goitre*, *centre* and *metre* become AmE *goiter*, *center* (but the adjective form is *central*) and *meter* (hence levelling the distinction between *metre* '39.37 inches' and *meter* 'instrument for measuring'). This rule applies everywhere in AmE except where the letter preceding the ending is a <c> or a <g>. In these cases <-re> is retained as in *acre*, *mediocre* and *ogre* in order to prevent the misinterpretation of <c> as 'soft' /s/ or <g> as /dʒ/. The AmE spellings *fire* (but note *fiery*), *wire*, *tire* etc. are used to insure interpretation of these sequences as monosyllabic. The fairly widespread use of the form *theatre* in AmE runs parallel to *glamour* and *Saviour*, as mentioned above: it is supposed to suggest superior quality or a more distinguished tradition for many people.

Derivational uniformity BrE writes *defence*, *offence*, *pretence*, but *practise* (verb) (all are also possible alternatives in AmE), while AmE alone has *defense*, *offense*, *pretense*, but *practice* (verb). What appears to be arbitrary (sometimes <c> and sometimes <s>) is really the application in AmE of the principle of derivational uniformity: *defense* > *defensive*, *offense* > *offensive*, *pretense* > *pretension*, *practice* > *practical* (see *connexion* vs *connection* under 'Simplification' above.) In another case BrE observes this principle and AmE violates it, namely *analyze* and *paralyze*. Here BrE *analyse* and *paralyse* (also possible in AmE) share the <s> with their derivational cognates *analysis* and *paralysis*.

Reflection of pronunciation The forms *analyze* and *paralyze*, which end in <-ize>, may violate derivational uniformity, but they do reflect the pronunciation of the final fricative, which is clearly a voiced-lenis /z/. This principle has been widely adopted in spelling on both sides of the Atlantic for verbs ending in <-ize> and the corresponding nouns ending in <-ization>. The older spellings with <-ise> and <-isation> are, however, also found in both AmE and BrE. *Advertise*, for example, is far more common than *advertize* (also *advise, compromise, revise, televise*). The decisive factor here seems to be publishers' style sheets, with increasing preference for <z>.

In AmE, when an ending beginning with a vowel (<-ing>, <-ed>, <-er>) is added to a multi-syllabic word ending in <l>, the <l> is doubled if the final syllable of the root carries the stress and is spelled with a single letter vowel (<e, o>). If the stress does not lie on the final syllable, the <l> is not doubled, for example:

re'bel	>	re'belling	'revel	>	'reveling
re'pel	>	re'pelled	'travel	>	'traveler
com'pel	>	com'pelling	'marvel	>	'marveling
con'trol	>	con'trolling	'trammel	>	'trammeled
pa'trol	>	pa'troller	'yodel	>	'yodeled

While BrE uniformly follows the principle of regularization and doubles the <l> (*revelling, traveller* etc.; also accepted in AmE), AmE spelling reflects pronunciation. The AmE spellings *fulfill, distill* etc. may be favoured over simplified BrE *fulfil, distil* etc. because they indicate end stress. A similar principle may apply to AmE *installment, skillful* and *willful*, where the <ll> occurs in the stressed syllable. In a few cases BrE doubles the final <p> where AmE does not, e.g. *worship(p)er, kidnap(p)er*. Both varieties accept both *biased* and *biassed, busing* and *bussing*.

Perhaps the best known cases of spellings adapted to reflect pronunciation are those involving <-gh->. Here AmE tends to use a **phonetic spelling** so that BrE *plough* appears as AmE *plow*, BrE *draught* ('flow of air, swallow or movement of liquid, depth of a vessel in water') as AmE *draft* (BrE has *draft* in the sense of a bank draft or a first draft of a piece of writing). The spellings *thru* for *through* and *tho'* for *though* are not uncommon in AmE, but are generally restricted to more informal writing; however, they sometimes show up in official use as in the designation of some limited access expressways as *thruways*. Spellings such as *lite* for *light*, *hi* for *high* or *nite* for *night* are employed in very informal writing and in advertising language. But from there they can enter more formal use, as is the case *lite* in the sense of diet drinks and the like.

Individual words which differ in spelling   For a number of words there are alternatives between <in-> and <en-> without there being any clear principle involved except for a slight preference in AmE for <in-> and in BrE for <en->, e.g. BrE *ensure, enclose, endorse* and AmE *insure, inclose, indorse*, but common *envelop* and *inquire* (beside BrE *enquire*).

The practice of writing compounds as two words, as a hyphenated word, or as a single unhyphenated word varies; however, there is a marked avoidance of hyphenations in AmE. Hence while BrE writes *make-up* ('cosmetics'), AmE uses *make up*; BrE *neocolonialism*, but AmE *neocolonialism*. Usage varies considerably from dictionary to dictionary; and no more can be said than that this is a preference; but there does seem to be an increasing tendency towards uniformity in the form of single unhyphenated words. Many Americans (and Australians) write compound numbers without a hyphen (e.g. *twenty five*), but most Americans retain one (*twenty-five*), as do most British writers.

In a similar vein, AmE drops French accent marks in some words (*cafe, entree*) while BrE may be more likely to retain them (*café, entrée*). However, the tendency towards Anglicization (= no accent marks) is great in both varieties.

The following list includes the most common differences in spelling, always with the BrE form listed first: *aluminium/aluminum, (bank) cheque/check, gaol* (also *jail*)/*jail, jewellery/jewelry, (street) kerb/curb, pyjamas/pajamas, storey* (of a building)/*story, sulphur/sulfur, tyre/tire, whisky/whiskey*.

In addition, informal spellings, especially in advertising, can probably be found more frequently in AmE than in BrE, e.g. *kwik* (*quick*), *do-nut* (now almost standard for *doughnut*), *e-z* (*easy*), *rite* (*right, write*), *blu* (*blue*), *tuff* (*tough*) and many more.

12.2.2 Punctuation

Aside from the lexical differences in the designations for some of the marks of punctuation, there are only a few differences in practice worth mentioning here. But first, some different names: a BrE *full stop* is an AmE *period*; BrE *brackets* are AmE *parentheses*, while BrE *square brackets* are AmE *brackets*. AmE and BrE *quotation marks* are frequently *inverted commas* in BrE. Note also that BrE uses single quotation marks ('. . .') in the normal case and resorts to double ones (". . .") for a quotation within a quotation ('. . . ". . ." . . .'). AmE starts with double quotation marks and alternates to single ones for a quote within a quote. Common British-American *exclamation mark* is also called an *exclamation point* in AmE. And the *slash*, /, may be termed an *oblique (stroke)* in BrE and a *virgule*, a *solidus* or a *diagonal* in AmE.

Simplification vs regularization AmE opts for simplification whenever closing quotation marks occur together with a period or a comma: The period or comma always comes inside the quotation marks whether or not it 'belongs' to the material quoted or not. BrE places its full stops and commas inside if they belong to what is quoted and outside if they do not. See, for example, (a) below where the punctuation belongs to the quotation vs (b) where it does not:

a) BrE: *'He belongs to the club,' he told her.* Or: *He answered, 'She left an hour ago.'*

AmE: Usage is identical here except that AmE sets double quotation marks instead of single ones.

b) BrE: These may be called 'corruptions', 'degradations' and 'perversions'.

AmE: These may be called 'corruptions,' 'degradations,' and 'perversions.'

The principle of regularization is observed in AmE usage (as in BrE) for all other marks of punctuation, i.e. question marks and exclamation points come inside the quotation marks if they belong, but are placed outside if they do not belong to the quotation itself.

Note also that in lists AmE usage is more likely than BrE usage to use a comma before the conjunction joining the final item in a list (AmE *x, y, and z* vs BrE *x, y and z*). On the other hand, (conservative) BrE usage sets a comma between the house number and the street name in addresses, e.g. *331, High Street*, something which is not practised in AmE.

The use or not of a dot (period, full stop) after abbreviations, especially titles, also differs. While AmE opts for simplicity, always using a dot, BrE distinguishes abbreviations which end with the same letter as their unabbreviated form and which therefore have no dot, e.g. *Mister > Mr, Missus > Mrs, Colonel > Col, Lieutenant > Lt* etc. In contrast, abbreviations which end with a letter different from the final letter of the full form have a dot, e.g. *General > Gen., Captain > Capt., (the) Reverend > Rev.* etc. Note that in the bibliographical information in this book *editor* is abbreviated as *ed.* (as is *edited*), but *editors* as *eds* (without a dot).

Miscellaneous differences in punctuation   In business letters, the salutation (*Dear Sir, Dear Madam*) is followed by a colon in AmE, but by a comma in BrE. Informal salutations have a comma in AmE. The colon, when used as punctuation between two main clauses, is followed by a small (lower case) letter in the second clause in BrE. In AmE, there may be capitalization, e.g. *One solution is quite evident: check* (BrE)/*Check* (AmE) *the credit-worthiness of the client carefully.* When a colon is used to introduce lists it may sometimes be followed by a hyphen in BrE; this is never the case in AmE, e.g. *Several commodities have fallen in price significantly:- coffee, cocoa, tea and tobacco.* The symbol <%> is written out as two words in BrE (*per cent*), but is a single one in AmE (*percent*). In addition, BrE uses the abbreviation *p.c.* or *pc*, as in *16 pc drop in unemployment*, but AmE does not.

Dates can be the source of serious misunderstanding between the two varieties since BrE goes with European usage in placing the date before the month between oblique strokes or separated by (raised) dots: *2 April 2003* is *2/4/03* or *2·4·03*. In AmE *2/4/03* (oblique strokes only) is *February 4, 2003*. In cases of possible confusion it is best to write out the name of the month or its abbreviation. The raised dots just mentioned are unknown in AmE, but are also used for decimals and times in BrE, e.g. *3·1416* or *10·43 a.m.* A normal period/full stop may also be used in BrE. Clock times use a dot in BrE (*3.45 p.m.*), but a colon in AmE (*3:45 p.m.*). Both varieties abbreviate *number(s)* as *No.* or *Nos* (capitalized or not, with a dot or not according to AmE and BrE rules, e.g. *No. 8* or *nos 5 and 8*); however, only AmE uses the symbol # (*# 8*).

12.3 GRAMMAR AND MORPHOLOGY

12.3.1 The verb

Morphology   A number of verbs ending in a nasal (*dream, lean*) or an <l> (*spill*) have two forms for their past tense and past participle; one is regular, adding {-ed}; the other adds {-t} (sometimes with and sometimes without a change in the vowel in pronunciation). These verbs include the following: *burn, dream, dwell, kneel, lean, learn, spell, spill* and *spoil*. In each case, AmE is more likely to have the regular form and BrE to have the form in *-t*. For example, *leant* /lent/ is rare in AmE in contrast to *leaned* /liːnd/. Note, however, that there are verbs ending in <m, n, l> which do not have two forms; for example, there is only irregular *meant* /ment/ in both varieties, just as there is only regular *quelled* and *teamed*. A further widespread phenomenon is the greater tendency in AmE for non-standard past tense forms to be used higher up in the scale of stylistic formality. This is especially the case with the pattern *sprung* for *sprang* (see also simple past tense *rung, shrunk, sung, sunk, stunk* and *swum*).

Most other differences in the past tense and past participle forms are singular, incidental ones, including the differing pronunciation of the past tense forms *ate* (BrE /et/, AmE /eɪt/) and *shone* (BrE /ʃɒn/; AmE /ʃoʊn/) or AmE past tense *dove* and *snuck* (beside common *dived* and *sneaked*) or BrE *quitted, betted* and *fitted* (beside common *quit* and *bet* and AmE *fit*). AmE also sometimes uses *proven* and *shaven* as past participles next to common *proved* and *shaved*. Furthermore, AmE has the past participles *beat, shook* and *swelled* (beside normal *beaten, shaken* and *swollen*) in the expressions, *to be beat* 'completely exhausted', *all shook up* 'upset' and *to have a swelled head* 'be conceited'. *Slay* (itself more common in AmE) has two past tenses, literal, though archaic, *slew* 'killed' and figurative *slayed*, as in *That slayed me* 'caused me to laugh vigorously'.

Get and have   *Get* has two past participle forms in AmE, *got* and *gotten*, each used with a different meaning. *Have got* is used for possession, obligation or logical necessity in both varieties (for example: possession, *I've got a book on that subject*; obligation, *you've got to read it*; logical necessity, *it's got to be interesting*). *Have got* for logical necessity, familiar in AmE, is apparently a more recent and less widespread phenomenon in BrE. *Have gotten*, which does not occur in BrE at all, means 'receive', as in *I've just gotten a letter from her*. In its modal sense *have gotten* means 'be able, have the opportunity', as in *I've gotten to do more reading lately*. These distinctions must be made lexically in BrE. In addition, the past form *had got* is not a real option for expressing possession in either variety, but it is just barely possible in the modal meaning of obligation in BrE (e.g. *They had got to reply by yesterday*).

Do and have   Further differences in the ways of expressing possession and obligation (but also events) involve *have*. AmE treats *have* in these uses as a lexical verb and therefore uses periphrastic *do* for negation and inversion; only the perfect auxiliary is an operator in AmE, which means that only it inverts and negates directly (see 5.1.3). In BrE this seems to be increasingly the case as well; however, lexical *have*, especially in the broad sense of possession, may also be treated as an operator, e.g. *I haven't any idea*; *Have you a book on this subject?*; or *Hadn't she any news?* This use, which is as good as unknown in AmE, is becoming rarer in BrE, especially in questions and even more so in past tense use. Note that *do*-periphrasis is obligatory in both varieties for events such as having lunch, having a good time, having trouble etc.

Pro-form do   A further difference involves *do* as a pro-form. This is the use of one of its forms (*do, does, did, done, doing*) to replace a lexical verb instead of repeating it, e.g. A: *Did you write to the hotel?* B: *Yes, I have done.* This type of construction is exclusively BrE; in AmE B's reply would be: *Yes, I have* or *Yes, I have done so*, both of which are also possible in BrE.

Modal auxiliaries   Other differences between AmE and BrE in the area of the verb concern the frequencies of the modal verbs. *Should, shall, ought to, dare, need* and *must*, all of which are relatively infrequent in BrE, are even more so in AmE. *Dare* and *need*, furthermore, are more likely to be used as blends between operators and lexical verbs in AmE. This means that they will use *do*-periphrasis, but an unmarked infinitive, e.g.

I don't dare think about it. The use of *ought* without *to* in questions and negations (i.e. non-assertive contexts) is an increasingly frequent pattern not only in AmE and BrE, but also in AusE. Modal *must* is losing ground to *have (got) to* in its obligation meaning, especially in AmE; and also in its epistemic use for logical necessity ('*must* is very much alive and is now met with also in clauses negated by *not*, a usage that appears to be fairly recent in origin' (Jacobson 1979: 311)). Quirk *et al.* consider negated *must*, as in *His absence must not have been noticed*, to be particularly American (1985: §4.54).

The modal *used to* still has direct negation relatively frequently in BrE (*used not to*, *usen't to*); in AmE (as well as in BrE) the preferred form of negation is with *do*-periphrasis (*didn't use(d) to*). The modal *would* is normally used in the *if* clause of a conditional sentence when it indicates willingness (e.g. *If you would agree, everything would be fine*). Here the two varieties agree. However, AmE extends the use of *would* to *if* clauses where no volition is involved (e.g. *If it would rain, everything would be okay*). A further point involving the *would* is that the expression *'d rather*, which is a contraction of *would rather*, is sometimes re-expanded to *had rather*, chiefly in AmE. The growing use of the modal *will* with first person pronouns (*I/we will*) instead of traditional *shall* is an instance where British and American usage are converging: 'Increasingly even in Southern Standard BrE the forms formerly associated with AmE are becoming the norm' (Quirk *et al.* 1985: §4.50). *Shall* is heard in AmE almost only in questions inquiring about the desirability of the speaker's doing something, e.g. *Shall I get you an ashtray?* More common, however, would be the phrasing, *Would you like me to?*, *Should I?* or *Can I?* The semi-modals *(had) better* and *(have) got to (gotta)* are more common in conversation in BrE than in AmE, but *have to* and *be going to* are more common in AmE than in BrE (Biber *et al.* 1999: 488f.).

The subjunctive In AmE the subjunctive is far more common than in BrE. This is less the case with the so-called formulaic subjunctive (e.g. *I wish I/he/she/it were*; *If I were you*), which is becoming less and less current in both varieties. Rather, what is typically American usage is the so-called **mandative subjunctive**, used after predicates of command or recommendation and other predicates which mark something as desirable future action, e.g. *we suggest/recommend that you be on time tomorrow*; *it is important/mandatory that you not misunderstand me*. While this is somewhat formal usage in AmE, it is by no means unusual in the everyday language. In BrE, on the contrary, it is largely restricted to formal written usage, though it seems to be making a comeback due to American influence. What BrE uses in its place is either what is called **putative *should*** (*it is mandatory that you should not misunderstand me*), which is also available in AmE, or the indicative (*it is mandatory that you don't misunderstand me*). This latter option is impossible in AmE. See also 5.7.4 'Suggest'.

The perfect The use of the perfect is interpreted somewhat differently in the two varieties. While there is basic agreement, AmE speakers may choose to use the past in sentences with the adverbs *yet*, *just* or *already*, all of which would almost automatically trigger the use of the present perfect in BrE, e.g. AmE *He just/already came* for BrE and also, but less stringently, AmE *He has just/already come.*

Complementation Of the more important differences in the patterns of complementation used in AmE and BrE one has already been discussed: the use of a *that* clause with the subjunctive after verbs of command, suggestion and desirable future action. A second pattern which differs is the use of an infinitive complement whose subject is introduced by *for* after verbs of emotion such as *love, like, hate* and *prefer*, e.g. *They would like for you to come*. While adjectives take such *for . . . to* complements in both varieties (e.g. *They would be happy for you to come*), the occurrence of the *for . . . to* construction after verbs is more typical of AmE. Note, however, that this pattern is not employed all the time in AmE, nor is it completely unknown in some varieties of BrE. When something separates the main verb from the infinitive complement, *for* will occur in both varieties, e.g. *They would like very much for you to come*.

The third case involves copular verbs. These may be classified as ascriptive (*be, become*: *he is silly*), as cognitive (*seem, appear*: *he seems silly*) or sensorial (*look, sound, feel*: *he looks silly*). So long as what follows is an adjective, the two varieties follow the same pattern (as in the examples). When, however, a noun follows, there are divergences. Both allow nouns following ascriptive *be* and *become*: *he is a fool*. The case is quite different with *appear* and *seem*, however, which may take noun predicative complements directly in BrE, but require *to be* in AmE (also possible in BrE): *he seemed (to be) a fool*. With sensorial copulas, finally, BrE once again allows a noun to follow directly while AmE requires intervening *like* (also possible in BrE): *he looked (like) a fool*. Note that even in BrE not every noun may follow directly (i.e. without *to be* or *like*); this seems to be possible only when the noun is more or less adjectival in nature (*to seem/look a fool* = *to seem/look foolish*). This practically dictates that the indefinite article be used, for then reference is general and serves the purposes of characterization just as an adjective does. In addition, the noun used must be gradable in the sense of more or less (someone can be *very much a fool*).

Concord   This is the final point concerning the verb. As elsewhere in the grammar the two varieties agree here almost completely. The one important divergence has to do with the greater degree to which *notional concord* is applied in BrE. While both types of English construe words like *people* and *police* as plurals, a large number of collective nouns for groups of people are often seen as plural in BrE while they virtually never are in AmE, e.g. *government, team, committee, council, board* etc. Hence BrE frequently has *The council have decided to make further inquiries*, where AmE (but BrE as well) has *The council has decided*. A minor point of concord is the BrE use of interrogative *aren't I* for the non-existent contracted form of *am*. This is rare in AmE.

Tag questions   **Tag questions**, at least those which show grammatical change according to the subject and auxiliary of the preceding main clause, are probably more common in BrE than in AmE; certainly ones without reversed polarity and especially those in which both main verb and tag are negative are rare or virtually unheard of in AmE, e.g. *They aren't leaving tomorrow, aren't they?*

12.3.2 The noun, the pronoun and the article

The noun   Besides the difference in interpretation of some collective nouns as notional plurals, as just discussed, it is perhaps of interest to note that some words appear regularly in the singular in the one, but in the plural in the other variety: plural pre-modifiers such as *the drugs business* or *the trades union* are more common in BrE than in AmE even though both share many such combinations such as *arms race* or *sales talk*. Also, BrE has the plural *(traffic)lights* and *maths* where AmE has singular *light* and *math*; on the other hand, AmE has plural *accommodations* and *sports* where BrE has abstract and non-count *accommodation* and *sport*. In AmE *inning* (as in baseball) is a count noun with a singular and a plural; in BrE there is only the unchanging singular and plural form *innings* (as in cricket). BrE can (but need not) give words like *fish* or *shrimp* a plural ending (*fishes, shrimps*), while this is strange in AmE. Furthermore, numbers are also sometimes treated differently: when a noun follows a number ending in *thousand, million* etc. no plural {-S} is added to it (*five thousand books*); when the noun is elided BrE may add a plural (possible BrE *five thousands*); AmE may not.

The pronoun   In addition to what has been said about collective nouns and notional concord we can note that both varieties agree in frequently, but not necessarily, using plural pronoun reference for 'group' nouns, e.g. *their* in the following: *The council is/are considering this at their next meeting*. A second point reveals greater divergence: a singular interpretation of a collective noun like *committee* or *council* will lead to the use of the relative pronoun *which*, while the BrE plural interpretation will be more likely to take *who*, e.g. *The Committee, which is considering the move* vs *The Committee, who are considering the move* (see generic pronouns in 9.1). There is a tendency in AmE to use the relative pronoun *that* in restrictive relative clauses noticeably more often than *which*, which is less conversational and more academic in style.

Two additional pronoun differences are first the greater preference for *-body* (e.g. *anybody*) over *-one* (e.g. *everyone*) in AmE and, second, the widespread use of a distinct second person plural pronoun in Southern AmE, *you all*, sometimes shortened to *y'all* (possessive *you all's* or *y'all's*). Although a few other second person plural forms exist in both BrE and AmE such as *yous(e)*, none of them have the relative acceptance which *you all* has.

The article   A few differences in article choice include the following well known difference: BrE *to/in hospital* vs AmE *to/in the hospital*. While all the seasons (*spring, summer, autumn, winter*) can be used with or without the article in both varieties, the usual AmE word for *autumn*, namely *fall* cannot occur without it (*in the fall*, not **in fall*). Although there are other differences in usage, none of them are of great significance.

12.3.3 The preposition, the conjunction and the adverb

Prepositions   While BrE and AmE both prefer *while, among* and *amid*, BrE also uses the forms *whilst, amongst* and *amidst*, which are rare in AmE. BrE sometimes also employs *in regard of* where both normally have *in regard to*. Common to both is *behind, apart from* and *on top of*, but AmE also has *in back of, aside from* and *atop* respectively, which are unfamiliar in BrE. AmE uses *in behalf of* in addition to shared *on behalf of*. Next to common *off, opposite* and *alongside*, AmE also has *off of, opposite of* and *alongside of* without any difference in meaning. AmE prefers *different than* next to BrE *different from* and *different to*. Furthermore, AmE usage is much more prone to leave the preposition out altogether in time expressions such as *Tuesdays*, where BrE has *on Tuesdays*. AmE also omits prepositions more freely in time expressions, e.g. *She starts work (on) Monday*.

The preposition *out* (AmE, informal BrE) is not used in the same way as common *out of*. The former may only be employed with two-dimensional objects which designate paths of exit, as in *out the window, door* etc. *Out of* may be used here as well in both varieties and indeed usually is in BrE.

The pair *round* and *around* also overlap in much the same way except that here it is AmE which has no choice since the form *round* is scarcely found there. In BrE, on the other hand, *round* may be distinguished from *around* as in *to go round the earth* 'in a circular movement, as for example a satellite' vs *to go all around the world* 'to travel to various places anywhere in the world'. This distinction is missing in AmE.

The preposition *through* as in AmE *Volume one of the dictionary goes from A through G* is not current in BrE, where the ambiguous *A to G* or the cumbersome *A to G inclusive* might be found.

The present perfect of verbs expressing continuous activity regularly has *for* to introduce periods of time in both varieties, e.g. *I've been working for an hour*. For individual events within a period both varieties use *in*, e.g. *I have gone twice in (the past) two weeks*. Usage differs when a verb expressing individual events is negated. Here BrE uses *for*: *I haven't gone for (the past) two weeks*, while AmE prefers *in*: *I haven't gone in (the past) two weeks*. In other words, BrE usage is generalized from the continuity of non-action while AmE usage is generalized from the non-occurrence of individual acts.

An additional difference in the application of generalities is the preference for *at* (BrE and common) vs *over* (AmE) for longer holidays and weekends (*at/over Easter*). Here *at* usage stresses the relatively punctual nature of the time unit, while AmE usage underscores its longer absolute length. The use of *at the weekend* (BrE; impossible in AmE) fits this pattern and treats *weekend* punctually. AmE *on* (beside *over*) *the weekend* treats *weekend* in the same way as a weekday (*on Monday*).

To indicate a fixed time in the future, the time of reference will always follow *from* in AmE while BrE may omit the preposition and even invert the elements, e.g. common *We'll meet two weeks from Saturday* and BrE *We'll meet Saturday fortnight*.

For clock time, informal AmE uses *of* or *till* for common *to* as in *It's quarter of/ till ten*. This usage with *of* is unknown in BrE; *till* is rare there. Informal BrE, on the other hand, has the preposition *gone* 'past' as in *It's gone eight*, which would puzzle an AmE speaker. Equally hard to understand for this speaker is the time expression *It's half eight* for 'eight-thirty'. AmE frequently uses *after* (*It's twenty after nine*), while BrE uses only the shared form *past*; however, AmE demands *past* in combination with *quarter* and *half* (*a quarter/half past ten*). A final preference worth mentioning is the use of time expressions without a preposition, which is more common in AmE than in BrE as in *The meeting started seven-thirty*.

Conjunctions   A few usages show preferences in the one or the other direction, for example, *lest* is more common in AmE (e.g. *Be quiet lest he call the police*). In BrE this counts as somewhat archaic. Instead the informal *in case* might be used in much the same sense, e.g. *Be quiet in case he should call the police*, a usage which, however, is not possible in AmE. Note that both could have . . . *so that he won't call the police*.

In AmE the prepositions *plus*, *like* and *on account of* are sometimes used as conjunctions, e.g. *I don't feel like we should go out on account of it's late, plus I'm tired* (*plus* as a conjunction seems to be gaining ground in BrE). In BrE, on the other hand, the adverbs *directly* and *immediately* can also be conjunctions, e.g. *Immediately/Directly you came, he left*. Furthermore, in BrE *nor* may be an adverbial conjunct and co-occur with the conjunctions *and* or *but*, e.g. *I don't like French cheese, but nor do I like cheddar*.

Adverbs   Perhaps the most noticeable difference in the use of adverbs is the greater tendency in AmE, especially in speech, informal writing and sports journalism, to use adjectives rather than adverbs as in *You did that real good*. While the use of an adjective in the function of a manner adverb (*good* in the example) is rejected in more careful usage, adjectives as intensifiers (*real* in the example) are used much further up the stylistic scale. The use of adverbs formed from nouns plus the ending *-wise* (e.g. *time-wise* 'from the point of view of time' or *word-wise* 'as far as words are concerned') is considered more typically American. A further morphological difference is the partiality of AmE to the ending *-ward* (without a final *-s*) as in *toward* or *backward*. AmE has both *someplace* and *somewhere*; BrE has only the latter.

12.3.4 Word order

BrE has *Will you give it me?* for common *Will you give me it?* or *Will you give it to me?* In the complimentary close to business letters American usage has *Sincerely yours* while BrE uses *Yours sincerely*. In BrE inversion such as *Monday last* can be found, but hardly in AmE. See also *the River Thames* (*Humber*, *Avon* etc.), but *the Mississippi* (*Missouri*, *Hudson* etc.) *River*. Pre-modifiers in journalistic style are more frequent in AmE than in BrE, for example, *British novelist Graham Greene*, where more formal styles would have *Graham Greene, the British novelist*.

12.4 LEXIS

The lexical relations between BrE and AmE have been analysed in many different ways of which only the most important can be mentioned in this section.

12.4.1 The developmental approach

What might be called the developmental approach takes the criteria of use, intelligibility and regional status to set up four groups which can be seen as the stages through which regional words have to pass before they are fully accepted in StE. The first category consists of words that are neither understood nor used in the other variety, e.g. AmE *meld* 'merge' or BrE *hive off* 'separate from the main group'. Group two contains items that are understood but not used elsewhere (AmE *checkers*, *cookie*, *howdy* or BrE *draughts*, *scone*, *cheerio*). In the third there are items that are both understood and used in both, but which still have a distinctly American or British flavour to them (AmE *figure out*, *movie*; BrE *niggle, telly*). The last group, finally, includes lexical material that is not only completely intelligible and widely used in the other variety, but has also lost whatever American or British flavour it may once have had (originally AmE *boost, debunk, hi*; originally BrE *brass tacks, semi-detached, pissed off*). There can be no doubt that many items start in group one and end up in the last group. It has to be added, however, that there is often no agreement on where an item should be grouped. *Student*, for example, in the (broader than university) sense of 'young person at school' used to be usual only in AmE, but is now commonly heard in BrE as well. Conversely, the BrE word *trendy* may have overtaken AmE *chic* in America. Finally, though almost all dictionaries say that *bag lady* 'a homeless woman who carries everything she owns around with her' is an AmE word, it is frequently found in newspapers in Britain, where the phenomenon is also widespread. This lack of consensus does not, however, mean that the criteria and the four groups have no value.

The national flavour of a word can be important in determining whether it is accepted or not. Some people in Britain seem to resent the great number of Americanisms in BrE. The controversy around the word *hopefully*, as in *hopefully, he will be back soon*, has frequently served as a call-to-arms for purists who condemn it by pointing out that it came from across the Atlantic. Other speakers in Britain, on the other hand, especially younger people, might perhaps welcome transatlantic items simply because they are AmE. Overall, Americans show a more tolerant attitude towards British loans than vice versa; however, there are far fewer of them in AmE than the other way (a)round.

12.4.2 The causal approach

Scholars have also enquired into the less subjective and more linguistic reasons why items are or are not borrowed from the one variety into the other. In the causal approach, the vivid and expressive nature of a number of words and phrases is held to have helped them expand, for example many of the informal or slang items from AmE like *fiend* (as in *dope fiend* or *fitness fiend*), *joint* 'cheap or dirty place of meeting for drinking, eating etc.' and *sucker* ('gullible person'). Secondly, many borrowings are short and snappy and often reinforce the trend in common StE towards the monosyllabic word, such as AmE *cut* (next to *reduction*) and *fix* (in addition to *prepare, repair*) or BrE *chips* (beside AmE *french fries*). The third reason has to do with the fact that some loans provide a term for an idea or concept where there was none before, called a **lexical gap**. When the idea itself is missing, this is known as a **conceptual gap**. Examples of lexical-conceptual gaps are originally AmE *boost, debunk, know-how* and *high, middle* and *low brow* or originally BrE *brunch, smog, cop, tabloid* or *gadget*.

Finally, part of the attraction of many loans may lie in their morphological make-up. When they conform to productive word formation patterns of English, they are more likely to be borrowed. This may include phrasal verbs or zero derived items (see Chapter 2). Examples of phrasal verbs: originally AmE *be into something* ('be passionately interested in'), *bone up (on)* ('study intensively'), *cave in* ('collapse, give up') or originally BrE *butter up* 'sweet talk' or *be cheesed off* 'annoyed'. Among zero derivations of American origin *brush-off, hairdo* and *showdown* can be mentioned.

Conversely, words current in the language of ethnic minorities in the United States, such as Blacks, Jews and people of Hispanic origin may provide other examples. The same is probably true of words borrowed into BrE from many of Britain's former colonial holdings, e.g. Anglo-Indian *pukka*, 'genuine, sound' or Arabic *shufti* 'a look at something'. Originally Yiddish words for instance, which are known and used especially on the east coast of the United States, like *schmooze* ('to converse informally'), *schlep(p)* ('carry, move slowly or with great effort') or *schlock* ('trash, cheap goods') are said to be unattractive to British ears and tongues perhaps because of the initial consonant clusters /ʃl/ and /ʃm/. But it would be rash to maintain that this type of word will 'remain firmly unborrowed in British English' (Burchfield 1985: 163); all the same, the latest edition of the *Concise Oxford Dictionary* does still mark *schlock* as (chiefly) colloquial American (but the regional label is not attached to *schlep(p)* any longer).

12.4.3 The semantic approach

Perhaps the most common way to deal with the lexis of the two varieties is what may be called the semantic approach. This method compares words and phrases with their referents or meanings in terms of sameness and difference. Despite varying approaches with sometimes numerous groupings, five different groups may conveniently be recognized.

First of all, most words and their meanings are the same, which explains the fact that British and American speakers rarely experience any difficulty in understanding each other. As a result this first group is seldom mentioned. The second group comprises words which are present in only one variety because they refer to something unknown in the other culture. This can be words for things in the natural environment such as BrE *moor* or *heath* and AmE *prairie* and *canyon*. It also may include social and political institutions, e.g. BrE *Yorkshire pudding* or *back bench* and AmE *succotash* or *favorite son*. Although cases in the second category make linguistic help necessary, they do not cause misunderstandings. A variant on this type of distinction involves lexical gaps. Here the referent or concept is known in the other variety but not lexicalized, i.e. only paraphrases are available, e.g. BrE *chapel* 'a local (branch) of a printers' union' or BrE (slang) *to tart up* 'to dress up in a garish manner'.

The third group covers those cases where different words and phrases are used to express the same meaning. BrE *petrol* is AmE *gas(oline)* and AmE *truck* is BrE *lorry*. In the fourth category the two varieties share a word/phrase, but with a fully different meaning, as with *vest*, which in AmE is what is called a *waistcoat* in BrE, but which in BrE is what is called an *undershirt* in AmE. A variation on this is the case in which the two varieties agree in the meanings, but one variety has an additional meaning not known or used in the other. For example, both agree in the meaning of *leader* 'someone who leads', but BrE also uses it in the sense of AmE (and shared) *editorial*. Conversely, both understand the noun *fall* as 'downward movement', but AmE also uses this word in the sense of BrE (and shared) *autumn*. In many cases special words and meanings arise only in certain contexts. Examples in BrE are *sit* or *enter for* when they collocate with *exam*, while *freshen* has the extra meaning 'add more liquid etc. to a drink' in AmE only in collocation with *drink*. BrE *set an exercise* is *assign an exercise* in AmE. The final, fifth grouping is the very common instance in which both varieties share an expression and its meaning(s), but where one or both have a further expression for the same thing not shared by the other. Both AmE and BrE have *taxi*, while *cab* is AmE. Likewise, both share *raincoat*, but only BrE has *mac(intosh); pharmacy* is common, while *chemist's* is BrE only and *drug store* is typically AmE.

12.4.4 Relative frequencies and cultural associations

Many writers make absolute statements and do not take into account the evidence for relative frequencies. Too little use has been made so far of such large scale corpora as those assembled at Brown University for AmE (Francis and Kučera 1982) and at Lancaster, Oslo and Bergen for BrE (Hofland and Johansson 1982). It is not the case, for example, that *railroad* is found exclusively in AmE or *railway* only in BrE: 'in the Brown corpus *railroad* appears forty-seven times and *railway* ten; in LOB *railway* appears fifty-two times and *railroad* once' (Ilson 1990: 37).

Differences in cultural associations are almost wholly neglected. It is often pointed out, for example, that *robin* refers to two different birds, but it is hardly ever mentioned that the English bird is considered a symbol of winter while the American robin is a harbinger of spring (Ilson 1990: 40). Scholars have, furthermore, also been prone to take meaning in a narrow sense which excludes such use aspects as field, regional and social distribution and differences in personal tenor (see 1.6.2). AmE *vacation* is *holiday(s)* in BrE, as in *they are on holiday/vacation now*. But lawyers and universities in Britain use *vacation* to refer to the intervals between terms. AmE *pinkie*, an informal word for *little finger*, is an import from Scotland, where it is still the accepted word, as is borne out by the regional labels 'especially US and Scotland.'

Difficult and controversial, though of great importance in both the United States and Great Britain, are the social class associations that items can have in the respective variety. It is therefore not unimportant for Americans to know that in BrE *lounge* 'is definitely non-U; *drawing room* definitely U' [*U* = 'upper class'] (Benson *et al.* 1986: 36). Conversely, British people might be interested to hear about America that 'Proles say *tux*, middles *tuxedo*, but both are considered low by uppers, who say *dinner jacket* or (higher) *black tie*' (Fussell 1984: 152).

12.4.5 Lexis in the fields of university and of sports

Instead of listing further unconnected items we will now undertake a brief systematic comparison of two fields, universities and the two 'national' sports of cricket and baseball. For the sake of convenience our discussion of university lexis will come under the headings of people and activities.

University: people In *higher education* (common) or *tertiary education* (BrE) a division may be made into two groups: the first are those who teach (*the faculty*, AmE; *the (academic) staff*, BrE) and commonly include:

AmE		BrE	
	(full) professors		professors
	associate professors		readers
	assistant professors		senior lecturers
	instructors		lecturers

And there are those who study:

AmE	freshmen	BrE	first year students or freshers
	sophomores		second year students
	juniors		third year (also possibly: junior honours) students
	seniors		final year (also possibly: senior honours) students

Teaching and research is organized in departments (common) or faculties (BrE), and these are under the administrative supervision of heads of department (common) or deans (BrE). American colleges and universities also have deans, both deans of students, who are responsible for counselling, and administrative deans at the head of a major division in a college (which, in AmE, refers to undergraduate education) or a professional school (AmE, postgraduate level, for example, in a school of medicine, law, forestry, nursing, business administration etc.). At the top in the American system is a president. This is not unknown in the UK: however, a chancellor (honorary) or vice chancellor (actual on-the-spot chief officer) is more likely to be found there. On the other hand, a chancellor in America is often the head of a state university system.

University activities   Students in the United States go to a college and study a major and a minor subject; in the UK they go up and then study, or read (formal), a main and a subsidiary subject. While at college or university they may choose to live in a dorm(itory) (AmE), a student hostel (BrE) or a hall (of residence) (BrE). If they misbehave, their may be suspended (AmE) or rusticated (BrE); in the worst of cases they may even be expelled (AmE) or sent down (BrE). In their classes (common) they may be assigned (AmE) a term paper (AmE) or given a (long) essay (BrE) to write. At the end of a semester, trimester, quarter (all especially AmE) or term (common) they sit (BrE) or take (common) exams which are supervised (AmE) or invigilated (BrE) by a proctor (AmE) or invigilator (BrE). These exams are then corrected and graded (AmE) or marked (BrE). The grades (marks) themselves differ in their scale: American colleges and universities mark from (high) A via B, C and D, to (low = fail) F, which are marks known and used in the UK as well. In the US overall results for a term as well as for the whole of one's studies will be expressed as a grade point average with a high of 4.0 (all A's). In the UK a person's studies may conclude with a brilliant *starred first*, an excellent *first*, an *upper second*, a *lower second* or a *third* (a simple pass). Particularly good students may wish to continue beyond the BA (common) or BS (AmE) or BSc (BrE) as a graduate (especially AmE) or postgraduate (especially BrE) student. In that case they may take further courses and write an MA thesis (AmE) or MA dissertation (BrE). Indeed, they may even write a doctoral dissertation (AmE) or doctoral thesis (BrE).

Sports expressions   Idioms, idiomatic expressions and figurative language from all areas, but especially from the area of sports are used frequently in colloquial speech, perhaps because they tend to be colourful. Many different types of sports are involved (e.g. track and field, *the university's track record*; boxing, *saved by the bell*; or horse-racing, *on the home stretch*). Yet the two 'national sports', cricket and baseball, in particular, have contributed especially to the language of everyday communication.

The following is a useful, but not an exhaustive list of the idioms which come from these sports.

Since the two sports resemble each other (if ever so vaguely), they actually share some expressions: *batting order* 'the order in which people act or take their turn'; *to field* 'enter a competition as "to field candidates for an election"'; *to take the field* 'to begin a campaign'. The user should, however, beware of the seemingly similar, but in reality very different expressions (BrE) *to do something off one's own bat* 'independently, without consulting others' vs (AmE) *to do something off the bat* 'immediately, without waiting'. Most of the expressions are, however, part of only cricket or only baseball. Of these a couple from cricket are well integrated into both BrE and AmE without any longer being necessarily closely identified with the sport: *to stump* 'to baffle, put at a loss for an answer' (< put out a batsman by touching the stumps); *to stonewall* 'to intentionally draw out discussion and avoid giving an answer' (< slow, careful overly protective play by a batsman). Further expressions from cricket which are known, but not commonly used in AmE are *a sticky wicket* 'a difficult situation' and *(something is) not cricket* 'unfair or unsportsmanlike'. Less familiar or totally unknown in AmE are *to hit someone for six* 'to score a resounding success', *to queer someone's pitch* 'to spoil someone's plans', *to be caught out* 'to be trapped, found out, exposed', *a hat trick* (also soccer) 'three similar successes in a row', *She has had a good innings* 'a long life'.

Baseball has provided the following collection of idiomatic expressions, most of which have a very distinctly American flavour about them: *to play (political, economic etc.) hard ball* 'to be (ruthlessly) serious about something', *to touch base* 'to get in contact', *not to get to first base with someone* 'to be unsuccessful with someone', *to pinch hit for someone* 'to stand in for someone', *to ground out/fly out/foul out/strike out* 'to fail', *to have a/one/two strikes against you* 'to be at a disadvantage', *to play in/to make the big leagues* 'to work with/be with important, powerful people', *a double play* 'two successes in one move', *take a rain check* 'postponement', *a grand slam* (also tennis and bridge) 'a smashing success or victory', *a blooper* 'a mistake or failure', *a doubleheader* 'a combined event with lots to offer', *batting average* 'a person's performance', *over the fence* or *out of the ball park* 'a successful move or phenomenal feat', *out in left field* 'remote, out of touch, unrealistic', *off base* 'wrong'.

What have been illustrated here are only some examples of the many lexical and idiomatic differences between the two varieties. This also seems to be the case in government and politics, in cooking and baking, in clothing and in connection with many technological developments up to the Second World War (railroads/railways, trucks/lorries etc.). Nevertheless, as a matter of perspective, it is important to bear in mind that the vocabulary and idioms associated with national institutions such as the educational system and national sports will diverge more strongly than that of other areas. The vast majority of vocabulary used in everyday, colloquial speech as well as that of international communication in science and technology is common to not only AmE and BrE, but also to all other national and regional varieties of English.

12.5 FURTHER READING

Fisher 2001 is a general historical treatment. Useful literature on **pronunciation** includes: (for RP) Gimson 2001; (for GenAm) Bronstein 1960; and Wells 1982 (for both). Standard pronouncing dictionaries for RP are Jones 1997; for GenAm, Kenyon and Knott 1944; Wells 2000 gives both. **Spelling**: for more on internal variation within BrE, see Greenbaum 1986; for AmE, see: Emery 1975; Venezky 1999. Information on **punctuation** is found in a very concise form at the front or back of most modern dictionaries. Most good dictionaries, whether AmE or BrE in their orientation, provide alternative spellings, but they cannot always be counted on to include the standard spellings of the other side of the Atlantic. See also 4.7.

Quirk *et al.* 1985 make frequent comments on BrE–AmE differences in **grammar**. Biber *et al.* 1999 make highly illuminating corpus-based observations on such differences.

On sources of **vocabulary** including national differences in word formation and borrowing see Gramley 2001. A typical comparative list is Moss 1994. Examples of loan words can be found, for example, in McArthur 1996: 137ff. For collocations see Benson *et al.* 1997 (both AmE and BrE) and *Oxford Collocations* (2002) (BrE). Few writers and fewer word lists or dictionaries give help with aspects of social class, but the books by Buckle (mainly BrE; 1978); Cooper (BrE; 1981), Fussell (AmE; 1984; especially Chapter 7) provide some orientation.

Chapter 13

English in Australia, New Zealand and South Africa

These three countries have been grouped together for a number of reasons. First of all, they are the only large areas in the southern hemisphere in which English is spoken as a native language. This itself is related to the relatively large-scale settlement of all three by English speaking Europeans at roughly the same time (Australia from 1788, South Africa essentially from 1820, New Zealand officially from 1840). All three were, for a considerable period of time, British colonies and hence open to British institutions (government, administration, courts, military, education and religion) as well as the use of English as an official language. Other southern hemisphere places such as the Falkland Islands, South Georgia, Fiji or Samoa will not be considered. East and West Africa are included in Chapter 14 in section 14.1.2; Vanuatu and Papua New Guinea, in the section on pidgins and creoles (14.3).

Each section of this chapter starts with a short sketch of settlement history, which provides the background to the establishment of English as a local language. Mention is also made of the number of speakers of English and other important languages as well as official language policies and the status of English. Finally, there is a characterization of English in these countries, taking into consideration pronunciation, grammar and vocabulary as well as social, regional and ethnic variation.

13.1 AUSTRALIAN ENGLISH (AusE)

When the first European settlers reached Port Jackson (present day Sydney) in New South Wales in 1788 the continent was inhabited by the native or Aboriginal peoples. Since these peoples were linguistically divided and technologically far less advanced than the European newcomers, they had relatively little impact on further developments, including language. Today the Aboriginal population numbers about 0.25 million in a total of about 19 million.

Initially Australia served as a British penal colony and was populated chiefly by transported convicts. With the economic development of the country (wool, minerals) the number of voluntary immigrants increased, and it boomed after the discovery of gold in 1851. The convict settlers were chiefly Irish (30 per cent) and southern English. The latter had the strongest influence on the nature of AusE. Because of their largely urban origins the English they used contained relatively few rural, farming terms and perhaps a greater number of words considered to be less refined in polished English society. The pronunciation which has developed, while distinctly Australian, has a clearly urban southern English bias; and although it is often compared to Cockney, the similarities are only partial (see below).

Today the vast majority of the population speaks English; and over 80 per cent of them have it as their native language. Aboriginal languages are in wide use only in Western Australia and the Northern Territory; in the late twentieth century Aboriginal languages were used there by perhaps as much as a quarter of the population. Non-British immigration has been significant since the Second World War. The long practised 'white Australia' policy, which discouraged non-European, even non-British immigration (except for New Zealanders) has yielded to more liberal policies: by the 1970s a third of the immigrants were Asians and only a half were Europeans. Regardless of the presence of numerous immigrant languages the primacy of English has never been called into question; the influence of both immigrant and Aboriginal languages has been limited to providing loan words.

13.1.1 AusE pronunciation

AusE is most easily recognized by its pronunciation. The intonation seems to operate within a narrower range of pitch, and the tempo often strikes non-Australians as noticeably slow. Except for the generally slower pronunciations of rural speech, there is no systematic regional variation in AusE, but there are significant social differences. Frequently AusE pronunciation is classed in three categories. The first is referred to as **Cultivated** and resembles RP relatively closely; it may, in fact, include speakers whose pronunciation is 'near-RP'. It is spoken by proportionately few people (in one investigation of adolescent speakers approximately 11 per cent; see Delbridge 1970: 19); nevertheless, it is the type of pronunciation given in the *Macquarie Dictionary*. The second type is called **General**, spoken by the majority (55 per cent; Delbridge 1970); its sound patterns are clearly Australian, but not so extreme as what is known as **Broad** (34 per cent; Delbridge 1970), which realizes its vowels more slowly than General.

In the light of Australia's early history, in which two groups stood in direct opposition to each other, namely the convicts and the officer class which supervised them, the following remark seems fitting:

> In sum, Australian English developed in the context of two dialects – each of them bearing a certain amount of prestige. Cultivated Australian is, and continues to be, the variety which carries overt prestige. It is the one associated with females, private elite schools, gentility and an English heritage. Broad Australian carries covert prestige and is associated with males, the uneducated, commonness and republicanism. The new dialect is 'General' which retains the national identity associated with Broad but which avoids the nonstandardisms in pronunciation, morphology and syntax associated with uneducated speech wherever English is spoken.
>
> (Horvath 1985: 40)

Today teenage speakers tend to cluster in the area of General, perhaps being pushed there to distinguish themselves from the large number of immigrants who have adopted Broad (ibid.: 175f.).

Map 13.1   Australia

AusE intonation   In addition to the remark made above on the narrower range of pitch in AusE, one further comment is appropriate. This is the use of what is called the high rising tone (sometimes also called Australian Question Intonation), which involves the use of rising contours (tone 2, see 4.5.3) for statements. It is part of the turn-taking mechanism, and it is used chiefly in narrative and descriptive texts. 'And finally, at the heart of it all is a basic interactive meaning of soliciting feedback from the audience, particularly regarding comprehension of what the speaker is saying' (Guy and Vonwiller 1989: 28). Like adding, 'Do you understand?' to a statement it requests the participation of the listener (see CanE *eh* in 11.2.1). It is apparently a low prestige usage, favoured more by young people; it is also more common among females than among males and may be observed increasingly often, especially among young women, in other national varieties of English.

AusE consonants   There are only a few significant differences in the realization of AusE consonants when compared with RP and also with GenAm. Among these is the tendency to flap and voice intervocalic /t/ before an unstressed syllable in Broad and General, though rarely in Cultivated. T-flapping is very similar to the same phenomenon in GenAm. This necessarily means that there is an absence of the glottal stop [ʔ], which many urban varieties of BrE have in the same environment (e.g. *butter* is [bʌdə] = '*budder*' rather than [bʌʔə] = '*buh'er*'.

Unlike GenAm, but like RP, AusE is non-rhotic. As in Cockney there is also a certain amount of H-dropping ('*ouse* for *house*). However, Horvath's Sydney investigation turned up relatively little of this (ibid). In addition, the sound quality of /l/ is even darker than a normal velarized [ɫ]; it is, rather, pharyngealized [lˤ] in all positions. Furthermore, there seems to be widespread vocalization of /l/, which leads to a new set of diphthongs (see examples under NZE, which is similar).

AusE vowels   In the following the vowel system of General/Broad AusE is presented schematically in comparison with an unshifted RP point of departure. One of the main differences, noted by various observers, is a general raising of the simple vowels (see Figure 13.1). A counter-clockwise lowering and retraction of the first element in the diphthongs which move towards a high front second element, and a clockwise lowering and fronting of the first element of the diphthongs which move towards a high back second element are further changes (Figure 13.2).

To some extent AusE represents a continuation of the Great Vowel Shift, which began in the late Middle English period and which is continuing in the same sense in London English (Cockney) (see also 10.2.2, 10.4.1 and 11.2.2).

Beyond such differences in the phonetic realization of the vowels, it is notable that far fewer unstressed vowels are realized as /ɪ/ in AusE than in RP. This means that the distinction maintained in RP between <-es> and <-ers> (as in *boxes* /ɪz/ and *boxers* /əz/ or *humid* /ɪd/ and *humoured* /əd/) is usually not made. Indeed, it may be possible to say that there is a certain centralization of /ɪ/ which brings it closer to /ə/, but also sometimes to fronted [ʉ] as well. An Australia newsreader working for the BBC is supposed to have caused some consternation by reporting that the Queen had *chattered* /əd/ rather than *chatted* /ɪd/ with workers. In addition, note that the final unstressed RP /ɪ/ pronunciation of <-y> and <-i(e)> (*hurry, Toni, hurries*) is realized as /iː/.

The /æ/–/aː/ contrast in words of the type *ask, after, example, dance* etc. shows divided usage in AusE, reminiscent of the same type of contrast between GenAm and RP. Apart from the fact that vowel realization differs from word to word (i.e. does not affect this class of words as a whole), one recent study shows significant regional distinctions. In an identical set of words (e.g. *castle, chance, contrast, demand, dance, graph, grasp*)

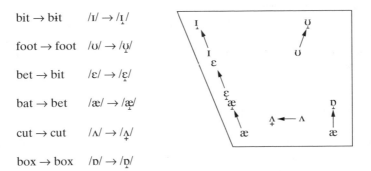

bit → bi̱t   /ɪ/ → /ɪ̝/

foot → foo̱t   /ʊ/ → /ʊ̝/

bet → bit   /ɛ/ → /ɛ̝/

bat → bet   /æ/ → /æ̝/

cut → cut   /ʌ/ → /ʌ̟/

box → box   /ɒ/ → /ɒ̝/

Figure 13.1   The Southern Hemisphere Shift (Australia): the simple or short vowels

fleas → fleas /iː/ → /əɪ/

who → who /uː/ → /əʊ/

bird → bird /ɜː/ → /ɜ̝ː/

face → fice /eɪ/ → /ʌɪ/

goat → goat /əʊ/ → /ʌʊ/

out → at /aʊ/ → /æo/

I'll → oil /aɪ/ → /ɒɪ/   start → start /ɑː/ → /aː/

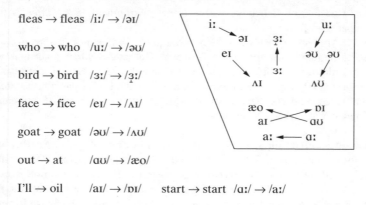

Figure 13.2 The Southern Hemisphere Shift (Australia): long vowels and diphthongs

Adelaide lies closest to RP with a preponderance of /aː/ (only 9 per cent /æ/) while Hobart is closest to GenAm with 72 per cent /æ/. Furthermore, working class speech favours /æ/ with the difference between working and middle class largest in Melbourne (33 percentage points) and least in Brisbane (3 percentage points) (Bradley 1991: 228–31).

Among the vowels there is, finally, also a tendency to monophthongize the centring diphthongs through loss of the second element. This levels the distinction, for example, between /eə/ and /e/ (*bared = bed*). Together with the fronting and monophthongize of /aʊ/ this can occasionally lead to misunderstandings such as the following one quoted in Taylor between himself and a postal agent in the outback (1973/74: 59):

Author: Do you sell stamps?
Agent: Yes.
Author: I'd like airmail [= *our mail* for Australian ears], please.
Agent: Sorry, but your mail hasn't come in yet.

Years of prescriptive schooling have not failed to have their effect on Australians, who have only recently begun to gain a more positive attitude towards their own variety of English (mostly pronunciation). Cultivated forms correlate 'strongly with sex (nine girls for every one boy), with superior education (especially in independent, fee-paying schools), and comfortable urban living' (Delbridge 1990: 72). Another linguist (Poynton) is quoted as remarking that Cultivated was 'good speech used by phony people whereas Broad was bad speech used by real people' (quoted in Horvath 1985: 24).

13.1.2 Grammar and morphology in AusE

There are no really significant differences in grammar between standard AusE and standard BrE or AmE although formal usage in all areas seems to tend more towards BrE. An investigation of the use of *dare* and *need* as modal or lexical verbs has shown, for example, that there are some differences in preferred usage, but no absolute ones (Collins

1978). Non-standard AusE usage is also very much like that of other countries in which English is a widely spoken native language. If there are any differences in non-standard AusE, they are in relative frequencies. For many AusE speakers, however, the use of the plural verb in existential *there* constructions, even with singular subjects, is virtually categorical (Eisikovits 1991: 243f.). Sex differentiation seems, for example, to be stronger in Australia than in the United States or Great Britain (especially in pronunciation, see Guy 1991: 222). A study of Inner Sydney usage reveals greater use of third person singular *don't* by males, probably 'as a marker of group identity, "maleness" and working-class values' (Eisikovits 1991: 238f.).

In morphology AusE reveals a preference for several processes of word formation which are less frequent in English at large. One of these is the relatively greater use of reduplication, especially in designations for Australian flora and fauna borrowed from Aboriginal languages (*bandy-bandy*, a kind of snake, *gang-gang*, a kind of cockatoo) proper names (*Banka Banka, Ki Ki, Kurri Kurri*) and terms from Aboriginal life including pidgin/creole terms (*mia-mia* 'hut', *kai kai* 'food'). In addition the endings {-ee/-y/-ie} /iː/ (*broomy, Aussie, Tassie, Brizzie, surfy*) and {-o} [ʌʊ] (*bottlo, smoko*) occur more often in AusE than in other varieties.

13.1.3 AusE vocabulary

AusE shares all but a small portion of its vocabulary with StE; however this small, Australian element is important for giving AusE its own distinctive flavour. Indeed, next to pronunciation it is the distinctively Australian words which give this variety its special character. Rhyming slang, though hardly of frequent use, is often regarded as especially typical of AusE, e.g. *sceptic tanks* 'Yanks'. In addition, there are a number of Australian words which originate in English dialects and therefore are not a part of StE everywhere, e.g. *bonzer* 'terrific', *chook(ie)* 'chicken', *cobber* 'mate', *crook* 'ill', *dinkum* 'genuine', *larrikin* 'rowdy', *swag* 'bundle', *tucker* 'food' (for much of the material in the following, see Turner 1994).

The specific features of AusE vocabulary have been affected most strongly, however, by borrowing (*kangaroo*) and compounding (*kangaroo rat; black swan; native dog, lyrebird* (bird), *ironbark* (tree), *outback* 'remote bush', or *throwing stick* 'woomera, boomerang'). Place names, of course, are often specifically Australian (*Wallaroo, Kwinana, Wollongong, Wagga Wagga*), including fantasy names such as *Bullamakanka* (fictitious place); *Woop Woop* (fictitious remote outback locality), both with Aboriginal-sounding names. Sometimes there is uncertainty even among Australians about how to pronounce them. So the anecdote about the train approaching Eurelia, where one porter goes through the cars announcing /juːrəlaɪə/ ('You're a liar') and is followed by a second yelling /juːriːliːaː/ ('You really are') (Turner 1972: 198). Regionally differing vocabulary is rare, but includes words for a bathing suit: *togs, cossie, swimmers* (East Coast, NZ: *togs*), *bathers* (South + Western Australia). Language Varieties Network at http://www. une.edu.au/langnet/ concentrates more on minority and stigmatized varieties, including pidgins and creoles from a sociolinguistic viewpoint.

There are, of course, words Australian by origin but accepted throughout the English speaking world because what they designate is some aspect of reality which is distinctively Australian. Chief among these are words for the flora, fauna and topography of

Australia as well as aspects of Aboriginal life. Many of these are borrowings from Aboriginal languages, of which some 40 words are still current in AusE and include: *billabong* ('dried out river'), *boomerang, budgerigar, dingo, gin* 'Aboriginal woman', *koala* (an animal), *kookaburra* (a bird), *mallee* (a tree, scrub), *nulla-nulla* 'Aboriginal club', *wallaby* 'small kangaroo', *wallaroo* 'mountain kangaroo', *wombat* 'burrowing marsupial', *woomera* ('throwing stick, boomerang'). There are a variety of words for Aboriginal hut: *gunya* (Port Jackson), *mia-mia* (Victoria), *humpy* (Queensland), *wurley* (South Australia). Some of these items have little international currency (except *kangaroo, boomerang*) and are not even universally known among Australians.

Other words are general StE, but may be applied somewhat differently in AusE. For example, early settlement gave AusE *station* for a farm (from earlier *prison station*). *Paddocks* are fields. A *mob* of sheep is a flock or herd. *Muster* for rounding up cattle is explained as due to the military arrangement of the convict settlements, as are *superintendent* of the *station* and *huts* of the men. *Squatter*, initially someone with small holdings but later large ones, took on a connotation of wealth. Further terms from this period include *outback, overlanders* 'cattle drivers', *stockman* 'man in charge of livestock', *jackaroo* 'apprentice on a station' (see *vaquero*), but also *cocky* 'small farmer'. *Mate/mateship* grew into its present legendary egalitarian male friendship and interdependence, first in the workplace and then more generally. Today an egalitarian mateyness contributes to the immediate use of first names, often abbreviated or given the Australian diminutive in {-o} as in *Stevo* from *Stephen*.

The convicts also contributed *flash* (or *kiddy*) *language*, e.g. *old hand, new chum, swag* 'bundle, rolled-up belongings' (today, 'a lot' as in *a swag of letters to answer, swagman* 'tramp', dated). AusE is well known for its slang, for example: *cadge, bash, croak, dollop, grab, job* 'robbery', *judy* 'woman', *fancy woman, frisk, move* 'action', *mug* 'face', *pigs* 'police', *quod* 'prison', *rattler* 'coach, train', *Romany* 'gypsy', *seedy* 'shabby', *sharper, snooze, stink* 'furore', *swell* 'gentleman', *dressed to the nines, whack* 'share'.

Borrowing was not only from Aboriginal languages and dialects, but also from both standard BrE and standard AmE. The former gives us *railway* (AmE *railroad*), *goods train* (AmE *freight train*), *guard's van* (AmE *caboose*), but AmE *cowcatcher* (not needed in Britain). Australians have *semi-trailers* or *semis* not BrE *articulated lorries*; and AusE has *truck*, not *lorry*; *station wagon*, not *estate car*. In the political arena we find *states* and *interstate*; *federalists* and *state-righters*; *Senate, House of Representatives* – all AmE in source, but each state upper house is called a *Legislative Council* and the lower, a *Legislative Assembly* (Queensland, New South Wales, Victoria, Western Australia) or *House of Assemby* (Southern Australia, Tasmania) – all more BrE. *Store* has the AmE meaning; other AmE borrowings include older *block* 'area of land for settlement etc.', *township, bush* 'the countryside as opposed to town' and more recently *french fries, cookies* and *movies*.

13.1.4 Ethnic groups and language in Australia

With the loosening of immigration policy Australia has ceased to be the almost totally English speaking country it once was. Immigrants from Asia, America and Europe use some 140 languages as their mother tongues, many regarded as 'community languages'. In her study of Sydney English pronunciation, Horvath found it useful to add to the

Cultivated, General and Broad division a further one which she terms Ethnic Broad (1985: 69). However, as is the case in the United States as well, the children of immigrants switch rapidly not only to English, but to an English virtually indistinguishable from that of their peers with native born parents (ibid.: 94).

It has already been mentioned that a number of Aboriginal languages are still spoken. Although about one per cent of the Australian population is aboriginal, only those in the more remote parts of the interior still speak these languages. Furthermore, in parts of Queensland and Western Australia as well as in the Northern Territory the mixing of Aboriginal people with mutually unintelligible mother tongues has led to the adoption of (Roper) Kriol, Torres Strait Broken (Cape York Creole) and Aboriginal English (see 14.3).

Kriol is spoken by at least 15,000 people in the north of Australia. Like Torres Broken, which is spoken on many of the islands between Australia and New Guinea and on Cape York, it is a pidgin for many speakers, but the first language, i.e. a creole, for numerous others. Aboriginal English, spoken especially in remote areas, denotes varieties located between standard AusE and one of the creoles.

> These Creoles are distinct languages. . . . They show an ingenious blend of English and Australian structural features, producing a language that seems quite appropriate to the bicultural milieu in which many Aboriginal Australians find themselves. Indeed, in some areas an increasing number of young Aborigines are speaking Kriol – instead of or as well as an Australian language – and it is coming to be thought of by them as 'the Aboriginal language'.
>
> (Dixon 1980: 73f.)

In most Aboriginal communities there is a continuum which runs from standard AusE to Aboriginal English. However, those Aboriginals who live in urban areas such as Sydney speak like their non-Aboriginal neighbours, though the variety of AusE they use tends to be on the non-standard side of GenE.

13.2 NEW ZEALAND ENGLISH (NZE)

The language situation in New Zealand resembles that in Australia in many ways. Virtually everyone can speak English, and most have it as their native language. The large minority of Maoris, the native Polynesian people of New Zealand, are rapidly losing their native tongue. At the end of the 1970s only about 20 per cent of them, which is approximately 3 per cent of the population of the country, were still fluent in it, and few of these speakers were younger people (Benton 1991: 187). The decision in 1987 to give Maori the status of official language is unlikely to change anything.

The historical development of New Zealand is closely related to that of Australia. Before British sovereignty over the territory was officially proclaimed in 1840 there were already some 2,000 English speaking people there. They had come, mostly via Australia, to establish whaling stations or to work as Christian missionaries to the Maoris. After 1840 European settlement was more closely regulated (but with no transported convicts and no penal stations) and grew gradually in the following decades, drawing on immigration chiefly from Great Britain and Australia. It was these people, Australians

Map 13.2   New Zealand

and many English immigrants with a London bias to their speech, who determined the linguistic character of New Zealand.

The English which the present day New Zealand population of almost 4 million (including approximately 15 per cent Maoris and 6 per cent other Polynesians) speaks is very much like AusE, suggesting a single dialect area with two major varieties. Indeed, it has sometimes been said that, linguistically speaking, New Zealand is to Australia as Canada is to the United States. The differences within each of the pairs are small, but for the smaller partner psychologically vital.

The pronunciation and the vocabulary of NZE is noticeably different for non-New Zealanders, but the grammar is fully standard, differing from other standard varieties only in preference for use of some forms:

> The differences between NZE and other varieties are to be found in matters of degree rather than in categorical distinctions, but NZE is not just the same as BrE or AmE: it is a distinct variety, in grammar as well as in lexis and pronunciation.
>
> (Bauer 1989: 82)

13.2.1 The pronunciation of NZE

For all practical purposes New Zealanders sound like Australians, at least to outsiders; of course, 'to New Zealanders the Australian accent seems quite different' (Gordon and Deverson 1985: 13). There seems to be little or no regional difference in pronunciation despite the fact that New Zealanders feel there is (but see remarks below on Otago and Southland). Social or class differences do, however, show up, though less than in Britain. It may also be the case that RP is still more a model in New Zealand than in Australia; certainly it is favoured in 'serious' broadcasting and the news. Investigations of attitudes show associations of RP with ambition, education, reliability, intelligence, higher income and occupational prestige, but association of NZE accents with friendliness and a sense of humour. While RP has high overt prestige, North American accents show the overall highest covert prestige. In contrast to AusE: 'A true New Zealand standard is still evolving' (Bayard 1990: 67). Note, too, that correction in the direction of the prestige sometimes results in such hypercorrect forms as /eɪ/ for /aɪ/ in such words as *I* or *like*.

The explication and figures presented above for AusE, apply to NZE as well. The shifts shown there include such items as the growing merger of /e/ and /eə/, which compounded with the raising of /æ/ to /e/ led to the following misunderstanding. A visiting American phoning a colleague at his house got one of the man's children on the line. The American heard, much to his astonishment, 'He's dead' rather than the intended 'Here's Dad' (Gordon and Deverson 1985: 82).

While much of NZE pronunciation is the same as in AusE, including the even more frequent use of the high rising tone, a few points are arguably different and merit pointing out. One of these is the greater retraction and centralization of /ɪ/ in NZE, a point which non-New Zealanders have often commented on. Hence the vowel of *kit* becomes [ɨ] or even a stressed schwa [ə]. This explains the surprise of an American hearing Flight 846 at Wellington Airport announced as follows: 'Flight ite four sucks' (Gordon and Deverson 1985: 82).

There is also a very noticeable tendency to vocalize /l/ in NZE. The result has had a far reaching effect on the vowel system because it has created a number of new diphthongs. This occurs more commonly after front than after back vowels and often involves **neutralization** (i.e. otherwise different vowels are no longer distinguished when followed by /l/), e.g. *bill* = *bull*, *fool* = *full* and *kill* = *cull*, or, even more extreme, *pool* = *pull* = *pill* = *pall*, all of which might be rendered as *pooh*. A related phenomenon is the neutralization of the /e/–/æ/ opposition in words like *helicopter*, *help*, *Wellington*, which then sound like *hallicopter*, *halp* and *Wallington*. The centring diphthongs /ɪə/ and /ɛə/ are merging (*beer* = *bear*) for more and more young people, as in AusE and SAE as well. On the other hand, young people show signs of increasing use of the glottal stop in words with final /t/ (Bayard 1991: 184).

13.2.2 NZE vocabulary

The vocabulary of NZE has been influenced by new flora, fauna, topography, institutions and the presence of a non-English speaking people. In addition, it shares many items with AusE that differ from other national varieties of English. Like AusE there is relatively little regionally different vocabulary, but note 'a certain type of large, smooth sausage', which in Auckland is called *polony*, in Christchurch *saveloy*, in Southland *Belgium*, *Belgium roll/sausage* (AusE uses *polony* and *saveloy*, Adelaide *fritz*, Brisbane and Sydney, *devon*) (Burridge and Mulder 1998: 4).

What distinguishes NZE most from AusE is the existence in NZE of a sizeable number of borrowings from Maori. Examples include the following: *hoot* 'money', *kiwi* 'a kind of (flightless) bird, the NZ symbol', *ngaio* 'a kind of tree', *Pakeha* 'white New Zealander', *wahine* 'woman', *whare* 'small house, hut', *yacker* 'work'. The fact that /aː/ as in *whare* /waːriː/ can become /ɒ/ in NZE led one schoolboy to make the following spelling mistake: 'Dad thought Mum looked tired so he hired a whore for the holidays' (Turner 1972: 129).

The following excerpt is taken from a newspaper review of the supplement on Australian and New Zealand vocabulary in *The New Zealand Pocket Oxford Dictionary* (1990). The passage makes highly intensive and unauthentically exaggerated use of NZE and AusE colloquial vocabulary; however, it also offers a little of the flavour of the language:

> Stone the crows, sports, but with no more bobsy-die than a dag-picking bushy claiming compo from out in the boo-ay, the sticky-beaks of the Oxford University Press have been taking a squiz at Aussie and Enzed slang. They've now published a beaut new supplement to the Pocket Oxford Dictionary – 1200 dinkydi words and expressions which are certainly giving the chooms something to chiack at.
>
> (quoted in Gordon and Deverson 1985: 51)

To help out, here is a short glossary:

stone the crows	–	expression of surprise
sports	–	'guys'
bobsy-die	–	'fuss, panic'
dag-picking	–	'sorting the wool from the dags'
dag	–	'wool around a sheep's hindquarters, often dirty with mud and excreta'
bushy	–	'someone from the countryside, from the bush'
compo	–	'worker's compensation'
boo-ay	–	'backblocks, remote country district'
sticky-beaks	–	'priers, meddlers'
squiz	–	'a look'
beaut	–	'fine, good'
dinkydi	–	'true, honest, genuine'
choom	–	'English person' (variant of *chum*)
chiach	–	'jeer, taunt, deride, tease'

13.2.3 Maori English

Although the Maoris (in contrast to the Aborigines of Australia) have a single language, it has not provided significantly more loan words to NZE than Aboriginal languages have to AusE, and it has been constantly giving way to English. Maori is now spoken by only about 12 per cent of the Maori, who themselves make up about 12.5 per cent of the population. These speakers are older (and bilingual) and even the traditional domain of the *marae* is giving way to English (Burridge and Mulder 1998: 275). Most Maoris have, in other words, adopted English, and they speak it virtually indistinguishably from Pakehas (New Zealand Whites) of the same socio-economic stratum. However, Maori English may have (marginally) more Maori words in it than NZE, e.g. *kai* 'food'. The frequent use of the high rise terminal intonation among Maori school children has also been remarked on (see Australian Question Intonation). 'The use of the tag question *eh?* [ay] is generally attributed to Maori and then Maori English as its source, but is today a general feature of New Zealand English' (Bauer 1994: 416).

> Maori-speakers often transfer terms and rules from the Maori address system to their English – for example, a three-way distinction in second-person pronouns *you* (singular), *youse* (dual), and *youse fullas* (plural), and address forms such as *cuz*, *sis*, *bro*, *aunty*, and *uncle*, which reflect Maori kinship relationships.
>
> (Burridge and Mulder 1998: 12)

Proportionately more Maoris speak a broad, working class type of NZE than their numbers would warrant. In an experiment recorded samples of Maori speech were rated lower in social prestige than samples from High and Middle Status Pakehas, but the Maori recordings were given high ratings on the 'warm' scale (as opposed to the 'hard working' and 'intelligent' scales). Overall, Maoris seem to be evaluated 'as if Low Status Pakehas' (Huygens and Vaughan 1983: 222).

13.3 SOUTH AFRICAN ENGLISH (SAE)

In this section only South African English (SAE) will be treated. A similarly oriented variety is said to be spoken in Lesotho, Swaziland, Botswana, Namibia, Zambia, Malawi, Zimbabwe and Kenya. When the first group of English speaking settlers arrived at Cape Town in 1820 there were not only black Africans living in the colony (principally the Khoikhoi or Hottentots, the San or Bushmen and the Xhosa), but also the descendants of Dutch settlers, called Afrikaners, who had begun arriving in 1652 and over whom the British had established permanent control in 1806. Both the Afrikaners and the British treated the native Africans much as the Europeans treated the Aborigines in Australia and the Maoris in New Zealand, for none of the native people were able to offer resistance to the Europeans or to influence the technologically significantly more advanced culture they represented. The British and Afrikaners, however, became rivals, and their subsequent history has been characterized by political, economic, cultural and linguistic competition.

After the Afrikaner National Party victory in the 1948 election English was no longer automatically the favoured language in South Africa. Despite its relatively small number of native speakers English did, however, retain considerable influence and prestige. It and Afrikaans had (and have) numerous advantages over the black African languages:

- they are not divided into dialects;
- they were the exclusive official languages of the country during apartheid;

Map 13.3 South Africa

- they are spoken by a culturally, politically and economically dominant white population;
- they offer access to technological and scientific knowledge (and here English has the advantage over Afrikaans)

The black population prefers English to Afrikaans both because of its utilitarian value and because it is more closely identified with liberal ideas than is Afrikaans. Indeed, English, in contrast to Afrikaans, is seen less as a group language and more as an 'out-group' language, one shared by various ethnic groups. This function is the result of the fact that English speaking white South Africans have relatively little group feeling, and it is strengthened by the fact that English is a widely used second language for all groups in South Africa including the Afrikaners.

Today about 8.5 per cent of the population of approximately 43 million speak English as their home language. This 'group' is made up of two fifths of the Whites (themselves one eighth of the population), somewhat more than one tenth of the Coloureds (of mixed black and white ancestry; one twelfth of the population) and virtually all of the Indian population (just over 2 per cent of the population), and totals altogether somewhat less than 5 million people. This makes it the seventh largest language of the country. About 33 million speak a black African language, 5 of which have more speakers than English

(Zulu, Xhosa, (South) Sotho, Pedi (North Sotho), Tswana (West Sotho)). Around 6 million are speakers of Afrikaans, the language of the Afrikaners and the vast majority (between 80 and 90 per cent) of the Coloureds.

The new, post-apartheid constitution of 1996 recognizes 11 languages as official (Afrikaans, English, the African languages mentioned above plus Tsonga, Swati, Ndebele and Venda) and further languages are to be promoted and developed (San, Khoi, Nama and South African Sign Language). A large number of European and Indian languages spoken by immigrants and their descendants have also been assured promotion and respect. This is a clear break from the predominant status of Afrikaans in the apartheid period. According to constitutional principles all the African languages should be available for use in education and court proceedings. However, there are neither the necessary teaching materials and trained teachers to conduct multilingual education on a large-scale basis, nor are there the necessary language skills among judges and lawyers to ensure the right all South Africans have to be tried in a language they understand. The Pan South African Language Board, established in 1996, is intended to help remedy this.

English, as a worldwide language of wider communication, offers the best chances for advancement. For this reason many black Africans are eager to learn it, despite their resentment of white hegemony in economic and political life. As a result English, with its generally high prestige and utility, has remained predominant in public life.

13.3.1 White SAE

The white English speaking community of approximately 1.8 million (not counting numerous Afrikaans-English bilinguals) in South Africa uses a variety of English which is close to StE in both grammar and vocabulary. Variation within this community is largely in the dimension of pronunciation: SAE is phonologically virtually identical with the English of southern England. However, phonetically there are numerous differences, most noticeably in the variety referred to as Extreme SAE, less so in what is called Respectable SAE and least so in Conservative SAE. These three distinctions correlate to some extent with class and, as comments will show, to region and to the gender of the speaker.

Conservative SAE   Conservative SAE is very similar to RP, and, indeed, it is said that most White SAE speakers cannot distinguish the two. Among the few differences between the two is vowel retraction after /l/ ([tʃʉldrən] for *children*), centralization of [uː], especially after /j/ and raising of /ɔː/ almost to [oː]. All of these features turn up in AusE and NZE as well. Conservative SAE correlates with the high socio-economic status and remains the widely accepted standard of pronunciation in South Africa as seen in its use in radio and television.

Respectable SAE   This is an informal, local standard and enjoys high social prestige though sometimes faulted for not being 'correct'. This type of SAE has developed from Natal English, is recognized as local in Natal and is therefore not so highly regarded there (Lanham 1985: 246); however, it is representative of 'upwardly mobile groups elsewhere' (ibid.: 243). Natal SAE differs from RP because of its tendency to monophthongize /aɪ/ to [a], especially before /l, m, n, v, z, s/.

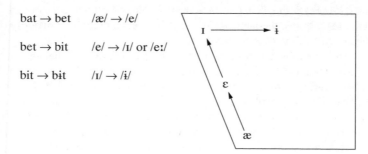

bat → bet   /æ/ → /e/

bet → bit   /e/ → /ɪ/ or /eː/

bit → bɨt   /ɪ/ → /ɨ/

Figure 13.3 The Southern Hemisphere Shift (South Africa)

SAE pronunciation is generally non-rhotic; however, because of the influence of rhotic Afrikaans, it is not consistently so. It may be characterized by the following eight features:

- /eɪ/ starts lower: [əɪ] (*may*);
- /əʊ/ starts lower as well: [ʌʊ] (*go*);
- /ɔː/ raised towards [oː] (*four* = *foe*);
- /e/ raised to towards [eː] (*yes* = *yace*) (see Figure 13.3);
- /æ/ likewise raised: [e] (*man* = RP *men*) (see Figure 13.3);
- /ɪ/ realized as [i] (*kiss*) in stressed syllables next to velars, after /h/ and initially; otherwise as [ɨ] or [ə] (*pin* = GenAm *pun*) (see Figure 13.3);
- final /ɪ/ is longer and closer: /iː/ (*city* = *citee*);
- /eə/ is monophthongized: /eː/ (*shared* = *shed*, except the latter is longer).

All of these characteristics, as well as the occasional occurrence of a flapped and voiced /t/ (*latter* = *ladder*), are reminiscent of AusE and/or NZE. In addition, /dj/ and /tj/ are palatalized /dʒ/ (*due* = *Jew*) and /tʃ/ (*tune* = *choon*).

Extreme SAE Extreme SAE has low social prestige, but is connected with the covert values of toughness and manliness, independence and lack of regard for what is considered refined. Its speakers are marked by gregariousness and unselective social relations, un-Englishness, strong local loyalties and Afrikaner patriotism (Lanham and Macdonald 1979: 25ff.). It shares some features with Afrikaans English and is associated with the Eastern Cape. These phonetic characteristics include the use of an obstruent, often trilled /r/, a retracted /ɑː/ (so that *park* is like RP *pork*) and fronted and glide-weakened /aʊ/ = [æʊ] as well as [ɒɪ] for /aɪ/. Yet even this 'broadest' of SAE varieties does not share such working class variables as /ɪn/ for <-ing> or H-dropping, which are typical of Cockney.

Although the influence of Afrikaans on SAE may be called into question, especially with regard to pronunciation, some evidence of grammatical influence remains. One such item is the construction, *I'm busy* Verb-*ing*, which is a kind of progressive form. In StE only an action verb may occur in the blank (e.g. *I'm busy working*). In SAE non-activity verbs are possible as well (e.g. *I'm busy waiting*). This construction seems to be modelled on the Afrikaans progressive with *besig* 'busy' (Lass and Wright 1986: 219f.). Other syntactic features include *no* as a sentence initiator (*No, that'll be fine. We can do that easily for you.*), third person address (*Will Doctor* [said to this person] *lend me two rand?*), incomplete predications (e.g. A: *I was looking for some shoes in town.* B: *And did you find?*), third person singular present tense without an {-S} (e.g. *I'm no musician but the wife play*), prepositions (e.g. *to be scared for* [= of] *something*; *explain me* instead of *explain to me*) (examples from Branford 1978: xv).

There are, of course, lexical items specific to SAE. These are largely loans from Afrikaans (e.g. *brak* 'salty, alkali water or soil', *lekker* 'pleasant, excellent, delicious', *trek* 'arduous trip', *veld* 'open country'), from Nguni/Zulu or Xhosa (e.g. *donga* 'river bank, gully', *kaross* 'skin blanket', *mamba* 'a type of snake') or from other languages (e.g. Portuguese Pidgin *brinjal* 'egg plant', Hindi *dhoby* 'washerman', Portuguese *kraal* 'native village'). In addition, there are further words which have entered World English, usually items reflecting South African, e.g. *apartheid* or its fauna and topography (*meerkat*, a kind of mongoose; *veld*, grassland).

13.3.2 Afrikaans SAE

Since English is recognized as extremely useful in business life and since English culture is attractive for numerous young Afrikaners, many of them use it widely. More than one in eight claims to be fully bilingual, while less than 10 per cent of white SAE native speakers know Afrikaans well enough to make a similar assertion (Lanham 1984: 335f.). Together with less fluent Afrikaans users of English a large number of white South Africans speak Afrikaans English. Generally, this variety carries little prestige and is associated closely with Extreme SAE, which it also resembles to a large extent. Additional linguistic features include de-aspiration of stops and /j/ for /h/ as in *hill* /jil/ or *here* /jə·/ (ibid.: 340).

13.3.3 Black SAE

Black South Africans speak a kind of English which is clearly identifiable as a second language variety. Despite the large number of English native speakers in South Africa, few teachers in black schools have a sufficiently good command of the language to offer a native speaker-like model. Nevertheless, a large portion, if perhaps less than half of the black population read, speak or understand English. This means that millions of South Africans use English, even though this English reflects 'Bantu-language phonology, idioms and fixed expressions, redefined semantic content, and peculiar grammatical structures' (Lanham 1985: 244). These are largely urban dwellers who read English language newspapers, listen to the English media and need English in education and in their work lives. Phonetically Black SAE is shaped by the pronunciation patterns of the African mother tongues of its users. Among other things this means that the long-short contrasts of English are not maintained (*tick* = *teak*; *head* = *haired*; *pull* = *pool*). Furthermore, there are no central vowels. This means that *bird* may be confused with *bed* and that there is no schwa. However, the higher a person is on the socio-educational scale, the more likely her/his English is to resemble White SAE.

13.3.4 Coloured SAE

The Coloured population has traditionally spoken Afrikaans. However, among the speakers of Coloured SAE the characteristics of this type of English are similar to (low prestige) Extreme SAE/Cape English. Yet its speakers seem to cultivate it as a symbol of group identity and solidarity.

13.3.5 Indian SAE

This variety of·SAE is spoken by approximately three quarters of a million South Africans of Indian extraction; most of them live in largely English speaking Natal. It is predicted that English will eventually replace those Indian languages which still are spoken not only in education and economic life, but also as the home language.

Linguistically Indian SAE, especially that of older speakers, has a number of characteristics of IndE (see 14.2.1), such as the merger of /w/ and /v/, the use of retroflex alveolar consonants, and [eː] and [oː] for /eɪ/ and /əʊ/. Yet Conservative SAE appears to be the overt standard of pronunciation and younger speakers seem to be shifting towards it.

Many basilect speakers of South African Indian English employ non-standard constructions to form relative clauses, using, for example, personal pronouns instead of relative ones (e.g. *You get carpenters, they talk to you so sweet*) or allowing the relative to precede the clause containing the noun it refers to (e.g. *Which one haven' got lid, I threw them away* 'I threw the bottles that don't have caps away') (Mesthrie 1991: 464–7). Furthermore, in basilect speech *that faller*, pronounced *daffale* in rapid delivery, is used as a personal pronoun. It is also reported that the area of topicalization (for example, the fronting of elements in a sentence to make them thematic) and the use and non-use of the third person present tense singular and the noun plural ending {-s} vary socially within the group of South African Indian English speakers. Despite the constructions and usages just mentioned, younger and better educated South Africans of Indian ancestry, who are usually native speakers of English, share most features of their English with other mother tongue speakers of SAE.

13.4 FURTHER READING

AusE Burridge and Mulder 1998 describe both **AusE** and **NZE**. Turner 1994 looks at AusE in general. For AusE regional differences in **pronunciation**, see Bradley 1989; for details on sociolinguistic distinctions, see Horvath 1985. Arthur 1997 deals with **Aboriginal English**.

AusE vocabulary. Baker's pioneering book, *The Australian Language* 1966, devotes most of its space to Australian words. This includes both slang and more formal usage; see also: Delbridge 1990; Turner 1972; 1994; Gramley 2001; and *A Dictionary of Australian Colloquialisms*. *The Macquarie Dictionary*, the *Heinemann New Zealand Dictionary* and the *Australian National Dictionary* all cater to both Australia and New Zealand; *The Australian Concise Oxford Dictionary* includes only AusE and not NZE. For a report on regional variation in AusE vocabulary, see Bryant 1985. Taylor 1989 provides a number of further items borrowed from AmE to which he adds comments on spelling, morphology and syntax. The Language Varieties Network at http://www.une.edu.au/langnet/ concentrates more on minority and stigmatized varieties, including pidgins and creoles from a sociolinguistic viewpoint.

NZE   Bell and Holmes 1990 give a general treatment of NZE; see also Bauer 1994; Holmes, Bell and Boyce 1991. For **vocabulary**, see *Heinemann New Zealand Dictionary* or *The New Zealand Pocket Oxford Dictionary* (and references under AusE above).

SAE   SAE in general is described in W. Branford (1994). **South African language policy** is treated very succinctly in Methrie *et al.* 2000. **SAE pronunciation**: Lanham and Macdonald 1979: 46f.; Lanham 1984: 339; Wells 1982. **SAE vocabulary**: Branford 1991 is an excellent source for SAE lexical items; see also Beeton and Dorner 1975.

Chapter 14

English as a second language (ESL)

The previous chapters in Part 3 have looked at those countries in which English is spoken as a native language, if not by the total population, at least by a significantly large group. This chapter continues the geographic survey of English by observing its use as a second language in Africa (14.1) and in Asia (14.2) and the use of English pidgins and creoles in 14.3.

The idea of **second language** is only slightly different from that of **foreign language**, for it is less the quality of a speaker's command than the status of the language within a given community that determines whether it is a second or a foreign language. In an unambiguous case, a foreign language is a language learned in school and employed for communicating with people from another country. A second language, in contrast, may well be one learned in school, too, but one used within the learner's country for official purposes and reinforced by the power of the state and its institutions.

As far as English is concerned, second language status is quite common. Not only are bilingual French-English Canada (Chapter 11), Irish-English Ireland (Chapter 10) and South Africa (Chapter 13) cases where English is, for some people, a second language; in addition, English is a second language in numerous countries in Asia and Africa, where it is the official or semi-official language, a status sometimes shared with one or more other languages. In these states English is typically not the native language of more than a handful of people. There are some 35 such countries, 26 in which English is an official language and 9 further ones in which it is so in reality. The first group includes Botswana, Cameroon (with French), Fiji, Gambia, Ghana, Hong Kong, India (with Hindi), Lesotho (with Sesotho), Liberia, Malawi (with chi-Chewa), Malta (with Maltese), Mauritius, Namibia (with Afrikaans and German), Nauru (with Nauru), Nigeria (with Igbo, Hausa and Yoruba), the Philippines (with Filipino/Pilipino/Tagalog), Sierra Leone, Singapore (with Chinese, Malay and Tamil), Swaziland (with Siswatsi), Tanzania (with Swahili), Tonga (with Tongan), Uganda, Vanuatu (with Bislama and French), West Samoa (with Samoan), Zambia and Zimbabwe. The second group consists of Bangladesh, Burma, Ethiopia, Kenya, Pakistan, Malaysia, Israel, Sri Lanka and Sudan.

The number of second language users of English is estimated at about 300 million (but see Crystal 1997: 61, who opts for 1 billion), i.e. roughly the same number as that of English native speakers. Whatever the exact figure may be, English is the present day language of international communication.

The circumstances that have led to the establishment of English, an outside language, as a second language in so many countries of Africa and Asia are not education and commerce alone, however important English is for these activities and however strong the economic hegemony of the English speaking world is. Quite clearly it is the legacy of colonialism that has made English so indispensable in these countries, of which only Ethiopia was never a British or American colony or protectorate. (Where the colonial master was France, Belgium, or Portugal, French and Portuguese are the second languages.) The retention of the colonial language is a conscious decision and may be assumed to be the result of deliberate language policy and language planning. Among the factors which support the use of English as an official language are the following:

- the lack of a single indigenous language that is widely accepted by the respective populations; here English is neutral vis-à-vis mutually competing native languages and hence helps to promote national unity;
- the usefulness of English in science and technology as opposed to the underdeveloped vocabularies of the vernaculars;
- the availability of school books in English;
- the status and use of English for international communication, trade and diplomacy.

In these countries English plays an important role in government and administration, in the courts, in education (especially secondary and higher education), in the media and for both domestic and foreign economic activity. English is, in other words, an extremely utilitarian, public language. It is also used, in a few cases, as a means of expressing national unity and identity versus ethnic parochialism (see especially Singapore). As a result second language English users are in the dilemma of **diglossia**: they recognize the usefulness of English, yet feel strong emotional ties to the local languages. English is the diglossically **High language**, used as official, public language vis-à-vis the indigenous languages, which are more likely to be diglossically **Low**, and therefore to be preferred in private dealings and for intimacy and emotion. Family life is typically conducted in the ethnic or ancestral vernaculars. Where the High language is the standard and the Low one is the variety of same language which is most divergent from it and where there are also a number of varieties along a continuum between the two, it is common to refer to the High language as the **acrolect**, the Low one as the **basilect** and the intermediate ones as **mesolects**.

English, in other words, is far from displacing the vernaculars. Historically, the conditions for language replacement have been, as the cases of Latin and Arabic show: (1) military conquest; (2) a long period of language imposition; (3) a polyglot subject group; and (4) material benefits in the adoption of the language of the conquerors (see Brosnahan 1963: 15–17). In modern Africa and Asia additional factors such as: (5) urbanization; (6) industrialization/economic development; (7) educational development; (8) religious orientation; and (9) political affiliation (Fishman *et al.* 1977: 77–82) are also of importance. Yet the period of true language imposition has generally been relatively short and economic development at the local level has been less directly connected with the colonial language, so that English has tended to remain an urban and elite High language.

All the same, where English is widely used as a second language there is often as much local pride in it on the part of the educated elite as there is resentment at its intrusion. As a result there has been widespread talk of the recognition of a 'local' standard, especially in pronunciation, either a regional one such as Standard West African English or a national one such as Standard Nigerian English. Some have emphasized the negative aspects of such '**nativization**' or '**indigenization**', which may sometimes lower international intelligibility, and, more importantly, preclude the development of the indigenous languages. A neglect of the vernaculars includes the danger of producing large numbers of linguistically and culturally displaced persons. On the other hand, the spread of English may be accompanied, for most of its users, by relatively little emotional colouring – whether positive or negative. Indeed, some would go so far as to maintain: 'The use of a standard or informal variety of Singaporean, Nigerian, or Filipino English is . . . a part of what it means to *be* a Singaporean, a Nigerian, or a Filipino' (Richards 1982: 235). As the following sections show, there is indeed room for a wide diversity of opinions on this subject, and the developments in one country may be completely different in tendency from those in another.

14.1 ENGLISH IN AFRICA

Second language English in Africa may be divided into three general geographic areas: the six anglophone countries of West Africa (Cameroon, Gambia, Ghana, Liberia, Nigeria and Sierra Leone plus Fernando Poo, where Creole English is spoken), those of East Africa (Ethiopia, Somalia, Uganda, Kenya, Tanzania, Malawi and Zambia) and those of Southern Africa (Namibia, Botswana, Zimbabwe, Swaziland, Lesotho and South Africa; see 13.3 on South Africa). English is an official language for millions of Africans in these countries, but the number of native speakers probably lies overall at around one per cent of the population of these countries.

The first group includes two countries which have native speakers of English (Liberia, five per cent) or an English creole (Sierra Leone, also five per cent) (percentages according to Brann 1988: 1421). All six are characterized by the presence and vitality of Pidgin English, used by large numbers of people. Neither Eastern nor Southern Africa has pidgin or creole forms of English. However, South Africa, Zimbabwe and Namibia all have a fairly large number of non-black native speakers of English (South Africa: approximately 40 per cent of the non-black population; Namibia, 8 per cent; Zimbabwe, virtually all the white population).

English in Africa, though chiefly a second language and rarely a native language of African Blacks is, nevertheless, sometimes a first language in the sense of familiarity and daily use. Certainly, there are enough fluent, educated speakers of what has been called African Vernacular English who 'have grown up hearing and using English daily, and who speak it as well as, or maybe even better than, their ancestral language' for it to serve as a model (Angogo and Hancock 1980: 72). Furthermore, the number of English users is also likely to increase considering the number of Africans who are learning it at schools throughout the continent, especially secondary schools.

Despite numerous variations, due in particular to the numerous mother tongues of its speakers, this African Vernacular English is audibly recognizable as a type and is distinct from, for instance, Asian English. It tends to have a simplified vowel system in relation to native speaker English. Furthermore, it shares certain grammatical, lexical, semantic and pragmatic features throughout the continent. These include different prepositional, article and pronoun usage, comparatives without *more*, pluralization of non-count nouns, use of verbal aspect different from StE, generalized question tags, a functionally different application of *yes* and *no*, semantic shift as well as the coinage of new lexical items.

Various expressions, such as the interjection *Sorry!*, are employed in a pragmatic sense unfamiliar to StE. For more details see the following.

14.1.1 West Africa

The six anglophone countries, Cameroon, Gambia, Ghana, Liberia, Nigeria and Sierra Leone (see Map 14.1) are polyglot. Nigeria has up to 415 languages; Cameroon, 234; Ghana, 60; and even Liberia, Sierra Leone and Gambia have 31, 20 and 13 respectively (Brann 1988: 1418f.). In this situation it is obvious that any government has to be concerned about having an adequate language for education and as a means of general internal communication. Where there is no widely recognized indigenous language to do this, the choice has usually fallen on the colonial language. In Cameroon both colonial languages, French (80 per cent of the country) and English (the remainder) were adopted when the two Cameroons were united. A bilingual French-English educational policy is pursued. Of the six states just mentioned only Nigeria has viable native lingua francas which are readily available for written use, most clearly Hausa in the north, but also the regional languages Yoruba in the west and Igbo in the east; all three are being developed as official languages. However, in Nigeria as a whole, as well as the other five, it is English which fulfils many or most of the developmental and educational functions. It is possible to speak of triglossia in these countries: at the lowest level, the autochthonous languages; at an intermediate level, the regional languages of wider communication; and superimposed on the whole, the outside or exogenous language, English (Brann 1988: 1416). For the most part the vernaculars and English are not in conflict, but are complementary, with English reserved for the functions of a High language in the sense of diglossia while the local languages are the Low languages. Note, however, speakers who do not share a native language prefer to communicate in a regional one. If that is not feasible, they will choose Pidgin English. English itself is likely to be the last choice in diglossically Low communication.

English in West Africa   English is present in West Africa in a continuum of types which runs from British StE with a (near-) RP accent (in Liberia the orientation is towards AmE), to a local educated second language variety, to a local vernacular, to West African Pidgin or one of its creolized varieties. This diversity of levels is one of the results of the history of European-African contact on the west coast of Africa.

Pidgins and creoles   Europeans went to the Atlantic coast of Africa in the first phase of European colonialism from 1450 on. Initial trade contacts gradually expanded as a part of the West Indian–American plantation and slave system, in which West Africa's role was chiefly that of a supplier of slaves. Throughout the era of the slave trade (Britain and the US outlawed it in 1808; other European countries slowly followed), Europeans and Africans conducted business by means of contact languages called **pidgins** (see 14.3). Pidgin English continues to be used today all along the West African coast from Gambia to Gabon though it is not always immediately intelligible from variety to variety. It is a diglossically Low language like most of the indigenous vernaculars and is, for example, said to be the most widely used language in Cameroon. It is perhaps so easily learned not only because it is simplified, but also because it is structurally so close to the

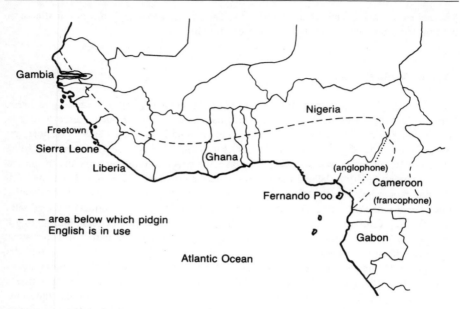

Map 14.1 West Africa

indigenous languages. Its spread and importance in Cameroon is influenced by its use on plantations and other work sites, in churches, markets, playgrounds and pubs. It is the regular language of the military and the police and is also commonly used in the law courts.

Standard English   StE was introduced in the second major phase of colonialism in the nineteenth century, when the European powers divided up as much of Africa and Asia as they could. As a part of this movement there was a wave of Christian missionary effort in Africa: 'English was to become the language of salvation, civilisation and worldly success' (Spencer 1971b: 13). Although the church made wide use of the native languages and alphabetized various of them for the first time, it had little use for Pidgin English. The result was the suppression of Pidgin and Creole English by school, church and colonial administration in favour of ' "correct" bourgeois English' (ibid.: 23). StE was and is used in education, in government, in international trade, for access to scientific and technical knowledge and in the media. It is a status symbol, a mark of education and westernization. While StE thus functions as the badge of the local elite, Pidgin English has little prestige, but does signal a good deal of group solidarity. Linguistically speaking, Pidgin and Creole English are often regarded as independent languages and hence outside the continuum of English; for 'throughout West Africa, speakers are usually able to say at any time whether they are speaking the one or the other' (Angogo and Hancock 1980: 72). Nevertheless, many people as well as the governments generally view pidgin and creole as English, albeit of an 'uneducated' variety. For speakers who have a limited command of the stylistic variations of native speaker English, Pidgin English may function as an informal register.

Whatever perspective is taken, it is a fact that only a local, educated variety may be regarded as a serious contender for the label West African StE. Such a form of English, which implies completed primary or secondary education, is available to perhaps ten per cent of the population of anglophone West Africa. A study of prepositional use in Nigerian English provides support for the view that an independent norm is growing up which contains not only evidence of mother tongue interference, but also of what are termed 'stable Nigerianisms'. (In addition, this study shows that a meaningful sociolinguistic division of Nigerian English is one which, reflecting the educational structure of the country, distinguishes the masses, the sub-elite and the elite (Jabril 1991: 536). Some of the characteristics of Nigerian English will be enumerated in the following section.

Linguistic features of educated West African English (WAfrE)   Within WAfrE there is a great deal of variation; indeed, the higher the education of a user, the closer his or her usage is likely to be to StE. In this sense standard WAfrE is perhaps less a fixed standard than a more or less well learned second language. At the upper end of the continuum of Englishes in West Africa there are few or no syntactic or semantic differences from native speaker English and few if any phonological differences from RP or GenAm. Although this variety is internationally intelligible, it is not widely acceptable for native Africans in local West African society. This is substantiated to some extent by the fact that a good deal of the difference between the StE of native speakers and that of educated West Africans can be explained by interference from the first language of the latter. All of this notwithstanding, there are features of educated WAfrE which form a standard in the senses that: (a) they are widely used and no longer amenable to change via further learning; and (b) they are community norms, not recognized as 'errors' even by relatively highly trained anglophone West Africans.

The pronunciation of WAfrE   Most noticeable to a non-African, as with all the types of StE reviewed in this book, is the pronunciation. Generally speaking, West Africans have the three diphthongs /aɪ, aʊ, ɔɪ/ and a reduced vowel system as represented in Table 14.1. What is noticeable about the list is the lack of central vowels. This means that schwa /ə/ is also relatively rare, which fits in with the tendency of WAfrE to give each syllable relatively equal stress (syllable-timed rhythm). In addition, the intonation is less varied. Important grammatical distinctions made by intonation, such as the difference between rising and falling tag questions, may be lost. Emphasis may be achieved lexically, by switching from a short to a long word, for instance from *ask* to *command* to show impatience (Egbe 1979: 98–101). In the same way cleft sentences are likely to be more frequent in the spoken language of Nigerian speakers than of non-African native speakers (Adetugbo 1979: 142). The consonant system is the same as in RP, but there is a strong tendency towards spelling pronunciations of combinations such as <-mb> and <-ng>; this also means that although WAfrE is non-rhotic, less educated speakers may pronounce /r/ where it is indicated in the spelling. There are, of course, numerous regional variations such as that of Hausa speakers, who tend to avoid consonant clusters, so that *small* becomes /sᵘmɔl/ (Todd 1984: 288). Among other things, for some speakers /θ/ becomes /t/.

The grammar of WAfrE   The syntactic features of standard WAfrE are difficult to define. A study of deviation from StE in Ghanaian newspapers reveals numerous syntactic

Table 14.1 The vowels of WAfrE in comparison with those of RP

WAfrE	RP	as in	WAfrE	RP	as in
i →	iː	bead	ɔ →	ɜː	bird
↘	ɪ	bid	↘	ʌ	bud
e →	eɪ	bayed	↘	ɒ	body
ɛ →	e	bed	↘	ɔː	bawdy
a →	æ	bad	o →	əʊ	bode
↘	ɑː	bard	u →	ʊ	Buddha
			↘	uː	booed

Source: Adapted from Angogo and Hancock 1980: 75.

problems, but very few general patterns (Tingley 1981). Among the points that are frequently mentioned and which therefore presumably have a fair degree of currency are the following:

1 the use of non-count nouns as count nouns (*luggages, vocabularies, a furniture, an applause*);
2 pleonastic subjects (*The politicians they don't listen*);
3 an overextension of aspect (*I am having a cold*);
4 the present perfect with a past adverbial (*It has been established hundreds of years ago*);
5 comparatives without more (*He values his car than his wife*);
6 a generalized question tag (*It doesn't matter, isn't it?*);
7 a functionally different use of *yes* and *no* (*Isn't he home? Yes [he isn't]*).

Most of these points (except 5) show up in Asian English as well, which suggests that their source may well lie in the intrinsic difficulty of such phenomena in English. Indeed, (6) may show up in BrE as in the following example:

'Yeah, well, we don't need strength,' said Millat tapping his temple, 'we need a little of the stuff upstairs. We've got to get in the place discreetly first, innit? . . .'

(Zadie Smith (2001) *White Teeth*, London: Penguin, p. 474)

The vocabulary of WAfrE   The English vocabulary of West Africa has special words for local flora, fauna and topography. In addition, special elements of West African culture and institutions have insured the adoption of numerous further items. This, more than grammar, gives WAfrE its distinctive flavour, reflecting as it does the sociolinguistic context of WAfrE. The words themselves may be:

•   English words with an extension of meaning, e.g. *chap* 'any person, man or woman';
•   semantic shifts: *smallboy* 'low servant'; *cane* 'bamboo';

- new coinages using processes of affixation, compounding or reduplication: *co-wives* 'wives of the same husband'; *rentage* '(house) rent'; *bush-meat* 'game'; *slow slow* 'slowly';
- new compounds: *check rice* 'rice prepared with krain-krain'; *head tie* 'woman's head-dress';
- words now outdated in Britain/America: *deliver* 'have a baby'; *station* 'town or city in which a person works';
- calques/loan translations, *next tomorrow* 'day after tomorrow' from Yoruba *otunla* 'new tomorrow';
- borrowings from a native language: *awujor* 'ceremony giving the ancestors food'; *krain-krain* 'a leafy vegetable';
- borrowings from pidgin/creole: *tai fes* 'frown'; *chop* 'food';
- borrowings from other languages: *palaver* (Portuguese) 'argument, trouble'; *piccin* (Portuguese) 'child'.

Most of these are restricted in use to West Africa, but some may be known and used more widely, e.g. *calabash*, *kola* or *palm wine*.

Some pragmatic characteristics of WAfrE   The cultural background of West African society often leads to ways of expression which are unfamiliar if not misleading for outsiders. This is surely one of the most noticeable ways in which second language English becomes 'indigenized'. A frequently quoted example is the use of *Sorry!* as an all-purpose expression of sympathy, that is, not only to apologize for, say, stepping on someone's toes, but also to someone who has sneezed or stumbled. Likewise, *Wonderful!* is used to reply to any surprise (even if not pleasant), and *Well done!* may be heard as a greeting to a person at work.

The difference in family structure between the Western world and West Africa means that kinship terms (*father, mother, brother, sister, uncle, aunt* etc.) may be used as in the West, but, because polygyny is practised in West African society, family terms may also be extended to the father and all his wives and all their children, or even to the father and all his sons and their wives, sons and unmarried daughters. The terms *father* and *mother* are sometimes also applied to distant relatives or even unrelated people who are of the appropriate age and to whom respect is due. When far away from home, kinship terms may be applied to someone from the same town or ethnic group, or, if abroad, even to compatriots (see also 8.3). One further example of such culturally constrained language behaviour concerns greetings, where different norms of linguistic politeness apply: 'the terms *Hi, Hello*, and *How are you* can be used by older or senior persons to younger or junior ones, but not vice-versa. Such verbal behavior coming from a younger person would be regarded as off-hand' (Akere 1982: 92).

14.1.2 East Africa

The main countries of East Africa to be reviewed are Tanzania, Kenya and Uganda (see Map 14.2). All three share one important feature: the presence of Swahili as a widely used lingua franca. Structurally speaking, this language is therefore somewhat parallel within East African society to Pidgin English in West Africa. However, while Pidgin

Map 14.2   East Africa

English is almost totally without prestige, the same cannot be said of Swahili, which is the official language in Kenya and Tanzania (in Tanzania together with English). In each of these countries English is used widely in education, especially at the secondary and higher levels. However, in Tanzania, despite the continued prominence of English in learning and much professional activity, Swahili is the preferred national language; it is also probably slowly displacing the autochthonous mother tongues.

The situation in Uganda is more ambiguous because of the ethnic rivalries between the large anti-Swahili Baganda population and the anti-Baganda sections of the population, who favour Swahili. While Swahili is used in the army and by the police, English is the medium of education from upper primary school (Year 4) on. In all three countries English is a diglossically High language in comparison to Swahili; but Swahili itself is

High in regard to the various local mother tongues. In Tanzania and in Kenya the (local) mother tongues provide ethnic identity and solidarity; Swahili contributes to national identity; and English serves to signal modernity and good education (Abdulaziz 1991: 392, 400).

English in East Africa   A survey of the domains of English reveals that it is used in a full range of activities in Uganda, Zambia, Malawi, Kenya and Zimbabwe, namely high (but not local) court, parliament, civil service; primary and secondary school; radio, news-papers, films, local novels, plays, records; traffic signs, advertisements; business and private correspondence; at home. In Tanzania, where Swahili is well established, English is used in the domains mentioned and the image which English has is relatively more positive than Swahili over a range of criteria including *beautiful, colourful, rich*; *precise, logical*; *refined, superior, sophisticated*, at least among educated Tanzanians (Schmied 1985: 244–8).

Kenya and Tanzania are, despite many parallels, not linguistic twins. After independence the position of English weakened in Tanzania as the country adopted a language policy which supported Swahili. In Kenya, where Swahili was also officially adopted, English continued to maintain a firm role as second language and attitudes towards the language are generally positive, being associated with high status jobs; English has even become the primary home language in some exclusive Nairobi suburbs; and many middle and upper class children seem to be switching gradually to English. In Tanzania, in contrast, attitudes vary considerably from a high degree of acceptance to indifference. In Kenya, in particular, multilingualism has led to a great deal of mother tongue/Swahili/English code-mixing among urban dwellers. This has even given rise to a mixed language jargon called **Sheng**. In Tanzania school students use an inter-language called **Tanzingereza** (< Swahili *Tanzania + Kiingereza* 'English language').

Linguistic features of East African English   The heading of this section is somewhat doubtful, for it is not clear whether Kenya, Uganda and Tanzania – with their different historical, political and linguistic characteristics – share enough to support the idea of East African English. Nonetheless, these three countries share a colonial past which included numerous common British East Africa institutions (the mass media, university education, the post office and governmental enterprises) and free movement of people and goods. In addition, many of the ethnic languages are closely related: over 90 per cent in Tanzania and over 75 per cent in Kenya speak a Bantu language. All this notwithstanding, many of the same types of interference and nativization processes described for WAfrE apply here as well. This includes a simplified five-vowel system as outlined in Table 14.2.

All the consonants of English except /ʒ/ have counterparts in Swahili though some speakers do not differentiate /r/ and /l/. /r/ may be flapped or trilled; /l/ is usually clear; /dʒ/ may be realized as /dj/; /θ, ð/ may be [t, d], [s, z], or even [f, v]; /p, t, k/ are likely to be unaspirated. Rhythm is syllable-timed, and there is a tendency to favour a consonant, vowel, consonant, vowel syllable structure, i.e. there are no consonant clusters.

Beyond syntactic and lexical differences, which are similar in type to those in West Africa, there are culturally determined ways of expression that reflect the nativization of English as a second language. For example, a mother may address her son as *my young husband*; and a husband, his wife as *daughter*. A brother-in-law is a *second husband*.

Table 14.2 The vowels of EAfrE in comparison with those of RP

EAfrE	RP	as in	EAfrE	RP	as in
i →	iː	bead	o →	ɒ	body
↘	ɪ	bid	↘	ɔ	bawdy
e →	eɪ	bayed	↘	əʊ	bode
↘	e	bed	u →	ʊ	Buddha
a →	æ	bad	↘	uː	booed
↘	ɑː	bard			
↘	ɜː	bird			
↘	ʌ	bud			

Source: Adapted from Angogo and Hancock 1980: 75.

Differences in the social reality associated with a language function can be seen not only in the differing prestige and domains of English and Swahili, but also in the behavioural roles associated with each:

> Certain socio-psychological situations seem to influence language maintenance among the bilinguals. One of the respondents [in a group of 15 informants] said that whenever he argued with his bilingual wife he would maintain Swahili as much as possible while she would maintain English. A possible explanation is that Swahili norms and values assign different roles to husband and wife (socially more clear cut?) from the English norms and values (socially less clear cut, or more converging?). Maintaining one language or the other could then be a device for asserting one's desired role.
>
> (Abdulaziz 1972: 209)

14.2 ENGLISH IN ASIA

In this section three Asian countries in which English plays an important role will be reviewed: India, Singapore and the Philippines. In none of these countries is English a native language but it is a part of the colonial legacy. In other former colonial possessions in Asia in which English once had a similar status, such as Sri Lanka or Malaysia, its role has gradually been reduced to that of an important foreign language.

14.2.1 India

In India, the largest of the South Asian countries, English plays a special role. The remaining countries which were, like India, also once British colonial possessions are Pakistan and Bangladesh, Sri Lanka and Nepal. Each of them has a certain amount of linguistic diversity and each continues to use English in some functions. The most data, however, are available on India, which dwarfs its neighbours with its ethnic diversity, its large geographic size and its enormous population of one billion. The three to four per cent who speak English make up a total of perhaps 35 million speakers, most of them in positions of relative prestige.

English has been used in India for hundreds of years, but it was an outsider's language for most of this time. The British colonial administration used it, and colonial educational policy encouraged its wider use for the creation of a local elite. To a limited extent, this goal has been reached, for English is well established as one of the most important diglossically High languages of India. The National Academy of Letters (Sahilya Academi) recognizes literature by Indians in English as a part of Indian literature. It is a 'link language' for the Indian Administrative Service (the former Indian Civil Service); it is a medium in the modernization and westernization of the country; it is an important language of higher education, science and technology.

The role of English is due, in part, to the general spread and use of English throughout the world, especially in science and technology, trade and commerce. However, English also has an official status. Fifteen 'national languages' are recognized in the Indian constitution; one of them, Hindi, the language of over one third of the population, is the official language. In addition, English is designated the 'associate official language'. Its status is supported by continuing resistance in the non-Hindi parts of India to the spread of Hindi, which automatically puts non-Hindi speakers at a disadvantage. Where everyone must learn English, everybody is on a par linguistically.

One of the practical results of this linguistic rivalry has been the application, in secondary education since the late 1950s, of the 'three language formula', which provides for the education of everyone in their regional language, in Hindi and in English. (If the regional language is Hindi, then another language, such as Telugu, Tamil, Kannada or Malayalam is to be learned.) The intention of this not completely successful policy has been to spread the learning burden and to create a population with a significant number of multilingual speakers. Sridhar remarks:

> The Three Language Formula is a compromise between the demands of the various pressure groups and has been hailed as a masterly – if imperfect – solution to a complicated problem. It seeks to accommodate the interests of group identity (mother tongues and regional languages), national pride and unity (Hindi), and administrative efficiency and technological progress (English).
>
> (quoted in Baldridge 1996: 12)

The weaknesses of the policy lie in the failure of the Hindi states to carry it out; likewise, Madras failed to institute Hindi teaching in Tamil Nadu.

English has maintained a kind of hegemony in several areas: English language newspapers or magazines are published in all of the states of India and the readers of the English language newspapers make up about one quarter of the reading public. A large number of books appear in English, as do scientific and non-scientific journals.

One of the most important motivations for learning English is that people feel it significantly raises their chances of getting a good job. One survey in Karnataka (South India) reveals that two thirds of the students investigated felt their job prospects were very good or excellent with an English medium education (vs only 7 per cent for Hindi and 28 per cent for their mother tongue) (Sridhar 1983: 145). Note that this group of students was aiming at jobs like bank manager, university or college teacher, high level civil servant

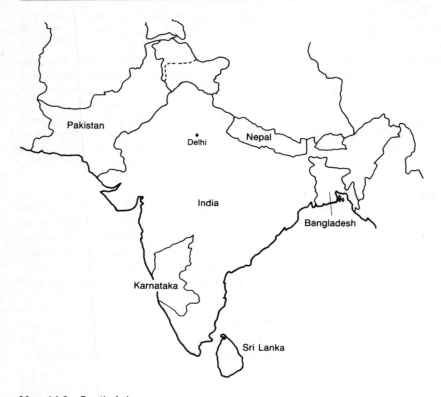

Map 14.3 South Asia

or lawyer. 'English is felt to be the language of power, a language of prestige' (ibid.: 149). It is, in other words, the language of the classes, not the masses.

English is more the language of the intellect, but not of the emotions. The language intrudes less on intimate areas such as communication with family or neighbours than on domains of business, politics, technology, communication with strangers or pan-Indian communication. Where English is used it signals not only a certain level of education; it also serves to cover over differences of region and caste. Through a judicious use of code-switching and code-mixing various speaker identities can be revealed. English, for example, is used not only for certain domains and to fill in lexical gaps in the vernacular, but also to signal education, authority, and a cosmopolitan, Western attitude.

Indian English (IndE)   IndE is for most Indians not a native, but a second language. Yet it is far too entrenched in Indian intellectual life and traditions to be regarded as a foreign language. Furthermore, a local standard IndE seems to be developing (sometimes referred to as nativization), though it is not universally acknowledged. Kachru quotes a study in which two thirds reported a preference for BrE and only just over a quarter accepted Indian English as their preferred model (1986: 22). Some, while realizing that IndE is not and cannot be identical with its one time model, BrE, have fears of a chaotic future in which 'English in India . . . will be found disintegrating into quite incomprehensible dialects' (Das 1982: 148). All the same there seems to be little doubt that IndE has established itself as an independent language tradition. While most of the English produced by educated Indians is close to international StE, there are obvious differences in pronunciation, some in grammar and a noticeable number in vocabulary and usage. In looking briefly at each of these areas, it is the English of the majority of educated Indians that we will be looking at.

The pronunciation of IndE offers the most difficulties for native speakers unfamiliar with this variety. Although there is a great deal of local variation (depending on the native language of the user) and although spelling pronunciations are common, there do seem to be a number of relatively widespread features in the pronunciation of IndE. What is perhaps most noticeable is the way words are stressed in IndE. Often (but not universally) stress falls on the next to last syllable regardless of where it falls in RP or GenAm. This produces, for example, *Pro'testant* rather than *'Protestant* and *'refer* rather than *re'fer*.

The effect of education is often evident. Among the segmental sounds one of the most common features is the pronunciation of non-prevocalic <r> in words like *part* (a non-standard feature), at least among 'average', i.e. especially the young and women, as opposed to 'prestigious' speakers. A further (though again not universal) difference is the use of retroflex [ṭ] and [ḍ] (produced with the tongue tip curled backwards) for RP/GenAm alveolar /t/ and /d/. The dental fricatives /θ/ and /ð/ of RP/GenAm are often realized as the dental stops [t̪] and [d̪], and the labio-dental fricatives /f/ and /v/, as [pʰ] and [bʰ]. The latter sound or [ʋʰ] is also frequently used for /w/, which does not seem to occur in the phonology of IndE. For Hindi/Urdu speakers initial consonant clusters are difficult and may be pronounced with a pre-posed vowel so that *school* becomes /ɪskul/, *station*, /ɪsteʃan/ and *speech* /ɪspitʃ/. As we see in *station*, unstressed syllables often have a full vowel.

Many of these points as well as numerous differences (always as compared with RP/GenAm) in the vowel system (phonemics) or in vowel realization (phonetics) are due, in the end, to the phonetic and phonological nature of the varying mother tongues of the speakers of IndE. Even within the IndE community there can be difficulties in communication. Hence the panic among the guests at a Gujarati wedding when the following was announced over the public address system, 'The snakes are in the hole'. The subsequent run for the exit could only be stopped when someone explained that, actually, the refreshments (snacks) were in the hall (Mehrotra 1982: 168).

The grammar of IndE is hardly deviant in comparison to general StE; yet, here, too, there are differences. Some of the points commonly mentioned, whether due to native language interference or the result of patterning within IndE, include

- invariant tag questions: *isn't it?* or *no?*, e.g. *You went there yesterday, isn't it?* (see also 14.1.1);
- the use of the present perfect in sentences with past adverbials, e.g. *I have worked there in 1990*;
- the use of *since* + a time unit with the present progressive, e.g. *I am writing this essay since two hours*;
- a *that*-complement clause after *want*, e.g. *Mohan wants that you should go there*;
- *wh*-questions without subject-auxiliary inversion, e.g. *Where you are going?*

The vocabulary of IndE is universally recognized as containing numerous characteristic items. For convenience they can be classified as follows:

- English words used differently, e.g. *four-twenty* 'a cheat, swindler';
- new coinages: e.g. *black money* 'illegal gains'; *change-room* 'dressing room';
- hybrid formations: e.g. *lathi charge* 'police attack with sticks'; *coolidom*;
- adoption of Indian words, which often 'come more naturally and appear more forceful in a given context than their English equivalents. *Sister-in-law* is no match for *sali*, and *idle talk* is a poor substitute for *buk-buk*' (Mehrotra 1982: 160–2).

The use of Indian words in English discourse is said to be more common in more informal, personal and relaxed situations; nevertheless, there may be the need to use Indian terms in formal texts as well, e.g. *Urad and moong fell sharply in the grain market here today on stockists offerings. Rice, jowar and arhar also followed suit, but barley forged ahead* (Kachru 1984: 362).

Style and appropriacy are the final areas to be reviewed. It has often been pointed out that IndE diction has a bookish and old-fashioned flavour to it because the reading models in Indian schools are so often older English authors. Certainly, the standards of style and appropriateness are different in IndE as compared to most native speaker varieties. There is a 'tendency towards verbosity, preciosity, and the use of learned literary words', a 'preference for exaggerated and hyperbolic forms' (Mehrotra 1982: 164); 'stylistic embellishment is highly valued' (Kachru 1984: 364). While, for example, profuse expressions of thanks such as the following are culturally appropriate and contextually proper in communication in India, they would seem overdone to most native speakers:

> I consider it to be my primordial obligation to humbly offer my deepest sense of gratitude to my most revered Guruji and untiring and illustrious guide Professor [. . .] for the magnitude of his benevolence and eternal guidance.
>
> (Mehrotra 1982: 165)

In an effort to use the idioms and expressions learned, an IndE user may, as a non native speaker, mix his/her levels of style (and metaphors) as did a clerk who, in asking for several days leave, explained that 'the hand that rocked the cradle has kicked the bucket' (ibid.: 162). Likewise the following wish: 'I am in very good health and hope you are in the same boat' (Das 1982: 144).

Less easy for a native speaker to penetrate are differing communicative strategies, for example *yes-no* answers, where the IndE speaker may agree or disagree with the form of a statement while the native speaker will agree or disagree with its content. IndE can, therefore have the following types of exchanges:

> A: Didn't I see you yesterday in college?
> B: Yes, you didn't see me yesterday in college.
>
> (Kachru 1984: 374)

Equally difficult for the outsider to comprehend is the way power differences may find subtle expression as in the following active-passive switch:

A subordinate addressing his boss in an office in India writes, 'I request you to look into the case,' while the boss writing to a subordinate will normally use the passive, 'you are requested to look into the case.' If the latter form is used by a subordinate, it may mean a downright insult.

(Mehrotra 1982: 166)

14.2.2 Singapore and Malaysia

The English language plays a special role in both Singapore and Malaysia, a role, however, which is developing in two very different fashions. The demographic situation in each state is comparable inasmuch as both have major ethnic elements in the population consisting of Malays, Chinese and Indians. In Peninsular Malaysia this is 53 per cent Malays to 35 per cent Chinese to 10 per cent Indians. In Singapore (population 3.3 million), which lies at the tip of the Malay Peninsula, the relationship is 14 to 77 to 7 per cent. Both states were formerly under British colonial administration, and in both English was an important administrative and educational language. For a short period in the 1960s the two were federated and shared the same 'national language', namely Malay (or Bahasa Malaysia). After Singapore left the Federation, it retained Malay as its national language along with its further 'official languages', English, Mandarin Chinese and Tamil. Malaysia, on the other hand, abandoned English as a second language (National Language Policy of 1967) and became officially monolingual in Bahasa Malaysia.

Singapore upholds a policy of maintaining four official languages; however, the de facto status of each has been changing. The Chinese ethnic part of the population, which is divided into speakers of several mutually unintelligible dialects, above all, Hokkien, Teochew and Cantonese, has been encouraged to learn and use Mandarin, and indeed, younger Singaporeans of Chinese descent do use more Mandarin, especially in more formal situations. Malay remains the 'national language' and it is widely used as a lingua franca; yet, it is English which is on the increase, so much so, in fact, that it is sometimes regarded as a language of national identity. In general, Malay is associated with the ethnic Malays, just as Mandarin and the Chinese vernaculars are associated with the ethnic Chinese, and Tamil with the ethnic Indians. In contrast, English is viewed as an inter-ethnic lingua franca (Platt 1988: 1385). As such English plays an important role in modernization and development in Singapore.

The pre-eminent position of English in Singapore is most evident in the area of education. Since the introduction of bilingual education in 1956, the teaching medium was to be one of the four official languages; if this was not English, English was to be the second school language. Consequently, virtually 100 per cent of the students in Singapore are in English medium schools (Platt 1991: 377). This means that about 60 per cent of teaching time is in English. Yet with 40 per cent for Mandarin or Malay or Tamil, literacy in these languages is assured. This is important in the case of Malay because the neighbouring states of Malaysia and Indonesia both use forms of Malay as their national languages. Mandarin is obviously useful because of the size and importance of China. Tamil – never the language of more than about two thirds of the ethnic Indians – is apparently losing ground, largely to English.

All four languages are also prominent in the media, both print and electronic. In both cases English is gaining proportionately and it alone draws on a readership/audience from all three major ethnic groups. Most parliamentary work is conducted in English, and it is the sole language of the law courts. Naturally, it is predominant in international trade.

Nevertheless, English is not a universal language. Rather, it is generally the diglossically High language, reserved for more formal use, though a local Low vernacular variety of SingE, sometimes called Singlish (not to be confused with Sinhalese English also sometimes referred to as Singlish) is used in a wider range of more informal situations including both inter-ethnic and intra-ethnic communication. Despite its increasing spread English is seldom a home language. Nevertheless, Platt does see English in Singapore as 'probably the classic case of the indigenisation' because its range of domains is constantly expanding and this includes its use among friends and even in families (Platt 1991: 376), thus making it a 'semi-native variety'.

Singaporean and Malaysian English (SingE)   Within SingE there are several levels. At the upper level (the acrolect) there is little difference in grammar and vocabulary between SingE and other national varieties of StE. As in any regional variety there are, of course, local items of vocabulary, more of them as the level broadens to the mesolects and basilect.

Map 14.4   Malaysia and Singapore

The vocabulary of SingE   Borrowings from Chinese and Malay are especially prominent, e.g. Malay *jaga* 'guard, sentinel', *padang* 'field', *kampong* 'village', *makan* 'food' and Hokkien *towday* 'employer, business person'. But other languages have also contributed to SingE, e.g.: *dhobi* 'washerman' from Hindi; *peon* 'orderly, office assistant' from Portuguese; *syce* 'driver' from Arabic via Hindi; or *tamby* 'office boy, errand boy' from Tamil. SingE vocabulary also includes different idioms. *To sleep late* means, on the Chinese pattern, to go to bed late and hence possibly to be tired. This, of course, stands in contrast to StE *to sleep late*, which indicates longer sleep in the morning and probably being refreshed. The loan translation of Malay *goyang kaki* as *shake legs*, rather in contrast to StE *shake a leg* 'hurry', means, in SingE, 'take it easy' as in '*stop shaking legs and get back to work la*' (Tay 1982: 68). The element *la*, just quoted, probably comes from Hokkien. It is almost ubiquitous in informal, diglossically Low SingE: 'Perhaps the most striking and distinctive feature of L [= Low] English' (Richards and Tay 1977: 143). Its function is to signal the type of relationship between the people talking: 'there is a positive rapport between speakers and an element of solidarity' (ibid.: 145).

The grammar of SingE   SingE grammar is virtually identical with that of StE in the formal written medium. In speech and more informal writing (including journalism) and increasingly at a lower level of education, more and more non-standard forms may be found, many of them reflecting forms in the non-English vernaculars of Singapore (and Malaysia).

The verb is perhaps most central. Since the substratum languages do not mark either concord or tense, it is no wonder that the third person singular present tense {-S} is often missing (*this radio sound good*) and that present forms are frequently used where StE would have the past (*I start here last year*). This tendency is reinforced by the substratum lack of final consonant clusters, but it also includes the use of past participles for simple past (*We gone last night*). On the other hand, the StE progressive is overused (*Are you having a cold?*), and *used to* is employed not only for the habitual distant past as in StE, but also for the present habitual as in:

> *SingE speaker*:   The tans [military unit] use to stay in Serangoon.
> *Non-SingE speaker*:   Where are they staying now?
> *SingE speaker (somewhat sharply)*:   I've just told you. In Serangoon.
> (from Tongue 1974: 44)

Numerous other points including modal use, the auxiliary *do*, the infinitive marker *to* and the deletion of the copula might be added.

The noun may lack the plural {-S} in local basilect forms, probably due to the different nature of plural marking in Chinese (a plural classifier) and Malay (reduplication), hence *how many bottle?* There is also a tendency to have fewer indefinite articles (*You got to have proper system here*) and to use non-count nouns like count nouns (*chalks, luggages, fruits, mails, informations* etc.).

Sentence patterns also sometimes differ from those of StE elsewhere. Indirect questions often retain the word order of direct questions (as they do increasingly often in GenE as well) as in *I'd like to know what are the procedures?* Both subjects, especially first person pronoun subjects, and objects may be deleted where StE would have them:

A: Can or cannot?
B: Cannot
C: Why cannot?

> (Tay 1982: 65)

One last point is the widespread use, also mentioned for IndE and WAfrE, of the invariant tag question: *is it?/isn't it?*, e.g. *the Director is busy now, is it?*

Pronunciation   The **pronunciation of SingE** is what is most distinctive about it. Once again this is the result of interference from the non-English vernaculars.

   The vowels of SingE are generally shorter or less tense than in RP/GenAm, and diphthongs are often monophthongized, for example /əʊ/ → [oː], /eɪ/ → [eː], /eə/ → [ɛː].

   The consonants of the acrolect are distinguished by a lack of voiced obstruents in word-final position; furthermore, there is less frequent release of all final stops and affricates. In the mesolects final consonant clusters are simplified to the first consonant only (see above *this radio sound good* with *sound* for *sounds* as a third person present tense form), and often the final stops are replaced by a glottal stop. /θ/ and /ð/ are commonly realized as [t] and [d]. In the basilect, finally, Chinese speakers realize /r/ as /l/ (*rice = lice*); Malay speakers may replace /f/ with /p/ (*face = pace*); and Indian speakers may fail to distinguish between /v/ and /w/ (*vary = wary*).

   The rhythm of SingE, which is staccato-like and syllable-timed, is one of its most noticeable features. This means each syllable gets approximately equal stress, where RP, GenAm and most other native speaker varieties have a rhythmical pattern which places the stressed syllables at approximately equal intervals often separated by one or more unstressed syllables. This has the effect of levelling the distinction made in RP and GenAm between the noun '*in-crease* and the verb *in-'crease*. In SingE both sound more like the latter. Furthermore, SingE has less range in pitch and fewer distinctive intonational patterns, due perhaps to the fact that Chinese, as a tone language, does not use word stress as English does: stress is signalled by greater length and loudness in SingE, while native speaker type stressing also includes pitch change.

The future of SingE   While it is evident that the role of English will continue to decline in Malaysia as Bahasa Malaysia extends its domains, it is clear that Singapore is and will remain a multilingual state in which English has a position of increasing preeminence. In Singapore, speech patterns are polyglossic. This means, concretely, that there is more than one High language (usually English and Mandarin) and several Low ones (usually Bazaar Malay, Hokkien and, increasingly, Singlish). English is seldom the first language in the sense of the first learned; it is, however, the first school language of practically everybody who has entered Singapore schools since the early 1980s. It has also grown to be the language of national identity, of work and of inter-ethnic (and even some intra-ethnic) communication.

14.2.3 The Philippines

Aside from the very size (approximately 75 million) and the regional significance of the Philippines, they are the major example in this chapter in which the tradition of AmE is of importance. The islands had been a Spanish colony for well over 300 years when the American government took possession of them as one of the results of the Spanish–American War (1898). Despite considerable Filipino resistance (1898–1901) to the new colonial master, the United States was soon firmly in control and established English as an official language beside and fully equal to Spanish in 1901. English was given favourable treatment (government jobs were more readily available to those who could use English) and soon began to displace Spanish. By 1936, when the Constitution of the Philippines provided for a national language (Filipino, a modified form of Tagalog), English had in fact become pre-eminent in education.

After independence (1946) little changed at first, but in the early 1950s a policy of vernacular education in Years 1 and 2 of school with a later shift to English was implemented. In 1974 the new Bilingual Education Policy was initiated, in which Pilipino/Filipino and English were to be the shared languages of education. This policy provided for the teaching of science and mathematics in English and the use of Pilipino/Filipino in social studies and the arts. The revised Bilingual Educational Policy of 1987 seeks to maintain English since this language is highly important for science and technology and international relations (trade, worker flows in and out of the Philippines). The Philippines continue to pursue the goal of establishing a national language, Filipino, which is approximately 80 per cent Tagalog/Pilipino and Spanish (Gonzales 1988: 47). The Bilingual Education Policy has served to spread Pilipino/Filipino (vis-à-vis other Philippine languages); however, it has also furthered the elite, who have access to English, while lessening access to English for the talented among the masses, thus slowing social mobility and increasing language-based social stratification (Gonzalez and Bautista 1985: 119).

In addition to Tagalog there are seven to eight other major languages spoken in the Philippines and over a hundred all told. The largest are Cebuano and Tagalog, each with approximately a quarter of the population. Ilokano and Hiligaynon together make up perhaps another 20 per cent. Filipinos and Filipinas are, as a rule, at least bilingual, often trilingual or quadrilingual (in their vernacular, the regional language, Filipino/Pilipino and English).

The vernacular is the language of emotion and is used for swearing and for dreaming. English is used in banks and book stores and especially for numbers and counting, which reflects the influence of schooling. At markets, in the popular press and on radio and TV Pilipino/Filipino and the vernaculars predominate, except for the news, which is generally in English. Books and the serious newspapers and magazines are in English; technical reports are in English; communication upwards – with a department head or boss – will tend to be in English. The more formal the occasion is and the higher the level of education, the more likely it is that English will be used. English remains predominant in government administration, legislation, the law and the judiciary, higher education and the professions, business and commerce, science and industry. The bar exams, Certified Public Accountant exams, engineering and medical board exams and the National College Entrance Examination are all in English; the Senate and the House of Representatives are conducted mostly in English; laws are passed in English with a Filipino translation. The Philippine population is obviously quite aware of the advantages of English, and parents want their children to learn it because of the advantages it offers, namely social mobility, higher paying jobs, power and prestige.

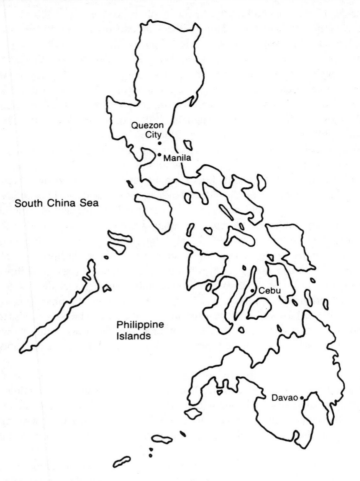

Map 14.5 The Philippines

Philippine English   After the immediately preceding remarks it is not surprising to read:

> The better educated [people are], the better the approximation (in lexis and in morphology and syntax though not in pronunciation) to Standard American English; the less educated, the more the discrepancies in word usage and especially in morphology and syntax (with likewise a more varied pronunciation) as compared to Standard American English.
>
> (Gonzalez and Bautista 1985: 25)

Pronunciation   The **pronunciation** of Filipino English is strongly characterized by the native language of the speaker. For this reason it is no surprise when a speaker says *as a matter of pact*, since this reflects that fact that Pilipino has no /f/. Among the differences in pronunciation are: the absence of aspiration of /p, t, k/; more stress on schwa; a tendency towards syllable-timing; spelling pronunciations; dental [ṯ] and [ḏ]; lack of release of all final stops.

Grammar   **Filipino grammatical features** include 'local rules for agreement, tense, tense sequence, article usage and prepositional usage as well as localized usage of the progressive, present perfect and past perfect tenses' (Llamzon 1969: 48).

Lexical items which are specific to the Philippines are often patterned on Tagalog expressions. Examples are *I will go ahead of you* as a leave taking formula; *my head/tooth is painful* 'I have a headache/toothache'; *close/open the light* 'turn the light off/on'; or *I slept late yesterday* 'I went to bed late yesterday' (as in SingE; see 14.2.2).

Code-switching   In a society in which two languages, English and Pilipino/Filipino, play such a prominent role it is not astonishing that a great deal of code-switching occurs. The use of English may be functional and prestigious, but the intermixture of Tagalog/Filipino establishes sender-receiver solidarity and may mark the speaker as a (westernized) nationalist. This mixing is pejoratively referred to as Mix-Mix (or *Halo-Halo*). If there is more Tagalog it is sometimes called *Taglish*; if more English, *Engalog* (ibid.: 214). The following illustration of it comes from the beginning of a short story:

> Maniwala ka kaya, pare, kung sabihin ko sa iyo that a mere whisper can cause death. It may even create chaos.
> Tipong heavy and intro ko, pero it happened one night dito sa destitute place namin. Ganito iyon, listen carefully. . . .

> [Can you believe it, friend, if I were to tell you that a mere whisper can cause death. It may even create chaos.
> It looks like my introduction is heavy [too serious], but it happened one night here at our destitute place. It was like this, listen carefully.]
>
> (quoted from Gonzalez 1982: 213)

Outlook   Although there is a steady move to Filipino in all domains, English will remain important for economic reasons – both because widespread knowledge of English may induce foreign employers to move to the Philippines and because it facilitates the ability of Filipinos and Filipinas to find jobs abroad (half a million go every year, see Gonzalez 1988: 10). However, despite claims of a standard variety of English in the Philippines, this applies only to the better educated parts of society. In general the level of Philippine English is and will remain relatively low and may even fall to the status of a foreign, rather than a second, language, albeit an important one.

14.3 PIDGIN AND CREOLE ENGLISH

No consideration of modern English is complete without taking into account the varieties of English which emerged, above all, as one result of European exploration and colonization. Over a period of some 350 years (from the beginning of the seventeenth century) Great Britain was a world power which exerted enormous influence on the economies and the societies of many parts of the world. This influence can be seen in the wide spread of the English language in all parts of the world today. Among its numerous varieties are the so-called **mixed languages**. This frequently used term comes from the assumption that such languages derive their lexicon from a prestigious **superstrate** or **lexifer** language, usually a European language such as English spoken by outside traders or by plantation owners. In contrast, the syntax is possibly strongly influenced by the **substratum** languages, the less prestigious vernaculars of the local population or of the plantation workers. While this conception has been called into question (see 14.3.2), contacts between English speaking seamen, merchants, plantation owners and overseers, missionaries, colonial magistrates and officers and many others, on the one hand, and native colonial populations, on the other, did lead to new languages whose

> very existence is largely due to the processes – discovery, exploration, trade, conquest, slavery, migration, colonialism, nationalism – that have brought the peoples of Europe and the peoples of the rest of the world to share a common destiny.
>
> (Hymes 1971b: 5)

Two kinds of mixed languages, pidgins and creoles, will first be defined. In a second step some of the theories about the possible origins and historical development of those pidgins and creoles which have an English-based vocabulary will be outlined. They will then be reviewed according to major geographic areas and illustrated with some of their linguistic features.

14.3.1 Definition of pidgins and creoles

The attempt to explain what pidgin and creole languages are leads in three different directions: the linguistic, the social and the historical.

Pidgins   From the **linguistic point of view** pidgins are second languages; no one has a pidgin as their mother tongue. This is so because pidgins grow out of contact situations in which none of the people who need to communicate with each other have an established language in common. (If an already existing language is chosen, possibly in a simplified form, this is known as a **lingua franca**.) Motivated by the necessity of communicating, pidgin speakers make do by taking the majority of the vocabulary from the **lexifer** language and resorting to grammatical patterns which may be either a common denominator of sorts or the result of universal processes of language acquisition which are innate in every human (see 14.3.2).

In comparison with the native languages of their speakers, pidgins are less elaborated. This means that they have a smaller vocabulary, a reduced grammar and a less elaborate phonology. Furthermore, pidgins are used in a much more limited set of circumstances and are stylistically less varied than first languages are. In Melanesian Pidgin English (now often called Tok Pisin) or in Hawaiian Pidgin English (Hawaiian PE), for example, this looks as follows:

- Reduced vocabulary leads to extensive use of paraphrase and metaphor, e.g. in Tok Pisin: /skru biloŋ arm/ 'screw of the arm' is the word for elbow just as /gras biloŋ hed/ 'grass of the head' means 'hair'.
- As compared to StE there is a simplified and changed phoneme inventory: often missing are, for example, /ð/ and /θ/, e.g. Hawaiian PE [tʰri ijá] 'three years'. Often mentioned is also the lack of consonant clusters and the resultant sequences of consonant, vowel, consonant, (vowel), as in early Tok Pisin *pelet* < *plate*.
- Inflections are rare as compared to StE; for example, there is no plural {-S} in Hawaiian PE /tʰri ijá/ 'three years'.
- Syntactic reduction as compared to StE frequently leads to the lack of the copula, prepositions, determiners and conjunctions, e.g. Hawaiian PE: *I think one year me school teacher* 'I think that I was a school teacher for one year'; *Baby name me no like* 'I did not like the baby name'.

When **historically**, from the fifteenth century on, Europeans ventured out into the (for them) newly discovered lands of Africa and Asia, they met with and had to communicate with peoples all the way down the coast of West Africa around the Cape of Good Hope and across the Indian Ocean to India, the Spice Islands and China. To do this they relied largely on pidgins, in their more reduced form sometimes called **trade jargons**. The same need for communication with a polyglot population grew with the establishment of plantations. Those established in the Caribbean area as well as Brazil and what is now the southern United States relied on the massive importation of slaves from West Africa. Later plantation systems employed contract labour and also moved workers from their homelands, sometimes for a set period of time (e.g. the Queensland sugar growing area), sometimes as permanent immigrants (the sugar and pineapple growing areas of Hawaii). In all of these places pidgins which drew on English for their lexicon came into existence.

The social situation in which these pidgins were spoken was characterized by the very limited needs and circumstances in the trading posts in West Africa. Consequently, it is no wonder that the registers which developed were equally limited: fewer contexts, fewer topics, more limited social relations.

Pidgins have sometimes been referred to as **marginal languages** because they are indeed marginal in regard to the conditions under which they came into existence and the attitudes of their users towards them, especially the speakers of the European lexifer languages. Nevertheless, quite a number of pidgins have been able to survive long enough to develop beyond the stage of a trade jargon. This was especially the case in the plantation situation, where pidgins were used not only to facilitate communication between master and servant, which was surely very limited, but also between the various labourers, who seldom shared a common mother tongue. These pidgins gained in stability and entered into a process of linguistic and functional elaboration.

Creoles   At the 'end' of this process of elaboration lies the creole, which is a pidgin which has become the first language of its speakers. This means that it may be either a mother tongue or a **primary language**, i.e. the speakers' dominant language. A creole is an enriched, expanded and regularized language; it has the full complexity characteristic of any natural language. This seems to have happened quite rapidly on the plantations of the New World. African slaves who were only able to communicate with each other in a pidgin had children for whom this language was the only or the main medium available. They clearly added to the vocabulary and they gradually established a relative stability of grammatical forms and phonological norms. In West Africa Pidgin English is the home language of some people (and the mother tongue of children in these homes) in urban areas. When it is used so constantly in the routines of daily life, it may be expected to be relatively more greatly expanded. However, pidgin is also widely employed as a market language. Here it may be considerably simpler. Pidgin and creole, in other words, can stand at the two ends of a linguistic continuum which stretches from true, elaborated creole to a minimal pidgin/trade jargon. Tok Pisin, the pidgin-creole of New Guinea, is a native language in the towns and is becoming progressively more elaborated. It exists, however, in ever more simplified and pidgin-like forms as one moves into the rural and mountainous areas. It is this continuum and the historical relationship between a pidgin and its creolized form which distinguish a creole from any other natural language. Viewed on its own, as an independent linguistic system, there is nothing about a creole which is essentially different from any other natural language.

14.3.2 The origins of English pidgins and creoles

A great deal of discussion by linguists has centred round the question of how pidgins and creoles come into existence. One of the intriguing points of departure for the various considerations involved is the high degree of structural similarity between many of the English pidgins and creoles (for examples, see 14.3.3). These pidgins and creoles are too different from StE to be related to it as the regional dialects of Britain are. The pidgins and creoles were presumably the result of necessarily rapid change in a contact situation involving obviously different languages. Furthermore, not only are the English pidgins and creoles similar as a group, but there is also an astonishingly high degree of structural correspondence between them and the pidgins and creoles which have lexicons based on French, Spanish, Portuguese and Dutch. The similarities are too great to be the product of pure coincidence. Three different views are offered to explain the similarities:

1   These languages all share a common source (the **monogenetic hypothesis**).
2   The historical conditions for the genesis of each were similar and hence they developed in a similar way (the **parallel development hypothesis**).
3   All pidgins are subject to the same principles of reduction and simplification, and all creoles expand according to the same principles of elaboration and extension of grammatical categories (the **hypothesis of universals of language acquisition**).

The monogenetic hypothesis   This hypothesis assumes that the first Europeans who came into contact with West Africans in the fifteenth century, the Portuguese, used a simplified language for their contacts. This may have been a form of the original lingua franca (Latin: 'French language'), which had been in use for trade throughout the Mediterranean for centuries. This language was then employed by the Portuguese in West Africa and along the trade routes in the Indian Ocean to China. Its grammatical structure remained basically unchanged, but its vocabulary drew heavily on Portuguese. This language would then have been firmly entrenched in the ports of West Africa so that when the Dutch began to make incursions on the Portuguese slave trade from 1630 on, they would have made use of the same language; however Portuguese words would begin to be replaced by Dutch ones, and, instead of **Portuguese Pidgin**, *Negerhollands* developed. Where the French established themselves, the same process resulted in *petit négre*.

In the seventeenth century English, too, became a party to this process. The English began participating in the slave trade which they dominated by the eighteenth century. In addition, they were also intent on acquiring colonial territories in the Caribbean. The first settlements were in the Lesser Antilles (St Kitts, 1624; Barbados, 1627; Nevis and Barbuda, 1628; Antigua, 1632; Montserrat, 1633; Anguilla 1650). In 1651 they began a colony on the mainland of South America in Surinam, which they ceded to the Dutch in 1667. At about the same time (from 1655) the English captured the Greater Antilles island of Jamaica from the Spanish. In all of these territories and in the slave trade Pidgin English would have come to be used.

The actual mechanism by which the originally Portuguese Proto-Pidgin vocabulary is supposed to have become Dutch or French or English is referred to as **relexification**, a process in which words originating in one language are replaced by those of another without there being any comparable change in the grammatical structure. This can be illustrated in the following manner. Perfective aspect (i.e. the designation of an action as completed) drew on the Portuguese marker *acabar de*. It was adopted as Proto-Pidgin *kabe*, which was relexified as French Pidgin/Creole *fèk* (from *faire*) in Haiti and as English Pidgin/Creole *done* (as in *ain't I done tell you 'bout dat*). The word changed, but what remained was perfective aspect, referring to something completed in the past. Not all the Portuguese words were replaced; this would explain the presence in English pidgins and creoles of such words as *pickaninny* 'small child' (from Portuguese *pequenino*) or *savvy* 'know' (from *saber*).

The parallel development hypothesis This hypothesis postulates that pidgins came into existence under a set of conditions so similar that languages with comparable structures were bound to be the result. The most important of those conditions include the similar grammatical structure of many West African languages, the influence of Pidgin Portuguese and possibly similar processes of simplification, for example, something like baby talk for communication with slaves on the part of the European native speakers who provided the language model.

There is evidence that many non-linguistic features of shared West African culture survived under New World slavery, including elements of folklore, religion, family structure, music and performance styles. Some linguistic features can also be traced fairly directly back to African languages. Dalby sees African influence when he defines Black English as 'all those forms of speech in which an English or English-derived vocabulary is used with a grammatical structure divergent at a number of points from so-called "standard" English, but reminiscent at those same points of certain widespread features in West African languages' (1971: 116).

The hypothesis of universal processes of language acquisition This hypothesis is based on the assumption that people everywhere simplify language in the same way, for example, by:

1   using a simplified phonology such as the sequential structure consonant, vowel, consonant, vowel (e.g. Nigerian PE /filag/ 'flag' with an intrusive vowel or /tori/ 'story' with one consonant deleted from the initial cluster;

2   placing markers directly in front of the propositions they apply to; this involves the markers for negation, past, aspect and irrealis (conditional); as an example, note the pre-posed negative particle *no* in Neo-Solomonic *no kæčĭm ɛni ples i-kwajtfɛla* (literally: no catch-him any place he-quiet-fellow) '[we] did not come to any place which was quiet';

3   leaving off inflectional endings, for example Australian PE *aj* 'eye' or 'eyes'.

In a converse procedure, in accord with universal principles, people are then said, under certain circumstances, to enrich and expand pidgins to creoles. One of the pieces of evidence adduced is the presence of similar categories of tense, modality and aspect expressed as particles (e.g. Sranan *ben* for past tense, *sa* for modality-future and *e* for progressive aspect). All three appear in pre-verbal position, and all three always appear in the same relative order, as listed above, when they occur simultaneously. This approach, relying as it does on universal, innate processes, is sometimes referred to as **bioprogram hypothesis** (Bickerton 1988; Fasold 1990: 202–7).

All three hypotheses have something to recommend them, and currently there is little chance that conclusive evidence can be produced for any one of them. Perhaps factors involved in all three have had some effect on the English pidgins and creoles presently spoken in the world.

14.3.3 English pidgins and creoles

At present English-based pidgins and creoles are spoken in three general areas, the Caribbean, West Africa and the Pacific. Although the social situation of each is in some way different from that of every other, there are three important variations in regard to the political, cultural and linguistic framework which affects them all, and these differences have an important effect on the status and the stability of the pidgins/creoles of each of the regions to be reviewed:

1   The pidgin/creole is spoken in a country in which English is the official language and is in general use. This is the case throughout most of the Caribbean, in Australia and Hawaii.

2   The pidgin/creole is spoken in an officially English speaking country, but one in which there are few native speakers of English. This is the case in most of West Africa and in Papua New Guinea and Vanuatu.

3   The pidgin/creole is in use in a country in which English is neither the official language nor the diglossically available High language. Surinam is an example of this, and the same applies on a smaller scale in parts of West Africa, such as the francophone part of Cameroon.

The Caribbean   No pidgins are present in the Caribbean, but English creoles are spoken throughout the Caribbean basin as well as on the mainland of South America (Surinam and Guyana), in Central America (above all in Belize, but see Holm 1983) and, though not part of the Caribbean, along the Georgia–South Carolina coast in the United States (see 11.5–11.7 and Map 11.3). In most of the Caribbean countries there is a

continuum between the creole and StE. This is a series of more or less closely related forms ranging from the broadest creole (the basilect) at one extreme to StE (the acrolect) at the other. Although broad creole is structurally very different from English, its speakers usually consider themselves to be speakers of English, however 'bad' or 'broken' they may regard their 'patois' as being. Furthermore, English is the public language of government, school and most of the media and is regarded as a means of social advancement. As a result of all this there has been a continuous pull towards the standard, and this has a de-creolizing effect on the creole (see 11.6 on the continuum).

Some people believe that American Black English is a de-creolized form of an earlier Plantation Creole, which was allegedly spoken throughout the American South (see 11.4.3). Gullah, the creole still spoken along the coast and on several of the islands off the coast of South Carolina and Georgia is possibly related to this putative Plantation Creole. Today it is spoken by fewer and fewer people as it gives way to local forms of English. Among the more extensively treated creoles of the Caribbean are Jamaican Creole, Guyana Creole and Belize Creole, all of which are de-creolizing in varying degrees. Some of the anglophone territories in the Caribbean have local basilect forms which have so few creole elements as to be considered more dialects of English than creoles, for example **Bajan**, as the vernacular of Barbados is called.

Only in Surinam is English completely missing as the diglossically High language. As a result there is no continuum and no process of de-creolization there. The major creole of the country, Sranan (earlier known as Taki Taki) is, consequently, only historically related to English and not in the least mutually intelligible with it. As an independent language it is meanwhile developing its own literary tradition.

Even where mutual intelligibility is not given, the English creoles of the Caribbean share numerous linguistic features. For example, all of them have lost the inflections of English, i.e. they do not use the noun plural morpheme {-S}, for example, Sranan *wiki* 'week' or 'weeks'. If the plural is marked (in mesolect varieties), this is done by adding *-dem* < English *them*, e.g. *boddem* 'birds'. This can even lead to a double plural as in Guyanese Creole *di aafisiz-dem*, 'the offices'; *di skuulz-dem*, 'the schools'. Possession is marked by juxtaposition *Mieri gyardan* 'Mary's yard'. There is a partially different set of personal pronouns (Jamaican Creole *yu* 'you (sing.)' and *unu* 'you (plur.)'), often without case distinctions (Jamaican Creole *wi* 'we, us, our').

Likewise, the past tense marker {-D} is typically missing from the basilect, e.g. Sranan *bribi* 'believe' or 'believed'. Yet past may optionally be marked with the pre-verbal particle *ben/bin*, e.g. Sranan *ben de* 'was somewhere, existed' or Guyanese *bin gat* 'had' or Bajan *been walk* (in standard spelling) 'walked'. The particle *ben/bin* is found throughout the Caribbean and, indeed, elsewhere as well (e.g. Nigerian PE *been meet* (standard spelling) 'met'; Australian PE *bin si* 'saw'). In mesolect varieties creole *bin* may be replaced by forms closer to StE such as *had* or *did* in Bajan or *did* or *woz* in Guyanese.

The Caribbean creoles also share the durative aspectual marker *a* or *de/da* + verb, e.g. Belizean Creole *de slip* 'is/was sleeping'. In Belizean this is de-creolized to either absence of the marker *de* in the mesolect or to an inflected form of *be* in the upper mesolect/acrolect. Much the same sort of thing takes place in the other Caribbean creoles as well.

The future and irrealis (conditional) marker *sa* from English *shall* (Sranan, Guyanese Creole, but rare in the latter) or its more general West Indian equivalent *go* or de-creolized *gain* or *gwain*, e.g. *ju gwain fáin óut* 'you will/are going to find out' is a further form common to the Caribbean creoles. Likewise, past perfective or completive *done* (already mentioned) is found in these creoles.

The verb does not have to be marked for tense, although the particle *been* (or *did* or *had*) + verb is available for marking the past and *go* or *gain* + verb are used for the future. However, aspect is always expressed, whether *process* (e.g. *da* or *duz* + verb, sometimes with the ending *-in*), *completive* or *perfective* (e.g., *dun* + verb), or *active* of a dynamic verb or *stative* of a state verb (zero marking). These particles can also be combined in various more complex structures. These examples of verb usage are taken from Bajan, the Barbados basilect (Roy 1986). In addition, the creoles make use of serial verbs, such as *come* or *go*, indicating movement towards or away from the speaker (*carry it come* 'bring it') or instrumental *tek* (*tek whip beat di children dem* 'beat them with a whip') (Roberts 1988: 65). The passive is widely expressed by the intransitive use of a transitive verb (*The sugar use already* 'was used'), but there is also a syntactic passive with the auxiliary *get* (*The child get bite up*) as well as the possibility of impersonal expressions (*Dem kill she* 'She was killed') (ibid.: 74f.).

All of these points make clear the close relationship within this 'family' of creoles. These correspondences have sometimes been strengthened and sometimes weakened by the one factor or the other such as population movement in the Caribbean (see 11.5). The single most important factor affecting almost all of these English creoles is the presence of Standard Caribbean English as the acrolect.

West Africa   The linguistic situation in West Africa is significantly different inasmuch as there is no large native English speaking population in this region. English is, it is true, the official language of Cameroon (with French), Gambia, Ghana, Liberia, Nigeria and Sierra Leone, but it is almost exclusively a second language. One of the chief results of this is that there is no continuum like that found in the Caribbean. Instead, English is the diglossically High language (as are such regional languages as Yoruba, Igbo and Hausa in Nigeria), and West African Pidgin English (WAPE) is diglossically Low (as are the numerous local indigenous languages). There are intermediate varieties of English and, therefore, a continuum of sorts. However, these forms are not like the mesolects of the Caribbean, but are forms of second language English noticeably influenced by the native languages of their various speakers. Note that in West Africa there are relatively few creole speakers and relatively many pidgin users. West African Standard English is in wide use by the more highly educated in the appropriate situations (administration, education, some of the media). WAPE is employed as a lingua franca in inter-ethnic communication in multilingual communities, sometimes for relaxed talk or joking and as a market language, even in the non-anglophone countries of West Africa.

However, because the pidgin has such a great amount of internal variation, some people feel that there is a need for some type of standardization of it. Sometimes the pidgin is a **marginal pidgin** or **jargon**, which is more severely limited in use, vocabulary and syntax; and sometimes, an **extended pidgin**, which has all the linguistic markers of a creole without actually being a mother tongue. Furthermore, creolized (mother tongue) forms of it are in wide use in Sierra Leone, where it is becoming more important than English, and in Liberia, both of which are countries to which slaves were returned – either from America, Canada and the West Indies or from slave ships seized by the British navy – from the late eighteenth century on. Their first language was or became a form of (Creole) English. This accounts for the approximately five per cent of Liberians who are native speakers of English and the two to five per cent of Sierra Leonans who speak Krio, the English-based creole of that country. Today, creolized forms of Pidgin English are continuing to emerge among the children of linguistically mixed marriages in many urban centres, especially in Cameroon and Nigeria.

Linguistically, WAPE has many parallels to the Caribbean creoles, due no doubt to the historical connections between the two areas. Here, too, for example, the past marker is *bin*; the aspect marker is *a* or *da/de/di*. The pronoun system is remarkably like that of the Caribbean creoles as well. Nouns may be followed by *dɛn* to mark the plural in Liberia, but they may also be followed by {-S}. Here, interestingly, the basilect–acrolect dimension is of less importance than semantic considerations since *dɛn* is used most often to mark the plural of nouns designating humans (Singler 1991: 552–6). The pronunciation of WAPE is, however, distinctly African, reflecting the phonology of the first languages of its speakers. Furthermore, we also find in it numerous lexical borrowings from the local vernaculars.

The Pacific The major focus of interest in the Pacific has been on the pidgins and creoles of Melanesia, especially: Tok Pisin in Papua New Guinea; Neo-Solomonic or Solomon Islands Pijin; Bislama of Vanuatu (the New Hebrides); and Australian PE. There is also increasingly more information available about Fiji. Polynesia includes the major case of Hawaii, where Hawaii PE, Hawaiian Creole English and a spectrum of de-creolized varieties are in use.

Fiji and Hawaii are cases in which there is a continuum similar to that of the Caribbean, which means that there is a great deal of de-creolization. This is also the case in Australia wherever contact with speakers of AusE is strong. Solomon Islands Pijin, Bislama and Tok Pisin, on the other hand, are relatively independent pidgins/creoles despite the fact that they co-exist with English as official language. In the following Tok Pisin will be discussed in somewhat more detail.

In Papua New Guinea, Tok Pisin is the most widely used language even though English is the official language. It is 'the linguistically most developed and the socially most established variety' of the Pacific pidgins with between three quarters of a million and a million users among the two million inhabitants of the country; some 20,000 households have it as their first language (Mühlhäusler 1986b: 549). It is 'a complex configuration of lects [= varieties] ranging from unstable pidgin to fully fledged creole varieties' (Mühlhäusler 1984: 441f.). Creolization is relatively rapid both in the towns and in non-traditional rural work settlements. Even the majority of parliamentary business as well as university level teaching is conducted in it as well. It is, in other words, in the process of establishing itself independently of English.

Due to the fact that more and more people are learning English, there is some evidence of an incipient continuum. This is most noticeable in Urban Tok Pisin (or **Tok Pisin bilong taun** 'Tok Pisin of the town') or in Anglicized **Tok Skul**, where mixing and switching between English and Tok Pisin is more frequent and especially where borrowing from English is stronger. One of the results of this is that the mutual comprehensibility of Urban Tok Pisin and **Tok Pisin bilong ples**, or Rural Tok Pisin, is becoming less complete, to say nothing of the more distant **Tok Pisin bilong bus** or Bush Pidgin used as a contact language and lingua franca in remoter areas.

Tok Pisin ultimately derives much of its vocabulary from English, but there is also evidence of borrowing from other sources, both Melanesian (e.g. Tolai *tultul* 'messenger,

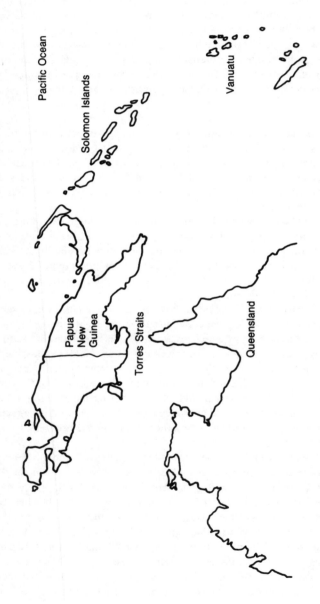

Map 14.6 The Pacific Region

assistant village chief') and European (e.g. *sutman* from German *Schutzmann* 'police-man'); however, the major source of new vocabulary lies within the language itself. In this way *vot*, which is both a noun 'election' and a verb 'vote' is semantically transparent; see also *hevi* (adj.) 'heavy' and *hevi* (n.) 'weight'. In urban varieties numerous loan words from StE are replacing Tok Pisin vocabulary and dispensing with native Tok Pisin means of word formation. Under the influence of English the nouns *ileksen* and *wait* have been introduced. Much the same thing applies when *smokbalus* 'jet' from *smok* 'smoke' and *balus* 'bird, airplane' gives way to *setplen* 'jet plane'. This process of approximation to English is sometimes referred to as **metropolitanization**.

As the forms of words borrowed into Tok Pisin from English reveal, the phonologies of the two languages differ considerably. This is most dramatically illustrated by the convergence of English /s, ʃ, tʃ, dʒ/ as Tok Pisin /s/, which together with the lack of a Tok Pisin /iː/–/ɪ/ distinction and the devoicing of final obstruents renders *ship, jib, jeep, sieve* and *chief* homophonous as Tok Pisin *sip*. Likewise, since /b/, /p/ and /f/ are not distinguished Tok Pisin *pis* may be equivalent to English *beach, beads, fish, peach, piss, feast* or *peace*. Here, of course, borrowing might profitably be employed to reduce the number of words which are pronounced identically. Too much homophony can lead to misunderstandings as when a member of the House of Assembly said: *les long toktok long sit nating*, meaning 'tired of talking to empty seats (sit nating)' but was mistrans-lated as saying 'tired of talking to a bunch of shits' (Mühlhäusler 1986b: 561).

The grammar of Tok Pisin has re-expanded, as is typical of elaborated and, especially, creolized pidgins:

Verbs

i	before predicates (except first and second person singular) (example: see next);
-im	marker of transitive verbs (from English *him*) (*samting i bin katim tripela hap* 'something divided it into three pieces');
i gat	existential *there is/are* (*i gat tripela naispela ailan* 'there are three nice islands');
i stap	progressive-existential marker:
	– *trak i stap long rot* 'The truck is on the road'
	– *mi stap we?* 'where am I?'
	– *mi stap gut* 'I am well'
	– *mi dring i stap* 'I am drinking';
pinis	completive or perfective aspect (after the predicate) (from English *finish*);
bin	past marker (pre-verbal) (*samting i bin katim* 'something divided it');
bai(mbai)	future marker (pre-clausal) *bai mipela i save* 'we will know';
save	modal of ability (*mi save rait* 'I can write');
laik	immediate future marker (*trak i laik go nau* 'the truck is about to leave');
laik	'want to' *em i laik i go long trak* 'he wants to ride on the truck'.

Adjectives

-pela	marker of attributive adjectives; only added to monosyllabic ones (*naispela* 'nice');
∅	no adjective marker = adverb (*gut* 'well');

móa   comparative marker (*liklik móa* 'smaller', *gutpela móa* 'better');
long ol superlative marker (*liklik long ol* 'smallest').

Nouns

ol   plural marker (*ol sip* 'the ships');
wanpela   singular article (*wanpela lain* 'a line').

Personal pronouns

Table 14.3   The personal pronouns of Tok Pisin

	singular	*plural*	
		exclusive	*inclusive*
first person	mi	mipela	yumi
second person	yu	yúpela	
third person	em	ol	

Conjunctions

na   and   *o*   or
tasól but, if only *sapós*   if

The following excerpt from the story, 'A Demon Made Three Islands', offers a useful illustration of some of the features just listed. Its narrator is Selseme Martina from Ais Island, West New Britain Province; the story was modified by Thomas H. Slone (ed.) in the collection *One Thousand One Papua New Guinean Nights* (*Wan Tausen Wan Nait bilong Papua New Guinea*, 1996).

Text

Long [p]asis bilong Kandrian long Wes Nu

Briten [Provins] i gat tripela naispela ailan

i sanap long wanpela lain tasol [Moewehafen

Pipel]. Tripela i wanmak na antap bilong

wan wan i stret olsem ples balus. I luk olsem

bipo ol i wanpela tasol, na wanpela samting

i bin katim tripela hap.

Glossary

bilong generalized genitive, ablative, dative 'of, from, for'
long generalized locative 'at, in, on, with, to, until etc.'
i sanap they stand
tasol also, however
tripela the three
wanmak the same
wan wan each, several
ples balus (place bird) airfield
olsem like
bipo before, once, used to
hap half/halves, part(s)

By the shores of Kandrian in West New Britain [Province], there are three nice islands that stand in a row [Moewehafen People]. The three islands are the same size. Each is flat on top like an airfield. Before, they did not look like this. There was just one island and something divided it into three pieces.

Na tru tumas, ol lapun i stori olsem. Wanpela

bikman bilong ples ol i kolim Ais [Ailan]

i sindaun stori long *Wantok* ripota [wokman

bilong niuspepa] i raun long dispela hap. Na

wanpela lapun meri tu i sindaun long dua bilong

haus bilong em long nambis na i stori tu. Nem
bilong lapun mama ya, em Selsema Martina.

tumas too much, very
lapun old
olsem this way
bikman leader
ples ol i kolim place that
   they call
stori long tell
wokman worker
raun about
meri woman
nambis coast, beach
ya here (= this)

This is the very truth. The old people tell the story like this. A leader from a place
called **Ais** [Island] sat down and told the story to a *Wantok* newspaper reporter [who
was around] this place. An old woman sat at the door of her house by the beach and
told it too. The name of this woman is Selseme Martina.

In Papua New Guinea as in other countries in which there is widespread use of a
pidgin/creole speakers seem to be in a permanent dilemma as to its status. The local
pidgin/creole is often not regarded as good enough for many communicative functions
and is rejected in education in favour of a highly prestigious international language such
as English. On the other hand, some people argue that such pidgins/creoles should be
espoused and developed because of their contributions to the internal integration of the
country and possible favourable effects on literacy if used in the schools. Pidgins and
creoles are certainly emotionally closer to local culture than StE. In most of the countries
reviewed in this section, there will probably be continued de-creolization. A few creoles
may stay on an independent course; most likely Sranan will, and possibly Tok Pisin,
Solomons Pijin and Bislama. Some will eventually disappear entirely: Gullah seems to
be going that way. And in many cases the status quo will surely be maintained much as
it is for an indefinite period in the future.

14.4 FURTHER READING

Ammon, Dittmar and Mattheier 1988 are a useful source on language use throughout the
world. For further details on **WAfrE** see: Angogo and Hancock 1980; Bamgbose 1983;
Todd 1984; for grammar: Tingley 1981; for vocabulary: especially Pemagbi 1989; for
pragmatics: Bamgbose 1983. On **EAfrE**: Abdulaziz 1988 gives a less Euro-centric view
than most authors; on interference from local languages see Schmied 1991; see Schmied's
website http://www.und.ac.za/und/ling/archive/schm-01.html.

IndE   Agnihotri and Khanna 1997 deal with the role of English. On pronunciation: Wells
1982; Sahgal and Agnihotri 1985; on grammar Verma 1982; on vocabulary: Nihalani
1989; Lewis 1992; Yule 1995. See also de Souza 1997. A useful, readable and comprehensive website on IndE (but without linguistic details) is http://www.thecore.nus.edu.
sg/landow/post/india/hohenthal/8.1.html.

SingE   See: Tongue 1974; Platt and Weber 1980 (vocabulary); Tongue 1974; Tay 1982; 1993; Platt 1984; 1991 (grammar); Platt and Weber 1980 (pronunciation). Ho 1993 looks at the language continuum and substratum influences.

Philippine English   Pronunciation is presented in Bautistia 1988 and Llamzon 1969 (also vocabulary).

Pidgin and creoles   Useful introductions are: Hall 1966; Hymes 1971a; Todd 1984; Mühlhäusler 1986a; Holm 1988, 1989; Fasold 1990; Singh 2000. On origins see Muysken 1988 for an annotated list of nine different theories. For extensive details on the language history of the Caribbean area, see Holm 1985. **Jamaican Creole** is treated in Cassidy 1961; **Guyana Creole** in Rickford 1987; **Belize Creole** in Dayley 1979. For a **comparison** between various pidgins and creoles see Taylor 1971 and Alleyne 1980. Linguistic and social details on individual varieties of WAPE are recounted in Barbag-Stoll 1983 for **Nigerian PE**; in Todd 1982 for **Cameroon PE**; Jones 1971 for **Krio**. The *Journal of Pidgin and Creole Languages* (*JPCL*) has its website at http://www.ling.ohio-state. edu/research/jpcl/; for *The Carrier Pidgin*, a newsletter see http://www.fiu.edu/~linguist/ carrier.htm. The *Creolist Archives* (formerly at http://creole.ling.su.se/creole/ is no longer available; see archived material at http://creole.ling.su.se/creole/creolist/Postings. html and http://listserv.linguistlist.org/archives/creolist.html and a re-start at http://groups. yahoo.com/group/CreoLIST/. The *Language Varieties Network* at http://www.une.edu.au/ langnet/ also deals with pidgins and creoles.

Bibliography of dictionaries

Note: 'CD-ROM' and 'Internet' after a title means that the work is also available on CD-ROM and on the Internet. Dictionaries are ordered chronologically, giving the most recent first, except for Section I.1, which is ordered by region.

I NATIVE-SPEAKER DICTIONARIES

1 National dictionaries on historical principles

The Shorter Oxford English Dictionary (2002), 5th edn, edited by W. Trumble and L. Brown, Oxford: OUP (CD-ROM).

The Oxford English Dictionary Online (2000ff.), 3rd edn, edited by J.A. Simpson, Oxford: OUP http://www.oed.com.

The Oxford English Dictionary (1989), 2nd edn, edited by J. Simpson and E. Weiner, Oxford: OUP (CD-ROM).

The English Dialect Dictionary (1898–1905), edited by J. Wright, 6 vols, London: Frowde.

Dictionary of American Regional English, edited by F.C. Cassidy, vol. 1 (1985), vol. 2 (1991), vol. 3 (1996), vol. 4 (2002), Cambridge, Mass.: Belknap Press of Harvard University Press.

A Dictionary of Americanisms on Historical Principles (1951), edited by M.M. Mathews, 2 vols, Chicago, Ill.: Chicago University Press.

A Dictionary of American English on Historical Principles (1936–44), edited by W.A. Craigie and J.R. Hulbert, 4 vols, London: OUP.

A Dictionary of the Older Scottish Tongue (1937–2002), edited by W.A. Craigie, J. Aitken and M.G. Dareau, Chicago: Chicago University Press; Aberdeen: Aberdeen University Press; and Oxford: OUP.

The Scottish National Dictionary (1931–76), edited by W.W. Grant and D.D. Murison, Edinburgh: The Scottish National Dictionary Association.

The Gage Canadian Dictionary (1973), edited by W.S. Avis, P.D. Drysdale, R.J. Gregg and M.H. Scargill, Toronto: Gage.

A Dictionary of Canadianisms on Historical Principles (1967), edited by W.S. Avis, Toronto: Gage.

Dictionary of South African English on Historical Principles (1996), edited by P. Silva, Oxford: OUP.

The Australian National Dictionary (1988), edited by W.S. Ramson, Melbourne: OUP.

Dictionary of New Zealand English (1997), edited by H. Orsman, Auckland: OUP.

Dictionary of Jamaican English (1980), 2nd edn, edited by F.G. Cassidy and R.B. LePage, Cambridge: CUP.

2 Comprehensive, unabridged dictionaries

The Random House Webster's Unabridged Dictionary (1999), 3rd edn, edited by S. Steinmetz, New York: Random House (CD-ROM).

World Book Dictionary (1992), edited by C.L. and R.K. Barnhart, 2 vols, Chicago: World Book.

Webster's Third New International Dictionary (1961; reprinted 2000), edited by P. Gove, Springfield, Mass.: Merriam Webster (CD-ROM, Internet).

A Standard Dictionary of the English Language (1893), by I.K. Funk, New York. Later editions published (1977) as *Funk & Wagnall's Standard Desk Dictionary*, 2 vols, New York.

3 Dictionaries of new words

Oxford Dictionary of New Words (1998), 2nd edn, edited by Elizabeth Knowles and Julia Elliott, Oxford: OUP.

Oxford English Dictionary Additions Series, (vols 1 and 2, 1993; vol. 3, 1997), edited by J.A. Simpson, Oxford: OUP.

Fifty Years Among the New Words. A Dictionary of Neologisms 1941–1991 (1991), edited by J. Algeo, Cambridge: CUP.

Third Barnhart Dictionary of New English (1990), edited by R.K. Barnhart, Sol Steinmetz with C.L. Barnhart, New York: Wilson.

Oxford English Dictionary Supplement (1972–1987), 4 vols, edited by R.W. Burchfield, Oxford: OUP.

12,000 Words: A Supplement to Webster's Third New International Dictionary (1986), edited by F.C. Mish, Springfield, Mass.: Merriam Webster.

9,000 Words: A Supplement to Webster's Third New International Dictionary (1983), Springfield, Mass.: Merriam-Webster.

The Second Barnhart Dictionary of New English (1980), edited by C.L. Barnhart, S. Steinmetz and R.K. Barnhart, Bronxville: Barnhart/Harper & Row.

6,000 Words: A Supplement to Webster's Third New International Dictionary (1976), Springfield, Mass.: G. & C. Merriam.

The Barnhart Dictionary of New English since 1963 (1973), edited by C.L. Barnhart, S. Steinmetz and R.K. Barnhart, Bronxville: Barnhart/Harper & Row.

4 Desk, college dictionaries

a) From publishers in the UK

Collins English Dictionary (2003), 6th edn, Glasgow: HarperCollins.

The New Penguin Dictionary of English (2000), edited by R. Allen, Harmondsworth: Penguin.

Chambers Science and Technology Dictionary (1999), edited by P.M.B. Walker, London: Chambers.

Chambers 21st Century Dictionary (1999, updated edn), edited by M. Robinson, London: Chambers.

The Concise Oxford Dictionary (1999), 10th edn, edited by J. Pearsall, Oxford: OUP.

The Chambers Dictionary (1998), edited by E. Higgleton, Edinburgh: Chambers.

The New Oxford Dictionary of English (1998), edited by J. Pearsall, Oxford: OUP.

The Concise Scots Dictionary (1996), edited by M. Robinson, Edinburgh: Chambers.

The Concise Ulster Dictionary (1996), edited by C.I. Macafee, Oxford: OUP.

Larousse Dictionary of Science and Technology (1995), edited by P.M.B. Walker, New York: Larousse.

The Longman Dictionary of Scientific Usage (1988), edited by A. Godman and E.M.F. Payne, London: Longman.

b) From publishers in the USA

Merriam-Webster's Collegiate Dictionary (2003), 11th edn, Springfield, Mass.: Merriam-Webster (CD-ROM).

The New Oxford American Dictionary (2002), edited by F.R. Abate, New York: OUP.

The Random House Webster's College Dictionary (2001), 2nd edn, edited by R.B. Costello, New York: Random House.

Webster's New World College Dictionary (2001), 4th edn, edited by Michael Agnes, Boston: Wiley.

The American Heritage Dictionary of the English Language (2000), 4th edn, edited by J.P. Pickert, Boston, Mass.: Houghton Mifflin (Internet).

The Encarta World English Dictionary (1999), edited by K. Rooney, London: Bloomsbury (CD-ROM; Internet).

Flexner, S.B. (1982), *Listening to America. An Illustrated History of Words and Phrases From Our Lively and Splendid Past*, New York: Simon and Schuster (arranged according to subject matter).

c) Other dictionaries

The Australian Oxford Dictionary (1999), edited by B. Moore, Melbourne: OUP.

The Canadian Oxford English Dictionary (1998), edited by K. Barber, Toronto: OUP.

Gage Canadian Dictionary (1997), revised and expanded, Toronto: Gage Educational.

The Macquarie Dictionary (1997), 3rd edn, edited by A. Delbridge *et al.* Sydney: The Macquarie Library, Macquarie University.

The New Zealand Dictionary (1995), 2nd edn, edited by E. and H.W. Orsman, Auckland: New House.

A Dictionary of South African English (1991), 4th edn, edited by J. Branford, Cape Town: OUP.

A Dictionary of Australian Colloquialisms (1990), edited by G.A. Wilkes, South Melbourne: Sydney University Press.

The New Zealand Pocket Oxford Dictionary (1990), edited by R. Burchfield, Auckland: OUP.

Heinemann New Zealand Dictionary (1989), 2nd edn, edited by H.W. Orsman and C.C. Ransom, Auckland: Heinemann.

The Australian Concise Oxford Dictionary of Current English (1987), 7th edn, edited by G.W. Turner, Melbourne: OUP.

The Dictionary of Newfoundland English (1982; with supplement 1990), 2nd edn, edited by G.M. Story, W.J. Kirwin and J.D.A. Widdowson, Toronto: Toronto University Press.

Hawkins, P.A. (1986) Supplement of Indian Words in J. Swannell (ed.), *The Little Oxford Dictionary*, 6th edn, Oxford: OUP.

5 Thesauruses

Bloomsbury Thesaurus (1997), edited by F. Alexander, London: Bloomsbury.

Webster's New World Thesaurus (1997), 3rd edn, edited by C.G. Laird, New York: Macmillan.

Bartlett's Roget's Thesaurus (1996), edited by E.W. Pitha, Boston: Little, Brown.
The Oxford Dictionary and Thesaurus (1996), American edn, edited by F.R. Abate, New York: OUP.
The Cambridge Thesaurus of American English (1994), edited by W. Lutz, Cambridge: CUP.
Roget's 21st Century Thesaurus in Dictionary Form (1993), edited by B.A. Kipfer, London: Hale.
The Scots Thesaurus (1990), edited by I. Macleod, Aberdeen: Aberdeen University Press.
Longman Lexicon of Contemporary English (1981), edited by T. McArthur, London: Longman.

McCutcheon, M. (2000), *Descriptionary*, 2nd edn, New York: Facts on File.
Glazier, S. *Word Menu* (1997), 2nd edn, New York: Random House.

6 Usage guides and dictionaries

The New Fowler's Modern English Usage (2000), 3rd edn, edited by R.W. Burchfield, Oxford: OUP.
Longman Dictionary of Common Errors (1999), 2nd edn, edited by N.D. Turton and J.B. Heaton, Harlow: Longman (for foreign learners).
A Dictionary of Modern American Usage (1998), edited by B.A. Garner, New York: OUP.
Modern American Usage: A Guide (1998), 2nd edn, edited by W. Follett, revised by E. Wensberg, New York: Hill & Wang.
Australian Writers' Dictionary (1997), new edn, edited by S. Purchase, Melbourne: OUP.
Guide to Canadian English Usage (1997), edited by M. Fee and J. McAlpine, Toronto: OUP.
The King's English: A Guide to Modern Usage (1997), edited by K. Amis, London: HarperCollins.
US News & World Report Stylebook: A Usage Guide for Writers and Editors (1997), 8th edn, edited by R.O. Grover, Washington, DC: US News & World Report.
The American Heritage Book of English Usage (1996), Boston: Houghton Mifflin.
The Cambridge Australian English Style Guide (1995), edited by P. Peters and G. Grayston, Cambridge: CUP.
Practical English Usage (1995), 2nd edn, edited by Michael Swan, Oxford: OUP (for foreign learners).
Bloomsbury Guide to Better Usage (1994), edited by M.H. Manser, London: Bloomsbury.
The Columbia Guide to Standard American English (1993), edited by K.G. Wilson, New York: Columbia University Press.
Modern Australian Usage (1993), edited by N. Hudson, Melbourne: OUP.
Webster's Dictionary of English Usage (1989), edited by E.W. Gilman, Springfield, Mass.: Merriam-Webster.

II NON-NATIVE SPEAKER DICTIONARIES

7 General dictionaries

Longman Dictionary of Contemporary English (2003), 5th edn, edited by D. Summers, Harlow: Longman (CD-ROM).
Collins COBUILD English Dictionary (2001), 3rd edn, edited by J. Sinclair, London: HarperCollins (CD-ROM, Internet).
Oxford Advanced Learner's Dictionary (2000), 6th edn, edited by S. Wehmeier; Oxford: OUP (CD-ROM, Internet).

Thorndike-Barnhart Student Dictionary (1998), edited by E.L. Thorndike and C. Barnhart, New York: Prentice Hall.

Longman Dictionary of American English (1997), 2nd edn, edited by D. Summers and A. Gadsby, White Plains, NY: Addison Wesley Longman.

Cambridge International Dictionary of English (1995), edited by P. Proctor, Cambridge: CUP (Internet); the second edition has been published as *Cambridge Advanced Learner's Dictionary* (2003), Cambridge: CUP (CD-ROM).

Longman Language Activator (1993), edited by D. Summers. Harlow: Longman (a mixture of the alphabetic and the thesaurus type; the first and only production dictionary on the market).

8 Dictionaries of word combinations

Oxford Collocations (2002), edited by J. Crowther, Oxford: OUP.

The LTP Dictionary of Selected Collocations (1999), 2nd edn, edited by J. Hill and M. Lewis, Hove: LTP.

The BBI Dictionary of English Word Combinations (1997), revised edn, edited by M. Benson, E. Benson and R. Ilson, Amsterdam, Penn.: Benjamins.

9 Dictionaries of phrasal verbs

Oxford Phrasal Verbs Dictionary for Learners of English (2001), Oxford: OUP.

Longman Phrasal Verbs Dictionary (2000), edited by A. Taylor, Harlow: Longman.

NTC's Dictionary of Phrasal Verbs and Other Idiomatic Verbal Phrases (2000), edited by R.A. Spears, Lincolnwood, Ill.: NTC.

The Cambridge International Dictionary of Phrasal Verbs (1997), Cambridge: CUP.

Oxford Dictionary of Phrasal Verbs (1993), edited by A.P. Cowie and R. Mackin, Oxford: OUP.

Collins COBUILD Dictionary of Phrasal Verbs (1991), edited by R. Moon, London: Athelstan.

10 Cultural dictionaries

Brewer's Dictionary of Modern Phrase and Fable (2000), edited by Adrian Room, London: Cassell.

Brewer's Dictionary of Phrase and Fable (2000), 16th edn edited by A. Room and T. Pratchett, London: HarperCollins.

Longman Dictionary of Language and Culture (2000), 2nd edn, edited by D. Summers, Harlow: Addison Wesley Longman.

The Oxford Dictionary of Phrase and Fable (2000), edited by E. Knowles, Oxford: OUP.

The Dictionary of Global Culture (1999), edited by A. Appiah *et al.*, London: Penguin.

Oxford Guide to British and American Culture for Learners of English (1999), edited by J. Crowther, Oxford: OUP (CD-ROM).

NTC's American English Learner's Dictionary: The Essential Vocabulary of American Language and Culture (1998), edited by R.A. Spears, Lincolnwood, Ill.: NTC.

And Now for Something Completely Different: Dictionary of Allusions in British English (1997), edited by R. Sampson and C. Smith, München: Hueber.

The Oxford Dictionary of Phrase, Saying and Quotation (1997), edited by E. Knowles, Oxford: OUP.

NTC's Dictionary of the United Kingdom (1996), edited by E. James, Lincolnwood, Ill.: NTC.
Encyclopedia of Britain (1994), edited by B. Gascoigne, London: Macmillan.
The Dictionary of Cultural Literacy (1993), 2nd edn, edited by J.F. Kett *et al*. Boston: Houghton
    Mifflin.
British English for American Readers (1992), edited by D. Grote, Westport, Conn.: Greenwood.

11 Some Internet sites for references and links to dictionaries

http://www.bartleby.com
www:yourdictionary.com
www.1000Dictionaries.com
www.elearnaid.com
math-www.uni-paderborn.de/HTML/Dictionaries.html

General bibliography

TOPICAL BIBLIOGRAPHY OF WEBSITES GIVEN IN THE FURTHER READING

African American Vernacular English, portal to: http://www.arches.uga.edu/~bryan/AAVE/.
American Dialect Society, link to: http://www.americandialect.org/.
Black English Vernacular, portal to: http://www.arches.uga.edu/~bryan/AAVE/.
British Black English, link to: http://www.ling.lancs.ac.uk/staff/mark/cwbc/cwbcman.htm [Sebba's *Corpus of Written British Creole*].
Dictionary of American Regional English (DARE), links to: http://us.english.uga.edu/ and http://polyglot.lss.wisc.edu/dare/dare.html.
English in Africa [1995], link to: http://www.und.ac.za/und/ling/archive/schm-01.html.
English creoles and pidgins, links to: www.fiu.edu/~linguist/carrier.htm *The Carrier Pidgin*; http://www.ling.ohio-state.edu/research/jpcl/ *Journal of Pidgin and Creole Languages*; http://creole.ling.su.se/creole/creolist/Postings.html (archived material); and http://listserv.linguistlist.org/archives/creolist.html (archived material) http://groups.yahoo.com/group/CreoLIST/ (a re-start); http://www.une.edu.au/langnet/ *Language Varieties Network*.
English in India, links to: http://www.thecore.nus.edu.sg/landow/post/india/hohenthal/8.1.html and http://www.ling.upenn.edu/ jason2/papers/natlang.htm.
English in Singapore, link to: http://www.uni.edu.au/langnet/singlish.htm (A.F. Gupta)
Jamaican Creole, links to: http://www-user.tu-chemnitz.de/~wobo/jamaika.html and http://www.jamaicans.com/speakja/glossary.htm.
Language Varieties Network, link to: http://www.une.edu.au/langnet/.
Phonological Atlas of North America, link to: http://www.ling.upenn.edu/phono_atlas/home.html.

BIBLIOGRAPHY BY AUTHOR/EDITOR

Abdulaziz, M.H. (1972) 'Triglossia and Swahili-English Bilingualism in Tanzania', *Language in Society* 1: 197–213.
—— (1988) '150. A Sociolinguistic Profile of East Africa', in U. Ammon, N. Dittmar and K.J. Mattheier (eds), *Sociolinguistics Soziolinguistik*, Berlin: Walter de Gruyter, pp. 1347–53.
—— (1991) 'East Africa (Tanzania and Kenya)', in J. Cheshire (ed.), *English Around the World. Sociolinguistic Perspectives*, Cambridge: CUP, pp. 391–401.

Abrahams, R.D. (1970) *Deep Down in the Jungle: Negro Narrative Folklore from the Streets of Philadelphia*, Chicago: Aldine.

Addington, D.W. (1968) 'The Relationship of Selected Vocal Characteristics to Personality Perception', *Speech Monographs* 35: 492–503.

Adetugbo, A. (1979) 'Appropriateness and Nigerian English', in E. Ubahakwe (ed.), *Varieties and Functions of English in Nigeria*, Ibadan: African Universities Press, pp. 137–66.

Agnihotri, R.K. and A.L. Khanna (1997) *Problematizing English in India*, New Delhi: Sage.

Aitchison, J. (2002) *Words in the Mind, An Introduction to the Mental Lexicon*, 3rd edn, Oxford: Blackwell.

Aitken, A.J. (ed.) (1979) *Languages of Scotland*, Edinburgh: Chambers.

—— (1984) 'Scottish Accents and Dialects', in P. Trudgill (ed.), *Language in the British Isles*, Cambridge: CUP, pp. 94–114.

—— (1985) 'Is Scots a Language?', *English Today* 3: 41–5.

Akere, F. (1982) 'Sociocultural Constraints and the Emergence of a Standard Nigerian English', in J.B. Pride (ed.), *New Englishes*, Rowley, Mass.: Newbury House, pp. 85–99.

Akinnaso, F.N. (1985) 'On the Similarities between Spoken and Written Language', *Language and Speech* 28: 323–59.

Alexander, L.G. (1988) *Longman English Grammar*, London: Longman.

Alexander, R. (1978/9) 'Fixed Expressions in English: a Linguistic, Psycholinguistic, Sociolinguistic and Didactic Study', *Anglistik und englischunterricht* 6: 171–88; 7: 181–202.

—— (1987) 'Problems in Understanding and Teaching Idiomaticity in English', *Anglistik und englischunterricht* 32: 105–22.

Algeo, J. (1978) 'The Taxonomy of Word Making', *Word* 29: 122–31.

—— (ed.) (1991) *Fifty Years Among the New Words*, Cambridge: CUP.

—— (1998), 'Vocabulary', in S. Romaine (ed.), *1776–1997*, vol. 4, *The Cambridge History of the English Language*, Cambridge: CUP, pp. 57–91.

—— (2001a), 'External history', in J. Algeo (ed.), *English in North America*, vol. 6, *The Cambridge History of English*, Cambridge: CUP, pp. 1–58.

—— (ed.) (2001b) *English in North America*, vol. 6, *The Cambridge History of English*, Cambridge: CUP.

Allen, H.B. and M.D. Linn (eds) (1986) *Dialect and Language Variation*, Orlando: Academic.

Alleyne, M.C. (1980) *Comparative Afro-American: An Historical-Comparative Study of Some Afro-American Dialects in the New World*, Ann Arbor, Mich.: Karoma.

American Speech 62 (1987) 'Are Black and White Vernaculars Diverging?' [various contributors]: 3–80.

Ammon, U., N. Dittmar and K.J. Mattheier (eds) (1988) *Sociolinguistics Soziolinguistik*, Berlin: Walter de Gruyter.

Angogo, R. and I. Hancock (1980) 'English in Africa: Emerging Standards or Diverging Regionalisms', *English World-Wide* 1: 67–96.

Arthur, B., D. Farrar and G. Bradford (1974) 'Evaluation Reactions of College Students to Dialect Differences in the English of Mexican-Americans', *Language and Speech* 17: 255–70.

Arthur, J.M. (1997) *Aboriginal English*, Melbourne: OUP.

Augustin, J. (1982) 'Regional Standards of English in Peninsular Malaysia', in J.B. Pride (ed.), *New Englishes*, Rowley, Mass.: Newbury House, pp. 249–58.

Austin, J.L. (1962) *How to Do Things With Words*, Oxford: OUP.

Ayto, J. (1999) *Twentieth Century Words*, Oxford: OUP.

Bach, K. and R.M. Harnish (1979) *Linguistic Communication and Speech Acts*, Cambridge, Mass.: MIT.

Bailey, G. and M. Bassett (1986) 'Invariant *Be* in the Lower South', in M.B. Montgomery and G. Bailey (eds), *Language Variety in the South*, Tuscaloosa, Ala.: University of Alabama Press, pp. 158–79.

—— and Erik, T. (1998) 'Some Aspects of African-American Vernacular English Phonology' in S.S. Mufwene, J.R. Rickford, G. Bailey and J. Baugh (eds), *African-American English*, London: Routledge, pp. 85–109.

—— and Thomas, E. (1998) 'Some Aspects of African-American Vernacular English Phonology', in S.S. Mufwene, J.R. Rickford, G. Bailey and J. Baugh (eds), *African-American English*, London: Routledge, pp. 85–109.

Bailey, R.W. (1984) 'The English Language in Canada', in R.W. Bailey and M. Görlach (eds), *English as a World Language*, Cambridge: CUP, pp. 134–76.

—— (1990) 'English at Its Twilight', in L. Michaels and C. Ricks (eds), *The State of the Language*, 2nd edn, Berkeley, Calif.: University of California Press, pp. 83–94.

—— (2001), 'American English Abroad', in J. Algeo (ed.), *English in North America*, vol. 6, *The Cambridge History of English*, Cambridge: CUP, pp. 456–96.

—— and M. Görlach (eds) (1984) *English as a World Language*, Cambridge: CUP.

Baker, C.L. (1995) *English Syntax*, 2nd edn, Cambridge, Mass.: MIT.

Baker, S.J. (1945, 1966) *The Australian Language*, 1st and 2nd edns, Sydney: Currawong.

Baldridge, J. (1996) 'Reconciling Linguistic Diversity: The History and the Future of Language Policy in India', http://www.ling.upenn.edu/jason2/papers/natlang.htm [August 1998].

Ball, P., C. Gallois and V. Callan (1989) 'Language Attitudes: A Perspective from Social Psychology', in P. Collins and D. Blair (eds), *Australian English: The Language of a New Society*, St Lucia: University of Queensland Press, pp. 89–102.

Bamgbose, A. (1971) 'The English Language in Nigeria', in J. Spencer (ed.), *The English Language in West Africa*, London: Longman, pp. 35–48.

—— (1983) 'Standard Nigerian English: Issues of Identification', in B.B. Kachru (ed.), *The Other Tongue. English Across Cultures*, Oxford: Pergamon, pp. 99–111.

Barbag-Stoll, A. (1983) *Social and Linguistic History of Nigerian Pidgin English*, Tübingen: Stauffenberg.

Barltrop, R. and J. Wolveridge (1980) *The Muvver Tongue*, London: Journeyman.

Barry, M.V. (1984) 'The English Language in Ireland', in R.W. Bailey and M. Görlach (eds), *English as a World Language*, Cambridge: CUP, pp. 84–133.

Bartsch-Parker, E., S. Burgen, R. Crowe, R.O. Maolalaigh and D. Watt (1999) *British Phrasebook*, Hawthorn, Vic.: Lonely Planet.

Bauer, L. (1989) 'The *have* in New Zealand English', *English World-Wide* 10: 69–83.

—— (1992) *Introducing Linguistic Morphology*, 2nd edn, Edinburgh: Edinburgh University Press.

—— (1994) 'English in New Zealand', in R. Burchfield (ed.), *English in Britain and Overseas: Origins and Development*, in *The Cambridge History of the English Language*, vol. 5, Cambridge: CUP, pp. 382–429.

Baugh, A.C. and T. Cable (2002) *A History of the English Language*, 5th edn, London: Routledge.

Bautista, M.L.S. (1988) 'Domains of English in the 21st Century', in A. Gonzales (ed.), *The Role of English and Its Maintenance in the Philippines*, Manila: Solidaridad, pp. 71–7.

Bayard, D. (1990) '"God Help Us If We All Sound Like This": Attitudes in New Zealand and Other English Accents', in A. Bell and J. Holmes (eds), *New Zealand Ways of Speaking English*, Clevedon: Multilingual Matters, pp. 67–96.

—— (1991) 'Social Constraints on the Phonology of New Zealand English', in J. Cheshire (ed.), *English Around the World. Sociolinguistic Perspectives*, Cambridge: CUP, pp. 169–86.

Beattie, G.W. (1981) 'Interruption in Conversational Interaction, and its Relation to the Sex and Status of the Interactants', *Linguistics* 19: 15–35.

de Beaugrande, R. and W. Dressler (1981) *Introduction to Text Linguistics*, London: Longman.

Beier, R. (1980) *Englische Fachsprache*, Stuttgart: Kohlhammer.

Bell, A. (ed.) (1999) *New Zealand English*, Amsterdam: Benjamins.

—— and J. Holmes (eds) (1990) *New Zealand Ways of Speaking English*, Clevedon: Multilingual Matters.

Benson, M., E. Benson and R. Ilson (1986) *Lexicographic Description of English*, Amsterdam, Penn.: Benjamins.

Benton, R.A. (1991) 'Maori English: A New Zealand Myth?', in J. Cheshire (ed.), *English Around the World. Sociolinguistic Perspectives*, Cambridge: CUP, pp. 187–99.

Berk, L.M. (1999) *English Syntax. From Word to Discourse*, New York: OUP.

Bertz, S. (1975) 'Der Dubliner Stadtdialekt', Freiburg: dissertation.

Bhatia, V.K. (1993) *Analyzing Genre*, London: Longman.

Biber, D. (1988) *Variation Across Speech and Writing*, Cambridge: CUP.

—— S. Johansson, G. Leech, S. Conrad and E. Finegan (1999) *Longman Grammar of Spoken and Written English*, Harlow: Longman.

Bickerton, D. (1988) 'Creole Languages and the Bioprogram', in F.J. Newmeyer (ed.), *Linguistics: The Cambridge Survey*, vol. II, *Linguistic Theory: Extensions and Implications*, Cambridge: CUP, pp. 268–84.

Bliss, A. (1984) 'English in the South of Ireland', in P. Trudgill (ed.), *Language in the British Isles*, Cambridge: CUP, pp. 135–51.

Blundell, J., J. Higgens and N. Middlemiss (1982) *Function in English*, Oxford: OUP.

Bodine, A. (1975) 'Androcentrism in Prescriptive Grammar: Singular "they", Sex-indefinite "he" and "he or she"', *Language in Society* 4: 129–46.

Bolinger, D. (1971) *The Phrasal Verb in English*, Cambridge, Mass.: Harvard University Press.

Bradley, D. (1989) 'Regional Dialects in Australian English Phonology', in P. Collins and D. Blair (eds), *Australian English: The Language of a New Society*, St Lucia: University of Queensland Press, pp. 260–70.

—— (1991) '/æ/ and /aː/ in Australian English', in J. Cheshire (ed.), *English Around the World: Sociolinguistic Perspectives*, Cambridge: CUP, pp. 227–34.

Branford, J. (1978, 1991) *A Dictionary of South African English*, 1st and 4th edns, Cape Town, Oxford: OUP.

Branford, W. (1994) 'English in South Africa', in R. Burchfield (ed.), *English in Britain and Overseas: Origins and Development*, in *The Cambridge History of the English Language*, vol. 5, Cambridge: CUP, pp. 430–96.

Brann, C.M.B. (1988) '159. West Africa', in U. Ammon, N. Dittmar and K.J. Mattheier (eds), *Sociolinguistics Soziolinguistik*, Berlin: Walter de Gruyter, pp. 1414–29.

Braun, F. (1988) *Terms of Address. Problems of Patterns and Usage in Various Languages and Cultures*, Berlin: Mouton de Gruyter.

Brazil, D. (1985) *The Communicative Value of Intonation in English*, Birmingham: English Language Research.

——, M. Coulthard and C. Jones (1980) *Discourse Intonation and Language Teaching*, London: Longman.

Brend, R.M. (1975) 'Male-female Intonation Patterns in American English', in B. Thorne and N. Henley (eds), *Language and Sex: Difference and Dominance*, Rowley, Mass.: Newbury House, pp. 84–87.

Brinker, K. (1988) *Linguistische Textanalyse*, 2nd edn, Berlin: Schmidt.

Brinton, L.J. (2000) *The Structure of Modern English. A Linguistic Introduction*, Amsterdam, Penn.: John Benjamins.

—— and M. Fee (2001) 'Canadian English', in J. Algeo (ed.), *English in North America*, vol. 6, *The Cambridge History of English*, Cambridge: CUP, pp. 422–40.

Bronstein, A.J. (1960) *The Pronunciation of American English. An Introduction to Phonetics*, New York: Appleton Century Crofts.

Brosnahan, L.F. (1963) 'Some Historical Cases of Language Imposition', in J. Spencer (ed.), *The English Language in Africa*, London: Longman, pp. 7–24.

Brown, G. and G. Yule (1983) *Discourse Analysis*, Cambridge: CUP.

Brown, P. and S. Levinson (1978) 'Universals in Language Usage: Politeness Phenomena', in E.N. Goody (ed.), *Questions and Politeness*, Cambridge: CUP, pp. 56–289.

—— and —— (1987) *Politeness: Some Universals in Language Usage*, Cambridge: CUP.

Brown, R. and M. Ford (1964) 'Address in American English', in D. Hymes (ed.), *Language in Culture and Society*, New York: Harper and Row, pp. 234–44.

—— and A. Gilman (1972) 'The Pronouns of Power and Solidarity', in P.P. Giglioli (ed.), *Language and Social Context*, Harmondsworth: Penguin, pp. 252–82.

Bryant, P. (1985) 'Regional Variation in the Australian English Lexicon', *Australian Journal of Linguistics* 5: 55–66.

Buckle, R. (1978) *U and Non-U Revisited*, New York: Viking.

Bugental, D.E., L.R. Love and R.M. Gianetto (1971) 'Perfidious Feminine Faces', *Journal of Personal and Social Psychology* 17: 314–18.

Burchfield, R. (1985) *The English Language*, Oxford: OUP.

—— (ed.) (1994) *English in Britain and Overseas: Origins and Development*, in *The Cambridge History of the English Language*, vol. 5, Cambridge: CUP.

—— (ed.) (1996) *New Fowler's Modern English Usage*, Oxford: OUP.

Burger, H., A. Buhofer and A. Sialm (1982) *Handbuch der Phraseologie*, Berlin: de Gruyter.

Burling, R. (1973) *English in Black and White*, New York: Holt, Rinehart and Winston.

Burridge, K. and J. Mulder (1998), *English in Australia and New Zealand*, South Melbourne: OUP.

—— and —— (1999) *English in Australia and New Zealand*, Melbourne: OUP.

Butters, R.R. (1989) *The Death of Black English*, Frankfurt: Peter Lang.

—— (2001), 'Grammatical Structure', in J. Algeo (ed.), *English in North America*, vol. 6, *The Cambridge History of English*, Cambridge: CUP, pp. 325–39.

Cacciari, C. (ed.) (1993) *Idioms: processing, structure, and interpretation*, Hillsdale, N.J.: Erlbaum.

Cameron, D. (1985) *Feminism and Linguistic Theory*, London: Macmillan.

—— (1995) 'Rethinking Language and Gender Studies: Some Issues for the 1990s', in S. Mills (ed.), *Language and Gender. Interdisciplinary Perspectives*, London: Longman, pp. 31–44.

Cannon, G. (1987) *Historical Change and English Word-Formation*, New York: Lang.

Carey, C.V. (1972) *Mind the Stop*, Harmondsworth: Penguin.

Carney, E. (1994) *A Survey of English Spelling*, London: Routledge.

Carter, R. (1998) *Vocabulary*, 2nd edn, London: Routledge.

—— and M. McCarthy (1997) *Exploring Spoken English*, Cambridge: CUP.

—— and W. Nash (1990) *Seeing Through Language*, Oxford: Blackwell.

Cassidy, F.G. (1961) *Jamaica Talk: Three Hundred Years of the English Language in Jamaica*, London: Macmillan.

—— (1986) 'Etymology in Caribbean Creoles', in M. Görlach and J.A. Holm (eds), *Focus on the Caribbean*, Amsterdam, Penn.: Benjamins, pp. 133–9.

—— and J.H. Hall (2001), 'Americanisms', in J. Algeo (ed.), *English in North America*, vol. 6, *The Cambridge History of English*, Cambridge: CUP, pp. 184–218.

Catford, J.C. (1957) 'The Linguistic Survey of Scotland', *Orbis* 6: 105–21.

Chambers, J.K. (1986) 'Three Kinds of Standard in Canadian English', in W.C. Lougheed (ed.), *In Search of a Standard in Canadian English*, Kingston, Ont.: Queen's University, pp. 1–15.

—— (1991) 'Canada', in J. Cheshire (ed.), *English Around the World. Sociolinguistic Perspectives*, Cambridge: CUP, pp. 89–107.

—— and M.F. Hardwick (1986) 'Comparative Sociolinguistics of a Sound Change in Canadian English', *English World-Wide* 7: 23–44.

Charteris-Black, J. (1999) 'The Survival of English Proverbs: A Corpus Based Account', at http://www.deproverbio.com/DPjournal/DP,5,2,99/black/survival.htm.

Cheepen, C. and J. Monaghan (1990) *Spoken English: A Practical Guide*, London: Pinter.

Cheong, K.L. (1978) *Syntax of Scientific English*, Singapore: Singapore University Press.

Cheshire, J. (1978) 'Present Tense Verbs in Reading English', in P. Trudgill (ed.), *Sociolinguistic Patterns in British English*, London: Edward Arnold, pp. 52–68.

—— (ed.) (1991a) *English Around the World. Sociolinguistic Perspectives*, Cambridge: CUP.

—— (1991b) 'The UK and the USA', in J. Cheshire (ed.), *English Around the World. Sociolinguistic Perspectives*, Cambridge: CUP, pp. 13–34.

—— and P. Trudgill (eds) (1998) *The Sociolinguistics Reader*, vol. 2, *Gender and Discourse*, London: Arnold.

Chishimba, M.M. (1991) 'Southern Africa', in J. Cheshire (ed.), *English Around the World. Sociolinguistic Perspectives*, Cambridge: CUP, pp. 435–45.

Chomsky, N. and M. Halle (1968) *The Sound Pattern of English*, New York: Harper & Row.

Christie, P. (1989) 'Questions of Standards and Intra-Regional Differences in Caribbean Examinations', in O. García and R. Otheguy (eds), *English across Cultures, Cultures across English. A Reader in Cross-cultural Communication*, Berlin: Mouton de Gruyter, pp. 243–62.

Clark, J. and C. Yallop (1995) *An Introduction to Phonetics and Phonology*, 2nd edn, Oxford: Blackwell.

Clarke, S. (1991) 'Phonological Variation and Recent Language Change in St John's English', in J. Cheshire (ed.), *English Around the World. Sociolinguistic Perspectives*, Cambridge: CUP, pp. 108–22.

—— (ed.) (1993) *Focus on Canada*, Amsterdam, Penn.: Benjamins.

Close, R.A. (1975) *A Reference Grammar for Students of English*, London: Longman.

—— (1988) 'The Future in English', in W.-D. Bald (ed.), *Kernprobleme der englischen Grammatik*, München: Langenscheidt-Longman, pp. 51–66.

Coates, J. (1986) *Women, Men and Language*, London: Longman.

—— (1993) *Women, Men and Language*, 2nd edn, London: Longman.

—— (1995) 'Language, gender and career', in S. Mills (ed.), *Language and Gender. Interdisciplinary Perspectives*, London; Longman, pp. 13–30.

—— (1996) *Women Talk. Conversation between Women Friends*, Oxford: Blackwell.

—— (1998) *Language and Gender: A Reader*, Oxford: Blackwell.

Coleman, H. (ed.) (1989) *Working with Language. A Multidisciplinary Consideration of Language Use in Work Contexts*, Berlin: Mouton de Gruyter.

Collins, P. (1978) '"Dare" and "Need" in Australian English: A Study of Divided Usage', *English Studies* 59: 434–41.

—— (1989) 'Divided and Debatable Usage in Australian English', in P. Collins and D. Blair (eds), *Australian English: The Language of a New Society*, St Lucia: University of Queensland Press, pp. 138–49.

—— and D. Blair (eds) (1989) *Australian English: The Language of a New Society*, St Lucia: University of Queensland Press.

Comrie, B. (1976) *Aspect*, Cambridge: CUP.

—— (1985) *Tense*, Cambridge: CUP.

Condry, J. and S. Condry (1976) 'Sex Differences: A Study of the Eye of the Beholder', *Child Development* 47: 812–19.

Cook, G. (1989) *Discourse*, Oxford: OUP.

—— (1992) *The Discourse of Advertising*, London: Routledge.

Cooper, J. (1981) *Class*, London: Corgi.

Coser, R.L. (1960) 'Laughter among Colleagues', *Psychiatry* 23: 81–95.

Coulthard, M. (ed.) (1985) *An Introduction of Discourse Analysis*, 2nd edn, London: Longman.

—— (1987) 'Intonation and the Description of Interaction', in *Discussing Discourse*, Birmingham: English Language Research, pp. 44–62.

Coupland, C.H. (1990) *English in Wales*, Clevedon: Multilingual Matters.

Cowie, A. P. (ed.) (1998) *Phraseology: Theory, Analysis, and Applications*, Oxford: Clarendon Press.

Crawford, M. (1995) *Talking Difference. On Gender and Language*, London: Sage.

Crowley, T. (1989) *Standard English and the Politics of Language*, Urbana, Ill.: University of Illinois Press.

Cruse, D.A. (1986) *Lexical Semantics*, Cambridge: CUP.

Cruttenden, A. (1986) *Intonation*, Cambridge: CUP.

—— (2001) *Gimson's Pronunciation of English*, 6th edn, London: Arnold.

Crystal, D. (1975) *The English Tone of Voice*, London: Edward Arnold.

—— (1997) *English as a Global Language*, Cambridge: CUP.

—— and D. Davy (1969) *Investigating English Style*, London: Longman.

—— and —— (1975) *Advanced Conversational English*, London: Longman.

Dalby, D. (1971) 'Black through White: Patterns of Communication in Africa and the New World', in W.A. Wolfram and N.H. Clarke (eds), *Black-White Speech Relationships*, Washington, DC: Center for Applied Linguistics, pp. 99–138.

Das, S.K. (1982) 'Indian English', in J.B. Pride (ed.), *New Englishes*, Rowley, Mass.: Newbury House, pp. 141–9.

Davies, E. (1986) *The English Imperative*, London: Croom Helm.

Dayley, J.P. (1979) *Belizean Creole*, Brattleboro, Vt.: Action/Peace Corps.

Delbridge, A. (1970) 'The Recent Study of Spoken Australian English', in W.S. Ramson (ed.), *English Transported*, Canberra: Australian National University Press, pp. 15–31.

—— (1990) 'Australian English Now', in L. Michaels and C. Ricks (eds), *The State of the Language*, 2nd edn, Berkeley, Calif.: University of California Press, pp. 66–76.

de Souza Filho, D.M. (1985) *Language and Action: A Reassessment of Speech Act Theory*, Philadelphia, Penn.: Benjamins.

de Souza, J. (1997) 'Indian English: Some Myths, Some Realities' *English World-Wide* 18: 91–105.

Dijk, T.A. van (ed.) (1985) *Handbook of Discourse Analysis*, London: Academic Press.

—— and W. Kintsch (1983) *Strategies of Discourse Comprehension*, New York: Academic Press.

Dillard, J.L. (1972) *Black English. Its History and Usage in the United States*, New York: Random House.

—— (1993) *A History of American English*, London: Longman.

Dirven, R. and G. Radden (eds) (1987) *Concepts of Case*, Tübingen: Narr.

Dixon, R.M.W. (1980) 'The Role of Language in Aboriginal Australian Society Today' (Chapter 4), in *The Languages of Australia*, Cambridge: CUP, pp. 69–96.

Dovidio, J.F. and S.L. Ellyson (1985) 'Patterns of Visual Dominance Behavior in Humans', in S.L. Ellyson and J.F. Dovidio (eds), *Power, Dominance and Nonverbal Behavior*, New York: Springer, pp. 129–49.

Dubois, B.L. (1982) 'The Construction of Noun Phrases in Biomedical Journal Articles', in J. Høedt *et al.* (eds), *Proceedings of the Third European Symposium on LSP*, Copenhagen: LSP Centre, pp. 49–67.

Dubois, B. and I. Crouch (1975) 'The Question of Tag-Questions in Women's Speech: They Don't Really Use More of Them, Do They?', *Language in Society* 4: 289–94.

Dudley-Evans, T. (1989) 'An Outline of the Value of Genre Analysis in LSP Work', in C. Laurén and M. Nordman (eds), *Special Language*, Clevedon: Multilingual Matters, pp. 72–79.

—— and M.J. St John (1999) *Developments in English for Specific Purposes*, Cambridge: CUP.

Dušková, L. (1971) 'On Some Functional and Stylistic Aspects of the Passive Voice in Present-Day English', *Philologia Pragensia* 14: 117–43.

Eakins, B.W. and R.G. Eakins (1978a) *Sex Differences in Human Communication*, Boston, Mass.: Houghton Mifflin.

—— and —— (1978b) 'Verbal Turn-Taking and Exchanges in Faculty Dialogue', in B. Dubois and I. Crouch (eds), *The Sociology of the Languages of American Women*, San Antonio, Tex.: Trinity University, pp. 53–62.

Eble, C.C. (1977) 'If Ladies Weren't Present, I'd Tell You What I Really Think', in D.L. Shores and C.P. Hines (eds), *Papers in Language Variation*, Birmingham, Ala.: University of Alabama, pp. 295–301.

Edelsky, C. (1979) 'Question Intonation and Sex Roles', *Language and Society* 9: 15–32.

Edmondson, W. (1981) *Spoken Discourse*, London: Longman.

—— and J. House (1981) *Let's Talk and Talk About It*, Munich: Urban & Schwarzenberg.

Edwards, J. (ed.) (1998) *Language in Canada*, Cambridge: CUP.

Egbe, D.I. (1979) 'Spoken and Written English in Nigeria', in E. Ubahakwe (ed.), *Varieties and Functions of English in Nigeria*, Ibadan: African Universities Press, pp. 86–106.

Eggins, S. and D. Slade (1997) *Analysing Casual Conversation*, London: Cassell.

Eisikovits, E. (1991) 'Variation in Subject-Verb Agreement in Inner Sydney English', in J. Cheshire (ed.), *English Around the World. Sociolinguistic Perspectives*, Cambridge: CUP, pp. 435–55.

Ek, J.A. van and N.J. Robat (1984) *The Student's Grammar of English*, Oxford: Blackwell.

Elyan, O., P. Smith, H. Giles and R. Bourhis (1978) 'RP-Accented Female Speech: The Voice of Perceived Androgyny?', in P. Trudgill (ed.), *Sociolinguistic Patterns in British English*, London: Edward Arnold, pp. 122–31.

Emery, D.W. (1975) *Variant Spellings in Modern American Dictionaries*, 2nd edn, Urbana, Ill.: National Council of Teachers of English.

Enkvist, N. (1987) 'Text Strategies: Single, Dual, Multiple', in R. Steele and T. Threadgold (eds), *Language Topics*, vol. 2, Amsterdam, Penn.: Benjamins, pp. 203–11.

Erdmann, P. (1990) *Discourse and Grammar. Focussing and Defocussing in English*, Tübingen: Niemeyer.

Ervin-Tripp, S. (1974) 'Sociolinguistics', in B.G. Blount (ed.), *Language, Culture and Society*, Cambridge, Mass.: Winthrop, pp. 268–334.

——, M.C. O'Connor and J. Rosenberg (1984) 'Language and Power in the Family', in C. Kramarae, M. Schulz and W.M. O'Barr (eds), *Language and Power*, Beverly Hills, Calif.: Sage, pp. 116–35.

Everaert, M., E-J van der Linden, A. Schenk and R. Schreuder (eds) (1995), *Idioms: Structural and Psychological Perspectives*, Hillsdale, N.J.: Erlbaum.

Fasold, R.W. (1972) *Tense Marking in Black English*, Washington, DC: Center for Applied Linguistics.

—— (1986) 'The Relation Between Black and White Speech in the South', in H.B. Allen and M.D. Linn (eds), *Dialect and Language Variation*, Orlando, Fla.: Academic, pp. 446–73.

—— (1990) *The Sociolinguistics of Language*, Cambridge, Mass.: Blackwell.

Feagin, D. (1979) *Variation and Change in Alabama English*, Washington, DC: Georgetown University Press.

Fenn, P. (1987) *A Semantic and Pragmatic Examination of the English Perfect*, Tübingen: Narr.

Fernando, C. (1996) *Idioms and Idiomaticity*, Oxford: OUP.

Fillmore, C.J. (1972) 'The Case For Case', in E. Bach and R.T. Harms (eds), *Universals in Linguistic Theory*, New York: Holt, Rinehart and Winston, pp. 1–88.

Filppula, M. (1991) 'Urban and Rural Varieties of Hiberno-English', in J. Cheshire (ed.), *English Around the World. Sociolinguistic Perspectives*, Cambridge: CUP, pp. 51–60.

Finegan, E. (1998) 'English Grammar and Usage', in S. Romaine (ed.), *1776–1997*, vol. 4, *The Cambridge History of the English Language*, Cambridge: CUP, pp. 536–88.

Fisher, J.H. (2001), 'British and American, Continuity and Divergence', in J. Algeo (ed.), *English in North America*, vol. 6, *The Cambridge History of English*, Cambridge: CUP, pp. 59–85.

Fischer, J.L. (1958) 'Social Influences on the Choice of a Linguistic Variant', *Word* 14: 47–56.

—— (1977) 'Chancery and the Emergence of Standard Written English in the Fifteenth Century', *Speculuum* 52: 870–99.

—— (1996) *The Emergence of Standard English*, Lexington: University Press of Kentucky.

Fishman, P.M. (1983) 'Interaction: The Work Women Do', in B. Thorne, C. Kramarae and N. Henley (eds), *Language, Gender and Society*, Cambridge, Mass.: Newbury House, pp. 89–101.

Fishman, R.A., Cooper, R.L. and Y. Rosenbaum (1977) 'English Around the World', in J.A. Fishman, R.L. Cooper and A.W. Conrad (eds), *The Spread of English*, Rowley, Mass.: Newbury House, pp. 77–107.

Flexner, S.B. and A.H. Soukhanov (1997) *Speaking Freely*, New York: OUP.

Flowerdew, J. (1988) 'Speech Acts and Language Teaching', *Language Teaching* 21: 69–82.

—— and M. Peacock (2001) *Research Perspectives on English for Academic Purposes*, Cambridge: CUP.

Fortanet, I., S. Posteguille, J.C. Palmer and J.F. Coll (eds) (1998) *Genre Studies in English for Academic Purposes*, Castellin: Publicacions de la Universitat Jaume.

Foulkes, P. and Docherty G. (1999) *Urban Voices: Accent Studies in the British Isles*, London: Arnold.

Fox, B.A. (1987) *Discourse Structure and Anaphora*, Cambridge: CUP.

Francis, W.N. and H. Kučera (1982) *Frequency Analysis of English Usage: Lexicon and Grammar*, Boston: Houghton-Mifflin.

Fraser, B. (1970) 'Idioms within a Transformational Grammar', *Foundations of Language* 6: 22–42.

—— (1973) 'Some "Unexpected" Reactions to Various American English Dialects', in R. Shuy and R.W. Fasold (eds), *Language Attitudes*, Washington, D.C.: Georgetown Roundtable in Linguistics, pp. 28–35.

Fries, C.C. (1952) *The Structure of English*, New York: Harcourt Brace.

Fudge, E. (1984) *English Word-Stress*, London: Allen & Unwin.

Fussell, P. (1984) *Class*, London: Arrow.

Gallegos, B. (ed.) (1994) *English – Our Official Language?*, New York: H.W. Wilson.

García, O. and R. Otheguy (1988) 'The Language Situation of Cuban Americans', in S.L. McKay and S.C. Wong (eds), *Language Diversity. Problem or Resource?*, Cambridge, Mass.: Newbury House, pp. 166–92.

Gardner, R. (ed.) (1994) *Spoken Interaction Studies in Australia*, special volume of *Australian Review of Applied Linguistics*, Series S, no. 11.

Garner, J.F. (1998) *Politically Correct, The Ultimate Storybook*, New York: Smithmark.

Gerbert, M. (1970) *Besonderheiten der Syntax in der technischen Fachsprache des Englischen*, Halle: Niemeyer.

Giles, H. (1990) 'Social Meanings of Welsh English', in N. Coupland (ed.), *English in Wales*, Clevedon: Multilingual Matters, pp. 258–82.

—— and P.F. Powesland (1975) *Speech Style and Social Evaluation*, London: Academic Press.

——, N. Coupland, K. Henwood, J. Harriman and J. Coupland (1990) 'The Social Meaning of RP: An Intergenerational Perspective', in S. Ramsaran (ed.), *Studies in the Pronunciation of English*, London: Routledge, pp. 191–211.

Gimson, A.C. (1980) *An Introduction to the Pronunciation of English*, 3rd edn, London: Edward Arnold.

—— (2001) *Gimson's Pronunciation of English*, 6th edn, edited by A. Cruttenden, London: Arnold.

Gläser, R. (1986) *Phraseologie der englischen Sprache*, Tübingen: Niemeyer.

—— (1990) *Fachtextsorten im Englischen*, Tübingen: Gunter Narr.

Gleason, J.B. (1987) 'Sex Differences in Parent-Child Interaction', in S.U. Philips and A. Reynolds (eds), *Language, Gender and Sex in Comparative Perspective*, Cambridge: CUP, pp. 189–99.

—— and E.B. Greif (1983) 'Men's Speech to Young Children', in B. Thorne, C. Kramarae and N. Henley (eds), *Language, Gender and Society*, Cambridge, Mass.: Newbury House, pp. 140–50.

Glowka, A.W. and D.M. Lance (eds) (1993) *Language Variation in North American English*, New York: MLA.

Goffman, E. (1967) *Interaction Ritual. Essays in Face-to-Face Behavior*, Chicago: Aldine.

Goodwin, M.H. (1988) 'Cooperation and Competition across Girls' Play Activities', in A.D. Todd and S. Fisher (eds), *Gender and Discourse: The Power of Talk*, Norwood, N.J., pp. 55–94.

Gonzalez, A. (1982) 'English in the Philippines', in J.B. Pride (ed.), *New Englishes*, Rowley, Mass.: Newbury House, pp. 211–26.

—— (ed.) (1988) *The Role of English and Its Maintenance in the Philippines*, Manila: Solidaridad.

—— and M.L.S. Bautista (1985) *Language Surveys in the Philippines (1966–1984)*, Manila: De La Salle.

Gopnik, M. (1972) *Linguistic Structures in Scientific Texts*, The Hague: Mouton.

Gordon, E. and M. Abell (1990) ' "This Objectionable Colonial Dialect": Historical and Contemporary Attitudes to New Zealand Speech', in A. Bell and J. Holmes (eds), *New Zealand Ways of Speaking English*, Clevedon: Multilingual Matters, pp. 21–48.

—— and T. Deverson (1985) *New Zealand English*, Auckland: Heinemann.

Görlach, M. (2002) *Still More Varieties*, Amsterdam: Benjamins.

—— and J.A. Holm (eds) (1986) *Focus on the Caribbean*, Amsterdam: Benjamins.

Graddol, D., D. Leith and J. Swann (eds) (1996) *English. History, Diversity and Change*, London: Routledge.

Graham, A. (1975) 'The Making of a Nonsexist Dictionary', in B. Thorne and N. Henley (eds), *Language and Sex: Difference and Dominance*, Rowley, Mass.: Newbury House, pp. 57–63.

Gramley, S.E. (2001) *The Vocabulary of World English*, London: Arnold.

Green, L. (1998) 'Aspect and Predicate Phrases in African-American Vernacular English' in S.S. Mufwene, J.R. Rickford, G. Bailey and J. Baugh (eds), *African-American English*, London: Routledge, pp. 37–68.

Greenbaum, S. (1970) *Verb-Intensifier Collocations in English*, The Hague: Mouton.

—— (1974) 'Some Verb-intensifier Collocations in American and British English', *American Speech* 49: 79–89.

—— (1986) 'Spelling Variants in British English', *Journal of English Linguistics* 19: 258–68.

—— (1991) *An Introduction to English Grammar*, Harlow: Longman.

—— (1996) *The Oxford English Grammar*, Oxford: OUP.

—— and R. Quirk (1990) *A Student's Grammar of the English Language*, London: Longman.

Grice, H.P. (1975) 'Logic and Conversation', in P. Cole and J. Morgan (eds), *Speech Acts*, vol. 3 of *Syntax and Semantics*, New York: Academic Press, pp. 41–58.

Grimshaw, A.D. (1971) 'Some Social Forces and Some Social Functions of Pidgin and Creole Languages', in D. Hymes (ed.), *Pidginization and Creolization of Languages*, Cambridge: CUP, pp. 427–45.

Guy, G. (1991) 'Australia', in J. Cheshire (ed.), *English Around the World. Sociolinguistic Perspectives*, Cambridge: CUP, pp. 213–26.

—— and J. Vonwiller (1989) 'The High Rising Tone in Australian English', in P. Collins and D. Blair (eds), *Australian English: The Language of a New Society*, St Lucia: University of Queensland Press, pp. 21–34.

Hall, R.A. (1966) *Pidgin and Creole Languages*, Ithaca, N.Y.: Cornell University Press.

Halliday, M.A.K. (1967a) *Intonation and Grammar in British English*, The Hague: Mouton.

—— (1967b) 'Notes on Transitivity and Theme in English', *Journal of Linguistics* 2: 37–81.

—— (1970) *A Course in Spoken English: Intonation*, London: OUP.

—— (1973) 'The Tones of English', in W.E. Jones and J. Laver (eds), *Phonetics in Linguistics*, London: Longman, pp. 103–26.

—— and R. Hasan (1976) *Cohesion in English*, London: Longman.

Hamblin, C.L. (1987) *Imperatives*, Oxford: Basil Blackwell.

Hampe, B. (2002) *Superlative Verbs*, A corpus-based study of semantic redundancy in English verb-particle constructions, Tübingen: Narr.

Hanania, E.A.S. and K. Akhtar (1985) 'Verb Form and Rhetorical Function in Science Writing: A Study of MS Theses in Biology, Chemistry, and Physics', *ESP Journal* 4: 49–58.

Harper, R.G., A.N. Wiens and J.D. Matarazzo (1978) *Nonverbal Communication: The State of the Art*, New York: John Wiley.

Harris, J. (1984) 'English in the North of Ireland', in P. Trudgill (ed.), *Language in the British Isles*, Cambridge: CUP, pp. 115–34.

—— (1985) *Phonological Variation and Change. Studies in Hiberno-English*, Cambridge: CUP.

—— (1991) 'Ireland', in J. Cheshire (ed.), *English Around the World. Sociolinguistic Perspectives*, Cambridge: CUP, pp. 37–50.

Hausmann, F.J. (1984) 'Wortschatzlernen ist Kollokationslernen', *Praxis des neusprachlichen Unterrichts* 31: 395–406.

—— (ed.) (1989–91) *Wörterbücher/Dictionaries: Ein Internationales Handbuch zur Lexikographie*, 3 vols, Berlin: de Gruyter.

Heinemann, W. and D. Viehweger (1991) *Textlinguistik*, Tübingen: Niemeyer.

Henley, N. (1973) 'The Politics of Touch', in P. Brown (ed.), *Radical Psychology*, New York: Harper & Row, pp. 421–33.

Herbert, R.K. (1998) 'Sex-based Differences in Compliment Behavior', in J. Cheshire and P. Trudgill (eds), *The Sociolinguistics Reader*, vol. 2, *Gender and Discourse*, London: Arnold, pp. 53–75.

Herbst, T. (1996) 'On the Way to the Perfect Learner's Dictionary: A First Comparison of OALD5, LDOCE3, COBUILD2 and CIDE', *International Journal of Lexicography* 9: 321–57.

Heslot, J. (1982) 'Tense and Other Indexical Markers in the Typology of Scientific Texts', in J. Høedt et al. (eds), *Proceedings of the Third European Symposium on LSP. 'Pragmatics and LSP'*, Copenhagen: LSP Centre, pp. 49–67.

Hill, R.J. (1982) *A Dictionary of False Friends*, London: Macmillan.

Ho, M.L. (1993) *Dynamics of a Contact Continuum. Singaporean English*, Oxford: OUP.

Høedt, J. et al. (eds) (1982) *Proceedings of the Third European Symposium on LSP. 'Pragmatics and LSP'*, Copenhagen: LSP Centre, pp. 83–104.

Hoey, M. (1983) *On the Surface of Discourse*, London: Allen & Unwin.

—— (1991) *Patterns of Lexis in Text*, Oxford: OUP.

Hoffmann, L. (1987) 'Syntactic Aspects of LSP' *Fachsprache* 9: 98–105.

Hofland, K. and S. Johansson (1982) *Word Frequencies in British and American English*, Bergen: The Norwegian Computing Centre for the Humanities.

Hofman, T.R. (1989) 'Pragmatics and Anaphora', *Journal of Pragmatics* 13: 239–50.

Holm, J.A. (ed.) (1983) *Central American English*, Heidelberg: Groos.

—— (1986) 'The Spread of English in the Caribbean Area', in M. Görlach and J.A. Holm (eds), *Focus on the Caribbean*, Amsterdam: Benjamins, pp. 1–22.

—— (1988, 1989) *Pidgins and Creoles*, vol. 1, *Theory and Structure*, vol. 2, *Reference Study*, Cambridge: CUP.

—— (1994) 'English in the Caribbean', in R. Burchfield (ed.), *English in Britain and Overseas*: *Origins and Development*, in *The Cambridge History of the English Language*, vol. 5, Cambridge: CUP, pp. 328–81.

Holmes, J. (1995) *Women, Men and Politeness*, Harlow: Longman.

——, A. Bell and M.T. Boyce (1991) *Variation and Change in New Zealand English*, Wellington: Department of Linguistics, Victoria University.

Hook, D.D. (1984) 'First Names and Titles as Solidarity and Power Semantics in English', *IRAL* 22: 183–9.

Hopkins, A. and T. Dudley-Evans (1988) 'A Genre-based Investigation of the Discussions Sections in Articles and Dissertations', *ESP Journal* 7: 113–21.

Horvath, B.M. (1985) *Variation in Australian English*, Cambridge: CUP.

Huddleston, R.D. (1971) *The Sentence in Written English: A Syntactic Study Based on an Analysis of Scientific Texts*, Cambridge: CUP.

—— (1984) *Introduction to the Grammar of English*, Cambridge: CUP.

—— (1988) *English Grammar: An Outline*, Cambridge: CUP.

Hughes, A. and P. Trudgill (1996) *English Accents and Dialects*, 3rd edn, London: Arnold.

Hughes, G. (1988) *Words in Time: A Social History of the English Vocabulary*, Oxford: Blackwell.

—— (2000) *A History of English Words*, Oxford: Blackwell.

Hutchinson, T. and A. Waters (1987) *English for Specific Purposes*, Cambridge: CUP.

Huygens, I. and G.M. Vaughan (1983) 'Language Attitude, Ethnicity and Social Class in New Zealand', *Journal of Multilingual and Multicultural Development* 4: 207–23.

Hymes, D. (ed.) (1971a) *Pidginization and Creolization of Languages*, Cambridge: CUP.

—— (1971b) 'Preface', in D. Hymes (ed.), *Pidginization and Creolization of Languages*, Cambridge: CUP, pp. 3–11.

—— (1972) 'On Communicative Competence', in J.B. Pride and J. Holmes (eds), *Sociolinguistics*, Harmondsworth: Penguin, pp. 269–93.

Ilson, R. (1990) 'British and American English: Ex Uno Plura?', in L. Michaels and C. Ricks (eds), *The State of the Language*, 2nd edn, Berkeley, Calif.: University of California Press, pp. 33–41.

Jabril, M. (1991) 'The Sociolinguistics of Prepositional Usage in Nigerian English', in J. Cheshire (ed.), *English Around the World. Sociolinguistic Perspectives*, Cambridge: CUP, pp. 519–44.

Jackson, H. and E.Z. Amvela (2000) *Words, Meaning and Vocabulary*, London: Cassell

Jacobson, B. (1979) 'Modality and the Modals of Necessity *Must* and *Have to*', *English Studies* 60: 296–312.

James, D. and S. Clarke (1993) 'Women, Men and Interruptions: A Critical Review', in D. Tannen (ed.), *Gender and Conversational Interaction*, New York: OUP, pp. 231–80.

—— and J. Drakich (1993) 'Understanding Gender Differences in Amount of Talk: A Critical Review of Research', in D. Tannen (ed.), *Gender and Conversational Interaction*, New York: OUP, pp. 281–312.

Jespersen, O. (1940–42) *A Modern English Grammar on Historical Principles*, Copenhagen: Munksgaard.

Johansson, S. (1975) *Some Aspects of the Vocabulary of Learned and Scientific Englis*, Göteborg: Gothenburg Studies in English.

Johnson, S. and U.H. Meinhof (eds) (1997) *Language and Masculinity*, Oxford: Blackwell.

Johnson-Laird, P.N. (1983) *Mental Models*, Cambridge: CUP.

Jones, D. (1950) *The Pronunciation of English*, Cambridge: CUP.

—— (1969) *Everyman's English Pronouncing Dictionary*, edited by A.C. Gimson, London: Dent.

—— (1997) *English Pronouncing Dictionary*, 15th edn, edited by P. Roach and J. Hartman, Cambridge: CUP.

Jones, E. (1971) 'Krio: An English-based Language of Sierra Leone', in J. Spencer (ed.), *The English Language in West Africa*, London: Longman, pp. 66–94.

Jonz, J.G. (1975) 'Situated Address in the United States Marine Corps', *Anthropological Linguistics* 17: 68–77.

Joos, M. (1962) 'The Five Clocks', *International Journal of American Linguistics* 28: 9–62.

—— (1968) *The English Verb. Form and Meanings*, 2nd edn, Madison, Wis.: University of Wisconsin.

Jordan, R.R. (1997) *English for Academic Purposes*, Cambridge: CUP.

Kachru, B.B. (1966) 'Indian English: A Study in Contextualization', in C.E. Bazell (ed.), *In Memory of J.R. Firth*, London: Longman, pp. 255–87.

—— (1984) 'South Asian English', in R.W. Bailey and M. Görlach (eds), *English as a World Language*, Cambridge: CUP, pp. 353–83.

—— (1986) *The Alchemy of English*, Oxford: Pergamon.

Kallen, J.L. (1991) 'Sociolinguistic Variation and Methodology: *After* as a Dublin Variable', in J. Cheshire (ed.), *English Around the World. Sociolinguistic Perspectives*, Cambridge: CUP, pp. 61–74.

—— (ed.) (1997) *Focus on Ireland*, Amsterdam, Penn.: Benjamins.

Katamba, F. (1993) *Morphology*, Basingstoke: Macmillan.

Kennedy, C.W. (1980) 'Patterns of Verbal Interruption among Women and Men in Groups', (quoted in B. Thorne, C. Kramarae and N. Henley (eds) (1983) *Language, Gender and Society*, Cambridge, Mass.: Newbury House, p. 282).

Kenyon, J.S. (1969) *American Pronunciation*, Ann Arbor: Wahr.

—— and T.A. Knott (1944) *A Pronouncing Dictionary of American English*, Springfield, Mass.: Merriam.

Kingdon, R. (1958) *The Groundwork of English Intonation*, London: Longman.

Kjellmer, G. (1994) *A Dictionary of English Collocations: Based on the Brown Corpus*, 3 vols, Oxford: OUP.

Knowles, G. (1987) *Patterns of Spoken English*, London: Longman.

Kochman, T. (1970) 'Toward an Ethnography of Black American Speech Behavior', in N.E. Whitten and J.F. Szwed (eds), *Afro-American Anthropology*, New York: Free Press, pp. 145–62.

Kramer, C. (1975) 'Sex-related Differences in Address Systems', *Anthropological Linguistics* 17: 198–200.

Kroch, A. (1996) 'Dialect and Style in the Speech of the Upper Class of Philadelphia', in G.R. Guy, C. Feagin, D. Schiffrin and J. Baugh (eds), *Towards a Social Science of Language*, Philadelphia: Benjamins, pp. 23–46.

Kuo, C. (1999) 'The Use of Personal Pronouns: Role Relationships in Scientific Journal Articles', in *English for Specific Purposes* 18: 121–38.

Kurath, H. *et al.* (ed.) (1939–43) *Linguistic Atlas of New England*, 3 vols, Providence: American Council of Learned Societies.

Labov, W. (1972a) *Sociolinguistic Patterns*, Philadelphia, Penn.: University of Pennsylvania.
—— (1972b) 'The Study of Language in Its Social Context', in J.B. Pride and J. Holmes (eds), *Sociolinguistics*, Harmondsworth: Penguin, pp. 180–202.
—— (1987) 'Are Black and White Vernaculars Diverging?', *American Speech* 62: 5–12.
—— (1998) 'Co-existent Systems in African-American Vernacular English' in S.S. Mufwene, J.R. Rickford, G. Bailey and J. Baugh (eds), *African-American English*, London: Routledge, pp. 110–53.
——, M. Yaeger and R. Steiner (1972) *A Quantitative Study of Sound Change in Progress*, Philadelphia. Penn.: US Regional Survey.
Labrie, N. (1988) 'Canada', in U. Ammon, N. Dittmar and K.J. Mattheier (eds), *Sociolinguistics Soziolinguistik*, Berlin: Walter de Gruyter, pp. 1307–13.
Lakoff, R. (1976) *Language and Woman's Place*, New York: Harper & Row.
Landau, S. (1984) *Dictionaries: The Art and Craft of Lexicography*, New York: Scribner.
Lanham, L.W. (1984) 'English in South Africa', in R.W. Bailey and M. Görlach (eds), *English as a World Language*, Cambridge: CUP, pp. 324–52.
—— (1985) 'The Perception and Evaluation of Varieties of English in South African Society', in S. Greenbaum (ed.), *The English Language Today*, Oxford: Pergamon, pp. 242–51.
—— and C.A. Macdonald (1979) *The Standard in South African English and its Social History*, Heidelberg: Groos.
Lass, R. and S. Wright (1986) 'Endogeny vs Contact: "Afrikaans Influence" on South African English', *English World-Wide* 7: 201–23.
Lattey, E. and A.E. Hieke (1990) *Using Idioms in Situational Contexts: A Workbook*, Tübingen: Francke.
Lawton, D.L. (1984) 'English in the Caribbean', in R.W. Bailey and M. Görlach (eds), *English as a World Language*, Cambridge: CUP, pp. 251–80.
Leap, W.L. (1986) 'American Indian English and Its Implications for Bilingual Education', in H.B. Allen and M.D. Linn (eds), *Dialect and Language Variation*, Orlando: Academic, pp. 591–603.
—— (1993) *American Indian English*, Salt Lake City, Utah: University of Utah Press.
—— (1996) *Word's Out: Gay Men's English*, Minneapolis, Minn.: University of Minnesota Press.
Lee, A., N. Hewlett and M. Nairn (1995) 'Voice and Gender in Children', in S. Mills (ed.), *Language and Gender. Interdisciplinary Perspectives*, London: Longman, pp. 194–204.
Lee, W.R. (1983) *A Study Dictionary of Social English*, Oxford: Pergamon.
Leech, G.N. (1969) *A Linguistic Guide to English Poetry*, London: Longman.
—— (1983) *Principles of Pragmatics*, London: Longman.
—— (1987) *Meaning and the English Verb*, 2nd edn, London: Longman.
—— and M.H. Short (1981) *Style in Fiction*, London: Longman.
——, M. Deuchar and R. Hoogenraad (1982) *English Grammar for Today*, Basingstoke: Macmillan.
Lehrer, A. (1984) 'The Influence of Semantic Fields on Semantic Change', in J. Fisiak (ed.), *Historical Semantics – Historical Word-formation*, Berlin: Mouton, pp. 283–96.
Leisi, E. and C. Mair (1999), *Das heutige Englisch*, 8th edn, Heidelberg: Winter.
Leith, D. (1983) *A Social History of English*, London: Routledge.
Levine L. and H.J. Crockett Jr (1966) 'Speech Variation in a Piedmont Community: Postvocalic *r*', in S. Lieberson (ed.), *Explorations in Sociolinguistics*, The Hague: Mouton, pp. 76–98.
Levinson, S.C. (1983) *Pragmatics*, Cambridge: CUP.
Lewis, I. (1992) *Sahibs, Nabobs, and Boxwallahs. A Dictionary of the Words of Anglo-Indian*, Delhi: OUP.
Lighter, J.E. (2001), 'Slang', in J. Algeo (ed.), *English in North America*, vol. 6, *The Cambridge History of English*, Cambridge: CUP, pp. 219–52.

Linguistic Society of America (1995) 'LSA Guidelines for Nonsexist Usage', *LSA Bulletin* (each issue).

Lipka, L. (2002) *English Lexicology*, Tübingen: Narr.

Lippi-Green, R. (1997) *English with an Accent*, London: Routledge.

Lipski, J.M. (1986) 'English-Spanish Contact in the United States and Central America: Sociolinguistic Mirror Images?', in M. Görlach and J.A. Holm (eds), *Focus on the Caribbbean*, Amsterdam: Benjamins, pp. 191–208.

Llamzon, T.A. (1969) *Standard Filipino English*, Manila: Ateneo University Press.

Lorimer, W.L. (1983) *The New Testament in Scots*, Edinburgh: Southside.

Lyons, J. (1977) *Semantics*, Cambridge: CUP.

—— (1995) *Linguistic Semantics*, Cambridge: CUP.

Macafee, C. (1981) 'Nationalism and the Scots Renaissance Now', *English World-Wide* 2: 29–38.

—— (1983) *Glasgow*, Amsterdam, Penn.: John Benjamin.

—— and I. Macleod (eds) (1987) *The Nuttis Shell. Essays on the Scots Language*, Aberdeen: Aberdeen University Press.

McArthur, T. (1986) 'The Problem of Purism', *English Today* 6 (April): 34ff.

—— (ed.) (1996) *The Oxford Companion to the English Language*, abridged edn, Oxford: OUP.

—— (2002) *The Oxford Guide to World English*, Oxford: OUP.

Macaulay, R.K.S. (1977) *Language, Social Class and Education. A Glasgow Study*, Edinburgh: Edinburgh University Press.

—— (1978) 'Variation and Consistency in Glaswegian English', in P. Trudgill (ed.), *Sociolinguistic Patterns in British English*, London: Edward Arnold, pp. 132–43.

—— (1997) *Standards and Variation in Urban Speech: Examples from Lowland Scots*, Amsterdam, Penn.: Benjamins.

McCarthy, M. (1991) *Discourse Analysis for Teachers*, Cambridge: CUP.

MacCarthy, P.A.D. (1965) *A Practice Book of English Speech*, Oxford: OUP.

—— (1972) *Talking of Speaking: Papers in Applied Phonetics*, Oxford: OUP.

McClure, J.D. (1980) 'Developing Scots as a National Language', in J.D. McClure, A.J. Aitken and J.T. Low (eds), *The Scots Language, Planning for Modern Usage*. Edinburgh: Ramsay Head, pp. 11–14.

—— (1994) 'English in Scotland', in R. Burchfield (ed.), *English in Britain and Overseas: Origins and Development*, vol. 5 of *The Cambridge History of the English Language*, Cambridge: CUP, pp. 23–92

McCoard, R.W. (1978) *The English Perfect: Tense-Choice and Pragmatic Inferences*, Amsterdam: North Holland.

McCrum, R., R. MacNeil and W. Cran (1992; 3rd edn, 2002) *The Story of English*, London: Faber & Faber.

McDavid, R.I. Jr et al. (1980) *Linguistic Atlas of the Middle and South Atlantic States*, vols 1ff., Chicago: University of Chicago Press.

McIntire, M.L. (1972) 'Terms of Address in an Academic Setting', *Anthropological Linguistics* 14: 286–92.

McIntosh, A. (1952) *An Introduction to a Survey of Scottish Dialects*, Edinburgh: Nelson.

MacKay, D.G. and T. Konishi (1980) 'Personification and the Pronoun Problem', in C. Kramarae (ed.), *The Voices and Words of Women and Men*, Oxford: Pergamon, pp. 149–63.

McKay, S.L. and S.C. Wong (eds) (1988) *Language Diversity. Problem or Resource?*, Cambridge, Mass.: Newbury House.

MacKinnon, K. (1997) 'Minority Languages in an Integrating Europe: Prospects for Viability and Maintenance', in B. Synak and T. Wicherkiewicz (eds), *Language Minorities and Minority Languages in the Changing Europe*, Gdansk: Wydawnictwo Uniwersytetu Gdanskiego, pp. 93–108.

Maidment, J.A. (1990) 'Focus and Tone in English Intonation', in S. Ramsaran (ed.), *Studies in the Pronunciation of English*, London: Routledge, pp. 19–26.

Marchand, H. (1969) *The Categories and Types of Present-day English Word-formation*, Wiesbaden: Harrassowitz.

Martin, J.R. (1992) *English Text: System and Structure*, Philadelphia: Benjamins.

Martin, S. and W. Wolfram (1998) 'The Sentence in African-American Vernacular English', in S.S. Mufwene, J.R. Rickford, G. Bailey and J. Baugh (eds), *African-American English*, London: Routledge, pp. 11–36.

Martyna, W. (1980) 'The Psychology of the Generic Masculine', in S. McConnell-Ginet *et al.* (eds), *Women and Language in Literature and Society*, New York: Praeger, pp. 69–78.

Master, P. (1987) 'Generic *The* in *Scientific American*', *ESP Journal* 6: 165–86.

Mather, J.Y. and H.H. Speitel (eds) (1975–77) *The Linguistic Atlas of Scotland*, London: Croom Helm.

Matthews, P.H. (1981) *Syntax*, Cambridge: CUP.

Mehrabian, A. (1972) *Nonverbal Communication*, Chicago, Ill.: Aldine, Atherton.

Mehrotra, R.R. (1982) 'Indian English: A Sociolinguistic Profile', in J.B. Pride (ed.), *New Englishes*, Rowley, Mass.: Newbury House, pp. 150–73.

—— (1989) 'Indian literature in English', in O. García and R. Otheguy (eds), *English across Cultures, Cultures across English. A Reader in Cross-cultural Communication*, Berlin: Mouton de Gruyter, pp. 421–39.

—— (1998) *Indian English: Texts and Interpretation*, Amsterdam, Penn.: Benjamins.

Mesthrie, R. (1991) 'Syntactic Variation in South African Indian English: The Relative Clause', in J. Cheshire (ed.), *English Around the World, Sociolinguistic Perspectives*, Cambridge: CUP, pp. 462–73.

Methrie, R., J. Swann, A. Deumertes and W.L. Leap (2000) *Introducing Sociolinguistics*, Edinburgh: Edinburgh University Press.

Michaels, L. and C. Ricks (eds) (1990) *The State of the Language*, 2nd edn, Berkeley, Calif.: University of California Press.

Mieder, W. (1989) *American Proverbs*, Bern: Lang.

—— (1993) *Proverbs Are Never out of Season*, New York: OUP.

Mihailovic, L. (1962/63) 'Some Observations on the Use of the Passive Voice', *English Language Teaching* 17: 77–81.

Miller, J. (1993) 'The Grammar of Scottish English', in J. Milroy and L. Milroy (eds), *Real English: The Grammar of English Dialects in the British Isles,* London: Longman, pp. 99–138.

—— and K. Brown (1982) 'Aspects of Scottish English Syntax', *English World-Wide* 3: 3–17.

Milroy, J. (1981) *Regional Accents of English: Belfast*, Belfast: Blackstaff.

—— (1991) 'The Interpretation of Social Constraints on Variation in Belfast English', in J. Cheshire (ed.), *English Around the World. Sociolinguistic Perspectives*, Cambridge: CUP, pp. 75–85.

Milroy, L. (1984) 'Urban Dialects in the British Isles', in P. Trudgill (ed.), *Language in the British Isles*, Cambridge: CUP, pp. 199–218.

—— and S. Margrain (1980) 'Vernacular Language Loyality and Social Networks', *Language in Society* 9: 43–70.

—— and L. Milroy (1993) *Real English. The Grammar of English Dialects in the British Isles*, London: Longman.

Montgomery, M.B. and G. Bailey (eds) (1986) *Language Variety in the South*, Tuscaloosa, Ala.: University of Alabama Press.

Moon, R. (1998) *Fixed Expressions and Idioms in English: A Corpus Based Approach*, Oxford: OUP.

Moss, N. (1994) *The British/American Dictionary*, 2nd edn, London: Arrow.

Mufwene, S.S. (1998) 'The Structure of the Noun Phrase in AAVE', in S.S. Mufwene, J.R. Rickford, G. Bailey and J. Baugh (eds), *African-American English*, London: Routledge, pp. 69–81.

——, J.R. Rickford, G. Bailey and J. Baugh (eds) (1998) *African-American English*, London: Routledge.

Mühlhäusler, P. (1984) 'Tok Pisin in Papua New Guinea', in R.W. Bailey and M. Görlach (eds), *English as a World Language*, Cambridge: CUP, pp. 439–66.

—— (1986a) *Pidgin and Creole Linguistics*, Oxford: Basil Blackwell.

—— (1986b) 'English in Contact with Tok Pisin (Papua New Guinea)', in W. Viereck and W.-D. Bald (eds), *English in Contact with Other Languages*, Budapest: Akadémiai, pp. 549–70.

Murison, C. (1977) *The Guid Scots Tongue*, Edinburgh: William Blackwood.

Muysken, P. (1988) 'Are Creoles a Special Type of Language?', in F.J. Newmeyer (ed.), *Linguistics: The Cambridge Survey*, vol. II, *Linguistic Theory: Extensions and Implications*, Cambridge: CUP, pp. 285–301.

NCTE (National Council of Teachers of English) (1977) 'Guidelines for Nonsexist Use of Language in NCTE Publications', in A.P. Nilsen *et al.* (eds), *Sexism and Language*, Urbana, Ill.: NCTE, pp. 181–91.

Newmeyer, F.J. (ed.) (1988) *Language: The Socio-Cultural Context*, vol. 4 of *Linguistics: The Cambridge Survey*, Cambridge: CUP.

Nichols, J.C. (1984) 'Networks and Hierarchies. Language and Social Stratification', in C. Kramarae, M. Schulz and W.M. O'Barr (eds), *Language and Power*, Beverly Hills, Calif.: Sage, pp. 23–42.

Nihalani, P. (1989) *Indian and British English. A Handbook of Usage and Pronunciation*, Delhi: OUP.

Nilsen, A.P. (1977) 'Sexism as Shown through the English Vocabulary', in A.P. Nilsen *et al.* (eds), *Sexism and Language*, Urbana, Ill.: NCTE, pp. 27–41.

Norrick, N. (1985) *How Proverbs Mean*, Berlin: Mouton.

—— (1988) 'Binomial Meaning in Texts', *Journal of English Linguistics* 21: 72–87.

Nunberg, G. (1983) 'The Decline of Grammar', *Atlantic Monthly* (December): 31–46.

O'Connor, J.D. and G.F. Arnold (1961) *Intonation of Colloquial English*, London: Longman.

O'Donnell, W.R. and L. Todd (1991) *Variety in Contemporary English*, 2nd edn, London: Routledge.

Orton, H., W.J. Halliday, M.V. Barry, P.M. Tilling and M.F. Wakelin (eds) (1962–71) *Survey of English Dialects*, Leeds: E.J. Arnold.

Palmer, F.R. (1987) *The English Verb*, 2nd edn, London: Longman.

—— (1990) *Modality and the English Modals*, 2nd edn, London: Longman.

—— (2001) *Mood and Modality*, 2nd edn, Cambridge: CUP.

Partridge, E. (1963) *You Have a Point There*, London: Hamish Hamilton.

Pascasio, E.M. (1988) 'The Present Role and Domains of English in the Philippines', in A. Gonzales (ed.), *The Role of English and Its Maintenance in the Philippines*, Manila: Solidaridad, pp. 114–24.

Pätzold, K.M. (1997) 'The New Generation of Learner Dictionaries', *Fremdsprachen Lehren und Lernen* 26: 184–218.

—— (1998) 'English Proverbs and Their Treatment in English-German Dictionaries', in J. Wirrer (ed.), *Phraseologismen in Text und Kontext. Phrasemata I*, Bielefeld: Aisthesis, pp. 169–96.

Pedersen, K. (2001) 'Dialects', in J. Algeo (ed.), *English in North America*, vol. 6, *The Cambridge History of English*, Cambridge: CUP, pp. 253–90.

Pellowe, J. and V. Jones (1978) 'On Intonational Variability in Tyneside Speech', in P. Trudgill (ed.), *Sociolinguistic Patterns in British English*, London: Edward Arnold, pp. 101–21.

Pemagbi, J. (1989) 'Still a Deficient Language?', *English Today* 17: 20–4.

Petöfi, J.S. (ed.) (1988) *Text and Discourse Constitution*, Berlin: de Gruyter.

—— (1990) 'Language as a Written Medium: Text', in N.E. Collinge (ed.), *An Encyclopaedia of Language*, London: Routledge, pp. 207–43.

Philp, A.M. (1968) *Attitudes to Correctness in English*, Programme in Linguistics and English Teaching, Paper No. 6, London: Longman.

Pike, K.L. (1945) *The Intonation of American English*, Ann Arbor, Mich.: University of Michigan Press.

Platt, J.T. (1984) 'English in Singapore, Malaysia, and Hong Kong', in R. Bailey and M. Görlach (eds), *English as a World Language*, Cambridge: CUP, pp. 384–414.

—— (1988) 'Singapore', in U. Ammon, N. Dittmar and K.J. Mattheier (eds), *Sociolinguistics Soziolinguistik*, Berlin: Walter de Gruyter, pp. 1384–8.

—— (1991) 'Social and Linguistic Constraints on Variation in the Use of Two Grammatical Variables in Singapore English', in J. Cheshire (ed.), *English Around the World. Sociolinguistic Perspectives*, Cambridge: CUP, pp. 376–87.

—— and H. Weber (1980) *English in Singapore and Malaysia*, Kuala Lumpur: OUP.

Poldauf, I. (1984) *English Word Stress*, Oxford: Pergamon.

Potter, S. (1979) *Our Language*, Harmondsworth: Penguin.

Poynton, C. (1989) 'Terms of Address in Australian English', in P. Collins and D. Blair (eds), *Australian English: The Language of a New Society*, St Lucia: University of Queensland Press, pp. 55–69.

Pride, J.B. (ed.) (1982) *New Englishes*, Rowley, Mass.: Newbury House.

Pringle, I. and E. Padolsky (1983) 'The Linguistic Survey of the Ottawa Valley', *American Speech* 58: 325–44.

Quirk, R., S. Greenbaum, G. Leech and J. Svartvik (1985) *A Comprehensive Grammar of the English Language*, London: Longman.

—— and J. Mulholland (1964) 'Complex Prepositions and Related Sequences', *English Studies* 45: 64–73.

—— and G. Stein (1990) *English in Use*, Harlow: Longman.

Ramsaran, S. (ed.) (1990a) *Studies in the Pronunciation of English*, London: Routledge.

—— (1990b) 'RP: Fact *and* Fiction', in S. Ramsaran (ed.), *Studies in the Pronunciation of English*, London: Routledge, pp. 178–90.

Redfern, W. (1989) *Clichés and Coinages*, Oxford: Blackwell.

Richards, J.C. (1982) 'Rhetorical and Communicative Styles in the New Varieties of English', in J.B. Pride (ed.), *New Englishes*, Rowley, Mass.: Newbury House, pp. 227–48.

—— and M.W.J. Tay (1977) 'The *La* Particle in Singapore English', in W. Crewe (ed.), *The English Language in Singapore*, Singapore: Eastern Universities Press, pp. 141–56.

Rickford, J.R. (1987) *Dimensions of a Creole Continuum*, Stanford: Stanford University Press.

—— (1998) 'The Creole Origins of African-American Vernacular English: Evidence from Copula Absence', in S.S. Mufwene, J.R. Rickford, G. Bailey and J. Baugh (eds), *African-American English*, London: Routledge, pp. 154–200.

Riper, W.R. van (1986) 'General American: An Ambiguity', in H.B. Allen and M.D. Linn (eds), *Dialect and Language Variation*, Orlando, Fla.: Academic, pp. 123–35.

Roach, P. (1991) *English Phonetics and Phonology*, 2nd edn, Cambridge: CUP.

Roberts, P.A. (1988) *West Indians and Their Language*, Cambridge: CUP.

Robinson, P.C. (1989) 'An Overview of English for Specific Purposes', in H. Coleman (ed.), *Working with Language. A Multidisciplinary Consideration of Language Use in Work Contexts*, Berlin: Mouton de Gruyter, pp. 395–427.

Romaine, S. (1984) 'The English Language in Scotland', in R.W. Bailey and M. Görlach (eds), *English as a World Language*, Cambridge: CUP, pp. 56–83.

—— (ed.) (1998) *1776–1997*, vol. 4, *The Cambridge History of the English Language*, Cambridge: CUP.

Rosenberg, B.A. (1970) *The Art of the American Folk Preacher*, New York: OUP.

Rosewarne, D. (1994) 'Estuary English: Tomorrow's RP?', *English Today* 10: 3–8.

Ross, A.S.C. (1954) 'Linguistic Class-Indicators in Present Day English', *Neuphilologische Mitteilungen* 55: 20–56.

Roy, J. (1986) 'The Structure of Tense and Aspect in Barbadian English Creole', in M. Görlach and J. Holm (eds), *Focus on the Caribbean*, Amsterdam: Benjamins, pp. 141–56.

Rubin, R. (1981) 'Ideal Traits and Terms of Address for Male and Female College Professors', *Journal of Personality and Social Psychology* 41: 966–74.

Russ, C.V.J. (1984) 'The geographical and social variation of English in England and Wales', in R.W. Bailey and M. Görlach (eds), *English as a World Language*, Cambridge: CUP, pp. 11–55.

Sachs, J. (1975) 'Cues to the Identification of Sex in Children's Speech', in B. Thorne and N. Henley (eds), *Language and Sex: Difference and Dominance*, Rowley, Mass.: Newbury House, pp. 152–71.

—— (1987) 'Preschool Boys' and Girls' Language Use in Pretend Play', in S.U. Philips, S. Steele and C. Tanz (eds), *Language, Gender and Sex in Comparative Perspective*, Cambridge: CUP, pp. 178–88.

——, P. Lieberman and D. Erickson (1973) 'Anatomical and Cultural Determinants of Male and Female Speech', in R. Shuy and R.W. Fasold (eds), *Language Attitudes*, Washington, D.C.: Georgetown Roundtable in Linguistics, pp. 74–84.

Sacks, H., E.A. Schegloff and G. Jefferson (1974) 'A Simplest Systematics for the Organisation of Turn-taking for Conversations', *Language* 50: 696–735.

Sadock, J. (1978) 'On Testing for Conversational Implicature', in P. Cole (ed.), *Pragmatics*, vol. 9 of *Syntax and Semantics*, New York: Academic Press, pp. 281–97.

Sager, J.C., D. Dungworth and P.F. McDonald (1980) *English Special Languages*, Wiesbaden: Brandstetter.

Sahgal, A. and R.K. Agnihotri (1985) 'Syntax – The Common Bond. Acceptability of Syntactic Deviances in Indian English', *English World-Wide* 6: 117–29.

Salager, F. (1984) 'Compound Nominal Phrases in Scientific-Technical Literature: Proportion and Rationale', in A.K. Pugh and J.M. Ulijn (eds), *Reading for Professional Purposes. Studies and Practices in Native and Foreign Languages*, London: Heinemann, pp. 136–45.

Salmon, V. (1988) 'English Punctuation Theory', *Anglia* 106: 285–314.

Samuels, M.L. (1972) *Linguistic Evolution with Special Reference to English*, Cambridge: CUP

Schank, R. and R. Abelson (1977) *Scripts, Plans, Goals, and Understanding*, Hillsdale, N.J.: Erlbaum.

Schegloff, E. and H. Sacks (1973) 'Opening up Closings', *Semiotics* 8: 289–327.

Schiffrin, D. (1987) *Discourse Markers*, Cambridge: CUP.

—— (1988) 'Conversation Analysis', in F.J. Newmeyer (ed.), *Language: The Socio-cultural Context*, vol. 4, *Linguistics: The Cambridge Survey*, Cambridge: CUP, pp. 251–76.

—— (1994) *Approaches to Discourse*, Oxford: Blackwell.

Schmied, J.J. (1985) 'Attitudes towards English in Tanzania', *English World-Wide* 6: 237–69.

—— (1991) 'National and Subnational Features in Kenyan English', in J. Cheshire (ed.), *English Around the World. Sociolinguistic Perspectives*, Cambridge: CUP, pp. 420–32.

Schneider, E.W. (ed.) (1996) *Focus on the USA*, Amsterdam, Penn.: Benjamins.

Schrock, E.F. Jr (1986) 'Some Features of the *Be* Verb in the Speech of Blacks of Pope County, Arkansas', in M.B. Montgomery and G. Bailey (eds), *Language Variety in the South*, Tuscaloosa, Ala.: University of Alabama Press, pp. 202–15.

Schulz, M.R. (1975) 'The Semantic Derogation of Woman', in B. Thorne and N. Henley (eds), *Language and Sex: Difference and Dominance*, Rowley, Mass.: Newbury House, pp. 64–75.

Scott, K.P. (1980) 'Perceptions of Communicative Competence: What's Good for the Goose is Not Good for the Gander', in C. Kramarae (ed.), *The Voices and Words of Women and Men*, Oxford: Pergamon, pp. 199–208.

Scragg, D.G. (1974) *A History of English Spelling*, Manchester: Manchester University Press.

Searle, J.R. (1969) *Speech Acts: An Essay in the Philosophy of Language*, Cambridge: CUP.

Sebba, M. (1986) 'London Jamaican and Black London English', in D. Sutcliffe and A. Wong (eds), *The Language of Black Experience*, Oxford: Basil Blackwell, pp. 149–67.

Shaklee, M. (1980) 'The Rise of Standard English', in T. Shopen and J. Williams (eds), *Standards and Dialects in English*, Cambridge, Mass.: Winthrop, pp. 33–62.

Shane, S.A. (1973) *Generative Phonology*, Englewood Cliffs: Prentice-Hall.

Shopen, T. and J.M. Williams (eds) (1980) *Standards and Dialects in English*, Cambridge, Mass.: Winthrop.

Shuy, R. and R.W. Fasold (eds) (1973) *Language Attitudes*, Washington, DC: Georgetown Roundtable in Linguistics.

——— , W.A. Wolfram and W.K. Riley (1967) *Linguistic Correlates of Social Stratification in Detroit Speech*, East Lansing, Mich.: Michigan State University.

———, ——— and ——— (1968) *Linguistic Correlates of Social Stratification in Detroit Speech*, Washington, DC: US Department of Health, Education, and Welfare, Office of Education, Bureau of Research.

Sibayan, B.P. (1988) 'Social Engineering Strategies for the Maintenance of English', in A. Gonzalez (ed.), *The Role of English and Its Maintenance in the Philippines*, Manila: Solidaridad, pp. 91–6.

Silveira, J. (1980) 'Generic Masculine Words and Thinking', in C. Kramarae (ed.), *The Voices and Words of Women and Men*, Oxford: Pergamon, pp. 165–78.

Singh, I. (2000) *Pidgins and Creoles. An Introduction*, London: Arnold.

Singler, J.V. (1991) 'Plural Marking in Liberian English', in J. Cheshire (ed.), *English Around the World. Sociolinguistic Perspectives*, Cambridge: CUP, pp. 545–61.

Smith, G. (1985) *The English Companion*, Harmondsworth: Penguin.

Sommerstein, A.H. (1977) *Modern Phonology*, London: Edward Arnold.

Spencer, J. (ed.) (1971a) *The English Language in West Africa*, London: Longman.

——— (1971b) 'West Africa and the English Language', in J. Spencer (ed.), *The English Language in West Africa*, London: Longman, pp. 1–34.

Sperber, D. and D. Wilson (1995) *Relevance: Communication and Cognition*, 2nd edn, Oxford: Blackwell.

Sridhar, K.K. (1983) 'English in a South Indian Urban Context', in B.B. Kachru (ed.), *The Other Tongue. English Across Cultures*, Oxford: Pergamon, pp. 141–53.

Stanley, J.P. (1977) 'Paradigmatic Woman. The Prostitute', in D.L. Shore and C.P. Hines (eds), *Papers on Language Variation*, Birmingham, Ala.: University of Alabama, pp. 303–21.

Stein, G. (1979) *Studies in the Function of the Passive*, Tübingen: Narr.

Stewart, W.A. (1964) 'Urban Negro Speech: Sociolinguistic Factors Affecting English Teaching', in R.W. Shuy (ed.), *Social Dialects and Language Learning*, Champaign, Ill.: National Council of Teachers of English, pp. 10–18.

Strang, B.M.H. (1970) *A History of English*, London: Methuen.

Strevens, P. (1964) 'Varieties of English', *English Studies* 45: 20–30.

——— (1972) *British and American English*, London: Collier-Macmillan.

Stringer, D. (1973) *Language Variation and English*, Bletchley: The Open University.

Sutcliffe, D. (1984) 'British Black English and West Indian Creoles', in P. Trudgill (ed.), *Language in the British Isles*, Cambridge: CUP, pp. 219–37.

Svartvik, J. (1966) *On Voice in the English Verb*, The Hague: Mouton.

——— and R. Quirk (1980) *A Corpus of English Conversation*, Lund: Gleerup.

Swacker, M. (1978) 'Women's Verbal Behavior at Learned and Professional Conferences', in B. Dubois and I. Crouch (eds), *The Sociology of the Languages of American Women*, San Antonio, Tex.: Trinity University, pp. 155–60.

Swales, J. (1981) 'Aspects of Article Introductions', *ESP Research Reports*, 1: Aston University.
—— (1990) *Genre Analysis*, Cambridge: CUP.
Swann, J. (1992) *Girls, Boys and Language*, Oxford: Blackwell.
Tadros, A.A. (1989) 'Predictive Categories in University Textbooks', *ESP Journal* 8: 17–31.
Talbot, M.M. (1998) *Language and Gender. An Introduction*, Cambridge: Polity.
Tannen, D. (1993) 'The Relativity of Linguistic Strategies: Rethinking Power and Solidarity in Gender and Dominance', in D. Tannen (ed.), *Gender and Conversational Interaction*, New York: OUP, pp. 166–88.
Tarone, E., S. Dwyer, S. Gillette and V. Icke (1998) 'On the Use of the Passive in Two Astrophysics Journal Papers', *English for Specific Purposes* 17: 113–32.
Tay, M.W.J. (1982) 'The Uses, Users, and Features of English in Singapore', in J.B. Pride (ed.), *New Englishes*, Rowley, Mass.: Newbury House, pp. 51–70.
—— (1993) *The English Language in Singapore*, Singapore: UniPress, Centre for the Arts, National University of Singapore.
Taylor, B. (1989) 'American, British and Other Foreign Influences on Australian English since World War II', in P. Collins and D. Blair (eds), *Australian English: The Language of a New Society*, St Lucia: University of Queensland Press, pp. 225–54.
Taylor, C.V. (1973/74) 'Ambiguities in Spoken Australian English', *English Language Teaching* 28: 59–64.
Taylor, D. (1971) 'Grammatical and Lexical Affinities of Creoles', in D. Hymes (ed.), *Pidginization and Creolization of Languages*, Cambridge: CUP, pp. 293–6.
Thomas, A.R. (1984) 'Welsh English', in P. Trudgill (ed.), *Language in the British Isles*, Cambridge: CUP, pp. 178–94.
—— (1985) 'Welsh English: A Grammatical Conspectus', in W. Viereck (ed.), *Focus on: England and Wales*, Amsterdam, Penn.: Benjamins, pp. 213–21.
—— (1997) *Issues and Methods in Dialectology*, Bangor: University of Wales.
Thomas, J. (1995) *Meaning in Interaction*, Harlow: Longman.
Thomson, A.J. and A.V. Martinet (1983) *A Practical English Grammar*, Oxford: OUP.
Thorne, B. and N. Henley (eds) (1975) *Language and Sex: Difference and Dominance*, Rowley, Mass.: Newbury House.
——, C. Kramarae and N. Henley (eds) (1983) *Language, Gender and Society*, Cambridge, Mass.: Newbury House.
Tingley, C. (1981) 'Deviance in the English of Ghanaian Newspapers', *English World-Wide* 2: 39–62.
Todd, L. (1982) *Cameroon*, Heidelberg: Groos.
—— (1984) *Modern Englishes: Pidgins and Creoles*, Oxford: Basil Blackwell.
Tongue, R. (1974) *The English of Singapore and Malaysia*, Singapore: Eastern Universities Press.
Toon, T.E. (1984) 'Variation in Contemporary American English', in R.W. Bailey and M. Görlach (eds), *English as a World Language*, Cambridge: CUP, pp. 210–50.
Tournier, J. (1985) *Introduction Descriptive à la Lexicogénétique de l'Anglais Contemporain*, Paris: Champion-Slatkine.
Trager, G.L. and H.L. Smith (1951) *An Outline of English Structure*, Washington, DC: American Council of Learned Societies.
Trimble, L. (1985a) *English for Science and Technology. A Discourse Approach*, Cambridge: CUP.
—— (1985b) (ed.) *Handbook of Discourse Analysis*, 4 vols, New York: Academic Press.
Trudgill, P. (1972) 'Sex, Covert Prestige, and Linguistic Change in the Urban British English of Norwich', *Language and Society* 1: 179–95.
—— (1974) *The Social Differentiation of English in Norwich*, Cambridge: CUP.
—— (1975) *Accent, Dialect and the School*, London: Edward Arnold.

—— (ed.) (1978) *Sociolinguistic Patterns in British English*, London: Edward Arnold.

—— (ed.) (1984) *Language in the British Isles*, Cambridge: CUP.

—— (1999) *The Dialects of England*, Oxford: Basil Blackwell.

—— and J.K. Chambers (eds) (1991) *Dialects of English*, London: Longman.

Turner, G.W. (1972) *The English Language in Australia and New Zealand*, London: Longman.

—— (1994) 'English in Australia', in R. Burchfield (ed.), *English in Britain and Overseas: Origins and Development*, in *The Cambridge History of the English Language*, vol. 5, Cambridge: CUP, pp. 277–327.

Valdés, G. (1988) 'The Language Situation of Mexican Americans', in S.L. McKay and S.C. Wong (eds), *Language Diversity. Problem or Resource?*, Cambridge, Mass.: Newbury House, pp. 111–39.

Venezky, R.L. (1970) *The Structure of English Orthography*, The Hague: Mouton.

—— (1999) *The American Way of Spelling*, New York: Guilford.

Verma, S.K. (1982) 'Swadeshi English: Form and Function', in J.B. Pride (ed.), *New Englishes*, Rowley, Mass.: Newbury House, pp. 174–87.

Viereck, W. (ed.) (1985) *Focus on: England and Wales*, Amsterdam, Penn.: Benjamins.

Waggoner, D. (1988) 'Language Minorities in the United States in the 1980s: The Evidence from the 1980 Census', in S.L. McKay and S.C. Wong (eds), *Language Diversity. Problem or Resource?*, Cambridge, Mass.: Newbury House, pp. 69–108.

Wakelin, M. (ed.) (1972) *Patterns in the Folk Speech of the British Isles*, London: Athlone.

—— (1983) 'The Stability of English Dialect Boundaries', *English World-Wide* 4: 1–15.

—— (1984) 'Rural Dialects in England', in P. Trudgill (ed.), *Language in the British Isles*, Cambridge: CUP, pp. 70–93.

Wardhaugh, R. (1986) *An Introduction to Sociolinguistics*, Oxford: Basil Blackwell.

Wekker, H.C. (1976) *The Expression of Future Time in Contemporary British English*, Amsterdam, Penn.: North Holland.

Wells, J.C. (1982) *Accents of English*, Cambridge: CUP.

—— (2000) *Pronunciation Dictionary*, Harlow: Longman.

Werlich, E. (1983) *A Text Grammar of English*, 2nd edn, Heidelberg: Quelle & Meyer.

West, C. (1990) 'Not Just "Doctor's Ordered": Directive-response Sequences in Patients' Visits to Women and Men Physicians', *Discourse and Society* 1: 85–112.

West, G.K. (1980) 'That-Nominal Constructions in Traditional Rhetorical Divisions of Scientific Research Papers', *TESOL Quarterly* 14: 483–8.

Whitcut, J. (1980) 'The Language of Address', in L. Michaels and C. Ricks (eds), *The State of the Language*, Berkeley, Calif.: University of California Press, pp. 89–97.

Wijk, A. (1966) *Rules of Pronunciation for the English Language. An Account of the Relationship Between English Spelling and Pronunciation*, London: OUP.

Williams, F. (1973) 'Some Research Notes on Dialect Attitudes and Stereotypes', in R. Shuy and R.W. Fasold (eds), *Language Attitudes*, Washington, DC: Georgetown Roundtable in Linguistics, pp. 113–28.

Williams, R. (1984) 'A Cognitive Approach to English Nominal Compounds', in A.K. Pugh and J.M. Ulijn (eds), *Reading for Professional Purposes. Studies and Practices in Native and Foreign Languages*, London: Heinemann, pp. 146–53.

Wolfram, W.A. (1971) 'Black-White Speech Differences Revisited' in W.A. Wolfram and N.H. Clarke (eds), *Black-White Speech Relationships*, Washington, DC: Center for Applied Linguistics, pp. 139–61.

—— and N.H. Clarke (eds) (1971) *Black-White Speech Relationships*, Washington, DC: Center for Applied Linguistics.

—— and D. Christian (1976) *Appalachian Speech*, Arlington, Tex.: Center for Applied Linguistics.

Wolfson, N. and J. Manes (1980) 'Don't "Dear" Me!', in S. McConnell-Ginet, R. Borker and N. Furman (eds), *Women and Language in Literature and Society*, New York: Praeger, pp. 79–92.

Woods, H.B. (1991) 'Social Differentiation in Ottawa English', in J. Cheshire (ed.), *English Around the World. Sociolinguistic Perspectives*, Cambridge: CUP, pp. 134–49.

Wright, P. (1981) *Cockney Dialect and Slang*, London: Batsford.

Wyld, H.C. (1934) *The Best English: A Claim for the Superiority of Received Standard English*, no. 39, Oxford: Society for Pure English.

Yule, H. (1995) *A Glossary of Colloquial Anglo-Indian Words and Phrases: Hobson-Jobson*, 2nd edn, edited by William Crooke, Richmond: Curzon Press.

Zentella, A.C. (1988) 'The Language Situation of Puerto Ricans', in S.L. McKay and S.C. Wong (eds), *Language Diversity. Problem or Resource?*, Cambridge: Newbury, pp. 140–65.

Zimmerman, D.H. and C. West (1975) 'Sex Roles, Interruptions and Silences in Conversation', in B. Thorne and N. Henley (eds), *Language and Sex: Difference and Dominance*, Rowley, Mass.: Newbury House, pp. 105–29.

Index

Bold is used to indicate section numbers.